# DUTY, HONOR AND A LOAF OF BREAD

## Portrait of An American Family in World War II 1944 - 1946

Compiled and Edited

by

Jan (Waldron) and Ed Votroubek

with

Dr. Monte Smith

**Cover Photos**
Main Street, Waukon, Iowa courtesty of
*Allamakee Historical Society*
and
Battle of the Bulge in Belgium near St. Vith with permission from
*Historylink101.com*

and are greatly appreciated

Order this book online at www.trafford.com
or email orders@trafford.com

Most Trafford titles are also available at major online book retailers.

© Copyright 2012 Jan (Waldron) & Ed Votroubek.
All rights reserved. No part of this publication may be reproduced, stored in a retrieval system, or transmitted, in any form or by any means, electronic, mechanical, photocopying, recording, or otherwise, without the written prior permission of the author.

Printed in the United States of America.

ISBN: 978-1-4669-6193-7 (sc)
ISBN: 978-1-4669-6192-0 (e)

Library of Congress Control Number: 2012918415

*Trafford rev. 10/02/2012*

www.trafford.com

**North America & international**
toll-free: 1 888 232 4444 (USA & Canada)
phone: 250 383 6864 ♦ fax: 812 355 4082

This book is dedicated in four parts:

William | Marjorie

First, to Bill and Marge, the foundation of the Waldron family. The examples set for their progeny have been indelible and distinct. Hard work, integrity, and intensity have been hallmarks for the Waldron way of life. We all took for granted that what Bill and Marge displayed as husband and wife, parents, and business owners was natural and expected. The reality for these traits is that the aforementioned became a foundation for each child's own development.

Second, to ten children spanning sixteen years, who have carried on for Bill and Marge.

| | |
|---|---|
| Janice | Dennis |
| Greg | Kathy |
| Rick | Suzanne |
| Wendy | Peggy |
| Gwen | Jane |

Dedicating themselves to an Irish/English/German heritage, steeped in the Catholic religion, and recognizing family values, this group has revered every facet of the examples set for them by their parents.

The food service industry (Bill and Marge's locally owned bakery and catering business), became a guiding light for employment opportunities at one time or another for eight of the ten children.

All ten of the Waldron children followed an expectation of Bill and Marge that they pursue higher education.

The joys and the accompanying trials and tribulations of parenting have been passed along to their children, by virtue of the fact that there are twenty-four grandchildren, direct descendants.

Bill and Marge may have preferred what is considered a simpler life. Not venturing far from Waukon, Iowa after World War II, they enjoyed family gatherings, playing cards, fishing, dancing, and always socializing; their life together was full and complete. They worked hard, played hard, and prayed. Bill said if he made it home from the War, he wouldn't venture far from home again. Marge and Bill were never away from Waukon for more than three weeks for the rest of their lives, even though they visited Europe, Canada, Mexico, and much of the United States.

Third, with this book, it is hoped that the grandchildren will have another level of familiarity with their Waldron grandparents.

| | |
|---|---|
| Chris Votroubek | Drew Votroubek |
| Nikki Votroubek (Langer) | Ashlee Votroubek |
| Dacey Waldron | Mandy Waldron (Samford) |
| Grady Waldron | Dusty Waldron |
| Tasha Waldron (Morris) | Bill Waldron |
| Nolan Waldron | Ben Waldron |
| Brenda Marlowe (Long) | Michael Fossum |
| Courtney Waldron | Amy Waldron (Benne) |
| Kate Waldron | Lindsay Snitker |
| Andrea Snitker | Sarah Snitker |
| Leeta Sivesind | Lars Sivesind |
| Landon Sivesind | Leslie Sivesind |

For the above listed Waldron grandchildren all but four were born before Bill's passing in 1992. As the number of grandchildren grew with each year beginning in 1969, Marge and Bill seemed to be prideful of the ever growing number gathering at the farm for special occasions.

Although this book covers only a nineteen month period, reading the letters sent and received by Bill and Marge, there will be a clear affirmation of what they stood for in terms of their integrity, their marriage vows, and their devotion to each other.

It is hoped that each grandchild will be able to read between the lines of these letters and decipher a theme for how to emulate these values in their own pursuits.

As proud as Bill and Marge were of their children, they were equally excited in the presence of their grandchildren. The grandchildren now can make a bonafide declaration that many good characteristics they possess have emanated from their grandparents.

Lastly, this book is dedicated to the ten great grandchildren of Bill and Marge.

Coral Votroubek — Dan Votroubek
Jake Votroubek — Lily Langer
Lucy Langer — Nickolas Votroubek
Madilynn Benne — Leighton Benne
Liam Samford — Kennedy Waldron ...
. . . and all those to come in the future.

Much is known in respect to the genealogy of the Waldron and Leet families. This book becomes a fundamental piece to the short term genealogy existence of these newest, and most recent additions to the Waldron family. Although only one great-grandchild was born before Bill's passing, one can only imagine how proud he and Marge would have been as each appeared.

To all in the Waldron family, to the present three generations, know that you can share in a proud heritage.

Marge and Bill Waldron, 1944

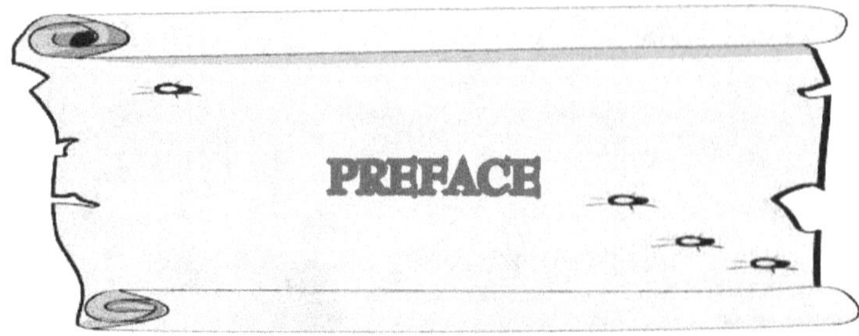


This project has been a long time coming.

Amongst the Waldron family, everyone knew that Bill served during the Battle of the Bulge in World War II. It was a given that Marge ran the Waldron owned bakery during Bill's military service.

Marge had saved Bill's letters. She also had what letters Bill saved during his basic training. He must have returned those to her before he shipped out.

When Bill passed away in 1992, the Waldron family gathered, and went through many boxes of "stuff" to be divided amongst the ten siblings, sold at auction, given to St. Vincent's, etc.

In Marge's memorabilia (sacks, boxes, loosely distributed in closets, etc.) the family rediscovered tens of letters that had been sent to Bill and received by Marge during Bill's time spent in the U.S. Army during World War II.

Their children sat around Wendy's dining room table and read aloud many of these letters with laughter and tears. They each kept any letters that they wished. Sibling Wendy retained the bulk of these letters.

Several years after Bill's passing, eldest child Jan began reading letters that she had in her possession. Besides the meaningful nostalgia, having been born while Bill was a member of the Germany Occupational Forces, Jan had a desire to learn more about this period of her parents' life. She gathered letters from all her siblings.

Jan began reading the letters. This was an opportunity for her to have part of her past revealed through the separation of Marge and Bill during this nearly twenty-month period. The letters sent by Marge and Bill pointed out a strong and loyal love between the two.

During this period, Marge was running the Waukon Bakery, although her experience as a baker and business person were limited. The letters point out the many travails that she had to work through. (Remember, also, that she conceived Jan when she traveled to be with Bill, while he was in training in Texas, and just prior to him being shipped overseas to Europe.) Many of the letters point out the fact that Marge struggled to staff the bakery and showed genuine concern and angst for the "proper" operation of the business. This became a focal point of Marge's letters. Plus, Bill showed concern for how Marge was getting along as she put a lot of energy into the business. Also, the letters make constant mention of the role that Amanda Waldron and Uncle Stan played in maintaining the integrity of the bakery.

As Jan became serious about reading the letters, the thought evolved to transcribe them to the computer, with the idea that they would be easier for others to read. Over the past year Jan has worked tirelessly to enter these letters (over 500) into our computer. Not an easy task, since all of them are hand-written in Marge and Bill's handwriting. Plus, Jan had to decipher much of the verbiage. This was compounded by the condition of some of the letters. Some letters were tattered with age, others water stained from the elements Bill encountered in combat. All were written in pencil on whatever paper he could find. And, all were worn over these past sixty-some years. With much perseverance, all letters in her possession were entered by mid-January, 2009.

Over the past three years, Jan and Ed have been researching Bill's Army Infantry Division and have been gleaning several web sites for information about the 90th Division, the 357th Regiment and Company F. At that point they decided to share this information with the family in the form of this book.

As they developed the narrative in respect to Bill's service and combat in the European Theatre of Operations, another element evolved. The obvious piece was that Marge's story needed to be incorporated in the narrative. For Bill, the dangers of war, combat and the threat of becoming a casualty was everyday stress.

For Marge, there were monumental stress factors as well. She was operating the bakery while pregnant with her first child; often experiencing car problems and having to walk to work at 2 AM from their home near the present day bowling lanes to the bakery on Main Street. She also had to deal with recurrent help issues. Plus, she had to be constantly fearful for Bill's safety.

Through the content of the letters and the experiences shared by the Waldron family, this book becomes a validation of what each of the family knows for sure and accepts as truth - a strong bond between husband and wife.

Thanks to all those who have participated in bringing this to fruition. The donation of pictures, inclusion of items that Bill transported from Europe and the oral history imparted by siblings have become important facets of this narrative.

## BILL & MARGE'S IMMEDIATE FAMILY

This could probably be called "the cast of characters." Many of the letters that follow were written by family members and friends of Bill and Marge Waldron; others contain references to family. The following list should be a guide to who is who.

### Bill's Family

Amanda and Jim Waldron, parents
Aunts:
- Tillie, lived in Waukon
- Stella, lived in Minneapolis
- Bessie, lived 2 houses up the street,
  - Her daughter, Marcella Robinson, lived next door to Amanda and Jim. She worked for a law firm and did Dad's business and personal taxes and filed the papers required for him to come home

Uncle:
- Frank, married to Gladys, lived in Minneapolis

Siblings:
- Vernon: Army, Quartermaster in Europe
- John: Army, also worked at Bakery after discharge
- Stan: 16-17 yrs old, worked at Bakery
- Max: about 12-13 yrs old
- Jeanne: about 10 years old
- Marie: about 3-4 years old
- Butch: about 1-2 years old

### Marge's Family

Viola and George Leet, parents
Aunt:
- Cecil Uhl, lived in Waukon (Lulu May's mother)

Uncles:
- Horace Gordinier, lived in Postville
- Lynn Gordinier, wife, Matilda; lived in Kalamazoo, MI- Rick Waldron's (Bill/Marge's son) middle name came from this uncle and he passed it down to his children Courtney, Amy, and Kate

Siblings:
- Ethyl, married to Aulger Paulsen, Clermont, IA.
  - Her daughter, Veryle, a few years younger than Marge, worked at the Bakery after high school and lived with grandparents George and Viola Leet in Waukon during war.*
- Albert, married to Dorothy, farmed near Waukon
- Lulu, married to Bryon Livingood, farmed outside Waukon.

* Marge also lived with her parents when Bill was in the service. After the war they lived in an upstairs apartment in the same house. This was a house up the street from the bowling alley on Spring Ave.

Jan (Waldron) Votroubek for her foresight to begin this project. For her diligence to input the letters into the computer. And for her knack to research for pertinent information.

Ed Votroubek for cultivating a passion to see this project to its fruition.

Kathy (Waldron) Fossum, Sue (Waldron) Smith, Wendy Waldron, Peg (Waldron) Thomas, Gwen Waldron, Jane (Waldron) Sivesind for contributing the letters they had in their possession to this project.

Den Waldron, Rick Waldron, Gwen Waldron, Jan Votroubek for providing pieces to an oral history of events that Bill had related to them.

Kathy (Waldron) Fossum, Wendy Waldron, and Peg (Waldron) Thomas for contributing family pictures and documents that have brought a personal touch to this project.

Monte Smith, for contributing his editing and publishing expertise, Sue for proofing, and Denise E. Knight for reading, editing and making suggestions. Also Ann Cutrubus and Lou Leetch for the final proof. All errors are, of course, our own.

Dedication ... iii
Marge and Bill Waldron 1944 ... v
Preface ... vi
Bill & Marge's Immediate Family ... vii
Acknowledgements ... viii
Table of Contents ... ix
Background and Setting ... 1
Normandy Campaign ... 1
Campaign of Northern France (The Breakout) ... 2
Battle of the Falaise Pocket ... 3
Pursuit Across France ... 4
Moselle-Saar Campaign ... 4
Duty and Honor ... 5
August - September 1944 ... 8
Company A, 172nd IRTB ... 40
October - December 1944 ... 41
The Rocket 507 ... 50
Picture of Veryle ... 66
Photo of Viola and George ... 68
Recipe for Pecan Pie ... 72
January - May 1945 ... 75
3rd Army, 90th Infantry Division, 357th Regiment, Company F ... 76
The Siegfried Line ... 84
Movement of the 357th Regiment ... 101
Hitler Dead ... 124
V-E Day ... 127
A Letter from Bill ... 129
Central Europe Campaign ... 131
Note to the Waldron Famly ... 136
June - August 1945 ... 155
German Sectors ... 160
3rd Army Area of Occupation ... 170
Hiroshima ... 237
Japan Surrenders ... 244
Permission to Carry ... 248
September - December 1945 ... 249

Therese Neumann . . . . . . . . . . . . . . . . . . . . . . . . . . . . . . . . . . . . . . . . . . . .250
Application for Discharge . . . . . . . . . . . . . . . . . . . . . . . . . . . . . . . . . . . 273-274
Response from Congressman Talle . . . . . . . . . . . . . . . . . . . . . . . . . . . . . .289
Map of Bill's assignments . . . . . . . . . . . . . . . . . . . . . . . . . . . . . . . . . . . . .296
Property Authorization . . . . . . . . . . . . . . . . . . . . . . . . . . . . . . . . . . . . . . .300
Photo of Jim and Amanda with Butch . . . . . . . . . . . . . . . . . . . . . . . . . . . .305
Photo of Vern with Jimmy and John . . . . . . . . . . . . . . . . . . . . . . . . . . . . .324
Response from the War Department . . . . . . . . . . . . . . . . . . . . . . . . . . . . .337
January - February 1946 . . . . . . . . . . . . . . . . . . . . . . . . . . . . . . . . . . . . . . .356
Letter to Congressman Talle. . . . . . . . . . . . . . . . . . . . . . . . . . . . . . . . . . . .364
Photo of Beck, Vernon, Jimmy with Ruth and John . . . . . . . . . . . . . . . . . .366
Phone call from Munich . . . . . . . . . . . . . . . . . . . . . . . . . . . . . . . . . . . . . . .368
Note from Representative Talle . . . . . . . . . . . . . . . . . . . . . . . . . . . . . . . . .369
Communique from Representative Talle . . . . . . . . . . . . . . . . . . . . . . . . . .374
Bill's orders home . . . . . . . . . . . . . . . . . . . . . . . . . . . . . . . . . . . . . . . . . . .377
Thank you note from Congressman . . . . . . . . . . . . . . . . . . . . . . . . . . . . . .380
Duty - Honor - A Loaf of Bread . . . . . . . . . . . . . . . . . . . . . . . . . . . . . . . . .385
Discharge Record No. 3 . . . . . . . . . . . . . . . . . . . . . . . . . . . . . . . . . . . . . . .387
Troop Levels . . . . . . . . . . . . . . . . . . . . . . . . . . . . . . . . . . . . . . . . . . . . . . .388
Acronyms used in Bill's letters . . . . . . . . . . . . . . . . . . . . . . . . . . . . . . . . . .388
Bibliography . . . . . . . . . . . . . . . . . . . . . . . . . . . . . . . . . . . . . . . . . . . . . . . .389
The Waldron Brothers . . . . . . . . . . . . . . . . . . . . . . . . . . . . . . . . . . . . . . . . .389
Post Script . . . . . . . . . . . . . . . . . . . . . . . . . . . . . . . . . . . . . . . . . . . . . . . . . .390

Bill arrived in Europe on January 13, 1945 where he, and the other replacement troops for the 90th Infantry Division, quickly moved across France and joined the 90th Infantry Division during the Battle of the Bulge. The Ardennes Campaign, the battle for the Siegfried Line and the Battle of the Bulge incurred high casualties for American and Allied forces. The fighting conditions during these bitter winter weather months made it that much more difficult and there was a desperate need for replacement troops.

In order to understand the setting into which Bill was placed, it will be useful to explore the history of the 90th and what they had accomplished.

The 90th Division entered WWII combat in Normandy on D-Day and fought across Europe continuously until V-E Day. During those eleven months, it served under six different division commanders. The first two (Brig Gen Jay W. McKelvie and Maj Gen Eugene M. Landrum) swiftly proved themselves inept and were deservedly relieved.

By the end of July, 1944 the following division commanders proved to be able military leaders: Brig Gen Raymond S. McClain, Brig Gen James A. Van Fleet, Maj Gen Lowell W. Rooks, and Brig Gen Herbert L. Earnest. (Gen Earnest was the division commander while Bill served his time from January, 1945 to February, 1946.)

Bill served in Company F of the 357th Infantry Regiment. The succession of regiment commanders are as follows: Col Ginder, Col Sheehy, Lt Col Schwab, and Col Barth. During Bill's time in Europe regiment commanders included Col George and, from February 1945 on, Lt Col John H. Mason.

The 90th Infantry participated in the following Campaigns while in Europe (a *Campaign* being a major offensive in a specific area): Normandy, Northern France, Ardennes, Rhineland and Central Europe. Bill served in three of these Campaigns - Ardennes, Rhineland, and Central Europe for which he received three battle stars.

The following is a Casualty Report for the 90th Division: Killed – 2,963, Wounded – 14,009, Missing – 1,052, Captured – 442, Battle Casualties – 18,460. While suffering these losses, the 90th Infantry took a total of 83,437 prisoners!

The following, in a bit more detail, is an accounting of the 90th Infantry Division as it fought its way across Europe. This is included so that the reader understands the peril that existed as the Germans fought to repel the Allied troops.

*Normandy Campaign....June 6-8, 1944*

The 1st and 3rd battalions of the 359th Regiment were attached to the U.S. 4th Division and were part of the Utah Beach assault force on D-Day, June 6, 1944 (Operation Overlord). The 2nd battalion and the other two regiments, 357th and 358th, landed on Utah

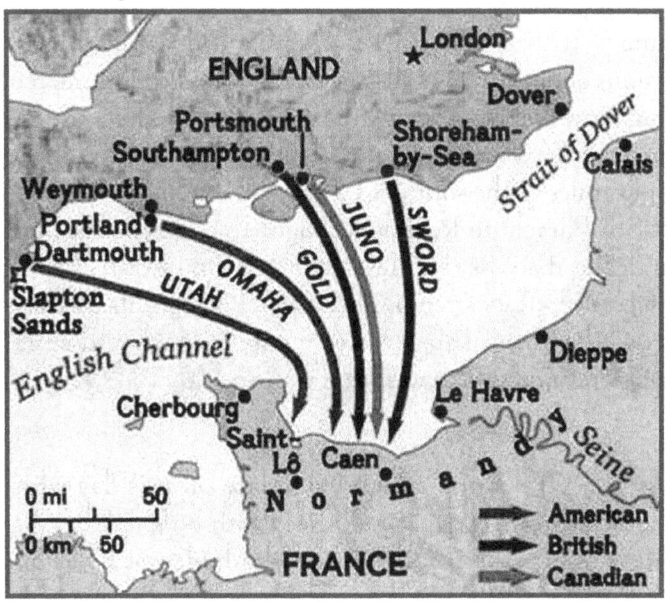

Beach on June 7 and 8.

Fortunately, resistance was very light on Utah Beach. This is in contrast to bloody Omaha Beach, where the U.S. 1st Division met murderous resistance and nearly had to withdraw from the beach.

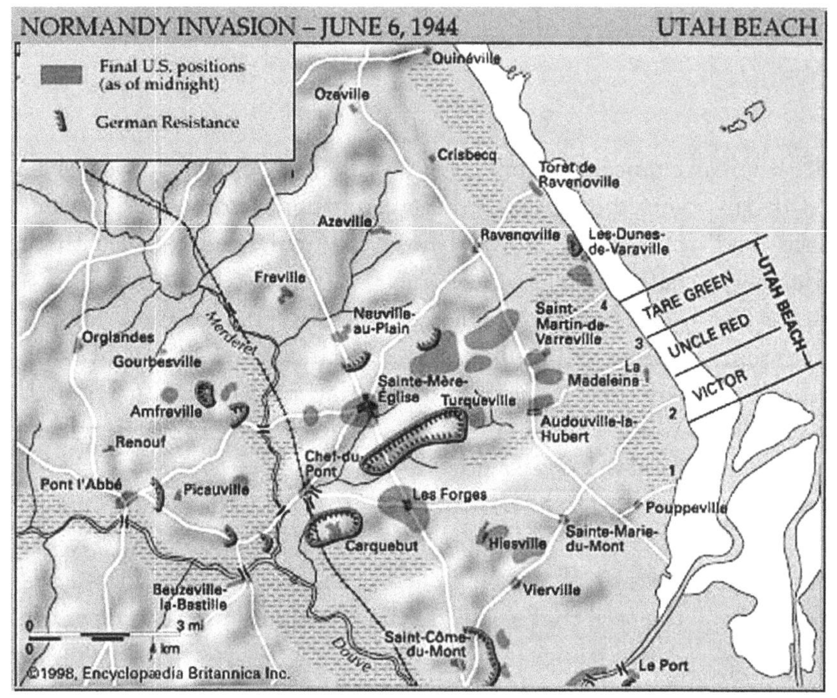


### *June 9*

By the end of D+2 (the third day of the D-Day landing) most artillery battalions and infantry battalions were ashore, but it would be several days before the Division could be organized and deployed for combat. The first offensive action for the 90th however, happened on June 9, with the 344th and 345th Field Artillery Battalions supporting an all-day attack across the Merderet causeway by the 82nd Airborne's 325th Glider Regiment at La Fiere, four miles west of St. Mere Eglise. Four miles to the south of La Fiere, the 82nd Airborne's 508th Parachute Regiment fought to establish another bridgehead across the Merderet at Chef du Pont. These successful attacks removed critical choke points and allowed the 90th's Infantry Regiments to move across the Merderet and attack westward on June 10.

### *June 10*

The 90th's first attack took place on this day with the 357th on the right and the 358th on the left. At 0400 hours, the 358th crossed the bridge at Chef du Pont, headed for Picauville moving just south of Hill 30 and passing partially through elements of the 508th Parachute Regiment on Hill 30. Just beyond this point the 358th was met with fierce resistance. The 357th, with the 2nd Battalion leading, started crossing the causeway at La Fiere towards Cauquigny at 0515. Both attacks found the going tough, with casualties heavy throughout the day. Meanwhile, the 359th remained attached to the 4th Division.

### *June 11*

Both the 357th and 358th Infantries continued their attacks with heavy casualties. The 357th on the right made little progress toward Amfreville. The 358th on the left, with two battalions abreast, was more successful, moving through Picauville toward Pont l'Abbe. The 359th Infantry was released to the 90th and moved during the night from positions near Freville, south to the 90th's sector. It was inserted in the line near Barneville between the 357th and the 358th. During the move, the 359th was severely shelled, which affected its readiness to attack the next morning.

The Normandy battle had just begun in earnest at this point and the 90th was very green. The 90th was an important part of the overall Normandy strategy. They were assigned to fight across the Cotentin peninsula and seal it off while Cherbourg was seized. This would eliminate German resistance in the Mahlman Line and prepare for the breakout (Operation Cobra).

Although not widely publicized then or later, those six weeks of combat involved some of the most difficult, demanding and costly fighting of the entire war (as depicted in the movie The Saving of Private Ryan). The battles at Beau Coudray and Mont Castre rank with the toughest. It was there that they faced and conquered, at great cost, the Mahlman Line, which was the German's main line of resistance for the peninsula.

### *Campaign of Northern France (The Breakout)*

July 24 was spent mostly in preparing for the 90th's role in COBRA, which was scheduled to jump off the next day. The 90th launched a coordinated attack on

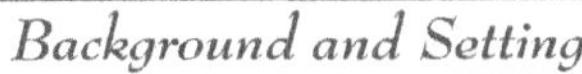


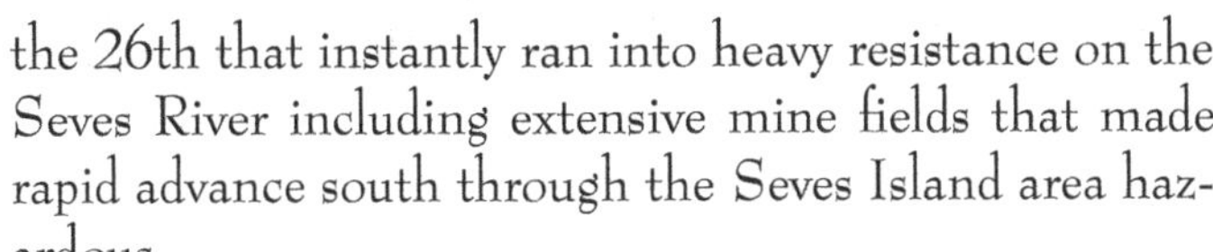

the 26th that instantly ran into heavy resistance on the Seves River including extensive mine fields that made rapid advance south through the Seves Island area hazardous.

During the night of the 26th-27th, the enemy in front of the 90th pulled out, enabling the Division to move farther south to liberate Periers on the 27th and then St. Sauver Lendelin the same day.

On the 28th, the 4th Armored Division passed through the 90th while the 6th Armored passed through the 83rd Division to the left (See *Appendix* for *Troop Levels*). The 90th continued to push some elements southward. However, late in the day, both the 90th and the 83rd were directed to stand fast so that the 8th and 79th Divisions could pass through and follow close behind the 4th and 6th Armored Divisions in order to exploit the breakthrough towards Avranches and beyond. It was during this brief halt for rest and reorganization that Gen Landrum was relieved and replaced by Brig Gen Ray McClain.

On the 1st of August, the Division again got under way, this time by motor, and moved south through Coutance and Avranches. The mission was to set up blocking positions east of Avranches, between the See and Selune Rivers, to protect the dams on the Selune River, and to capture Louvigne and make contact with the 79th Division on the 90th's right.

On the 5th of August, the 90th was ordered to seize and secure crossings over the Mayenne River, between Mayenne and Leval, some 30 miles distant. To accomplish this, task force Weaver was formed. The 90th was finally gaining resounding success in battle. The opportunity was rapidly forthcoming, for they were to play a key part in devastating the German Seventh Army in the Falaise Pocket. It was the 90th's 359th Regiment that fought north and closed the Falaise Pocket by meeting the Polish forces that were fighting their way south.

Bill at this time was about to be inducted into the U.S. Army at Fort Snelling, Minnesota. He would then be dispatched to Camp Hood, Texas where he would undergo extensive basic training. He and the men with him learning close order drill, extended order drill, hasty field fortifications, field sanitation, weaponry maintenance, markmanship, military courtesy, map reading, potato peeling, and dishwashing.

### *Battle of the Falaise Pocket*

*Nothing is as strong as the heart of a volunteer.*
LTC Jimmy Doolittle

Hitler's order directing Von Kluge's Seventh Army to attack Mortain and cut off the twelve American divisions that had passed through the area not only failed but it led to the German Seventh Army's virtual destruction in the Falaise-Argentan region. The Seventh was partly encircled by the American 1st and 3rd Armies. British and Canadian forces slugged their way south in an effort to close the trap. Von Kluge, realizing his predicament, on August 21st ordered his divisions to make their way out of the trap as best they could. He then committed suicide.

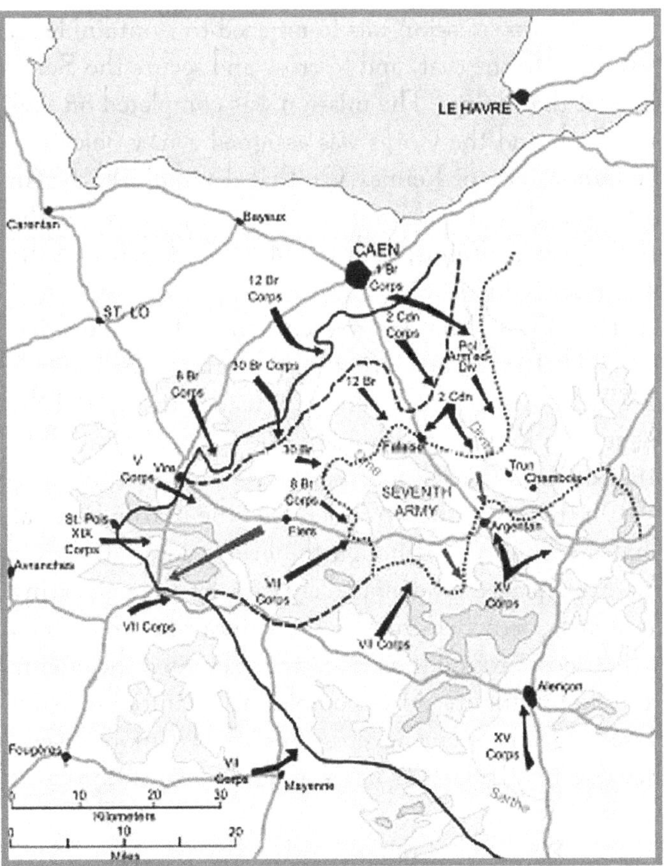


The major route of retreat was a road running southeast from Falaise through Chambois, twenty-five kilometers away. The road ran through a valley and on both sides the high ground provided excellent observation of any actions and movements the enemy made. In a period of four days, the 90th took more than 13,000 prisoners, killed or wounded an estimated 8,000 Germans, but suffered less than 600 casualties. More than 300 enemy tanks, 250 self-propelled guns, 164 artillery pieces, 3,270 vehicles, and a variety of other types of equipment and weapons were destroyed.

### *Pursuit Across France*

*May God have mercy upon my enemies, because I won't.*
Gen. George S. Patton (General of the Third Army to which Bill would be attached)

After a few days of rest near Chambois, the 90th was reassigned to XX Corps and the Third Army. The American Seventh Army and the French First Army landed at Marseilles in southern France on August 25th, so the enemy was either surrounded or overwhelmed at every turn. The Germans were in a state of confusion.

XX Corps' mission was to proceed to Fontainbleau, 176 miles to the east, and to cross and secure the Seine River at that point. The mission was completed on August 26th and the Corps was assigned a new objective, the famous city of Reims. On that day the 90th began to move. The 7th Armored Division spearheaded the attack towards Reims, with the 90th on its left and the 5th on its right.

The 357th Infantry was chosen to lead the Division. The drive carried it through famous battlefields of WWI, through the Marne, Chateau Thierry, and the Aisne – to Reims. Verdun and the River Meuse fell to other units of the XX Corps.

On the 28th, the 357th crossed the Marne River at Chateau Thierry. Although the bridge across the river had been placed under artillery fire by the retreating Germans, French Forces of the Interior had remained at their post around the bridge and prevented the enemy from destroying it. After completing its initial mission of seizing and securing crossings of two more rivers, they covered the last 23 miles on foot. The 90th was in the Reims area until September 6. The pursuit across France was over. The next task was to close to the Moselle River and attack the Maginot Line.

### *Moselle-Saar Campaign*

Continuing eastward against ever increasing German resistance, this campaign involved several of the 90th's most important and difficult battles. The greatest obstacles in their path were the Moselle and Saar Rivers, backed by the Maginot and Siegfried Lines. Their successful surprise crossing of the Moselle near Thionville, at a point where the river was to expand in width from less than 300 feet to over a mile because of flooding, was perhaps the most renowned of all their operations. This was followed by the epic fight to seize Fort Koenigsmacher, breaking the ring of defenses around Metz and leading to the first capture of Metz in modern history. Then, in November, on to battles at the Siegfried Line, which involved a most difficult crossing of the Saar without bridges. Further progress against the Siegfried was abruptly interrupted by the German attack in the Ardennes, the Battle of the Bulge.

On January 13, 1945 Bill was in a contingent of soldiers sent as replacements for the 357th Regiment. He was a member of Company F. Although he had an M.O. (Military Occupation) as a cook, he had volunteered to be a scout for his company. It must be noted that infantry riflemen suffered the bulk of war casualties. And, further noted, that the designation as a scout meant that he, alone or sometimes in concert with one other scout, would precede the company into hostile territory in an attempt to locate enemy positions. The scout became a prime target for enemy snipers and was often the first to experience combat conditions as elements of the unit moved toward an objective.

*Who is a hero? My heroes are the young men who faced the issues of war and possible death, and then weighed those concerns against obligations to their country . . . not for fame or reward, not for place or for rank, but in simple obedience to duty as they understood it.*

James Webb, Secretary of the Navy (1944-1947)

Bill was owner of the Waukon Bakery, a business he had bought in 1938 when he was 18 years old, and on February 22, 1944 he married Marge Leet.

His profession as a baker was considered an "essential trade" during World War II and thus, he was exempt from military duty (if he so desired). The production and distribution of bread and bread products was extremely important to the American economy. At that time in history, there were no commercial bakeries, as we know them today. Nearly every small town had a local bakery. Large cities had neighborhood bakeries to serve the various areas of each city.

When Bill and Marge got married in 1944, Marge must have had the feeling that she and Bill would be safe from the ravages of war. Little did she know that Bill would have a patriotic urge to join the military.

That urge was exacerbated by the urgent Call to Arms by the United States government for young men to join the war effort. The June invasion of Europe by Allied troops at Normandy (D-Day) precipitated the need for more manpower. Certainly the fighting in North Africa, Italy, and the Pacific added to the need for more men and women; the death and wounded toll ever increased because of the heavy fighting taking place.

When the call came for young men to enlist, Bill decided that he too would join several of his friends and brothers who were already serving the military in Europe and the Pacific.

One can only imagine the fear that must have gripped Marge when it became apparent that her husband of

only a few months would place himself in harm's way.

On August 17, 1944, Bill was inducted into the U.S. Army at Fort Snelling, Minnesota. From there he was sent to Camp Hood, Texas for his Basic Training.

The trip to Basic Training in Texas was a three day (non-stop) train ride that apparently was quite uncomfortable for the troops. He arrived at Ft. Hood on August 30, and then faced the trials of Basic Training.

Bill also wrote a letter to his brother, John, on August 31, shortly after arriving in Texas. Of note in this letter is the fact that Bill writes strictly about the military experience; John having served his tour of duty already and more able to understand what Bill was experiencing at this time. John, therefore, agreed to help Marge with the bakery. Her only other ally was Amanda, Bill's mother, who worked there and knew a lot about the business.

Following the six to seven weeks of basic training he was assigned to Cook Training and served there until his orders to ship to Europe came through in late December, 1944. Dedication to each other prompts both Bill and Marge to write daily. This makes their lives bearable during this period of separation.

We are fortunate to have a written history of Waldron life and grateful that first Marge, and later the Waldron children, preserved the family letters. As you read, it is possible to feel the anticipation of what was to come from Bill's letters and sense the fact that he was not receiving a stream of letters from Marge because he was unable to provide an address until late August or early September.

Marge continues to communicate to Bill about the goings-on at the bakery. Often she will recite the day's receipts to Bill, e.g. $185 one days sales, $428 for a week's receipts. Not only does Marge keep Bill apprised of what is going on at the bakery but she relates some of the local news about friends and family.

Bill started receiving Marge's letters around September 3. One of the issues of military (APO - Army Post Office) mail is that delivery was not regular. Sometimes several letters arrive on the same day. And that situation existed in both directions. Both Bill and Marge note, in some of their letters, that they "had not received a letter" on specific days, but then they happily state that they received multiple letters a few days later. The receipt of letters from loved ones weighs heavily on all soldiers. That is the one thing that is greatly anticipated. There is disappointment when a letter does not arrive at mail call. And there is apparent euphoria when those letters and packages do arrive. Letters are read over and over until the next arrives.

During Bill's basic training period at Fort Hood, Texas there were frequent time lapses where he was unable to correspond with Marge. Long days of training and periods of fatigue made it difficult for him to take the time or muster the energy to write. This is pointed out in several of his letters home.

Marge notes frequently in her letters, what a hard worker Stan is in the bakery. Stan is still a high school student. He obviously took to the bakery work, as he opened his own bakery a few years after graduating from high school. He was a lifesaver for Marge and he often skipped school to help Marge get the baking done.

Bill is able to sufficiently keep Marge and Jim and Amanda (his parents) informed about his life as a soldier in basic training. He is specific about several phases of the training. One can ascertain that Bill has taken well to the training, and is able to withstand the short hours of sleep, the physical part of the training and the loneliness of being away from Marge, family and friends. Not only does Bill show compassion to Marge, as she toils at the bakery, but he makes sure that his parents know that they can count on him to help them financially in these trying times.

It is important to note the tone of Bill's letters to his parents, as compared to the tone in letters to Marge. Much uncertainty surfaces in the content of the letters that Bill has begun to write.

He appears to be informative with what is contained in the letters to Jim and Amanda, yet more specific with information in Marge's letters. Bill is trying to be somewhat complacent in the letters to Marge, obviously trying not to worry her any more than she already is.

Summer 1944 prior to joining up, Bill, Dorothy Luther and Harold Kosbau on the steps of the original bakery.

The weight of having to operate the bakery is certainly a burden that Marge is facing.

Marge is hopeful, in her letters to Bill, that he will get a furlough following his six-week basic training period. Bill has a tendency to be somewhat pragmatic about getting that leave time. Surely, he wants that furlough as much as Marge does, but it appears he is preparing himself for the disappointment in the event that leave time is not granted. He mentions this in a letter to Jim and Amanda but does not mention it to Marge.

As the month of September gets closer to that of October, Bill states an assumption that he will be in the occupation forces once he arrives in Europe. The war has progressed well for the Allied Forces, as they continue to drive Hitler's troops out of France and back to the German borders. Of course, little did they know in September that Hitler's forces would begin to see the end and fight ferociously in an attempt to save their homeland from Allied victory. Once the replacement troops, of which Bill would be a member, arrived in Europe, they would be faced with some of the war's fiercest combat.

It became more inevitable that Bill would be shipped to the European Theatre of combat. During the month of December his letters became more subdued with a touch of anxiousness, as the uncertainty of a shipping date approached. Marge expressed a strong desire to travel to Texas to visit Bill before the inevitable. In reality, it could be the last time they might see each other.

Marge was able to join him in Texas during the Thanksgiving holiday and part of November. She was able to make arrangements to take the train from Oelwein to Camp Hood, Texas. She left Waukon/Oelwein on, or about, October 29 and arrived in Texas around November 1. Marge was able to connect with Waukon friend Sis Goltz in Oklahoma during a stop-over. In a letter from Sis, dated November 20, she informed Marge that her husband, Dale, was being sent to Ft Hood in late November. That was bound to excite Marge, as she would have a good acquaintance from home for a period of time. The bakery was left in the dedicated hands of Grandma (Amanda) Waldron with capable workers Stan Waldron (brother) and Veryle Paulson (Marge's first cousin).

Because of the uncertainty of Bill's ship date to Europe (the US Army offering no information to soldiers or their families about when they would be shipped overseas. This is with good cause, as the military was aware of possible leaks about troop movement that the enemy could get their hands on) it was decided that Marge would return to Waukon. She had been able to spend over a month in Texas with Bill.

They were able to share New Years Eve in Kansas City, Missouri before he shipped overseas. A footnote to this is that Janice (Jan), their first child, was born in September of 1945, while Bill served as part of the Occupation Forces in Germany.

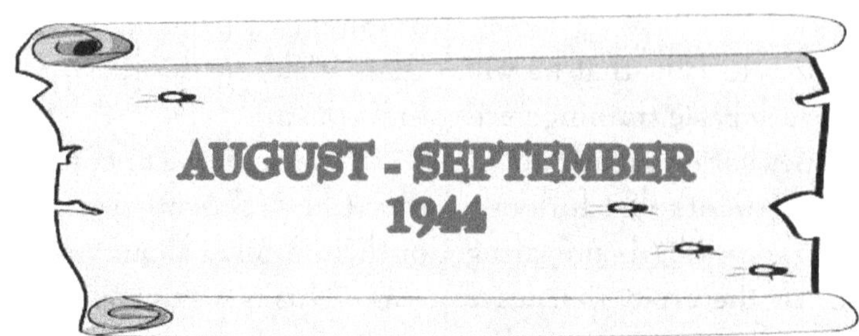


*June 16, 1943 - From Bill & Marge to John, Serving in Africa*

*Dear John,*

*Bill asked me to write to you as he just can't find time too. Isn't that a laugh? He said they got a couple of letters from you last week and believe me, they really are glad to hear from you.*

*I suppose you don't have much time to yourself out there. Bill worked pretty hard this winter but now that he has Stan working in the bakery, it is a lot easier for him. Of course he makes the rest of them work.*

*Boy, is the town ever dead. Most of the kids are gone now. Ralph Anderson, John Luther, Tommy Collins were inducted this week so they will have to do some celebrating.*

*There are a few dances around yet but not so many people to go. The Luther girls usually go to all of them. We went over to Matter's last night for a while. It's nothing like it used to be. We were talking to Phyllis Ramlo and she said Veneda has a swell job in Florida. That's plenty O.K. We hear she had left Decorah but didn't know where she was.*

*Do you hear from Danny? Bill got a letter soon after he left but has never heard since.*

*What did you think about Vernon and Beck getting married? Your mother said you didn't expect him to do it. She really is a grand girl. She was coming up but if Vern goes to Peoria, she probably won't.*

*Cowan is in Crowder, Mo. Lila is working at the Polar Bear (Black and White now) but she says she's going to quit. We picked her up after work Monday nite and we buzzed out to the Mark and drank a couple beers. It's the same old place but all farmers now and believe me they get drunk. Bill says I keep him out too late Sat. nites to go out there anymore and does he ever feel bad. Maybe there would be someone like Lorna Wilde out there.*

*We never hear from Harold Kosbau cause we never got around to writing until this week. He is in Idaho, flying and I guess he really likes it so Goldie says.*

*Riley is out to Churchtown in the creamery. You know him, believe me, he runs the place. He went to Matters with us last nite and got sort of full.*

Editor's Note: Side bar text that appears in the color blue indicates information pertaining to the letter next to it.

---------

The United States had been at war for just over a year and a half and this letter, from 1943, gives a sense of small town America in those days.

Prices at local Waukon stores at that time:

| | |
|---|---|
| Men's wool suit | $32.50 |
| Men's business shirt | 2.50 |
| Girl's cotton blouse | 1.80 |
| Hershey candy bar | .05 |
| Coke | .05 |
| Kelloggs Corn Flakes | .08 |
| Gasoline | .21/gal |
| Bread | .08/loaf |
| Milk | .62/gal |
| Postage Stamp | .03 |

| | |
|---|---|
| Average Annual Salary | $2,600.00 |
| Car | 1,220.00 |

*New cars were becoming impossible to buy.*

| | |
|---|---|
| House | $8,600.00 |

Stock Market 152

Minimum Wage
$ .30 cents per hour

*We don't drink much - just once a week or so. The limit is a quart a week here. How about you? Do you ever get a chance to get stewed?*

*There are some things I told Bill I wouldn't write so he said he'd finish.*

*Be sure and write, John*

Bill's additional note

*I had Marge write you all the gossip because she's pretty good at it.*

*Write soon.*

*Bill*

John had been honorably discharged from the Army due to health reasons; he had been wounded (shrapnel in the knee) in North Africa and later contracted malaria. He returned home, via Chicago. He was to play an important part in the bakery while Bill was in the Service.

On this date in 1944, the Battle of Eniwetok Atoll began and would end in an American victory on February 22.

Feb. 17, 1944 Chicago - From John to Bill

*Dear Bill,*

*Just a couple of lines to let you know when I am coming home. I was going to leave Sun but they wanted me to work and if I do I'll make about $19 from Sun alone so I am going to work Sun. and will be there Mon.*

*I will call the bakery when I get to Prairie. I leave here at 9:00 o clock in the morning so I'll call around 1:00. I have been sick all week but have been working it same as hell when you have to work as when you are sick.*

*Well, I am going to close, will see you Mon. So long till then.*

*Your Broth,*

*Johnie*

Bill reported to Ft. Snelling (St. Paul, Minnesota) for induction into the Army.

He is finding out, in short order, about the Armies' "hurry up and wait" philosophy.

Billboard's Number One Song on this date was *Swinging on a Star* by Bing Crosby.

August 17, 1944 - From Bill to Marge

*Dear Marge,*

*We took our exam today. Two or three didn't pass theirs. I don't know when we'll leave here, maybe not till next week.*

*I'm going in to see Aunt Stella tonight. I'll call you before I leave here. The grub and bed has been good so far. We got up here about eight last night and have been waiting most of the time since.*

*With love*

*Bill*

Recruits are able to leave the Reception Center at Ft. Snelling in the evenings and on weekends.

In a joint venture by Harvard and IBM the first computer is unveiled. The whole apparatus measured 55 feet long.

On or about this date, an insurrection starts in Paris.

August 17, 1944 (Second Letter) - From Bill to Marge

*Dear Marge, I went down to Minn last night and found Aunt Stell at the Curtis Hotel. She got off work at seven o'clock. Grant Allison was with me and we went across the street and had a few bottles of that 1.6 point beer. Then she took us down to another place where they had a floorshow. Nothing like the one in Milwaukee though. We had our pictures taken there. She'll give you mine when she comes down. We sure had a swell time though. We can go out ever night until 12 but I think that will be the only night I go out. I was split up from Grant this morning. He's quite a ways behind some of the boys and here a week or so behind when they get sworn* in.

I was this afternoon. Larry Brown, Thoma and Klemme from ---- also were. We're all in the same barracks. The guys sure can't kick about the grub or anything here except they make you hurry like Hell to wait. We'll probably be here a week or two before we're shipped out. They're sending them to Texas, Arkansas and Alabama.

I made a few bucks yesterday so I've still got as much as when I left. No pinochle though.

I've a kid from North Dakota bunking with me. I sure hope the bakery is getting along all right. It seems kinda funny sleeping alone. I suppose you kind of miss your husband being home at night too eh?

Some of these guys are here from last week yet and haven't been sworn in.

After you try figuring out my scribbling you won't be quite as anxious to hear from me. You won't be able to write me when I get shipped out because they say they don't know when we leave here. We get shots tomorrow. I guess I suppose Veryle and that lover of hers are still sitting out on me. You letting them use the upstairs on Sat. night? Tell John I haven't heard them whistles yet but there's been ------ -bellowing over the microphone half the night

Lots of love,

Bill

August 21, 1944 - From Bill to Marge

Dear Marge,

We made it back to camp by 9:30 Sunday night. Got our dog tags today and seen a few shows (training) and heard a few lectures. In the morning looks like some of us will go on K.P. from 3:30 to 4:30.

They shipped out a bunch here and hard telling how long we will be here from a few days to a month. Some guys have been here for a month. They take a few from each bunch and not ship any of them from the same place together. You can start writing to me now.

We got moved to Co 1 today.

They didn't have hardly any draftee's coming in today. I'll probably be home again Sat night if I don't get stuck for detail work. I made 4 o'clock chow so I'm getting a -----.

Klemme and me are going to the 6 o'clock show. I sent my clothes home today. You'll probably get them before this letter.

We spent about an hour down in the sand pile this afternoon cleaning our canteens and mess kits. I hope things in the bakery are still going all right.

I hope you catch a few fish for me too If you go this week. Sunday if I get home, I'm figuring on going back on the Zephyr at 8 o'clock if I can make it. I would get in at Eleven. I

Bill mentions trying to figure out his "scribbling," and, while Jan did a fantastic job of transcibing the letters and putting them on the computer, there are places where it was impossible to tell what some words were. When that occurs, it will be indicated with the symbol "-----."

**Waukon Locals**

William Waldron and Arthur Klemme, both of whom were inducted into the army at Ft. Snelling, Minn., last week, were given a weekend furlough and spent it with home folks here, the former's wife meeting them at Cresco Saturday night. "Billy" is owner of the Waukon Bakery and would have been granted a deferment had he asked for same but refused to do so, being loyal to his country.

Mailed from the Reception Center at Fort Snelling, MN this letter is written in pencil and is very faint.

Bill is planning on taking the train to Prairie du Chien to spend a day or two in Waukon.

On August 20, American forces successfully defeat Nazi forces at Chambois, closing the Falaise Gap.

On August 22, *Tsushima Maru*, a Japanese unmarked passenger/cargo ship is sunk by torpedoes launched by the submarine USS Bowfin off Akuseki-jima, killing 1,484 civilians.

could catch a taxi and make it to Snelling before 12. We'll go down to the river in the afternoon.

Say Hello to everybody for me. There's nothing else I can think of except I'll be remembering tomorrow.

Lots of love

Bill

This letter is not dated but the postmark is August 24 from St. Paul.

On this date, the Allies liberated Paris, successfully completing Operation Overlord.

Oscar was the nickname of Bill's brother, Stan.

On August 25, Hungary decides to continue the war together with Germany.

Vernon was drafted in December, 1942 and became a member of the 359th Engineers. He served until two months after the war ended.

August 24, 1944 - From Bill to Jim and Amanda

Dear folks,

Well, I'm getting around to writing again. I hope everyone is OK. How's Dad's arm coming? Is he going to be back to work before long? I'm going to have to break down and get my hair cut one of these days. They have got good barbers here to. They will cut it the way you want it. There is one civilian barber, boy, I think they really make the money. They work from the time they come till they leave. Are you keeping John & Oscar on the ball teams? I would of liked to seen John's girl when I was home.

There are sure a swell bunch of fellows here, of course there are a few of the boys so homesick, they cry themselves to sleep. The guy next bunk to me goes to bed about 6:30 every night and lays awake most of the night. I've got an upper bunk and I expect to wake up some morning and find myself on the floor. I still sleep as sound as ever. It rains like hell here all night and I never heard it. The guy that comes around to wake us in the morning usually has to just about tip the bunk over to wake me up. When you write to Beck, say hello to her and the young dad for me. Tell her to keep him out of the beer taverns till his old man comes home to take him on a good one. Tell Vernon they told us up here as (that as) quick as we finish our basic training, we'll be shipped overseas. Never can tell. I might get a chance to see him yet. I'll be waiting to hear from you folks.

Your son,

Bill

Postmarked Ft. Snelling but probably written in transit to Texas.

On August 29, the Slovak National Uprising against the Axis powers begins.

August 28, 1944 - From Bill to Marge

Dear Marge

We won't get there till Tuesday. I'll call then. We don't have a chance to write a line. It is so goddamn rough just like a box car. We got off here for 1/2 hour. I'll write soon.

Bill

This letter is postmarked Ft. Hood, TX and Bill begins his basic training.

August 30, 1944 - From Bill to Marge

Dear Marge,

I thought I'd write again. It will probably be longer yet before I hear from you. I got moved over to a rifle co. today. All the new guys, they sure make sure you don't stay with anyone you know but I'm getting acquainted with a new guy that came through and all guys are starting basic Monday. Only have 6 weeks basic and then are transferred to another camp so I guess I won't be here near as long as I thought. The Sarg. just told us a few minutes ago. This basic training now don't mean we'll be in the infantry after we are through. It sounded like they will send us anywhere - field artillery, Eng (?) or any of those branches.

I don't think you had better figure on coming down here because it would take you a week to get here and go back and we can only get a pass for weekends from 6 Sat to 11 Sun and you are never sure of getting one. When you plan on it you might get stuck on night detail or K.P. Sunday morning. The K.P. here is nothing like at Fort Snelling. Only for 1/2 day at a time and they are not near as particular. Everybody has to do it every so often. I haven't had it yet but I'll get it. I've been taking John's advice about the not volunteering for anything. Some of these guys that volunteer get some crap to do and then find their name on K.P. in the morning. There is one guy in our barracks here that is going to start with us, I guess. He came in about 3 months ago but went over the hill for 24 days and just came back. He hasn't been court marshaled yet. Tell John a PFC is a big man around this place. He does a hell of a lot more bossing and hollers more than the Sarg. or Liet. Say when are you going to sent that letter of Luther's? I'd like to see what she has to say. Is she still as much in love with her husband or do you think she's out getting a little strawtail? There are a pile of things I need but I suppose I better wait and see if I can get them at the P.X. when we get to go there. The cadre men get our cigarettes and things like that for us. You can keep on sending the paper as it is a pretty good pastime. We don't get a chance to see a magazine or paper yet. A guy don't hardly get time here to get homesick but I still don't think it's near as hard as working in a bakery.

Lots of Love

Bill

On August 31, the *Mad Gasser of Matton* struck again.

In 1933-34 a number of incidents occurred in Virginia wherein some 15 people reported seeing suspects in the process of spreading gas and fumes. Nobody was ever caught nor convicted on these crimes.

The second report of these incidents happened in Matton, Illinois on August 31. There were 26 reports of smelling gas and seeing suspects spreading fumes. Often, the suspect was described as a man dressed as a woman. The reported sightings lasted until September 13.

Again, no-one was ever caught by the authorities and two credible explanations were given by the experts.

First, that these were the work of Axis sympathizers working to disrupt civilian life in the U.S.

The more plausible explanation was that, given the times, this was an example of mass hysteria. Daily, the civilian population was warned of Nazi sympathizers, called 5th Columnists, doing dirty deeds for the Fatherland. Many thought that someone started the first rumor of the gasser and the idea simply caught on.

We'll probably never know.

## August 31, 1944 - From Bill to John

Dear John,

Well I've got time so I suppose I'd better write. I was in an antitank Co. the final couple days but they split up most of them up and sent them to different rifle battalions for the last couple weeks. The Sarg. told us tonight that the Basic was cut to six weeks and then we get sent out of here. The battalion I was in sure served rotten grub and no butter but over here it's just the opposite. Lots of butter and good food. We were out drilling most of the day yesterday. I didn't have any trouble with my right or left. You can't walk outside of the barracks hardly without meeting an officer. If you don't

John, who had served and been discharged, would enjoy and understand the military references. He was working at the bakery and helping Marge at this time.

Bill uses both the designation "Camp Hood" and "Fort Hood" in different letters.

salute them, they take your name and see to it that you do a little K.P. or detail.

I don't know whether you were ever in Texas or not but it sure surprised me. The country isn't much different than around home except lots hotter. I guess we just missed the hot weather. It's been raining ever since we came Mon. but that's a lot better than the hot weather. This camp is all wood and mud here, no grass but they have just build this camp in the last two years. There is supposed to be between 165,000 and 200,000 men here now. The barracks I was in before you couldn't play cards of any kind but we can here. I've still got just about as much money as I had when I left and I bought cigarettes and everything. Even loaned a little money which I suppose I'll never see but its pretty tough on some of these guys who haven't been able to have any sent. Some of them, their mail don't get a chance to catch up to them.

Say hello to Ray and Stan for me.

Brother Bill

September 1, 1944 - From Viola to Bill

Written from Waukon by Marge's mom, Viola.

Dear Bill,

Hello, this is Friday morning and the sun is shining. It seems like the first in days. It has rained for days and been so cold, do hope we have nice warm weather this month.

We are the same as usual but pretty lonesome around here.

How are you with the shots you have been getting? Do you have to work when you don't feel well?

On this date, King George VI promoted Bernard Montgomery to the rank of Field Marshall.

Dad went to farm to start putting the tin roofing on the shed. He has the potatoes (?) about dug but not many.

How is the weather there? I hope not so cold and rainy.

Lula and Byron up yesterday for dinner. They are painting their house.

Are you with any of the boys that you know? Marge just came to get coat hangers to send to you.

Lots of Love,

Mother and Dad

September 2, 1944, 12:20 AM - From Marge to Bill

Throughout the letters of September, 1944 there is a sense of disappointment from both Bill and Marge as they have not yet realized that APO mail did not come on a regular basis. This creates angst from both ends of the postal delivery system.

In these letters, one can feel that loneliness is now, and will continue to be, a haunting fact during their separation.

Dearest Bill,

What is the matter honey? Have you forgotten your wife already? I feel so badly because I didn't get a letter from you today. Sent Veryle up after the mail this afternoon but no soap - I hope you wrote to but gee, from Fri aft. till Monday aft. is a long wait. I hope you have received my letters by now. When you once get them, they should come regular cause I send them all the time.

This is really a long day and talk about work to do - it was terrible. Had white cakes and etc. but we got thru. I came home at six and went back at eight. Jeanne Fitz came home *today so of course she came in. She wanted me to go out with her and have a coke so we went to the S + D. Bill Daugherty, Kenny Neubauer and Chilton Loedes asked us to sit with them so we did. I had a little drink of whiskey, the first since you left.*

*Then after we went back to the bakery, Riley and Bill were in there. I drank a glass of beer with Veryle and Jeanne then. Marie and Ray were there - I am going to spend my time up there this winter. I have to learn to drink beer. So......I know I won't. (And she never did)*

*What did you have today? I've been wondering what you are doing tonight. The weather is simple wonderful here tonight and the moon is so bright it makes me awful lonesome for my man. It has been two weeks tonite since you were home. Gee, I wish you were here with me tonite but wishing doesn't help.*

*John, Stan, Mother, Jeanne and Marie went to Monti (Monticello) about 6:00 this afternoon in our car. I really miss it too - had to walk home after we locked up tonight. $185 today but we have quite a bit of stuff left. Sold so darn many cookies tonight.*

*The folks are going to the (Waukon) Junction tomorrow so Veryle and I are going. Guess I'll ask Char too. Dad wants to go fishing but we won't catch any. Kreeb's wanted me to come up for dinner but I called her tonite and said I would some other time.*

*Stan really put in a day and worked till almost three this aft. But then he and Bobbie played a lot. I really don't know what to make of Bob. He can't do anything without being told and he doesn't remember from one day to the next what to do. I had to scrape and sweep the floor tonight after he had said he did it.*

*Mass is at 8:00 and 10:00 from now on so I won't have to get up quite so early. Guess I'll go early tomorrow. Will you have any chance to go? You can say your rosary at least and I'll pray for you too honey (for the day I can see you).*

*I tried to get some white washcloths and an iron but there aren't any. Can you see any other color? I'll keep trying to get them tho. Anything else you want or need?*

*Well, darling, guess I will retire for the nite. I'm really pretty tired tonite. I'll be thinking about you waiting for the mailman. Please write to me honey as that is all I have of you now. Do you still love your wife a little: She surely does you and how.*

*Your loving wife,*

*Marge*

Marge and Bill had committed to each other to try to write letters every day.

For Bill, this would be difficult, what with all of the physicals, the basic instructions for their military order, and the "hurry up and wait" attitude of military life. During his basic training at Ft. Hood, there would be little leisure time fit in between constant marching/drilling, rifle training, more physicals and shots, and learning military discipline; the free hours were very limited.

And, once Bill was sent to Europe, he entered combat immediately.

However, to his credit, Bill found, or made, time to write Marge nearly every day.

Marge did likewise, despite long and tedious hours at the bakery.

The reader of Marge's letters will notice a different tone than what comes across from Bill's letters.

The woman's touch in her words; that of a more tender, endearing tone. Marge has a tendency to be more explicit in respect to goings-on in Waukon, plus she tried to keep Bill aware of issues and progress at the bakery.

From Bill, a more matter-of-fact tone. Of course, it is Bill's nature to try not to worry Marge, especially during the months of heavy combat he faced in Europe.

On this date, The Holocaust diarist Anne Frank and her family were placed on the last transport train from Westerbork to Auschwitz, arriving 3 days later.

**IMMUNIZATION REGISTER[1]**

| LAST NAME | FIRST NAME | ARMY SERIAL NO. |
|---|---|---|
| WALDRON, | WILLIAM K | 37 772 525 |

| GRADE | COMPANY | REGT. OR STAFF CORPS[1] | AGE | RACE |
|---|---|---|---|---|
| Pvt. | | | 23 | W |

**SMALLPOX VACCINE**

| DATE | TYPE OF REACTION[6] | MED. OFFICER[4] |
|---|---|---|
| AUG 2 9 1944 | [illegible] | |

**TRIPLE TYPHOID VACCINE**

| SERIES | 1ST DOSE | 2D DOSE | 3D DOSE | MED. OFFICER[3] |
|---|---|---|---|---|
| 1st | 19 Aug | AUG 2 9 1944 | SEP 11 | |
| 2d | | | | |
| 3d | 9-10-45 | | | [illegible] |

**TETANUS TOXOID**

| INITIAL VACCINATION | DATE | MED. OFF.[3] | STIMULATING DOSES | DATE | MED. OFF.[3] |
|---|---|---|---|---|---|
| 1st dose | 19 AUG '44 | [illegible] | | | |
| 2d dose | SEP 11 '44 | | | | |
| 3d dose | OCT 9 '44 | | | | |

**YELLOW FEVER VACCINE**

| DATE | LOT No. | AMOUNT | MED. OFF.[3] |
|---|---|---|---|
| | | | |

**OTHER VACCINES**

| TYPE OF VACCINE | DATE | MFR'S. LOT No. | AMOUNT | MED. OFF.[3] |
|---|---|---|---|---|
| | BLOOD TYPE A | | | [illegible] |
| Typhus | 6 Jan 45 | | | [illegible] |
| " | 17 Jan 45 | | | [illegible] |
| Typhus Stim. | 5-18-45 | | | |

*Bill's Immunization Register*

Even today, only in small town America would you think of asking the local cop to stop in at 2 AM and start your oven. Wonder if he had a key or if he even needed one?

As a footnote, the cop was asked and helped out. In later years, if Bill wasn't open in the wee hours of the morning, when he was supposed to be, the cops would call him and wake him up. Not completely altruistic, they would stop in to have coffee during their early morning shifts.

The family had to be concerned about Vernon as he was in Europe at the time. He was supposed to be at Normandy but wasn't involved as he was transfered to the 1301[st] Engineers just prior to the invasion.

<u>September 3, 1944, Sunday - From Bill to Marge</u>

*Dear Marge,*

*Well, Marge I got the first letters from you this noon and was I ever glad to get it. You ought to see the look on some of these boys' faces that hadn't got any mail yet. I get down to the P.X. last night to get stuff for our barracks but I didn't have enough time to call. I didn't get to church this morning either. They moved us all around and put us in different barracks and in platoons. I'm in the fourth and our address will still be the same now tho. We had a good dinner here today. Chicken, ice cream and different vegetables. They really feed us good here.*

*I did my washing again a little while ago. It only takes it about an hour to dry here when the sun is shining. Tomorrow we are supposed to start drilling with combat pack and rifle, and then we won't have a minute to ourselves. I sleep on an upper bunk now. I sure hate to crawl out of there in the morning. This morning we didn't have to get up till seven because of it being Sun. I guess in a week or two, I'll be able to start going to church although some of the guys who have been here 5 months told me they never had a chance to go in camp.*

*I'm glad to hear you've got everything under control. If the oven don't heat up fast enough for them at night, I think you can get the cop to start it about an hour early. Is Doris still staying with Veryle? Have you been down to the cabin lately or done any more work on it.*

*Has Hank been over to help any days yet? We do all of our writing here in our bunks. This is a pretty quick day here - everybody is shaving, washing clothes, writing letters, reading and taking showers. What do the folks hear from Vernon? Is he still in France? I thought I would really be stiff today from the exercises yesterday but they didn't stiffen me at all. Some of these older guys get so stiff they can hardly move. We won't know for a while just how many weeks we'll have here but most of the non-coms say 6. I hope they're right but I guess there are a lot of worse camps. That's pretty good about Marg. Luther. What does Maggie have to say about it? I think I better write (a) letter to the folks. I haven't wrote to them here yet.*

*Lots of love*

*Your Husband*

<u>September 3, 1944, Sunday - From Bill to Jim and Amanda</u>

*Dear Folks,*

*I'm finally getting around to writing again. I hope everybody is all right at home.*

*How's Vernon coming? Have you been down to see Beck's baby yet? When you write to Vernon tell him you never can tell, I might get a chance to see him there yet. All the compa-*

*nies that have left here went to Maryland and then overseas, they tell us. We would make up the army of occupation but they don't know hell of a lot more about it than anyone else, I guess.*

*Tell John these cadre men are mostly all back from the South Pacific for rest but they get worked harder than anyone else. I guess we are finally settled in on permanent bunks. The Army can sure figure out more ways to waste time than anyplace you ever saw. These guys here run all the way from 18 to 50 in age, I think. There are a couple fellows look to be 50 I suppose. You can just about imagine me working all (of the) time and shaving every day. Our officers all seem like nice guys. Of course, there are some of these guys who never did a days work who get their ass ate out. We might only get six weeks training here and then get a furlough. All the Co. before all got furloughs when they finished. Some of them had to lay around here for two or three weeks when they finished before they got theirs. I think the Army sure will make chiselers out of a lot of men. I've been writing to Marge every day since I've been down here. I guess things are going pretty good in the bakery, aren't they?*

*I got my first letter this noon from her. It takes a long time for mail to catch up with you here. This Texas isn't such bad country if it weren't quite so hot. I was really lucky not getting in until now instead of a month or two ago. I guess they dropped like flies in the heat. There have been a few in our Co. that did this week but it wasn't any hotter than at home. It cools off pretty good here at night. We are about 40 min. from the closest decent size town. Well, write when you folks have time.*

*Your son,*

*Bill*

September 4, 1944 - From Ens. Harold Kosbau to Marge

*U.S. Naval Auxiliary Air Station*
*Green Cove Springs, Florida*

*Dear Marg,*

*I sort of feel guilty for not writing before but if you know how I hate to write letters, that might help.*

*I heard Bill was some place in Texas and would sure love to have his address. I imagine you are pretty busy woman now that he is gone but I'd appreciate a letter now and then informing me about Waukon. I don't hear from anyone in Waukon any more except the folks and they don't get down town much.*

*I've been in Florida 3 weeks and haven't flown an hr. since I got here but I'm going to start this week. I'm going to fly Corsairs' when we get started.*

*I haven't heard from Jim since I was home. Is he still in North Carolina? I heard Lila was home. Say hello to her if*

On this date, word was received that an American patriot "may" be alive.

Idaho-born Marine aviator Gregory "Pappy" Boyington, 31, shot down three Japanese planes January 3, 1944 but was himself shot down in Rabaul harbor, picked up by a Japanese submarine, and taken to a prison camp. A veteran of Gen. Claire Chennault's Flying Tigers who saw service in China, Boyington rejoined the Marines in 1942, organized the 212 (Black Sheep) Squadron, had shot down 28 enemy planes, and was awarded the Medal of Honor.

It was not known whether or not he was actually alive until he was liberated from Japanese custody at Omori Prison Camp near Tokyo on August 29, 1945. - *Time Magazine*

John before his discharge.

This letter from Ensign Kosbau illustrates again how important letters and news from home were.

At one time, Harold worked in the bakery.

Of note to the Waldron family is the reference made in this letter to Marge about her wonderful chicken dinners. Legendary even in 1944!

On September 5, the Soviets declared war on Bulgaria.

At the end of 1942 there were about 45,000 living and training at Camp Hood. Its peak population was reached in June 1943 with 95,000 troops. This strength was maintained until early 1944.

In 1944 the number of tank destroyer battalions in training at Camp Hood declined. Field artillery battalions and the Infantry Replacement Training Center replaced them in March 1944. By September, the Infantry Center was the largest post, reaching a peak of 31,545 troops.

The total camp population on the last day of 1944 was 50,228.

*Time Magazine*

*you see her for me and I'd love to have Jim's address too. Tell Lila to write to me.*

*Sure seems like ages since I was home and imagine it seems like ages for you that Bill has gone but buck up, it won't be long now.*

*Suppose Luther and O'Riley are pretty ancient at this married life by now. I was out on a party with "Handy" when I was in Corpus and he sure feels bad about it. He's sure a good guy but so is Fred.*

*I've been into Jacksonville several times and get out to the beach occasionally. If I never see any action, I can at least say I've swam in both oceans.*

*By the way I'd sure love to have some of those pictures you took when I was home if you have any extra ones handy.*

*Goldie was down to Corpus when I graduated. She got out to the base a little too late to get in on the graduation but we had a good time, still a single man tho. I can't talk her into it and no one else will love me so I guess I'll be an old bachelor.*

*Suppose the old man is cooking like hell for the army now. He'll probably have them all killed off in a month. Maybe he's taken some lessons from his wife tho. Those chicken dinners were sure wonderful. I'm looking forward to a lot more of them.*

*Well Marg I have to hit the hay so until the next time, hope everything is going OK and don't forget to send me Bill's address right away and in the meantime say hello to him for me.*

*Your friend*

*Harold*

September 6, 1944 - From Bill to Jim and Amanda

*Dear Ma and Dad,*

*I was sure sorry to hear that Dad's arm is troubling him. How long before you think he will be able to go back to work? If you are running short of money and don't want to get it from Marge, I put $200 on my own checking account before I left that you can write checks on. Tell them at the Bank I said it was all right. If they won't, then send me a check blank and I'll sign it for you.*

*I was sure glad to get your letter and hear that Vernon is in pretty swell quarters. You've never seen hot weather up there till you get down here. We had a big speech from the General and Col. yesterday morning. They said at present this is the largest camp in the U.S. I'll have about 10 min to walk to church here when we get out of quarantine. There is only one Catholic priest in the whole Company. There are Jewish and every kind of Protestant chaplain here. They might have a few more Catholic chaplains later on they said.*

*I wrote John and Stan last week. I suppose they have heard from me by now. You said Stan sold his chickens in that let-*

*ter. I think we must have had them for dinner here Sunday. You ought to see this beautiful haircut. It's only about 1/2 in long now and I had it cut about a week ago. In the rifle co. we are in now, we don't need a G.I. (haircut) but in the anti-tank, they make them all get their hair cut. And that's where some of us were the final few days. Those guys that stayed there got in on that 7 weeks training because it started a week ago. I kind of like the haircut. Here though, these guys with long hair, it's plenty bad for them.*

*Well write soon again.*

*Your son,*
*Bill*

On September 6, *Double Indemnity* opened at theaters. Starring Fred MacMurray and Barbara Stanwyck, the price of a ticket was $ .32.

On September 7, the Belgian government in exile returns to Brussels from London.

September 8, 1944, 10:14 PM - From Marge to Bill

*My dearest Bill,*

*How are you tonite, honey? Did you have a pretty hard day? I'm glad you don't seem to mind the hard work they make you do or are you just putting up a big front?*

*Honey, I feel so badly about your not getting my mail that I had to sit down and cry today. I'm sure by now you must have. I got your first letter on Thursday afternoon after you got in Texas. I called your Mother and she wanted your address. She had that letter ready to mail. I was working so I couldn't get mine mailed till that night at the hotel. It was airmail. (It used to cost more to airmail a letter. You needed special thin stationary and envelopes that were lighter weight.) Then Friday morning I mailed an airmail, a three cent one and the package and one or two every day since then. Gee, honey, that is all I can think about. I'm praying you have some by now. After this week, I'll write more often as I won't have so much to do. Your mail comes fast here. You mail it on Wed. morn. And I get it on Fri. aft. That isn't too bad.*

*Am I ever tired and sleepy tonite. It must be because I am finally a little more relaxed. If I ever have to put through another week like this one without you, honey, I don't think I could take it. Everything went just fine and we didn't have much bother, but it was the worry and responsibility. I don't have much trouble with the orders at nite anymore though. If Ray gripes, let him gripe. He yelled around there this morning for hours. Gee, I wish you could have said what to give them all for fair week. This is what your Mother and I decided. To give Ray and John $10 more and Stan the same as John, $22 plus his cookies. He has worked hours and hours and hasn't gone to school all week. He was so tired tonight when he left, he didn't know what to do. He worked over 12 hrs. every day, honey. He was up to the fair for about two hours last nite (and) was*

The time is often noted on letters written from Marge to Bill and most of the time they are written late at night after an exhausting day at the bakery.

Marge's emotions are clearly enunciated in this letter. There is a lot of discussion, in this letter, about the business and the Allamakee County Fair.

On this date, London was hit by a V2 rocket for the first time.

The French town of Menton is liberted from Germany by the Allies.

all the whole week. There aren't many kids who would do that.

Veryle and I are sitting up here writing letters and eating. Seems like we have eaten a lot this week. We got egg salad sandwiches and cake at the fair grounds and brought them home with us to eat.

In the food business, getting "stuck" referred to having stock left over at the end of a day or event. Regardless of how much was sold, if there was too much product left at the end of the day, you lost money and were "stuck."

Honey, We didn't get stuck. (bakery) Aren't you happy? I'm afraid some of the (food) stands are going to though. Mason has a terrible lot of them. I would think he would soon learn. Ray left the lard out of the first 32 qts of buns last nite so they weren't the best. I took them to the fair this morning. Then he made a barrel this morning and took the big ones off of it.

Eitzen has a big order - 60 sandwich bread and 30 doz. hamburger buns besides their regular order. I'll have to take part of it up. More fun. Remember those Sat. mornings when we used to take the order up and go over for a drink or two? Those were the days.

Fitz introduced me to that Donny Donlon from McGregor last nite. Remember he was the one Mary Luther (Fitz's wife) went with for so long and that she almost married. He surely seemed to be a nice guy. Brophy went to New York for a week leaving today so she is on the loose. Donny called her up last nite for a date but she already had one. Now tonite she was pretty burned up because he had Phyllis Grinegar.

Bill Conners and Donny Howes are home on furloughs now. Will you get a furlough in 6 weeks, honey or don't you know.

It is not unusual in the military, even today, to get news (sometimes even correct news) from family and friends. The other method to find out what was happening is/was "scuttlebutt." This is/was usually rumors started by other soldiers and usually not all that reliable.

No, darling, the war in Germany is not over. Your Capt must have been feeding you a line of bull because the last two days, the Americans haven't gotten very far. There is some fierce fighting. Sure hope it will soon be over though.
Did it rain, as you had to march in the mud? It looks very much like rain here tonite. I'm surely glad it waited till the fair is over.

Honey, how much does the fair usually run? I have figured this year to be pretty close to $160 up there. What do you think of that? Is it much, little or a lot?

Paragraph ripped from bottom of page and missing

It is evident from this letter, and in other places, that some of Bill's letters are missing. Still, it is amazing that so many of them were saved or found.

What is the matter with you? I thought you could at least keep your barracks clean. Bet you do from now on, won't you.

You should have seen us delivering at the driveway of the fairgrounds. It was really funny. I think I'm getting pretty good. Ha!

Oh, Lilia was working in the church stand this morning so I got Jim's address. It is at the Bakery now. She said he is expecting to be sent overseas at any time and she wasn't worked up about it at all. When I asked her, she said she doesn't care - he would go sometime. I asked her if she was *going to see him first and she said no. "She is too busy to do that." I don't quite get it, do you?*

*Today was JeanAnne's birthday so I got her a sweater. My husband soon has one too, doesn't he?*

*Well darling, I am just about asleep - it is 11:15 and I must go early in the morning. I'm going to really love your pillow up tonite. I miss you so much. How is your money holding out? Write to me and keep thinking about me.*

*All of my love*

*Your wife,*
*Marge*

<u>September 8, 1944 - From Amanda to Bill</u>

*Dear Bill*

*Well we really got a letter from you yesterday. Did we ever go around in circles this week. The boys really worked. Hank didn't show up or call but got along fine without him. Will see buns and more buns for a while.*

*Today is JeanAnns birthday. Have a cake in the oven now. Told her she could have 6 or so girls over tomorrow and that was all right. Marge got her a brown sweater from you. She wants a bathrobe so will see what I can get. Will be after Dad goes to work. I don't know what he's doing. Left yesterday noon to go to the fair with Uncle Frank. Went to Bessie's for supper and then they went down to Marcella's. Red Robinson, Earl's brother, from Italy is back. He is in limited service now. When his elbow really pains, he walks around with Baxter. Dad came home at 6 this morning. I was working when he got up about 9:30 and went down town and that's the last I saw of him. Don't write I told you this for it sure makes him hot under the collar.*

*Had a letter from Vernon yesterday. Said they were doing a lot of moving. He wrote that he got the cablegram the 23rd and he got a letter I mailed on the 25th so the cablegram is not much faster. He said to say hello and that you would get any ------ by the time this war is over. I see Billy Connor is home on leave. Marge was saying she will take in around a $160 when they all get paid up. But there are a lot of them go and (get) stuck with loans. And Mason wouldn't let Mrs. Keefe run the fair stand. She had to stay in town. Did that ever burn her up.*

*Did your hands ever swell from rolling buns? John thought that's what his came from. They were just puffed up. They may be all right after he makes a few more buns.*

*Eitzen has an order for tomorrow. There is a big creamery opening up there Sun. They have buns, 30 or 40 doz and a lot of bread but the rest runs about the same. I hate to call Stan at 1 for he is tired. He didn't get to the fair - only about an hour and 1/2 last night late. Marie said today "Bill comes home on the bus Sunday."*

Bill's mother often wrote informative letters to Bill.

She had a tendency to keep Bill posted about family and how things were going at the bakery (ever the protective mother).

It is soon apparent that in addition to Marge's leadership and efforts, Amanda and Stan were keys to keeping the bakery functional.

British anti-aircraft and RAF fighter planes destroy 80 percent of incoming German rockets by August (De Havilland Mosquito planes are credited with downing more than 600 of the missiles), and the rocket attacks stop in early September, but they are succeeded September 8 by faster and deadlier V-2 rockets (buzz bombs with warheads of nearly one ton each); they also hit Antwerp, killing hundreds. These V-2 rockets take an increasing toll in Britain despite efforts by Allied bombers to destroy launching sites at Peenemünde and knock out the German factories producing the bombs.

The film, starring Pat O'Brien, that Amanda went to was probably either *Marine Raiders*, released in June or *Secret Command* released in July. Both were patriotic movies and typical of the war effort undertaken by Hollywood in those days.

Yes, we were down to Monticello last Sunday and had to use your car. Of course Johnnies was and still is in the garage. I think he said a cylinder head cracked. Decker was going to try and weld it. He has it at Matilles. Dad was going to try and work a little tomorrow but he won't now. I went to church tonight then went to see Pat O'Brien. Thought I'd enjoy that more than going to the fair. My mind is wandering so think I'll go to bed. I'm sure glad you (seem) to like it. It is a lot different than you're used to. Must write Vernon tomorrow. He said they sure have been moving. Write.

With Love

Mother

This is his address if you want to write him:
S/Sgt Vernon J Waldron 36672493
301 Eng G. S. Regt Co RS
APO 403
Postmaster, New York, N.Y.

The Number One Song on this date, according to Billboard Magazine, was still *Swinging on a Star* by Bing Crosby. It would hold this distinction for nine weeks.

Prior to the war, Dorothy (Luther) worked at the bakery for many years. After the war, Fritz made a career of the military and they lived in Texas.

September 8, 1944, Tampa, FL - From Dorothy & Fritz O'Reilly

Dear Marge,

Never know where I'll be next, Marge. Always did want to go to Florida though.

We'll only be here about a week I guess until they decide where they will send us. Hope its close to home because your next stop will be for a long time.

Freddie gets off most of the time, so we are together now more than we ever were and Gosh, it's really been nice too. We have been going to some nite spots and also swimming and fooling around. Just like a honeymoon. We have a room in a nice home close to the field.

Where did they send Bill? Bet you really are lonesome Marge. I can just imagine how dull everything is to you now. I'll probably have the same thing happen to me - never know I guess. If he did have to go across again, I'll come home and we can be in misery together. O.K.?

Better not write me until I send you our new address. Might take ages to catch up. I have a lot of letters to write today Marge, so I'll sign off. After we move and get settled I'll start in again and keep up with my letters.

Bye for now and be good. Send our regards to Bill

Love,

Dot and Fritz

One of the most difficult things for a couple separated because of military service is the delay in receiving letters from a spouse or loved one. The APO mail delivery service was suspect at best. Although Marge and Bill may write a letter every day, they do not always receive a letter every day - there was either none or a bundle of letters.

September 9, 1944, 12:00 AM - From Marge to Bill

My darling Bill,

Gee, honey, I know how you must feel if you haven't heard from me. I feel almost as badly as if it were me not hearing from you. I just can't understand why you haven't gotten any. Your Mother thought maybe it was because I didn't put the K. in your name but I don't see why that should make any *difference as long as your number is on it. Lord if you don't get them pretty soon, I'm going to pack up and go to Texas. I'm so darn lonesome for you I could die. Another Sat nite and you know how that is. Here it has been three weeks since you were home. How much longer is it going to be? I'm praying it won't be too many weeks, aren't you?*

*Gee, I keep thinking that as long as you haven't heard from me, you will think that I'm not writing to you and well, honey, I do all the time but next week I will twice a day so maybe you will get some of them. I still love you so much that it hurts, honey and I don't want you to think that I'm slow writing or anything. I'm afraid this letter won't amount to much because it is all I have been able to think about since I got your letter.*

*What did you have to do today? I'm surprised you even keep writing. They are getting shorter tho, aren't they? Please write even if you don't get any cause they should be coming.*

*This was a pretty busy day. Stan and I went to Eitzen this morning and believe me it was a short trip. I drove up and then let him drive all of the way home. He sort of likes that. I was terrible busy today and was I ever glad to see 6:00 o'clock come. Ethel, Aulger, and Judy came up and are staying all nite so Veryle is sleeping with me. Oh, if it were only you, I would be so happy! We got those pictures back so I'll send you some. They are pretty good. I sure have a good-looking soldier, don't I? How is your haircut?*

*Marie came downtown tonite so we went over to the Grill for a while. Drank a glass of beer with her too, believe it or not. (Marge didn't like beer.)*

*I'm going up there for dinner tomorrow. It will be something to do. I haven't any desire to go to the river tomorrow. Maybe you will call me. If you ever get the chance, Bill, please call. Reverse the charges. After Marie went home, Connie, John and I sat talking. Connie (Quillan) is home for the weekend. She still hears from Wayne everyday and boy is he in love with her! Then Ray and his wife came in and sat with us so we had a couple drinks on him. Gee was he ever drunk and is he ever sickening. Sure wants to fight with all of the farmers because they aren't in the Army. It is sort of sickening. John and Riley are using the car for a while tonite.*

*Claudie Lane died this afternoon, I guess. In a way it was a good thing as he has suffered so.*

*I'm so glad you have a nice Sarg. Have you gotten the box I sent you yet? I hope so. I'll send another the first of the week.*

*I'm pretty tired tonite. I will have to get up and go to early Mass in order to get this letter out tomorrow. See how you rate?*

*I lay here reading the verse on the pillow thinking if you really could mean what is written on it. Honey, this is going*

On this date, an insurrection breaks out in Sofia, Bulgaria. As word of the Allied invasion spread, the light of freedom was rekindled in the hearts of many. As these people stepped up their behind the front activities, it meant that the Nazi war machine had to expend men and other resources to quell these outbreaks when they were needed on the front to fight against advancing Allied forces.

*The Road to Serfdom* by Vienna-born economist Friedrich (August) von Hayek, 45, is published this day. The book attacks Keynesian economic theories, pointing out that state planning is both dangerous and inefficient, and that internal contradictions in all collectivist societies not only doom them to failure but also lead logically and inexorably to tyranny. Marxists have called Fascism (and Nazism) "the last dying gasp of capitalism," but Hayek, writing in Britain, creates a sensation by asserting that Hitler is actually the direct and inevitable consequence of socialism.

to be short tonight but I'll write two tomorrow.

Will you be about to go to Mass tomorrow? I'll be praying for you and I always am thinking about you. Do you miss me and love me a little? Sat. nite is about the worse as that was always our nite to howl. I am going to try to sleep and maybe I can write a long one tomorrow.

Gee I love my husband so much!!!

Wish I could kiss you goodnite instead of writing it but it is impossible so.........

All of my love
Your devoted wife

Marge
XXXX

On this date, Northern and Southern France invasion forces link up near Dijon.

Dutch physician Willem J. Kolff, 33, devises the first kidney machine to filter noxious wastes out of the blood of patients with kidney disease. He uses the clinical apparatus in secret to save the lives of Dutch partisans in German-occupied Holland. A surgical operation is required to insert the machine's large tubes into an artery and vein, and the machine is used only for brief emergency treatment of waste-product buildup.

September 11, 1944, - From Marge to Bill

Hi, Honey,

How are you by this afternoon? I didn't get a letter from you but I'm looking for one this aft. Unless you are so mad because you didn't get any from me that you are going to divorce me--- Are you? Ha

I just finished writing to Harold so I'll send his letter. Also got one from Luther. I'll send as long as I can't write to her. Say, Fritz was telling us the other day that Glenn Beardmore washed out and is now at the Great Lakes. What a laugh?

Dad wants to go to the cabin tomorrow and get some of the boards so guess I'll go along and see what I can do. He wants to use them in his coal bin. He said he could work on the car down there then.

Dad said Aulger was looking at our car yesterday morning and said that it ran good. Said the carburetor wasn't any good tho. I wish he would do some work on it when he is up here sometime. John thinks he will get his back this week.

Guess I'll go up to see Helen and the baby this afternoon and pay some bills and do a lot of work I have been putting off for so long.

Marie ran away this morning and was up by the courthouse and then down town. Some lady found her in the dime store and brought her over to the bakery. She is surely a little brick. Dad went to work this morning but I don't know how he got along. Your Mother said she forgot to ask him.

Boy, is it ever cold today. It rained all night and it is so damp now. Sis and Dale didn't get any squirrels yesterday. They said there are too many leaves on the trees yet and that there aren't too many squirrels. Are you going to get home in time to go, do you think?

Well, darling, this is all for now. Surely hope you are getting my mail by now. I will write again tonite.

All of my love
Your wife

Marge

President Roosevelt and Prime Minister Churchill meet at Quebec from September 11 to 16 (the Octagon Conference) and decide to advance against Germany on two western fronts rather than making a concerted drive on Berlin. The decision will later be criticized as having permitted Soviet troops to take the German capital.

*September 16, 1944, - From Bill to Marge*

*Dear Marge,*

*I got your letter with the pictures in today with Dorothy and Harold's letters in it. I don't care if I don't get any letters from anyone else except the folks if you keep them coming. Hegeman seemed glad to see someone from home. I don't think I would have the ambition to walk over as far as he did. He's clear down the line from here. We have 2 hrs free time again this afternoon. I'm not going to care too much about the 5 day bivouac next week.*

*I'm getting all your mail regular now. I guess you know that by now. Are you keeping Mickle pretty well in line? Marge, I don't think you should let John use the car too much. Did you have any luck fishing or haven't you tried? Have any of you used the throwlines since I left? Dale must of slipped out a little ahead of the season being open, didn't he? It don't make any difference to them here if you sprain an ankle here. If you can stand on it, you march. I'm sure hoping I don't mine. I used to have a lot of trouble with it. We don't have much of any idea if we get a leave after our 6 weeks or not. I haven't read a newspaper for so long, I hardly know what they look like. They read us war news direct from Washington every day.*

*I never realized that it was so far from home until I tried to call you last night. It sure seemed funny when I went to church Sunday to see them all sitting around reading papers and things like that. They have Catholic church in a big theater here and you are kneeling down on tile. If your knees get some tired during church, you ought to be down here to try it.*

*How much flour have we got booked there yet anyway? These Mexican Indians in this Co. seem like swell enough guys. A couple of the Indians are Yellow tail and Swan. Quite the names, eh? I still haven't read all of the Readers Digests. So that pussy of yours hasn't been bothering you yet, eh? I'll bet you've had a few wet dreams though. Know about it?*

*It still's hotter than hell down here yet. The stars are all out yet when we fall out in the morning. We usually have lemonade for dinner in the day. It goes plenty good. I suppose I should write to Vernon. Ma sent me his address. Those pictures were sure*

This letter was undated but post-marked September 16.

A hurricane was first detected on 9 September, northeast of the Lesser Antilles. It moved west-northwest and steadily intensified to a 140 mph major hurricane on the 12th, northeast of the Bahamas. Around that time, the Miami Hurricane Warning Office designated the storm The Great Atlantic Hurricane to emphasize its intensity and size. It was rated as a Category 4.

'Eia ke ola . . . Have a Coke

. . . or winning a welcome in Wailuku

clear. That looks like a big fish there that Connie and Mary Lou had.

Maybe you could have a different carburetor put on the car. That one might have been just a bad one. Take it over to Matille and ask him. Don't forget you have to take it over and have the filter changed every 2 or 3000 miles, I think. I spend about 1/2 the time thinking about you but I'm still glad I'm in here instead of home because after it all is over, it's going to be tough on some of the guys who have been dodging it. Are they drafting many there now? They keep the camps all pretty well filled up with guys coming in yet.

On this date, Lauren Becall celebrated her 20th birthday and David Niven with Primula Rollo celebrated their 4 year anniversary.

Hegeman told me they are releasing the guys over 35 where he is after this week. I don't know how true it is. You can't believe only about -- of what you hear, I guess.

Don't worry about your Husband not loving you even if I don't say it, you should know that pretty well or I wouldn't be writing every day.

Lots of love,

Your Husband
Bill

Parliament adopts an Education Act creating two basic classes of school, grammar and secondary modern, based on the ideas of University College, London, psychologist Cyril Burt who has determined that some pupils have high levels of academic intelligence while others can benefit more from practically-based education.

September 16, 1944, - From Bill to Marge

Dear Marge,

I sure hope you are not mad because I didn't write last night but it was way to late when I got off K.P. to write. I got a letter and the box from you yesterday and today 2 letters from you and one from your folks and one from Swede. I'm making use of the stationary you sent. I didn't open that box until tonight and had a chance for a little of it myself. We ate that fudge in a couple min. - 4 of us. Red, he's the guy that bunks next to me, told me to tell you it was the best fudge he ever ate. Homemade candy is one thing that really tastes good here. I don't think I'll eat the cheese and crackers until some night after we come in from a march when it will really go good. Was down to the P.X. tonight after something and had a bottle of beer - Budweiser. First I've had of that in 3-4 yrs.

*Seventeen* magazine begins publication at New York in September. Publishing heir Walter H. Annenberg, now 36, has started the periodical for young girls.

Don't ever send me any more cigarettes because I can buy them here for 12 cents a package and get any kind. I tried to look up Brown tonight but I can't tell much by Co. C. unless I have the rest of his address because there are hundreds of Co. C. here. We haven't had hardly any rain here at all and this is supposed to be rainy weather. I'm sorry to hear the fish aren't biting. You must really be getting the cabin to look like something. How about Stan? Don't he ever go down with you? Most of the guys here are gone on pass tonight. Our Co had cleanest barracks in the Battalion this week so most of them could have passes. We can buy whiskey right here in Camp if we want to but I think I'll drink mine after I get home. There are some of the Cadre that bottle it. Cadre

As Bill later explains, *Cadre* referred to soldiers who had seen action and were sent back to train recruits.

*is one of the non commissioned officers who trains us. Most of them are back from overseas. I think I'll be able to write next week when we are out on bivouac at least I'm going to try. I could use about 3 undershirts and shorts. I've tried to buy them down to the P.X. but they don't have any. I was coming out of the Mess last night and seen a white flash coming out of the barrack and here comes a guy across the street without any clothes on to mail a letter. We aren't allowed out of the barracks without our field shirts on.*

*They use all fresh eggs in the mess halls here and no powdered because I cracked 40 dozen last night for breakfast this morning. I'm going to try the arch supports in the morning. I don't know if I'll be able to wear them now or not. It feels like my feet are about flat. There were about 10 whose feet gave out on them today but I'm still going pretty good on mine. Today we were out in foxholes and every time a tank or plane came, we had to hit the foxholes. The planes dived down to within 3-4 ft of the ground and the tanks came right over the holes. It felt like they were coming right down on you but they would be about 3-5" to a foot above you. We seen a show on Hitler's coming to power this morning and all the different advancements he made. It was just about like a propaganda show you would see at home. Pretty interesting. The cooks were telling me I had a good chance of getting in the bakery as quick as I'm done training, because they are so short on cooks and bakers all over in the army but these cooks down here are the best you would ever find.*

*I suppose Sis hated to see Dale leave. Is he still in the same camp? I didn't think the squirrel season opened till the 15, you were wrong about me leaving a month ago the 12 because it was the 15 when I left. This is another of those Sat. nights we are not going to be together and there will be lots more of them, I guess but I'll still be thinking of you and the good ones we used to have. I'll try calling again tomorrow after church. I don't know if I'll have any luck though. I doubt if I'll even be able to call on the 22 of this month (Bill's birthday). I'll be on bivouac the 22 so that will be about 10 mi. out in the country.*

*Lots of Love*

*Your husband*
*Bill*

French authorities arrest poet-political theorist Charles Maurras September 16 for having given strong support to the Pétain government; now 76, he will be sentenced in January to life imprisonment and excluded from the Académie Française, into which he was received in 1938.

Coppertone Suntan Cream is introduced by Miami Beach pharmacy owner Benjamin Green, who has seen tourists rubbing homemade concoctions on their skins to prevent sunburn. Having used his wife's coffee pot to cook up a batch of cocoa butter, he has tried it on his bald head, found that it worked, and markets it with a picture of a Native American saying, "Don't be a paleface."

September 16, 1944, 3:00 PM, - From Marge to Bill

*Hi Bill*

*I said I would write again this afternoon but I really don't have much to say. What are you doing today? Is Saturday the same as any other day or do you get off early in the afternoon?*

*We have been very busy today. Veryle is working with me this afternoon so it isn't nearly so bad. But then by the* time I get Bobbie out of here, I'm a nervous wreck. He is even worse than Ray if you get what I mean.

Irene Graham was just in to tell me that Charlotte Rumph died this morning. Guess Jake came in from the field and found her. I wonder what was the trouble.

I don't feel a hell of a lot better today but I've kept going all day. I haven't been sitting back behind the oven but I have a funny feeling in my stomach. Hope to hell I get over it pretty soon.

I just talked to Marie (Kreeb). Honestly she is the craziest thing I ever saw. I don't get a chance to say much when I'm around her.

Mrs. Raymond over to Helen's just called me and said they have suits in so I'm going over to see if I like them.

Marie asked me to go to the show with her tomorrow nite so I guess I'll either do that or stay with the kids while she and Ray go - Can't you see me doing that?

I'm going up to the post office now and see if I get a letter from you. I'm surely hoping as I didn't get one this morning. I still owe so many letters but I never have the ambition to write. I wish you could have some of the sleep that I get. I might just as well hibernate, as I don't think I would sleep any more if I did.

Fitz came home from Rochester yesterday but she leaves for school tomorrow. We are going to confession tonite and up to see Helen Baxter for a minute. Then I think I will feel like going to bed again.

Well this will be all for now, honey. I'll write again tonight. I hope you are feeling OK and that your feet aren't bothering you.

All of my love

Your wife
Marge

September 16, 1944, 11:00 PM, - From Marge to Bill

Dearest Bill,

How are you tonite, honey? I'm surely wondering what you are doing your first Sat nite with a pass. I only wish I could be there to spend it with you but wishing doesn't help any.

I'm down stairs watching the folks and Veryle do away with a quart of ice cream and a cantaloupe. I couldn't even taste it. Dad just picked a bug out of the ice cream but Veryle said that couldn't beat the hornet Mom fried in the potatoes a couple weeks ago down at the cabin. Mom said to tell you she wished you were here to help them eat it. She also said that I must write all of the news so there wouldn't be much for her to write about.

Riley came in tonite about six so he, Veryle, and I had a coke and then went over to Hales. He was feeling pretty good

The new Kentucky Dam on the Tennessee River creates the largest reservoir in the Tennessee Watershed—a 160,000-acre body of water with 2,380 miles of shoreline to provide a Land Between the Lakes recreation area for anglers, boaters, campers, hikers, riders, and swimmers. Even more than the other dams on the river, it provides effective flood control, protecting 6 million acres of land in the lower Ohio and Mississippi River valleys from inundation.

The average yield per acre in U.S. corn fields reaches 33.2 bushels, up from 22.8 in 1933.

U.S. soybean acreage reaches 12 million as new uses for the beans are found in livestock feed, sausage filler, breakfast foods, enamel, solvent, printing ink, plastics, insecticides, steel-hardening, and beer.

U.S. farm acreage will decline by 7.3 percent in the next 20 years, dropping by 1.3 million acres per year. Some 27 million acres of non-croplands will be converted to farm use (mostly in Florida, California, Washington, Montana, and Texas), but 53 million acres of croplands will go out of production and be used for home and factory sites, highways, and the like.

*Time Magazine*

*or I don't think he would have gone but he wanted to buy a present for Mits Wilde's baby before he went up to the hospital to see Genevieve. You would have split if you could have seen him. He got the cutest little comb and brush set and a little thing to carry a bottle in. At the time I was thinking about you cause I could feature you doing that.*

*I went to confession tonite and said the rosary for you while I was there. I didn't have any sins to confess but I want to go to communion often while you are gone. I hope you will get to go to Mass in the morning. I'm going to early as usual and Jeanne is going to meet me at the bakery so I won't have to go to communion alone. I'm still a baby about that aren't I, but then I'll get over it soon, I hope.*

When Marge married Bill, she converted to the Catholic faith. Apparently her receiving communion was somewhat intimidating.

*When I came from church tonite Jeanne and I went up to see Helen (Wiltgen) and the baby (Maralyn). She went home today. Gee, her baby is so nice. We had to watch her change her and dress her and then nurse her. Seems funny to see her nurse the baby as most of them get put right on the bottle now. She is surely proud of the baby but I think she was terribly lonesome for Viv tonight and how I can understand that. It would be so much different for her if he was home tonite, her first nite at home with the baby.*

*I hope you got your arch supports and the fudge by now. It was funny but I thought maybe you would like that. I'll send another box the first of the week so you will get it by your birthday.*

*Gee, honey, I do hate to think of your being gone from camp for those five days. You won't even get any mail then, will you? Well, I'll try to write a lot so they will be waiting for you when you get back. I'm really going to miss getting your letters those days as I surely wait for them. Write to me as soon as you can though.*

*I hope you are able to get the call through tomorrow as I'll surely be waiting for it. I guess it is hard to get through like that tho.*

*I'm glad that Hageman guy came over to see you. I gave his mother your address so I thought he might look you up although I didn't know you knew him. Is he going to get a furlough now? Do you know any more about your plans for the future after this 6 wks?*

British airborne troops landed September 17 at Eindhoven and Arnhem are unable to outflank the German Westwall defenses and sustain heavy losses before the survivors are withdrawn; by September, the U.S. 1st Army under Gen. Bradley has breached the Siegfried Line and is fighting on German soil—the first invasion of Germany from the west since Napoleon's time.

*We should have had a pretty good day, I think. We all worked hard enough anyway. I wasn't over town tonite tho except to have a coke and then we came right home. I sure hate these Sat nites and how I used to look forward to them.*

*I bet you are out drinking beer tonite, aren't you? Hope it tastes good if you are. Do you get to play any cards now? How is the money holding out? I don't know if I should send a dollar now and then or not, should I? Well, darling I better sign off again. I'm surely thinking about you, missing you and loving you. Your wife, Marge*

On this date, waves of paratroopers landed in the Netherlands during Operation Market Garden.

In Holland, Dutch workers began railroad strikes in order to hinder the German invaders.

September 17, 1944 - From Marge to Bill

Dearest Bill

Well, honey, I went off without your letter this morning and didn't have time to come back and get it before Mass. However, Jeanne said she will mail it at Dubuque tonight so you will get it a little sooner. I thought maybe if you saw the postmark was from Dubuque you would think I was there but I'm not, honey, I'm right here at home.

Veryle and I just finished eating steaks. The folks are gone so we're here alone. She was still in bed when I came home at noon. I worked this morning for a change and I took in about $13. Not bad, eh? Yesterday was $188, best in quite a few weeks.

Gee, but this is a wonderful day. I only wish you were here to enjoy it with me. I bet we would either be fishing or hunting, one of the two. The barp (?) went about 11:30 again so I suppose Stan won't get any cookies baked and he should, as there are only a few butter left. He hasn't been making very many the last few wks since school started.

I'll make some candy this aft. to send to you. I will surely be worrying about you this wk as I think that will be plenty tough.

I should go up to your folks but I just don't get around to it. Mary Olson was in this morning and she said to tell you hello.

All for now darling but I'll write tonite.

All of my love,

Your wife
Marge

This letter is not dated but the postmark is from Camp Hood, September 18.

September 18, 1944 - From Bill to Marge

Dear Marge,

Well, we are getting our packs ready and everything for a little hike. I don't know whether I'll be able to write out there or not - I guess they will keep us busy as hell out there. We weren't told we could bring any paper or envelopes along but I got some in my pocket in case I can write. These damn calisthenics get rougher every day. Boy, one hour of them and we're about ready to drop. We get 1 hour about every morning. This is Mon. morning, we mailed in (a) card to get voting ballots this morning.

I hope everything is all right at home. Both our folks and you are well. How about it, you still miss me? What I wouldn't give for a weekend together but I guess that won't be for a while yet. I sure hope I get out of here in 6 weeks. I think I'll have a pretty good chance of getting in the Bakery. Boy, I'm sure hoping any way. We have to do a lot of running in the infantry and I can't run worth a damn. I suppose you have got your fifth of whiskey from this month already?

How about it? Maybe I should mail you my book?

They issued steel helmets to us this morning. They feel like they weigh about a ton. We've got 2 guys they shipped here from Alaska to take their training. Think how far them poor devils are from home! We'll get plenty of chances to fire our rifles this week, I guess.

How is Sullivan coming anyway? Say Hello to him for me and tell him it is easy to see why they don't want guys over 26 in the infantry. It is pretty rough training. Tell Ma I haven't had a hell of a lot of time to write and that I couldn't get one of these pillow covers up to Fort Snelling for our Mother. They were just for wives. Down here they haven't got any at all. I might go down to a military store at Kileen here some night to get a belt, cap and a few other things and I'll try to get one there. It is about 2 mi. out of camp and we need a pass to go there. I'm not supposed to be writing now, I'm supposed to be getting ready. I'll get my ass in a jam if the Lieut. happens to come in. Marge, keep up with the writing cause I sure wait for the letters from you. I haven't wrote to Harold yet. I should of yesterday but we had about a 2 hr. bull session by my bunk last night and I didn't write to anybody. Mostly everybody talked about hunting, fishing, going home and the war. They get to be some pretty good arguments, sometimes. I guess everyone thinks their town and state is the best.

How's John behaving anyway? Is Stan still turning out the work? Did you pay for the icebox yet? Is it working all right? If Bobby isn't any good, you will probably have to get a bigger kid.

All my love,

Your husband,
Bill

September 18, 1944, 10:30 PM, - From Marge to Bill

My darling Bill,

Well dear, how are you by now? I was very disappointed today when I didn't receive any letters from you but maybe I will tomorrow, I hope.

I am wondering what they are having you do now. Maybe you are out sleeping in the country tonite. I don't know why but I've been having such a scared feeling lately. I'm scared to death to come in the house alone at nite and I know I could never stay alone at nite at all any more. Guess it is because everybody is always talking about the prowlers, etc. I surely hope I get over it soon as I don't like it.

I didn't get around to writing to you at noon. The morning went by so quickly just doing the same old things. Then I packed your box at noon and when I went back up this aft. I banked $428. Is that a pretty good week? Deduct $55 from that for fair tho. Ha. Say honey while I think of it, I still take out the $10 you know. What do you want me to do with that

Britain cuts her food imports to half their prewar levels. Domestic wheat production has increased by 90 percent, potato by 87 percent, vegetable by 45, and sugar beet by 19 despite the manpower shortage. *Land Girls* and others have worked to achieve the agricultural production gains, and the Ministry of Food has economized on shipping space by importing dried eggs and milk, dehydrated vegetables, and boneless and compressed meat, recommending what foods may be produced at home and what deficiencies can best be met by imports. Far more cheese, dried milk, canned fish, and legumes such as peas, beans, and lentils are imported than before the war, while imports of nuts and fruits other than oranges have been sharply reduced.

Bread, flour, oatmeal, potatoes, fish, fresh vegetables, and fruit other than oranges remain unrationed in Britain. Prices are controlled so that the average householder has about half the food budget available for unrationed foods after buying rationed foods plus foods whose distribution is controlled or allocated on a "points" basis.

Dutch civilians survive in many cases only by eating sugar beets and sometimes flower bulbs. A poster put out by the underground shows a prisoner in a German uniform with a ball and chain attached to one foot as he sits at a wooden table eating with a spoon from a bowl labeled "Pulp." The legend says, "Don't shoot a single Jerry. Let them eat pulp for 20 years."

Britain requires bakers to make the "national loaf," comprised about 85 percent of whole wheat flour, partly to provide the nutrients found in enriched U.S. white bread; U.S. authorities find it more reasonable to restore certain food factors to the refined bread and cereal products that people want. Britain's rich do not eat as well as they did before the war, but the poorer third of the population enjoys better nutrition than it has in decades. British per-capita calorie consumption is actually slightly higher than it was in 1939, and intake of vitamins and minerals is substantially higher, thanks to higher wages and efforts by the Food Ministry to maintain stable prices.

*Time Magazine*

*money? There is $300 now. Send it to you, I suppose? Ha. Be sure and tell me.*

*I picked some babe up at the post office today and gave her a ride home. She was going in at the same time I was and had her arms full of packages so I was helping her. When she heard I was mailing your package to Camp Hood, she started jabbering. She just came from the Southern part of Oklahoma and visited your camp a lot. Her husband has gone overseas now and she has come here to live with her brother, the new coach. She is going to work at Penney's. Gad, she had a fifth and a pint of whiskey in her sack too. I was sure surprised to see her flinging that around.*

*I stopped up to Marie's (Kreeb) a minute this aft. And then brought Patsy (Kreeb) downtown and down home with me. She was the best darn kid so I kept her here till 7:30. I surely do like her only I wish she would learn to talk.*

*I talked to Vonnie (White) for a long time this afternoon. Bob is so sure he will get a discharge as soon as the war in Germany is over. You must have been right when you said what you did about he and his family.*

*Sis Campbell went with me up to Rumphs tonite to see Charlotte. She surely looked nice but it just doesn't seem like she died. Jake and Ma Iule are taking it very hard. I felt so sorry for him. I can imagine how he feels can't you honey? I think I'd feel like there wasn't much left to live for.*

*Then Leona, Char, Eunice S. and Sis and I went down to the Grill for a coke and sat and gossiped (I might as well say it) for an awfully long time. Really got in on a lot of dirt then too but none very important.*

*Sis heard from Dale today and he will be in Fort Sill Wed. I don't think that is very far from where you are, honey. She wants to go down before very long to see him.*

*Say, honey, Ray and Marie are going to Monte (Monticello) Sunday morning and coming back that night. They asked me to go along as long as I didn't get to go down when your folks went. I know you will get this letter in time so you won't try to call me this Sunday. Marie has to go to the Dr. again. I'm going to write Beck so we can meet her after 10:00 o'clock mass. I suppose I will go out with her then. Gee, honey, I wish you could be here to go too as we talked so much about doing.*

*I'm going out to Char's school tomorrow noon - (going) after her to come in to go to the funeral in the afternoon.*

*Well, SEARGINE (?) told Marie all about her having to get married, etc. She is to have the baby in November which would make it 2 mo too early. George feels terrible about it and of course Marie does too but it is done now so there isn't much to do. She isn't very happy tho, I don't think, and still Bub is just crazy about the idea of it. His mother is just perfect to them now even if he did join the church. Marie said she hates to think of what her mother will say when she finds it out. Of course it will be a "premature" baby but who will believe it. Marie gave her all of the clothes she wore before Billy was born so she doesn't have to get any.*

*The kids got seven squirrels yesterday. Ray and Bob were out too and they got six. I would surely love to go but it wouldn't be any fun without you.*

*Marcella stopped in this morning to help me on that income tax business so I sent in a check for $40.32. Is that OK?*

*Veryle said there was some guy in the bakery today asking for you. She told him that you were in the army. He said the last time he saw you was the day before Vonnie and Bob were married which was just three years ago. She asked his name but he wouldn't tell her as no one would know him, he thought. Sort of mysterious, isn't it? Vonnie was telling me yesterday of a darling dress Bob sent her for their anniversary. They are worrying about where they are going to live when he comes home. He is very fed up with the army, I guess.*

*Well, honey, I better sign off for now. You'll probably get this on your Birthday so Happy Birthday, honey with all my love. I wish we could be together to celebrate it and our wedding anniversary but I'll be thinking of you. I don't think your present has arrived from the factory yet, honey. I'm so sorry but you will be getting it soon.*

*In case you are short of money, I'll send this to go out and celebrate on Fri or Sat? Only please think of me when you are, will you.*

*Good nite, honey—*
*All of my love*

*Your wife*
*Marge*

On September 19, an armistice was signed between Finland and the Soviet Union, thus ending the Continuation War.

Hershey Chocolate increases the size of its nickel Hershey Bar from 1 1/4 oz. to 1 5/8 oz. G.I.s in Europe hand out Hershey Bars to children and use them as a medium of exchange.

September 22, 1944 - From Bill to Marge

*Dear Marge,*

*I got your box tonight and two letters, one of them was dated the 16. I don't know how it was held over. The rest of your letters get here in 2 days now. We just about cleaned out most of the cookies. Some were mashed but the guys ate every crumb of them. The candy stayed in good shape but it disappears pretty quick. I got about 10 or 15 pieces out of it though. Say, I'd sure like some of that peanut butter candy. Ask Ma how to make it. I thought I would be able to write you this afternoon but I didn't get a chance. We didn't do a hell of a lot but we still couldn't write. They have been easier on us this week than any week since I started. It stays around 100 in the shade here. I suppose you have noticed it on the letters I write. You have asked me about my snoring and talking in my sleep. Nobody has said anything to me about it but some of the guys get razed about it. You take a bunch like this*

and when a few of them get to sleep you have a hell of a job with all the snoring. A lot of the guys got poison oak and ivy on them from being on bivouac. Their hands swell up so they can't shut them. Their arms are all swelled and blistered and the yellow puss runs out of them and it keeps spreading. They just started getting medical attention tonight. A guy would pretty near be dead before they would take care of him here. I'm sure lucky I didn't get any because it was all around our tent. The kid I slept with got it bad. He is the guy who sleeps under me. He's a polack, Al Wochiliski, seems like a nice kid. I found out he's supposed to be a Catholic but he hasn't been to church the last 2 or 3 years much so I told him starting Sun, I'm going to roll his ass out of bed and take him to church with me on Sundays.

I was down to the P.X. tonight about 20 minutes. Had a bottle of beer and got some razor blades and tonic. We carried our bed outside to air out. We do that about twice a week. Take them out in the morning and bring them in at night. We didn't get up till 7:15 this morning. That was pretty nice for a change. You can sell that donut machine for $25 and make them take it out if you can.

I've got a lot of letters to write but I just can't find time to do it. They give a couple hrs free time every now and then but we have to clean our equipment and things like that. Then there was a guy in 2 barracks from here hung himself the other night about 11:30. One of the Sergeants happened to come in and cut him down. They took him to the hospital and brought him around and the next night they found him hanging with his necktie and it still didn't kill him. The Sergeant says the next time he's going to tackle him to make sure they aren't penning him up or anything. Well, Marge, I'll be thinking of you. I still love you.

Your Husband

Bill

Only 10 U.S. grocers have completely self-service meat markets. The figure will increase to 5,600 by 1951, 11,500 by 1956, and 24,100 by 1960, when 35 percent of all meat sold at retail will be from self-service cases.

September 22, 1944 - From Bill to Jim and Amanda

Dear Ma and Dad

I just got that letter you wrote the 10th the other day. You want to be sure to put CO down on it or it takes about a week longer to get. We have had it pretty nice this week. We went out in the country on bivouacs. It was a lot of fun. We were out scouting, map reading, going through barbwire in any climate in the day and night. I also got your birthday cards.

*I hope all the kids are still fine. I got the box from Marge today. I guess you had a hand in it. It was sure good and got about 10 or 15 pieces out of it myself and that is something unusual around here. I hear from Marge a couple times a day. I've been writing her about every day but some days we don't get much chance to do anything except what they want us to. One thing we really get is a lot of marching and hikes from 5-10 miles. We were supposed to have one tonight but I guess they changed their mind. We were out for an hour tonight marching in Regiment formation. That is about 11 or 1200 men marching all together. It really takes a lot of num (?) We had one guy take off with his rifle and all his equipment when we were out on bivouac. They still haven't found him. He was over the hill once before and he started his training over with us and now he's gone again. I guess he will really get a good rap this time.*

*It really stays hot down here. It's around 100 all the time. When we come in at noon there isn't a dry place on our clothes. We have to rinse them out every night to take the salt out of them. They turn just white from the salt in your sweat when they dry out if we don't wash them. I don't have any trouble sweating down here.*

*I wrote to Vernon after you sent me his address. I sure hope he is all right. We start having bayonet practice this week. Pretty tough, I guess. I hear Stan and John have been having a pretty good luck hunting. I doubt like hell if we will get a chance to come home after we finish here. I might have a chance to get in the bakery after I'm done with basic. I sure am hoping anyway. My hair is only about a -- inch long now and I've had to have it cut over the sides. I don't suppose Dad will be able to do any hunting this year, will he.*

*Well I guess I better quit for now. I have to write Marge yet and shave, take a shower and get a little sleep. 5 o'clock rolls around pretty early.*

*Your son,*

*Bill*

Chiquita Banana is introduced by the United Fruit Company in a move to make bananas a brand-name item rather than a generic commodity. The bananas are advertised on radio with a tune composed by Len MacKenzie and performed by Ray Bloch's orchestra with vocalist Patti Clayton singing Garth Montgomery's lyrics: "I'm Chiquita Banana/ And I've come to say,/ Bananas have to ripen in a certain way:/ When they are fleck'd with brown and have a golden hue/ Bananas taste the best and are the best for you. / You can put them in a salad/ You can put them in a pie-aye/ Any way you want to eat them/ It's impossible to beat them/ But bananas love the climate of the very, very tropical equator/ So you should never put bananas in the refrigerator."

### September 24, 1944 - From Bill to Marge

On this date, the US Army 45th Infantry Division took the strongly defended city of Epinal before crossing the Moselle River and entering the western foothills of the Vosges.

*Dear Marge,*

*I got the paper and a letter from you today. That's the quickest I ever got it. I went in to Killeen last night. We left the barracks at 6:30 and went down to the bus station and waited for a hour and still didn't get a ride so we walked it about 5 miles from the bus stop. Can you imagine me doing that in civilian life? Red Watts and myself went in. We got a ride back. We were back at 10 o'clock so we weren't there very long, not even in a tavern. Went to the Army store. I got a belt, undershirts, knife, cap, dog chains and some pillow covers. I sent them to you and both folks. They mailed them for us. I hope you got it. Went into the drug store and*

Moscow publishes edicts in September aimed at replacing the millions of war dead suffered by the nation. The edicts reward mothers with cash payments that increase according to the number of their children, confer decorations on those with especially large families, and erect obstacles to divorce.

Otto Hahn of Germany wins the Nobel Prize in chemistry for his discovery of atomic fission.

An analog to coumadin, synthesized by Mark Arnold Stahmann, is patented and named *warfarin* (after the Wisconsin Alumni Research Foundation, which had financed research on coumadin). It is a potent poison for rats and mice, and is still used for that purpose, although now also administered to humans in smaller doses as a generic form of coumadin.

*Time Magzine*

*got some bandages and medicine for the guys. I bought a qt. of ice cream and came home. It cost me about $12.00 though. Everything is pretty high. We get paid Sat. Everybody will be going to town then. Most of them go to Temple or Austin but I guess I'll stay in camp from now on. I got up about 6:45 this morning and cleaned up and went to breakfast. Then I went to church. I wrote to Herold, Verle and Ethel today too. And I've still got a lot to write but I'll have to put them off for a few days. I went down to go to the show this afternoon. Waited about an hr and the film didn't come on so I came back and slept till 6. One guy here got a letter from his wife the other day that she was going to have a baby. He hasn't seen her for a year. Boy, but was he ever mad. He showed the letter to all of us guys. He really wrote her a good one back. There is a hell of a lot of dirty talk around here though. It has really surprised me.*

*Say, I don't know what the hell I would of done without these arch supports. My feet haven't bothered me a bit since I've started wearing them. They sure hurt like hell before though, usually when we double-timed or long marched. Our training here depends a lot on how the war goes, it ends in Germany pretty quick, I guess we will be occupational troops. That's what they tell us anyway but everyone that goes overseas from here gets 10 days and travel time at home. It's better than most camps for that. About everyone is broke around here now. I've got $2 left but we get paid Sat. Some of these guys got 2 1/2 or 3 months pay coming. Last night one guy offered $10 for someone to work K.P. for him today and had a hell of a job getting anyone. Everybody likes to lay around on Sundays. Some kids went to bed at 9:30 last night and never got up until supper time tonight. Not even for breakfast or dinner. I haven't missed a meal yet though. I haven't got weighed yet though but I think I'm putting on weight. My muscles are getting hard as can be. I guess our pack weighs about 50 or 60 lbs and rifles weighs 8 1/2#. Nice to carry around all day, eh? I've still got all the letters I've got from you in my locker. It is getting about full. On Sat. and Sunday is when I really miss you the most. They were the two days we were always together. God, but I'd sure like to spend a couple days down to the cabin hunting and fishing. It should be good hunting down around there, I think.*

*When does the hunting season close anyway? Just in case we do get home after 6 weeks here. When I send for money, I guess I'll have to wire for it because you can't call me or get checks or money orders cashed too quick here.*

*Has Hank made any cookies or anything for you yet? When the business slacks up in the fall, you can put a batch on the order every now and then for John and Mickle to make. How is John getting along with Ray anyway? Have you been able to get supplies of every kind, all right? You can order that cold filled jelly if you want to, but be sure they don't use it for rolls because it runs all over the pans. Did you get Clare's business or is he a little too big for small town stuff now? Tell John I met a guy who was in the Third Division in the infantry who was wounded on the Anzio beach head. He's got shrapnel in his arms and back. He's a cadre man and only a buck private. These guys in the infantry don't make any rating unless they are in 3 to 5 years. Have you even been down to the cabin lately? Why don't your dad use those throw lines of mine when he goes fishing.*

*I sure hope you get rid of the donut machine. It sure has been an eyesore there long enough.*

*Well, I guess I better quit. I've got to shave yet. We have to every night. This about kills me after shaving twice a week.*

*Lots of love*
*Your Husband*
*Bill*

On September 26 Operation Market Garden ended in an Allied withdrawal.

On the middle front of the Gothic line, Brazilian troops took control of the Serchio valley region after 10 days of costly fighting.

Evangelist Aimee Semple McPherson dies of a sleeping-powder overdose at Oakland September 27, 1944 at age 54. Despite accusations of adultery, alcoholism, fraud, hypocrisy, perjury, grand theft, and physical assault, she has never been convicted and an estimated 45,000 weeping mourners file past her coffin between October 6 and 8. She is buried with great ceremony October 9.

<u>September 28, 1944 - From Bill to Marge</u>

*Dear Marge,*

*I got two letters from you yesterday but I didn't get a chance to write so I'm writing this morning. I guess you will get it just as quick. We fell out at 4 o'clock yesterday morning and didn't get in till 12. Then we worked on our rifles, took a shower and a few other little things. It was about 2 or so when we got to bed and up again at 5:15 this morning. They are really pushing us now. Tonight we have a forced march of 4 mi. in 50 min. and that really is cutting it. Yesterday we were on booby traps and mines. They had us clear mine fields in the afternoon and then 4 hrs of it at night. It rained like hell all day again. A raincoat didn't do a hell of a lot of good. Crawling around in the mud, our rifles and equipment were in terrible shape. We have 3 hrs today to get everything cleaned up. I haven't been gigged on anything yet but there is always the first time. They told us yesterday and today, the reason they are pushing us so fast is because they are pretty certain we only get 6 weeks. Maybe we can find some way of getting together after it is over. If we go to an embarkment camp we get a 10-day delay in route and travel time but if not, we go to the next camp.*

*I'm glad they heard from Vernon again. I guess we hear the war is getting pretty rough over there. Glad to hear you had a good time at Monticello. I suppose Beck is getting a little smaller by now. Where in the hell does Ray get all the guts to go down there so much? Don't forget to send a little more candy again because I sure like it. Last night I could of ate the ass off a shark but we didn't get anything to eat except a few cookies that my bed partner had. All of these boys are getting broke now. Most of them haven't been having cigarettes the last few days. It takes me about 2 or 3 packs a*

The Greenwich Royal Observatory installs its first quartz-crystal clock, providing ten times the accuracy of the previous pendulum system.

In September, the Germans introduce a rocket-powered airplane, the Me 163B-1 Komet, into World War II, but its habit of exploding spontaneously makes it a poor weapon. Development also starts in Germany on the Ba 349 Natter, a semi-expendable rocket plane that is to be launched vertically. In the air, the Natter will launch unguided rocket missiles at enemy aircraft; the pilot, rear fuselage, and rocket motor are to return to Earth with separate parachutes. During the one known piloted launch in February 1945, test pilot Lothar Siebert will be killed, and World War II will end before the craft becomes operational.

Igor Sikorsky builds the first modern helicopter, the VS 36 A; it has an enclosed cockpit for the pilot and adjustable pitch for the rotor blades.

day now figuring all that are bummed but we get paid Sat. and some of these guys have 2 or 3 months pay coming. One guy is supposed to have a court martial for letting his rifle go all rusty. The Captain told us to be sure to dry and oil them before we went to bed. Have Stan and John taken you along hunting yet? I'd sure love to go hunting but I kind of doubt it.

One thing we don't have many of here is mosquitoes. I haven't had any bites yet. I've seen my first buzzards down here though. There are usually 3 or 4 circling around all the time when we are out in the field.

I guess we walked out about 6 mi yesterday and 6 mi back and ate out in the field.

I think you know how much I miss you and love you. It sure seems like a long time since I've last seen you and I'm just as anxious as you are.

Lots of love,

Your Husband,
Bill

September 28, 1944, 11:45 PM, - From Marge to Bill

Dearest Bill,

It's me again. Gee I've done right well the last couple days haven't I? Just making myself take the time I guess.

I've (been) up to Vonnies (White) and we are in bed doing our writing. We have really had the old gab session and I'm not kidding. I've really been learning a lot, honey. Maybe I'll be a bright girl some day, suppose?

The afternoon flew after I got your letter in the mail. I left a lot of work until late today so it really kept me jumping the latter part. $65 today. HOW Is THAT?

I wrote so much this afternoon that I haven't much to say but I'll write a long letter tomorrow containing my tales of tonite. Hadn't better write much with her sitting here - ha.

I took material up to Marie (Kreeb) and she is making my jacket so I'll have to try it on tomorrow.

Oh, honey Dorothy and Al (Leet, her brother and his wife) are leaving the farm. Really I don't see it. What they are going to do, I mean. Of course the folks are so upset about it. Mom said they don't know what they will do if they can get a renter or if they will have to try and sell. I hate to think of the worry this all places on the folks. Dad will surely age under it all.

How were you after your shots? I do hope they didn't make you sick again. Honey your not lying to me are you about that poison oak? If you have it and don't tell me . . .

I'm sure glad "my Man" is smart and not letting himself in for any of that details work. It will go a lot easier on you if you behave, I imagine.

You really think a lot of that Sergeant of yours don't you.

*How old a guy is he? He is the one you said was married and has one baby isn't it?*

*I haven't heard any more about Brown's wife but I know I never would be able to like her, honey. I can imagine her really settling down, oh, yeah.*

*I was up to Marie's when I read your letter so I let her read that last part about the guy getting his wife pregnant. That really is good, isn't it? You really must gab about a lot of things.*

*Well, dear, Vonnie is ready to go to bed so I'll quit for to-night.*

*I sure love you, honey and miss you so much.*

*All of my love,*

*Your Wife*
*Marge*

*Fri. Morning*
*Hi Honey,*

*There are some things Vonnie gave me (jokes). She had gotten them from Bob. She wanted me to send them to you.*

*I'm sure sleepy today. I'm getting so I can't sleep at all unless I'm in my own bed. Terrible aren't I?*

*I'll write this aft. dear.*

*All of my love*
*Marge*

September 30, 1944 - From Bill to Marge

*Dear Marge,*

*I didn't get any mail from you this Friday. Are you starting to ease up? God, but I'm really tired today. We went out practicing position with our rifles again and it isn't any snap. I'm going to bed as quick as I get this letter wrote. Next week we go on the range from Tues until Sat. We shoot around 2 or 3 hundred rounds. Get up at 4 every morning and march out about 5 mi. and then back in at 8 at night so I guess we won't get much sleep next week in our march. Last night we went on a little one, 4 mi in 53 minutes. We were running most of the time. The last bunch made it in 58. The best it has ever been done here is 52 min, I guess. I hope we don't get anymore of them cause it really takes the wind. It has been kinda cool here the last couple days. It feels kind of good for a change. How's our bed coming? Are you having any wet dreams on my side of the bed? I'll sure raise hell with that if I ever get home. What do you think? We have a chance for a pass again tomorrow night but I didn't put in for one. They have dances and shows at the service club just about every night. Lot of the guys go down. I guess they have some pretty good actors there sometimes. I've never been down there yet. I go past there every Sun to church, as well as I like shows, I haven't been to only one and I haven't played cards for a*

Plays released included:

*Storm Operation*. Maxwell Anderson's war drama depicts U.S. soldiers in combat in North Africa. It fails with both the critics and the public.

*Jacobowsky and the Colonel*. S.N. Behrman has a popular success adapting Franz Werfel's comedy about a Jew and an anti-Semitic Polish officer during the fall of France.

*Harvey*. Mary Chase's amiable comedy about alcoholic Elwood P. Dowd and his imaginary six-foot rabbit companion is the surprise winner of the Pulitzer Prize. Conceived by the playwright as wartime escapism, it has a run of 1,775 performances and would be adapted as a 1950 film starring James Stewart.

*Goldbrickers of 1944*. African American actor, playwright, and producer Ossie Davis writes and directs this play based on his army experiences. It is first performed in Liberia, West Africa, where Davis is stationed.

*Deep Are the Roots*. This effective social drama looks at what a black war hero faces when he returns to his Southern hometown. The romantic relationship between the black protagonist and the white daughter of a senator adds to the controversy stirred by the play.

Some books that were being read at this time:

Saul Bellow - *Dangling Man*. Bellow's first novel uses the netherworld between civilian and military life to explore modern alienation and existential freedom. It focuses on a young man who quits his job and waits to be drafted. With overtones of Kafka and Dostoyevsky, the novel turns the wartime home front into an occasion for serious moral and philosophical meditation.

*Something for which Bill probably did't have time, energy nor inclination.*

Harry Brown - *A Walk in the Sun*. The writer of humorous sketches in Yank about a Brooklyn G.I. (collected in Artie Greengroin, Pfc., 1945) offers a more serious depiction of war in this realistic story of an American army platoon during the invasion of Italy. Brown would win an Academy Award for his screenplay for the 1945 film version.

Erskine Caldwell - *Tragic Ground*. This book recounts how a Georgia backwoodsman is stranded in a wartime boomtown when a munitions factory closes. Obscenity charges are brought against a Boston book dealer for selling the novel, but twelve days later, all charges are dismissed when Boston judge Elijah Adlow rules that the book is not obscene.

John Hersey - *A Bell for Adano*. Hersey's first novel presents the moral ambiguity of war, viewed through the American military occupation of a Sicilian village. A U.S. major helps replace the village's ancient bell, winning the respect of the inhabitants but the wrath of the commanding general. The novel would win the Pulitzer Prize in 1945 and be dramatized by Paul Osborn.

*month so you see they keep us pretty busy. How are you getting along with Miekle anyway? Does he still bitch as much as ever? I suppose with basketball on you will have a hell of a time keeping Stan working enough. Does he get down in the morning to make anything?*

*How's the cabin or haven't you been down lately? I suppose I will hardly know it the next time I see it. Sure hope I get a letter from you tomorrow. I probably will though. The mail that you mail at the Hotel don't come any faster than the other I don't think.*

*Lots of love,*

*Your Husband*
*Bill*

<u>September 30, 1944 - From Bill to Jim and Amanda</u>

*Dear folks,*

*I got your letter last night. It came a little quicker than the other one. That box I got was really all right but the jam was cracked and I didn't notice it till a week later when I went to get it for some ice cream. It had run all over everything in my locker and made quite a mess.*

*Sorry to hear they aren't getting many squirrels. I suppose John is quite the boy now with that new car. Just so he don't go cracking it up. Marge writes that every thing has been going pretty good at the bakery. How's John getting along with Miekle? I suppose Ascan (?) is starting to get a lot of eggs from her chickens by now or has she sold them? I'm sorry to hear Marie is sick. It kinda sounds like you will have to keep her tied up all the time, won't you?*

*There is pretty nice weather down here now. It has cooled off a little so it is just about right. I guess it never gets very cold here in the winter. They had one snow in 18 years but when it rains, it is the stickiest stuff you've ever seen. You have about 1 or 2 inches of mud every step you take. We don't get time for much of anything to do. We had a 4 mile speed march the other night and we made it in 53 min. We were about played out when we got in.*

*We are practicing positions with rifles now. Next week we go on the rifle range for all week. We get up at 2 in the morning and get in about 9 or 10 at night so we won't have much time for anything. We shoot 2 or 3 hundred rounds of live ammunition. These are really nice rifles. If we break one or lose any parts, we have to pay for them. They cost $85.00 or so. One guy in the next Co. dropped his and jumped in a foxhole and a tank ran over it so he'll be out $85 bucks. We get paid today and everyone's broke here. I am too but I don't think I'll get a hell of a lot. Some of these guys have 2,3, and 4 months pay coming. It seems funny some of these guys being in 6 or 7 weeks and just taking their basic now. This camp re-*

*ally filled up. We have about 300 in our Co and that is about 100 over what they usually have.*

*Well, write soon.*

*Your son,*
*Bill*

Bill as a member of Company A, 172nd IRTB (Infantry Replacement Training Battalion)
Camp Hood, Texas

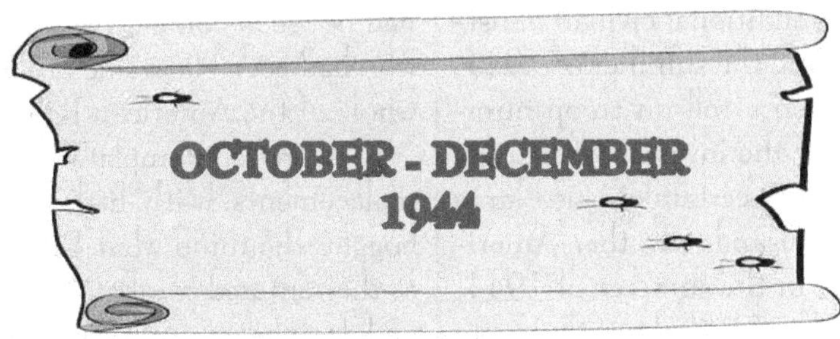


By the middle of October Bill had completed his infantry basic training and was assigned to Cook/Bakery training school. In his letters home, it sounds as if his training in Cook/Bakery school was more on-the-job type than being taught the basics of cooking and/or baking. Of course, Bill knew a lot of what went on in this phase of his training because of his background at the Waukon Bakery. During this training there were still times when he had to join other infantry troops on marches and at the rifle range as it is always a certainty that in combat zones, everyone must be equipped to handle combat warfare situations.

Letters sent by Bill to Waukon and those received from Marge are much more calming than what were being exchanged in August and September.

Marge's letters to Bill are full of anticipation (and hope) that she will soon go to Texas before Bill ships overseas. There is a strong sense of loneliness and yearning in Marge's letters. Bill presents a calming aura for Marge to cling to.

Marge was able to make arrangements to take the train from Oelwein to Camp Hood, Texas. She left Waukon/Oelwein on, or about, October 29 and arrived in Texas around November 1. Marge was able to connect with Waukon friend Sis Goltz in Oklahoma during a stop-over. The Bakery was left in the dedicated hands of Mother (Amanda) Waldron with capable workers Stan Waldron (brother) and Veryle Paulson (Marge's first cousin).

November's letters are mostly from Veryle to Marge and Bill, as she keeps them apprised of every detail about the workings of the Bakery. This had to fill Bill and Marge with considerable confidence, knowing that Marge had established a day-to-day operation of the Bakery to the point that Amanda and Veryle would have little difficulty running the business.

Marge's letter of November 23 (Thanksgiving Day), to Jim and Amanda, is very poignant....Amanda, realizing how important it was for Bill and Marge to be together during this time, had mentioned to Marge that it would be fine if she decided to stay in Texas longer. Reading Marge's letter of response to Amanda, and the rest of its' content brings this period almost to life. Marge talks about Amanda sending a huge fruit cake to the people who had rented Marge a room during her stay in Texas ("a four pounder"). Plus, she also included a recipe for pecan pie!!

In reflection, Marge and Bill continued to be acutely aware of their Bakery business and the dedicated obligation they both felt for its' success. And this is one of the redeeming attributes of ownership that Bill and Marge showed for the entirety of time that they operated their small town business.

Because of the uncertainty of Bill's ship date to Europe it was decided that Marge would return to Waukon. She had been able to spend over a month in Texas, with Bill.

Based on the few letters written in December, 1944 that are available, the assumptions are as follows:

Marge was back in Waukon sometime before December 10.

Bill left for Europe from Kansas City shortly after the New Year; it is known that Marge and Bill spent New Years Eve, 1944 together in Kansas City. Apparently Bill received a leave prior to shipping to Europe and that leave time was most certainly spent in Kansas City with Marge. Obviously, the troops received leaves immediately after Christmas, in preparation to receiving their shipping orders for Europe.

These replacement troops for the 90th Infantry Division left Kansas City shortly after the New Year, 1945, proceeded to New York City, received their shipping orders on January 4, 1945, and left New York on the ship Queen Elizabeth January 8, 1945.

As mentioned, there had been an urgent call by the United States government for additional civilian enlistments to the armed forces during the summer of 1944. The war in the Pacific had been a toll on troop numbers. Plus, the anticipation for the invasion of Europe by the Allied Forces would most certainly cause large casualties. Thus, Bill and thousands of other Americans joined the military ranks in the summer of 1944. Combat at Normandy (D-Day) and all along the route from the English Channel to Germany was heavy with casualties. Replacements became the life-blood of maintaining troop strength. Most of those replacements during the fall, winter, and spring of 1944 and 1945 had not seen combat before. By the end of the war men who had been state-side on D-Day made up virtually the whole of the American fighting army.

As one contemplates what was to happen to these replacements, with little or no combat experience, it boggles the mind what Bill and his fellow soldiers faced as they entered combat under severe weather conditions, and facing an enemy who was fiercely fighting a last ditch battle at the Bulge, along the Siegfried Line, and in their Fatherland.

---

*October 1, 1944 (Sunday) - From Bill to Marge*

*Dear Marge,*

*This is the day we like to see roll around. No work, get up at seven or stay in bed all day if you want. I always get up at seven to eat. We have church at nine. I took my bed partner with me this morning. There has been crap games and poker games going steady ever since supper last night. Going all night and still going now. There are 3 big games going now. Some of the guys who got 60 or 70 bucks yesterday are broke already. Others are really making the dough. I haven't got into any of them yet. I would just as soon lay around today. Did we ever get a surprise when we went in the Mess hall for dinner. The Captain and his wife and daughter were sitting at the head of one table eating with a quart of whiskey on the table and mixed drinks. This has really surprised me here because they aren't supposed to have any in the camp. All the officers came up here in our barracks and got shots from the 1st Sarg and Field Sarg. I still haven't had a drink down here yet and I sure have a lot of chances. Doing pretty good, eh?*

*We haven't had any mail call today yet. They will probably have it tonight. It seems funny to go to church and no collection. They furnish magazines, paperbacks, Catholic magazine of all kinds. I'd get to the show today only I don't like the idea of waiting for a couple hours to get in so I guess I'll go down to the P.X. for a while. It's only 4 blocks from our barracks. I still haven't seen Brown or Kleme here. I don't know for sure if they are in the same company or not. There was a big bunch that came in here from Fort Snelling yesterday that are down to 171 Battalion, but I didn't see any one from home in them as they marched by our barracks. They were really loaded down with barrack boys so it was hard to tell. Some of the fellows went down this morning to see if there were anyone they knew but not me. I haven't got that much ambition.*

*I really don't miss being away from home but it is hell to*

On this day, Scott McKenzie, rock vocalist, was born. His most famous hit would be in the 1960s with *If You Come to San Francisco.*

be away from you and not getting to see you. If I do get a chance to come home after the cycles' over, one kid from Iowa is going to have his car brought down and drive home. At that rate it would only take a day or two to get home. I'm sure hoping we do but you never can plan on anything in the Army. They change their minds every 10 min.

It's plenty warm down here again today. You can be just walking around in your clothes and be all wet with sweat. Can you imagine me sweating like that? I never knew it was possible. There are guys here from Kentucky that are sure dumb bastards but they sure think they know it all. The boys from up North don't get along very well with the Texans or Kentuckians. The other states don't seem to make much difference.

Is Lila still around there? What does she hear from Jim or aren't they getting along too well?

Lots of love.

Your Husband,
Bill

This letter is written from Monticello, Iowa. Beck is Bill's brother Vernon's wife and, of course, Jimmie is their son.

The letter gives another glimpse of home while husbands served their country.

October 2, 1944 - From Beck to Marge and Amanda

Dear Mom, (Amanda)

Just wanted to drop you a line and send you this letter from a friend of Verns. He is the one who wrote for Vern's address in August. I thought it was a nice letter and they both brag about their children, I think.

I said to Mother you might think I'd gone as crazy as several other married women down here and started to write to other men. Now I'm only kidding. By the way one is having a baby I hear and her husband has been overseas two years. I believe a good thing to do would be to hang them. When they are over there fighting, bet they wonder what they got to fight for when their wives can't behave.

When you write again send it back as I'd like to keep it and show them to Vern. I keep all my letters.

Don't you hate this rain? It makes me so lonesome and lazy.

Jimmie is fine and so good when he gets all the attention in the world. That's all I got to do and he sure gets plenty.

Sure would like to come up so Dad could see him. Will as soon as he is a little older.

Write when you can -

Lots of Love,
Beck and Jimmie

One of the rare Jewish revolts and attempts to fight back against the Germans happened in Warsaw, Poland. It was known as the *Warsaw Uprising*. On this date, Nazi troops overwhelmed the fighters and ended the uprising, killing some 250,000 people.

October 3, 1944 - From Gene Hoberling to Bill

For the first time, USAA B-17s drop propaganda pamphlets on Watchenen, Germany.

Dear Bill,

I imagine you can give the same answer about "how do you like the Infantry?" that was given by a Private on Bob Hawk's "Camel" program last night by saying "What do you *think?" Anyway I hope you are getting along fine and as long as you are a baker, I imagine they are probably making a mechanic out of you - this fellow last night on Hawk's program was a radio engineer in private life and I believe they had him driving a truck.*

*Secured your address from Marge while Frank Herzog was talking to her over the phone the other evening about flour. From all reports, things seem to be running pretty smoothly at your shop, and I am sure they will be able to carry on fairly well until you get back. Haven't been down to Waukon in quite some time, but plan on making a trip down that way with Frank sometime within the next thirty days.*

*Looks like fall and winter are really on the way the last few days around here, with cold, drizzly rain and some snow in the northern part of the state. Suppose you are finding quite a contrast in the weather down in Texas from what we have up North, but don't let too much sand blow into your eyes.*

*If you get time, drop me a card some day and let me know how you are.*

*Best regards,*
*Gene Hoberling*

This letter was written from Bay State Milling Company, located in Winona, Minnesota. Gene Hoberling was one of the vendors to the bakery; in this case, he sold them flour.

The Royal Air Force bomb West Kapelse.

October 5, 1944 - From Bill to Marge

*Dear Marge,*

*I got 3 letters from you today, one from your Mother and Ethel and Harold. You know when I came in the Army, I had the good intention of not doing any drinking or running around because I figured you wouldn't like it, but it kinda seems you are doing your share so I might just as well start. I heard it before I got any letters from you. It kinda sounds like you were pretty well paired off over at the Berg. But don't worry, I'll tell you when I do go out.*

*We went out to the range at 4:15 this morning and got in about 8 tonight. I worked in the pits pulling targets up and down and this afternoon we were fixing rapid fire. That is standing up and going into kneeling, prone, or sitting position and firing 9 rounds in 51 seconds. I like to shoot that way. I really picked off a lot of bull eyes today. It will probably be 11 or 12 before we get to bed tonight and up again at 4.*

*Those forced marches Ralph was telling you about are really a bitch. We had one I wrote you about and once and awhile that's what we have going out to the rifle range.*

*You can do what you want about John. If I was there, I would know what to do. We don't know how in the hell long we'll be here. It's beginning to look like 17 weeks though. If the war with Germany would of ended, we would only have been here six but I think we probably will be just as well staying here or getting shipped to some other camp. If you are planning on coming down, you'll have to see about Ma or someone*

Kerkrade, Netherlands, is liberated.

One cannot but wonder if Marge had a chat with Mom, Ethel and Harold about what they write in their letters to Bill.

On this date, Royal Canadian Air Force pilots shot down the first German jet fighter over Holland.

Suffrage is extended to women in France.

*taking care of the Bakery. I'd have to know two weeks ahead of time to get into Killeen and see about a room unless you want to take a chance coming in the middle of the week and getting one. We have to put in for our passes on Friday and aren't sure of one about every other weekend.*

*Lots of Love,*

*Your Husband,*
*Bill*

<u>October 6, 1944 - From Marge to Bill</u>

On this date, German submarine U-168 was attacked and sunk by the Dutch submarine Zwaardvis near Java.

The Soviet army marches into Hungary and Czechoslovakia.

The Battle of Debrecen starts on the Eastern Front and will end in an Allied victory on October 29.

*My dearest Bill,*

*Hello, dear - how are you tonite? I received a nice long letter from you this afternoon. My you really are falling for that rifle in a big way aren't you? To think that a rifle is taking my place. Ha! Of course I don't understand all of that 'rounds' stuff but I get the general idea.*

*I'm up to Marie's (Kreeb) now. She is putting up her hair and Ray has gone to the show. I came up about 4:30 and Marie washed my hair and fixed it. Then she wanted me to stay for supper so I did. We had the best oyster stew. I went down and decorated the cake and it looked pretty darn nice if I do say so myself. Made out the order and checked up. $81.00. Not bad, eh, but tomorrow probably won't be so big then.*

*Pat Campbell got his notice to leave the 24th. I haven't heard who else has to yet. Guess Hazel can't do anything about it. They still haven't heard anything from Bill. When I told Marie about your shooting and the different positions you do it in she said to tell you she didn't know you could do it squatting and standing.*

*She was to some old hen's sewing party last nite at one of the neighbors so she is going around with her nose in the air. Today she got Mrs. Land to take care of the kids. So now when you come home, darling, we're going out on a real good one.*

*I'm so anxious to see if it will be longer now. If it is do you really want me to come down or were you just saying that? Gee, what I wouldn't give to be with you home now and in bed. Still miss you when I come up to this darn bedroom and go to bed. Ray made popcorn when he came home and so we had to eat it. Boy, was it good. I could pop you some and send some but then I suppose you wouldn't like it if it didn't have butter on it.*

*Guess the folks must not have come home tonite. I don't hear Dad snoring downstairs so I woke Veryle to see if she let Tao (dog) in. I left him out at noon and was sort of wondering if she let him in but she did so I won't lose any sleep over that now.*

*There is quite a lot of stuff to make tonight. I can usually remember if there is much stuff left over or anything.*

*Sis still wants me to go as far as Kansas City with her if you are still there when she goes. It is pretty definite that when you leave and you will be sent across isn't it? Lord I don't even want to think about that.*

*I wrote to Luther again today. The third in a week. Think I'm doing pretty good. That is all I've written except you. I promised Connie I'll write her but I just didn't get around to it. She is coming home this weekend any way though.*

*In case you are there longer than 6 weeks, how long would I be able to stay and how much would I get to see you? When the time comes to leave I'll probably be too scared to (illegible).*

*Well, honey, all for tonite. I'm sure thinking about you and I still love you so darn much. I'll be waiting for your letter tomorrow.*

*All of my love and kisses XX*
*Marge, your little wife*

The reference to Kansas City at the bottom of the last page and " . . . how long would I be able to stay . . ." on the left, refer to the possible up-coming trip to Texas to see Bill before he ships out.

This letter is as real as it gets.

October 7, 1944 - From Marge to Bill

*My dear Bill,*

*I'm going to try and jot a line. Have been kept pretty busy-you know the usual Saturday rush. Just got a small package ready to send to you. Will send another the first of the week that might be a little better. The candy in the box is some your Mother made. We have such a time finding boxes to put stuff in.*

*Sis (Goltz) is in here wrapping packages to send Billy and Mike. It is quite a job.*

*Guess they got word today that James McMarrow (married to Jean Welch) was killed in action. Bet she will take it hard as they always got along so good.*

*The folks still aren't home so we didn't go home for dinner. Kreebs left for Monticello this aft. Marie called and wanted to use my suitcase. I told her she could just so she brought it back to me before I went to Texas. Sure presuming a lot, aren't I?*

*Stan made 480 doz. cookies this week so he felt pretty good. He made coconut krispies today, first time ever. He sure cussed them but they are nice.*

*Max said she was in last nite. She was eating a cracker out of a box I had on the bench and Ray said, "You better look out or Marge will break your neck."*

*Max said, "Oh, I'm not worried."*

*Then she said that Ray said he wished I would fire him cause he'd like to quit. Said the flies were too damn thick around here for him, but boy, he has never said a word about them since he broke that fly spray. I told Stan I'd get some more and he said John told Ray he didn't want me too. Guess John is sort of shutting him once in a while.*

*Time out. Stan was just in and wanted me to give him a push. He had John's car and got stalled with it. You should*

Vlissingen ( Flushing in English) is a municipality and a city in the southwestern Netherlands on the former island of Walcheren. With its strategic location between the Scheldt River and the North Sea, Vlissingen has been an important harbour for centuries. On October 7, the Allies bombed the sea dikes of that city turning it into a swamp.

On this day, Fieldmarshal Rommel got his orders to return to Berlin.

Uprisings happen in both Auschwitz and Birkenau concentration camps as Jews attempt to burn down crematoriums.

have seen us - it was pretty good.

Well, darling, there are people in all of the time so I better quit and get this mailed. Guess Connie and Fitz are both here but I haven't seen them yet.

Sure hope I get a letter from you this aft. I sure wish you could be here for the week-end.

All of my love and kisses

Your wife,
Marge

October 8, 1944 - From Bill to Jim and Amanda

Dear Mother,

I got your letter the other day so am answering. I hope everyone is all right at home. I was sorry to hear Marie is so sick. Does she miss Bill yet? I wrote to Vernon about a month ago. I suppose he don't get much mail or anything now. We only can get 2 packages of cigarettes at a time now. We don't get a hell of a lot of time to write except on Sunday.

On this day, *The Adventures of Ozzie and Harriet* radio show debuts in the United States.

The Number One Song in the US was *You Always Hurt the One You Love* by the Mills Brothers.

I just came from Mass a little while ago. We have church in a big theater here. I've been going every Sunday. We were out on the rifle range all week getting up at four and getting in at 9 or 10 at night. Haven't had much sleep this week but caught up on it last night. Slept about 10 hrs. I suppose John is really putting the miles on that new car of his. Some days we haven't been getting much to eat but as a rule, they put out good meals. I usually hear from Marge twice a day, I guess. She has been keeping things going all right. We don't know for sure yet how long a training we will get here. Some of the Lieuts. say 6 weeks, others say 7 weeks, so we don't know where in the hell we stand. We go on an 18 mile hike Wed. I don't think I'm going to care for it too much. I made marksman all right on the rifle range so I don't have to take it over. Lots of them have to finish 3 or more times to make it. This week we have a moving targets, shoot the carbine, bazooka, rocket launcher and grenades. We usually have chicken every Sunday for dinner.

On October 9, British Prime Minister Winston Churchill and Soviet Union Premier Joseph Stalin begin a 9-day conference in Moscow to discuss the future of Europe.

I just took time off to go eat and go to mail call. I got a letter from you and 2 from Marge. I thought Stan got rid of all of his chickens by now. I got Bessie's (Aunt) letter but I just haven't had the time to answer it. We really don't have anytime of our own except on Sundays and then I usually write to you and Marge and maybe a couple others but then a guy likes a little time to lay around because the training ain't ever that easy here. There is sure a lot of gambling that goes on in the building on Sundays but I have enough to do without it.

Love,

Your son,
Bill

October 10, 1944 - From Marge to Bill

*Hi Honey,*

*Well how are you today. Hope you aren't too - too mad after having received yesterday's mail. I feel some better today but as yet I haven't received a letter from you. You aren't too mad to write are you? I'm keeping my fingers crossed so maybe I'll get some this aft.*

*This was a long morning. Just the usual routine. Went over and had a cup of coffee and Sis and I talked over our trip plans. I drink about as much coffee now as you used to. You said once you were going to send home some coffee and hand grenade pieces. What happened, did you forget?*

*I have Vern's package ready to send now all but for getting his address from Mother. It is surely a job to do it.*

*I went home to dinner today as Lu and Byron were up. She had dinner about ready when I got there.*

*Fleming was just in. He said to tell you hello. I never liked that guy very well. I ordered some jelly, cupcake liners and a box of currants for sale.*

*Everything is going just fine. If anything business is better the last couple weeks. There are surely more orders. Leona asked me today if we would bake the potatoes for their Farm Bureau fish fry next Tues nite. They are going to get rolls too and plan to serve about 500. What did you usually charge for baking the potatoes for something like that. Give me some idea if you can.*

*I just put three 15 lb. raw hams in the oven. The ladies wanted them started on a slow oven today and finish them in the morning. I talked to Ray and John about the 5 dozen panrolls they have ordered and they were just swell about it. Ray thought they better make a -- bl (?) and then use the rest for buns.*

*Ray even bought a 4 lb fruit cake this morning to send to Jimmie. I almost asked him if he was sick. Bobbie is doing pretty good on the panrolls now so they don't have much to gripe about.*

*John got a letter from one of the kids in his outfit who is in France now. I don't know what he said but John was very happy about the letter. Gee, I don't think he takes girls out very much anymore.*

*Vonnie was in this morning and was wondering if that old desk lamp of Bobs was still here so I gave her the top part of it but I'm sure I don't know where the rest is.*

*How is your money holding out, honey? I suppose you don't have too much to spend it on. Is your clothes supply big enough now? My, I sure hope I get a letter this afternoon.*

*I just happened to think if I go down there in Nov. I'll get out of the work for our unit but Veryle has volunteered to take my place and give them whatever they want. Pretty nice, eh?*

On this day, 800 Gypsy children are systematically murdered at the Auschwitz Nazi death camp. During The Holocaust, it is estimated that somewhere between 250,000 and 500,000 Gypsies are murdered in death camps. This became known as *The Porajmos* which means the *Devouring* in the Romani language.

The German occupying Army turned off the electricity in Amsterdam as a defensive move.

Fleet Admiral William Frederick Halsey's *Task Force 30* bombs Okinawa killing 700 Japanese.

On October 12, the Allies land in Athens, Greece and the Germans retreat.

Flage just came in with an order for the church in Dorchester for 700 parkerhouse and 2 white sheet cakes for Thursday. Guess the boys won't have a chance to loaf this week.

Well, honey, I have to go to the bank, city hall and make out my application for another "B" book and deliver to the Tydol and hospital so I better start doing it.

Remember honey that I love you with all of my heart and I'll try not to do anything to hurt you again. I can hardly wait until I can see you - Sis and I are counting the days by making an X thru each one. Hope I won't be disappointed now and can't come. Please write all of the time dear. I hope you are feeling fine. I have a honey of a sore throat today but it will be O.K. by then. Ha!

All of my love and kisses.

Your little wife,
Marge

<u>October 12, 1944 - From Marge to Bill</u>

Hi honey!

I received three wonderful letters from you this afternoon. Fri, Sat, and Mon. Gee honey, I get all the more lonesome for you, I think I could pack up and leave tomorrow. I don't know what to do though - What do you think? Should I wait till Nov 7 and come with Sis or come sooner. I'm afraid she will get mad if I don't wait for her. She hasn't enough money to go any sooner as she won't have her allotment check. Say we could leave the 6th tho - on Monday and get there one day sooner. The reason we planned to leave on Tues was that I would probably get there Fri and wouldn't have such a long wait till I got to see you. I thought it wouldn't be till Sat see, but if I could see you sooner than that we could leave as soon as she gets her check. I can't wait, honey.

I think my husband is getting a little lonesome too, don't you? You talked more about it this time then ever anyway. Everything is going O.K. here. Miekle was ornery this morning and that sort of made John mad but they will be all over it again tonight.

Helen B. was in this afternoon and wants me to come up for a little while tonite. I asked her if she wasn't afraid of my cold but she said she wasn't. I would much rather go to bed right when I get home tho.

Got a letter from Ralph A (Anderson) today. I'll send it on to you. I couldn't make much sense out of it. Say, you are really getting good at the letter writing, Bill. The army changed you, didn't it? How you used to always kid me and say that you weren't going to write very often. You sort of surprised me and it makes me feel good to have you write every day.

I suppose you are confirmed to the fact that I'm crazy as much as I write to you but gee, I feel so much closer to you then - almost like I'm talking to you. Of course I was always *pretty good at the talking wasn't I? As soon as I got the mail this afternoon I wanted to sit right down and write to you.*

*I haven't heard from Luther for almost a week but I think she is still pretty much in love with her husband. She is terribly lonesome tho. I hope she's home when I come down to see you cause I'd sure hate to miss her.*

*Uncle Frank (Waldron - Jim's brother) was just in. He said they are going to have a little card game tonite. Mother and Dad are going over, I guess. Maybe Gladys (wife) isn't going to think she is as much as the rest of you all thought. Suppose?*

*Sis and I are going to write to Oelwein to get information on the trip. Mrs. Ray Brandt went that way. Leave here on the afternoon bus for Oelwein and then take a train out of there at 8:00 at nite. Get in to Kansas City the next morning and take the Rocket from there to Oklahoma City - from there on, I don't know what I would be doing yet. I think you have to have reservations for the Rocket tho. I'm afraid if we asked old Fred, he probably would have us in California or some place.*

*I too thought Winona gave a pretty high price on the flour but of course I didn't know too much about it either.*

*Well, honey I'll finish writing tonite. Gee, I can hardly wait to see you. I love you so much, honey. I'm wondering if you will be sent to another camp. I sure hope not cause it might be still longer before we could get together.*

*All of My Love and Kisses XXXXXXX*
*Your wife - Marge*

<u>October 15, 1944 10:30 PM - From Marge to Bill</u>

*Hi Honey-*

*How is my husband tonite? Bet you are all tired out after your hard days work, aren't you? Oh, yes, this is your day of leisure so I suppose it is the loafing that made you tired.*

*I'm sleepy but that is nothing unusual. Veryle and I just got home from the show. I didn't care too much for it - Betty Grable in "Pin Up Girl." Sis went with us and then I made out the order and we had a coke.*

*Oh, yes, we also are walking. I don't know what's wrong with the car but I think it must be the battery. John pushed me from the back of the bakery down to the Tydol this morning and it wouldn't even think of starting. I'm going to have Rusty put in a battery in the morning and see if that's the trouble - if not, I'll call Metille to look at it.*

*This has been the longest day. The folks went fishing this morning. They got several little sunfish about three inches long and Mom caught a nice carp - about a lb. in all. Dad is rather disgusted with the fishing for this year.*

*Veryle and I ate dinner at the Model. It was the first Sunday I've eaten there since you left. Seemed sort of funny.*

The trip to Texas is becoming more of a reality. The *Rocket 507* was a more luxury-type train and was rumored to be faster than regular train service; one of the reasons was that it made fewer stops en route.

Rige, the capital of Latvia, is taken by the Red Army on October 13. Rumors would come out of the area of atrocities committed by the Communists and later there was proof of mass graves, but politics intervened and nothing ever came of the incident.

On October 14, German Field Marshal Erwin Rommel committed suicide rather than face trumped-up charges of conspiring against Adolf Hitler. Rommel had been a hero of the Fatherland, was awarded numerous medals and praise, and was Patton's greatest foe; he was a brilliant battlefield tactician and commander of tanks. His death is but one more example of the insanity that was Hitler.

*Time Magzine*

Gee, honey, it was two months ago today - the 15th- that you left for the Army. Really it seems like much, much longer than that to me. How about you?

We spent part of our afternoon in the Elite talking about our trip. We wrote a letter to the guy at Oelwein asking about train connections. I don't know if you remember me writing about the babe I gave a ride home from the post office one day or not. She used to live at Fort Sill. Well, she has been working in the Penny Store ever since she came here and is she ever a lot of fun. Her name is Hattie something and her husband has arrived safely at New Guinea. He is a Lieut. in the Air Corp, I think. She was down at the Elite with us too.

She had a film so we took pictures. I hope they are good. She was telling us all about her trips, etc, Her home used to be in South Dakota but she is living here with her sister and husband, the coach.

On October 15, the *Arrow Cross Party* (very similar to Hitler's Nazi Party) took over power in Hungary.

When we came home this aft. I wrote to Beck and slept awhile. I had the cramps all day so this bed felt pretty good.

We saw Lillian Brown on the street today and Sis says she heard that she really tears around a lot. Guess she goes up to LaCrosse for weekends and everything. Boy, wouldn't Guy like that - Honey, don't tell him tho cause I wouldn't want him to find out thru us. Have you seen him this week? He seemed like a nice guy from the way you talked but I always thought she was an old rip.

I'm anxious to get a letter from you tomorrow. They are all I wait for except the day when I get to see you.

Do you know Hazel Berger? Well, the other night Ray came home from bowling and said that she and some other gal had it all arranged with Steve that Ray and Steve were going to go out with them that nite. It sort of made Ray mad - he thought that took a lot of guts. Steve went with them tho and I guess he steps out all of the time and his wife is about to have her baby almost any time. Ray described the other gal but we couldn't figure out who it was. Today I found out it was Thelma Palmer-Broderick. Boy, I bet she does step high, wide, and handsome. Wonder what our darling Dorothy would say to that.

Sis said Margaret L. was in just cussing Mrs. O'Riley the other day. Mrs. O'Riley said she didn't know where the kids would stay when they came home. Guess one would have to stay one place and the other at the other. You know how Margaret likes her anyway. So she was raving.

Gee, Bill, I'm wondering if you got to be cook. It seems like it takes so long to write you a letter and get an answer. I surely hope you can, cause then you wouldn't have quite so much marching, etc. to do.

The wife of the New Waukon Lumber Co. comes in every day. I like her a lot. She is older than me and has a girl married, I think, but she is a lot of fun. Did you ever charge any-

thing down there?

Well, darling, I still love you, as you know. I'll say my prayers now and go to bed. Keep writing, honey.

All of my love,

Your wife
Marge

October 16, 1944 - From Marge to Bill

My dearest Bill,

I got a letter from you this morning. I'm glad you got out of going on that 18 mi. hike. Save your energy for something else. What did you have to do at the Mess hall? I hope that means that you will get to stay there if that is what you want. I really don't see why you wouldn't like it better.

Gee, is this ever a beautiful day. Sis and I are going over to Decorah with Marie this afternoon. Mom is going to keep Patsy and Billy (Marie Kreeb's kids)

Rusty hasn't gotten around to the car yet but he thought it was the battery. Gee, I hope it isn't shot cause it doesn't seem like so long since you got it.

My Aunt Matilda (her mother's brother's wife—married to Lynn Gordinier) from Kalamazoo Mich stopped in to see me a minute this morning. Gee, but I was surprised to think she'd stop up there cause I haven't seen her for years. She also stopped a minute to see mom so that made her feel pretty good.

I delivered to Owens this morning. Is that joint ever small. Guess he has the business though, cause he sold 16 1/2 doz. buns Sat.

John took me to the school with the bread this morning. He said that Mert told him Bernie is married to some guy who works in Lockheed Aircraft in Calif. Boy, there is another one out of circulation. I told John I could imagine what you would say when you heard it.

Mom just came in and sat again so its jabber-jabber. She said to tell you that they sure thought about you when they were fishing yesterday.

Marie said Ray and the guys got 9 squirrels yesterday morning.

I'm going to see if I can get some cake boxes from Hank. I ordered some but as yet they haven't come. We really were kept busy this morning.

I hope I get your letter to see what you think about getting that Baxter girl soon. I'd like to get her used to things while I'm still here. Ray was gone before I got to work at 7:00 this morning. John said they didn't talk much so that accounts for it.

I still haven't written to Dorothy. Veryle wrote to Ralph so I won't have to for a while. She sort of thought he was O.K., I think.

*I saw the rat when I was back sitting on the can this morning and it about scared me so I didn't have to go. I made Veryle come back till I got out of there. He sure is tame, too. Only hope we can catch him soon.*

*Honey, I'm anxious to see if you still want me to come down. I'm planning strong on it. I'm so anxious to see you that I'll even be brave enough to travel, I think.*

*Gee, I didn't know it got so cold you had to wear winter underwear. You'll have to tell me what kind of clothes to bring.*

*Well, darling, I sure miss you and love you more all of the time. Have to wipe dishes for Mom now so bye, bye.*

*All of my love and kisses,*

*Your wife*
*Marge*

October 17, 1944 - From Marge to Bill

This letter suffers from severe water damage. The reason that Marge's letters up to this date are available is that Bill saved them and they were either transported back home with Marge when she returned to Waukon from Texas or were boxed up and shipped back to Iowa before Bill shipped out.

The water damage on this letter and the fact that we do not have any letters written after this time might suggest that they were destroyed by water while in Bill's locker or wherever he stored them or, more probable, at some time after they were stored in Waukon as we lack many of Bill's letters from this same period.

*My dearest Bill,*

*Another beautiful day. This weather is surely too nice to last. It would surely be grand if you (water damage - 1/2 page)*

*I don't expect a letter from you today, dear. The mail evidently doesn't leave the camp on Sunday.*

*Everything is going fine at the bakery. There wasn't much work to do this morning so we cleaned showcases and woodwork. Everything gets dirty so quickly. I called Vonnie this morning. I was wondering if she was going (back of water damage page)*

*She said Bob thought he could get you into the mess hall and you wouldn't have to go across. He said he had sort of a pull or something. Had gotten a couple of other guys off from going across. Sis and I almost laughed in her face. Bob really thinks he is such a big shot no matter where he is.*

*I can hardly wait until I get down there, Bill. Sis hasn't been feeling very good the last couple days. She is afraid she might (water damage - page 2)*

It should come as no surprise that we lack any of Marge's letters while Bill was in Europe. Infantrymen, scouts and cooks lacked any means to keep and store much more than what would go in a backpack. Further, the Army mandated that all letters be burned after reading in case of capture by the enemy.

*I'm wondering what you are doing this week. Did a lot of the guys get shipped out at the end? Would you rather stay at the mess hall? I thought cook and bakery school was closed.*

*Campbells got a letter from the gov't this morning saying that they received word Sept 24 that Billy is convalesing. They can send a five word cablegram to him.*

*Well I'm going to do some work so I'll sign off for this afternoon, I still love you. (water damage back of page 2)*

October 17, 1944 - From Bill to Marge

*Dear Marge,*

*Still haven't got any mail yet but I guess it will be a few days yet. We get up at 5:30 in the morning here. This morning we had 4 hrs of lectures and 5 lessons on cooking, baking and meat cutting. They were pretty interesting but this afternoon we really had a treat. A truck rolled up to the barracks at one o'clock and took us down to the camp warehouse, packinghouse, and bakery. The bakery is all run by German war prisoners. Most of them were in the African campaign. I talked with 4 or 5 of them for about an hour. Some of them can speak pretty good English. They sure have a snap of it. They work about 2 - 3 hours a day and spend the rest of the time sitting around. I asked them what the hell they thought of Hitler and they sure think he's all right. They say they don't have any younger soldiers than we do in this country. Most of these guys were from 20 - 28. Really good-looking guys. They don't have any guard around at all. I think they are allowed more freedom than the guys in camp. They said they don't like the women in this country as well as their own because they use too much lipstick and finger nail polish and that over there they don't use any. One of them when he was sitting alone talking to me said he was damn glad he was here instead of over there but if another one is around, they will never say anything against it. Some of them still think they will win the war. They say this country right around here is just the same as it was in Africa. I've seen them around here a lot but I never had a chance to talk to any before. Some of them think they are still going to win the war.*

*The bakery was really modern. They had 2 big high-speed mixers. Then the dough went into the dough room for 2 1/2 hrs, then onto the dough divider and rounder. From there it went up overhead and raised for 10 min. Then came down into the moulder, panned, and run into the proofing room. From there it comes out and went into the oven. They hold 680 loaves of bread. They had 2 oven trays over but all automatic. It would go around and when it got around it was done - 32 min. to bake.*

*Honest, had a pack on all week and it sure feels funny without it. The old company I was in has a 25 mi one this week. I'd sure as hell hate to be on it. How's Veryle coming by now. Has she got herself a boy friend around town yet or is she still going with the cream hauler yet? How's about John? Has he got anything*

Written from Camp Hood.

On October 18, Generals Eisenhower, Bradley and Montgomery conferred in Brussels.

Soviet troops invade Czechoslovakia in the early morning on the 18th.

On October 18, the *Volkssturm* is founded by Adolf Hitler.

This was a German national militia of conscripted males between the ages of 16 and 60 years who were not already serving in some military unit.

Because the Wehrmacht was running out of men, Hitler ordered Martin Bormann to recruit six million men for this militia - that number was never attained.

On October 19, the US Navy begins accepting black women volunteers into the Waves.

On October 20, Belgrade was liberated by Yugoslav Partisans and the Red Army.

American forces landed on Red Beach in Palo, Leyte as General Douglas MacArthur returned to the Phillippines.

United States Marines and Filipino troops with Filipino guerillas begin the Battle of Leyte.

on the string yet? I suppose he's got quite a few dents in the car by now or has he been taking a little better care of it now. Stan, I suppose is still staying clear of the girls or has it started to bother him now?

I think this is really going to be all right here. We'll get home at the end of 7 weeks, the same as the rest, maybe. I suppose Ray is still bitching as much as ever but there will come a day when you won't have to put up with that shit. Well, I'll be waiting to hear from you.

Lots of love,

Your Husband
Bill

October 20, 1944 - From Bill to Marge

Dear Marge,

Well, I didn't get any mail tonight. I suppose it has to accumulate a little up there before the mail clerk will send it down. We signed the payroll tonight so I guess we will get paid this month after all. We seem to have a hell of a good First Sarg. And Captain. It means a little extra work for them by having it signed this late. A guy don't dare stay in fatigue clothes here after supper because after supper they usually pick a couple details for something and it is usually guys with their work clothes on yet.

We got up at 5:15 this morning but it wasn't a very tough day. We fire at airplanes they have that are radio controlled. There are about 12x9 ft in size. They have a regular motor in them and everything. They go about 150 mi./hr. Cost $1500. Just for trainees to shoot at. We knocked down one of them but they are sure hard to hit. They dive, loop, and everything just like a pilot was in them. When they get hit in the motor or radio, they cut out and a big parachute opens and they come down easy. It is really surprising how good they have them working. When we came in tonight, we passed a bunch of kids out at Hood village where cadets live. They were probably from 4-8 yrs old. The Captain said eyes right and we marched along and turned our heads to the right. These kids all snapped to attention and saluted all the officers as we went by. Everybody got a big kick out of it. The Captain said the kids really like it every time he brings a company by because he always gives them eyes right or left.

We had a swell supper tonight, all we could eat. Cake, mashed potatoes, gravy, salad, carrots & peas, duck, bread and butter and coffee. The duck was really good. The mess Sarg. said we were a little heavier eatin' than he figured so he would try to have plenty to eat from now on.

Well, how is everybody coming at home by now? I've sure been lucky. All I've had was a little cold. I thought I had some poison oak once but it was just a little on my fingers and it healed right up without spreading. I don't know what the hell we have on tomorrow. We have to wear our packs again though. Today we wore field packs this morning and combat packs this afternoon. This is sure a lot different than where we were before. They aren't telling us here all the time we are going right overseas like they did up at 196th. They got a thousand Japanese in here yesterday to start basic training. They are about 4 blocks up from here. I think there will be lots of fights here now. Write soon and let me know when you are coming down and I'll fix things up.

All my love,

Your husband
Bill

October 22, 1944 - From Bill to Marge

Dear Marge,

I got 3 letters from you tonight but one of them sure sounded screwy. You said you hadn't heard from me for 3 days, yet you had the letter addressed with my new address. I can't figure it out. Maybe you can tell me how you did it? That's pretty good about White getting me in a mess hall. Even a 1st Liet. ain't got a hell of a lot of say about keeping you in one. The one up in the old Co. tried his damndest to keep me there (as a cook) but he couldn't. I'm sure glad he couldn't do (it) because those boys are really getting hell worked out of them. I stopped up there after Mass for a couple of hrs and shot the bull with some of them. Then this afternoon Red came down and we went to the show. After waiting for 2 hrs to get in, it was "The Song of Bernadette." It was a religious picture all about Lourdes, France, a Catholic picture. I was surprised to see it here.

It is getting so we can't buy a damn thing at the P.X. anymore. They haven't had any candy or matches for 3 weeks now. When one guy lights a cigarette, there are about 40 around after a lite. These P.X.'s are just like a variety store only not so nice. They have counters and a line about 50 or so long to get up to them. Then on one side they have pop and beer and there is a really long line there. When you get your pop or beer, you go outside and they have a big pen all fenced in with tables where you drink it. No pop or beer can be taken out of the P.X. The help is all civilians. We have a lot of pretty girls working in them so we do see women down here. Most of the Texas girls are plenty good looking too and I guess the boys have them all pretty well broke in. I can't understand why you haven't been getting my letters because I write every day. I hope you try to see Jim and tell him about the letter I wrote you about the money. He must not of got mine. I kinda feel sorry for him now. This war is sure ruining things for him. By the way what rank is White anyway that he has so much pull? Is he in the infantry or what? If he is I bet it really kills him to do a little work. I'm sorry to hear

On October 20, a liquid natural gas explosion destroyed a square mile of Cleveland, Ohio. 135 people died and 3,600 became homeless.

On October 21, Aachen became the first German city to be captured by the Allies. Aachen was destroyed partially - and in some parts completely - during the fighting, mostly by American artillery fire and demolitions by fanatical Waffen-SS defenders.

*The Song of Bernadette* starred Jennifer Jones, Charles Bickford and Vincent Price and won 4 Oscars.

your dad isn't well but I would think Albert (her brother) could get things fixed up so he wouldn't need to be going to the farm all the time. I wish this war would be over just as much as you do and I could be home again but that's hard telling how long it will be. They really have some pretty hot arguments here about the war.

On October 22, the 1st Central Kitchen opens in Amsterdam bringing much needed food and sustenance to the starving population.

I hope Ray and Marie are not mad at me for not writing but you know how well I like to write and outside writing you and the folks, I'd just as soon not write anyone. I don't if I can get out of it.

All my Love

Your Husband
Bill

Page 5 & 6 -same paper but no 1st pages

. . . picked out of the different rifle co. they have been sending the fuckups and guys who can't take it in the rifle company to another camp in Georgia. Now I talked to some of the guys in the old Co. and they said they sent out 20 of the fuckups this week and got 20 guys from another rifle Co.

I wrote you about seeing Brown the other night but I think he is on pass this weekend. Somebody ought to take that bitch of a wife of his out and shoot her. I kinda think he knows she is whoring around from the way he talked but he didn't come right out and say so and I didn't say nothing to him. One guy in our barracks is trying every day to get a furlough so he can go home. He worked in Hollywood before he came in and his wife is an actress. His sister came down on the train to see him and told him about all the whoring around she is doing and I guess he is about nuts. He was on the detail with us last. I wrote you about the Broadway star we had with us over in the other Co. His pictures are a lot of these CocaCola advertisements showing 2 soldiers drinking Coke with a girl. The officers and non-comms really rode the hell out of him because he figured he could get out of most of the work.

Well, Marge I better quit now and get to church before it is too late. I'll be waiting to hear when you are coming. I can't hardly wait till you get here.

Lots of Love,

Your Husband
Bill

On this date, the Naval Battle of Leyte Gulf in the Philippines began and would end, on October 26, in an Allied victory.

October 23, 1944 - To Bill From His Mother Amanda

Dear Son Bill

Well, this is the 23rd - our Wedding Anniversary. Hope I can be here for another 27 years. Marge was up for supper. The first time she's been up since I don't know when. I mean for a meal but my chicken wasn't done enough. Stacks is taking the oil stove back and selling it. I got Stella Olson's, the oven is a little larger. We went out to Althea's tonight *but Dad has an awful cold. Just don't seem to get rid of it so only played one game and came home. How do you like the school? And what do you do? Suppose you are counting the time till Marge comes. Stan had a letter from Vernon today. Didn't say much, it was getting darn awful cold over there. Wishes he was back here. Dad said he saw Handy I. on the street today.*

*Was Bessie ever mad last week. Her and Leo won the prize waltz last Wed and she heard the prize was only going to be a dollar. She told Marie Veretien who is our leader. So Marie gave her $5.00 in defense stamps. I told Marie I didn't sell tickets to give it away. We have a food sale Sat. and then Marge's month starts. And then we have the bazaar and will be selling chances on pigs and sheep but they will be a quarter a chance this year. Haven't got you to get rid of a few chances to. How about sending you a book of chances?*

*Ed Helming plowed the garden this afternoon. Thought maybe it wouldn't be quite so hard next year. Oh, we have a pet down cellar chewing to get out. Stanley's pullets are starting to lay if he would just get rid of them –will be getting cold.*

*Had a letter from Beck the other day. Said she didn't think she'd bring Jimmy up till spring. Afraid he'd get a cold. Thought sure she'd be up in this nice weather. Bud White got home late night again. He sure is lucky.*

*How did you like the fruitcake? Dan Regan expected Danny home - 4 of their letters came back they wrote. Mrs. Keefe had a letter from Tommy that he had lost his hearing and thought he'd be home soon. Nobodys ever heard from Keefe since he left. Campbells haven't heard anything from Bill. Just a letter from the gov. that he was getting along all right. It's 6 weeks since he was hurt. I wonder if Pat is going tomorrow. Paper said he was working in Waterloo. Well, guess I'll hit the hay. Write.*

*With Love,*

*Mother*

*P.S. Marge brought the things up you sent and had on the pearls, honey t.*

October 30, 1944 - From Bill to Jim and Amanda

*Dear Ma and Dad,*

*Well, I got a letter from you last night so I better get writing this. Cooking has got the rifle Co. beat all to hell. Don't have to take much of the other training except a day a week and an hour drill in the morning. The rest of the time we spend cooking. We cook in one building and then take it to the mess halls. In another couple of weeks, we get farmed out to different mess halls for 3 weeks then we work with the regular cooks. We will be on for 24 hrs. and then off 24. They are going to open up another Co. of cooks here in 3 weeks so*

On October 25, the Red Army enters Kirkenes, the first town in Norway to be liberated.

The US Navy engaged the Japanese in the Straits of Surigao and destroyed their fleet located there.

On October 28, Russia and Bulgaria signed a weapons pact.

On October 29th, the 1st Polish Armoured Division liberated Breda, Netherlands.

On this date, Anne Frank and sister Margot Frank were deported from Auschwitz to Bergen-Belsen concentration camps.

On October 30, Scottish Highlanders liberated Waalwijk.

Sweden announced their intention to stay neutral in the World War and to refuse sanctuary.

Sally Kirkland, actress (Anna, Sting, Pvt Benjamin, Big Bad Mama), is born on this day.

*there will be 120 out of the whole camp going to cooks school. Not a hell of a lot, I think they are probably short more cooks than that in this camp alone. We don't get any rating here, not until we get assigned to a regular outfit so I guess they give us some kind of a cook school diploma. Most of these guys have had from 2 yrs to 10 at cooking, baking or meat cutting. We get all three of them but after I get out of here, I'm going to try to get in as a pastry baker because they have one in every mess hall.*

*I got up early this morning and called Marge but she had gone to church so I missed her. I talked to her mother though and gave her the address of the room I got for her. I think I'll be able to get out the first night she gets here but we can only get out till 11 o'clock. Lots of the boys go without passes so if I don't get any, I'll take one.*

*I've only been out of camp once since I've been here. There really isn't a hell of a lot of use. You can buy most stuff in here. Of course, you wait for 2 or 3 hours if you want to go to the show or anything. I've only been to two shows. This last week I was on guard duty and K.P. so I shouldn't catch either one again while Marge is here. I also had the G.I. shits for the first time since I've been in the Army. I really had the sore stomach for a few days. Some guys have them every couple weeks so I have been plenty lucky.*

*I went to Mass a little while ago. We had Mass and benediction this morning. I'm going to try going Wed. morning if I can slip away. I suppose John has quite a few miles on his car by now. If I'm lucky I might get home for New Years and get a ride in it. Then we come in off a 2-week bivouac Christmas eve and the next week they give us review and start shipping us out. But some of the cooks will be kept home but I hope I'm not one of them. About 50% of them leaving here have been going overseas right after their furlough. They are still sending most of them to Fort Meade, Maryland.*

*We got one French cook here who couldn't speak English until 3 months ago when he came into the army and he is sure a crazy devil. Came from Louisiana and half the time, no one knows what the hell he is talking about.*

*There are about 3,000 Japs and Whites shipped here from Hawaii to take their basic training. I wouldn't be surprised at all if they sent Pat Campbell down here because they have been sending a lot here from Snelling and Levenworth but I hear that Snelling is closed for induction station now and is going to be turned into a discharging station.*

*We have a lot of guys go over the hill here every day but they get them back in a week or two. Some of them go 2 and 3 times. They either get a dishonorable discharge, Sec. 8 or go to prison. Tell John I've seen and talked with a lot of these German prisoners that were all in the African campaign. They don't even have any guard over there. They run the bakery* here and things like that. They have more freedom than the trainee's, I think. Some of them speak pretty good English, others can't at all. It is really unbelievable the way they have it. They get radios and everything else to listen to. Some of them still think they are going to win the war.

I think I have missed Marie more that any of them at home. How is she coming now? Over being sick? I suppose she is still running away every chance she gets.

Well, I better quit now. It's just about dinnertime. I've put on about 10 lbs. since I've been here but I don't see how.

Write soon.

Lots of love,

Your Son,
Bill

November 1, 1944 - From Veryle to Bill and Marge

Dear Marge and Bill,

Well here I am again. It is about 2:15 and I just finished sweeping the floor out back.

Well, I suppose 'tonight's the night' for you kids, huh?

Well, last night was Halloween and boy did the kids ever do a good job of soaping every window in town, including the car windshield. It was over to the garage as Stan took it over yesterday noon and it wasn't done at 6 o'clock. At 8:30 I went out to see what I could do with the window and I bet every place clear down the street had somebody out washing windows. I took a razor blade and scraped the soap off and then later Max washed the rest of it off. Ruth and I are going to wash the inside after she comes down.

Hey, Marge was that lady there to meet you? Were you scared traveling alone?

Say, Harris Evans married Delila Halverson last night. Do you know her?

The fire whistle just blew, wonder where the fire is.

Oh, Marge my clock is OK now. I set it 15 min. fast last night in case the current went off but it didn't and I forgot I'd set it fast, so I came around the bank corner at 6:30 this morning.

Ray was in this afternoon. Didn't say much only that he wished Bobby would clean the steam box floor. Gee whiz is it ever hot around here today. Everybody says there is a storm on the way - Darn it!

The hospital gave me that slip today. The schoolhouse asked for their bill. I paid both milkmen and also Russell Miller for the last 2 boxes of Sweetex.

Some current news now. Schwartz's are selling out everything tomorrow. Going out of business. They had signs all over the front windows. So maybe I'll have a new dress again.

Grandma and pa (Viola and George Leet, Marge's parents)

It's apparent that Marge is on her way to Texas and that in Veryle's opinion she would have arrived this day.

These letters are rich in the savor of small town America during the War.

Also, the impression is that Veryle has the bakery situation well in hand.

On November 1, units of the British Army land at Walcheren in the Netherlands. This was known as *Operation Infatuate* and was necessary in order to capture the vital ports of Antwerp. The amphibious landing was accomplished against heavily fortified and entrenched German positions.

*Time Magazine*

*went up to Land's last night. Same relation was up there.*

*No mail except the "Rap-in Wax Gossip." In it was signs in a beauty parlor---"closed for the week-end, husband home on furlough"*

*Flags didn't leave an order for Pottratz for tomorrow so.........*

*Oh, yes and the cake boxes came in. I paid freight on them and also paid Kiesau for hauling that flour. It seems like all I did this morning was something extra. About 10:30 Grandma called and said the stuff for your unit was ready so I had to go over and get the car and get that stuff. They had a big crowd upstairs and a very good menu. Max and I ate dinner up there. Chicken and noodles, beans, cabbage salad, coffee, rolls, and apple pie. Sound good?*

*Have you found an iron to press your clothes yet? I suppose you'll be drinking some of your precious cargo tonight won't you?*

*I don't know exactly what it was Monday night about $60, I think and last night was a little better.*

*Have you noticed the beautiful full moon? It was really pretty last night. I walked home from town about 10:30 and it was as bright as day—almost.*

*Mrs. Waldron has the flu now. She said all she did this morning was sit on the can. Jean and Mr. Waldron are better. Stan and Husky went hunting today, I guess.*

*That lady that adopted that little boy - the one from the bank was in the other day. The kid is real cute.*

*Rath just brought a tierce of lard. Any paper I don't know for sure what to do with, I file away so I know where it is.*

*Where are you staying? How far from Camp? How often can Bill get a pass? Oscar (Stan) wants to take his drivers test today but he didn't know who's car he was going to use the last time I saw him. Wonder if he found one.*

*Did you know that we couldn't make "butter" cookies because the ration points on butter was so high we couldn't get enough any more? Well, that is what one woman told me yesterday.*

*I guess I'll have to write letters to you before I go to bed because if I write in the afternoon as you suggested, I hate to go back to work.*

*Well I guess I've told you all the news for now so bye until tomorrow.*

*"Veryle"*

*PS - Joe came and brought "the Witness" and a check from Eitzen.*

On November 2, according to German sources, "in order to save needed munitions," at concentration camp Auschwitz they began to gas inmates.

Canadian troops occupy Knokke on the Belgian coast.

US 28th Infantry Division opens an assault on Schmidt Hurtgenwald in Eifal's Kailital Valley.

Marie-Louise Osmont lived in a chateau overlooking the Normandy beaches with her husband, a physician. The occupying Germans appropriated the home for their own use after invading France in 1940 but allowed the Osmonts to stay in a few rooms. The house stood near the point on the Normandy coast designated for attack by the British forces - Sword Beach. Marie-Louis kept a diary of her experiences. "The Witness" is her story.

November 2, 1944 - From Viola to Bill and Marge

Dear Marge and Bill,

How are you by now? Suppose you were very tired, have you got rested some?

Did Bill have any trouble getting away? Seems like it will be a long time before we hear.

Veryle said that a card came today but she did not bring it home. Was nice that you had company after Sis left. Veryle heard that Harris Evans was married Tuesday eve. But I have not called Mae. Eardie just called and invited us up to supper tomorrow nite. Her birthday - will go if can, if not at farm. Rained some and looks awful dark now, Dad told Al to call and has not yet and its 9:30 now. Veryle gone with Stan. Dad gone to bed. Dad asked Al where Closse was. He said they had bought a place up in Minn. And sent him to take care of things until they go. He asked if they were going before school was out and he said no, but very careful to say no more.

Closse told Byron Monday that he was going to work for Harlin Herms, Al told dad that he would help Harlin so that is that.

I ironed today, cleaned cabinet and worked around. I cleaned your room and waxed the floors. Looks clean but will have time to get dirty again.

Veryle came home about 5 and dad came after so we got supper and we had a long evening. I crocheted some. Sure miss you - hope to hear from you this week.

Lots of love

Mother and Dad

Have a good laugh about the way Mom writes her letters! Do you have enough covers on the bed? Ha Ha

On November 3, two supreme commanders of the Slovak National Uprising, Generals Jan Golian and Rudolf Viest, are captured, tortured and later executed by German forces.

Allied commandos landed at Westkapelle in the Netherlands.

German troops in Vlissingen, Netherlands, surrender to superior Allied forces.

US 28th Infantry Division occuppied Schmidt Hurtgenwald.

November 4, 1944 - From Viola Leet to Bill and Marge

Dear Marge and Bill,

This Sat afternoon Veryle brought your letter at noon and am so glad to hear that you are there because I know how nervous you must have been and being so tired and about sick, but hope you are much better by now. Hope throat OK.

How are you, Bill? I know it must of seemed long after she got there before you got together and do hope you can be together over Sunday. It seems like ages since you left.

Well, Al (Marge's brother who farms the home place outside Waukon) called at 7 this morning and said the (corn) picker was on the way so we went down but they did not start until most 11, just had 7 men. Mrs. Bolds there yet. She did not say anything about coming back today so I did not go.

And to our surprise Ethyl (her sister) and Judy (niece) came to visit. Dot (Al's wife) was at school (teacher) and Aulger came to town to see Veryle (Ethyl and Aulger have

On November 4, German troops reconquered Schmidt Hurtgenwald.

On November 5, Canadian and British troops liberated Dinteloord in the Netherlands.

German troops blew-up the Heusden North Brabant city hall killing 134 Dutch civilians.

According to Billboard Magazine, the Number One Song in America was *I'll Walk Alone* by Dinah Shore

Lux Radio Theater was sponsored by Lever Bros. who made Lux soap. These hour-long radio programs were performed live before studio audiences. It became the most popular dramatic anthology series on radio, broadcast for more than 20 years (1933 - 1954) and continued on television as the Lux Video Theatre through most of the 1950s. The night Veryle was listening, Cecil B. DeMille was the radio host.

two daughters - Veryle who works at the Bakery and Judy. They are from Clermont, IA. Dot and Al had no children).

They came back by dark all there for supper. We got home about 10. They are still there. Ethyl brought pumpkin pie, loaf of bread, some grape jam. I think it is too much for Al, but they will get it all out today (the corn). Hard for Dad too. Al will have to help men back, don't think they will take pay.

They bought the house from the folks that they stayed with when up there. Those folks moved to town - a 3 room house and a cabin. Some difference, I say. He wondered if she could keep it clean, ha!

They bought 3 cows and Closse going to take care of things. He went on the train. So far he was afraid it would rain and he don't run his motorcycle in cold weather. And we could not go up for supper for Erdies birthday.

Veryle did not drive car home last nite. She said something did not sound right but she drove it down at noon so someone can drain it. Weather cooler but awful nice today.

I scrubbed the kitchen floor and waxed it this forenoon. Shirley came up this noon. Lula's (other sister) were up yesterday. I don't know how long here. She left a coal flatiron for Cliff.

Hope you are rented somewhere by now. Harris Evans married last Tues. Al's got a card for shower at hall Tues eve, but have not yet.

I don't know when V. will write. She said everything was OK at noon and she has just been home one eve. She did not come to eat yesterday when we were gone.

Hope you will be able to get to church somewhere. All for now.

Write soon

Lots of Love,
Mother and Dad

Veryle took the girls birthday presents up Thursday.

<u>November 6, 1944 - From Veryle to Marge with Bill</u>

Dear Marge,

Lux Radio theatre is on so if I make some mistakes please excuse them.

Well everything went ok today. We got the order off in time and I had 3 loaves of bread left to slice when Ruth came at noon. I didn't go home for dinner. Not time enough.

John wasn't at work last night and wasn't home all day today. Wonder if he'll be there tonight. I'm not in the mood for writing at all.

Today was Marie's (Waldron) birthday. Amanda wanted a cake decorated so I decorated one for her. A 39 cent one.

I got a long letter from Ralph this afternoon. He says he hopes you like Texas better than he did. I'm glad you're so *happy. It was worth the long trip down there, wasn't it?*

*What have you been doing lately?*

*Today was pretty good about 68 degrees. Quite a lot left though.*

*I asked Ray today if there was anything he wanted to order this week and he said no - except salt from Bob's. He said we have about 12 # of sugar on hand and not to loan any to any one.*

*I just finished washing my hair. I'm hoping on going out tomorrow night. If I do, I'll tell you about it later.*

*My clock runs just fine as long as the current is on. It usually wakes me up about 6 o'clock every morning.*

*Gee, the weather has taken a turn for the colder. It was sleeting when I came home tonight. I can't think of any more to write now.*

*Love,*
*Veryle*

On November 7, 1944 the United States held presidential elections. Franklin D. Roosevelt won reelection over Republican Thomas E. Dewey, becoming the only U.S. President elected to a fourth term. At a later date, the American people approved a constitutional amendment to ensure that no other person would serve more than two terms in that office.

Sometime in November, 1944 - From Marie and Ray Kreeb to Marge with Bill

*Dear Marge and Bill;*

*How's Texas and Bill by now? And you, Marge, are you getting used to it again? Practice makes perfect.*

*We went home Sat. afternoon. I stayed at Mom's in Hopkinton with Billie and Patsy and Ray took Jackie over to Monticello to his mothers. We tried getting rid of those damn bugs while we were gone. We burned sulfur and put mothball dust all over everything before we left Sat. It nearly killed Ray but it didn't hurt the bugs any. We didn't stay long in Monti. It was eleven before I got over there Sun. We went to Ray's folks for a while and had to eat dinner at Bob's folks. We took the baby to the church at two and by two thirty we were ready to start for home again. We had to get home early so we could air out the house and clean it out before we could bring the kids in. We took them over to Mrs. Lands until 8.*

On November 8, in a deal between the governments of Hungary and Germany, 25,000 Hungarian Jews were "loaned" to the Nazis to work as forced labor.

*Gee, George sure looks swell again. The baby is sure a tiny thing. George and Bob aren't getting along too hot. She said all she let him do now was look at her and he didn't like it. She cried when we left, poor kid, I feel sorry for her.*

*Veryle called tonight, first I've heard of her for a while. She is quite the kid, I like her.*

The last German troops at Walcheren surrendered. The next day, all of the Nazis were shot.

*Louise called from Anamosa tonight. She got home from Washington, D.C. on Friday and was to come home with us Sun. But real luck happened for her. Her brother John got home from the army too last week, so they had a big family dinner Sun. That's the first time she has seen him for almost 2 yrs. She is coming up here tomorrow on the jitney, I'm to meet her in Calmar. I wish you were here to go with me.*

A nickles was once called a *jitney* but the term was most commonly used for a bus that traveled a specific route. When Marie writes that Louise is coming up on the *jitney*, it is probably the Greyhound bus.

*Say, you bum, when are you going to come home? I bet*

you wish you could stay for good.

We are going on a party Sat. night to the Burg with Dutch Russel and Lee and his wife. Think I'll have any fun? I'll make it if there isn't any.

The sewing club is Thurs night again. I have fun now. They're going to take inventory at the yard tomorrow. Ray was working last night. I was along and we had the worse thunder and hailstorm. Boy was I scared.

On November 9, the American Red Cross was presented the Nobel Peace Prize.

We weighed Billie Sun. He weighs 13 1/2 lbs. So you can see he is still growing. I got him on all cows milk now. Never bothered him a bit.

I better go on something myself. I'm sure losing. I started drinking milk besides my beer. That should do something. I'm going to eat every thing this time to get fat.

Nita May (Robinson - Dad's first cousin) comes up some times now. She brought that ass she is going with along. Gee, I think he is a dope.

I'll be glad when your Willie can come home, then we can go on some good ones.

Helen Flage had some of the women over to her house last Thurs afternoon. Helen and Merle Sullivan and their families, Mrs Handgardner, Mrs Earl Kelley, two women I didn't know and Mrs Kreeb and her young ones. (all older ladies but her)

Billie woke up so be careful and write!

Love, Marie and Ray Kreeb

November 9, 1944 - From Viola Leet to Bill and Marge

Dear Marge and Bill,

How are you kids? We have not had a letter since Monday. Have you stopped writing or are we just not getting the mail?

Hope to hear today and that you are fine. If sick, Bill can send a word. I wonder if you are getting our letters.

On November 10, the citizens of Rotterdam/Schiedam rioted. After the Germans had put the riots down, they shipped 52,000 men to Germany. Most were never heard from again.

All O.K. here, Dad gone to the farm to fix things and I will not even have to get dinner. Think of that!

Well, did the cold spell get down there? No snow here and just down to freezing last night. Sun came out and is so nice and will warm up today. I just finished cleaning in here for Sat. I will make pies for the church unit. Think I will make fresh apple that will be as good as any. Wish you could have one.

Have you been in stores much? How are things? Suppose they have different things there than we do. Are the grocery (stores) about the same? Cecil (Marge's aunt - Viola's sister) called here from Ida's (Ida Cook-friend). She was not so good. She washed and ironed and that was too much for her.

The US 9th Army took Margraten cemetery.

Veryle went with Marie to Calmer to take a friend to the train this afternoon. She got Max and they got back about quarter to four and then she did not come home to supper until usual time.

Erdie (Mrs. Land, her friend and our babysitter) stayed with kids. She called and was going to stay with kids last nite to. I am going to try to write to Goldie (Goldie Burman, sister-in-law in Waverly, IA) now but I don't think they will be up any more this fall. I did not hear Veryle say when she wrote to you. Hope we get a letter today and that you are O.K.

Lots of love,

Dad and Mom

P.S. Veryle called and said we got a nice letter but I will mail this before I get that one so glad you are OK.

On November 12, the Royal Air Force sank the German battleship *Tirpitz* at Tromso Fjord Norway.

November 15, 1944 - From Veryle to Marge with Bill

Dear Marge,

I'll start this now and finish it later. I'm going to a dance in Waterville later.

Of all things to happen. The refrigerator didn't click in all morning so I was going to call Jay but he doesn't have a phone. So Amanda sent Stan to see him at noon. He came and monkeyed around for a while. Made it work and I asked him if it would, for any reason kick off and not on again. He said it had a reason this time -one of the plugs was wrecked. A piece chipped out and couldn't unscrew. Said it could have been too much electricity going through due to the storm last night. I paid him-$1.60.

Lightening struck a straw stack and burned. Quite a storm but I didn't hear any of it at all.

Well, dear, do you still see your husband every nite? Hope you can continue seeing him every day.

Oh, yes, another thing today. Ray said there had to be a plug put in the steam box before they could bake. The men from the plumbing shop were out in the country so they couldn't come until about 7. Amanda checked up and made out the order while they were there.

What about Thanksgiving? Do we stay open all day -same as any other day? Be sure to answer that.

Stub (Davis) took the bread to the schoolhouse today. John's car is in the garage. Asked Stub how much he wanted for the other 2 days and today and he said "Nothing, I'll do it for Bill." Pretty nice wasn't it?

Stan was all excited today because of the game tonight. Hope they win. Got a good start anyway.

What have you been having to eat lately? You have been eating, haven't you?

Grandpa had Metille come and get the car today. I'll call him tomorrow and see if he knows what's wrong.

Dennis gets along OK with the delivering all though except the Model K. Ann didn't come down today even after I'd called her at 9:30. But about 5 to 11 one of her sister's came.

Veryle Paulson pictured near the cabin in Harpers Ferry.

On November 16, US 9th Division and 1st Army attacked at Geilenkirchen, Germany situated on the Wurm River north of Aachen. This was part of *Operation Clipper*.

*Dorothy Hayes has been hollering about her buns but we've been taking fresh ones every day. I can't help it if she doesn't use them until they are old!!*

*Grandpa ran out of gas at the foot of the hill tonight coming back from the sale. Ain't that awful?*

*Your chairman came in today and said they wanted 2 pies-sandwich bread and 1 qt. salad dressing for the food sale upstairs Saturday. They are also having one the 22 and then they are through, I guess.*

*Eitzen has the usual order for tomorrow. Bread isn't selling very fast lately so we are only making 1/2 of a barrel tonite too. Otherwise they have been ok.*

*The Farm Bureau has 45 doz donuts (plain) ordered for Thursday nite. Quite a few donuts, huh?*

*Ferd Kain is due to come in the 22nd. So the card I got today said. Say, do you ever order anything from Jack's? Just asking, it is boiler compound and janitor supplies.*

*Say, what is Hattie's last name?*

*Is the wallpaper still on your ceiling or has the wind blown it off?*

*I had the best dinner today—ate at the Elite and had meatloaf, potatoes and gravy, beets, cabbage and carrot salad, bread and butter and coffee. Sound good?*

*I also got a box of Christmas cards while I was home- from the League- or did I tell you last nite?*

*Grandma says that Miss Flynn was over today for a long visit. Said to tell you hello and that she missed seeing your car leave every morning so regularly.*

*The cattle they took up all sold good. Al didn't stay for supper.*

*Erdie (Land) called to say that Lena and the kids were ok. I just tried to call Marie (Kreeb) but we were connected to the bakery and I got Amanda talking or waiting for Hausmanns to answer.*

*Wed. Morning - 11:15*

*I got Marie a little later but I didn't have any more time to write then. She said she got your letter. The kids are fine and Patsy is just as full of the devil as always. She said she made Patsy a dress from the rest of that red silk of yours - sounds like it is cute.*

*Bud Campbell is leaving today - 18 are going and most of them are married. It is another rainy day—rained all nite too.*

*Andy Schmitz of B & R is supposed to stop the 20th Monday.*

*Grandma called a while ago and said they were going to Lu's as long as it is raining. Ray said the refrigerator didn't click in all nite. It was 70 this morning but it has been running ok since I came.*

*Quite a few people in town - suppose there will be all day.*
*Have you had a chance to use your rubbers yet? Or hasn't it rained?*
*Well, if I intend to get this front end cleaned up before Ruth comes, I'd better get busy.*

*Bye*

*Veryle*

*Write soon.*
*P.S. The city clerk was in today and said our water bill was awful big and wondered if we had a leak somewhere. Only thing I could think of is in the stool. It runs sometimes. It's harder to stop than before. Do you suppose we could disconnect the box somehow? Because the flushing part doesn't work anyway. It does if it takes the notion, otherwise not.*

Veryle was a few years younger than Marge. She later married a man who retired from military service, L. D. Scott, and resides in Enterprise, Alabama. They had two children.

During her years working at the bakery, it is apparent that she was both a good worker and fun to be around.

November 16, 1944 - From Viola (The Leet Family) to Marge with Bill

*Dear Marge and Bill,*
*Know that you will be looking for a line, but no news, so will not be much of a letter.*
*We did not get a letter yesterday or today but hope to tomorrow.*
*How are you both? How is weather down there? It is raining hard now and all evening but just a drizzle today.*
*So we went down to Lula's and men worked on their framer for bridge and put it across, so he can work on it when has time. Has 9 days of husking yet, and they say it is going to snow.*
*Lula washed ceilings and woodwork in living room today. She would not let me help her so I patched all day. Baby is so good now. Cliff fine. He had company tonite, Bonny Ewing. Veryle wrote a letter but not to you that said she was to (illegible) last nite, but told me to tell you. Mother (Amanda) banked $390 today. She said she did not know about it but you would. His Mother has been sick but better today.*
*Bill's dad wore Aunt Bessie's glasses and his headache was better so maybe he will be getting glasses. Anyway, I hope he can get help.*
*How are you both? Was Bill out Sunday? It seems so long before we hear from the letter. Are you getting my letters yet? I hope so. She said being rainy, they sold a lot today so not so much for tonite (at the Bakery.)*
*We have not heard from Waverly but I must write them. Lula is still looking for Mervin and Jean near Thanksgiving. Their wedding anniversary but I have given all up.*
*What do you do to keep busy?*

*Bye, bye*
*Veryle, Dad and Mother (Leet)*

On November 17, Nazi troops mount an offensive by staging numerous raids against dikes north east of Polder in the Netherlands.

A rare photo of Viola and George Leet - Marge's parents.

On November 19, President Franklin D. Roosevelt announced the 6th War Loan Drive that was aimed at selling $14 billion dollars in war bonds to help pay for the war effort.

On November 20, Japan commits the first suicide submarine attack at Ulithi Atol in the Carolines. They were called *Kaiten* and were not really submarines but a manned torpedo.

The Japanese used this weapon for the remainder of the war with very little success.

## November 19, 1944 - From Amanda to Marge with Bill

Dear Marg and Bill,

Well, am scribbling a few lines. I think everybody is better or Dad seems to be getting there. He got his glasses about 1:30 yesterday and went to work after supper. He was still a little dizzy. Says he feels better now. I suppose it takes a little while to get used to the glasses. The eye dr. here said his eyes were terrible and said it was funny he didn't have a nervous breakdown before.

Say, Bill, Dad borrowed your overcoat for church this morning. Just seems can't get anything or satisfaction out of Oliver. Dad being sick last week but Butch, the laundry man, said the boiler down there broke and the boss couldn't get near him. Think Dad will be able to go down tomorrow. They wanted to cut a black overcoat to fit Dad. I can just see him wearing something like that but they been just stalling till it got colder, thinking whoever has it, hasn't opened it yet. Wish it were you here instead of your overcoat, Bill.

Danny Regan came home Friday night. He has a month. John took them to New Albin today. It was Mrs. Regan's mother's Birthday. They had a big turkey dinner. Danny stopped in yesterday but I was over to confession. They say he is a little thin. Dad thought he looked like he always did. You'll get the laugh on us now, Marg. Quillin don't like to get up so early.

Pecans could cost some thing by the time they got here. (Marge sent a recipe she got down south for pecan pie.) Was down this afternoon and got the money all ready. $384 and some cents. $380 last week. I didn't think this was going to be quite so much. One day we only had 1/2 lb. and made 1 lb Friday and 1 1/2 lb Sat and ran out about 9:30 last night. I cut the rolls to 30 qt. for yesterday and there still was a big tray left. Eitzen got 30 round.

We got a card to the wedding dance of Gladys Halverson and Floyd Beardmore Thursday night Thanksgiving night. They are only having one dance for the Fireman's Ball at the Opera House. They wouldn't let them use the K.C. hall on account no fire safety. Veryle said you got the jam and letter. Did the boys get the candy? Heard John telling Dad that Brant asked for a longer furlough because he was thinking about marriage. Don't know if they are or not.

Was talking to Margaret (Luther) last night. Said Dorothy (Luther, daughter married to Fred O'Riley) called Friday morning and wanted her to come there. Wouldn't cost her a cent. Margaret said the rest of the family didn't think much of it. Asked her when Dorothy was coming home and she said she didn't know - said they got Dorothy's wedding pictures and they were just swell. She said they had one for you and how Bill would like to see it.

*Marge, here are a few points if you want more, just say so (ration points). Must call and see what the green are and whatever they are for. They are sure gone, on one side mostly. Well, write. Dad is better though I'll let you know. He said it was tiring to walk (the rest is illegible).*

*With Love,*

*Mother*

*Oh, I have the mirror up and is it ever a honey. Thank you both very much again.*

*Love, Mother*

<u>November 20, 1944 - From Sis Goltz to Marge with Bill</u>

This letter was written from Lawton, Oklahoma on a Monday morning.

*Dear Marge,*

*Well, kid, I've got some news for you. I could hardly wait till this morning to write as I knew I'd better wait till I got a little more information. Well, anyway they told the kids the next place we're going to is - Camp Hood, Texas, that's for sure. So we're really thrilled more or less. So here goes: first of all, I'd like to know where the nearest town to Camp is. I mean how far is Belton from camp? Are there buses - I mean good bus schedules from Belton to Camp Hood or is Killeen closest to camp?*

*Find out for me, Marge, will you. All I know is we're leaving the 30th of Nov. That's about 10 days from now. I hope you stay so I can at least see you one day or so. Be sure and answer right away so I'll know if rooms are hard to find or not. We can leave here say Nov 30 at 9:00 and be in Belton or Killeen at 6:00 that same nite. Tell me which is the nearest town. I want to get as close to camp as I can and if you would happen to know of a place in Killeen if that's closer to Camp than Belton. See about getting it for me. I'd really appreciate it very much. But first tell me about our connections to camp and stuff.*

*I'll be waiting patiently to hear from you.*

*Love*

*Just Sis (Goltz)*

On November 22, Canadian Prime Minister, William Lyon Mackenzie King, introduced conscription in Canada. It became known as the Conscription Crisis of 1944.

The Duke of Cornwall's Light Infantry occupied Hoven at Geilenkirchen in the Netherlands.

<u>November 23, 1944 - From Beck to Marge</u>

As we know, Marge was with Bill when this letter arrived in Waukon.

*Dear Marge,*

*I'll take a chance on writing you now. You should be home from Texas by now. I suppose you had a wonderful time and are now home with your memories and darn lonesome. I know just how you feel.*

*Jimmie has been sick. He had an awful cold and I had to sit up for three nites and hold him up cause he couldn't breathe when I laid him down. I took him to Dr. and he gave me medicine for him. He is better now. I was nearly crazy. I was so worried about him.*

*I want to come up some Sat. and come back on Monday. I thought maybe if you and I went out together for just one*

Part of the appeal of this epistle is a look at life as it was for the women back home; kids, peer pressure, holidays alone, etc. and, in Marge's case, running a business.

nite, people wouldn't talk about us. I'm afraid to take Jimmie out now and I'd have to wait until my aunt is through picking corn and then she'd come and stay a couple days. Course I wouldn't leave Mom alone with Jimmie. Thought maybe we could go out on Sat nite if you could meet me at Calmer. Honestly, they talk so about all the war widows here, I never go any place. Jimmie will soon be four months old and I've only left him four times.

I wish you'd send me Bills address. I'd like to send him a Christmas card. I suppose he hated to see you leave. If we ever get them home again, I think I'll baby him worse than I do Jimmie.

I just hate to think of Christmas. I don't have the least bit of Christmas spirit. I'm sure getting lonesome and disgusted, but I'm only one in a million so I guess maybe if I went out and hung one on, I'd feel better.

Well, Marge, it's time for your nephew's bottle and he is starting to fuss. Write and tell me about your trip-

Love,
Beck and Jimmie

November 23, 1944 (Thanksgiving) - From Marge to Amanda

On this date, the US 7th Army, under General Patch, conquered Straatsburg (*Strasburg* in English) in the Alsace area of France. The 2nd Battalion, 324th Infantry, E Company was the first American unit to reach the Rhine.

Dear Folks,

Got your long letter yesterday and surely are glad to hear that Dad and all the rest are better again.

Bill called yesterday but I wasn't here so he told Mrs. Gerstenberg to tell me to meet him at 8:30 but he didn't get there till about a quarter to nine. He was a little tired. They had gone 9 miles in 1 1/2 hrs. I came back at 10:00 as he had to get up at 4:30 this morning. They are to be out in the range all day but he thinks he can get a pass tonite. He got the telegram about the money so I'm sure hoping.

You really must have had a time Sat. What was the matter with Dennis - was he sick or just didn't show up? Veryle or Ruth can help with the delivering then.

Gee, Bill was disappointed to hear Harold was home too now. They really were all home at once, weren't they?

On November 24, US bombers based in Saipan began the first attacks on Tokyo, Japan.

Thanks so much for saying I could stay longer but I don't know what to do. I surely would give anything to be with Bill those three days at Christmas. They told them yesterday that they won't have a weekend pass this week. They have to work out on the range all day Sunday because they get time off for Christmas. Wouldn't that frost you? If I knew Bill would be going across, I would stay for sure and then we could come home together but if he could be lucky enough to get assigned here, he wouldn't get a furlough until Feb. at least. So - I'm on the fence. He will have to decide today cause Mabel is going to take me to Temple tomorrow to look around and to see about train reservations.

Say, when you make your fruit cakes, do you suppose you

*can make one that weighs about 4 lbs. for me? I'd like to send it here to Mrs. Gerstenberg. Have you had any call for them yet?*

*I'll ask Bill about the spice cakes to see if he wants him to make any. I know they cost a lot more. I didn't read your letter out there last nite as I couldn't see it. I think Bill only got to read part of it. Stan will have to cut down on the cakes if he is having quite a few left. How many cookies does he make a week? (Note: Stan is a junior in high school.)*

*Bet Marie looks cute in her new outfit. Will be a lot cheaper than if you would have bought it.*

*Glad you like the junk I sent. It wasn't much but I hadn't been around much then. Guess I'll do quite a lot of Christmas shopping here.*

*So you have had a little snow. It surely is nice here today - only a little cold. The sun is surely nice though. As I said yesterday, this is Thanksgiving so they just left for the country for dinner and are invited out for supper too (Gerstenbergs, I mean).*

*I called Arlene and we are going downtown this afternoon anyway. Dale was to see Bill yesterday morning and afternoon too. He is anxious for Sis to get here but wish we wouldn't be so far apart.*

*Suppose you are thinking about the bazaar about now. Gee, thanks so much for fixing the beans and then Veryle said you sent down an angel food to one of the sales. You shouldn't have done that. I feel guilty having such a good time and having everyone else working for us.*

*Here is the recipe for pecan pie:*

*1 cup sugar*
*3 Tbls flour*
*1 c. white syrup*
*2 eggs - beaten*
*1 c. pecans*
*vanilla*
*butter*

*Mix it all together and put in a raw pie shell. (large tin). Bake in a real slow oven for an hour until the inside doesn't wiggle when you shake the pie.*

*Boy it is simply delicious.*

*I haven't picked out any pecans all week - sort of lazy, I guess. Made some peanut butter candy for Bill last nite and really had good luck with it.*

*Have you heard from Beck or Vern? I wrote Vern but still haven't to Beck*

*Well, guess I'll have to move my chair or bake by this stove. Write again soon - hope everything is still O.K.*

*Love from us both,*
*Bill and Marge*

On November 25, a German V-2 rocket hit a Woolworth store in Deptford, United Kingdom, killing 160 shoppers.

On November 26, Allied marines attacked the harbor at Antwerp.

Himmler ordered the destruction of crematoriums at Auschwitz and Birkenau concentration camps.

On November 27th, the US 121st Infantry Regiment opens an assault on Hurtgen Forest, northeast of the Belgium/German border between the Rur River and Aachen.

They would occupy Hurtgen on November 28 but the battle would rage until February 10, 1945 making this the longest battle on German ground during the war. It is also the longest single battle in the history of the US Army.

On November 29, Albania was liberated from Nazi control.

John Hopkins Hospital performs the first open heart surgery.

On November 30, Britain's biggest (and last built) battleship HMS Vanguard ran aground just after commissioning and did not see service in the war.

This is a Christmas Card written to Marge from San Francisco, California.

On December 3, fighting broke out between Communists and Royalists in newly liberated Greece which would eventually lead to a full-scale Greek Civil War.

December 6, 1944 - From Paul Anderson to Marge

*Dear Maggie:*

*Hello Maggie! How's all the loaves of bread coming? Okay I hope. I am enclosing a little letter that I wish you would give to Charlotte. By the way, what's the address of your Bakery? I don't even know your address. I'll just call it the Waldron Bakery, Okay? I understand it's getting a little chilly back there in Iowa now. I only wish I could be there. There isn't much news. In fact there isn't any. I still hear from "Jakie" ever once in awhile. I suppose you do too. Tell me Maggie, how do you like married life? I think I'll end up being a bachelor in the army at that. Ha! We have a good show tonight for a change. "Saratoga Trunk" with Gary Cooper and Ingrid Bergman. I can't even spell any more. Must close for now.*

*Write when you find time.*

*FFs ever,*
*Paul*

Sent from Gatesville, Texas.

December 7, 1944 - From Sis and Dale Goltz to Marge and Bill

*Dear Marge and Bill,*

*Dale brought in your letter tonight and so we're laying here on the bed and since Dale is getting kinda crazy, I decided it was about time we started to answer you letter afterwards. (Oh, Boy!!!)*

*I wrote you a letter the other day. You've most likely gotten it by now. I sure hope so anyway. I meant to call you, Marge but we live out in the country more or less and we don't have a telephone. When Dale comes home at nite we usually stay home in fact we've been in to Gatesville 1 nite together since I've been here. There's nothing in that town al all not even a good theater.*

*Bill starts on bivouac Sun, huh? Well Marge, Dale goes out tomorrow (Friday morning). He doesn't even plan on being here for Christmas but maybe the army will be tender hearted. I sure hope so anyway.*

*Well I really want to see you too, Marge. We tried to get down but Dale was either on K.P. over the weekend or some other damn thing.*

*So I'm going to McGregor Texas tomorrow with a girl. We're going to see about getting a job at a defense plant there. We're coming back tomorrow though, I think but I'll be home all day Sat and Sun so try and make it up. I know you will want to wait and see if Bill gets a few hours off Sat. so I'll be expecting you Sun if you can come in the morning around 9:00 or so and I'm not here, I'm at church out at camp. It's at 9:00 and you wait and I'll come right back after Mass. I'll leave the front door unlocked so you can come in and make yourself at home.*

*If you come though camp and into Gatesville, we live about 1 good block from the main gate - the first little white house*

On December 12 - 13, British units attempted to take the hilltop town of Tossignano, Italy but were repulsed by an entrenched German force.

On December 13, United States, Australian and Philippine troops landed on Mindoro Island, the Philippines to begin the *Battle of Mindoro*.

The Number One Song in the US for this week was *Don't Fence Me In* performed by Bing Crosby and The Andrew Sisters.

*on the left side of the road as you come by out of the gate. It's near the road, not back far. A small porch with a screen door and a little wood pile on the side of the house and a tub near the porch. You can't miss it.*

*(2 more pages, illegible due to water damage)*

*Love, Sis and Dale*

December 14, 1944 - From Bill to Marge

*Dear Marge,*

*Well, Marge, I got two letters from you tonight and one from Luther. It is pretty damn cold out here to be writing letters. I'm sitting on the edge of a foxhole that we each had to dig. After our march out here - we left at 4 o'clock in the morning and got out here about 11:30 - 23 miles. I guess it was I didn't mind it at all - thought it wasn't much rougher than the 9 mi. march. It's been freezing every night here but I would sooner have that than rain. We are all sleeping together. It is plenty warm in our tents but what we wouldn't give for a few candles. We got about 6 inches of leaves and grass under us for bedding and it sure makes it nice. I sleep like a log. I haven't much time to write because it is getting so dark I can hardly see. I have been through all the battle courses but we still go through the infiltration course at night. That's where they fire the live ammunition at night. Next week I probably (will) have more time to write.*

*Lots of love, Bill*

December 16, 1944 - From Bill to Marge

*Dear Marge,*

*I have a little time now so I thought I had better write. It sure is nice today except it was plenty cold this morning.*

*Wyscover got a box yesterday with the candy and canned heat. They are both really all right. He's says you had better send a cake too, I guess. I wrote you that we were through the infiltration course and the German Village. A little exciting but nothing to get scared about. We were out last night till about 11 o'clock and will be every night till Sun. Then we go to the other areas to cook. This ain't bad at all just so it don't rain. I suppose you are home by now and getting things under control this morning. We just screwed around all morning. Not a hell of a lot of work tonight. We go though that machine gun fire again. We have been having damn good meals but Fri. and Sat. we have C Rations but Lemaster stole some eggs so we'll have boiled eggs, and cheese and crackers.*

*Well there isn't much else I can think of to write. I probably won't have a chance to write again for a few days because we are kept plenty busy out here. I have to get my rifle cleaned up now to get it all mud again tonight.*

*Well, keep on writing.*

*All my love, Bill*

On December 15, a private airplane carrying bandleader Glenn Miller disappeared in heavy fog over the English Channel while flying to Paris.

On December 16, Germany began the Ardennes offensive, later known as the *Battle of the Bulge*. This would be the bloodiest battle of the war.

Bill would take part in this battle.

General George C. Marshall became the first Five-Star General.

On December 17, German troops carried out the Malmedy massacre. During the Battle of the Bulge, this was one of the worst atrocities committed against prisoners of war. 113 men from US B Battery, who had surrendered, were shot and clubbed to death.

On December 22, Brigadier General Anthony C. McAuliffe, commander of US forces defending Bastogne refused to accept demands for surrender by sending a one-word reply, "Nuts!" to the German command.

On December 24, the Bulge reached its deepest point at Celles.

On December 26, American troops repulsed German forces at Bastogne.

On Decembr 31, over hundreds of thousands of Japanese Imperial forces are killed in action at the *Battle of Leyte* by Filipo and American forces.

While correspondence is missing, we know that Bill and Marge spent New Years in Kansas City.

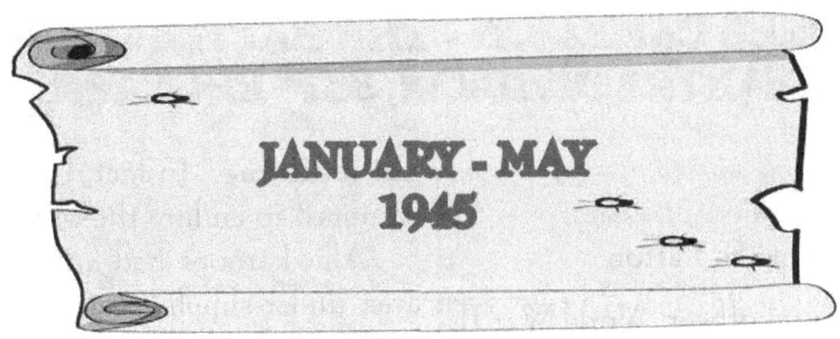


Bill spent New Years with Marge in Kansas City. Shortly thereafter, as part of the replacement troops for the 90th Infantry Division, he left there and proceeded to New York City by way of Indianapolis and Baltimore. There the replacements received their shipping orders on January 4, 1945 and left New York on the ship Queen Elizabeth on January 8; they would arrive on the 13th. Bill explained in a letter to Marge that there had been no time to make a telephone call to her prior to being shipped out. Marge had to endure that void of not knowing where Bill was and not knowing when, exactly, he had been shipped to Europe.

It is probable that this period for Bill and Marge was the most difficult of their nearly two year separation. For Bill, the rigors of combat could have taken a severe mental and physical toll. In fact, he arrived on European soil as an unseasoned combat replacement for the 90th Infantry Division. His Division had suffered 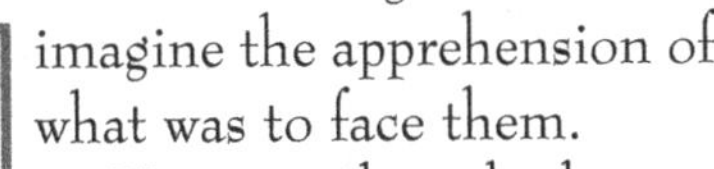 debilitating casualties to their numbers. As a company, regiment, or division replacement Bill, and his fellow comrades, had no combat experience. In fact, Bill mentions in a letter that many of those sent to the European Front had as little as 14 weeks of training. One must imagine the apprehension of what was to face them.

Upon disembarkation from the Queen Elizabeth troop carrying ship, they were transported directly to the scene of the Battle of the Bulge in eastern Luxembourg.

As Bill's company entered the fray in the Bulge, there would be little opportunity for him to write letters home. The combat was such that he would not have much of an opportunity until late in January, when his unit was moved from the "front lines" to a rear area. We know that although the Battle of the Bulge had been determined to be an Allied victory by January 16, 1945, there remained nearly two weeks of fierce German fighting.

We also know that Bill served as a *scout/rifleman* during this time. In that Bill's MOS was *cook/baker* it is probable that he became a scout/rifleman when the call went out for volunteers.

A scout was an easy target for German snipers, as a scout, alone or with another scout, would move toward the enemy at a distance apart from the squad or company of soldiers. Their objective was to locate the enemy in advance of the main body of moving troops, either by drawing the fire of the Germans, or by visually locating the enemy. There was also the occurrence when the Germans would allow the scout to pass their positions, and then ambush the forward moving troops. In those situations, the scout was alone and behind the concealed Germans.

Of note, in the letters Bill wrote home in late January, is a poignant statement at the end whereby he is asking Marge, and Amanda, for their "prayers". The severity of the combat situation certainly dictated that a good Catholic boy would seek protection and hold a reliance upon that higher being to keep him safe.

For those at home, anxiety had to be very stressful. And, of course, the next four months would fill Marge with apprehension about the safety and well-being of her husband. It is lamentable that we lack letters written by Marge.

# THE ARDENNES CAMPAIGN - THE BATTLE OF THE BULGE
# 3rd ARMY, 90th INFANTRY DIVISION, 357th REGIMENT, COMPANY F

*"....an imperfect plan implemented immediately and violently will always succeed better than a perfect plan."*

Gen George S. Patton

To many an Allied soldier and officer, World War II in Europe appeared near an end when in late summer of 1944 Allied armies raced across northern France, Belgium, and Luxembourg to the very gates of Germany. That this was not, in fact, the case was a painful lesson that the last months of 1944 and early months of 1945 would make clear with stark emphasis.

The fighting during these months belonged to the small units and individual soldiers, the kind of warfare which is difficult yet essential to ultimate victory.

By early December, 1944, the Germans were reeling as they had been pushed from France and Allied forces were on the brink of entering the German homeland in the west. Russian forces were advancing into Germany in the east.

In a last ditch effort, an attempt was made to divide Allied divisions along the west, and, hopefully, break through and take the port of Antwerp (which was a major American/Allied supply port/depot). Hitler concentrated his forces on the Ardennes Forest area of eastern Belgium/Luxembourg. This was done without Allied leadership fully understanding that this was taking place. Hitler's theory for the build-up of his forces in this area was to break through under cover of this heavily forested area during a period where the weather completely favored the Germans. This became known as the "Bulge".

The weather was a formidable foe as January winds swept through the exposed valleys; temperatures hovered around the zero mark. As to the cold, all suffered equally. The GI's and the Germans opposite them went through worse physical misery than the men of Valley Forge but, in this battle, the Germans were not retreating. In fact, the Germans were much better equipped to endure the winter weather conditions.

Allied troops had arrived in the Ardennes forested area under-supplied with ammunition and with inadequate clothing.

The early success of Hitler's massive assault in the Ardennes caused a severe disruption in the Allied battle plans. Gen. Patton ceased attacks to the east and redirected the 90th's effort northward to cut off the base of the German salient. The 90th secretly withdrew across the Saar, trucked north over 70 miles of road iced like skating rinks, and then immediately engaged the Germans in bitter, brutal fighting.

All of this was complicated by weather so severe that the infantry's losses from frostbite exceeded losses from wounds.

Here the 90th experienced some of their toughest times, both in the form of opposition and weather, but they overcame them. By January 16, the Germans launched nine counterattacks led by powerful armor; the battle raged for a 36 hour period. (This phase of the battle was depicted in the documentary *Band Of Brothers*.)

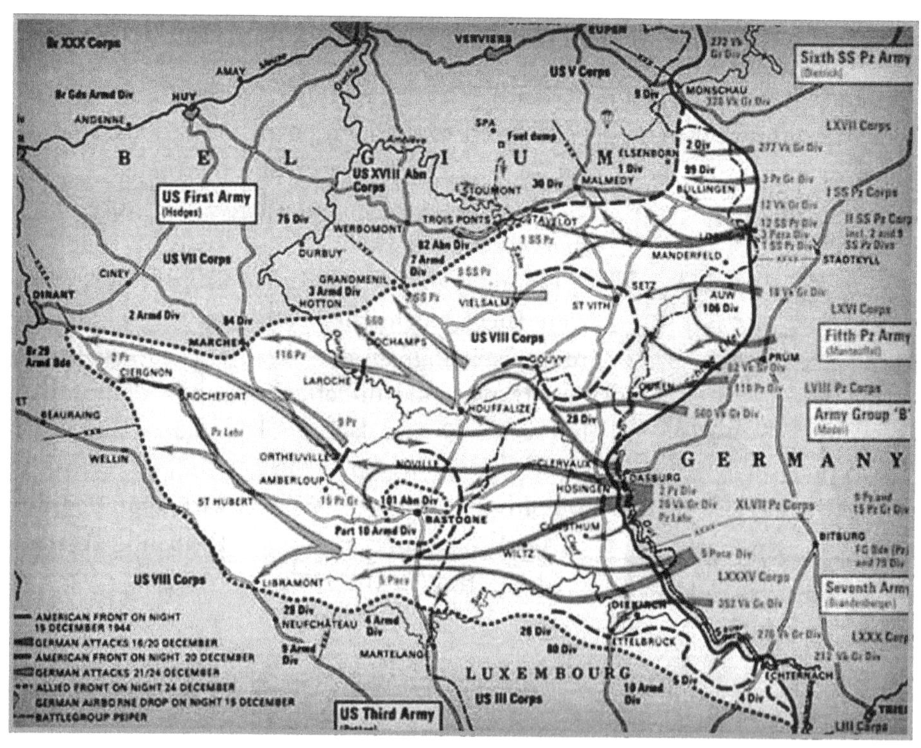

What had begun as an ambitious counterattack against elements of the 90th, ended in a dismal fiasco with the 90th in firm possession of Oberwampach.

The German forces and officer corps had great respect for the 90th Division. A captured directive from a German headquarters stated that, "It is imperative that steps be taken to ascertain whether or not the American 90th Infantry has been committed to battle. Special attention must be given to the numbers 357 (Bill's Regiment), 358, 359, 343, 344, 345, 915, and 315. American prisoners identified with these numbers will immediately be taken to the German Regimental G-3".

Bill was a member of the replacement forces being sent to the 90th Infantry Division, 357th Regiment, Company F. He arrived in Europe on January 13, 1945 and was deployed to where the Battle of the Bulge was in process (by way of Scotland, England and France). This was approximately 200 miles from his point of arrival on European soil.

Bill and his fellow replacements would join the fray with 3rd Army fighting for the town of Houffalize (approximately five miles north of Bastogne). From this point in Belgium, until the German surrender in early May, elements of the 3rd Army had to methodically capture one town after another against German forces fighting for their lives.

The German retreat out of the Bulge was slow, stubborn, and costly to both the Americans and to the Germans. Hitler, always insistent on holding captured ground, refused to consider pulling out of the Bulge and returning to the Siegfried Line. Thus, the Germans were fighting to the last man. The American forces were fighting not only the winter conditions but some of Germany's finest remaining soldiers who were struggling fiercely for personal survival and for that of the Fatherland.

The total toll of American casualties in the Bulge was 80,987. From the period January 3 through January 28, when the Americans were on the offensive, the losses were 6,138 killed, 27,262 wounded, and 6,272 missing. Thus January 1945 was the costliest month of the campaign in Europe for the US Army. Total German casualties in the Bulge are estimated from 80,000 to 104,000.

Although fighting in the Bulge area continued through the month of January, the 90th Infantry, including the 357th Regiment (and Bill's Company F) began their movement to The Siegfried Line.

---

Getting ready to ship out it seems the Army is the Army.

Germany staged air raids on Allied airports at Eindhoven, St Trond and Brussels.

On January 2, Allied aircraft attacked the city of Nuremberg, Germany.

<u>January 3, 1945 - From Bill to Marge</u>

*Dear Marge,*

*I've been trying to get a chance to call but they have kept us too busy to do anything drawing new clothes and equipment. They said we will be here about another day or two yet. We got in Tues. morning. When we left Kansas City, we flew to Indianapolis Ind. and stayed there all night. There weren't any phones there to call from. It was an army air base. We didn't have any heat in the plane we rode in. We were just about froze when we finally got here. They only go about 150 miles an hour. I haven't seen LeMaster or Wyscover yet and I don't suppose I will. There are guys here from every company in the U.S. and they are running them through in 2 or 3 days where they used to take a couple weeks so they keep you busy most of the night. I got two letters from you that were at Hood and one from Swede. And Klemmer is sleeping in the same bunk as I do. He's about the only one I know. Scavazzo is down a couple of barracks from here. I could of just as well stayed home a couple days longer because some of them took 2 or 3 days extra and they never said a thing or hardly knew the difference. They've got every thing in such a rush and muddle.*

*We have got about all our equipment now and the officer in charge of us said he had shipping orders on most of us all ready so we will be leaving for POE* (Port of Embarkation) *in a day or two. That's about 30 miles from here. This is only about 20 miles from Baltimore and Washington. We flew over the Capitol coming in.*

*We got our new boots issued to use in place of shoes and leggings. They are like Paratroop boots. They tell us the reinforcement depot over in England and France, are all empty and we are to fill them up. A lot of guys here got but 14 weeks of training.*

*I'll try to call you the first chance I get. I hope you don't worry to much about your husband because he takes good care of himself. The war don't sound too good yet (Battle of the Bulge) but I sure hope it starts looking better. I suppose the folks worry about Vernon now.*

*To get a cigarette we have a card they punched allowing us one pack a day so cigarettes must be getting harder to get overseas. They tell us we are allowed 2 packs a week. That is going to be kinda rough. We won't get assigned till we get overseas so I don't know whether I'll be a cook or a rifleman. I'm waiting to here from you.*

*All my love*

*Your Husband*
*Bill*

On January 3, the Allies landed on the west coast of Burma and conquered Akyab.

English Prime Minister Winston Churchill visited France.

In the Pacific, carrier-based aircraft attacked Okinawa.

On January 4, the US aircraft carrier *Ommaney Bay* was sunk after repeated kamikaze attacks.

*January 4, 1945 - From Bill to Jim and Amanda*

This was a Thursday and the letter is postmarked from Fort George G. Meade, MD.

*Dear Folks,*

*I wrote to Marge last night. I don't know whether she is coming here or not but if she does, I think I'll be gone. We got our shipping orders about 1 hr. ago so we leave sometime this afternoon or tonight. We have got all our clothes. Now there are about 25 leaving out of about 400 in this bunch leaving today. Mostly truck drivers, cooks, and anti tank guys. We go to P.O.E. from here. Maybe we will be there a few days yet to, after today.*

*I won't be able to write about anything so they tell us, anyway. Some of these boys here have had hardly any training.*

*I got your box today, with the cigarette lighter and candy. The lighter works good and I've been eating the candy ever since. If you can try to send me some a little later on maybe you can use this letter to mail it if we go to France. I'm going to sure try looking up Vernon. I was a damn fool for reporting back on time because everything's all mixed up. They really don't know when we were to report back and I've still got my furlough papers. They were supposed to take them the first day we got back but I guess we don't ever have to turn them in if we haven't.*

*I'll be waiting to hear from you. Your Son, Bill*

On January 5, the Australian Union recognized the new pro-Soviet government of Poland.

On January 7, British Gen Bernard Montgomery held a press conference at Zonhoven describing his supporting role at the Battle of the Bulge.

On January 9, the Soviet Union began the *Vistula-Oder Offensive* in Eastern Europe against the Nazi.

Bill would sail on January 8 and his daughter Jan recounted the following:

When we lived in California, Bill came for a visit after Marge passed away. We took him to visit the Queen Mary ship moored in Long Beach. That was the only thing he particularly wanted to see. Bill had made the crossing of the Atlantic Ocean from the U.S. to Europe on her sister ship, the Queen Elizabeth. The ships were built as exact replicas.

When he saw the ship, he told us how things were different on the Queen Elizabeth, which became a "troop ship". As he toured the Queen Mary, Bill said the wood floors were the same as on the Queen Elizabeth, as were the light fixtures. However, the troop ship had horizontal rows of hammocks attached to the walls. They were the "beds" for the troops. He said it was crowded, noisy, and not very comfortable during the crossing. He also said that he enjoyed seeing the Queen Mary as it was meant to be.

Bill called the disembarkment the scariest thing he had to do in the war. He was afraid of heights and getting off the ship required the soldiers to scale down nets thrown over the side, into boats below. The ship was rocking and the nets were swaying away from the ship. The soldier above him had a leg crushed when the net hit the side of the ship violently as it rocked. He was scared to death and thought nothing he faced from that point on could be worse.

Bill's Company was in Longvilly on January 16 and were probably somewhere between Oberwampach and Bastogne when this letter was written. Bill was either in England or France.

### January 13, 1945 - From Bill to Marge

*Dated Jan 13, 1945 - Postmarked Feb 13, 1945*

*Dear Marge,*

*I don't think you will find much of interest in any of my letters anymore, as I can't write much. I came over in one of the (censored) ships in the world. I've seen LeMaster and Wyscover (sp) every day. Le Master is acting Sarg. I just wrote a letter to the folks, too. I hope every thing is under control at the bakery. I wish you would send me a box as soon as you have time. I've got 3 cartons of cig. to last me a while. I'm going to wire for some money if I can because I'm just about broke and I'll only have $4 coming this month. I got overpaid at Hood. We left too quick for me to call you or anything. Send me Herald and Swedes address. I might get a chance to write them by and by. Keep up the writing even if it does take a long time for them to catch up. I sure miss my wife now but I have to make the best of it the same as others are doing.*

*All my Love,*

*Your Husband*
*Bill*

### January 13 - 20, 1945 - From Bill to Marge

*Place and Location cut out by censor*

*Dear Marge,*

*I got a letter from you yesterday. The one you wrote on the train, the telegram and a box that you sent me at Hood with the candy and cookies. We cleaned them up right away. I never did get the box with the watch in it and I don't suppose I ever will now. I was cooking with Scavazzo all day today. Wyscover was in to see me today but I wasn't here but I'll probably see him tonight. You can mail his wife that $10.00 I owe him because I'm pretty short now. I think that will be all right with him. All our mail is censored now so I guess there won't be a hell of a lot to write about anymore but I still keep on trying to do my best. I'm sorry to hear you're having trouble at the bakery but I guess there is nothing I can do to help things out now. Maybe John and Stan can take care of things till Meickle gets back.*

*If there is anything you can't find, invoices or when you are taking inventory, you can either call Hank or guess at the prices of them.*

*That bracelet you sent me with my name on, I am finally wearing it now. I was sitting around a couple days ago playing with it and took 3 links out of it. Fits swell now so I'll keep it on.*

*Have the folks heard from Vernon lately?*

*Love*
*Bill*

January 20, 1945 - From Bill to Marge

*Dear Marge*

*I hope you'll forgive me for not writing but it wouldn't do any good to because I couldn't mail them anyway. I've really covered a lot of ground since I've left. I was in the country where Meikle said he wanted to go on furlough when he was over here. I'm in Patton's 3rd army about 10 mi or so from where Vernon is. I'll see him if I get half a chance. I don't think I'll be assigned as a cook either. It's been about a week or so since I've seen Wyscover or LeMasters. I haven't any idea where they are now. Still with Scavuzzo though. I hope everything is going all right at home. You know how much I miss you. It will sure be a happy day when this is all over and we are back together again.*

*I had a nice ride in a 40+8 (Merci Boxcar, very small, could hold 40 men and 8 horses) over the country. Ask Miekle what they are like.*

*I didn't get a chance to call you before I left. It was in such a hurry. Say hello to the Kreebs and the rest of the gang for me. I suppose that Herald and Swede are both in the South Pacific by now. I told you before I left not to expect much mail from me and I guess that will be about right too. I don't expect to get any from you for a month or so yet but keep on writing.*

*All my love,*
*Bill*

January 26, 1945 - From Bill to Marge

*Dear Marge,*

*I'm sorry I haven't been able to write for the last week because I was sleeping in foxholes and I guess it was just as cold or as much snow as there is. I'm in a rifle co. and not as a cook neither.*

*I guess I'll never get a chance to look Vernon up till after it is over. I was within about 10 miles from him once. I've been in 4 different countries now since I've left the states. It will probably be a month or so yet before I get any mail from you and I sure do miss it.*

*You can send me a box with whatever you can put in it.*

*John knows what it is like at the front so tell him if Stan gets any ideas of coming here - to be damn sure not to let him. Well, I guess there isn't much else to write about except to tell you I am still loving you as much as ever. I hope everything is going all right at the bakery. Say hello to everyone for me.*

*All my love*

*Your Husband*
*Bill*

*My address - CO F 357 Inf. APO 90 % P.M., N.Y.-N.Y.*

From somewhere in France after joining up with Gen Patton's 3rd Army.

The 357th Regiment was in Asselborn on January 21, crossing the Clerf River on the 23rd, they took Heinersheld, Lausdorn and Harlange that same day.

On January 22, FDR is inaugurated to an unprecedented fourth term. No president before, or since, has ever reached a third term in office.

On the morning of January 24, elements of the 357th, having just occupied the town of Binsfield, bore the brunt of a vicious counterattack supported by overwhelming armor. Without anti-tank guns, without armor of their own, the doughboys slugged it out, matching their light machine guns with the direct fire laid down by the enemy tanks.

Succeeding days found the 90th wading eastward through the snow, warming itself where it could, as freezing winds numbed hands and feet. Security forbade the building of fires with which to warm the brick-hard cylinders of K-ration cheese, yet survival demanded fire and warmth. The Division buttoned its coat against the weather and pushed eastward over the "Sky Line Drive", grimly defended by the Germans.

From *www.hobbylinc.com* - *Italeri Battle of the Bulge Figures for Games.*

Still in Luxemburg. The 357th would be making its way to the Our River.

On this date, the Red Army liberated the Auschwitz and Birkenau death camps.

West African 82nd Division fights for and occupies Myohaung, Burma.

While people in the Netherlands are starving, Nazi occupiers forbid any import of food and supplies.

*January 27, 1945 - From Bill to Marge*

*Dear Marge,*

*If I stayed here very long I'd be right in the groove again writing every day but we'll probably move out sometime today. If we don't, I'm going to church in the morning. They have a nice little church here in the village. Most of these towns and villages, there isn't much left of them from the shelling and bombing. Hardly any of them have any windows left in them. We took quite a few German prisoners when we were on the front and lost quite a few of our own men. I guess the way they work it, you are up for from 6-15 days and then come back a few miles for a couple of days rest. The officers are really a lot different out here than they are in the states. They really treat you like you are just as good as they are. I got all washed and shaved up this morning and I feel like a new man now. You wouldn't even know me for the dirt and whiskers before. The meals we get back here are better than what I ever had in the states. As quick as you hear from Wyscover's wife, write that you sent me Bill's new address - the one with the small APO no.*

*I have been in Scotland, England, France, Belgium and now Luxemburg. I wonder where the next one will be. It sure seemed funny in France to see all the people go into the little bakeries and come out with their couple loaves of long French bread under their arms, not wrapped or anything. I've got plenty of money now. I was just about broke and I made a pretty good chunk when we were in England.*

*Those boxcars we rode across France in are really something to see. The houses over here are a lot better built and a lot prettier than in the States. I haven't seen a wood house since I left the States. Scotland has about the prettiest country and houses I've ever seen. I think Bill and all the rest of the boys are riflemen now. It kinda looks like they will wind this war up before to long.*

*I didn't think a guy could live out in the snow and cold day in and day out before but I'm finding out now that you can and there isn't a very big percent that got their feet froze or anything.*

*How's the Kreebs coming? You haven't moved up there yet, have you? It's a good thing you have somebody as nice as them to visit with. Tell Marie I could sure go for a bottle of that beer of hers here now. How's John doing now? Is he going with Merte? I suppose Verle is still taking out the milkman and getting fatter than ever. Tell her she better not marry the guy till after I get home. Well, Marge, I guess I better quit for now. What I wouldn't give to be home with you again but will make it up after the war is over.*

*All my Love, Your Husband Bill*

January 27, 1945 - From Bill to Jim and Amanda

Dear Folks,

I hope everyone is all right at home yet. I haven't had any chances to write till yesterday and I wrote to Marge and Vernon then. I'd sure like to see him. I'm fine except for a little cold that I had before I left. I had a chance to get myself washed up and shaved this morning. You wouldn't even of know me for the whiskers and dirt. We don't have any use for money here at all. There isn't one thing you can spend it for. Be swell and send me a box with some peanut butter candy in it. I just came off the front lines. We are getting a couple of days rest. I see there is a Catholic church in the village here and if we are still here in the morning, I am going to Mass. I haven't been to Mass now for about 2 months or so.

Some of these people over here really go through hell. It is just unbelievable till you see it. It don't sound like the war is going to last too much longer. I sure hope it don't anyway.

I think I make a hell of a lot better cook than a rifleman but they need riflemen so that is what I am. Well, there is not much else to write about except remember me in your prayers.

Love,

Your Son
Bill

January 28, 1945 - From Bill to Marge

Dear Marge,

I sure feel swell this morning. I didn't figure we would be here long enough to get a chance to go to church but we did. I went to Mass, confession and communion. It was sure a beautiful little church. 3 altars like ours at home only a lot prettier. Most of the windows have been blown out of the church so it was pretty cold but the guys would have been glad to go anywhere.

It is snowing a lot here again so it's hard to tell how deep the snow will be when it is done. The people around these countries are all Catholic. In the houses there is a crucifix hanging in every room and one or two Holy pictures. And some rooms have a holy water font. I think I'll write to Luther after awhile. I never had and I think her and Fritz probably would like to hear from me.

Did you ever hear where Cowan went to? (be sure and answer this) and Harold and Swede? I hope when this war is over we can have one of those good old times with all the guys there again. It sure seems funny over here to see the men sit around on their asses while the women do all the work. The women in the States better watch out when the men come home or the women will be doing all the work. But I guess you are really getting a workout anyway.

There isn't much of anything I need over here but you

On January 28, supplies began to reach China over the newly reopened Burma Road.

On January 30, the *Wilhelm Gustoff*, with over 10,000 mainly civilians from Gotenhafen in the Gdansk Bay, is sunk by three torpedoes from the Soviet submarine *S-13* in the Baltic Sea; 7,700 die.

121 American soldiers and 800 Filipino guerrillas free 813 POWs from the Japanese-held camp at Cabanatuan City, Philippines.

On January 31, Eddie Slovik was executed by firing squad for desertion. He was the first American soldier since the American Civil War, and the last to date, to be executed for this offense.

*Bathing Beauty* was a movie released in July of 1944 starring Red Skelton with Esther Williams in the title role. Featured was the music of Xavier Cugat and Harry James.

The day after this letter was written, the 357th would cross the Our River which was the boundary between Luxemburg and Germany.

From what Bill writes in his next letter, he was with them and, for the first time, set foot in Germany. Not so encouraging, however, was the realization that beyond the present lines lay the bulwark of the enemy defense, the Siegfried Line.

can send me a box with some candy in it. Yesterday I had 4 Milky Way candy bars and some chocolate ice cream. Last night I seen a show "Bathing Beauty" in Technicolor. It don't hardly seem possible they could have shows within 3 miles from the front lines but they do.

I've got some French money in my pocket. I'll send you a few francs' of French money. We are limited on what we can send. I've got a 1000 Franc note that I'd like to send but I can't so I'll hang on to it.

Keep on saying a prayer for me every now and then because this is one place a guy can use them.

With all my love

Your Husband
Bill

<u>February 4, 1945 - From Bill to Marge</u>

Dear Marge,

Well, another week gone and I'm back again. I hope you get the letters I wrote a week ago. My writing paper is getting pretty badly battered up but I guess you can make it out. We just came out of Germany so that makes another country I've been in. I went to Mass and communion this morning. The Heines took the priest with them from this village. We really eat good when we come back from the front. Better grub than you would get in a restaurant. We get mostly K. rations on the front. The first week I couldn't eat them very well but I sure go to town on them now. I could get lots of German things to send home, but it sickens a guy too much to even take it off them and then you don't know how long you'll have to pack it before you can mail it. Every thing we have, we pack on our back. If we want a blanket to sleep on at night, we carry it. The weather is starting to break now. 3 or 4 days ago there was 2 ft. of snow. Now there isn't anything but mud. It has been raining the last 3 days now. It's beautiful country over here but I'll take Iowa anytime. Some of the boys get letters in 10 or 12 days from the states so I should be getting some from you pretty quick. Send me a jar of Vicks and a pair of size 8 arch supports. I've got a jar of Vicks that I brought with me and it sure comes in handy. I changed clothes today for the first time since I left the states so you can imagine what they looked like. How's every one coming at home? I hope they are all well.

Tell John I'm finally learning what the Heine's 88 (see next page) are like.

I've got my combat rifleman's badge and ETO (European Theatre of Operations ) rib-

*bon now over a week ago. I got 2 stars coming for it too. The combat badge means 14 dollars a month more on top of overseas pay but money don't mean a thing here. I haven't spent one cent since I've got off the boat.*

*Well, Marge, I will quit now. I'll write you again tomorrow if we are still here.*

*With all my love*

*Your husband*
*Bill*

Heine's 88: One of the most deadly weapons the German's had was the 88 millimeter gun. It was the best gun of the war. It was a lethal and extremely versatile gun. It could appear on a tank, as an anti-tank gun, assault or as an anti-aircraft gun. It could knock out Allied tanks at ranges up to 2,000 yards and proved lethal as an anti-infantry weapon when it fired fused shells to create air bursts. It was easily hidden in the *bocage* or a fortified village.

February 4, 1945 - From Bill to Jim and Amanda

*Dear Folks,*

*I suppose you think I'm poor at the writing but it can't be helped. Do you hear from Vernon very often? I think he is back quite a ways from where I'm at from what I can gather. I'd sure like to get a chance to see him. I wrote him last week. He should of got it a couple days ago. Maybe I'll hear from him pretty quick. I'll bet he's surprised to know I'm over here. He thought the war would be over way before I finished basic. I'm doing all right. Washed up and changed clothes today for the first time since I left the states. I suppose, Ma, you could wring my neck for going a week or two without washing my face or hands but water is to precious to waste washing with. We drink water out of any shell hole or creek. Melt snow or any way we can get it.*

*I wrote to Marge a little while ago.*

*Well, folks, there isn't much else to write about except to send me a box, a few icebox cookies and some candy. We get all the cigarettes we need.*

*Lots of love,*

*Your son,*
*Bill*

*P.S. I went to Mass and Communion this morning.*

Written from somewhere in Luxemburg, probably near St. Vith. It is probable that the day after this was written, Company F would go up against the vaunted Siegfried Line.

On February 4, FDR, Churchill and Stalin met at Yalta.

On February 5, US troops, under General Douglas MacArthur entered Manilla.

After the Bulge was pushed back to the German border, the 90th regrouped for a few days and again turned east. Having lost the bulk of their best troops in the Ardennes, the Germans' principle defensive troops were now *Volksgrenadiers* (folk soldiers), but these troops made professional use of their defensive assets - the Siegfreid Line, bad weather and the Moselle, Kyll and Prum Rivers.

Hitler planned the Siegfried Line in 1936 and it was built between 1938 and 1940 after the Nazis had broken the Treaty of Versailles and the Locarno Treaties by remilitarizing the Rhineland. The Line was a defensive system stretching more than 390 miles with more than 18,000 bunkers (pillboxes), tunnels and tank traps.

Rain fell continually in February and things were a muddy mess. Each day featured cold, wetness, mud, hunger for much of the time and thirst. The Siegfried Line Campaign cost 140,000 American casualties.

Reaching the Line on February 5, the 357th Regiment picked its way undetected through minefields, barbed wire and pillboxes. Once the Americans were discovered by the Germans, the pillboxes came to life, pouring fire into Patton's tanks and reinforcements. A week-long fight ensued.

The early days of February also saw the abrupt departure of winter, and the equally abrupt arrival of the hated enemy of all troops... General Mud. The melting snows developed into countless streams which cascaded from the hills into the Our. And once more the 90th found it necessary to contend with rivers in flood.

Enemy opposition consisted chiefly of mortars, nebelwerfers (*smoke blowers*) and artillery. The enemy now comprised units of Volksgrenadiers (*People's Grenadier*). The troops, while not highly trained, nevertheless fought stubbornly now that the Fatherland was menaced.

Heckhuscheid fell on the first day of the month, and now the attack turned its direction again. Wheeling about almost at right angles, Corps now altered its course and aimed toward the southeast. New objectives were assigned. At H-hour, D-Day, the entire Corps would assault the Siegfried Line with the Prüm River as its objective. The 4th Infantry Division would attack toward the town of Prüm, while the 90th was to cut through the 4th and take Pronsfeld, southwest of Prüm. Nothing lay between Corps and its objectives but treacherous knee-deep mud, hills, and the desperate Wehrmacht anchored securely in the Siegfried Line.

(http://www.90thdivisionassoc.org/90thDivisionFolders/90thhistorybook/histbkmainframe.htm)

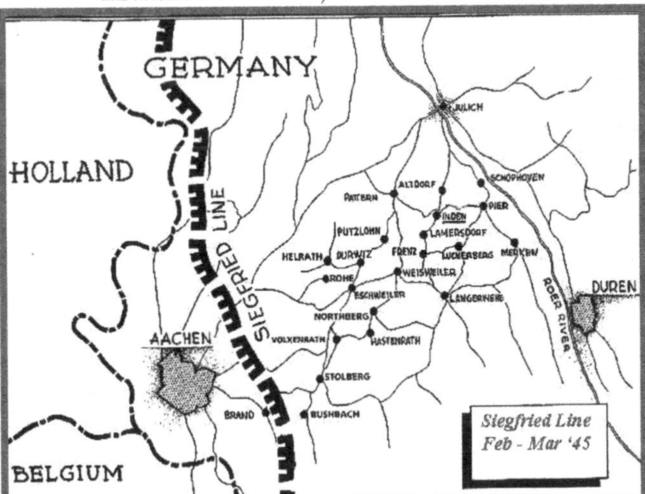


Siegfried Line
Feb - Mar '45

## *February 5, 1945 - From Bill to Marge*

*Dear Marge,*

*Well, Marge another day gone and I don't find it quite like Vernon does over here because the time seems to go fast. Too fast when we are back for a rest especially. How's everything coming at the bakery? In good shape, I hope. Say hello to the Kreebs and everybody for me as I don't get much time for writing. You can send me a tablet and some envelopes but not too many because I don't have the room to carry them.*

*We had chicken last night for supper and this morning we had cereal, French toast, and meat and coffee for breakfast. Are they still drafting a lot of them around home? According to the Stars and Stripes, everyone is going to have their turn at the front. Some of these Heinies fight till they fired their last round of ammunition and others surrender fairly easy. I'm sure glad most of them are poor shots or it would be a hell of a lot worse. The boys all got paid yesterday and the gambling is really going on around here. I played a couple hours and made a few hundred francs. You ought to see the brooms they have here. They take a stick and wrap a lot of small branches around it and that is supposed to be their broom. In these villages all the barns and chicken houses are attached to the house. The walls are from 1-2 ft thick made of sand and cement. All the farmers live in little villages like this and go out from the villages to do their farming. In the winter they keep all their livestock right in the village. The villages are only about 2-3 miles apart. That's why you read where they take so many towns in a day. They all have a little Catholic church in them. For lights when we are back this way (off the front), we use a bottle of gas and a sock in it for a wick. It works good too. I wrote to the folks yesterday. I hope they are all well. How are your folks coming? I suppose they are rid of the farm by now. I hope the fish are biting good this summer and maybe they will stay down at the cabin some. Tell them I didn't write them because you can tell them about every thing I have to say (Marge is living with her parents.) They were sure good to me all the time I lived there. How did those pictures turn out we had taken when I was home? I hope they were not to bad. I suppose Miekle is just as*

ornery as ever around there. (employee at the bakery)

Lots of love,

Your Husband
Bill

February 12, 1945 - From Bill to Jim and Amanda

Dear folks,

Have arrived safely. I can't write what ship I was on but it is one of the largest and fastest in the world.

I hope you have wrote Vernon that I am over here because I am going to try looking him up after we get moved a few times. Mother, will you get some flowers or something else for Marge for our wedding anniversary because I won't be able to. You can write a check on my account at the bank for it. Don't forget to send me a box, too. I suppose it will probably be a month or so before I get any mail. I hope everything is going all right at home. I didn't get sick on the ship coming over. It 's sure hell if a guy does. Well, write soon.

Lots of love,

Your son,
Bill

February 17, 1945 - From Bill to Marge

Dear Marge,

This is the first letter I've had a chance to write in 2 weeks now. The last time we were only back for a day and a half. I missed church last Sunday but I think I'll get a chance to go in the morning. I'm in good shape now. Rid of my cold and my feet are finally thawed out. They sure hurt like hell for a week when they were thawing out. About everyone froze them only some not as bad as others. A few weeks back we fought in 3 different countries in 6 hrs. I suppose you read about it in the paper. There was a big write up about it in the Stars and Stripes. I should soon start getting some mail from you. The guys who came in with me are starting to get their mail now. I can't wait till you start sending some candy. We get some every once in a while so send me a box but be sure you never put any cheese in it because we have cheese every day for dinner in our K rations.

I hope every one is all right at home and things are going all right at the bakery. Say hello to Verle and your folks for me. Marge you can really believe what you read in the paper about our planes bombing and strafing. I counted 820 planes in one bunch go over the

On February 6, the 8th Air Force bombed both Magdeburg and Chemnitz in Germany.

The Russian Red Army crossed the river Oder.

A great example of APO mail delivery. This letter was not dated but written sometime in the previous month. It is postmarked Feburary 13, 1945

On February 7, the US 76th and 5th Infantry Divisions begin crossing the Sauer River.

This letter was written from somewhere in Germany probably near Aachen after taking the towns of Winterspelt, Hurtgen and before they captured the town of Duren.

On February 9, in the *Battle of the Atlantic*, the HMS Venturer sunk U-Boat 864 off the coast of Norway.

On February 11, the Yalta agreement was signed by FDR, Churchill and Stalin. The backdrop for the *Cold War* is set.

From basic training through the end of the occupation, those "boxes" of candy and goodies were very important to Bill.

*lines where we were. That was just in the afternoon. Then there was planes going over all night and morning. We see them bombing and strafing every day. I'm sure glad the Heinies don't have an air force. We hardly ever see a Heinie plane. I'll write again later on today.*

*All my love*

*Your Husband*
*Bill*

*P.S. don't forget to send me a box.*

On February 13, armies of the USSR captured Budapest after a furious 49 day battle against German troops. 159,000 soliders died in this battle.

February 17, 1945 - From Bill to Jim and Amanda

*Dear Folks,*

*I just finished writing to Marge so I'm writing to you right away. I got all washed and shaved up today, first time in 2 weeks. It sure feels good. I hope you are all fine at home. I really feel good now, I'm rid of my cold and everything. It has rained and snowed every day here for 2 weeks except the last 2 days and the sun has been out nice. We are in tents back of the lines now for a couple days rest. I'm going to try going to church in the morning. We got a couple chickens on cooking now so I guess I have chicken to eat in a little while. It sure smells good. You can't imagine what things look like over here. Not a house or barn left standing hardly.*

In several letters Bill asks Marge if the censors had been "cutting anything out"? This was standard procedure, because there was always a chance that enemy forces could capture trucks or jeeps carrying mail bags. Thus, American censors would black out names of towns or areas where troop concentrations existed. Several of Bill's letters, that Jan transcribed to the computer, had lines and/or words blacked out.

*Everything is just about completely wrecked. Dead G.I.'s and Heinies laying around, mostly Heinies though. Things are sure going to start stinking before long. I got a letter from Vernon the other day but I won't hardly get a chance to see him till after the war is over here. From as much as I can gather, he is in a rear echelon so there isn't much danger of him getting hurt. The Heinies hardly even send any planes over. I guess they ain't got many left.*

On February 14, US 8th Air Force bombs Dresden. On the same day, Prague was bombed probably due to a mistake in the orientation of the pilots bombing Dresden.

*Boy, Ma, I'll sure appreciate home when I get the chance again. I could sure go for one of them dinners of yours again!*

*I get all kinds of Heine stuff but I have to throw it away because it gets too heavy to carry and we haven't any chances to mail it. That cigarette lighter I got from you sure works good. Send me a box of peanut butter candy if you have time to make it. There should be plenty of sugar at the bakery.*

On February 16, US forces landed on Corregidor. They would complete the conquest on March 3.

Venezuela declared war on Nazi Germany.

*Lots of love,*

*Your Son,*
*Bill*

February 18, 1945 - From Bill to Marge

Dear Marge,

Well Marge this makes the 3rd letter in a day and a half. Doing pretty good eh? This will probably be the last for a couple weeks again. I'm going to send a Heine rifle home the first chance I get. So far we've busted theirs all up but now we can send them back if we ever get back far enough. We get the Stars and Stripes to read a couple times a week. It is usually 3 - 6 days old but it is sure good to read. I'm sure hoping I get some mail from you pretty quick. I suppose when I do, I'll really get a bunch of it. Marge, if I ever forget to ask for a box when I write, don't forget to put a P.S. on the end of the letter asking for it. The boys over here are all worrying about going to the South Pacific after this is over. I told you before I left not to expect too much mail from me and it looks like I don't get much time to write. How have the censors been doing on my Mail? I hope they haven't been cutting any thing out. I've been writing on both sides because I'm a little short on paper. These Heinies sure have got the mines and booby traps all over. You can look about any place and see booby traps and mines.

You haven't heard anything where Wyscover or LeMaster are, have you? If so send me their addresses. Well, Marge don't forget to send a box, mostly candy. I still like sweets as well, and I love my wife more than ever.

All my love

Your Husband
Bill

Getting ready to go back to the front on the Siegfried Line and to take the town of Duren.

Weather conditions would be inclement with snow and rain and lots of muddy conditions.

On February 19, 30,000 US Marines launched the invasion of Iwo Jima.

980 Japanese soldiers die as a result of a killing spree by long saltwater crocodiles in Ramree, Burma.

On February 21, the US 10th Armour Division overthrows the Orscholz line.

February 22, 1945 - From Bill to Marge

Dear Marge,

I got my first mail from you today, 3 letters written the 11& 12 of Jan. Boy but I was sure glad to get them especially being our wedding anniversary. I wrote mother to get you something nice, I hope she did. It seems like a long time ago since we went up to the altar. I hope I'm able to spend our next anniversary together.

It is sure a swell day over here, the sun is out nice and bright. You should of seen us last night sitting in a pillbox having a few games of Pinochle with the Heinies

It's interesting in this letter to compare the attitudes of German prisoners he is meeting now with those of the guys he talked to in Texas from the African campaign.

They are taking pillboxes one at a time, probably between Duren and Bitburg.

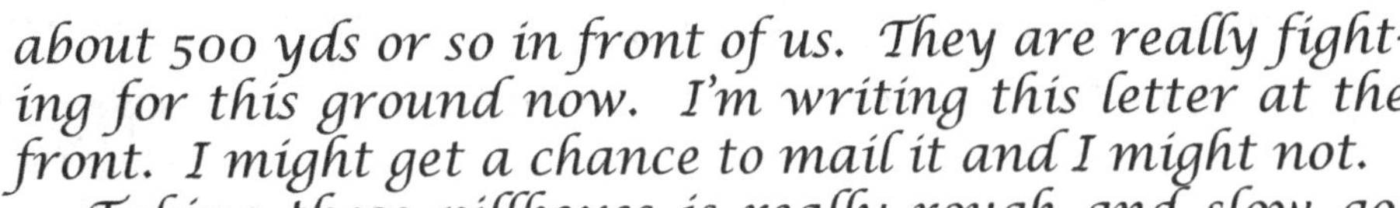

*about 500 yds or so in front of us. They are really fighting for this ground now. I'm writing this letter at the front. I might get a chance to mail it and I might not.*

*Taking these pillboxes is really rough and slow going. This is the roughest time and yet, I think it seems like the Lord is really with this army, most of the guys get hit in the ass, arms, or legs. Our Co. took 85 prisoners the other day. One of them a German medic hid in the basement until he heard the Americans and then came out and surrendered. He worked voluntarily all day long on Heinies & Americans wounded because there was a pile of them hit that day. We are starting to hit places now, where the Germans are using slave Russian labor. Some of them have been working for 3 yrs. as slaves. Practically all of the Germans are Catholic, the homes are full of holy pictures and crucifixes, most of the Heiny soldiers all have rosaries, medals and other religious articles. They are really sick of the war, but there is nothing they can do if they don't fight, the Gestapo picks them up and shoots them.*

*I can't began to tell you how much I miss you but I'm hoping it won't be to long before we are back together again,*

*All my Love,*
*Your Husband*
*Bill*

*P.S. Don't forget to send me a box*

<u>February 22, 1945 - From Bill to Jim and Amanda</u>

*Dear Folks,*

*I suppose you think I don't write very often but I do every chance I get. I'm fine and hope everyone is all right at home. You wouldn't hardly know me now for all the dirt, whiskers, and long hair. I'm still wearing some of the same clothes I had on when I was home. How would you like to wash them? It's starting to get warm here now so I guess I will be able to keep a little cleaner and shed a few clothes. I've got on 2 sets of winter underwear, set of a O.D. with 2 shirts, set of fatigues, sweater, and field jacket, snow pack boots, 2 pairs socks, P38 automatic, wool cap and helmet and rifle, rifle belt, bandoliers with 200 round of ammo, blanket shelter half, toilet articles, towel and pack. Do you think that's enough to*

Part of the defensive system were some 18,000 concrete bunkers called pillboxes; some had concrete 3 feet

thick. They varied in size large enough to hold two to fifteen soldiers. The pillboxes contained narrow openings, through which the enemy could engage Allied troops with their machine guns. These openings normally were situated on all visual sides from the pillbox. The construction was such that they were impervious to aerial bombing by Allied aircraft.

German pillboxes normally sat in open territory, the Germans having a clear view to advancing American troops. To conquer the entrenched enemy, troops had to overcome the intense firepower emanating from the pillbox and toss TNT satchels through the firing slits. They had to be taken one pillbox by one pillbox. It took courageous acts of heroism by American troops, ignoring their own safety, to eliminate each fortress. The Siegfried Line, constructed by the Germans to protect the western border of their country, became just one more formidable element which the Allied forces had to face in their march to Berlin.

On this date, British troops captured Ramree Island, Burma.

Canadian troops occupied Kalkar.

*pack, then I have all my rations and all my pockets full of cigarettes and junk of all kinds.*

*I got the P38 automatic out of a pillbox we took; it's worth $75 to $100 if I could get back a few miles. I could sell it easy but I'm going to keep it, even this paper and U.S. air mail envelopes the Heinies had in with there stuff. They had G.I. clothes of all kinds, our buttons, milk powder, cereal, and different things they had .We nearly ate all right for a little while. There were only 8 of us so we had all we wanted. We busted up about 15 or 20 Heine rifles and machine guns in case they break through they won't be able to use them. Some of those pillboxes were built back in 1921 to 31.*

*Boy, but this weather is sure getting me. Now if I was home and it was like this, I'd be taking off going fishing where I'm digging foxholes and running across the worms pretty thick. It sure makes me want to go fishing. I'm going to write a letter to Vernon yet today if we don't move again.*

*Lots of love*

*Your Son,*
*Bill*

*P.S. Don't forget to send me a box . It sure goes good over here.*

February 23, 1945 - From Bill to Marge

*Dear Marge*

*Well Marge I'm writing again. I told you in my letter yesterday that I got 3 letters from you. I read them over again this morning. I'm sitting here in a room writing a letter and in walks a guy from Caledonia, Minn that used to be around town a lot. Myers is his name. He's in the combat engineers. I thought I knew him and I asked him if he wasn't from Caledonia and he was. He used to run around with Bernice Folsom's husband and them guys. We had quite a bull session. I'm the first one he's seen from around home. He's been overseas for a year. From the looks of the Stars and Stripes they are moving right along in the South Pacific. I hope they keep it up. That sure is pretty good about Owen's. I suppose they are taking a lot of men at home yet. It looks like they still need them.*

It is possible that this is the Walther P-38 that Bill is writing about and he ended up sending it home. It is now owned by one of his sons. He would later capture a second pistol that he brought home, which is with another son.

His son, Rick relates:

Bill, later in life, gathered the boys (Den, Greg, and himself) to divide up his World War II captured guns. He had 2 rifles that he disassembled and shipped home in parts and a German Luger. They drew lots to make their choices.

Later that evening (somewhere around 1:00 AM, probably after a few beers) he told Rick and Greg that he had captured the German captain to whom the Luger belonged. The captain went for his gun and Bill had to shoot him in the head. As was a common thing by most American soldiers, Bill kept the gun.

Rick stated that this experience was one of the few things about the war that Bill ever told him.

(Note: The Walther P-38 and the Luger P-08 were the two pistols usually carried by German officers. G.I.s referred to both commonly as Lugers.)

On February 23, in Operation Grenade, General Simpson's 9th Army crossed the Ruhr River in Germany.

US Marines raised the Stars and Stripes over Iwo Jima. The famous photo, taken by Joe Rosenthal, won a Pulitzer Prize. The battle would continue to a US victory.

On February 24, Egypt and Syria declared war on Nazi Germany.

Manila, capital of the Philippines, is freed from Japanese occupation.

It is possible that the town captured was either Duren or some place very close to there.

*Boy if I only had half a chance I would send home some good souvenirs but don't get a chance to mail them. I've got a German P38 automatic that I wear. It's probably worth from $75 to $100. I got it when we took a pillbox. That is something to see when a bunch took a pillbox. Gets a might hot sometimes.*

*Say hello to Dorothy for me. Tell her I wrote her and Freddy about 2 weeks ago. How is everything coming at the bakery. I suppose business is pretty slack now. Making any money? I'm flat broke now. Lost the other playing cards but the only thing to use money for is airmail envelopes and PX rations. We should get paid in another 5-10 days.*

*I guess I wrote you that I thought Vernon was back quite a ways. I'm sure glad he isn't in the combat engineers because they have pretty rough going sometimes.*

*Well write and tell me what you did on our wedding anniversary. I haven't been to Mass the last couple of Sundays now but I go every chance I get.*

*All my love*

*Your Husband*
*Bill*

*P.S. Please send a box mostly candy. Still like candy as well as ever.*

February 24, 1945 - From Bill to Marge

*Dear Marge,*

*Well Marge I'm writing again and maybe I might be able to write a little more often. The rumor is we are going back for a couple weeks in the morning and I sure hope it's right. I'm the most tired today I've ever been since I've been in the army. Boy we advanced all day yesterday and took a pretty good-sized town. Stayed there a few hrs. and then pulled out and came back here for rest. We are supposed to get all clean clothes and showers. That is really going to be nice. We have been sleeping in Heine shit and every thing else. We slept in the woods for a few hours last night and shit or not, we laid our blankets down and went to sleep.*

*It seems like the farther into Germany we get the better the places are. We've cracked the Siegfried line in 3 different places now so it's about time the 90th gets a little rest. I'm sitting here in a room in a shell torn house with a bottle of gas sitting in front of me. Have a little light. I have to quit writing every now and then and shake it a little to make it burn bright again.*

I wrote a letter to Bessie (Aunt) and the Kreebs a couple of days ago. I haven't got any mail from you since the 3 letters I got a week ago. The guy I bunk up with all the time is from a little town up in the center of Minn. He's a pretty good guy too. He came in this co. the same day as I did but he put in 2 yrs and 8 months up in the Aleutian Islands before he came over here. You can stick an envelope and a couple sheets of paper in letters when you write me once in a while if you want to. We can usually get envelopes and paper someplace but once in a while it is hard to get.

Here it is Sat. night and how I do miss the one's we used to have. Have a few drinks and have Luther go a long to Butch with you and have a good feed.

All my Love

Your Husband
Bill

P.S. Send a box mostly candy

On February 25, US aircraft carriers mounted attacks on Tokyo.

Turkey declared war on Germany.

On February 26, very heavy bombing raids on Berlin were accomplished by the 8th US Air Force.

February 27, 1945 - From Bill to Marge

Dear Marge,

Well I am getting around to writing again. We've been off the front for a couple days but we are in a town where there isn't hardly a roof on the buildings. I went to Mass and communion last night. We had Mass in a room of one of the buildings. The church here hasn't got any roof on it. One wall left standing, just all knocked to hell. Yet the altar and statues in the front of the church weren't touched except the tabernacle was busted open. It must have been a beautiful church at one time. The Heinies had machine gun nests set up in it. That is why it got beat up as bad as it did.

I'm sure hoping we stay back for a few days this time. We had showers and clean clothes yesterday. We took showers in big tents they had set up for the whole Division. They really run a lot through to. I haven't got any more mail from you yet. I'll write soon again.

All my love

Your Husband
Bill

On February 27, the battle of the US 94 Infantry began in Germany.

February 27, 1945 - From Bill to Jim and Amanda

Dear Folks,

Just a line to let you know I'm all right. I haven't got any letters from you yet but I probably will pretty quick. We came back for a few days rest and I sure like

them. This is one of the hottest drives over here from what they tell me. We've cracked the Siegfried line in 3 different places now. It is sure thick with mines, booby traps, pillboxes and dragon teeth. Those are to stop tanks. For miles you can see them about 10 yds wide, reinforced concrete about 4 ft. high and about 4 ft. thick coming up in the shape of teeth. They have really spent a fortune building this Siegfried line. I've always heard the people were Catholic over here but every house in Germany I've been in so far is Catholic with a religious picture in the living room. Every village has a Catholic Church. Most of the Heine prisoners that we've took had medals, rosaries, or crucifix's on them.

Town captured is possibly Bitburg.

We took a big town in Germany a couple nights ago which was the nicest I've seen yet but we pull out again in a few hours. It wasn't shot up bad then but by now it is probably in ruins from shelling.

It seems like the Heinies have plenty left. We had wine, champagne, and everything to eat there. Wine and champagne was bottled back in '32.

The people in one house were in the basement having waffles, eggs, jam, cake and cookies and a few things like that when we took over.

Well, write when you get time.

Love,

Your Son,
Bill

P.S. Send me a box of peanut butter candy if you get time.

March 1, 1945 - From Bill to Marge

On this date, the British 43rd Division under General Essame occupied Xanten.

The Chinese 30th Division captured Hsenwi.

Fieldmarshal Kesseiring succeeded von Rundstedt as Germany Commander as a result of Allied victories.

US Infantry Regiment captured Munchengladbach.

Dear Marge,

I still didn't get any more mail since that one day but I'll get a bunch some one of these days. We played pinochle all day yesterday again. I won about $40 but will probably lose it the next time.

We didn't get paid yet. I should have a little (more) money coming now than when I was in the states.

How is the censor doing on my mail? I hope you are writing to Swede, Harold and Jim once in awhile for me. This is the first chance I've really had to do much writing and I haven't got any of their addresses.

Suppose by now all 3 of them are in the South Pacific. How about White - is he over here? If so what is he in? If he's a rifleman with the Infantry, I feel for him.

How long does it take for you to get my letters anyway? A guy sure can remember all the good times he used to have at home here. I'm hoping it won't be too long before I'm back with you again.

All my love

Your Husband
Bill

P.S. Please send me a box if you get time.

March 2, 1945 - From Bill to Marge

Dear Marge,

I wrote 2 letters to you yesterday and one to the folks. I still haven't got any more mail. We are getting a pretty good mist this time in. Even if it is a hell of a place we are in, we all got our room fixed fairly warm. A good stove made out of a gas barrel. There are 9 of us in a room about 8 by 12 so we stay warm when you are that close together. I wouldn't write some of the things I do, only I know you like to know what I'm doing. Anything I write you don't understand, ask John. He was in the army plenty long enough to know what everything means. I'm a scout and I don't come from the job much. You are out in the front of the rest, especially taking pillboxes. A guy expects a bullet to tear through him anytime but our scouts have been pretty lucky in our Co.

We have a Captain and a platoon Sergeant that really know their stuff. They've been through a lot of combat and are pretty careful. The Platoon Sgt. has been hit 3 times already.

We are having a U.S.O. show today about a couple miles from here. I don't think I'll go though. It's the National --- bunch from Tenn. I suppose it won't be long now before you'll be able to get to the cabin but, boy, I'd sure like to be home this summer to go fishing, maybe I'd be able to catch one of those big one's. Write and tell me all the news.

All my Love

Your Husband
Bill

P.S. Send me a box if you get time.

March 2, 1945 - From Bill to Marge

Dear Marge,

It is sure quiet here now - no guns firing or anything. All the guys went to a U.S.O show down the road a couple of miles. There are just 2 of us left here and we are

On March 2, King Michael of Romania gave in to the Communist government.

Anne Frank died in the Bergen-Belsen concentration camp, Lower Saxony, Germany of typhus.

His son Den remembers that Bill was reluctant to discuss, in detail, very much of his combat experiences.

However, he did mention that as a scout he was often behind German lines. His responsibility was to try to locate enemy positions, usually alone, or with one or two other scouts.

There were occasions when they took Germans prisoner. It was impossible to transport the prisoners to their headquarters or to a staging area. Their orders were to dispose of the prisoners.

Den stated that Bill had mentioned that if he made it home from the war, he vowed "never to leave home (Waukon) again".

Bill was very fortunate not to have been a casualty of World War II - given the fact that he entered combat during the Battle of the Bulge, and spent the next five months in some of the fiercest combat that occurred during the European Campaign plus the fact that he was a scout during these months. Bill had told Den that he had been slightly wounded in combat, yet refused aid. This wound would have qualified Bill for a Purple Heart. And he refused to fill out the paperwork related to the injury.

He, later, regretted not completing this paperwork because a Purple Heart added "points for separation" for an eventual early discharge.

*both writing letters. There was a big bunch of fighters and bombers (that) went over a little while ago. Last night is the first night in a couple weeks I heard a Heine plane flying around.*

*It turned out plenty cold today and the ground is froze and a good wind. I guess I'll wait a month yet before I start peeling off any clothes. I still wear 2 pants and shirts and a combat jacket and every one of my pockets are filled with junk—cigarettes, handkerchief, knife, can opener, toilet paper, socks, gloves, P.38 ammo, Heine heating unit for cooking coffee and rations and about everything else. I just finished reading the Stars and Stripes and it tells of a division that just took Winterspelt and we were in there a week ago but we didn't stay there. If we wouldn't of been pulled back, our Co. would have been the first Co. or men to cross the Prum into Germany and we wasn't but 15 ft from the other side. We have been getting oranges the last few mornings for breakfast and they are sure good. I've managed to get a couple extra that my buddy had. He don't eat them. Well, Marge, keep up the writing. I'll start to get them by and by.*

*All my Love*

*You Husband*
*Bill*

*P.S. Send me a box.*

As this letter is written, the 357th is preparing for the Kyll River crossing and the continued assault along the Siegfried Line.

On March 3, an RAF bombing error hit The Hague, Netherlands, killing 511 civilians.

US and Philippine forces recaptured Corregidor after over four years of Japanese occupation.

The US 7th Army occupied the last portion of Westwall.

A possible experimental atomic test blast occurred at the Nazi Ohrdruf military testing area.

March 4, 1945 - From Bill to Marge

*Dear Marge,*

*I'm getting run out of things to talk about but I'll still write every chance to.*

*We played pinochle most of the day yesterday. I won 5.00/none.*

*Today is payday so I suppose the games will really be going strong. How is everything going in the Bakery? Is John doing all right now with the cookies? There was a Red Cross truck with hot coffee and doughnuts here yesterday. I never expected to see them this close to the front, about 15 mi.*

*We were talking the other day and this kid with me said he was going to remind me of some of these things after it is over.*

*One day I filled my canteen out of a ditch and after I drank it, we went up the ditchways and there was a dead Heine laying in it. Appalling, isn't it? A guy sure sees and does things over here that would really get him*

On March 4, Finland declared war on Nazi Germany.

In the United Kingdom, Princess Elizabeth, later to become Queen Elizabeth II, joined the British Army as a driver.

*in the States.*

*It's been raining the last couple days here but it looks like it might be nice today.*

*All my Love*

*Your Husband*
*Bill*

*P.S. Send me a box*

On March 5, Generals Eisenhower, Patton and Patch met in Lineville.

March 7, 1945 - From Bill to Marge

*Dear Marge*

*Well Marge I am getting a chance to write again. I might carry it for a few days before I get a chance to mail it. This is Heine stationery and envelopes and pencil I'm using. I sent a Heine rifle and a few other things home today. I had another rifle here but I sawed it off too short. Boy but it made me mad. I walked way up a big hill where we were a while ago and got them. I've been really seeing the combat lately. I took my first prisoner. I went in one place with about 20 civilians hiding in it and behind them were two hiding. They threw up their hands right away. One of them gave me a P38 with full clip of ammo on it. This is the first street fighting I ever did. After we cleared the town, we moved to the hills the next day and 5 of us went out on patrol. Really had a battle with them. We got 33 prisoners and killed a few. They got one of us but he didn't get hit bad. He'll get the Silver Star for it because he kept on fighting with us till after they surrendered. Their men all got hit right through the head with their brains splattered all over. It was a bad enough sight to pretty near make anyone surrender. We were only about 10 yds from their trench before they seen us and we had the drop on them. Every time they would stick their heads up, we'd let them have it. I'm sure glad the Lord's on our side because we didn't have a man killed the last few days in combat and nobody hit very bad. I'm sure going to miss this one kid that got hit though because he was a hell of a good guy and could really handle a bar. We crossed the river here the other night. Say, was it ever cold! I got wet from head to foot. I lost my rifle when I fell crossing it and had to dig around the bottom. There it was only knee deep so it wasn't to bad. I poured the water out of my boots about 3 hrs later. I'll bet there were a couple qts left in them yet by night. My clothes were fairly dry. I'm sitting here eating plums and cherries and trying to write at the same time.*

The stationery is much better quality than his usual and is imprinted *J.P. Clarens-Lamort, Wiltz-Wiltz (G.-D. De Luxbg)*.

When Bill wrote, "... could really handle a bar," he is probably referring to the Browning Automatic Rifle. The weapon could be fired on full automatic and, because they were such a threat to enemy soldiers, the men who handled the BAR in a company had a life expectancy in combat shorter than any other duty save scout.

The river crossed was the Kyll; there were no bridges left standing so the infantry had to wade or swim across.

On March 10th the 90th stopped by direction of Corps to await further orders. The 343rd Field Artillery Battalion registered its guns, thus speeding the 90th's first rounds into the heart of Germany.

And now the direction of attack shifted once again. Transferring from VIII to XII Corps control, the Division recalled elements of the artillery and infantry which were already within sight of the Rhine. Swinging sharply south, the men of the 90th once more viewed the river they had decisively beaten four months before. Again the 90th was face to face with its erstwhile enemy... the challenging Moselle.

Plans called for a crossing to be effected by the 5th and 90th Infantry Divisions. The 90th would then drive southeast and seize a bridgehead over the Nahe River between Bad Kreuznach and Bingen. On the left, the 87th Infantry Division was to hold on the north side of the Moselle. At the same time, troops of the Seventh Army, held up by the Siegfried Line positions in the Saar area to the south, were to launch a powerful offensive. It was hoped that the twin drives would catch the Germans in a vise and thus clear for the Americans the entire area west of the Rhine.

www.90thdivisionassoc.org/

*We liberate a few chickens and canned goods quite often over here and don't think they don't go good. A guy can have a lot of fun in combat even if it does get kind of rough.*

*I haven't got but 2 letters from you since I've been over here but I'll get a bunch pretty quick, I'm hoping. How's everything going at the bakery. Does any of the old gang get home and come in? I'd sure love to go on some of them good old parties again. I suppose Riley is still taking care of all that Churchtown stuff? Whats John rushing now anyway? Well I better quit for now. I got time to write the folks yet. I don't know how long before I can write again, maybe tomorrow if I have a chance.*

*All my love*

*Your Husband*
*Bill*

*P.S. Send a box of candy and cookies*

March 7, 1945 - From Bill to Jim and Amanda

*Dear Ma and Dad,*

*It's been about a week now since I've written so I've got a chance and I'm writing. I wrote Marge just a few min. ago. If Dad could only see my hair now! It is curled up in back. I haven't had a haircut yet and it was plenty long at home so he can imagine what it looks like now. (Note: His dad is a barber.) It's plenty thin on top from wearing a cap and helmet 24 hrs a day, day in and day out, but plenty thick behind.*

*We sure took a nice town here a few days ago. 2 nice bakeries in it but all they make is brown bread. The bakery had about 200 or 300 loaves of bread just baked when we took the town. It didn't last long then. Their German women make good jams and jelly and coffee cake too. We can't do any looting but the combat troops do a lot of liberating, especially chicken and preserves. I've got a good wristwatch and a pocket watch that I got from a couple Heine prisoners. I turned down a 60 and 45 automatic for an extra P38 I had but I gave it to a buddy of mine. So you can see what a guy thinks of money over here. Everybody shares with the next guy over here. It would really be a hell of a place if they didn't do it. I get more cigarettes than I need but I bet they are still hard to get at home. We don't have to pay for our cigarettes or anything. P.X. rations are the only thing we pay for and we only got them once since I've been here. I buy a few airmail envelopes whenever I get a chance. I suppose Marge reads your letters and you read hers so I try not to write the same stuff in both of them. Tell John we get a kick out of the artillery boys just a couple of miles behind the lines. They dig their foxholes just as quick as they get their guns set up and us guys on the front just have to hope to hell it don't hit us when we are moving. We don't get a chance to dig in.*

*Well guess I better quite for now. I haven't heard from you yet.*

*Lots of Love*

*Your Son*
*Bill*

*P.S. Send me a box of cookies and candy.*

March 10, 1945 - From Bill to Marge

*Dear Marge,*

*I still didn't get any mail from you yet but I'm still hoping I get some. I hope you get the rifle and things I sent all right. I didn't get a chance to clean it or anything because I had to get it ready in a hurry. Have your dad or mine clean it up as quick as it gets there, will you? It is just about a new rifle but where we were fighting the Heinies I got it from, it was plenty muddy. It belonged to one of those 5 guys I wrote you about us taking. That is one time I really thought the end was coming because we thought they worked around behind us and were pinning us in the middle but the guy who got hit in the back was just firing from an angle and he just thought they were behind us. I really burned up a lot of ammo that day. I fell down where we waded the Kyll river and my rifle was full of everything but it still worked good. A guy's life sure depends a lot on his rifle. I'm going to send some more Heine equipment home a little later on if I get a chance. We are moving so fast now that there isn't time for much of anything. A while back we went 3 days and nights without bunking down and walking most of the time. Cold and snowing most of the time. It was sure good to get back in that town again for a night or two. The woods over here now are just streams of French, Poles, Russian, Italian prisoners of war and about every nationality going back that the Germans had some working around at farms, digging dugouts and foxholes for the Heinies and everything.*

*I sure hope I can take my automatic home with me after the war is over. It sure is a honey. I have a German*

On March 7, Josip Broz Tito begins to form a government for Yugoslavia.

On March 8, the Nazi occupiers executed 53 civilians in Amsterdam.

Phyllis M. Daley became the first black nurse to be sworn in as a US Navy ensign.

On March 9, 334 US B-29 Superfortresses attacked Tokyo with 120,000 fire bombs.

Japanese proclaimed the "independence" of Indo-China (Vietnam).

During this time frame, the 357th had also crossed the Rhine River at Ramagen, the only bridge into Germany left standing by the enemy.

All bridges across the Kyll had been destroyed by the retreating enemy. Thickly wooded hills on the other side of the stream commanded all approaches to the Kyll, and earth entrenchments were visible even through the rain and mist. The weather, however, was proving a handicap to the enemy as well as to the 90th, for the foxholes and the trenches soon were flooded and rendered untenable for the Germans.

Late in the evening of the 5th, elements of the 357th forded the Kyll River, meeting scattered small arms fire of negligible importance. On the following day other units of the Division affected crossings and continued their advance. Gerolstein, a strategically important enemy marshaling yard and former American POW (Prisoner of War) camp, was taken by the 358th after a brief fight in which five enemy tanks were routed.

www.90thdivisionassoc.org/

On March 10, Patton's 3rd Army made contact with Hodge's 1st Army.

Tokyo burns after night time US B-29 bombing. Approximatly 100,000 die, mostly civilians.

On March 11, 1,000 Allied bombers pounded Essen, Germany by dropping 4,662 bombs.

belt for it that holds 50 rounds and 2 clips in my holster. I was just looking out the window here and watching a few French soldiers that were prisoners' doing a little looting on their way back. If the Germans don't surrender before long, there won't be anything left at all. The Germans all are eating good and clothed good as far as we are.

All my Love,

Your Husband
Bill

PS. Send me a box - Icebox cookies and candy

March 11, 1945 - From Bill to Marge

Dear Marge,

I really hit the jackpot today. I got 25 letters from you and 3 from the folks. All old letters but they were sure good to get. 2 of them had the Camp Hood address on but I still must have a lot of back letters coming because you would write about one thing in a letter that you had wrote in another and I couldn't find the ones to match.

How do you like the war news now? Pretty good, eh? If you were over here you would really see sights, the way the prisoners are streaming in. Probably the next time I write you it will be from across the Rhine. I'm glad they got bridges across for we won't have to wade or swim it. When we crossed the Kyll River we waded it pretty deep in some places to. As quick as we hit the other side they opened up on us but it was still dark so we didn't make very good targets. We have a lot of fun in combat sometimes. We have damn good officers in our CO and it keeps the casualities lower than the other CO. I got that $4 and the stamps but don't send me any more or any cigarettes because I get plenty. I have plenty of money. I do all right when I gamble. I staked a friend of mine a few times now but he still goes broke every time. He's one of the guys who showed me the ropes the first couple of weeks.

I get to Mass and communion once or twice a week. Sometimes in morning , afternoon or night, whenever the chaplain gets a chance and we are free for an hour. Sometimes I miss a week or two but then we have it every day on a break. I'm sure glad my wife is saying the prayers for me because I need them here.

I could probably get to see Vernon but I'm going to wait till after the war is over because a guy missing from

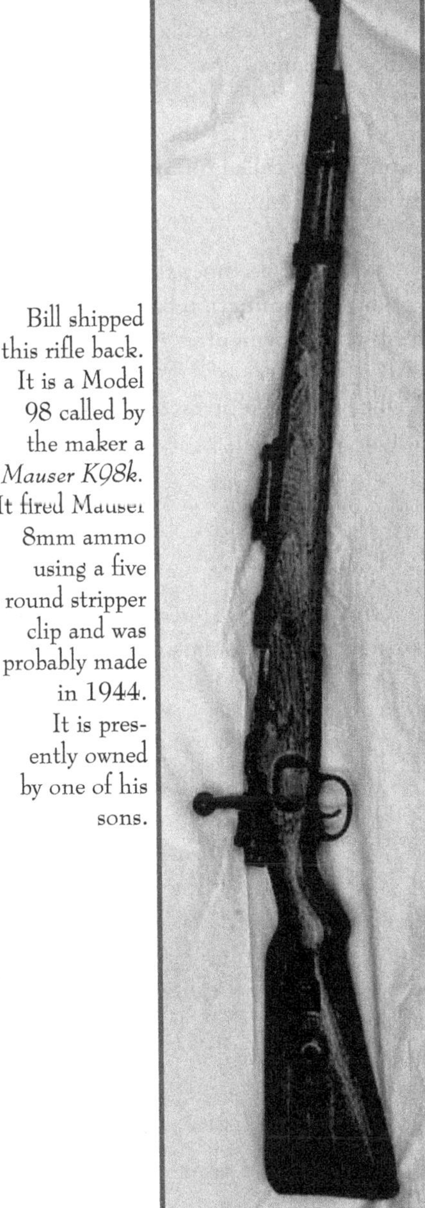

Bill shipped this rifle back. It is a Model 98 called by the maker a *Mauser K98k*. It fired Mauser 8mm ammo using a five round stripper clip and was probably made in 1944. It is presently owned by one of his sons.

*your squad over here is liable to get your buddy killed in that its much more of the load they carry. When we go into the attack it's never with a full squad of men. There are always some that have been evacuated and replacements don't come in too fast. We have only had 7 men since the day on the hill I wrote you about.*

*I hope you can read this. I can't hardly see the paper to write on but I'm doing my best. I guess you have been really getting a workout with the bakery. But Marge it won't be to long before I'm home again. Well, Marge, I guess I better quit for tonight. I still love my wife as much as I ever did and I know she loves me. I never worry about the bakery or you because I know my wife pretty good.*

*All my love*

*Your Husband*
*Bill*

*P.S. Send a box of cookies and candy if you get time.*

US Army Infantry Squad - 12 men: Squad leader (Thompson submachine gun 'SMG', M1 carbine, or M1 Garand rifle), 10 rifleman (M1 Garand rifle), 1 automatic rifleman (BAR). Organized as: Able Team (2 scouts); Baker Team (5 rifleman), Charlie Team (3 rifleman + BAR). One rifleman per platoon would generally carry a bazooka in addition to his personal weapon. There were 3 rifle squads per platoon in a rifle company.

March 13, 1945 - From Bill to Marge

*Dear Marge,*

*I got 10 letters from you today, 8 back letters and two 23 and 27 of Feb. I got one from Jim Cowen dated the 4th of Feb. He still thinks I'm back in the States. I'll write him as quick as I can. I don't think they need to worry about him. He's quite a ways back from the sound of White's address. He never gets any where near the front but I think when it is all over, I'll be just as glad I was up here. I know I'm doing my part now anyway. We took another town yesterday but we didn't hit any opposition. I was the second guy in it. I don't care much for this scout job but somebody has to do it. From the sounds of your letters you're doing enough praying for me at home to carry me through.*

*Every building in this town has a high brick wall about it, a foot or two thick and 7 or 8 ft high around it. These places are the cleanest homes we have run into yet. I guess our Co. took 3 or 4 towns altogether since yesterday. If we can keep on moving fast, this war shouldn't last too long. I visited Mayen a while back and that city has been really all bombed to hell. We stayed there for a couple of days. It should show it on a map of Germany. It isn't far from Coblenz (Koblenz). I'm sure glad I'm getting my mail from you now. I sure do miss you but I guess it won't do much good for a while. We'll make up for the lost time after I get home.*

On March 12, the Italian Communist Party called for armed uprisings throughout Italy.

New York becomes the first state to prohibit discrimination based on race or creed in employment.

The USSR returns Transylvania to Romania.

On March 13, Queen Wilhelmina returned to Netherlands.

There is a good description on the web at (http://www.b26.com/marauderman/ch/bridge.htm) of an American pilot hitting Mayen during the Battle of the Bulge on Dec. 23, 1944. He won the Silver Star for his participation in this battle where 6 of the 36 planes aircrews were lost and every plane received damage.

On March 14, RAF bombers cut the railroad link between Hannover and Hamm in Germany.

On March 16, US Marines secure Iwo Jima, fighting would continue with suicidal Japanese for weeks.

Bill had been in heavy combat between March 7 and March 17 crossing the Rhine and Moselle Rivers and fighting in the towns of Krefelt, Mainz and Koblenz.

On the next page he talks about burning Marge's letters which was mandated by the Army;

On March 16, in the sector of the 357th Regiment, the enemy counterattacked violently, apparently sensitive to the threat of an American advance northward toward Koblenz.

Wurzburg, Germany was 90% destroyed, with 5,000 dead, in only 20 minutes by RAF bombers.

On March 18, 1,250 US bombers attacked Berlin.

*All my love*

*Your Husband*
*Bill*

*P.S. Please send a box if you can get time. I should be getting it pretty quick.*

March 18, 1945 - From Bill to Marge

*Dear Marge,*

*Just got back from the front again. I hope it is for a couple days. We really had a tough week. We didn't get hardly any sleep all week. We have been fighting the SS troops and they fight like devils. They won't give up like the other Heinies. You have to wound them or kill them. We only got about 30 prisoners and a lot of them were wounded. Our Co. and another Co. took 2 towns about 800 yds apart and they must have had 5 or 6 Co. defending them. They took 60 prisoners out of the other Co and killed and wounded about 60 more just about wiped them out. We only had 10 wounded in our Co. and didn't have any boys taken prisoner. We really knocked hell out of them in our town. We were shut off from the rest of our lines for 2 or 3 days. They counter attacked after we got the town but we beat them off. We got 3 of their Captains prisoners.*

*We burnt 2 buildings down with Heinies in. I suppose they are still there because the building was still burn-*

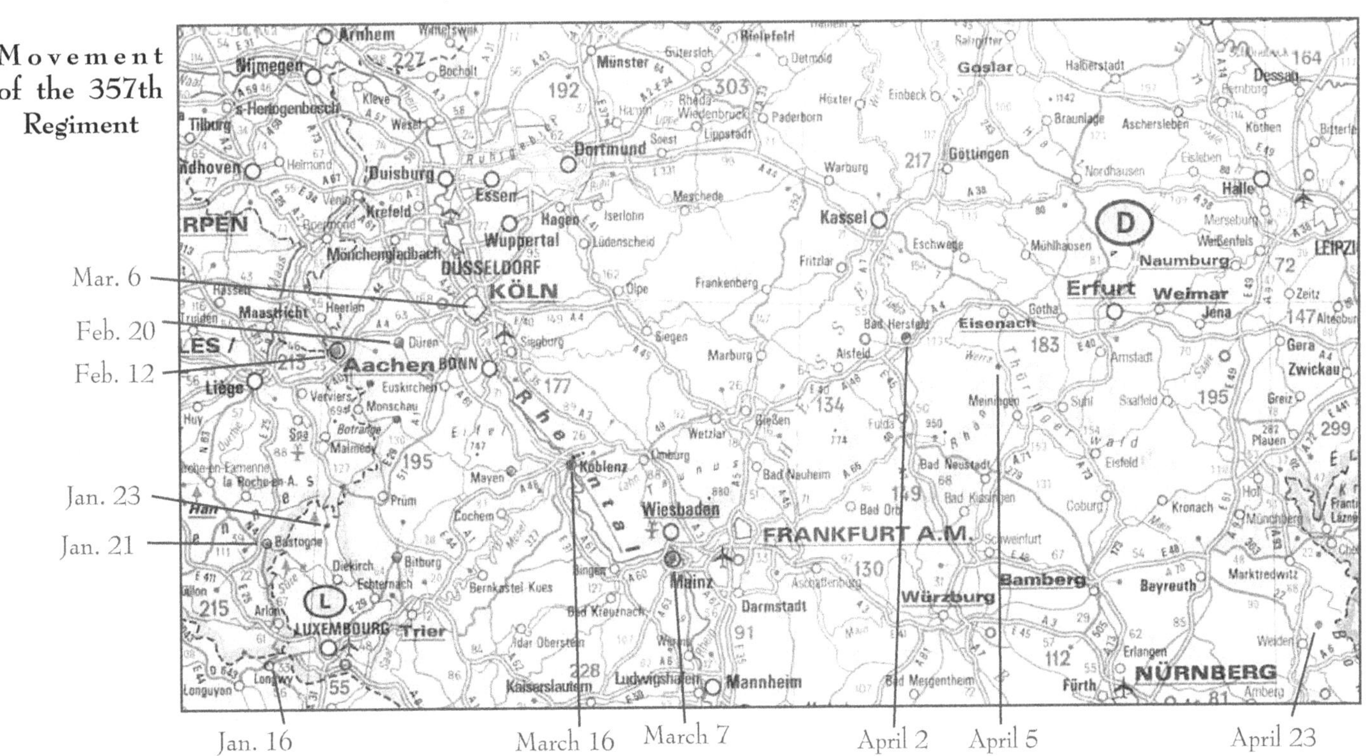

ing when we went into the attack again. I picked off a couple Heinies sitting up in a tree sniping. I've got 28 letters from home now. I can't write the dates because I had to burn the letters after I read them and I don't remember the dates. I got 2 letters from Vernon yesterday. He wants me to get him a P38. I wished I knew it a week ago. I gave a couple away. It's too much extra weight to pack when you don't know when you are coming back, but I'll get one as quick as I can. Mine sure comes in handy when we are taking houses and my rifle is out of shells I use it. I carry it right in my belt loose for it's easy to get at. Did you get the rifle and stuff I sent home yet? Let me know when you do. I got 2 letters from you with the school papers in, pretty good picture of Oscar. I'm sure sorry to hear about Quillin and Collins. I hope Collins is a prisoner and not one of the dead GI's laying around. I still didn't get the letter you wrote at the same time as one of the others I got from you.

Well Marge keep up the writing and praying and it might not be too long before I'm back with you again. I'll be the happiest guy in the world when that day comes again.

All my love

Your husband
Bill

March 18, 1945 - From Bill to Marge

Dear Marge,

Well Marge I went to Mass again this morning. I didn't have the least idea what day or date it was till today. I haven't got any mail from you for the last week now but as long as it is coming, I don't mind it because I'll get a bunch pretty quick again. I was in on that crossing of the Moselle river. We crossed it in a few boats. They just filled the river with mortar fire but we had just got across and only one guy got hit.

I'm sitting here drinking a bottle of Heine beer and it tastes pretty good. Well, Marge the boys are getting ready to play a little pinochle so I'll quit for tonight. Write and let me know all the news and everything.

All my love

Your Husband
Bill

P.S. Send me a box mostly candy.

Another soldier from the 357's account of the crossing:

Crossing the Moselle River

I am writing this experience because I have read in the newspapers and veteran magazines that 1200 WW11 veterans die each day.They all stress that we should tell our stories so that our children and others would realize that "WAR IS HELL."

Tonight is June 21, 2002 and it is 0200 hours and I cannot sleep thinking of WW11 (58 years ago).

I remember it this morning as if it were yesterday.

We were on the banks of the Moselle River and had been told earlier that we were to attack at 0500 and at 0400 the artillery, mortars, and machine guns would open fire on the enemy positions on the opposite bank.

At 0400 our firing began and it stopped at 0500 and my squad climbed into pontoon boats. There were 4 to 6 men in each boat and we had to paddle to the opposite shore and attack the enemy.

We paddled as fast as we could, all the while, the enemy sent flares into the sky, lighting up our crossing and firing mortar and artillery shells at us.

My boat and some others made it to the other side. Other boats overturned due to the swollen and swift current of the Moselle. Others were hit with mortar and artillery fire.

We jumped out of our boats and started to fire our rifles at the top of the bank. We received no return fire and climbed to the top of the riverbank.

There we saw one of the best sights and surprises of the war. In front of us was a trench about 5 ft.deep and about 2 ft.wide. It ran quite a long way, mostly to the left of where we were and at our right, it curved and went inland, on our right side front, were trees, probably 3 or 4 about twenty to thirty feet tall.

We jumped into the trench and knew that we would not have to dig a foxhole tonight.

The Germans had retreated and we were alone.

At 1400 word came down to us to be on the lookout for a counter attack and see if we can take any prisoners if they do counter attack.

Just before darkness the Germans counter attacked us. We didn't know how many of them there were. They had very little cover and we kept firing at them. Some of us who had German pistols and other stuff began to throw them into the Moselle River. I threw my German luger pistol into the river. We didn't want to be caught with them for fear of what they would do to us.

As it happened we stopped them cold and they turned and ran. As darkness came, one enemy soldier was wounded and kept moaning "Ma, ma, ma" all evening long. This was terrible to listen to all evening and if we could, we would have killed him. It was very demoralizing.

At midnight we could hear the enemy moving around. We surmised that the Germans were removing their wounded and dead.

As daylight arrived we saw two German medics waving a white flag and motioning to us that they wanted to remove their wounded and dead.

This, we let them do and it was a peaceful morning.

In the afternoon we had several bullets hit the dirt in our trench and looked to see if we were being attacked. No enemy was in sight. We figured it was snipers firing from the trees.

The three of us in the trench decided that I was closest to the trees. I would fire a clip of bullets into the trees and move to a new position, then the second man would do the same thing and then the third man would fire and hope we would hit the sniper.

We got lucky. A sniper fell from the branch he was tied to and hung there. All three of us emptied our clip into

<u>March 19, 1945 - From Bill to Marge</u>

*Dear Marge,*

*I wrote you and then I wrote the folks and still got time to write you another one. We had a party a few nights ago like one of the old ones at home. I parboiled 12 chickens and Don fryed them in a lot of fat. There was our whole platoon - 27 that's what we have in it now. Lots of liquor to drink and 4 or 5 instruments. Guys doing every thing - I only had a few drinks. I did the cooking and that kept me busy. We had fried potatoes too. Really a big time every one had a lot of fun.*

*There are sure a lot of good looking girls around over here but you don't need to worry about your Husband. He'll keep it in his pants till he gets home.*

*Write and tell me where all the different guys are now. What about Bud and Pat Campbell. Did they come over here too? I just seen a 1935 Ford go down the street (that) a bunch of GI's picked up. They ride the German motorbikes and everything else. Lucky things - most of these places have carbite (carbide) lights so we have better light. I just got a letter from you and one from Ma dated Feb 26 and was I ever glad to get them. The countries that I was in were Scotland, England, France, Luxemburg, Belgium, Germany. Well, it's getting pretty late now so I better quit now.*

*All my Love*

*Your Husband,*
*Bill*

*P.S. Send me a box.*

<u>March 19, 1945 - From Bill to Marge</u>

*Dear Marge,*

*Well Marge, I'll try it again. The last letter I wrote I had to cut it short because we moved in a hurry. So when I cut them short, you'll know why. I try to write every chance I get. I try to write whatever I can of interest to you. The civilians are really friendly to the Americans. I think they are glad to see the war coming to a close but we can't have anything to do with them except route them out of the houses and shove them all in one section of town. They really get pushed around but I guess they asked for it. I'm sure glad this fighting isn't going on back in the states because it sure does knock hell out of all the places. Every house I've been in both in Luxemburg and Germany, the people are Catholic. I haven't see anything but a Catholic church over here yet and they are the most beautiful churches inside that you ever seen. Along the roads in lots of places you see little church grottos with a small altar in it, just enough room for 5 or 6 people. We are between the Mosel and the Rhine now. I guess there are about 70,000 Heinies trapped in here. You can ask Mother to read her letters. I don't think she'll care because I'll write her a little I didn't write you. I hope you like this Heinie stationary. I guess I won't need any now. I got quite a supply now. The boys sure get plenty of cognac and wine to drink around here. I drink a glass or two of this sour wine once in a while. It tastes pretty good to but I'll wait till I get home before I'll ever hang one on.*

*The S.S. troops we were fighting a few days back were Himmler crack troops. The ones who killed all the people in the village of Littin or something like that in Yugoslavia. They counted 52 dead, 55 laying just along the road between the 2 towns we were in, besides all the dead ones strung around the building and those that got burnt up in houses and cellars. There is not much left of them 2 towns. The one we were in was Edinburgh. Maybe you read something about it.*

*Well Marge, I still love you as much as I ever did and am hoping it won't be too long till I'm home again.*

*All my Love*

*Your Husband*

*Bill*

*P.S. Send me a box if you have time.*

March 19, 1945 - From Bill to Jim and Amanda

*Dear folks,*

*Well it's been a week or so since I've wrote you but we don't get the chance very often. I was sure sorry to hear about Quillin and Collins and Ray Zoll getting wounded but a guy who gets wounded is pretty lucky most of the time because most of time that just means 3 months rest. Most of the guys don't get more than a good gash or a small hole in the arm or legs but I think I'd just as soon stay up here and fight these bastards as get hit. The last battle (See inside column, next page) we had was with the 11th Division of SS. It is supposed to be the best German Division and we sure knocked hell out them. We had a few guys wounded and none killed and I'd sure hate to count the dead Heinies around besides those that were wounded and we busted out of houses. We had 3 Captains and about 20 or 30 other prisoners.*

him. We wanted to make sure he was dead. A short time later another sniper jumped or fell from the trees.

We could not see him. A few minutes later I heard what sounded like a person running towards us. I backed away from the corner towards my men. The sniper came around the corner and I yelled "Hand De Hock" (meaning, put your hands above your head). He stopped and quickly did as I ordered him to. He was young and frightened. He did not have a rifle and I searched him for a pistol. He had none.

When he fell or jumped he must have become confused and ran right into us. We had our prisoner.

I led him down our trench to our Sargeant and he sent him to the rear for questioning.

That sniper never knew how lucky he was to be alive. All combat infantrymen hated and despised snipers. Snipers would hide and fire at us. Sometimes wounding or killing some of our men. We had no use for them.

I often think of that day and think how lucky that sniper was that we let him live. Then, I think of how lucky we were that we didn't kill him. I think that perhaps God spared me and I lived through the war. Strange things happen in a war. I am sure other soldiers have had strange experiences.

(http://www.savingprivatesheridan.com/Rocky/Story04.htm)

This letter was written on high quality German note paper with scenic pictures on 3 of the pages.

Bill mentions having *knocked hell out* of SS troops. That would probably have been on March 15 in Buchholz. It was becoming apparent to the German troops that their cause was futile and this resulted in some wholesale surrenders but many continued to fight furiously.

This is one account of the battle Bill is writing about:

"The next day saw the enemy resisting furiously, however, on the Division's left flank. Five companies of SS troops engaged the 2nd Battalion, 358th Regiment. The enemy lost heavily in the ensuing fight which continued throughout the day, and in the evening his remnants were forced to withdraw. The 1st and 2nd Battalions, 357th, fought last ditch SS defenders at a crossroad near Buchholz and at Pfaffenheck respectively, and forced the enemy to withdraw under cover of darkness. As an indication of the ferocity with which the SS fought, in one engagement 70 German defenders chose death rather than surrender, and only 9 were captured alive.

(http://www.90thdivisionassoc.org/90thDivisionFolders/90thhistorybook/histbkmainframe.htm)

On March 19, 800 were killed as Kamikaze fighters attacked the *USS Franklin* off Japan.

Adolf Hitler issues his *Nero Decree* to destroy all German industries, military installations, machine shops, transportation and communication facilities.

British 36th Division conquered Moguk and the ruby mines.

On March 21, the Japanese drop flying bombs (*ochas* - bomb filled with explosives and a human) in an attack on Okinawa.

Allied bombers began a 4-day raid over Germany.

*They should soon be running out of troops to fight with. Most of the regular German soldiers don't want to fight anyway but these SS troops are just like the Japs. Some of them shoot their buddies if they try to surrender but there was a whole Division of them wiped out the last week.*

*I got 2 letters from Vernon the other day so I wrote him yesterday. If you want, you can let Marge read my letter. There might be something in them she might like to see about what I have to say. She'll probably do the same. Then I don't have to write the same thing in them.*

*I got White's address from Marge and from the address he's back quite a ways but he's in the division on the right of where I'm at. You can tell Marge to tell Vonnie that she don't need to worry to much about him. The only way they get hurt back there is getting hit by a truck or something. Vernon is in about the same boat as White. I guess it's all right if you are lucky enough to be back there but I don't mind it much up here when I know I have a lot of them praying for me. I know now when I come home if any of them ever opens their mouth, I'll be able to shut them up. I've seen more combat than guys who have been over here since the start. Only a couple of guys in the platoon have had more combat. The one guy from Minn that I sleep with all the time came in this outfit the same time as me. He's been in the Army 5 years. We are sure getting to be good buddies. Every time we pull in some place where we are going to get a chance to sleep, we always get together. Well folks, I'll have to quit now because I guess we might be getting ready to move again.*

*Lots of Love*

*Your Son*
*Bill*

March 22, 1945 - From Bill to Jim and Amanda

*Dear Folks,*

*I haven't had any mail from you lately but I guess it is just slow in coming. I hope you are getting mine all right by now. Will you buy something nice for me for Marge's birthday because I haven't had a chance over here. I hope she remembers to get some for your birthday. How are the kids coming? I suppose when I get home Butch and Marie will be so big I'll hardly know them. I guess everything is going all right at the bakery.*

*I've been in a few bakeries over here. All they make is brown bread. One day we attacked a town just as the baker was baking his bread so we had hot bread and jam. I've never tried to get in the kitchen since I've been over here. I think I'm doing a better job here than in the kitchen. It isn't so bad once a guy gets used to it. I just got a letter from you and Stan and 5 from Marge. I haven't gotten any papers or boxes yet though. Marge was wondering whether I was at Prum or not. Well, I was at Prum, Our River, Kiel and Mosel crossings but the Kiel was the only rough crossing. I was in Moyen a couple weeks ago, that place is really knocked to hell. Marge said she read about the 4th Armored. We've been cleaning out pockets they bypassed the last week or so. We have been riding on trucks and tanks a lot since the push and it sure beats walking all to hell. If you'd just as soon I didn't write about things over here, let me know and I won't.*

*Tell Oscar I'll write to him pretty quick but I didn't think he should put a basket up in the bakery. It would get dirt into everything.*

*I'm in fine shape. I haven't lost any weight up here at all. We do quite a bit of night fighting in towns now but missing the sleep I don't mind because it is going to make the war that much shorter. Vernon never thought I'd ever be over here but I think I've seen a hell of a lot more combat now than he ever will. I was just writing for a few min. and went down in the basement and got a pitcher of wine. It's pretty good to. I usually drink a glass or two of it. Quite a few of the boys got quite a bum on tonight but not me. I'll wait till I get home and then the whole family can pitch in. It is getting dark now so I better quit. This weather here has been swell the last week, it sure makes me want to go fishing.*

*Love*

*Your Son*
*Bill*

*P.S. Send me a box if you have time.*

March 29, 1945 - From Bill to Marge

*Dear Marge,*

*I just got 2 letters from you, the 15th and 16th of March and one from Bessie (aunt) and the folks and 8 from you about a week ago. One was about the Mosel crossing but that didn't amount to much. We crossed the (censored) and the (censored) which were rough crossings. We got*

On March 23, the largest operation in the Pacific began when 1,500 US Navy ships bombed Okinawa.

*Operation Varsity* was the largest one-day airborne drop when 600 transports and 1,300 gliders were landed east of the Rhine by US and Canadian troops.

On March 27, Iwo Jima was occupied after 22,000 Japanese and 6,000 US had been killed in battle.

Crossing The Rhine

The 357th Regiment was immediately dispatched to the bridge site, crossed the Rhine on the afternoon of the 23rd, and was attached to the 5th Division until the remainder of the 90th arrived. By this time the enemy had begun to react to the disaster which had overtaken them. The Luftwaffe flew sorties against the bridging site, bombing and strafing in a furious attempt to destroy equipment and personnel, to halt at all costs the endless swarm of troops across the German river. Enemy artillery became active and disorganized groups counterattacked continuously in an effort to contain the bridgehead.

The 357th relieved elements of the 5th Division at once, and became involved almost immediately in a violent enemy counterattack of battalion strength. The attack was finally overcome with 250 prisoners taken. The Regiment moved forward rapidly, brushing aside resistance as it went.

The remainder of the Division crossed the Rhine via bridge throughout the day of March 24th and took its place in the line at once. The 4th Armored also effected a crossing, passed through the 90th's sector, and began a powerful lashing drive to the Main River to the North.

(http://www.90thidpg.us/Research/90thDivision/History/divhistch12.html)

pinned down in an open field after we crossed and I shed everything but my rifle and ammo so I'm traveling plenty light now. Nothing but pants, shirt, and field jacket and rifle and ammo, a P38 and ammo belt. I've been in on 3 counter attacks lately now - all at night and they are plenty rough too. One town they were driving an armor outfit out of it and we had to go in and clear it out. I've got my share of Heinies by now so this war can end any day and it don't look like it is far off. We have really been moving fast. I could write things for hrs to you but I haven't got the time now. It don't look like we will get a break until this is over now but we'll keep making bridgeheads and clean out the pockets without breaks if we can keep the armored rolling. We are really getting a long way into Germany now. We ride and walk both. When we crossed (censored), we walked about 7 miles and the (censored) about the same. It seems like I usually stumble in every river and get a little wetter. We walked about 20 yards in the (censored) river. After we got out of the river and to the bank on an island in the (censored), Our Co had to clean it out. We took 188 prisoners and in one of the counter-attacks, we got 211. Our division has taken more prisoners than any other division in the ETO.

On March 29, this was the last day of V-1 flying bombs attacking England.

I'm sure hoping we don't have any more S.S. to fight because they die too hard and fight till about the last man. The rest of these Heinies you throw plenty of lead at them and they give right up. I'm going to try writing a letter to the folks tonight. If we don't move again before then. Say hello to your folks and Veryle for me and keep on praying. Maybe I'll be home before to long. Say but do I every miss you. Every time I cross one of these rivers, I sure get the old urge to go fishing. The (censored) sure reminded me a lot of the old Mississippi. I hope you take the folks down with you sometime when you go down. Well, I'll write again as soon as I can.

All my Love

Your Husband

Bill

P.S. Send me a box when you get time. I should be getting one before long but it takes longer for mail and stuff now.

On March 30, 289 anti-fascists were murdered by the Nazis in Rombergpark Dortmund.

The USSR invaded Austria.

March 29, 1945 - From Bill to Marge

This letter is postmarked March 29 and part of a page had been cut out by the censors.

Dear Marge,

Well, Marge, I'll try to write again although I'll prob-

*ably be carrying this letter for a few days before I can mail it. I got 2 letters and an Easter card from you today dated March 5. That's getting here in pretty good time. One letter was about White being to Paris. Well, he can, he's back behind where they have it pretty soft. We never get to go any place. There is one guy every couple months from our platoon that gets to go to Paris.*

*We run into our first Heinie strafing the other day. I'm glad the Heinies haven't got many planes because that could be rough. We took a town the other day that had 11 G.I. prisoners. They said the Heinies had been treating them swell. It sure surprised me. We caught a Major and he rounded up the rest of the Heinies for us so it made it pretty easy. I hope you don't mind the different kinds of paper I write on but as long as we keep taking Heinies, I'll be able to keep in writing paper and envelopes.*

*I sure hope Ray (Kreeb) don't have to go because it would be really tough on them leaving the kids and everything and this isn't any picnic over here. Of course, we have a lot of fun sometimes on the front. We get a big kick out of talking over things that happen after they are over. It's funny how scared a guy gets before he starts fighting but you don't have time to be scared after you get started. As fast as things are moving now we should hit Berlin in another couple of months. That is if they keep on fighting. I seen my first church that wasn't Catholic the other day. I don't know what kind it was. I noticed from LeMaster's address that he is in the same division as Ray Zoll. I don't write any more V mail because they are hard to read and take longer to get there.*

*Marge when you send a box, don't put any cheese or cigarettes in it because I get plenty of both. We eat good now. We are in towns most of the time with lots of meat, potatoes and jams and fruit. Don't ever believe the people over here were starving because they really got a lot. I've seen 8 or 10 bottles of wine that hold probably 500 gallons in basements of some of the houses and potatoes to partly fill a cellar. At this time in the year, lots of hams and sausage.*

*Our Sarg. got a battlefield commission. He's been hit 4 times now, twice since I've been in his platoon. Well, Marge keep up the praying and writing and I'll be home that much sooner.*

*All my Love, Your Husband Bill*

Military combat has taught us that casualties are lumped primarily in the rifle platoons. For here are concentrated the handful of troops who must advance under enemy fire. It is upon them that the burden of war falls with greater risk and with less likelihood of survival than in any other of the combat arms. An infantry division of WWII consisted of 81 rifle platoons, each with a combat strength of approximately 40 men. Altogether those 81 assault units comprised but 3,250 men in a division of 14,000. In an army of 350,000, fewer than one out of seven soldiers stood in the front line. Some rifle platoons lost over 200 percent during the course of the war. That is, because of the replacement system, more than 80 men may have passed through a platoon's ranks during the eleven months of ground combat in the ETO.

On March 30th the 90th Division gained 30 miles, the following day 25 miles. Huge quantities of valuable military equipment were overrun in the lightning drive. White flags replaced the Swastika as the German national emblem. Village after village, town after town, displayed the banners of surrender, delighted that their community had been spared the ravages of war. As in France, the civilians pressed wine and champagne on their American conquerors, while chickens laid eggs exclusively for the delectation of the invading army.

http://www.90thdivisionassoc.org/90thDivisionFolders/90thhistorybook/histbkmainframe.htm

On March 30, the Soviet Union Army invades Austria and takes Vienna.

Alger Hiss is congratulated in Moscow for his part in bringing about the Western betrayal at the Yalta Conference.

March 29, 1945 - From Bill to Jim and Amanda

Dear Folks,

I got a little time so I guess I better write. I wrote a letter to Marge too. This is the first chance I've had to write for quite a while but I don't know if I'll be able to mail them or not for a while. I'm in good shape except the feet get a little sore once in a while. I wrote Marge to send me some ankle supports a while back. I hope she mailed them by now. I got a letter from you a week ago saying Vernon is probably in Germany now. Boy, but we are sure getting a long ways into Germany now. I haven't been to church now for 2 or 3 weeks but I'll probably get a chance before long again. If we are pushing the way we have been, it shouldn't be too long. Some of these people here think it will only last a couple weeks yet but I doubt it. These people all seem glad to see the American soldiers. I still don't believe all that shit about them all being Nazi and everything. Most of the people up to about (censored) across the Rhine are all Catholics. They aren't as thick now as they were.

The guy is here to pick up the mail so I guess I'll have to make this one short. I'm bumming paper now because I lost all my paper and envelopes and everything else or rather, I threw them away the night after we crossed the (censored). It's a pretty good sized river to. We got shelled by our own mortars and Heine machine gun fire both at the same time after we got across so things get screwed up over here once in a while to. You just ought to see the prisoners we take and the streams of them coming back from the armor. One we got was 67 yrs. old and then a lot of them 50-60 yrs. old.

Lots of love,
Your Son,
Bill

P.S. Send me a box of candy if you get time to make it.

Bill carried this case and deck of cards throughout the European Campaign.

April 1, 1945 - From Bill to Marge

Dear Marge,

I guess I wrote you I got 36 letters and the picture from you. I finally got them all read. It is sure good to get mail over here. I think by the time you get this letter, it will probably be over. I'd sure rather take occupation than go to the South Pacific. All the boys are sweating it out. I wouldn't know where we are in Germany but if we keep moving we'll be meet-

*ing the Russians pretty quick. Sure don't seem like there is any fight left in these Heinies anymore. They come out without firing a shot now. This don't seem much like Easter Sunday. I didn't .....*

Missing Page 2

*...beg to be taken in and fixed up. I let them lay because I wasn't getting my ass shot off pulling them in and it didn't bother me too much. We get --- I left the letter writing for a while and went fishing. I have got a nice string of them too, a little different than home. I used hand grenades and that sure brings them up then. We get them as they float down. I don't know what river it was but it was a little smaller than the Iowa River. We sure haven't had any fighting to do lately but we are on the march all the time. All the liquor that floats around over here...*

Next page is missing also

April 3, 1945 - From Bill to Marge

*Dear Marge,*

*Well Marge I am still in good shape. I hope every one is all right at home. I got a letter from you today of March 20 and 5 letters from Feb. and one from Ma. I don't think Beck would like to have Vernon getting all he can over here neither. "Like she says" you don't need to worry about your husband, he'll wait till he gets back home again. The war news is sure good now. I hope it keeps up. If it wasn't for these damned SS, this war would be over, even all their own people hate them. I hope you don't believe all the propaganda that you read and they feed us but I'm not blind and I still think the same about the German people as when I left. These people are really taking a beating now. I guess we are supposed to treat them rough but I can't go for that old shit. I'm sure hoping I stay here a while rather than go to the CB but you never can tell. That might not last so long either. We haven't been doing much the last week except ride and walk a few miles every day but one never knows where we will hit something. You should see the strings of French, Poles, and Russian prisoners going back that are released. Lots of them came from Hirschfeld, that city got beat up plenty.*

*What armored div. is Billy Campbell in? I see a lot of the 4th and 6th but never seen anyone in them I knew.*

*I haven't ever got any packages yet but in the next one, if you send some orange juice or pineapple juice it*

On April 1, Canadian troops free Doetinchem, Enschede, Borculo and Eibergen in the Netherlands.

US forces invaded Okinawa

On April 2, diplomatic relations between the Soviet Union and Brazil were established.

On April 3, the Nazi's began evacuation of death camp Buchenwald.

US 1st Army conquered Hofgeismar, Germany.

Bill's daughter Jan recalls . . .

Bill telling stories about the raping and looting that went on as the Americans captured small villages and towns. He said at one place his superior officer and two other guys were going to rape a girl and that Bill stood between them and told them they were not going to touch her. They did not touch her, but he thought for sure he would be suffering the consequences later from his fellow soldiers. Nothing ever happened about it.

would be all right. We get a hold of tomato juice every now and then. You can keep sending me a few stamps now and then too. I never ever got the watch you sent but I have two gold 15 jewel watches, one pocket and one wristwatch. I'm going to write Vernon if I get time tonight. I haven't heard from him for a few weeks. I suppose he's too busy moving the same as we are. We haven't had any hot meals from the kitchen for about 3 weeks now but I've been eating plenty of eggs, potatoes, and canned fruit. I probably weigh more now than when I was home. A guy would starve if he had to live on Krauts all together.

On those bonus', Marge, don't give them to John or Stan any week they don't deserve them and if they don't believe I said that you can show them this letter. I told them that before I left. I sure hope you can get by there without to much trouble till I get home. Don't forget what I told you to do when this war is over. Well, Marge, still missing you as much as ever but we'll both have to sweat it out for a while yet.

All my love

Your Husband
Bill

On April 4, Hungary was liberated from Nazi occupation and this day is now known as *National Day*.

April 4, 1945 - From Bill to Marge

First page of letter missing

... get a chance to go to church but I had some good sweet rolls and coffee that we liberated from a house. Raspberries and jam and hot cocoa and a few things we got out of a train with Red Cross supplies for prisoners of war.

US Forces liberated the Nazi death camp at Ohrdruf in Germany.

Patton's 3rd Army, with heavy use of tanks and reinforced infantry conquer Bielefeld.

Boy, Marge I hope to hell the people at home never have to go through the hell these people are going through from a conquering army. It isn't quite like you will read in the paper (I don't think). You wrote in one letter that you hoped this war wouldn't make a drunkard out of me like it has John. I guess you don't have to worry. I think I've seen a hell of a lot more blood and guys killed than John ever did now. I've seen Heinies lay 10 ft in front of me for from 2 to 9 hrs ...

Page 3 missing

And I never drink anything stronger than wine. There is whiskey, cognac, champagne and about everything. Well, Marge, I'm still as much in love with my wife as when I left. I can't wait till we get back together

A Nazi Cross that Bill took from a German officer. We don't know the condition of the officer when this cross was taken.

*again. Keep up the writing and taking care of everything at home till I get back.*

*All my Love*
*Your Husband,*
*Bill*

*P.S. Send me a box of candy if you get time.*

April 5 or 6, 1945 - From Bill to Marge

*Dear Marge,*

*Well, Marge, I got 6 letters from you today, one from Dorothy, Marcella, the folks, and Paulsons and also a box with recipes, socks, and candy in it. The candy was swell. You would think being 3 months old it wouldn't be any good but it was swell. The last time I wrote I told you we were doing much walking. Well, the next day we walked 12 mi taking towns and we really got hell shot out of us.*

*I can thank the good Lord for not getting hit because every one on both sides of me got it. I never seen so many bullets but all open in front of my head and both sides and not hit. Some of them just grazed my clothes. Times like this make the war look a long ways from being over but I hope not. These Heinies really use a lot of machine guns and bayonets. I haven't heard any war news the last few days so don't know how things are going. It is sure good to get the clippings in the letter you write because I never ever did get a newspaper. Marcella was telling me what a hell of a good wife I had but I think I knew that before I ever married you or what? I got the letters with Wyscovers address so will write him as quick as I get a chance. I'm glad he got in as a cook. He'll have things all right. We haven't seen our kitchen for 3 weeks now. I guess I wrote you about being fishing with grenades a couple of times. One day I got a nice bunch of big Pike and were they ever good eating. I got some flour and lard and frying pan and cooked them out in the field.*

*It is really unbelievable. The amount of slave labor these Heinies have. Every house has 2 or 3 of every nationality. We even ran into some Chinese.*

*I write to the folks about every time I write you but I won't have time today, I don't think. Say Hello to your folks and Veryl for me. Tell her she better not go marrying that milkman till after I get home.*

*It must seem funny to have everything closed so early at home now. I'll bet it's hard on a lot of those farmers,*

As mentioned before, some German troops still fight to their demise.

Bill mentions that "I can thank the good Lord for not getting hit", and that fellow soldiers "on both sides of me got it". This most likely in a battle for the town of Hersfeld on April 2.

On April 5, Almelo, in the Netherlands is freed.

Kuniaki Korso resigned as Prime Minister of Japan and was replaced by Kantaro Suzuki.

eh? Those prayers you and the folks have been saying are really bringing me through a lot of tough scrapes. I can't see anything else that does it so I know you'll keep it up.

It's raining pretty good out now. I sure wish it would quit because it slows things down that much more but Marge, it might not be too awful long before this is all over and we are together. Then I think I'll be about the happiest guy in the world. You never need to worry about your Husband chiseling on you because I really love my wife. And you know what I think about the chiseling. Boy, I could sure go for that old Miss. about now. I think I'd be worse than ever for wanting to go to the river. Well, Marge, keep up the writing.

All my Love

Your Husband
Bill

P.S. You can send a box if you have time.

April 6, 1945 - From Bill to Marge

Dear Marge

I wrote you yesterday that I got a lot of letters and the box with the socks and candy in it. Boy, the candy tasted swell to. I'm in a lot better mood today than when I wrote yesterday. I guess I was still a little jumpy yet from the day before. I got all washed up and got clean clothes today (that) makes a guy feel like a different man but I've still got the same combat jacket I had in the states. It is some waterproof now from the oil, dirt, and mud. We have been having a lot of rain the last week here but it is nothing like in the States. Here it just drizzles. I've never heard it thunder or lighting. Boy but I'm really sleeping in a swell place tonight. The electric lights work, running water, toilet and radio.

I just got 5 letters from you, one from Ma, Jean, and Lu and Byron. I got the one with the locket in it. Don't worry, I'll hang onto it, to. It is sure nice. Well Marge, I am going to quit now. Their having a show down the street so I'll guess I'll go. I haven't been to one for 1 1/2 months. Still loving you.

All my love

Your Husband
Bill

P.S. Please send a box.

This letter points out the pressure of combat and what battle fatigue can do to soldiers.

Bill's comment points that out, *I'm in a lot better mood than when I wrote yesterday. I guess I was still a little jumpy yet from the day before.* He was referencing the Hersfeld fire-fight.

On April 6, the Japanese giant battleship *Yamato* heads toward Okinawa.

Massive *kamikazi* attacks began on the US battle fleet near Okinawa.

The US Marines began a recon of Tsugen Shima near Okinawa.

April 7, 1945 - From Bill to Jim and Amanda

Dear Folks,

I wrote Marge last night but got a few minutes this morning so will write. I got a couple letters from you and one from Jeananne yesterday. I'll answer hers as quick as I get a chance. We are going to have Mass in a few minutes so I am going. We'll probably be on the move again after that.

We are in a swell house now, electric lights, with toilet and a good radio. We've been getting music from the states. It sure makes a man feel different when you get clean clothes on and washed up. We had a hot meal this morning, first in about 3 weeks. I seen a show last night. National Barn Dance, it was pretty good to. We haven't heard any war news lately so don't know how things are going. I hope this thing is soon over with. I haven't heard from Vernon for quite a while now but I suppose he is kept pretty busy. Did Marge ever get the rifle and things I sent home? We can't mail much of anything now because we are moving to fast and they don't bother with it. Well, guess I better quit for now. Keep up the writing and praying and maybe this will end before long.

Your son,
Bill

P.S. Send a box if you have time.

April 8, 1945 - From Bill to Marge

Dear Marge,

Well, Marge, I'm writing again. I got a lot of letters to answer but it don't seem like I get the time to do it. We have been through quite the Manufacturing places lately and they really have them camouflaged. Last night and today I was on 2 hrs and 2 hrs off guard duty. Guarding refugees from knocking off any more Heine civilians. I had quite a bit of fun today though. Did a little fishing the same way as I wrote about before with a few French, Russian and Poles. A nice bunch of trout, we were going to have them for supper but we moved just before. I don't remember the name of the city we was in. These refugees are sure raising hell with the Heine civilians now - looting and knifing them.

I got 3 letters from you today and one from Vernon. He didn't have much to say. Said he was a long ways from where I was but might be more near here before long. He can't write a hell of a lot of anything in a let-

This letter is postmarked *Stadtlengsfeld, Germany.*

Rammkommando "ELBE" was the name of a World War II Luftwaffe task force assigned to bring down Allied bombers by ramming German aircraft into the bombers. While the Luftwaffe had a ready supply of airplanes at this point in the war, well-trained pilots and fuel were two components in short supply. Despite the grim prospects of survival of such a mission, the unit was not a true "suicide unit" in that the pilots were expected to attempt to bail out just before colliding with the Allied aircraft.

Adding to the last ditch nature of this task force, the only mission was flown on 7 April 1945 by a sortie of 120 Rommkommando Bf 109s. While only 15 Allied bombers were attacked in this manner, eight were successfully destroyed.

On this same day, April 7, US planes intercepted the Japanese fleet heading for Okinawa and the *Yamato* (on a suicide mission) and four destroyers were sunk.

On April 8, Nazi Gen Christiansen fled the Netherlands as hundreds of his occupier troops were executed.

On April 9, a Liberty ship, in the harbor at Bari, Italy, carrying aerial bombs, exploded killing 360 civilians.

On April 10, Canadian troops conquered Deventer in the Netherlands.

Allied troops liberated Nazi concentration camp Buchenwald, Czech.

When Bill writes *P.T.A.* he refers to the Postal Transit Authority that incorporated the functioning postal system of the liberated part of Germany. In 1945 the stamp inscription *Deutsches Reich* was changed to *Grossdeutsches Reich* (Greater German Empire).

Field post stamps were issued to the military forces starting in 1942. The world's first postal code system was introduced on July 25, 1941 with a two-digit number system. This system was initially used for the packet service and later applied to all mail deliveries.

On April 12, US President Franklin D. Roosevelt (1933-1945) died suddenly at Warm Srings, GA and Vice President Harry S. Truman (1945-1953) becomes the 33rd President.

ter. I just remember I sent home $70 yesterday by P.T.A. so it takes a while to get there. It was about all I had in Belgium and Netherlands money so I thought I'd better get rid of it someways. We get paid in German money now so I still got between 50 and 100 dollars left, I don't know for sure. We stayed in a high Nazi officers house last night and was it ever swell. Lay in bed and ring a buzzer for the kitchen. It must have held 30-40 rooms in it. Only 8 of us guys in it. Pool tables, billiard tables, movie machine. We ran films most of the time. We went off guard and Boy, Marge, when I get home I'm going to buy some good champagne for you to try good champagne. I drank some last night and this afternoon and it was the best drink I ever had. A few of the boys got a little full but after a couple drinks I always leave it alone because we never know when we are moving or going on the attack. And I want to be safe and besides I'll wait to get home with you to hang one on. That bunch of pictures I sent you of the church and a few buildings were in one city or town I was in. There was one of only myself and another guy left out of the bunch. I came in with him - the same guy I wrote about from Minn. Our Sarg. got hit for his fifth time a few days ago. He got a couple slugs in the back so I guess he'll go back to the States now. We are sure going to miss him too. I listened to the war news over the radio today and it still sounds pretty good. Well, Marge, I'm still loving you.

All my Love

Your Husband

Bill

Send a box if you have time.

April 9 and 10, 1945 - From Bill to Marge

Dear Marge,

Well Marge I'll write again this morning. I hope to get some mail from you today. Been getting it now in pretty good time from 2 weeks on.

I should start getting a box or two pretty quick. I got one a week or so ago that was over 3 mo. old. I wrote and told you about that. I lost my Identification bracelet that you gave me about a week ago. It must of just come unhooked. I suppose Meikle is just as ugly as ever around the bakery. His day is coming yet so I guess we have to make the best of it till I get home. John should be pretty good on most of that stuff by now. Or is the booze bothering to much yet?

*April 10, 1945*

*Finishing this letter now. I suppose you read in the paper where we captured all Germany's Gold, 2 million in American money and about every other kind of money. It don't look like these Heines will ever give up until we take everything they have. Sure getting hell knocked out of everything by keeping on.*

*It is sure funny to see Coca Cola signs all over here. The Germans have mostly all Ford trucks and lots of Ford cars. I see lot of Fords like mine over here. I always thought before I came over here that there weren't much trees in Germany but there are a hell of a lot more than we have in the States. Mostly big pine just as straight as can be. When they cut down a patch they plant new ones so have them all the time.*

*The people in the refugee camps got rough treatment from the Heines and I guess about all they ever got to eat was potatoes. I've been getting plenty of mail now and my old mail is still coming. Its sure good to see our bombs go over ever day but some of the plants I've seen, they didn't knock out much of the equipment and a lot of them are so well camouflaged, you can't see them.*

*Well Marge I think I've wrote enough for now and keep up the writing and praying because I can use them both. I'll probably write again tomorrow.*

*All my love*

*Your Husband*
*Bill*

*P.S. Send a box with whatever you want to put in it.*

At this time elements of the U.S. Third Army, racing across Germany, stopped at the Kaiseroda Mine at Merkers, because they had been informed by some local residents that the German Reichsbank had, within the preceding weeks, stored gold and other valuables there. Upon entering the mine the soldiers found stacks of gold bars, bags of gold coins, millions of dollars worth of foreign currencies, art treasures, and other valuable assets.

When an accounting of the gold was undertaken by the Army, with the help of U.S. Treasury officials, it was determined that the gold was worth about $238.5 million (equivalent to some $2.5 billion today). During subsequent weeks the U.S. Army uncovered gold valued at about $14 million in Reichsbank branches as well as $9.7 million from other sources. In addition the U.S. Army uncovered other significant bodies of Nazi loot, including gold wedding rings found at concentration camps.
(http://www.archives.gov/research/holocaust/records-and-research/searching-records-relating-to-nazi-gold1.html)

April 15, 1945 - From Bill to Marge

*Dear Marge,*

*Well, Marge, I'm getting around to writing again. I've been doing pretty well, I think. I owe quite a few letters but they'll have to wait. I've never got around to writing Wgsuccen (Wyscover) or Le Master yet. We haven't got any mail for quite a while now. I guess it hasn't caught up to us yet. I've had a little beer lately, a couple bottles yesterday and some keg beer today. There is always lots of other stuff around but I'll just drink the beer. I have been fishing again the other day. I had 3 nice mountain trout for breakfast the other morning. I'm glad I'm able to go fishing once in a while. You know how well I like to fish. How's everything going at home now? I hope all right.*

Bill mentions in these letters that he caught several fish to eat. His favorite method of fishing was to toss a hand grenade into a stream or lake and harvest the fish that surfaced after the grenade detonated!!

On April 15, Bergen-Belsen concentration camp was liberated.

*The war now still sounds good but it looks like we will have to take every city and village over here before it ends. I've been trying to write now for an hr but I'm stopping to listen and get a few words in now and then.*

*I suppose the men are kind of getting cleaned out around there now. Has Ray heard anything yet? I sure hope he don't have to go. From the sounds of things they are going to take all the soldiers out of the States for the South Pacific before they take them from over here. We are seldom in the same place over one day but it really is all right as long as it will shorten the war. I just saw about 6 Heine prisoners go by. Now that is the way I like to see them. Well, Marge, I think I'll quit for now. I'm thinking of you always and you don't need to worry about me chiseling. I'll wait until I get back.*

*All my Love*

*Your Husband*
*Bill*

*P.S. Send a box when you get time.*

April 17 and 13, 1945 - From Bill to Marge

The dates on this letter are a bit confusing. We know that Bill wrote on April 15 and would write again on the 18th, so it's probable that this letter was written on April 16 and 17. As Bill stated earlier, dates tended to run together.

*Dear Marge,*

*I wrote a letter to you yesterday and just finished one to the folks a few minutes ago. I've been playing pinochle most of the morning so you know I still have my games wherever I go. There are quite a few around that play. I sent you $70 a week or so ago but it will take a little longer to get there. Are you still getting our bonds and allotment checks?*

*How much is there in the checking account at the bakery now? I suppose business is pretty slack now. I'm glad to hear the business held up during the winter. You probably should hire another girl to work steady if it is too much for you. We have been eating a lot better since we got into Germany than we did before. They seem to have quite a lot of everything. I think we will have deer for supper. Some of the boys got a few deer yesterday and the cooks are going to fix them. The kitchen is keeping pretty well up with us all the time now. I hope they keep it up. Lot of the old guys are coming back now. It seems funny to have so many again.*

On April 17, Brazilian forces liberated the town of Montese, Italy from German forces.

The US 8th Air Force bombed Dresden, Germany.

Mussolini fled from Salo to Milan.

US troops landed in Mindanao.

*How is the cabin? Have you been down there yet? When I get out of this army I think we'll spend a couple months there. I've been fishing quite a bit here with grenades. That's really the way to get them. Boy would I ever like to go over to Gun Lake in the spring with a few grenades.*

*I suppose Ray has been fishing a lot by now. We have been having pretty nice weather over here except for a little rain of course in the Mt. here. There is still snow around the tops.*

*April 13, 1945*

*Well, Marge, I'll continue now. Rode 20 miles on tanks since I started to write this so will finish this now. It's about 7 o'clock here now. We had a hard rain yesterday afternoon and last night. Just like one back in the States. This is the first time I've heard thunder and lightning over here. You can keep on sending me a few air mail stamps now and then. How is O'Riley coming now anyway? Is he still bragging about that thing as much as ever?*

*Well, Marge, I'd better quit now because I want to get this letter out with the mail. I think you are going to get one from me with this article taking out (that) I put in. I sure wished you could have read it. It was about this outfit but I heard it wouldn't go through. Loving you and missing you more than ever.*

*All my Love*

*Your Husband*
*Bill*

*April 18, 1945 - From Bill to Marge*

*Dear Marge,*

*Well, Marge, I'm getting around to writing a few lines again. Our mail is having a hard time catching up with us but I got 3 letters of the last of March and box with March 5 (Des Moines) Register and the candy, it has lasted about 10 minutes. Sure was good to me - got quite a kick out of the paper.*

*I got a card here at a place I stayed in a day and night. (Today is Marge's Birthday). We were Div. Guard for a couple days. It was pretty good. I was within a couple mi. of Czechoslovakia once but I don't know where in the hell I am at now. You ought to see the way they farm over here. Sometimes you see a horse and a cow hooked up together plowing or a couple cows or oxen, or horses. I've sure been fishing a lot in the last month. Have pretty good luck all the time, too and it only takes a little while.*

*How's everybody and everything coming at the bakery? I had some hot doughnuts a while ago. Some German people just got done making them when we came in. We*

Before the 90th Division lay the forests and mountains of Thuringia. Ordinarily, such terrain would have proved most difficult but the 90th had proved itself in difficult terrain time and again, and Thuringia held no terror for the men who had crossed the Eifel Hills in the cold of winter and the mud of Spring. Indeed the Germans themselves now called the 90th the "Forest and Mountain Division".

From Zella-Mehlis, home of the Walther small arms factories, the Division changed directions once again, this time to the southeast toward the communications centers of Hof, close to the Czechoslovakian border.

A news blackout had been imposed on the activities of the Third Army for several days. The news-hungry public read newspapers avidly for word of Patton's dramatic drive. For the Third Army nothing was impossible. For all they knew, spearheading elements might already be in Czechoslovakia. (Unreasonable, of course).

The answer was not long in coming. When the blackout was finally lifted, the 90th had taken Hof against fanatic but futile resistance, and elements of the Division, duly accompanied by press photographers and war correspondents (sent to immortalize the historic occasion), had indeed set foot upon the soil of Czechoslovakia. The 90th Division thus became the first unit in the ETO (European Theater of Operation) to slice across the German nation, to cut the land in half, to divide Bavaria in the south from the great industrial Germany in the north. The date was 18 April 1945.

(http://www.90thdivisionassoc.org/90thDivisionFolders/90thhistorybook/histbkmainframe.htm)

On April 18, American war correspondent Ernie Pyle was killed by Japanese machine gun fire on the island of Ie Shima of Okinawa.

Clandestine Radio 1212, after broadcasting pro-Nazi propaganda for months used their influence to trap 350,000 German Army Group B troops.

The US aircraft carrier *Franklin* was heavily damaged in a Japanese air raid in the Pacific.

The 90th Division and Bill's 357th Regiment is now in Czechoslovakia, moving rapidly, with little resistance.

On April 20, Soviet troops entered Berlin and the US 7th Army captured the German city of Nuremberg.

*run them out of a house and then took it. We aren't supposed to sleep in the same houses as they do.*

*I owe Vernon a letter yet. I'll answer in a few days.*

*Well Marge, I'm still missing and loving you so much if not more than ever. I guess I'd better quit for tonight. Now if I can borrow an envelope off one of the guys, I'll mail it.*

*Keep up the writing because I never get too many letters from you.*

*All my love*

*Your Husband*
*Bill*

*P.S. Send me a box if you have time.*

April 21, 1945 - From Bill to Marge

*Dear Marge,*

*I've been getting a lot of mail from you now - even 3 boxes the other morning but we moved right away so I passed it out in a hurry and carried one. I really got filled up on candy for one day. It looks like this war is going to last a few months more. It seems like we are going to have to take every village before it is over. I used to feel a little sorrow for some of these people but now I'd just as soon burn all the bastards up when they fire on us when we are taking a town. Now they just don't have a town left because they got them burnt to the ground. A couple days ago they fired on us going into town and we were on tanks in about 15 min. There was about 10-15 houses on fire.*

*I got your package and letters there the next morning. It was sure a mess around - dead cows and everything around but these bastards got to learn the hard way. I suppose you read by now where the 90th is in Czechoslovakia. I still haven't missed a day since I joined this outfit and I hope I don't have to. If the Lord stays with me, I haven't taken a thing out of a house over here yet except stuff to eat. Lots of the guys take rings, watches, everything. I still don't believe in that yet. We have a lot of new men in the co. now. And old ones coming back. It is the biggest now that I have ever seen it.*

*Does Vernon ever write where he is at? I think he is probably back along the Rhine. When we crossed and for about a week after we had a lot of Heine planes*

*over strafing us but never did much damage. I think I might get a chance to go to Mass and Communion in the morning.*

*Thank Ma for them boxes for me, will you? I forgot about it in the letter I wrote her. I haven't got any letters from you addressed April yet but I got 2 from Ma. Her's have been coming through quicker for some reason. I still haven't taken any of this Heine stuff yet and there is a lot of good looking stuff around. Some of them speak English. In the house we are staying tonight, there is one, but we ran them out a while ago.*

*I still love and miss my wife as much as ever, boy, what I wouldn't give to be with you again.*

*All my Love*

*Your Husband*
*Bill*

April 21, 1945 - From Bill to Jim and Amanda

*Dear Folks,*

*Well, folks, I'm going to make this a short letter. It seems that I never get around to writing much anymore but maybe it is because we are moving so fast. We ride on tanks, TD, trucks and about every way. I got myself another pistol a few days ago off a Heine. It is an Italian make 32. I wished I'd get a chance to see Vernon. I'd give it to him. We've been taking lots of towns. One day we took 6. I wished I had a picture of one town we took. We were on tanks about a quarter mile out of town when they opened up on us. We burnt the town down. It was sure a sight to see, just getting dark. It looks like these people got to learn the hard way.*

*I got a copy of the Stars and Stripes I'll send. This is about 1/2 as big as it usually is.*

*Well, write when you get time. I'm getting so I can understand these Heines pretty well.*

*Love,*

*Bill*

April 22, 1945 - From Bill to Marge

*Dear Marge,*

*I've got a little time so I'll write again. I haven't got any mail the last few days but I've been getting quite a bit. I just got done making some chicken and noodle soup and frying a few chickens and potatoes. They sure hit the spot too. I didn't make it to church today. I didn't find the right church but I sat in one and said a few prayers. It was sure a beautiful church with 5 big*

On April 21, Allied troops occupied a German nuclear laboratory.

He Shima, Okinawa is conquered by US forces after a battle of five days in which 5,000 Japanese died.

On April 22, Heinrich Himmler, through Count Bernadotte, put forth an offer of German surrender to the Western Allies, but not to the Soviet Union.

On April 23, US troops in Italy crossed the river Po.

On April 24, retreating German troops destroyed all of the bridges over the Adige in Verona, Italy including the historical Ponte di Castelvecchio and Ponte Pietra.

On April 25, founding negotiations for the United Nations began in San Francisco.

On that same day, US and Soviet troops linked up at the Elbe River.

On April 26, the last successful German panzer offensive ends in Bautzen, German with the city being recaptured.

On April 27, US Ordinance troops found the coffins of Frederick Wilhelm I, Frederick the Great, Paul von Hindenburg and his wife.

On that same day, the Western Allies flatly rejected any offer of surrender by Germany other than unconditional on all fronts.

In May 1938 a concentration camp was established at Flossenbürg, in the Oberpfalz region of Bavaria, near the Czech border. This camp was originally intended for criminals, "asocial" persons, and Jews, but it grew to include political prisoners and foreign prisoners of war. The largest number of the latter were Soviets. The site was chosen for its granite hills, and prisoners were put to work in a large quarry.

Flossenbürg was liberated by the U.S. Army on 23 April 1945. By that time, some 30,000 inmates had died in Flossenbürg and its subcamps. (Memorials at the camp state the number as over 74,000, but recent research indicates it was around 30,000.)

Among those killed were Admiral Wilhelm Canaris, Pastor Dietrich Bonhoeffer, General Hans Oster, and others involved in the plot to kill Hitler on 20 July 1944 (see the Berlin page for more details). These men had been arrested following the collapse of the plot, but they were held in various prisons and camps until being sent to Flossenbürg, where they were hanged on 9 April 1945, shortly before the liberation.

At Flossenburg, men of the 90th learned that propaganda and truth are sometimes the same. It was here that they saw with their own eyes a vivid example of the cruelties of which the enemy was capable. Flossenburg, one of the most infamous concentration camps in all Germany, was the first encountered by the 90th. Bodies were stacked grotesquely like cords of wood. The ovens used for disposing of the bodies were on display. More than 1,100 inmates, who had not been evacuated by the German SS, were liberated by troops of the 90th, to whom the nature of the enemy was now revealed fully and graphically.

www.90thdivisionassoc.org/

altars in it and holy pictures painted and statues every place you look. We are just running into the Catholic communities again. It is sure nice to get inside a Catholic church again. We've got about 6 or 7 Catholic guys in our squad now. We got a nice radio in the house we are in tonight so we get the news. It still sounds pretty good but I'm waiting to hear the war is over but I'm afraid it is going to last a few months yet. Boy I'll sure be glad when I get home with you again.

Well, Marge, guess I better quit for tonight.

All my Love

Your Husband

Bill

P.S. Send a box with anything you want to put in it.

April 23, 1945 - From Bill to Marge

Dear Marge,

I just got done writing a letter to John. I thought it was about time I wrote to him. How's he doing at the bakery anyway? I hope everything is going really good. I know its about enough to drive you nuts there but I don't think it will last forever. We are pretty close to the Russians now. Seen a bunch of their planes the other day. It was sure a pretty sight.

I'm waiting to get some mail from you tonight. I heard a lot came in tonight. There's nothing I like better than to get letters from you. In the next package you send me, see if you can't find some small packages of cups of Nescafe. That is one thing us guys really go for and we only get one package a day in our breakfast ration. And better send me a few more stamps - I'm all out again.

Just got 8 letters and a box from you. Boy, but the candy is hitting the spot. I'll read the letters after a while. Well, Marge, it is getting dark so I'll quit.

All my Love

Your Husband

Bill

P.S. Send me a box if you have time.

April 28, 1945 - From Bill to Marge

Dear Marge,

I got 4 letters from you last night and one from Verle's folks. I wrote one to the folks this morning. I'm as bad as ever for writing. I guess I played pinochle most of the day. I'm sitting here in the kitchen writing, nobody around. It's raining just like back in Iowa. Most of the boys are out trying to fig, fig for chocolate, if you get what that means. We have been having a lot of fun with some of these Heine civilians - making them shave off their kitten mustaches, boy but it makes some of their old bucks mad. When we took one town a ways back myself and another kid went into scout a house and a couple Jews were hiding in it, when they seen we were American they tried kissing our hand or any part of us. Then in a few minutes they were crying to beat hell. They had scars all over from being beaten. They said the German SS had killed 600 of them already at the concentration camp when they escaped. They were just about starved, bones sticking out of them all over. I'm hoping I get some mail from you again tonight. I sure am always waiting for that. I don't think I ever ate so many eggs in all my life as I do over here. I had 6 just before chow tonight and I fryed 3 after breakfast this morning. I don't think you have to worry about me losing any weight over here because I manage to liberate enough to eat. I'm sure waiting and praying for the day we can be back together again.

All my Love,

Your Husband
Bill

P.S. Send a box if you have time.

Daughter Gwen said that Bill talked to her about liberating a concentration camp in Czechoslovakia. His regiment/company had fought its way across Germany and into Czechoslovakia during the month of April and into May.

Bill told Gwen that he and 4 other soldiers were one of the first groups of Americans to liberate the Flossenburg concentration camp.

April 28, 1945 - From Bill to Jim and Amanda

Dear folks,

I was going to write last night when I wrote to Marge but I didn't get around to it so will write the first thing this morning. I got 2 letters last night from Marge, wrote the 12th and 13th so get mail finally good up here. I want to thank you for the box I got. It was swell. I forgot to thank you in the last letter.

I wished I would of known Bud Gavin's address sooner because back at the Rhine we were fighting in the same town as some of the fifth Div. And we always used to see a lot of them. If Klemme is the 26th that is a new Div. over here. We ran into them a couple of times on this side of the Rhine. We still have been pushing to beat hell. We walked 40 mi. in 2 days cleaning out towns and villages. I don't see where they get all the men. We run into kids that aren't over 14 years old along the Czech border. Here the people are all Catholic, the same as before we crossed the Rhine. I should be hearing from Vernon pretty quick. I think he is near Frankfort so it will be a long time before I ever see him. The boys are

On April 28, Benito Mussolini and his mistress, Clara Petacci were executed by Italian partisans as they attempted to flee the country. Their bodies were hung by their heels in the public square in Milan.

On April 29, in *Operation Manna*, British Lancaster bombers dropped food in the Netherlands to prevent the starvation of the civilian population.

Brazilian forces liberated the commune of Fornavo di Taro, Italy from German forces.

Patrols and limited objective attacks were the principal business of the 90th Division as April came to a close. The Sudeten hills as formidable a defensive line as the Eifels, ranged darkly and forbiddingly against the Tough 'Ombres. Patrols, venturing into the vast wooded areas before them, met sharp opposition as elements of the battle-wise 11th Panzer Division barred their way. It was determined, therefore, that the high ground on the Division's left flank must be cleared.

The attack was launched on April 30th northeast and southeast of Waldmunchen, and met stubborn resistance consisting of enemy small arms, artillery and armor. The dense woods made progress double difficult. On the following day the attack was continued, but still the almost impenetrable forests and the constant sniper fire made movement hazardous and difficult at best. On May 3rd the mayor of Vseruby surrendered the town after Germans had fled. The Division now held its objectives.

http://www.90thdivisionassoc.org/90thDivisionFolders/90thhistorybook/histbkmainframe.htmobjectives

getting ready to play a little pinochle so I guess I'd better get in on it. We have some real games. Well, write when you get time.

Love,

Your son
Bill

P.S. Send me a box with whatever you want to put in it.

April 29, 1945 - From Bill to Marge

Dear Marge,

Well, Marge, I got 4 letters from you last night and 3 from Ma. Sure is good to get mail. Ma wrote about Hadley sending so much stuff home. Well, them rear Echelon bastards.

Come but most of them have to steal it off of some wounded G.I. or guys who went back to the hospital. We haven't been any place where we can buy anything since I've been over here but if I ever get a chance, I'll send some things home. I'm going to try going to church in a little while but I have to go back a ways, I guess. The Red Cross was here with hot coffee and doughnuts today boy, they sure went swell and to think I'd never eat them when I was home. Ma said in her letter she heard I was to the hospital with frozen feet. Well, Marge, I haven't missed a day since I've been with this outfit so I couldn't hardly have been. Lots of guys froze their feet here in the winter that never went back with them.

I played a little pinochle again this morning. These Heinies are hiding there eggs on us now - they are kinda getting onto us.

I suppose by now you have been to the river. I'd sure like to be there to go with you. You asked me in one letter how many days I'd been in combat. Well, we were on the line most of the time. We are never off over a couple days at a time but there haven't been any mortars or artillery to sweat out since we crossed the Mainz River and that makes it a hell of a lot nicer. Most of the guys are getting lousier than hell from sleeping on these Heine beds and never changing clothes. I haven't got them yet but am expecting to be crawling with them pretty quick. I sprinkled yesterday with louse powder so that should keep them away for a while. I've worn the same field jacket everyday now for 4 months so you can imagine what it looks like. You ought to see how tight my ring is after walking about 20 miles. I've still never had it off. Well, I'm hoping I get a box and some mail from you again tonight.

All my Love,

Your Husband
Bill

P.S. Send me a box if you have time.

May 1, 1945 - From Bill to Jim and Amanda

Dear Folks,

I just finished a letter to Marge, so thought I would write you. I got a few letters from you a few days ago.. You and Marge are about the only ones I even write to. I got a letter from Vernon the other day. From as near as I can figure out, he is back around Frankfurt. I'd sure like to see him, but I doubt whether I will or not. You ought to see all the kids they have over here.

One little village I was in, they had about 1,000 Hitler youth. Where ever in the hell are they going to get the food to feed them with?

I have to quit now because we just got paid so we'll start a little game. I hope everybody is all right at home. I'm in good shape. I think I eat a doz. eggs a day. Good thing these people have a lot of chickens or we would about starve.

Lots of love,

Bill

May 2, 1945 - From Bill to Marge

Dear Marge,

Well Marge, I got a letter from you and one from Vernon and a box a couple days ago from you with the arch supports and candy in it. That was the best candy I got yet. Those chocolates were sure good to. I think I was in Czechoslovakia the other day but not for long. I sure hope we get out of these mountains pretty quick. It's been snowing the last couple days and it's pretty cold up so high.

Vernon said he thought his outfit was going to the South Pacific. I sure hope the 90th don't. These Heinies use a lot of bazookas now. They got 5 of our men the other day.

One of my buddies thought for sure one of those was me when he went by but lots of times they let the scouts go by before they open up. You are usually as good as dead when they fire bazookas at us because they fire from close range. I sure hope Ray don't have to go be-

EXTRA THE STARS AND STRIPES EXTRA

# HITLER DEAD

**Fuehrer Fell at CP, German Radio Says; Doenitz at Helm, Vows War Will Continue**

Churchill Hints Peace Is at Hand

On April 30, Adolf Hitler (56) and his wife of one day, Eva Braun, ate a vegetarian lunch and then committed suicide as the Red Army approached the *Fuhrerbunker* in Berlin. Karl Donitz succeeded Hitler as President of Germany and Joseph Goebbels became Chancellor of Germany.

On May 1, Hamburg Radio announced that Hitler had died in battle, "fighting up to his last breath against Bolshevism."

Joseph Goebbels and his wife commited suicide after killing their six children. Karl Donitz appoints Count Lutz Graf Schwerin von Krosigk as the new Chancellor of Germany.

Troops of the Yugoslav 4th Army, together with the Slovene 9th Corp enter Trieste.

Radio Budapest, Hungary re-enters shortwave broadcasting.

The Soviet army reaches Flensburg, Denmark.

A Nazi flag that Bill captured and sent home.

cause this is no place for a guy with kids. I just heard we are going to get paid today but that never interests me because it don't do you any good anyway. I seen a Heinie prisoner really saying his prayers the other day. He had his rosary and crucifix in his hands. He thought we were going to kill him. Of course some of the boys worked over a few of them.

I'm sure hoping I get some mail from you again tonight. The last dated mail was 2 letters of the 16th of April. The one I got yesterday was the 7th. I've never ever got the Democrat (Waukon paper) or any papers so you can send a clipping or two in letters of things I might like to read. I'll write again in the morning if I have a chance. I'm still loving and missing you as much as ever.

All my Love

Your Husband
Bill

P.S. Send a box.

May 2, 1945 - From Bill to Marge

Dear Marge,

Well Marge I'm writing again. I didn't get any letters from you last night but I got 2 from Ma and a box from Verle that she sent to Texas. It was plenty old but we ate all the candy and cookies. Tell her thanks for me. Yesterday I sent $50 home. We got paid. I draw $38.60 a month with my combat pay and overseas pay. Hitler's death has caused a lot more excitement over here than Roosevelt's. From the sounds of things, that must really have been quite a stew when Roosevelt died but over here the guys didn't think much about it. Some figured the war will be over soon.

A few of the boys are writing their wives not to get scared when they get the notice from the Army that they were wounded because they just got like a scratch but some didn't fare so well.

Went out on a patrol last night and brought back a case of beer so have had a couple bottles of beer today. There is a lot of cognac around but I never drink any of it. We are figuring the war to be over any day now. Sure hope it is. If it isn't pretty quick, they'll just get that

On May 2, the Soviet Union announced the fall of Berlin. Soviet soldiers hoisted the Red flag over the *Reich Chancellery*.

Troops of the New Zealand Army 2nd Division entered Trieste a day after the Yugoslavs. The German army in Trieste surrenders to the New Zealand Army.

Lubeck is liberated by the British Army.

On May 3, the prison ships *Cap Arcona, Thiebek* and *Deutschland* were sunk by the RAF in Lubeck Bay.

Rocket scientist Wernher von Braun and 120 members of his team surrendered to US forces.

much rougher treatment from the front line troops.

We all have to turn our pistols in on account of so many guys shooting themselves with them. Most of them are drunk when they do. I've got 3 P38's, a 32 German automatic and a Italian 32 so I suppose I'll turn in a couple of them. It's supposed to cost over $120 if we get caught talking to any German people.

Marge, I'm sorry I can't send you anything for your birthday but I haven't seen a single place since I've been over here where you can buy anything. Back aways the boys can buy everything to send home but not up here.

It seems funny with a couple inches of snow on the ground but it will go quick now. The sun is out for the first time in about a week. I think I'm heavier now than I ever was at home but couldn't tell for sure but can't wait to find out. I'm getting so I can understand these Heines pretty well now. Well, I'm hoping I get some mail from you tonight. What I wouldn't give to spend a few days with you again but it might not be to long from the sound of the news.

All my love

Your Husband
Bill

May 7, 1945 - From Bill to Marge

Dear Marge,

I suppose by now you know I'm in Czech. We just got the news a while ago the war is over, boy, but we sure were waiting for it. We had rough going the last few days in Sudatinland. The people were really Nazi but here it is really swell. When we crossed the border, guys standing there with schnapps and the women with cookies and rolls. Today when we rolled through villages on tanks, they came out with everything for us. I'm sure glad I'm not one of these people that helped the Germans because they are really catching hell. They are having people count now and going kinda rough on some of them.

They are getting things all fixed up. It looks like they are going to put on a celebration tonight. It's a good thing I'm married or I'd sure be playing some of these girls but you needn't worry. I haven't yet and I ain't going to start.

I finally shed my fatigue pants today. The guys have been kidding me about them for the last month about getting rid of them, but I told them I was keeping them

On May 4, the North German army surrendered to Marshal Bernard Montgomery.

Holland is liberated by British and Canadian troops.

Denmark is liberated.

On May 5, Admiral Karl Donitz orders all U-boats to cease offensive operations and return to their bases.

A Japanese balloon bomb kills five children and a grown woman, Elsie Mitchell, near Bly, Oregon when it explodes as they drag it from the woods. They are the only people killed by enemy attack on the American mainland during WWII.

On May 6, Axis Sally delivered her last propaganda broadcast to Allied troops (the first was Dec. 11, 1941).

On May 7, General Alfred Jodl signed unconditional surrender terms at Reims, France, ending Germany's participation in the war. The document takes effect the next day.

The Sudetenland is the western region of Czechoslovakia inhabited mostly by ethnic Germans. Named after the Sudeten Mountains.

As you read Bill's letters dated during the month of May, you will note a more relaxed tone. The war is over, combat has ceased, personal hygiene improves, and supplies are forthcoming.

Note, also, that at the bottom of nearly every letter Bill writes home, he asks Marge to "send a box if you get time".

He will gladly accept anything from home....candy (he loves Amanda's peanut butter fudge), chocolates, newspapers, toiletries, even cookies that may get stale or crumble.

on till the war was over.

The rumor is we are going to be occupation and I sure hope it's true (vs. going to the South Pacific). I haven't had any mail for quite a while now but I'm hoping I get a lot tonight. I guess we have been moving too much again for it to catch up.

I got all washed and shaved up today. I don't feel right being clean for a change. It's going to be rough when I get back home to have to take my clothes off to go to bed. I haven't taken off anything but my shoes since I joined the 90th.

I still am loving and missing my wife more than ever. Well, I will be writing more often now.

All my Love

Your Husband
Bill

On May 8, V-E Day (Victory in Europe) commemorated the end of World War II in Europe with the final surrender being to the Soviets in Berlin, attended by representatives of the Western Powers.

Canadian troops moved into Amsterdam after German troops surrendered.

The British 8th Army, together with Slovene partisan troops and a motorized detachment of the Yugoslav 4th Army, arrived in Carinthia and Klagenfurt.

May 8, 1945 - From Bill to Marge

Dear Marge,

Well, Marge, I'm writing again tonight. I got one letter yesterday but it was an old one, April 3. The mail just came in now and I got one letter from you and one from Mother dated the 30th of April. The quickest I've ever got any letters. I sure am sorry to hear you have been having so much trouble with help. I can't wait till I get home again and then you will have things a lot easier. Boy, were we a happy bunch when they halted us and said the war was over. We were driving across Czech.

Boy, this place where we are staying really treats us swell. The old lady has been baking cakes and rolls for us yesterday and today - all we want to eat, making our beds and everything. They had a little celebration here last night. All kinds of beer and music but I had one glass of beer and came down to the house and played. We played ball most of the day and a while tonight. Boy, but the Lord was sure with me that I didn't pick up a few slugs over here or get it with a bazooka. They were really using the bazooka at the last. Those --- in Sudatenland were really fighting the last while before it was over. I seen all the fighting and killing and blood I ever want to see. I hope I won't have to stay over here too long now. Vernon thinks he'll go to the Cbs. I hope not though and me to. I'm going to write to the folks yet tonight. So I'd better quit for now. Still loving and missing you. Your Husband, Bill

Vernon is in a supply unit and when Bill writes Cbs he is referring to the CBI - -China, Burma India Theatre.

The goal of the Allies in the CBI theater was to supply and reinforce the Chinese forces in their fight against the Japanese invaders. Japanese occupation of China's seaports had cut off the normal supply route. Therefore, the Allies moved equipment, personnel and supplies to China through India (by flying the "Hump Route" over the Himalayas) and Burma (through construction of roads and pipelines).
http://thompsonian.info/ben-cbilinks.html

May 8, 1945 - From Bill to Jim and Amanda

*Dear Folks,*

*Well, folks, the good news has finally come that the war is over. Don't think there aren't a happy bunch of boys around now but they are all sweating out the South Pacific. What kind of shape was that rifle in when it got home? It was a new rifle I think, but it got pretty muddy there where we had the battle.*

*I finally got a Democrat today but it is March 21st. I'll try to pick up a bayonet when I go into Germany again which will probably be in the next couple of days. I've got 3 nice pistols that I've taken off prisoners. I'm going to take them home with me when I come home. We can't send them by mail. Two of my old buddies just came back from the hospital. Boy but am I ever glad to see them.*

*Well, folks, I think I'll quit now. Getting anxious to shoot the shit with them.*

*All my love,*

*Your Son,*
*Bill*

On May 8, Chinese troops countered attacks at Tsjangte with support from the US 14th air fleet.

May 9, 1945 - From Bill to Marge

*Dear Marge,*

*I just came back from Mass. We had Mass out in the open today. I got a couple cards here I'm sending, give one to Ma. We were out playing ball again this morning. I think over here (it) is the first ball I've played since I was about 18. Lots of fun to. When you send boxes again, you can stick a magazine or two in it. I might get a chance to read once in a while now. I hope I get some mail tonight. I know I must have some coming someplace but it will catch up before too long. There are lots of things I've seen over here I'd like to write to you about but I can't so I'll wait till I get home. I still don't like to write any better than I ever did. I write you, the folks and Vernon is about all. I'm glad to hear Lemaster got in the Air Corps. He probably got put there on account of being hit. He won't have to do so much work. I've had one bath since I've been over here, nice and clean, eh? But we'll probably get clean clothes and a bath pretty quick now.*

*All my Love*

*Your Husband*
*Bill*

*P.S. Send a box if you have time.*

On May 9, the Soviet Union marked V-E Day.

Hermann Goring is captured by the United States Army and the Norwegian resistance movement in Oslo, Norway, arrested the traitor Vidkum Quisling.

The Red Army entered Prague.

General Alexander Lohr, Commander of German Army Group E near Topolsica, Slovania, signed the capitulation of German occupation troops.

The German occupation of the Channel Islands ends with their liberation by British troops. Amazing that islands in the English channel had remained occupied for so long. Alderney, an annex of the concentration camp *Neuengamme*, is also liberated.

A typical letter that Jan transcribed. Written in pencil, this example has been computer enhanced to make it more readable.

Somewhere in Germany
March 18, 1945

Dear Marge,
Just got back from the front again I hope it's for a couple days. we really had a tough week. we didn't get hardly any sleep all week. We have been fighting the SS. troops & they fight like devils they won't give up like the other heinies you have to wound them or kill them. we only got about 30 prisoners & lot of them were wounded. our CO & another Co. took 2 towns about 800 yds apart & they must of had 500 or 600 defending them. they took 60 prisoners out of the other Co & killed & wounded about 60 more just about wiped them out. we only had 10 wounded in our Co. & didn't have any boys taken prisoner. we really knocked hell out of them in our town we were shut off from the rest of our lines for 2 or 3 days. they counterattacked after we got the town but we beat them off. we Got 3 of their Captains prisoner

See Pages 101-102 for transcribed letter.

May 10, 1945 - From Bill to Marge

On May 10, Allied forces captured Rangoon from the Imperial Japanese.

Russian troops occupied Prague.

Dear Marge,

I got 2 letters from you tonight, 2 or 3 and one from Ma and your Mother. I had to saw the stock off the rifle so it would fit in the mailbag. In regards to hiring help, you have who ever you want. I left you to run the place and Ma to help you any way she could. I know you are doing a hell of a good job of it too. Maybe you should have a couple girls steady and you can have a little off. Sure wish I could come home to do it but I think it will be quite awhile yet. From what we hear, we are going to be Occupational.

I came over on the Queen Elizabeth in 4 days, landed in Scotland, went to England, France, Belgium, Luxemburg, Germany, Czechoslovakia, Sudateland, and Czech again. I wrote you about the Queen Elizabeth a long time ago but you must never have got those letters. I can write about anything I want except a few things - that I wouldn't have written about if someone happened to get a hold of the letters.

On May 11, US Marines conquered Awatsha Draw in Okinawa.

I just went broke playing cards thats the second time for me since I've been over here.

Might have to sell a pistol to raise a little money. I've never sold or bought any of that crap yet. I made Pfc the first week I was in combat, the last part of January.

I've still got my ETV ribbon and combat badge but have never worn them. Don't know what the hell I kept them for anyway but I guess we'll soon have to start wearing them. Those that don't.

My hair is finally getting long in front again. I had it all butchered off in front a couple months ago. Boy, but I sure get lonesome for you now. More than I ever did before because (I) have more time. I'm sure glad I've got a good wife. It's kinda rough on some of the boys when they are getting divorces and everything. Well it's getting dark so I quit for tonight.

All my Love

Your Husband
Bill

P.S. Send a box if you got time.

May 11, 1945 - From Bill to Marge

At the top of this letter, Bill notes that it is written from *Czech*.

Well, Marge, I'll try writing again. I guess we will stay in Germany a little while yet but will wind up in the Pacific by and by. The old men will stay here and I haven't been in the Army long enough. Lots of these

With this letter begins a lot of uncertainty. Bill is not certain where he will be stationed as an Occupational Force (and this will change several times over the next nine months). He is bored, lonely and desires to get home to Marge.

**Central Europe Campaign**

The long anticipated Rhine crossing was no problem at all as the 90th followed the 5th Division over its bridge, proceeded east to capture Darmstadt and cross the Main at Hanau, and then rolled up light German resistance toward Czechoslovakia. The 90th still encountered small groups of fanatical, vicious, unprincipled SS troops, but overcame them with light but regrettable U.S. losses.

Three memorable actions during this period did not involve combat: Seizure of the German national treasure in the Merkers salt mine, acceptance of the surrender of the entire 11th Panzer Division at Hof, Germany, and liberation of the infamous Flossenburg concentration camp. These were fitting preludes to the unconditional surrender of the German Armed Forces at 0001 hours, 9 May 1945 (V-E Day has since been recognized as 8 May).

www.90thdivisionassoc.org/

replacements that came in after me had 2 or 3 years in the Army but then, one never knows. We haven't been able to take any prisoners lately because I guess we have taken over our quota. All we could do was take their arms and turn them loose. This is the Russians territory to take but we came in to shorten the war. The Russians will probably be in town sometime today or tomorrow. The next letter I write, I'll probably write from Germany. I know the name of the city we are going to but I'll be able to write that later, I think. Boy, but I'm sure getting sick and fed up with this war and army life. I've never been so lonesome for you as I have been this week. Have had a lot of time to ourselves for a change. I guess you used to figure from my letters when we had a couple days break. We were in a rest camp. But I haven't seen one yet. We usually are a couple miles behind the lines or in a holding position.

I've been having a hell of a job getting any paper to write on. Lost the tablet you sent me but still have the envelopes.

A Heine plane came over the other night just skimming the town but a P51 and 47 went after him and knocked him down. There are still a lot of Heinies that haven't given up yet. Well Marge, be sure to keep up the writing because I really wait for your letters. I'd sure love to be home with you now. I bet we'd spend a little time at the river.

All my Love

Your Husband

Bill

P.S. Send a box if you have time.

May 12, 1945 - From Bill to Marge

Dear Marge,

How am I doing? Writing every day now. You should start getting a little more mail by now. I suppose a lot of letters I wrote you were lost during the push.

The Heinies still come in every day but we just let them go now. These Czech people really treat us swell. The old gal where our squad stays bakes us rolls and cakes every day. We've been here longer than we ever were any place. I've still got a German Pauatnays knife that I never sent home but will some one of these days. I got one letter from you last night, May 1. Hope I get a box and some mail tonight. One of the boys wrote you a letter today. They all kinda wait for my boxes. If any of

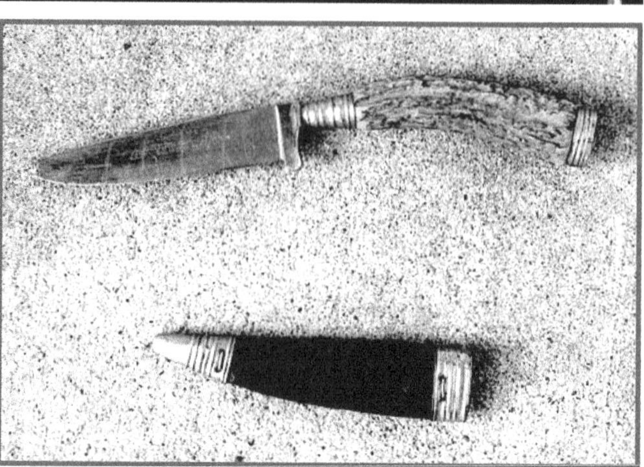

This is probably the knife that is mentioned in this letter. In any event, it was sent home and now belongs to one of Bill's sons.

Stamped into the blade is *Gottlieb Hammesfahr, Solingen Foche* and below that *Nirosta*. Also there is an emblem of a pyramid with a Cross on it

*the old fellows go home before long, I'm going to send a couple of my pistols with them because we can't mail them and that will be about the only way I'll get them home for awhile. Maybe you should have an extra man in the backend now if there is getting too much (to do). I got a letter from Ray the other day. Good to hear from him. It seems like the women in all these countries do all the work. The men just lay around.*

*How are your folks coming? Say hello for me. I borrowed $10 this morning and made $25 so I'm not broke any more! You should be getting the money I sent home pretty soon. I sent $120 all together. We had a show here last night out in the open with the picture showing on the side of a house. It was good to see again. Keep up the writing.*

*All my Love*

*Your Husband*
*Bill*

*P.S. Send a box if you get time. Can use a little hair oil now too.*

May 12, 1945 - From Bill to Jim and Amanda

*Dear Folks,*

*Well, folks, I'm still in Czech. These people really treat us swell. They were really glad to see us come. They have taken out a lot of the German collaborators and shot them all ready. Girls 18-20 year old too, of their own people. I sure hope we never have a war in the states like this. I'm really getting caught up on my sleep lately. I think I weigh more than I did when I left the states. I'd sure like to weigh sometime. It sure seems funny to see the people with a couple (of) cows hooked up pulling their wagons plowing with them and everything else. Most of the people in all the different countries over here are Catholics.*

*How's every one coming at home. I suppose by the time I get home again the kids will be so big I'll hardly know them. I suppose dad is still making pretty good money. Vernon wrote he thought he would go to the CBI. I guess most will (go) over there. It will sure be a happy day when this thing is finally over. It never caused too much excitement here when Germany surrendered because most of the guys figure they would just go CBI. anyway.*

I guess about everybody is getting cleaned out around home by now. We have a lot of 18 yr. old boys with us now. Some of them are plenty good boys to. I've been getting mail pretty good from home. I had a letter from Marge yesterday dated May 1, that was good time getting here. Well, write when you get time. I went to Mass the other day. We had mass out in the open.

Love,

Bill

P.S. Send a box if you have time.

May 13, 1945 - From Bill to Marge

This is the first letter in which he talks about *points*.

To be sent home (for discharge or reassignment in the United States) each soldier must have accrued a certain number of points.

Points are determined by rank, time in service, time in combat (being *on the line*), being awarded a purple heart, receiving a bronze or silver combat star, and/or receiving campaign stars.

As you read several of Bill's letters written from this point forward, there will be mention of his points and about how many points he needs to be sent home.

Well, Marge, I got 3 letters from you last night, April 14 and 16 and one May 3, also one from Ma. I think Angscauen is lying to his wife about cooking because no cooks are suppose to have a Pfc. Rating but between a T-5 or T-4 which is a little more money. The boys are all figuring up their points around here and most of them are really mad about it. We don't get any points for combat and a guy who has been on the line all along don't get as many as guys who were hit because lot of them got bronze or silver stars. I don't need to figure mine for a long time yet for the sounds of it. The guys in Paris and England get just as many if not more than the front line troops. Our squad leader's been with this Co. since June and has never been hit or got any decorations and is one of the best men in the Co. and has only got about 40-50 pts the way they figure. I've still haven't got buzzed up over here yet - sure have had plenty of chances too but I guess I'll still wait till I get home with you. Vernon kinda lost a stripe for getting full, but up here I never seen anyone getting busted for getting drunk and there was plenty of it.

On May 13, US Marines conquered Dakeshi Okinawa.

We have Mass at 4 o'clock this afternoon so I'll be going pretty quick. I got 2 sheets of paper left - don't know what I'll write on after that. I got the watch you sent me last night. It was too nice to wear here but I'm going to after we move because if I sent it home it probably would never get there. The package was sure beat up.

Well, Marge, I sure wish this thing would end so we could be back together again.

Here's one time I have plenty of time to think of all the good times we have had together and I hope it won't be too long before we can have them again.

All my Love

Your Husband, Bill

<u>May 14, 1945 - From Bill to Marge</u>

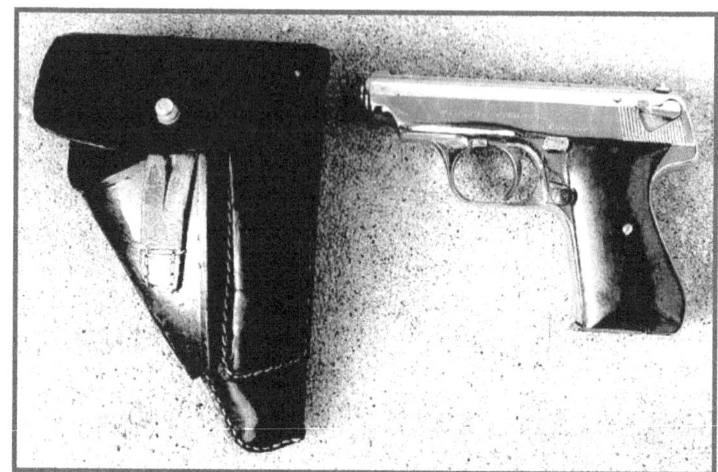

Dear Marge,

Well, Marge, How do you like me writing every day? We are starting training again just like in the States. It's been so long since I've did any drilling, I don't think I'll like it to well. I didn't get any mail last night but I sure hope I get some tonight. Are you getting my mail any better now? I sent my P-38 pistol home today with Marquardt from Vesta, Minn., a good buddy of mine. I guess he'll get discharged. He spent 2 1/2 years in the Aleutians Is. But came in when I did over here. He is sure a good guy. He said if he couldn't get where we live, he would call you and let you know where he'll leave it. Be sure to get it if he leaves it someplace for you to pick up because they are worth $150 bucks in France. Over here these guys in rear echelons just jump at the chance to buy one. I've been having a hell of a time getting any paper to write on but managed to find a couple pieces again today. I'm going to get a hair cut in a few min. The old guy here is the community barber. If Marquardt brings my pistol, then be sure to have a couple qts. of good whiskey to give him because he kind of likes his liquor.

Is everything still going at the bakery or are you still running into a little trouble?

Still loving my wife and missing you.

All my love

Your Husband

Bill

PS Send a box if you have time.

This may not be the pistol mentioned in this letter; however, he does mention carrying it with him in his letter of May 2.

It was known as the Sauer 38H but was actually a 7.65 caliber which equates to a .32 ACP. It was made by J.P. Shuer & Sohn of Suhl, Germany.

Sauer 38H pistols presented to Nazi officials often featured custom engraving, ivory grips, and often gold inlay as well. This one originally had pearl hand grips but they were broken and replaced with the brown ones as seen above.

<u>May 15, 1945 - From Bill to Marge</u>

Dear Marge,

I got 4 letters from you and one from Ethel last night also the Democrat so it was pretty good. That article of White's, I think I read in the Stars and Stripes. The 89 Div. was near us for a while back a ways but where he is at, is always quite a ways behind the line troops. I don't know whether I ever told you before or not but our platoon was Div. Guard for about 4 days that.

Antpasting for guys who are in Div. headquarters. Kind a snap because it is usually back 20 or 30 miles behind the INF. I wrote him once, kinda ribbing him

On May 14, a *kamikaze* Zero struck the US aircraft carrier Enterprise.

US Marines mounted a major offensive in Okinawa and conquered Sugar Loaf mountain.

On May 14-15, the last battle of World War II in Europe is fought at Poljanak near Slovenj Gradec, Slovenia. Known as *The Battle of Poljana*.

about he better be careful or he might get hit by a truck back there or something. I sure am hoping I get some mail from you again tonight. You can't imagine how much I look forward to getting your mail but I guess it's the same both ways. I've had my first drink today since I went into Czech. We got a lot of wine and beer but I'm just drinking a little wine. We have been having a lot of fun here batting the ball. Fat baby, the guy who wrote you a while ago said to tell you he is getting pretty hungry. We had a long ride today and most of us are pretty tired. We are at Nurstadt. I guess it don't make any difference now this is over. The people in Czech really treated us swell and were sorry to see us leave but the Russians are pretty well all over there so they didn't need us any more. To my opinion the Russians are pretty crumby looking. They wear uniforms that are just about like the Heinies. I'm sure hoping they start fighting the Japs pretty quick though it will make it that much quicker I get home to you. Am I ever waiting for that day. Still never chiseled on you but have had plenty of chances. The boys have quite a few gang jobs but I'll wait till I get home with you. "Remember Kansas City." Oh, boy, but what I wouldn't give for a night like that now. Marquardt left for home today. Hope you get a chance to talk to him. He's a good boy. We had a lot of fun together over here. I'll sure miss him now.

All my Love,

Your Husband
Bill

P.S. Send a box if you have time.

On May 17, two US Air Force P-47 Thunderbolts bomb Kyushu, Japan.

May 17, 1945 - From Bill to Marge

Dear Marge,

No mail from you last night but I got one from Wyscover's wife. How are you doing by now? I hope things are running a little smoother at the bakery. Say Hello to your folks and everybody for me. You should be getting my mail a little better by now. I wrote every day for the past 2 weeks. I think we are in a town now - 12 of us. All the G.I.s that are in it are guarding a factory.

We got a beer tavern right across the street where we get a beer now and then. Will only be here a couple days and then go back where we were, I think. I was talking with a few English Leut's a while ago and they are sweating out the CBI (China, Burma, India Theatre of War) too.

I've been in or seen hundreds of these prison camps over here and have never seen anything like what White wrote about. I didn't know that the 3rd Army ever ran across any like that. They were all up North where that went on from what I read in the Stars and Stripes. We liberated a few Jews but they knocked most of them off but not (those) of other nationalities. Some of them we liberated - don't even want to go back to their own countries.

I sent you a picture of myself and some of the fellows that was taken about a month ago one night when we stopped at a house for the night. I'll send one later, if I get it, that we had taken when we were driving through Czech our last day of combat before the war ended. We were riding tanks when the order came to hold up. Well, Marge, still loving and missing you. Can't wait till the day comes we'll be together again. Keep up the writing

All my Love

Your Husband
Bill

May 18, 1945 - From Bill to Marge

Dear Marge,

Well, Marge, I got 2 letters from you again last night, April 28 and 30. That's pretty good about Stan. I wonder how he acts when he is out with women. Do you suppose he is anything like his brothers? Do you remember that trip to LaCrosse the first time I was out with you? I sure wish we could spend some of those times again before too long. I don't know what to tell you to do with the money there. I guess just leave it.

We have to pay for our cigarettes now. I guess I won't be able to get them like we did before so I wish you would send me a good pipe and some tobacco. I guess I just have to learn to cut down. The last month I've been smoking more than I ever did - sitting around so much, I guess. I sure got so going without sleep don't bother me. I pulled 4 1/2 (hours) guard night before last and then had breakfast at 4:30 so I only got about 1 hr. (sleep). It don't get dark over here now till about 10 and gets light about 4. The weather has been swell the past week and 1/2, just like summer at home. I won't be able to go fishing much anymore. We had to turn in our Grenades. I wrote a letter to Vernon a little while ago - been quite a while since I wrote to him. I'll have to write on the

To the family: Read all of the letters. You will get a feeling for how Bill is opening up to Marge. He knows he is safe and will be home eventually. He shows genuine concern for Marge and all that she is enduring.

He shows respect to Marge for her efforts to do what is right at the bakery. And, he professes his moral integrity to Marge frequently...."no chiseling".

No more fishing for Bill as he had to turn in his grenades!! He does some fishing with his M1 Garand but it's much more difficult.

other side because this is all the paper I got. Managed to get hold of a few sheets every day. The Army is keep us fucked up as usual. We don't know how long we will be here. Whether we go CBI or what but we take physicals in about 1 hr but I guess that is just a short time.

I think you know what that is. School should be out pretty quick now for Stan, can work steady. John must be pretty good about letting him have the car if he takes his girl out riding. How about John? Who is he going with or is he still shopping around.

Keep up the writing because I sure wait for them.

All my Love

Your Husband
Bill

May 18, 1945 - From Bill to Marge

Dear Marge,

Was I every glad today to get 4 letters from you - May 3, 7, 8, and one from Ma.

It is getting so there isn't a hell of a lot to write about here any more. I'm in a nice little town here with just a few G.I.'s but there are quite a few English - pretty nice fellows, too.

I was up buying some cigarettes off of them last night and they had coffee with us today. They like it the way we make it but I guess their cooks can't. We've been getting 10 in one rations so we do our own cooking. The beer here isn't near as good as ours but it tastes pretty good for a change.

I sure wish Verle wouldn't leave. Isn't there anyway you can talk her into staying? She's a good girl and I hate to see her leave.

Ma told me you have really been getting the work out since Miekle got home. It shouldn't be too awful long before this thing finishes and I can be home again if those Japs would only know enough to quit and not lie (down) like the Hienies. I hear our air force is starting to go to town there now. It's too bad about Junior Luther getting hit, but maybe he's lucky that's where. Guys used to pray we'd get hit in the ankle or legs if we were going to get it because doctors now can do wonders. I don't think Maggie need worry too much about it just so he was hit bad enough to keep him off the line a couple months. I was out shooting a few fish today but it is a lot harder getting them that way than with grenades.

How come Swede (Paul Anderson?) never wrote to

The "Ration, 10-in-1" was designed to feed groups of men, primarily motorized infantry or tank crews in armored units. Inspired by the success of British 14-in-1 "compo" rations, and the first 5-in-1 ration, the 10-in-1 ration offered one day of meals — breakfast, evening supper, and a midday snack — for 10 soldiers. The 10-in-1 was introduced in mid-1943 and over 300 million rations were produced by the end of World War II.

The possibility of packaging a field ration in units of 10, with an approximate weight of 50 pounds, was suggested as early as 1941. But little or nothing was done about this suggestion until the spring of 1943. At that time, conditions in the battle areas called for such a type of ration. The purpose of this ration was to serve as the principle ration for subsistence of troops in all areas in advance of the field kitchen, but prior to engaging in actual combat, for troops isolated in small groups, and for highly mobile troops. The general specifications for the ration were set in early 1943, and by the end of April of the same year the project had been completed. Several late changes were effected on the ration before it was finally adopted in the fall of 1943.

www.olive-drab.com

*me? I'd sure like to hear from him. Where is Kosbau now? I wrote him about the same time I did Cowan.*

*I don't remember whether I put anything in it about Lila or not. I doubt it though or he wouldn't of sent it to here. I didn't know she was knockers again. The old boy must be on the ball. I hope they have better luck this time or do you suppose one of the boys helped him out?*

*Do you know I'm going to have a hard job learning to talk when I get home again. Yesterday I walked in the tavern and some of the boys were sitting there talking to a babe that used to live in Milwaukee. I got a beer and sat down and talked a while and in come one of the boys who got lost in the factory that I walked off and left when I was on guard. He said something, so without thinking I says, 'Fuck you - I told you to go through alone."*

*See how it is - we are so used to saying anything around women because most of them don't know what the hell we are talking about any way. I can tell you some good ones that happened to some of the boys when I get home. You see we aren't supposed to fraternize. Marquette, the guy who is bringing my pistols home is quite a skin man. He can talk good German but I've still never stayed around any of them. I ain't going to but just wait till I get home. You better be in good shape. How about it?*

*Keep up the writing.*

*All my Love*
*Bill*

<u>May 19, 1945 - From Bill to Marge</u>

*Dear Marge,*

*How do you like this - me writing you every day? I don't think I've missed a day since the war ended. The only bad thing when it comes to writing is (that) I can't think of a hell of a lot to say. I can't write the old line like lots of these fellows can.*

*How's the cabin? Have you been down there yet? I hope I get home before winter so I get a chance to go down. The Rhine reminded me a lot of the Miss. I hear I'm going to the kitchen as quick as the Co. gets settled all together but I don't care much weather I do or not. I don't seem to care much for the cooking or baking any more. I've been lots of places I could of baked stuff but never had enough ambition. I'm getting lazier than hell over here but I guess when I get home I'll get over that.*

In March, Brigadier General Herbert L. Earnest assumed command of the Division, and about the same time the 90th received warning orders.

In the north the American First and Ninth Armies and the British had launched a powerful drive which was carrying them to the Rhine River and the famous Remagen Bridge. Just to the south of VIII Corps zone the 4th Armored Division was preparing to drive through the Eifel Hills, also to the Rhine. The mission of the 90th was to move through the advancing 6th Armored and seize a crossing over the Kyll River, where, intelligence reports revealed, the enemy was digging in and planning to hold whatever the cost.

http://www.90thdivisionassoc.org/90thDivisionFolders/90thhistorybook/histbkmainframe.htm

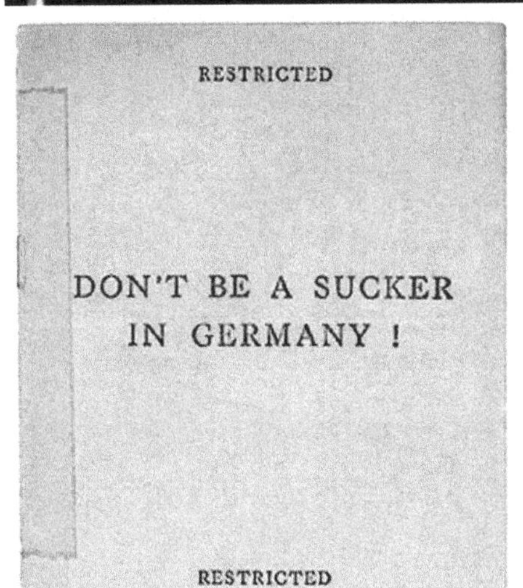


Germany Occupation Booklet 1945
*Don't Be a Sucker in Germany*

Distributed to 3rd Army troops in May, 1945, shortly after the German surrender, this 15-page booklet was the 12th Army Group's basic primer for GI's as occupiers. It was then "Restricted" (Classified) info that makes very interesting reading now. As one short example, a section on "Women" included: "German women have been trained to seduce you. Is it worth a knife in the back?"

Another example: "Don't believe there are any 'good' Germans in Germany. Of course you know good Germans back home. They had guts enough and sense enough to break away from Germany long ago because they couldn't go along with German militarism and intolerance. Don't believe that it was only the Nazi government that brought on this war. Any people have the kind of government they want and deserve. Only a few people bucked the Nazis. You won't meet them; the Nazis purged them long ago."

And: "Toward children, you are wrong again. You've generously given them chewing gum and candy all across Europe. Don't do it now. All kids aren't friendly. Yell "Achtung" (attention) at a bunch of these kids and watch them snap-to. That's how they're trained."

When I stay in a place over a few days any more, I'm usually always ready to move because we are getting so used to it. I was out practicing up with one of my pistols yesterday for awhile. Of course, we are supposed to have them turned in but I always carry one in my pocket and 2 in my pack. I sure hope Marquardt brings that one of mine there because I think a lot of that pistol. He's about the only guy I would trust sending it home with.

How are they still drafting them at home? I hope so it will mean that much quicker some of these guys can get out. I'm sorry to hear your dad isn't very well. I don't suppose he'll do much fishing this summer then. Say hello to them both for me. I've still got my first officer to salute since I've been overseas but I suppose I'll have to soon one of these days. I've seen Gen. Ernest a lot of times here but we never saluted him. That was before the war ended but the officers sure snap the salute.

Well, Marge, keep writing me and tell me all the news. I hope you are having a little better time of it in the bakery by now.

All my Love

Your Husband
Bill

May 19, 1945 - From Bill to Jim and Amanda

Dear Folks,

I got a letter from you the other night. I sure like to get mail here but I don't like to write any better than I ever did. I haven't been doing much lately mostly guard duty is about all. I finally got the watch that Marge sent me. I'm wearing it now. I busted both of my other ones so I guess I got it just in time. I haven't got my packages for quite a while now. You'll have to do something about that.

We heard the rumor this morning that the Japs are trying to make peace. I sure hope that is true but I don't think I'll be able to pick up a bayonet now because most of that stuff has been picked up and turned in and besides what ever we pick up, we have to carry it a week or so before we get a chance to mail it. I sent a P38 pistol of mine home with a kid who went home on furlough. It was brand new when I got it but I used it a lot. But it still's worth $150 in France. I've still got a Italian pistol and a German 32 that I intend to bring home with me. I am (in) a little town for a couple days where there were a few English soldiers. We got along pretty well with them. Even had a cup of tea with them. I hear Oscar (Stan's nickname) is starting to chase the women a little? I'll bet he really gets razzed around the house now.

I wrote to Vernon a few days ago. I should hear from him soon. I told him the name of the town I'm staying in for a week or so. It's hard to tell how long and to ask if he could get a pass to come see me. I sure hope he can because I'd sure like to see him. I guess he can't write much about where he is at or what he is doing. Well write when you get time and send a box if you have time.

Love

Your son
Bill

May 20, 1945 - From Bill to Marge

Dear Marge,

Well, Marge, haven't got any mail the last 2 nights now so should get a little again tonight. I sure hope we get some clean clothes pretty quick. I've been wearing these for 2 months now. We all figured when the war was over we would get clean ones but we haven't yet. Didn't get to Mass yet today but they might have it someplace tonight. There are sure a lot of Catholics in our Co. Just finished playing a little pinochle. Haven't been having too good of luck lately but have still got a few dollars left and pay isn't far off. Do you ever have any games there anymore?

How's Bob Anderson coming? I think I'll write him today if I have enough ambition. Haven't been doing anything the past 2 days but lay around. Marge, you know if any of them there should have more money, give them a raise. I suppose summer now it will give you quite a workout. Is Stan still chasing the girls? That sure's a surprise to me. Do you suppose he tries to get a little of it? We got a gal staying here with us that the boys been trying to make but I've been leaving it alone. The married guys in our squad, they don't any of them chisel - four of us now. One guy's wife just got a divorce.

They are starting to give trips to Paris now. I should be in line to go before too long but a lot of the old men that were in the hospital are back now and I guess they go first.

I'd sure hate to try living on what these people do over here. All I ever see them have for a meal is pota-

On May 21, according to Time Magazine:

In Akronism. In Akron, a thoughtful bus driver drew up at a grocery, announced, "They've got cigarettes today," and waited while all 16 passengers made their purchases.

Cash & Carry. In Des Moines, a war bride, fresh from New Zealand, labored under a pocketbook heavy with coins, and the notion that she had to change a bill every time she bought something.

Sliver My Timbers. In Garden City, Kans., Daniel L. Osborn sued the oil company where he works, claimed that while on the job his wooden leg had been fractured.

Tally Hole! In the course of the Third Army's advance, Lieut. Jack Bradford jumped into a foxhole, found a real live fox in it, sent the pelt home to Atlanta as proof.

Read more: http://www.time.com/time/magazine/article/0,9171,852197,00.html#ixzz0ke0tbIWd

toes, bread and barley coffee which is lousy. I've drank it a few times when I couldn't get any thing else. They just have the dark bread, heavy as hell about 5 or 10 lb. to a loaf. Back along the Rhine and Moselle, the people ate better than here but I don't think they do now after we went through.

On weekdays lots of the women and kids run around barefooted or with wooden shoes on.

Well, Marge, better quit for now.

All my Love

Your Husband
Bill

May 21, 1945 - From Bill to Marge

Dear Marge,

Well, Marge, I got one letter, May 1, and the Des Moines paper of April 14 today. It sounds like you are still really getting a workout. How long has Miekle been off anyway? He must of gotten a pretty good burn.

On May 21, Lauren Bacall and Humphrey Bogart were wed.

Well, we moved into our new place yesterday - a big schoolhouse. We haven't got any bunks in it yet but I guess we will. We are supposed to be here for a month but we are never sure of anything. The guys are sure bitching more every day about the points system. The line men who landed here on D Day and went through the hell all along haven't near enough points. I wrote you a few days ago and told you to send me a pipe but don't bother because I got a good one today in rations. We got candy and orange juice, cigars and a few other things. I've been smoking about everything since I've been over here. Even chew once in a while but I'll quit that when I come home. I can imagine how well you would like that.

I suppose we will start training again in the next couple of days. We have been having good chow now the last 2 days. I sure hope they keep it up. Boy, Marge, but I sure do miss you a lot more than when the war was on because we were kept pretty busy then and I'm still loving you. Have to quit now because they are taking the mail.

On May 22, the 6th Marine Division reached the suburbs of Naha Okinawa.

Love

Bill

May 22, 1945 - From Bill to Marge

Dear Marge,

Well, Marge, I got 3 letters from you yesterday, May

*6,7, and 10 and one from Ma. It is sure good to get mail from you. The letters were all stamped the 10th so it only took 11 days for me to get them. Are you getting my mail any sooner now? I'm glad to hear you have been able to keep things going at the bakery. If you think John is better than Miekle, maybe you better let him keep on mixing and things like that and let Meikle be second man. I suppose all the men are getting pretty well cleaned out of town by now. We haven't got any idea how long we will be in Germany but I'd a hell of a lot sooner sweat it out here than in South Pacific. I'm glad to hear Danny (Donny?) finally got a break and is going to stay in the States awhile. Our line medics really used to have some pretty tough spots to take care of men.*

*We got a bunch of films down at the Hienies getting them developed. I'll send a couple as quick as we get them back. We have to trade chocolate or gum for things like that. We got some covers last night to fill with straw to sleep on. That was a little better than on the floor. I guess we'll get bunks in a week or so. When you send me a box, you can stick in a couple of magazines. Anything to pass the time away. I was out playing ball for a while yesterday.*

*There are a lot of White Russian refugees around here who will be going home in the next day or so - ones scared to go back. The White Russians are mostly Catholic and don't get along with the Russian government from what I gather. When I think of all the propaganda and shit they fed us back in the States about over here, it sure makes me disgusted. I suppose it is the same with the Japs. I hope this thing ends pretty quick so we can be together again. I sure do miss you. How's John - is he chasing anyone in particular or is he still shopping around? Keep up the writing because I sure wait for them.*

*All my Love*

*Your Husband*
*Bill*

May 22, 1945 - From Bill to Marge

*Dear Marge,*

*Here I go again. I wrote you this morning but have plenty of time so am writing again. I'm sending a couple pictures. They were both taken in Czech about 3 days before the war ended, about 2 or 3 hrs after we cleaned this town. I had my equipment laying on the tank. The peo-*

The time-honored precedent of making a top party politician the Postmaster General of the U.S. got its bow from President Truman. To replace Postmaster General Frank C. Walker, the President appointed jut-chinned, 42-year-old Bob Hannegan, who had risen to the top of the Democratic National Committee in twelve years from a start as a Committeeman in St. Louis' 21st Ward.

But the precedent of appointing professional Army & Navy officers as Presidential aides was broken. President Truman had already replaced Colonel Richard Park Jr. of the regular Army with Colonel Harry H. Vaughan, emergency officer and World War I comrade of Captain Harry S. Truman, Battery D, 129th Field Artillery. Last week the President announced that his new Naval aide (replacing Vice Admiral Wilson Brown) was Captain James K. Vardaman.

Reserve Officer Vardaman, 50-year-old son of the late rabble-rousing Senator James K. Vardaman of Mississippi, is a St. Louis lawyer, banker and shoe manufacturer (Vardaman Shoe Co.). He was also commander of Battery A, 335th Field Artillery, A.E.F. For onetime Artilleryman Harry Truman, that was a recommendation too.

Read more: http://www.time.com/time/magazine/article/0,9171,792089,00.html#ixzz0ke270k10

ple were bringing us everything to eat and milk. That's the first milk I drank since I've been overseas and it sure made me sick and gave me the G.I.'s.

When I get home I will have to go easy on it for awhile. After eating these K rations for so long, milk usually makes a guy sick. Say hello to your folks and Verle for me. Well, Marge, you know I still love you just as much and always will. I'm waiting for the day we can be together again.

All my love

Your Husband
Bill

May 22, 1945 - From Bill to Jim and Amanda

Dear Folks

I wrote a couple days ago but I guess it won't hurt me to write a little more often now that the war is over. We are getting it a little better now. We got straw ticks to sleep on. We are having good meals and today they got regular plates and cups for us to eat out of. The next thing will be the silverware. Most of the guys only have a spoon that serves the purpose all around. We got a keg of beer tonight. One of the boys usually hooks one every day. I'm enclosing a snapshot we had taken about a month before the war was over. I'm also sending Marge a couple we took in Czech about 3 days before the war was over.

What do you hear from Vernon? I haven't heard from him for about a month now. The last letter I got from him he thought he would be going to South Pacific. We still don't know how we stand. I guess most of the heavy stuff will be moved first but one never knows what they'll do. I suppose by the time you get my letter school will be out and you'll have the kids home to help a little. I suppose they are really growing. By the time I get home little Marie will be so big I'll hardly know her. I should be getting a trip to Paris before long and if I do have any money, I'll try to send you something. We can't buy anything in Germany here to send home and are not supposed to even talk to the people but I have bought a little beer and a few things like that.

Well Ma write when you get time and tell Jim it wouldn't hurt him to break down and write me a few lines. All the booze that floats around over here and I haven't got a buzz on yet.

Love

Your Son, Bill

Freed from the German police a fortnight ago, two former Vichy officials were arrested by the French police last week. When ex-Sports Director Jean Borotra and unsuccessful General Maxime ("They have given me a disastor") Weygand got to Paris, their first stop was the Ministry of the Interior. There a police commissar and three inspectors arrested them as "dangerous to national security."

Borotra, the Bounding Basque of tennis, slapped his chest, cried derisively: "Me dangerous? Come, come." Said lean, sickly General Weygand: "Je m'en fou" ("I don't give a damn"). He added: "This animal isn't vicious, but when attacked it defends itself."

Then guards drove Weygand to a private room at the Val-de-Grâce military hospital, Borotra to an elegant residence at 35 Avenue Foch, to await the charges against them.

Time Magazine
May 21, 1945

May 23, 1945 - From Bill to Marge

Dear Marge,

Well, Marge, I got 3 Des Moines papers and one letter from you, one from Ma and one from Ethel yesterday. Your letter was the 14 of May. Coming through pretty fast now but I haven't had a package for about 1 1/2 months. How are you doing anyway? Do you ever get any of those ornery streaks of yours any time? How are things at the bakery. Have you ever been able to raise the prices on anything since I left? You should be able too by now. Is the equipment still in fairly good shape? I sure wish you were over here with me. This is beautiful county. Sometimes it just seems like a dream but then a guy thinks of all the hell of last winter. You could never imagine the way things were for the Infantry then. Most of us were sick and feet half froze but we still had to keep on pushing. One night back in Belgium we stood around in the snow and cold all night waiting to go into the attack. Didn't dare take out our blanket because we had to move in a minute's notice. We were lucky having a good Platoon Leader. He was just a T Sgt. but really knew his stuff. He got hit 3 times since I've been with the outfit. The last time about 1/2 months ago. He got about 3 or 4 machine gun slugs in him. He'll probably be on his way home by this time. We've been sitting here for about an hour now talking over individual things that happened so I quit writing for a while.

I made a few dollars playing hearts this morning but I'll probably lose it tonight but I guess you know how I like to gamble. Well, Marge, think I'll quit for now. I hope I get some mail from you again tonight.

All my Love

Your Husband
Bill

On May 23, President of Germany Karl Donitz and Chancellor of Germany Count Lutz Graf Schwerin van Krosigk are arrested by British forces at Flensburg. They are respectively the last German Head of state and Head of government until 1949.

Heinrich Himmler, former head of the Nazi SS, committed suicide while in British custody.

On May 23, the German island of Heligoland in the North Sea surrendered to British troops.

May 24, 1945 - From Bill to Marge

Dear Marge,

Well, Marge, I didn't get any mail from you today either but got a letter from Marcella. Some of the boys got

On May 23, Winston Churchill resigned as British Prime Minister.

letters today that were only 6 days old. I was on K.P. today for the first time since I've been overseas. We got a pretty nice mess hall or rather they are getting it fixed up pretty good. We got wooden beds today with board bottoms that should have a lot of spring to them, eh? We don't get hardly any cigarettes anymore since the war is over. I'm out about 1/2 of the time now. Pretty quick I'll be out swiping butts like these Heine kids do.

I see by the Stars and Stripes where the First Army has arrived in the States. I'll bet there will be some big times there for the next month. We still don't know for sure weather we will be Occupational or not but I sure hope so. I've got a Rehl paper I'm sending. They are just starting it. I've got about 6 copies of the (Des Moines) Register but they are all April ones 12-20. I was figuring today and Vernon should have just about enough points to get discharged. I'm sure hoping I get a chance to see him before he goes home. I haven't any idea where he is at now but he might be close to me. I wrote him and told him the town I was in.

I just got a hold of a package of cigarettes. One of the boys was going back to his old outfit. I bought a couple cartons back. I guess I'll always manage all right but you don't catch me volunteering for anything anymore, even in the kitchen.

On May 25, Arthur C. Clarke proposed relay satellites in geosynchronous orbit around the earth.

Well, Marge, guess I'll quit for now. I'm still always thinking of you and loving.

All my Love

Your Husband
Bill

May 25, 1945 - From Bill to Marge

Dear Marge,

Well Marge, here I go again. Hope you are all right. I'm still in as good a shape as ever. I see by the Stars and Stripes where we get some more Stars for over here. That will make me 3. Boy, I can sure use all the points I can get. Still got 55 to go. Long time, eh? I suppose Beck is pretty happy because that should give Vernon enough to get out.

I just got washed and shaved up but am still wearing the same pants and shirt I've had on for the last 2 or 3 months. I started this letter this afternoon but quit and went to the show. Am finishing it tonight. The show wasn't any good. They didn't have the camera working right. I found out where Vernon is - he's about 260 mi.

*from here, in Southern Germany, near Switzerland. We had a couple kegs of beer today but they don't last long - about 2 glasses apiece. But it is not near as good as old American beer.*

*I see by the paper where 4 more Div. are slated for Cbi next month. This is one of the oldest outfits over here so it might stay, never can tell. Marquette should be getting home in a couple more weeks. I sure hope he stops in to see you. He's my buddy. He thought I got killed one day back a way and he pretty near bawled. He couldn't hardly believe it when he seen me standing in the woods a little while later.*

*The mail just came in but I didn't get any. I'd sooner have you let the work go to hell at the bakery than have you let up on writing to me because I sure wait for your mail. There isn't a hell of a lot for me to write about over here anymore. I'm sending a picture I had taken after the war was over. The guy with his arm on my shoulder was the one got hit back at Birresborn when the 5 of us got the bunch of Heines. The one on the other side next to me is a buck Sarg. in our squad and the other is the platoon leader.*

Birresborn is a municipality in the district of Vulkaneifel, in Rhineland-Palatinate, Western Germany. It is located on the Kyll River between Mürlenbach to its south and Gerolstein to its north. It has a train station on the line Cologne-Gerolstein-Trier. There is a bike path along the Kyll River. Temperature is very cold in the winter and very rainy and cold most of the other times.
http://en.wikipedia.org/wiki/Birresborn

*All my Love*

*Your Husband*
*Bill*

*P.S. Send some tobacco and papers. I guess you can still buy that back there, can't you? Running mighty short.*

May 26, 1945 - From Bill to Marge

*Dear Marge,*

*Well, writing again. I haven't had any letters from you for 3 days now but been getting the Republic and I got the Readers Digest, May Edition but got it all read already.*

*Been playing lot of cards lately. Some days I got quite a bit of money and next day I'm about broke but am still way ahead of the game. We play hearts, poker and pinochle.*

On May 26th, the US Air Force dropped fire bombs on Tokyo.

*I usually go to bed about 12 and get up about 6:30 or 7 o'clock. I guess we are going to have a P.X. open here in a couple days. Its sure good to see the way the German girls strut by here. Kinda like they are trying to do a little business. I guess they do all right to. We've got a nice church in the town here and if we don't have Mass anyplace tomorrow, I'm going to it. I see 10-15 nuns go-*

The Germans managed their surrender with a skill which will plague the victors for years to come. No Wehrmacht campaign was ever planned to deadlier purpose, executed with greater cunning.

The Mission. The twilight rulers of Germany preached to the last that the German people and armies were the enemies of Russian Bolshevism, the defenders of western civilization. Upon this powerful and insidious theme, they based the whole edifice of surrender.

The Strategy. To a disturbing degree, they succeeded in their strategy of separate surrender. True, a Russian signed the first general surrender at Reims; British and U.S. officers signed the second in Berlin (see WORLD BATTLEFRONTS). But Reims was General Eisenhower's show. Berlin was Marshal Zhukov's.

British and U.S. army commanders in the west had no choice but to accept the "field surrenders" of German armies a process climaxed by the surrender of The Netherlands, Denmark and northwestern Germany to Field Marshal Montgomery. The fact that U.S. armies had been deliberately halted in their advances toward Berlin and Prague, so that the Red Army could take them, was so much grist for the German mill.

The scheme of separate surrender was no artificial fabrication; it had its roots in the fears and beliefs of the German soldiery and people. On the U.S. First Army front, many German units seriously expected to join the U.S. battle line, march with the Americans against the Russians. An entire German regiment had kept its arms with this end in view, was genuinely astonished when the Americans declined to cooperate.

Time Magazine May 27, 1945

*ing to church every morning.*

*We are really beginning to have a big Co. All the old guys are coming back from the hospitals. It sure seems like a long time since we spent New Years together. I'll never forget that day and night as long as I live. How about you? Sure lucky I found you that day, eh?*

*Marge I don't think you'll ever have to worry about me chiseling. Course I've passed up a lot of nice stuff over here. Still think to much of my wife. How things going at the bakery? Maybe it won't be to long before the Japs quit. I hope so anyway.*

*Well Marge, keep up the writing because I sure wait for them.*

*All my love*

*Your Husband*
*Bill*

*P.S. Send a box if you have time. You know how much I like chocolates so you don't have to make any candy.*

May 27, 1945 - From Bill to Marge

*Dear Marge,*

*I sure hope by this time you are getting some of my mail because I wrote everyday since the war ended here. I got 2 Democrats, 2 Registers of April and a letter of May 19 from you tonight. I went to Mass this afternoon in a beautiful church not quite as big as ours at home but it was sure nice, 4 big altars in it. I guess it must have been one of the nuns playing the organ but our priest said mass and had 2 little kids for altar boys just like back in the States. Haven't done much all day except lay around read and played a few hands of hearts. We started doing physical exercise and close order drill starting tomorrow. Haven't done any drilling or any of that crap since I was down in Texas. Sure seems like a long time ago. We sure had some swell weekends there thou, even if I did have to sweat out all week whether I was going to get a pass or not. I should get a trip to Paris or England next month unless I get screwed out of it.*

*They are letting lots of the old men who just came back go first but I think I should still make it. I think I was lucky getting into the 90th. It's one of the Crack Inf. Div. over here and even the replacements have from 2 to 4 years in the army. This watch you sent me sure works swell, my other one quit a couple days after I got this one so I started wearing it. I guess all my other one needs is cleaning. It will sure seem funny when I get home to take my clothes off to go to bed. I haven't slept without my clothes on ever since I came over here. If I even get a hold of a blanket I might but the last time I carried a blanket was when I crossed the Mainz River and I threw about everything away. How is the cabin, been down to do any fishing? I sure wish John or Stan would take the folks down sometime. It would do them good once in a while. I haven't heard from Vernon for a long time now. I sure hope he can come up and see me. 260 miles is quite a ways over here though. I suppose Meikle doesn't know what to think when the bakery has been running without him. How much compensation does he get a week anyway?*

*Well Marge there isn't much more to write about except I love you. So will quit for tonight. Keep writing because I sure wait for them.*

*All my Love*

*Your Husband*
*Bill*

May 28, 1945 - From Bill to Marge

*Dear Marge,*

*I got a letter from you tonight dated May 12. I can't figure out how come I don't get any more mail but I guess it is because of them moving so many troops. I sure hope you start getting my mail pretty quick. We had our first day of training today but it didn't amount to much. A talk of military courtesy and one on venereal diseases. We were supposed to have a hike this afternoon but they called it off on account of the ball game. I fell asleep about 1 o'clock and never woke up till supper time so I suppose I won't sleep to much tonight. It's sure funny the way the money goes here. A week ago I had to borrow $10 and today I got a little over a hundred so that's the way it comes and goes over here.*

*I still got that $5 you sent me 3 or 4 months ago. I'm glad you are giving John a little more money now if he is working so good. You know you can order that substitute for lard which will save from 25-50 percent.*

*They finally got around to checking up on how much equipment we've left but I haven't anything except rifle, ammo and clothes I got on. So I guess we get new clothes and things pretty quick but will have to pay for anything we lose or throw away. It won't be like it used to be if you got tired of carrying anything, toss it away.*

On May 28, William Joyce (*Lord Haw-Haw*) was captured. He was later charged with high treason in London for his English language wartime broadcasts on German radio, convicted and then hanged in January 1946.

*I guess this is Bavaria we are in now but didn't know that till I happened to see it on a plate and know I'd been in the town where they made them. Our old Platoon leader came back today - sure good to see him again but he got 100 points so I suppose he will be going home shortly. He's got a Purple Heart with 4 clusters on it. In other words, he's been hit 5 times. Well, Marge, still love you as much as ever and hope you keep up the writing and praying we will be together before too long.*

*All my love*

*Your Husband*
*Bill*

May 29, 1945 - From Bill to Marge

*Dear Marge,*

*Well, Marge, I didn't get any mail yet today but am still hoping. I hope you are getting my mail by now. I see by the papers that food is getting harder to get all the time back there. Well, that isn't the only place. We'll never get fat on what we eat now and we can't go into these houses and help ourselves any more. I sure used to eat a lot of eggs and canned fruit then. I finally broke down and got a bar of G.I. soap and washed and ironed my clothes today. They look pretty nice now but before I washed them, you should of seen them. You can imagine wearing the same clothes for a couple months without never taking them off, what they would look like.*

*How old is Stan getting to be now? Anyway I hope he don't get any ideas of getting in the service. He could probably get in quick enough. How is he coming with his romance? Has he forgotten about being a priest or does he think he should get a taste of that stuff first? Who's this gal from Decorah John has been going with and how long has he been going with her? Do you suppose he'll ever settle down and get married like his brothers? I suppose Waukon is getting deader all the time. Do the farmers still make up for all the guys in the service? I suppose Verle has left by now. I sure hated to hear that she was leaving. How come she didn't wait till after the war ended before going to college? A lot of people back home don't realize that this war would of ended sooner if they would have had the gas and ammunition over here. Well, Marge, better quit for tonight.*

**COOPERATE WITH YOUR GOVERNMENT**

**USE LESS GAS**

**HERE'S HOW YOU CAN HELP:**

**If You Cook with Gas, Use One-Fourth Less**

1 Don't use the gas range to heat the kitchen.
2 Cook with a blue flame (not yellow), and use less water in the pot.
3 Use oven as little as possible. When you do, plan to cook whole meals in it. Don't open door often.
4 Plan more "one-dish" meals. Cook more than one thing in a pot, if possible.

**If You Heat Water with Gas, Use Half as Much**

1 Have leaky hot water faucets repaired.
2 Don't let hot water run while washing hands, shaving, or washing dishes.
3 Use as little as possible for a bath. Take showers if you can.

**If You Heat Your Home with Gas, KEEP IT BELOW 65°**

1 Put weather stripping around doors and windows. Install storm windows.
2 Close off rooms you don't need. Keep bedroom doors closed at night and when rooms are being aired.
3 Use fireplace if you have one. Close fireplace damper when the fire is out, to keep heat from going up the chimney.

**If You Have a Gas Refrigerator**

1 Cool cooked foods before placing in refrigerator.
2 Never leave refrigerator door open.

CONSOLIDATED EDISON

SERVICE

Hoping I hear from you soon
All my Love
Your Husband
Bill

May 29, 1945 - From Viola to Marge

This letter is written by Marge's mother, Viola from Bemidji, MN on Monday, probably the 27th but the postmark is May 29, 1945.

Dear Marjorie,

Hello, Veryle has gone home? When did she go? Did her folks and Doris come and did they stay one nite?

Who is going to stay with you or will you stay some place?

Please tell us because it will be so lonesome without Veryle.

Hope you have heard more from Bill.

How are you? Hope you got more sleep and hope Ray will work tonight. Did the rain wash much of the garden out?

Dad said he wondered how much garden washed out at breakfast. (Thurs morn) Hope you have talked to Mrs. Palmer after they got home.

Sat. men had to take cream and some bottles of cream up town to pay the light bill so we went and did a little shopping but I did not go in a grocery store.

We called on Mrs. Krog, the ones they bought this place of. We had dinner about 3 then went out in boat. Had a nice ride but did not get any fish but was so nice and warm, I wonder what the weather is there. Dad talking to an old man right close said that we did not know how to fish. Said they would come over and he would show them how to catch all they wanted but raining this afternoon so maybe will turn cold then. Is everything looking like we should be getting back?

We had water on to wash and I guess it was hot and then they wanted us to go ride around Lake Bemidji and Itasco State Park, source of the Mississippi River. We crossed it on a plank. Do not work too hard and get sick. Write if you can find time.

Love,
Mother and all

We had chicken and noodles for dinner. Dot opened chicken the nite her folks left. I made the noodles. Was very good. Al some better. We are O.K.

Monday afternoon:

Did not get letter mailed yet. They are 1/2 mi. from mail so will write a line. Got a letter from you. I do hope

On May 29, German communists, led by Walther Ulbricht, arrived in Berlin.

The Dutch painter Han van Meegeren was arrested for collaboration with the Nazis but the paintings he had sold to Hermann Goring (Koch) were later found to be his fakes.

The US 1st Marine Division conquers Shuri-castle Okinawa.

Ray worked last night. How are you? Did Ethyl's come and stay overnight? I know it will be hard for you alone but don't just know when we'll get there but if you want any thing just say so. Did Mrs. Palmer call you? Dot got a card from them. They were very tired when they got home on the bus to Decorah. Sun is nice and bright today. Dot not much better so she did not want me to wash. Men have been working here at the river. Just got it done at 4:30 now. I don't know just when C. is going, a day or to, I think. I have not done much today. They got Waukon paper and some other papers today.

The men planted a lot of sweet corn this forenoon. Al said cows could eat it anyway. Will plant more potatoes a little later. He is resting now. They did not sleep very good, Dot so sick.

Is it warm there? We had company for dinner. The folks they got the place from are awfully nice. Dad said tonight he wished we were home. He is dreading the ride home.

I wonder who is staying with you or where are you. Dad has not said when we will leave.

Well, bye, bye,

Love

Mother and all

It don't get dark until between 10 and 11. Seems so funny. Did you get to the cabin yet?

On May 30, the Iranian government demanded that all Soviet and British troops leave the country.

May 30, 1945 - From Bill to Marge

Dearest Marge,

Well, Marge, got 2 letters from you today and one from Paulsons. The letters from you were 9th and 21st of May. You should have lots of mine by now. One of the guys wife has been getting mail but one guy got a letter last night that his wife just got a couple of his from May. I hear you can't send any packages now for awhile. We'll probably be pretty hungry around here then. This morning for breakfast we had tea, powdered eggs, dehydrated potatoes. For dinner: a wiener, a 1/2 slice of bread, a few dehydrated carrots and beets, and a cup of lemon. For supper 1/2 slice of bread, cream soup, corn and potatoes. So you can tell by that we aren't eating too heavy and (get) small portions of whatever we get, but that still beats K rations.

Haven't heard from the folks lately so I'd better get busy and write them tonight. I sure hope every one is still okay at home. I think I'm just about the same as *when I left, never missed any day with the Co. yet but I was sure sick enough sometimes in the winter. I think about half of the guys were sick all the time then, but we still kept going. We had a memorial service today for all the guys killed in the Battalion since D Day and (had) the Col. over for inspection this afternoon. We haven't been doing a hell of a lot of anything since the wars over. It sure seems funny to see the hundreds of Heinies going home with discharges and us guys still sweating it out. Say Hello to Luther for me and tell her while she is laying around on her dead ass and getting kicked in the belly, she just as well scribble a few lines to me. I'll bet she sure hates to strut up the street now like she used to. How are the Kreeb's coming? I suppose Ray is starting to go fishing a lot by now. Wouldn't I like to be down at the cabin now. I'll bet I'd get some of them big ones over in Gun Lake, one way or another. I shot a few nice ones over here a couple weeks ago but they are pretty hard to hit. I never seen any like them before. They look something like a carp only they were black. Some of the guys ate them and said they were good, but I was getting too much other food to eat them so I didn't eat any of them. I guess we'll probably get paid tomorrow. Have you been getting our bonds all right now? How much have we got in them anyhow?*

*Well, guess I'll quit for tonight, be sure and keep writing whenever you can.*

*All my Love*

*Your Husband*
*Bill*

<u>May 30, 1945 - From Bill to Jim and Amanda</u>

*Dear Folks,*

*I hope everyone at home is still all right. I'm still doing all right and I guess Vernon probably is to. I just got a letter from him now. I'll read it to see what he has to say.*

*He said he is near Munich, but would move in the next few days. He thinks he will eventually wind up in the South Pacific. I'm going up in the morning to see if I can get a pass to go see him. Where he's moving to is about 60-70 miles from here. Boy, but I'd sure like to see him. The only trouble is transportation is sure poor here.*

*I got a letter from Marge and also the Democrat tonight. I don't know who's been sending that and the*

From Prague General Bohumil Bocek, Czechoslovak Chief of Staff, broadcast last week that henceforth the organization, armament and training of the Czechoslovak military forces will be identical with the Russian Army's. Czechoslovak officers will be trained in Soviet military schools.

Said General Bocek: "Only thus will it be possible for the new Czechoslovak Army not only to make full use of the great fighting experience of the Red Army but also to be formed in the shortest period, without loss of precious time. Our Army, which is destined for fighting, will be formed and grow in battle, and the bureaucratic conception of an army living in barracks while millions of our brothers-in-arms, men of the Red Army and of our other allies, are still fighting will be abandoned.

"The Army is destined for battle, battle is her aim."

Army orders for cigarettes have been cut by one-third, thus releasing 200 million packages of cigarettes a month for civilians. In addition, the civilian supply of book matches will be increased by June and civilians will get approximately two million books a month.

Read more: http://www.time.com/time/magazine/article/0,9171,775706,00.html#ixzz0ke54nvic

Register but I'm sure glad to get it. I hear Stan's getting to be quite the ladies man. He hasn't started to dance yet, has he? I'll sure rib him when I get home.

The supply of woolens and worsteds in this year's third quarter may not be large enough to keep everybody warm. Last week the War Production Board slashed Army requests 26%, slashed Office of Civilian Requirements requests 65%. At this rate, civilians will get approximately one-quarter of their normal supply.

We haven't been doing much since the war's been over. A little guard duty, play ball, and that's about all. The only thing we don't get too much to eat or smoke but I don't mind. I'm just thankful I'm not in the first army. It sounds like they are the first from over here to go home and the CBI.

I don't care for that over there unless I have to. We have sure been getting a pile of our old men back now who were in the hospital.

Well folks, guess I'll quit now. Keep writing.

Love,

Your Son,
Bill

P.S. Send a box whenever they start letting them again.

May 31, 1945 - From Bill to Marge

This letter is the first mention by Bill that Marge may be *in a family way*.

Dearest Marge,

I got a letter from Vernon last night and one from you of May 22. It kinda sounds like you are in the family way. I kinda figured it from your letters before. I'm glad too, except I'd like to be with you. So you better ease up on the work there at the bakery and if nothing better, lock up the bakery or let Ma and John try to run it.

In the letter I got from Vernon, I found out he is only about 60 mi. from here so I went to see the Co and he called Battalion and they said I had to go to Regiment so this morning I caught a ride to Regt. And they sent me to Major Bradley, Regimental (M.Y.?) And then he told me I had to get a written pass from my CO and then it had to go to Battalion from there to Regt, then Div. And if it was Okay there, I'd get it. Well, by that time it would probably be a month or so. I'm leaving it go. I wrote him and told him the town I was in and to come up with a jeep and I'd go back with him for a day or two. So I hope he comes. I pretty near took off any way today but it was raining to beat hell so I didn't. I was never so pissed off at this army as I was today. Another kid with me went to get permission to talk to his Grandparents here but "no cooperation" because that is fraternizing. This is really a bad day for me. Lost about $60 playing poker today too.

Another kid in this squad used to be a baker back in

*Philadelphia so every now and then we get going on the bakery business. Sure like to be back in it at home. I'm glad to hear Ray won't have to go to the Army because I think it's more horseshit every day I stay in it. This country is sure pretty out here but we can't go out of the Co. ground now. The weather had been nice except for today. It rained all day.*

*Well, Marge, guess I'd better quit. Keep up the writing.*

*All my Love*

*Your Husband*
*Bill*

Why be Irritated?
Light an Old Gold
Apple "Honey" helps guard O.Gs from Cigarette Dryness

HE WANTS TO HEAR FROM YOU—
Write that boy in service today!
Loft
FRESH CANDY
It's good taste and . . . it tastes good

On V-E Day, Gen. Eisenhower had sixty-one U.S. divisions with 1,622,000 men in Germany, and a total force in Europe numbering 3,077,000. When the shooting ended, the divisions in the field became the occupation troops, charged with maintaining law and order and establishing the Allied military presence in the defeated nation. This was the *army-type occupation*. A counterpart of the *military government carpet*, its object was to control the population and stifle resistance by putting troops into every nook and cranny.

As Bills' letters reflect, the occupation troops manned border control stations, maintained checkpoints at road junctions and bridges, sent out roving patrols to apprehend curfew and circulation violators, and kept stationary guards at railroad bridges, Army installations, DP (Displaced Persons) camps, jails, telephone exchanges, factories, and banks. In the first months troops were plentiful and almost everything of importance-and some not so important-was guarded. In effect, the combat forces became military government security troops.

The most obvious defect of the blanket occupation was its impermanence. The vast majority of the troops were going to be redeployed either to the Pacific or home for discharge. Their work in Germany was finished the day the war ended. Some troops would be there for weeks, some for months, but all would be almost constantly on the move outward.

The ban on fraternization had been in force eight months by V-E Day; long enough in the opinion of those who had to enforce it and, no doubt, too long to suit those required to observe it. Three days after the surrender Generals Bradley and Smith talked about modifying the policy.

For two months thereafter SHAEF (Supreme Headquarters Allied Expeditionary Force) wrestled with itself, trying desperately to enforce the non-fraternization policy and, just as desperately, to get rid of it. Meanwhile, arrests were being made, cases were being tried, and good combat soldiers were getting bad records.

A curious myth associated with the non-fraternization problem was the belief that the ordinary soldiers objected most to the ban on friendliness to young children. On 2 June, Eisenhower reported to Marshall, "Continuing surveys among our troops show that non-fraternization rules are fairly well observed except in the case of small children."

After some discussion as to what constituted a small child (Eisenhower proposed twelve years as the age limit, but Marshall wondered "how a soldier is going to tell the age of a child before being kind to it?") and after Marshall decided that public reaction would be favorable, Eisenhower announced the lifting of the ban on fraternization with children on 11 June.

As Bill points out numerous times, the soldier's urge to befriend small children was not the real issue. Of five provost marshals interviewed in June, none mentioned children as figuring in his fraternization cases, or, for that matter, any other Germans except women. Maj. Hal N. Briggs, 35th Infantry Division, added, "There is a lot of fraternization going on and we know it, but to catch them is a different thing." Exactly how widespread fraternization was, no one in authority seemed to know or want to know.

One thing could not be ignored: In attempting to force on its troops a wholly artificial standard of conduct, the Army was putting itself in a position that was both ludicrous and potentially dangerous. No amount of pious exhortation could, once the fighting had ended, convince the soldiers that they were not the chief and possibly intended victims.

Fittingly non-fraternization did not end, it disintegrated. On 19 June in Washington, Eisenhower said that there could be no fraternization in Germany until the last Nazi criminals had been uprooted. On 10 July,

Eisenhower announced, "In view of the rapid progress which has been made in carrying out Allied de-Nazification policies . . . it is believed desirable and timely to permit personnel of my command to engage in conversation with adult Germans on the streets and in public places."

Although non-fraternization had still not positively been pronounced dead, from then on the SHAEF staff was concerned only with arranging the funeral.

< < < < > > > >

Wartime planning had assumed that a large part of the forces required to defeat Japan would come from Europe after hostilities ended there. By the third week in March 1945, SHAEF anticipated having to release a million and a half troops for the Pacific and having to send another 600,000 men home for discharge.

What would determine whether a man stayed in the occupation forces in Germany, went to the Pacific, or went home to be discharged was the Adjusted Service Rating; what Bill refers to as points. The rating was calculated individually for every enlisted man in the theater on the basis of one point for each month of service since September 1940, one point for each month of overseas service since September 1940, five points for each decoration or battle star, and twelve points for each child under eighteen up to a maximum of three.

The critical score was 85 for enlisted men (44 for enlisted women). Those with 85 or more points on the Adjusted Service Rating were eligible for discharge. Those with fewer points would serve either in the occupation or be redeployed to the Pacific.

No matter how high the rate of departure, hundreds of thousands of men were going to have to wait months before their turns came. Since they could have constituted a monumental morale problem, especially while the non-fraternization policy was in force, the redeployment plans included provisions for training, education, and recreation programs throughout the theater.

The training program, which was to have prepared the low-score units for combat in the Pacific, never started. The education program, aside from sustaining morale, was conceived also as a means of smoothing the transition to civilian life and of compensating soldiers who had had their educations interrupted by the war.

Entertainment and recreation programs, considered important to morale during the war, were continued after the German surrender. The sixty-six USO (United Services Organizations) shows in the theater on V-E Day played to three-quarters of a million men a month. Stars such as Jack Benny, Bob Hope, Raymond Massey, and Shep Fields continued to perform, but the lesser known professionals became noticeably more temperamental after the war was over and career opportunities at home beckoned.

Furlough travel appeared to be the best prop for morale. It offered contact with civilian society, relief from the military routine and the supposed strain of non-fraternization, instructive experience, and a taste (with a marked GI flavor) of what had formerly been the life of the privileged. The US zone in Germany, in spite of the war damage, offered a variety of tourist attractions.

Bill and his fellow soldiers were surrounded by some of Germany's most scenic countryside.

By mid-summer 1945, the search for morale-sustaining devices was being stretched to, and perhaps somewhat beyond, the limits of feasibility. In July, General Marshall visited Paris and the Berchtesgaden center and pronounced the efforts being made there for morale "splendid," but he came away worried that the enlisted men were still not getting the "feeling of independence which all Americans crave."

In spite of the offerings in education, entertainment, and recreation, surveys conducted in July indicated that the high-score men wanted above all to go home. As Bill makes evident, so did the low-score men.

Postmark on this letter is "Germany (Neustadt)."

Bill mentions being *"about 60 miles from Nuremberg"* but it turns out to be more like 100 miles. Nuremburg was the location for the War Crimes Trials of German officers.

He also begins one of many discussions of the *points* that he has attained and what is needed to be released from military duty.

*Neustadt (Aisch)-Bad Windsheim* is a district in Bavaria, Germany. It is bounded by (from the west and clockwise) the districts of Würzburg, Kitzingen, Bamberg, Erlangen-Höchstadt, Fürth and Ansbach, and by the state of Baden-Württemberg (district Main-Tauber).

*Nuremberg* (German: Nürnberg) is a city in the German state of Bavaria, in the administrative region of Middle Franconia. It is situated on the Pegnitz river and the Rhine-Main-Danube Canal and is Franconia's largest city. It is located about 170 kilometers north of Munich.

http://en.wikipedia.org/wiki/

June 1, 1945 - From Bill to Marge

Dearest Marge,

Well, Marge, just got back from getting paid. $38.50 - lot of money but I'm not going to send any home this month because I might get a trip to Paris the last of the month. But I kinda doubt it because they are only giving a couple a (furloughs a) week out of the Co. At this rate, I'll probably be in CBI before my turn comes around. This Div. is Occupational here for 17 months but that don't mean (much). The rumor is you have to have 50 points or 3 battle stars in order to stay here. I'll have the 3 battle stars but not the 50 points. If these last 2 stories are official and I guess they are, they also say we will get 10 points for our Inf. Combat badge which will make me 42 points. But then a guy never knows for sure where he stands. I suppose there have probably been 100 or more come in the Co. since I have but a lot of them aren't here now. We didn't get our mail yet today. We usually get it about suppertime. I'm hoping I get some letters tonight. I haven't gotten a package now for 2 months or better. We really got good chow for dinner today for a change and all we wanted to eat. Good coffee for breakfast and dinner. I don't know whether I ever wrote you where I was at or not but it is 7 mi. from Nvestadt (Neustadt) or about 60 mi. from Nuremberg and Vernon is about 12 mi. from there. I'm sure hoping he can come over here. I only ever met the one guy from Caledonia here that I know but lots of guys from Chicago, Minn. and Missouri in this outfit. And one of the cooks is from Cedar Rapids. He is going home before long because he's got 100 points. There is Mass here at 4:30 this afternoon so I guess I'll go. I usually go every chance I get. Well, I can't think of anything else to say so I better quit.

Keep writing
All my Love

Your Husband
Bill

June 2, 1945 - From Bill to Marge

Dearest Marge,

Well, Marge, I got two letters from you today, the Democrat (Waukon paper) - May 2 and the Register (Des Moines). This is the best day I've spent in the ETO. We got a pack of cigarettes and candy bar today - first in 3 days and chow is getting better. This afternoon I rode about 20 mi. or so and saw a Russian Stage show put *on for the G.I.'s. It was sure good singing and dancing - lasted about 2 hours. They had the best looking Russian girls I ever saw. Most of these slave labor ones are hard lookers but those gals were really good. You've seen some of those Russian dancers in Monier (?) but these were better than in any show I've ever seen. All different kinds of costumes, then tonight I went back over to the same town and saw a movie "Hollywood Canteen" and for once the film worked good and didn't break or anything. If they had shows like this right along over here, life wouldn't have been half bad.*

*But they couldn't be anything like being home with you. I sure do love you, Marge, and you'll never have to worry about me chiseling on you. I suppose they all tell you I will but you won't need to worry. I'm sure glad I got a good wife waiting for me and the bakery. Lot of the boys are starting to wonder now what they (will) do when they finally get out of this army. Lots of them will never be satisfied staying in one place very long. Being used to moving so often - it was wondering if the next town was always a little better. New supply of eggs, wine, and everything else but it would probably be a few less of your buddies there to enjoy it. But we figured most of the time they were better off going to the hospital because we never had many men killed. Boy, Marge but the Lord and your prayers sure were with me a good many times. I still can't figure out how I got missed a couple of times. Tonight riding home from the show, I was thinking of all the times we came home from the river about that time just getting dark and the air getting a little chilly. Oh, boy, for them days again.*

*We've new Co. commander tonight. That makes the fifth different one that we've had since I've been with the Co. I'm just hoping he isn't too strict because it will take awhile to make garrison soldiers out of us guys.*

*They didn't have Mass yesterday but are having it tomorrow so I'll be going to Mass and Communion. Do you know the last bath I've had was back in Feb? But I'm going to break down one of these days and take a bar of soap and go down to the creek. Well, it is getting close to Midnight so guess I'd better quit. But the guys got a big poker game on in the room so I probably won't sleep anyway.*

*Keep writing*
*All my Love*

*Your Husband Bill*

*Hollywood Canteen* (1944) was a movie about two soldiers on sick leave who spent three nights at the Hollywood Canteen before going back to active duty. Nominated for 3 Oscars, it starred almost everyone including The Andrew Sisters, Jack Benny, Eddie Cantor, Betty Davis, John Garfield and Alan Hale among others.

On June 1, the British took over Lebanon and Syria.

The Government's sudden 50% increase in A gas coupon values had a catch to it - tires. President A. L. Viles, of the Rubber Manufacturers Association, announced that the June quota of passenger tires to be released (1,500,000) will be 33% short of the number needed to keep essential civilian cars on the road through the summer months.

U.S. industry has more working capital than at any time in its history. Reason: War. The Securities & Exchange Commission survey revealed that in December 1944, industry's ready money (much of it invested in Government bonds) had reached a staggering $45.5 billion - 85% more than was available in 1939.

http://www.time.com/time/magazine/article/

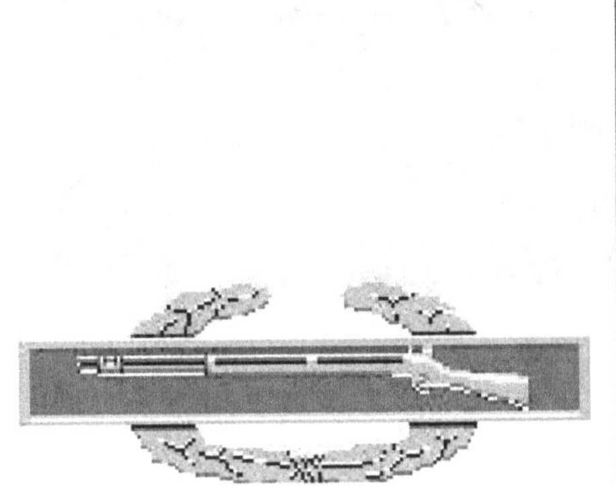

Combat Infantryman's Badge

The first, confused days of moving and readjustment were past. The official mourning for Franklin Roosevelt was over. Now a new pattern of life in the White House took shape. Once again, as under the Roosevelts, the White House was a home for an active, happy family.

President Truman still seemed a little startled at the furor he caused on personal expeditions in the capital. Last week, when he hustled out to open his safety deposit box at a Washington bank, he virtually tied up noon-hour traffic in the street outside. But his informality, his habit of early rising had begun to seem natural. So did the folksy atmosphere which visitors imparted to White House anterooms. Newsmen now rated callers as OFs (Old Friends) and PRs (Payers of Respects).

The President got most of his relaxation from occasional swims in the White House pool, had little time for outside entertainment. But Mrs. Truman took her place in the Washington social whirl, proved herself equal to the rigors of teas, dinners and receptions.

Time Magazine
June 4, 1945

*June 3, 1945 - From Bill to Marge*

Dearest Marge,

Well, Marge I really got the mail tonight. 2 letters from you - May 26 and one from Ma. 2 (Des Moines) Registers and a letter from Jack Whitlinger. He wrote last Feb. I was glad to get them all. I went to confession, Mass and Communion today. We had high Mass with a Children's choir. They were really good, too. Our Mass is in the afternoon and theirs in the morning. We aren't allowed to sit by them in Church unless there isn't any other place. Our restriction is lifted now so we can go out around the town now but I suppose it will last till they catch a couple in bed with some of their women again.

I'm out of paper so I'll have to write on both sides now. I sure get a kick out of reading in the Democrat where different ones have been awarded the Combat Badge. Mostly all of the Inf. Soldiers get it after they hit combat and don't turn out yellow or make themselves a hindrance rather than doing good. I got mine in Jan. but never wore it till a couple weeks ago when they told us anyone that had one would wear it and then we get 10 extra points for it so I guess it is all right. Most of the questions in your letter I find by the time I get them, I have wrote (the answers) a few days before. What ever you are asking about, Marge, I wrote you before about getting another girl or whatever help you need. There is no use of you killing yourself even if you have to pay them plenty.

I see in the Democrat where James Henderson was killed over here. He went to the Army in the same bunch as me - went to Ft. Hood and came home on leave the same time and came across about the same time. The paper was wrong about him being over since June. I think there are a lot of the boys I took training with that aren't here today. I seen a few photos last night that a kid had of one of those concentration camps up north. Boy, they are just like you see in the paper and I still don't think White seen them unless his Div. got switched to the First Army. I haven't seen any of those men for the last 1 1/2 months and we used to see them every time we got a couple days rest. They were usually behind us or on our flank. I wrote you along time ago about losing that bracelet with my name on it in the Mainz River but I don't think you ever got the letter because I put in it about making the bridgehead for the 6th Armored.

We wiped out a pocket that the 4th Armored left over here for a while but the last month they were behind us up till the day before the war ended. Then they went through us after we cleaned the Highway through Sudatenland and into Czech for them. The next morning they took off one way and us another but then we were held up to wait for peace to be confirmed. I've shot enough over here to last me a long time. I don't think I'd care for any more of it, but then sometimes a guy used to just wish he'd see a few too for the excitement and it really comes time pretty quick. It's a lot of fun when you get them pinned but it sure is hell when they get you pinned down. I used to think it was funny sometimes how they would take our guys prisoners because in order to take any guys in this Platoon, I think they would have to kill or wound us first.

I got a letter from the nuns in Dubuque asking for a donation. I guess it wouldn't hurt if you sent them a $100 because it is for a pretty good cause and they have a plenty rough life. We got a couple kegs of beer today but there is still one left. I just had one cup but I guess I'll have a little more tomorrow if the other keg is left till then.

We had a movie tonight at the theater downtown so I went. Betty Davis, but I don't know what the name of it was. It didn't say. Pretty good though. This life in ETO (European Theatre of Operations) is heaven now since the war is over compared to want it was back in Jan and Feb.

We really haven't done a hell of a lot since it's been over. Pull a few hrs. guard a week and that's about it or play horseshoes and ball. We have been going to start drilling different times but it is usually called off for something or other. A couple of the boys got guitars and they are all singing and having a good time. Played a little poker today, made a few dollars but will probably lose it again tomorrow but I manage to keep between $50 and $200. A few times I've gone broke but borrow a few bucks and always come back. There are about half dozen that borrow from me right along. That's one thing over here, if you got any money and another guy needs it, they'll always give it to him whether they ever see it again or not. Have you heard from

On June 4, the 6th Marine Division occupied the Orokoe Peninsula, Okinawa.

The United States, Russia, England and France come to a preliminary agreement to split occupied Germany into Sectors.

On June 5, the Allied Control Council, the military occupation government body of Germany, formally takes power.

A little wearily, WPB (War Production Board) announced the war shortages that the U.S. public - judging by its complaints - has found it hardest to bear: 1) window screens, 2) alarm clocks, 3) wash tubs.

http://www.time.com/time/magazine/article/

Vernon was overseas for twenty months and his son, Jim was eighteen months old before Vernon saw him.

Marquardt yet? That's the guy I sent a pistol home with. I suppose he's probably still sweating it out about over here yet.

My best buddy here now is a little wop from Philly. We get along swell. He came in about a month before me. I got him started going to church after I came in. He went to confession about 2 weeks ago the first time in a year or two. He's got a beautiful wife and he sure thinks the world of her. He writes 10-15 pages to her some nights. I don't see how he does it. He's sitting across from me now but he can't think of anything to write.

I'm glad to hear you got the neon sign fixed. It's been on the blink enough. It probably would be all right to have them paint it too if they don't want too much.

Well, Marge, I'll quit for tonight. I'm still loving and missing you more than ever but some one of these days, we'll be together again.

All my Love

Your Husband
Bill

June 5, 1945 - From Bill to Marge

Dearest Marge,

Well, Marge, I didn't get any mail from you last night because I wasn't there. Vernon came up in the afternoon and I came back with him. Sure good to see him again. He looks just the same as the last time I saw him. Those guys sure think the world of him. Some of them were telling me he was the best supply Sarg. in the Regt. I didn't get a chance to write last night - we were so busy talking about everything.

He's taking me back again in the morning. It's about 135 miles by the road we came. I guess I figured it out a little off when I said 60 miles. That's what it would be straight across. You can write Beck (that) he looks just the same as the last time I saw him but he thought I was heavier and it seemed funny for him to see me so brown because when he was home, I was always working indoors so much. They're kept plenty busy from the looks of things. They sure have a lot of more things to take care of than our supplies. He fixed me up with a few clothes and cigarettes so will get by awhile longer. They still have their mail censored but as you know, mine never was to amount to anything. He thinks they will be going to CBI without a furlough in the States but I sure hope he don't. Well, Marge, I'd better quit for now *but will write as quick as I get back in the morning or afternoon.*

*All My Love*

*Your Husband*

*Bill*

June 6, 1945 - From Bill to Marge

*Dearest Marge,*

*I just got back so will write. I had a box and a letter waiting for me from you and we've finished it off already. It was great to see Vernon. I guess we talked over about everything. He really fixed me up with clothes, cigarettes, tobacco and even a table. His mail is all censored now. I guess he is leaving before long but not for home. He said to write and tell Beck. I put in for a transfer to his outfit. I don't know whether I'll get it or not. It has to go through in the next week or it won't do me any good. I hope I get it. I'd sooner go over with them without a furlough home than get a furlough home and go with the Inf. You can write Beck and tell her that they are never in too much danger or maybe I might write her myself tonight. They sure have things good in that outfit. A barrack boy, full of clothes, plenty to eat, chance to sleep in. I was there for 2 days and it sure went quick. When I got back I found out we had one guy killed and 2 wounded monkeying around with guns while I was gone. Vernon sure has a lot of responsibility. I never realized before how much stuff he had to take care of. I guess he really knows his stuff too. They left to go back about 2 hours ago and it just started to rain to beat hell. I bet he really gets soaked (jeep).*

*Well, how's my little wife doing by now "getting big and fat" or staying about the same? I'd sure like to be home with you now but I guess we have to keep praying it ends over in that CBI pretty soon, Marge. If you could get Lucille Dayton to work for you, you would have a good one. I used to work with her and she's good and honest, too, I think. I remember seeing where Hubert died and maybe she might want to work. You sure are doing a swell job of it there but there is no sense in killing yourself doing it. I'd as soon see it locked up if you have to keep on like you have been.*

*Well, Marge, keep up the writing. I'm still loving and missing you more than ever.*

*All my Love*

*Your Husband, Bill*

On June 6, King Haakon VII of Norway returns to power in Norway.

Wetting his finger and holding it to the U.S. breeze, New York's aging, ailing Senator Robert F. Wagner, a shrewd weatherman of public opinion, thought the wind last week favored a revised and expanded Social Security bill. Promptly, he introduced one in Congress.

Wrinkling his emotional nose, Columnist Samuel Grafton wrote: "There isn't any meat; that's war. There isn't any curfew; that's peace. The price of steel scrap is going down; that's peace. Try and get sugar; that's war."

All across the U.S. there were signs of this curious transition period: half war and half peace. The Army cut back its plane production program by 17,000 planes, saving $4 billion, and temporarily throwing thousands out of work. The next day, fire bombs from 500 Superforts set flames that roared and crackled through Tokyo, licking the edge of the Emperor's palace.

http://www.time.com/time/magazine/article.html

June 7, 1945 - From Bill to Marge

Dearest Marge,

Well, Marge, I got 3 letters from you tonight, 2 of May 31 and one of June 1st. That is really making good time. I hope you start getting my mail just as fast. I'm glad to hear you are going to have a baby, but I think you could do just as well picking out the name for him or her. Then I'd be able to have something to razz you about when I do get back. How about it? But then again I might be home before that from what we've been hearing. That is if my transfer don't go through. I hope you don't think I'm crazy like everybody here does for putting in for it. Even the officers think I'm foolish for doing it but the way I figure, I'd sooner go direct with an outfit like that than get a furlough home and go with the Inf. I don't think my luck would hold out forever and I had plenty of close ones. One of the officers who likes me pretty well is doing all he can to get it through. If I do get it and go there, I don't think you'll ever get the letters with stuff in them like I wrote over here. I think Vernon was a little surprised at the way we lived and everything when he heard the boys around here talking. You asked me about the lice here in your letter. Well, I was one of the lucky ones that never had them. I don't see how unless it was because I used to dust myself with louse powder every now and then. Most of the guys have had them. They aren't too bad to get rid of if you can get a bath and some clean clothes and a little powder. They'd get them sleeping in straw, dirty houses, and blankets and wearing clothes so dirty and rotten they'd about fall off.

I think Vernon was kind of surprised when he brought me back yesterday. I didn't even know my way to this building from downtown and it's only about as big as Lansing or a little bigger. So you can tell how much I've been out and around. But tonight me and the little wop I hang around with went out walking for a couple hours and covered the place from one end to the other. I guess we've been here about 3 weeks now. I gave Vernon a pistol and $50 when I was down there because he was broke. He only gets $4.20 and he was broke because he didn't cut his allotment which is $140 a month so I guess Beck should be able to live all right on that. I think this is the hottest day we have had over hear yet, just like back in Iowa in July. It's 9:45 now and still light out. I guess pretty quick we only have a few hours of darkness.

On Okinawa last week, a Jap shell fragment seriously injured LIFE Photographer W. Eugene Smith, just as he was shooting a final picture for a layout on "A Day with a Front-Line Soldier." Commented Smith, a veteran of 13 Pacific actions and 23 combat bombing missions, at a field hospital afterwards: "I forgot to duck, but I got a good picture of those who did."

Time Magazine
June 4, 1945

Japanese Communique: Our Giretsu (unsurpassed Japanese loyalists) special attack airborne units, commanded by Captain Michio Okuyama, daringly landed amid the enemy in Kita and Naka airfields on the main Okinawa Island. . . . Upon landing they promptly blasted grounded enemy aircraft, munitions depots and airfield installations in rapid succession and are achieving great war results by throwing the enemy into confusion.

Time Magazine
June 4, 1945

*Good thing the war is over or they would be working us 24 hrs. every day. What the hell is Riley doing now? Still out to Churchtown, I suppose. He still brags about that big tool he carries and all the work he's doing with it.*

*Lots of these guys were in the beauty parlor today and got their hair curled. I don't know weather they were permanents or what but we sure been razzing the hell out of them tonight. I think there are going to be a lot of little American babies left over here from the U.S.Army but here is one who isn't monkeying around. I'm still loving and staying true to my wife. Remember what I told you, if I ever chiseled, I'd tell you but never have and don't intent to, but a lot of the boys do.*

*Keep up the writing.*

*All my Love*

*Your Husband*
*Bill*

June 8, 1945 - From Bill to Marge

*Dearest Marge,*

*I didn't get any mail from you tonight but probably will again tomorrow. I hope you are getting mine good now. It was just 5 months ago today that I left New York harbor on the Queen Elizabeth. Took 3 1/2 days, I guess it was to get to Glasgow, Scotland. Then I went to South Hampton, England and from there to France, the port of LeHavre. Then they loaded us on 40+8's there and went just about to Metz. That's where I joined the 90th. Left there on trucks and met their company at Bastogn. (Belgium) where we pushed off from there as you know pretty well where I was all the time. This Co. has had 700 men since D day. Quite a lot, eh? And now is the first time there has ever been over 150 since I've been in it (Note: Normal compliment was 200 men).*

*Vernon couldn't figure out how come I didn't know the guys in the Co. or they didn't know me but that explains it. You usually just know the guys in your platoon and then they usually go by their last name. There are a few of us they call by the first name but not many. We had a big parade today. Probably about 5 or 6 thousand guys in it. Lot of fun marching when we had a good band but they usually fuck around so much before we ever got started. They're having a show over to Battalion tonight about 20 miles from here. I guess I'll go. It is Betty Hutton in "Over the Waves." Or something like*

The schools closed at noon. Most of the stores locked their doors. At 1 p.m. three big transport planes plumped down at the airport and a thin, tired-looking man stepped out on Georgia soil.

A four-star veteran of the European campaign was coming home. General Courtney Hicks Hodges had flown the Atlantic, stopped briefly in Manhattan, then had flown to his native South.

His Georgia neighbors were primed to give him the reception he deserved. His First Army had made history. His men had been first in France, first across the Rhine, among the first through the Siegfried Line. Now Washington made his command the first to be redeployed to the Pacific.

Read more: http://www.time.com/time/magazine/article/

The Forty plus Eight boxcar is described earlier in this narrative. It is interesting that the government of France donated one to each State in the US after WWI in appreciation for our efforts in that war.

When Bill was writing letters to Marge during the months that he was in combat (January through May) in Europe, there was a considerable amount of censorship. He was not allowed to mention geographical areas or towns where he was located during this period. Occasionally Marge would receive letters that would have words blacked out or cut out.

Now that the war is over Bill is able to refer back to battles and/or locations where he had been. This letter is a great example.

Stunned and bleeding, T/5 Louis F. Korineck Jr. of Manitowoc, Wis. turned up at a battalion aid station of the 38th Division on Luzon this week, demanding to know all the details about his wound. A doctor told him a bullet had penetrated his helmet above his left ear, creased his scalp and passed out of the helmet above his right ear. Then Korineck remembered something more important than treatment: "Call the sergeant right away," he shouted. "Tell him that sniper is right where we thought he was."

http://www.time.com/time/magazine/article.html

that.

Who is the babe Paul Anderson is marrying and how long has this romance been going on? I wish you would send me his address. I'd sure like to hear from him. I haven't heard from Harold or Jim either. I wrote them both a long time ago. The people over here are all doing their haying now and pretty quick they will be cutting their grain. It seems funny over here not to see any of the land with fences around. The only place they have them is around their house and they are usually cement walls about 10 ft high and 2 ft. thick. They must not trust one another much, house doors and everything are always locked. When we were to be cleaning houses, we really had to shot off the locks or bust the door with a rifle or knock out a window and go in.

Well, Marge, I guess this is enough shit for tonight. Take good care of yourself. I'm still loving you and figuring on being home with you again some one of these days.

All my Love

Your Husband
Bill

P.S. Have the girls wrap me up a box - any kind of candy. Don't go to the trouble of making it. You know how well I like it.

June 9, 1945 - From Bill to Marge

On June 9, Australian troops landed in Brunei Bay in North Borneo.

Eddie Arcaro, racing in the 71st Kentucky Derby aboard Hoop Jr wins in 2:07 minutes.

Dearest Marge,

I just got back from Neustadt where they had a circus for the 90th tonight. It was Austrians and Czech's. It was pretty good to. I guess before the war it was really a big outfit over here. They just came from Austria, I guess.

It's sure good when a guy can get away once in a while and see a few shows. If I had you over here with me, I could stay here for a long time and not mind it. It's sure pretty country, too but I'll take good old Iowa anytime. They had a lot of nurses there with their officer boy friends tonight, too.

I didn't get any mail the last 2 nights, now sure do miss it. That's one thing that keeps the boys going, I think. How is my little wife coming now or should I say, my fat little wife? Be sure and take good care of yourself. The war news sounds pretty good today. I'm hoping those Japs have brains enough to surrender pretty soon but I can't see why they don't give them some other peace terms. All they gained by unconditional surrender over here was lost a lot of lives. I think if the German people would of known it was going to be this easy on them, it would of ended long ago. Things are starting to go on just like if there never was a war. Their crops look good, the railroads are mostly all running now. Factories are going and the brewery must really be turning it out because we usually have a barrel on tap in our room. I don't drink too much of it though - nothing like the beer back home.

I got 2 shifts of guard to pull tonight. I rolled with a kid to see whether he stood mine or I stood both and I lost but this is the first time I've lost so I shouldn't kick.

We haven't done hardly any drilling since this war's been over. And I'm sure glad too, but then drilling over here is nothing like the States anyway. I just read your letter over again tonight and you wrote you thought I wouldn't like you going to Rominger (Dr). Well, I'm not that foolish Marge. Rominger is a good Doc, a little more serious than Dillon and you were the one going. I know if it would have been me, I would want to go to the one I wanted to.

Well, Marge, keep up with the writing.

All my Love

Your Husband
Bill

June 10, 1945 - From Bill to Marge

Dearest Marge,

Well, Marge, I didn't get any mail tonight, that's 3 nights I haven't gotten any now.

When the war was on, we only used to get mail once a week or so. A guy never used to be looking forward to it so much and we get it every night now. That's why we notice it so much. I went to Mass this afternoon. We had high Mass the same as last Sunday. I always go every time we have Mass. We are supposed to start our training schedule again tomorrow but it's liable to be like other times. Something happens and they call it off but even if they do, we only have 1/2 drill like hiking and things like that so it is nothing like them in the States where your officers set themselves up like little gods. I think I'll probably be home in a couple of months if that transfer don't go through because they have stopped all the passes and the high points men haven't been going home. I'd sure love to go home again too. I'll bet the

From a building in the disciplinary area of Indiana's Ft. Benjamin Harrison last week rushed an irate mob of G.I. prisoners. They snatched up the whitewashed boulders lining the paths and flower beds and rushed the guards. Suddenly, the compound became a battlefield.

The prisoners were Army recalcitrants and out-&-out criminals: everything from AWOLs to arsonists, rapists and murderers. Some 2,700 are housed in the Ft. Harrison disciplinary barracks.

Time Magazine
June 11, 1945

On June 10, the United States destroyer William D. Porter (*Willie Dee*) was sunk by Japanese kamikaze aircraft.

Cecylia Mikolajczyk, 42, wife of the former premier of the London Polish Government, rejoined her husband in London after nearly three years in Nazi prison camps. Tattooed on her left arm, for permanent remembrance, is her slave number: 64,023.

Inga Arvad, sightly Danish film writer, thought it over for two days, then broke her engagement to British M.P. (Conservative) Robert Boothby - because she felt that the stigma of having once been described by Adolf Hitler as "the perfect Nordic beauty" would hurt her M.P.'s career.

http://www.time.com/time/magazine/article/

*first place I'd be after I got home would be down to the cabin if it is still warm enough. The fishing isn't any good right around here. Got a few grenades one day and tried it but just got some little ones. I don't know whether I'd even have the patience with a pole and line any more or not.*

*Does Emmy still go down to the river as much as ever? How about Ray? Does he still go and has he went to our cabin yet to try his luck?*

*I suppose you folks are really enjoying it up to Albert's (Leet, Marge's brother) if the fish are biting. How long before they are coming back? Say hello to them for me. I wrote you a few days ago to try getting Lucille Dayton to work, I think. If you offered her enough, she would. How's John? Is he still staying sober on the job and how's that namanne (?) of his coming? I'll bet Stan really gets razzed by everybody, now he always said he wasn't going to be foolish enough to spend any money on the girls. What does Sis hear from Dale (Goltz). I kinda figure he is in that 5th Army. Has he ever wrote and said?*

*They issued us all rubbers today and we are supposed to carry them all the time but I let one of the boys have mine. I won't be needing them. It sure is pretty good, not supposed to fraternize and then they issue rubbers, but I suppose it will stop a lot of clap and babies born. But I think there will be plenty of them around Germany here without German fathers anyway.*

*I hear these Russians are quite the cunt hounds too. They say when they come through towns, if they seen any thing they wanted, they would just roll it over and help themselves. Some fun, eh?*

*I'm sure glad this war never reached the States but some of the people it would probably do some good. I think I'll write the folks yet tonight. I still don't care about writing letters any more than I ever did. I write a few lines and listen to the guys shout the shit, then have to join in now and then. Well, there ain't anything else I can think of to write so I guess I better quit for tonight.*

*Be sure and keep on writing because I'm a waiting for you letters.*

*All my Love*

*Your Husband*
*Bill*

The U.S. Navy, biggest in world history, had almost as many ships in commission last week as it had sailors in 1938. In that year its establishment numbered 109,065 officers & men. Last week the Navy announced that it had added 100,000 vessels (above the size of boats) to the 7,695 it had in commission on Dec. 7, 1941. The breakdown: 1,150 combatant ships; 557 auxiliaries; 82,266 landing ships and landing craft; the balance, patrol and mine craft.

Philadelphia's Evening Bulletin last week hoisted a new kind of service flag. The flag was official, having received the approval of Major General James A. Ulio, Adjutant General. At the top it carried a gold star with the number 6 (for war dead); below it a blue star with the number 396 (for employees in service); at the bottom the eagle emblem of the honorably discharged, with the number 28 (for veterans who have been employed or re-employed by the Bulletin).

http://www.time.com/time/magazine/article/

June 10, 1945 - From Bill to Jim and Amanda

*Dear Folks,*

*I haven't had any mail the last few days but before that I was getting it. About every night been getting the Democrat and Register. They really are pretty old but I'm glad to get them.*

*I got the Readers Digest a couple weeks ago. That was the first one I ever got out here. I don't remember weather I wrote you I was down to see Vernon for a few days or not. He came up after me Mon. and brought me back Wed. I guess they'll be leaving pretty quick for CBI without a furlough but it is hard to tell. I put in for a transfer to his outfit but I don't know weather it will go through or not. If it don't I'll probably be home in a couple months if the rumors are right that are going around. Vernon sure looked good. Just the same as the last time I saw him. I wrote Beck a letter too.*

*The boys all sure like him good in his outfit. I guess he gets them about every thing. He fixed me up with clothes, cigarettes and tobacco so I still got enough to last a couple weeks. We usually have a keg of beer on tap in our room but it's nothing like the beer we get at home. The only way I could ever get dad any razors over here would be steal them and I don't think he would want them that way. I was in one place where there were 8 brand new ones but I passed them up. The other guys all took them and sent them home. I've passed up a lot of beautiful watches, rings, and everything but I never could believe in taking them like most of the guys did, very seldom would we ever go in a house when the guys wouldn't loot it from top to bottom. I could of made plenty over here that way if I wanted to. I seen one guy get 60 thousand dollars and it wasn't German money either so some guys have made a small fortune over here. One of the machine gunners sent home about 200 rifles and shotguns, all new ones. They have jeeps to haul their stuff in though.*

*How's all the kids coming. I suppose getting so big I'll hardly know them. Marge wrote that dad was sick. I sure hope he's better by now.*

*I got a letter from Jack Whitlinger about a week ago that he wrote me in Feb. If you can get his address, send it to me because I would like to answer it. I just finished writing Marge a little while ago. We usually don't go to bed till 12 or 1 o'clock and get up about 6:30. Play a lot of cards. I manage to stay pretty well ahead all the time*

A Letter From The Time Magazine Publisher, Jun. 11, 1945:

You get a new appreciation of America's power in the Pacific these days when you talk with TIME'S Gilbert Cant.

Cant first went out to the Pacific in the summer of 1943 when Guadalcanal was newly won and Munda, Salamaua and Lae were the next stops on the road to Tokyo and he remembers those months as "one foxhole after another everywhere the skies were filled with Japs."

Now Cant has just flown home from an eye-popping tour of the whole Pacific front. He covered 27,210 miles of land and water, visited every important news spot from Pearl Harbor to Manila, from Iwo Jima to New Zealand and "not once did I see a single Jap plane in the air. There are plenty of them on the ground, though on Saipan and Guam and Iwo Jima our airfields are walled with their wreckage. At Clark Field on Luzon there's so much Zero metal laying around that our men use it for signposts and you can bet it did my heart good to see all those U.S. squadron numbers painted over the Rising Sun on the wingtips."

Two years ago Cant flew with the men of our Thirteenth Air Force when they took off from Guadalcanal through Zero-infested skies to soften up Bougainville for the landings (the 424th Bombardment Squadron made him an honorary member after that job). When he flew with them again on this trip the 6-17 was not even armed as they went over to blast Jap targets on Mindanao with "the best precision bombing I have ever seen."

Up at the front on Luzon he met other old friends and joined the men of our 43rd Division as they cleaned the Japs out of the caves northeast of Manila. ("The 43rd has come a long way since I was with it last, sloshing our way through foot-deep mud in the jungles of New Georgia — and I don't mean just geographically. At Munda we half starved on the cookie unit of C rations; but on Luzon, even at a forward observation post as near the Jap lines as you could get, we drank hot coffee, ate home-fried potatoes and shell eggs sunny side up.")

Bill is hoping to be home and out of the Army by the time their baby is born in September.

Little did he know that he would not see his first child until nearly five months after her birth.

William Lyon Mackenzie King is re-elected as Candian prime minster.

The Franck Committee recommends against a surprise nuclear bombing of Japan.

*but of course I went broke 2 or 3 times, borrowed a few dollars and made it back the next day though.*

*Well, write when you have time.*

*Love,*

*Your Son*
*Bill*

*P.S. Send a box if you have time.*

June 11, 1945 - From Bill to Marge

*Dearest Marge,*

*Well, Marge I got 2 letters from you tonight of June 2 and the Register for May 9. I was sure glad to get them too.*

*So Marie wants to be the godmother, eh? (sister, Marie, age 4) Well, I couldn't think of anyone better. You never can tell, I might be home by that time but you know the Army, we are never sure of anything from one day to the next. It rained here today so we didn't have any training. Back in the states though we would of still had to do everything. I haven't shaved for about 4 days now but I guess I'll break down tomorrow. I'm still using my Schick razor yet. That's one thing I'd never throw away.*

*How's Stan doing? Is he making many cookies and cakes now? I suppose he should be working steady by now. I suppose in about a week, Miekle will be doing as much bitching as ever. Maybe John don't realize it, but I think he's got some good experience by Miekle being away.*

*I don't know whether I would be any good any more or not. It's been so long since I've done any baking and I've sure got lazy as hell since I've been in the Army. The day this war ends can't come too quick for me because if I ever get out of this Army, I'll know enough not to get in it again, even though I have had a lot of fun sometimes. We still have our pinochle games every day. I lost about $50 or $60 bucks tonight but I'll make it back again tomorrow, I hope. What does White's wife hear from him or is he home already?*

*I kinda figured he left with the First Army but maybe I'm wrong. I guess most of the First Army is home by now or are on their way. It seems like a lot more than a month since the war ended and its beginning to look like it won't last too long in the Pacific if some of them fuckers in Washington will give them a little better terms. If not, I suppose it will be the same as over here - have to*

take every bit of it but I sure hope not.

What do the Luthers hear from Junior? Is he back on the line again? Toward the last of the war over here, a man could get hit pretty bad and they would have them back in a month or two. Have you heard from Marquardt yet? He should be home by now if they haven't kept him in these Rep Depo over here. I gave one of my pistols to Vernon when he was up here and got one left yet. We are getting a pack of cigarettes just about every day now so I'll have plenty because I smoke a pipe a lot now and cigars when we can get them. Can't you just see me at home chewing, smoking a pipe and cigars? It's been about a month now since we have had any wine and then we had a little over a hundred qts. we got out of a cellar in a tap room where we were staying. Boy, but the old gal that owned the place was sure pissed off when she found out but believe it or not, I've never even been tight over here yet but just wait till I hit the States. Well, Marge, I'll be looking for some mail again tomorrow night. Still loving and missing you.

All my Love

Your Husband
Bill

Bill refers here to the Army Reinforcement Depot. Men were often assigned to these places to await shipment back home or assignment to the War in the Pacific. The Army restricted a stay in such a depot to fifty days or less.

June 12, 1945 - From Bill to Marge

This letter was received by parcel post in Waukon Aug. 13, 1945

Dearest Marge,

Well, Marge, here it is 9:30 at night. The sun just came out a little while ago. It's rained all afternoon but I went to a show at Schweinfurt anyway. Kay Kaiser and Ann Miller but I don't remember the name of it. This morning we did a little close order drill, physical exercises, and an hour march but it was all easy. If it don't get any rougher, I won't mind it too much. I didn't get any mail tonight, now don't you do like lot of the guys wives are doing, writing that they think their husbands are probably on the way back or getting ready to leave so they quit writing and it will probably be a long time yet before they will be back home. I see by the Stars and Stripes where the 3rd and 7th Army are going to be occupational but that don't mean us guys will stay here. Lots of

3rd Army Area of Occupation

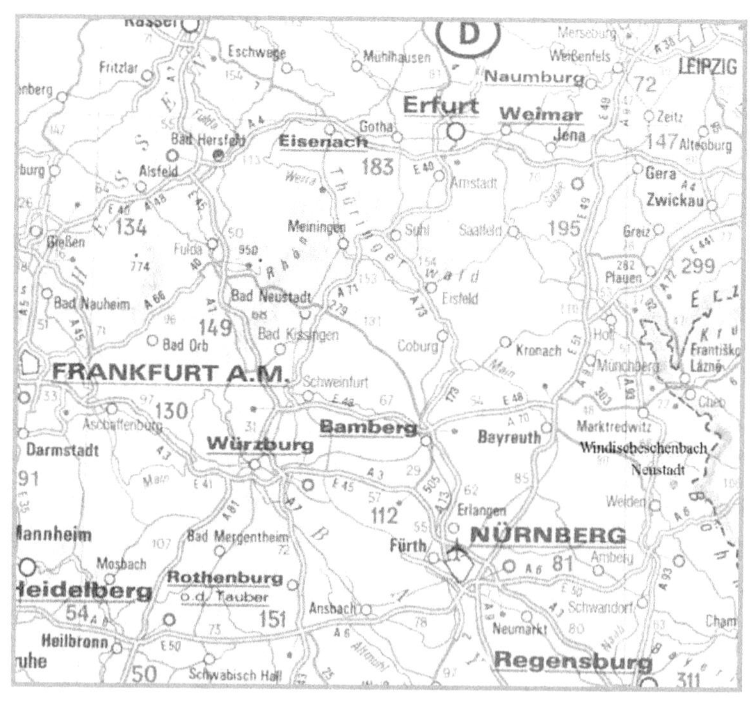

The movie Bill saw was *Carolina Blues* made in 1944 and was the only time Kaiser starred with Ann Miller.

On June 12, the Yugoslav Army leaves Trieste which left the New Zealand Army in control.

US 7th Marine Regiment conquered the summit of Kunishi Ridge, Okinawa.

The first trickle became a stream, and by this week upwards of 100,000 men had trooped off the grey ships and out of the big grey airplanes. The great migration of U.S. soldiers from Europe was on.

There were many *Kriegies*, former prisoners of war, bitterly unforgiving of the Germans. There were sick and wounded. There were 1,700 airmen in one day at Connecticut's windswept Bradley Field. One jubilant man jackknifed to kiss the good, solid U.S. runway. Most of them were pretty certain to be off to the wars again soon.

At New York City, Boston and Charleston, thousands of men piled down the gangplanks, lugging barracks bags, German sabers and helmets. They wolf-howled at the WAC bands, kneeled to make the sign of the cross. One G.I., debarked to a bus, impetuously obeyed his resolve to kiss the first American girl he saw. The bus de-bussed them before they could even exchange names.

Time Magazine
June 14, 1945

*us will be transferred to other outfits, I think. Haven't heard from Vernon since I was down there so I don't know whether he is still here or not. If they drop these points to 75 and he don't go to the Pacific, he'll have enough to get out. I'm hoping he does because he'd sure like to see Beck and the baby. I don't think he gets the time to write like I do.*

*We had the Civil War fought again over here last night. The guys were arguing about it and Negroes till 2 - 3 o'clock this morning. Everybody had a word in it and there are about 30 in our room.*

*How is the new girl going to be? Do you think she will be any good and will stay awhile? I hope so anyway. How's everything working at the bakery? Does John Dotseth ever come in?*

*Well, Marge, I can't think of anything else to say except I love you and take good care of yourself.*

*All my Love*

*Your Husband*
*Bill*

*P.S. Have the girls at the Bakery wrap up a box of any kind of candy and a couple packages of Velvet tobacco.*

June 13, 1945 - From Bill to Marge

*Dearest Marge,*

*Was I ever glad to get 2 letters from you, June 3 & 4 and 3 Registers but they were old, May 3,8,9.*

*I'm glad to hear Miekle is back to work and you can take it a little easier. I suppose John will really go on a good spree in Minn. Do you suppose he will lay up with that stuff. I remember one night he did, don't you?*

*The Third Army came out with an order today restricting all G.I.'s to the Co. at all times unless they have a pass. I don't know whether they are trying to get volunteers for the CBI or what but it don't make me no difference anyway because I never leave it except to go to a show or something like that. But a lot of the boys who have acquired girlfriends are really pissed off so I suppose there will be a lot of court martials coming up. They tell us lots of boys with 85 points or over have got V.D. so it is going to stop them going home for a while. I guess they have got prostitution in all the Co or Battalions now.*

*Our old platoon Sarg. left for the States today. He has quite a bit over a hundred points. You wanted to know* the name of the town I am in. It is Windischeschenbach. Little one, eh? I thought I had wrote you that before. It is about 100 miles north of Nurnberg.

We didn't do much today - had 1/2 hour exercises and 1 hr march and played ball this afternoon and then we got double deck wood bunks that we set up with board bottoms and we have our own straw mattresses and pillows so it isn't so bad. I got a bottom and the little diago from Philly sleeps above. He is sure pissed off at his wife for writing those v. mail or as we call it dehratrated shit all the time so he wrote and told her to throw all of it away that she's bought. If she sends any more of them, he's going to quit writing. The guys sure hate to get them and I think they take longer to come anyway. I found out today that I'm 7th in line to go to Paris or England so if they start taking them again, I'll be going that is, if I don't get the transfer or we don't move. But if they don't get transported any better, I won't get there till Christmas. In the Army, it's always "if" and "I hope".

We have guard again tonight and tomorrow but there are four of us who don't have to stand any. I think a few of the boys are getting kind of pissed off about it because we don't catch any of the details either. But I don't give a damn because when the war was on, we went on all the patrols when none of the others volunteered. Boy, but it has been cold here the last couple of days with a little rain mixed. Are you still having the cold weather at home or is it warming up? I suppose if it is you'll be able to go to the river once in a while. I wish you would take the folks down sometime too. It would do them good to go down. When this war finally ends and I get out of the Army, we'll sure spend a lot of time down there - more than we did last summer anyway.

Well, Marge, keep up the writing and a little more if you get time because I sure love to hear from you.

All my Love

Your Husband
Bill

*Windischeschenbach* is a town in the district of Neustadt (Waldnaab), in Bavaria, Germany. It is situated 14 km north of Weiden in der Oberpfalz. http://en.wikipedia.org/wiki/Windischeschenbach

On June 13, Orokey Peninsula, Okinawa was captured by the US Marines after killing 6,000 Japanese.

An overwhelming majority of the U.S. is against any compromise whatsoever in the Pacific war, according to the latest FORTUNE Survey of Public Opinion. More than 80% of the people questioned declared they would not settle for withdrawal of Japanese forces from China, Malaya, The Netherlands East Indies, etc. as a condition of leaving the Japanese homeland unoccupied. Like their Government, they stood for unconditional surrender - everywhere.

http://www.time.com/time/magazine/article/

June 14, 1945 - From Bill to Marge

Dearest Marge,

Well, Marge, got a letter from Ray tonight and a Register, May 5. Haven't got the Democrat for a long time now. I got a box from Ma to. It is the first one I got that was moldy but we ate about 1/2 of the candy and cookies. I sure put in another hard day today play-

With victory in sight at Okinawa, Fleet Admiral Chester W. Nimitz made a routine switch in his command team last week. Cold, calculating Admiral Raymond Ames Spruance and his Fifth Fleet staff were given a respite after four months of continuous sea duty, during which Iwo Jima was taken and Okinawa all but secured. Out with Spruance came hard-driving Admiral Richmond Kelly Turner, commander of the Fleet Amphibious Force, and gnomish Vice Admiral Marc Andrew Mitscher, the wizard of carrier war.

While Spruance and Mitscher set up temporary headquarters alongside Nimitz at Guam, to plan future operations, ebullient Admiral William Frederick (Bull) Halsey, Third Fleet boss, again took over the command at sea. With him as amphibious force commander went lean Vice Admiral Harry Wilbur Hill, and as commander of the fast carrier task forces, pint-sized, peppery Vice Admiral John Sidney McCain.

Halsey's Calling Cards. Halsey and McCain lost no time in throwing their first punch: the big battleships were promptly ordered to fire a few salvos of one-ton shells at Japanese positions on Okinawa. Said Halsey: "I just wanted to leave my calling card." Aircraft from McCain's carriers pounded airfields on Kyushu, closest of the Jap islands to Okinawa, and a nesting place for Kamikaze aircraft flying to attack the U.S. fleet. The first day the weather was atrocious; by the second day, the weather improved—but so did Jap fighter opposition. U.S. flyers reported that the enemy had a new, fast plane of high performance, and "very experienced pilots employing aggressive tactics similar to the Americans."

http://www.time.com/time/magazine/article/0,9171,775827,00.html#ixzz0keJlKSDt

ing pinochle all morning and slept all afternoon. Pretty rough, eh? I was supposed to go out on 24 hr outpost but one of the boys wanted to go in my place so I let him take it. He'll get a chance to do a little fraternizing that way. I read an article in the Stripes where the women in the States aren't going to like these fraternizers when they get home. Well, they had better stop and figure it out. Pretty damn hard to walk down the street and have some little kid or even grown up say Good Morning and then snub them. Besides everyday they get letters from their girls that say they are in love with someone else or are getting a divorce. So you can't blame a lot of them for taking out these girls. We've been in Germany now for nearly 5 months and hardly any of the guys have had passes to go to France or someplace where they can ever talk to anybody but G.I.'s. I know myself, I've talked with plenty of people here and really enjoy it. They are a lot of innocent people in my opinion - getting punished for what they didn't do. But Marge, you need not worry about me playing any woman while I'm away because I've found out it isn't too hard to get along without. I wrote you about this fraternization so you could see the guys side of it over here. They say because they killed our buddies, we should hate them but I think we killed more of them. If any thing, these people will really hate the Americans after this occupation if (it) going on awhile the way it is. I think as a whole most Germans like the Americans. I've got one of our Regimental papers that we get every day. I'll stick that in this envelope.

Well, Marge the guys want to turn the lights out so I better quit for tonight.

All my Love

Your Husband
Bill

June 15, 1945 - From Bill to Marge

I got 3 letters tonight, one from Arlene Wyscover, Paulsons, and one from you of June 7.

But you are cutting them kinda short, aren't you? How about a little of that gossip now and then. Don't tell me you don't know any because I know better. Arlene didn't have much to say except that Bill was back along the Rhine near Frankfort. Which is quite a long ways from here. He was sure lucky he stayed in the Regiment pool when we came over - about 2 weeks from *what LeMaster said in the letter I got from him. (He said) that both of them did and I was just there over night.*

*We haven't done much today, went to a ball game this morning and a movie this afternoon. "Humphrey Bogart" but I don't remember the name of it. By the way where did Verle go to school and what kind. You never did write and say anything about it except that she was leaving and she left. Maybe she won't like it and you can get her back a little later on. I'll have to quit writing now for a little while. The boys want me to take a little of their money. I'll tell you how it came out.*

*Well, I'm back again 3 hours later and 18 bucks ahead. Playing pinochle again how about it - do you ever play any more? We have a big inspection and parade tomorrow. I should be getting showered and washed up instead of playing cards. My rifle is plenty dirty too so I'll have to work like hell in the morning to get ready in time. We don't have anything to do from Sat. noon until Mon. though unless we catch guard again Sunday. I think only about half the guys go to church but I go to church every chance I get. We have a swell chaplain too. He really gives the sermons on morals and stealing. I would have probably had a lot of souvenirs if it weren't for him, he always told us the only thing we could take without it being stealing was off a prisoner or food or drink so that's what I went by. But as far as our orders were at first we could take anything we wanted to. Well, Marge, I sure do miss you and love you but I guess we'll be sweating it out for a while yet.*

*All my Love*

*Your Husband*
*Bill*

June 15, 1945 - From Bill to Marge

*Dearest Marge,*

*I got 2 letters tonight, one from the folks and one from you of May 31. It kinda sounds like you and the little one are having quite a time. I suppose you'll be taking him down fishing some one of these days, eh. I hope you take care of yourself now and let the bakery get along the best they can.*

*I hope they figure up the critical score the last of the month here, then we are supposed to know if we come home, stay here or go CBI or go to other outfits. I don't have very many points now but if they give credit for*

Joseph Clark Baldwin, dapper socialite New York Congressman, made a straight-faced proposal that U.S. film actors be "lend-leased" to Europe to re-educate the enemy: "Overnight they would be able to do more good in inspiring confidence in the Nazi and Fascist-trained youth of Europe than all of the unknown professional educators we are now contemplating sending abroad."

Fiorello H. LaGuardia, New York's fractious little Mayor, looked forward to a monthly radio broadcast over WJZ, and looked over his shoulder at one of his pet projects, the New York City Center of Music and Drama. Admitting that he had never attended a ballet performance there, he explained: "I'm so prejudiced against ballet. I can't be fair about it. It's the male ballet dancers I can't stand."

Mae West, always good for a quote or two, first told a Variety reporter that "a lot of loving is coming back from the war," then shook an admonishing finger at her sisters in arms: "Many wonderful men are already on the way home to their wives and sweethearts, and the lady who has been stepping out had best begin to polish off her low talk and shifty ways before he arrives."

http://www.time.com/time/magazine/article/

This letter is dated June 15 but was probably written on the 16th as he writes herein about the inspection that was supposed to happen the day after his last letter (above) and there is no letter dated June 16.

Paced by tanks, 38th Division infantrymen were storming a narrow gorge, its 500-ft. walls honeycombed with Japanese caves, leading to Wawa Dam east of Manila. The tanks stalled in the bouldered terrain. So they called up lanky Charles R. Oliver Jr., who a year ago was a Wortham, Tex. high-school student, gave him a bazooka and appointed him spearhead.

The bazooka was borrowed and Charlie noticed that the sight was broken. A runner started back to battalion headquarters for a new sight, but the attack could not wait. With two scouts on his flanks to protect him, Charlie and his bazooka loader moved forward, the men of A Company trailing cautiously behind.

They rounded a bend, started up a concrete path and saw a pair of 20-mm. Jap guns aimed down the trail. Charlie got them with a squirrel-hunter's "bark" shot, hitting the rock wall beside the guns and splattering them with shell and rock fragments. Next he blasted open the heavy steel doors of a Jap tunnel and set off a store of enemy ammunition.

Charlie moved nearer the dam, firing again & again: He saw four Jap huts half hidden by boulders on a hill across the river. He fired four rounds, demolished four huts. At the very end Charlie Oliver spoiled his record. He saw a small cave far up the opposite cliff, fired twice and missed both times. That brought his day's score down to 28 hits in 30 shots. When he reached the dam Charlie said that next time he wanted a bazooka with a sight on it.

http://www.time.com/time/magazine/article/0,9171,775828,00.html#ixzz0keLS0eOG

combat it helps like hell and if I don't have enough to stay here, I'll probably be home in a couple months. But then Marge, we can pray that it ends pretty quick. I remember you in my prayers every night to. I never realized when I was in the States how much I would miss you. Maybe I'll appreciate a good wife when I get home a little more, eh?

I'm getting where I smoke my pipe most of the time now. We only get a pack of cigarettes every 2 or 3 days now and I always have plenty left. We had inspection and a parade through town this morning. That's about all this afternoon. Glen Millers Band played at Div. Hq. A lot of the guys went but I didn't go because I figured there would be so many there, you wouldn't be able to get near it but tonight I went to a movie over to Battalion. I don't know the name of it but Barbara Stanwick was the main actor in it.

It is sure good the way these people pick up English. Tonight we went by 2 girls and one of the guys bellowed Hi, Kraut and she said "Kiss my ass" and most of the kids swear in English but don't know what they are saying.

Well, Marge, it is getting late now so guess I had better quit for tonight. I'm still loving and missing you.

All my Love

Your Husband
Bill

June 17, 1945 - From Bill to Marge

Dearest Marge,

I didn't get any mail yet tonight. I guess it hasn't come in yet but I'm still hoping I do. How do you like getting mail from me about every day now. A little better than when we were fighting, eh? A guy never got much time to think about home and mail then but we sure do now. I didn't do anything today except go to church. We had a high Mass at four o'clock this afternoon - with the Children's Choir again. I still can't get used to it, it seems just like being home. These people really go in for making their church's beautiful inside. The crucifix right above the tabernacle, usually, has a big reflective light in back of it. We had a big sermon today on married men choosing pussy over here and then expecting their wives not to go out. He was telling how it was the same for both of them, neither one had the right to. "You know - for better or worse!" Remember, it seems like a long time ago but when I get home again we'll sure make up for it.

How are your folks coming? Are they still up at Alberts (Albert Leet, Marge's brother in MN.) I suppose your Dad will be wanting to go to the river pretty quick.

Well Marge, I quit writing for about 2 hrs (ago) and am back again. Made $10 playing pinochle. And I also got 4 letters from you June 8, 2, 5, and 7th. I read the one the 8th but will read the others in the morning or after I get off guard. I go on in about 15 min. for 2 hrs and then again for 2 hrs. in the morning. When we have guard, we don't have any drill or any thing else that day. You wrote about Coppersmiths. Well, we used to try getting his business but never succeeded. I'm glad to hear you got it and tell Miekle you are running the business and whatever you do there is okay with me. I sure wish there was a chance to get somebody else for you. Wouldn't have to put up with his gripping and maybe it would be best if you have John keep on with some of the main things. In case Miekle gets the idea he is to good for that place again.

It kinda sounds like you are really doing the baby shopping. I'm glad to hear your folks are home again. How about it - are you getting quite a stomach on you now and widening out in the rear? I'll bet in one way you are glad I'm not home because I suppose I'd be kidding hell out of you. But I guess I'll wait until I get home. I see by the Stars and Stripes where 9 Divisions are leaving during June and July but the 90th still isn't scheduled to go. That we know of. We were issued Battle jackets today. They are pretty sharp looking. I suppose you have probably seen them at home by now. They are a dress jacket with a short waist. Well, better quit for now. I sure do love you with all my Heart and am hoping it will be over before long.

All my Love

Your Husband
Bill

June 18, 1945 - From Bill to Marge

Dearest Marge,

Well Marge, I got a letter from you again tonight. Boy, but I like to get them from you. You asked me about cable. We never used to have any and they haven't ever said anything lately about it. I know none of the guys

General Dwight D. Eisenhower, whose successes have not distorted his perspective, held up a restraining hand to 40,000 cheering, liberated American prisoners, and said: "Say, I'm just a G.I., not a movie star." Ike's response to an ovation in a London theater: "I wonder if you people realize what it means to me to be back here among friends, among people whose language I can almost speak."

http://www.time.com/time/magazine/article/

The US Army Battle Jacket was introduced in 1945, first to officers and later to the troops. It was more popularly known as the *Eisenhower Jacket*.

On June 18, William Joyce (*Lord Haw-Haw*) British radio traitor was charged with treason.

*ever got a cable or sent them. Now our mail will probably go faster. This letter I got from you today was postmarked the eleventh and this is the 18th so it only took 7 days to come. We had a young kid 20 years old with us that got killed the last of April. He just got a letter the day before he was killed that his wife had a baby. Boy, Marge, I think they are the kind that really hit me hard. Never getting a chance to see the baby or anything. He'd been with us about 1 1/2 months when he got it. Most of the guys usually got hit in the first 2 weeks and if they got through that, they usually lasted quite a while but there are very few men who last on the line 6 months in a infantry outfit.*

*I see by the Stars and Stripes out of 187,000 killed in this war that 116,000 of them were out of the Infantry. I could of got the purple heart when we crossed the Kiel (Kyll) River but I didn't know at the time they were going to count points so I didn't have the medics put me in for it.*

*About 3 of the Co. have them. We haven't been doing much all day today. I pulled a couple hrs guard this morning and went to a movie this afternoon but I had seen it about a week ago. We have to fall out for reveille and retreat every day and tonight at 5:30 when we fell out, I was asleep so they got me for being absent so I suppose I'll be on a few details tomorrow.*

*You said in your letter you could see I was wearing a ribbon in that picture. Well, if you look close you'll be able to see it is the Combat Badge. I've a got a ribbon here with one star on it that I got in Jan and it has been in my billfold ever since so I'll stick it in this letter. Well, I'll be getting a new one now with 3 stars on it. Vernon will only have 1 more than me. John only had one. They are issued for being in an attached to an outfit which fought in different sections. I guess the most anyone can have for the campaign is 5 and they count 5 points apiece as you probably know. I'm sure hoping we get points for our Combat Badge and time on the line. I don't know what I'm going to use to write on in a few more days because I'm just about out of paper and so are all the other guys. We can't go into houses and get it the way we used to. Have Luthers ever heard anything more from Junior? These doctors can sure fix guys up in a hurry now.*

*What's Riley doing now? You haven't mentioned in your letters whether he still is around and comes in*

In this letter Bill mentions that he *could of got the purple heart when we crossed the Kyll River*, but *didn't have the medics put me in for it*. He also mentions that he was awarded the Combat Badge and a ribbon with three stars.

The three stars signify having served in the campaigns of the Ardennes, Rhineland, and Central Europe.

U.S. and Chinese authorities coped with a new problem last week - "jeep girls," a slightly more commercial version of the U.S. bobbysoxer.

The people of Chungking were shocked even by the customs of the modernized coastal Chinese who retreated to the province six years ago. Chungking people believe that woman's place is in the home, that no nice girl goes out publicly with a man, that only a trull plays and drinks with a man, that marriages are arranged by parents and no nonsense.

In Chungking the U.S. Army employs many English-speaking Chinese girls, mostly from Hongkong, Shanghai and Tientsin. They have been brought up under Western influences. They like to dance, date boys, kid around. But when they dated U.S. soldiers, Chungking confused them with the jeep girls who ply their trade with great zest and professional abandon.

http://www.time.com/time/magazine/article/

*the bakery when he gets to town. I suppose with summer now they'll keep him pretty busy if he still is at the creamery. I suppose he is still trying to find himself a woman.*

*Have you ever heard from Marquardt yet? He should be home by now. I guess they are starting to fly the guys home in C5's now. I still don't know where in the hell I stand but I think I'll probably be home by August or a little later.*

*I quit writing for a couple hrs and went over to 3rd Battalion and took a good shower. I stayed under it about an hr, it sure felt good. That is the first one I've had since in Feb. Long time, eh? I think I'll write the folks yet tonight. Keep writing.*

*All my love*

*Your Husband*
*Bill*

June 18, 1945 - From Bill to Jim and Amanda

*Dear Folks,*

*Well folks, I'm getting around to writing again. I got a letter and a box of yours the other day. Sure swell to get them to. I've been getting mail about every day. We are still in Windischeschenbach about 100 miles north of Nuremberg near the Czech border in Bavaria. I'm kinda figuring on being here in August or along in there but we will never know anything for sure over here, I guess. I see by the Stars and Stripes where there are 9 more Divisions leaving here this month and (the) first of next month for home and then CBI. I haven't heard from Vern since I was down there so I don't know whether he is still there or not.*

*I sure hope they don't go direct (to the Pacific Theatre) anyway, if they lower the points, he will have enough to get out, I think. We don't do a hell of a lot here. A little drill and go on a few hikes. We usually get to go to a movie about 3 times a week. I was down and took a good shower tonight. The first I've had since in Feb. We still only have one pair pants and shirt and we've had them 3 months but Vernon fixed me up with some extra clothes when I was down there. I gave him one of the pistols I had so I only got one left anymore and I hope to bring it home with me when I come.*

*I suppose a lot of the guys are starting to come home on furlough now and will be for the next few months. I sure play a lot of pinochle over here. We play for 2 dol-*

U.S. railroads now face the war's worst jam. In his message to Congress last week, President Truman said: "Troop movements on the nation's railroads will become increasingly heavy from now on. I ask for full public cooperation in preventing any aggravation of this burden on domestic transportation, for it would slow down the rate at which soldiers can be reunited with their loved ones." But the President had described the picture in the mildest of terms.

Many of the 2,000,000 soldiers in U.S. camps are already shifting to the West Coast. Troops from Europe are already arriving and moving toward their homes with their parents, wives and sweethearts going to meet them. By the end of the month many of the same men will be moving over western roads toward the Pacific. And these movements will mount like a swelling flood.

The outlook, as far as Washington officials could see it at the moment :

For troop movements and furloughs, the Army now uses half the Pullmans in the country (total 8,753) and one-third of the coaches (total 39,244). To handle the load at its peak, some Office of Defense Transportation officials thought 4,000 to 5,000 more passenger cars would have to be taken from civilians.

In the first quarter after V-E day (to Aug. 8), an estimated 280,000 men will come back from Europe each month (to speed westward, go to various camps, scurry home on furloughs). In the second quarter (to Nov. 8) the figure will run around 395,000, possibly reaching a peak of 500,000, then tapering off to 270,000.

When the movement is in full tide, 25 full troop trains a day will be shuddering over the rails into San Francisco, Los Angeles, Seattle (at Midwest terminals they will be made up from 140 trains daily).

http://www.time.com/time/magazine/article/html

The Coat, Wool Serge, OD (olive drab) of the U.S. Army was also called the *service coat* and evolved during WW II from an all-purpose coat to one used in garrison only, not in the field.

However, it is questionable that the Army would issue wool serge in June for summer use and Bill may have been referring to summer uniforms that were also, of course, olive drab.

*lars a game and a dollar a bump. Most of the time but we only play to 100 instead of 150 so it makes it a pretty fast game. I've sent Marge home $120 since I've left the States and burned out quite a bit here and still got about $75 bucks but I've went broke a few times to. It's nothing to borrow money over here. Most any guy will loan you a hundred or so. Usually when the guys go to Paris and places, they have to borrow the money.*

*Liquor there is about 18 or 20 dollars a quart so it usually takes them quite a lot.*

*I started this letter last night but didn't get to finish it. We started playing cards and didn't quit till around 12 o'clock. I lost a little last night. We got issued new battle jackets yesterday. They are a dress jacket with a short waist. I hear we are going to get new O.D. to but I'll have to see that first. I was sure lucky, never getting lousy over here. Most of the boys did but they aren't to hard to get rid of them. Well folks, I better quit now. We are going to have a little game this morning.*

*Love*

*Bill*

June 19, 1945 - From Bill to Marge

*Dearest Marge,*

*Well, Marge, the mail hasn't come in yet tonight but I'm sure hoping I get some. I got a copy of our paper here. I'll send it to you. This town of Nuestadt is only 7 miles from here. Sure a pretty placc too. It turned out plenty hot here today for the first time in quite a while. The kind of weather I like to go fishing in.*

*When you get down to the cabin sometime, why don't you have the Wagner boy cut the weeds and finish the privy. I suppose they are getting plenty high by now. How's Stan coming with his romance by now. Does he ever get time to go fishing. I seen a swell place to fish today when we were on a hike so I'm going to try getting some grenades and try my luck.*

*The mail just came in. I got the Readers Digest, Democrat, and a Register but no letters so I'll have a little something to read now. I lost my ass playing cards today but still have enough left to make if back again in the next few days. We didn't do much today except go on a hike, take a little exercise, and played cards the rest of the day. Do you know I've still never had my ring off since you slipped it on that day. The watch sure keeps good time. I've been wearing it ever since I got* it. I don't suppose you have figured out where we are going to build our house yet after this war is over, have you? I guess we should have enough money to build it with, shouldn't we? I sure hope that day ain't too far away. Don't forget to get Dad something for his birthday. Maybe buy him a $50 bond he'll have it put away for ins. Is he still getting full now and then or is he leaving it alone? He should be able to save some money now if he is ever going to. John and Stan should both be kicking in at home. They are making enough anyway. Is John still spending it as fast as he makes it?

Well, Marge, keep saying a prayer now and then and maybe I'll be home with you some one of these days again. Still loving and missing you.

All my Love

Bill

June 20, 1945 - From Bill to Marge

Dearest Marge,

I sure hit the jackpot tonight. Got about 7 Registers but they were all a month old and the Democrat of May 23 and one letter from your mother, 2 from you and one from the folks. Dad even wrote a page in it. He says he hasn't taken a drink since I left. I'm sure glad to hear that but he said when Vernon and me got home he was going to take on a few. We still haven't heard anything more so I don't know whether I'll stay here or go home.

If they do let wives come over here, I don't think it will be for a year yet anyway. If there was a chance of having you come, we wouldn't let the bakery stop you. But by the time they start letting them come over, I'd probably have enough points to go to the States. Like some of the boys say only 10 or 12 months more overseas and they'll have enough points to get out. Oh, by the way I just happened to think I see a lot of the lakes here with pond lilies just starting to bloom. Remember you said they just grew around home. I was walking by a farmhouse the other day and saw a bunch of peacocks. Boy but they are sure a pretty bird. I've seen them a few other places in Germany before. Just about every family in Germany has rabbits, chickens, geese and some ducks. I was even in a few towns where the storks were on the nest on the tops of the chimneys. That was sure funny to see.

I went to the show this afternoon, mostly all newsreels of the war so I didn't care much for it - showing the

For Technical Sergeant William L. Brown of De Witt, Ark., it all began in New Guinea, where the 32nd Division commander badly needed a Jap prisoner to question, and promised a furlough as payment. Brown scurried off into the bush, brought back a live Jap, spent his leave in Australia and got married there.

When the division moved to Luzon, there were new terms: For every live Jap, one case of beer and a three-day pass to Manila. Sergeant Brown took a prisoner in a cave by persuading him to discard his hara-kiri grenade and come out. Then Brown picked up his beer and went to Manila.

Twenty-four hours after his return, Brown ran into a Jap officer who went after him with his saber. The Sergeant wrestled him down, took the saber as a souvenir, again collected his beer and went to Manila.

Two days after this return he copped one live prisoner with a flying tackle, turned him over to a second soldier to hold, then chased a second Jap, who promptly sat down and pulled out a hara-kiri grenade. Thoughtfully Sergeant Brown stopped, took out a cigarette and lit it. The Jap's face brightened. Brown replaced his .45 in its holster, walked up to the Jap and offered him a cigarette. The Jap put down his grenade for a moment to accept the gift. Brown went to Manila again.

http://www.time.com/time/magazine/article/0,9171,775914,00.html#ixzz0keUod3FV

At his headquarters on a Guam hilltop, Major General Curtis Emerson LeMay added up the results of three months massive B-29 attacks on Tokyo. Tough-minded, realistic Curt LeMay claimed nothing of which he could not be sure. The things of which he could be sure:

51.3 sq.mi. of Tokyo (46% of the built-up area) had been burned or bombed to ashes.

4,500,000 people who had lived in the area were now homeless.

50 Superforts had been lost—one per sq.mi. of devastation.

"We have destroyed all the target areas we have set out to destroy."

http://www.time.com/time/magazine/article/

Produced in 1944, *Between Two Women*, is an adaptation from a *Dr. Kildare* episode. Though Kildare is nowhere to be found, Lionel Barrymore is very much in evidence as Dr. Leonard Gillespie, crusty chief surgeon of Blair General Hospital. Gillespie's assistant is Dr. Red Adams (Van Johnson), who spends the early part of the film fending off the romantic advances of social worker Ruth Edley (Marilyn Maxwell). Adams is also romantically involved with ailing socialite Cynthia Grace (Lucille Bremer), who suffers from a life-threatening blood clot.

Unless Bill picked up another pistol before coming home, he failed to obey this order.

Frustration. It is remembered that less than two weeks ago they heard the 90th was part of the occupation.

weather and the fighting of the Belgium bulge, I think. Most of us guys remember it plenty well without them having to show it to us again. I busted the crystal on my watch getting on the truck but I think I can get a new one put on it at the jewelers in town. If I can fraternize for a few minutes. It cost $65 for fraternizing if you get caught so I hardly ever talk to any of these people any more.

Ma writes that John is broke and had to wire for money. What the hell is he doing with his money, anyway? He better start saving something. Times aren't going to last forever. It kinda sounds like from your mother's letter that they are figuring on taking the boat down to the river after the war. We'll have to buy a good motor and boat. I think I'm going to be lazy as hell when I get out of the Army. Well, Marge, I'd better quit for tonight. Take good care of yourself now.

All my love

Your Husband
Bill

June 21, 1945 - From Bill to Marge

Dearest Marge,

Well Marge I didn't get any letters tonight but got 3 Registers. I've been sure glad to get as much mail lately. We didn't do much today except we had a Battalion parade this afternoon. I don't mind the parades but we usually monkey around 3 or 4 hrs first. I went to the show tonight "Between Two Women" was the name of it. Good too.

When I got back, was it ever a mess. Everybody drunk and puking and raising hell. This place will really be a mess in the morning. They got about 4 or 5 barrels of beer and a couple barrels of whiskey so you can imagine what that would do to a company of men. I had one cup of beer and that is all. I don't get much kick out of drinking over here but I'll bet when I get home with you, we'll really tip a few. I had to quit for awhile to pull an hour guard. It sure was a mess around here. They were carrying guys in all the time.

We got orders today to turn in all our pistols. A couple more guys got killed with them, I guess. I just got the one left and I was going to bring it home when I come home. They had a list of the Divisions that were going to stay for occupation and the 90th wasn't listed on it but as I said before they change their minds about every *day on what they are going to do. I'm liable to be home yet before the baby comes. The days are going by pretty quick. It will be July and the old man's birthday. (Jim's birthday is 4th of July.) I'll bet he'll have to take on a few then. The day will never come soon enough for me to be home with you again. I sure pray every night that it ends soon. There is a pile of good boys getting killed every day it keeps on. I see by the paper they are burning hell out of all the cities. I sure hope the Japs haven't got any factories set up like the Germans did. We come through a lot of them that were never touched. Built in small towns on the side of big hills and forest and like that.*

*I'm still loving you with all my heart and missing you to beat hell. I'll be waiting for a letter from you again tomorrow.*

*All my Love*

*Your Husband*
*Bill*

June 22, 1945 - From Bill to Marge

*Dearest Marge,*

*I'm writing a little earlier today than I usually do. It's about one now and I usually won't (write) till after supper when the mail comes in. I see by the Democrat where they are still taking the guys. I suppose there are hardly any of the young guys around any more. There should start to be some of them getting out now or discharged. Maybe they'll grab a few of them good farmers now. I don't know whether I ever wrote you this before or not but we took a town one day and found a bunch of conscientious objectors. I didn't even think before they had such ones here.*

*The boys around here are sure pissed off at only getting a pack of cigarettes every 2 or 3 days and the Seniors (?) get 10 packs a week and come over and sell to us for a dollar or so a pack. Nice, eh? When we come out of the mess hall here there are about 8 or 10 kids standing there with little pails so if you have any coffee left in your cup, they hold out the pail for it. They like our coffee. Theirs is sure bad. The only way it is halfway fit to drink is with a little cognac in it. The nuns have a pretty nice strawberry patch here and I see they are ripe. Sure tempting but the guys have been leaving them alone. I slept just about all morning except for an hour guard and after I finish this letter, I will probably sleep this*

The enemy on Okinawa had been compressed into a minute fraction of the island's area - no more than 20 of its 485 sq. mi. - and U.S. ground forces called for fire support from the fleet's guns to soften another stubborn line, the last on which the enemy could stand. Along the Yaeju-Dake escarpment, 3,000 yds. long, 600 ft. high, including a 300-ft. cliff, perhaps half of the 15,000 or so surviving Japanese were dug in. They had scores of fortified caves, from each of which they would have to be burned by flamethrowers or blasted by grenades and satchel charges.

The U.S. fighting men doing the job had to face a curtain of fire from rifles, rockets, machine guns, 20-and 40-mm. guns and mortars. The balance of the enemy remnants fought with the same stubbornness on Oroku Peninsula.

As ever, the Japanese were relying on hopeless stratagems. With a group of seven soldiers, killed while trying to infiltrate Marine lines south of Naha, were two women, each armed with hand grenades.

Navy doctors reported that stores found in caves included large stocks of morphine, opium, heroin and cocaine, evidently for morale-building.

But Naha field, best air base on Okinawa, had been captured by the 4th Marines under husky, soft-voiced Colonel Alan Shapley, former Annapolis football star.

It was being repaired to give U.S. air forces room enough to take over the air defense of the island, and release the fleet for other projects.

Time Magazine
June 18, 1945

On June 21, the Battle of Okinawa ended.

Married. Judy Garland, 23, snub-nosed cinemingenue and Vincente Minnelli, 38, who directed her in *Meet Me In St. Louis*; she for the second time, he for the first; in Los Angeles; one week after she divorced Bandleader-Composer David (*Holiday For Strings*) Rose.

Married. Deanna Durbin, 23, round-faced cinema songstress and Felix Jackson, 43, German-born producer of her current film (*Can't Help Singing*); she for the second time, he for the fourth; in Las Vegas, Nev.

http://www.time.com/time/magazine/article/

On June 23, Eddie Arcaro riding aboard *Pavot* won the 77th Belmont Stakes with a time of 2:30.2.

In Tarakan the last organized Japanese defiance was broken.

Finally, The Word from on high but, as it turns out, not exactly prophetic.

afternoon because there is no show or anything. A lot of the guys went out to another town where we have a ball game. Well, here it is about 5 hours later. They made us all get out of the building for inspection and I took a tour around town. Had reveille and ate some then, and got the mail a little while ago. A letter from the folks and one from LeMasters and 2 from you - one letter with the pictures in. They are all right to. It's probably better that (illegible girls name) quit now than a little later on. I wrote you about Lucille. Did you try getting her or do you know of someone else to get? We should have quite a bit in bonds by now if you have been buying. We've been having a bond drive here but I didn't buy any tonight. We have to go to the show on venereal diseases. I suppose it will be the same one they showed us about 5 other times in the States. I guess there isn't any way of getting out of going either. I guess we are finally going to get a pack of cigarettes again tonight. We haven't had any for 3 or 4 days now. We get P.X. rations about once a month which is usually a candy bar, can of juice, bar of soap and razor blades and sometimes a couple cigars so you can see as quick as the fight is over, they started fucking the infantry a little more. So if you can have the girls fix me a box now and then.

Well, Marge, better quit for tonight. Keep on writing.

All my love

Your Husband
Bill

June 23, 1945 - From Bill to Marge

Dearest Marge,

Well Marge I borrowed a few sheets of paper so I'll be able to write a few more. The mail hasn't come in yet tonight but by the way, the more I look at them pictures, the more I think you should burn that hat. You don't look very big in that picture. We finally had to start buying our cigarettes today. We can buy 6 packs a week, a can of fruit juice, package of gum and bar of candy for a week at the PX.

We went to hear General Ernst talk today and he just came back from the States. He told us about the best news we have heard since we've been over here. He told us we were in Category II and he thought we would be home before the first of the year and we would either go to a base in China or stay in the States as strategic re-

*serve. He thought it would be the latter. Sounds pretty good, eh? And he should know what he is talking about. He is a 2 star General now.*

*All we did today was listen to him and they had the orchestra play for about a hour. I'm sticking in the re-bill (digest of Gen. Ernst's remarks) so you'll be able to tell a little more about it. I'm in the 2nd Battalion. The 773rd TD are the TD's (Tank Destroyer) attached to us in combat. We had about from 2 - 5 of them with our Battalion. There are historical places they write about. I've been to about all of them. Tomorrow we can go to Nuremberg if we want but I was there once so don't care to go again. Here it is Sat. night and me just sitting here writing a letter. I'll bet if I was home we'd be taking in a few about this time but it don't sound like it will be to long before we will again. Most of the guys here figure the only reason they aren't discharging more than they are now, is because they are afraid of unemployment if they left to many out now. I hear there is going to be a new point system come out next month. Maybe we'll get some points for time on the line and for our combat badges. There will be a lot of bitching if we don't any-way. By the way, a little later or if my mail is censored, you'll know I'm getting ready to go to redeployment and then it takes a month or more to get to the States. The mail just came in but I didn't have any but you've been doing all right. If I start getting a few boxes once in awhile. I haven't heard from Vernon since I was down there so I'm kinda beginning to think he has left. I'd just as soon the transfer don't go through now after hearing the news today. The order came out from our Captain today that he didn't care how drunk the guys get just so they didn't wreck the place. They did a good job of it here the other night. Have you ever heard anything from Marquardt yet? I'm sure wondering whether he got home yet or not. That pistol of mine I sent home with him takes a 9 mm shell in case anybody goes firing it. I had 2 clips full of ammo in it when I sent it but he might have had to take it out.*

*Well, Marge, keep up the writing.*
*All my love*

*Your Husband*
*Bill*

It was just after midday, on June 23 when thousands of Osaka workers had paused to bolt down meager lunches in the partly ruined Chicago of Japan. High in the heavy overcast the U.S. planes rode in - more than 400 B-29s and 150 escorting P-51 Mustang fighters. For three hours the planes were overhead. High-explosive bombs fell first, driving Japanese air-raid workers to the shelters. Then the fire bombs fell, destroying without interruption.

Sister city Kobe, 20 miles northwest, was still smouldering from an earlier attack. Flyers had driven through snow, fog, thunderheads, antiaircraft fire and fairly strong fighter opposition - but they had left Kobe "one hell of a hot place."

At week's end the planes came again, and this time added Nagoya in a three-way simultaneous rain of demolition bombs. Next day Superforts made their fourth strike of the week, bombing five Japanese industrial plants and repair bases in the Tokyo area.

The Superfortress teams had now hit most of Japan's large cities, and were preparing variations on their attack pattern. Tons of British pathfinder bombs had been shipped to the Marianas and would soon permit the 21st Bomber Command to bomb at night with greater precision. U.S. Army officers announced that fleets of 1,000 planes would soon smite Japan. Tokyo warned its medium and small-size cities to expect the worst. The big bombers were not the only planes that struck Japan. Kyushu Island, whence enemy planes attack Okinawa, was worked over for several days by U.S. fighters from carrier decks and land bases.

First-line flyers reported that Japan had a new defense fighter, faster, more maneuverable and better handled than anything they had seen before. Promptly the U.S. answered by unveiling the Grumman F-7F Tigercat.

Time Magazine - June 4, 1945

On June 24, a Victory Parade is held in Red Square in Moscow by the Soviets.

Little did Bill know what an important part of his life the VFW and the Vet's Club would become.

*Cinderella Girl* doesn't appear in Miss Leslie's bio but she did star with Ronald Reagan and George Murphy in the 1943 hit, *This is the Army*. As we know now, Murphy would become a US Senator and Reagan one of our greatest Presidents.

June 24, 1945 - From Bill to Marge

Dearest Marge,

I got 2 letters from you today, the 14th and 15th. The one with the paper about the V.F.W. and you joining. I didn't know they had it in Waukon yet. I know it is a good organization but I can't see much sense to me belonging while I'm over here but I'll probably be home before long so you can put me in if you want to.

I didn't know they had a woman's part of it though. It kinda sounds like they are getting all the fat women to join. How about it? I went to the show this afternoon. Joan Leslie in "Cinderella Girl". I didn't care much for it though but I didn't get back on time for Mass so I missed it. That's the first time since before the war ended so I guess after this I'll just have to forget about going to the show on Sunday.

I had my first coke today since I've left the States. I guess we will get 2 a week. It sure seems funny to have to pay for everything now. A lot of the boys are broke so they have been hitting me up. I still got $85.00 so not bad off. Liable to lose a little of it playing cards the next time but I usually come back a little stronger than before.

I doubt whether I'll ever get that trip to Paris or U.K. The way they are taking them only about one or two a month and I'm 5th or 6th on the list. Of course there are about 40 behind me that are still planning on going. I would of got a chance by now if it weren't for some of the old Staff Sgt.'s coming back and they went first. I see by the papers where about all the Generals over here are home or just came back. I see where Patton gave some of his prize speeches again, mostly bullshit the guys all think, but I guess he knows his stuff when it comes to directing troops but he sure drives the hell out of them. He always gave so many days to do a thing in and it had to be done. He took the big swastika from the Stadium at Nuremberg home for a souvenir, I guess.

Does Dorothy still think Freddy will have to go back overseas or will he be getting out before long? What do Harold's folks hear from him? I'd sure like to hear from him. I suppose Goldie is still taking care of her share of liquor and men around Clinton. I kinda doubt whether they will ever get married.

The letter I got from Ma the other day, she said John was home. I suppose he's pretty well fucked out after the Minn deal. Did he make it to Marshfield or not? Most *of the guys are laying around sleeping now. On Sunday we don't have anything to do. Well, here it is about 4 hrs later. I went to chow and read the Stars and Stripes and the Yank Magazine since I quit writing. We only get a few so the first ones to get them read it. You wait a day to get a hold of the Stripes because we don't get much of anything to read.*

*Well, Marge keep up the writing and say hello to Jack Wittlinger for me if he is still there.*

*All my Love*

*Your Husband*
*Bill*

June 25, 1945 - From Bill to Marge

*Dearest Marge,*

*Well, here goes again. There isn't even anything to write about anymore. The mail hasn't come in yet so I won't know for awhile whether I get any or not. I see by the S & S where most of our air mail letters are going by boat because of so much more since the war is over but I'm still getting yours in quick time so don't think I haven't been writing because it will eventually get there. Just got all washed and shaved up and am finally running out of blades. I'm still using the ones I brought from States so you can buy me a couple clips of blades and send them will you? I don't ever see any over here. Didn't do much again today. A little physical exercise and an hour march and we laid out in the woods most of that time. The mail just came in. I got one letter from you of June 6th. You still never wrote me where Veryle went to school or what kind.*

*We seen a training film "On to Tokyo". It only lasted a few minutes and then they answered a lot of questions all the G.I.'s were wondering about.*

*I hope the Japs surrender pretty quick or otherwise it probably will take a long time if the Infantry has to clean them all out. There shouldn't be a lot of guys from town coming home for CBI (China, Burma, India campaign) now with enough points for discharges. I would think all the Kosbau boys would have enough points.*

*I'm on K.P. tomorrow for the 2nd time since I've been over here. I've been pretty lucky staying off of it. Everyone gets there turn at it but some guys get it a little more often for fucking up. We got fatigues finally issued to us today that are work pants and shirt.*

*I bought some air mail envelopes tonight but don't*

Bill refers often to *Stars and Stripes* newspaper. Founded on 9 November, 1861 during the Civil War, this newspaper from, to and for our men in uniform has been in operation ever since.

It is now available both digitally and in print.

On June 25, with the Allied landing at Ternate Molukkas, the Imperial General Headquarters in Tokyo announce the final fall of Okinawa.

After his tumultuous European receptions, "Ike" Eisenhower invited correspondents in for a chat. For nearly an hour he stood, ramrod straight, answering all questions. Like a coach holding a post-mortem on a football game, he explained some plays and straightened out some disputed points.

Time Magazine
June 25, 1945

know where in hell I'll get paper to write on. They sure as hell never issue any for us to buy. I'm going downtown tomorrow and try my luck. Just so the S.G. don't pick me up because we aren't supposed to go in any place. Great life, eh? But it still beats going to the South Pacific all to hell.

Do you still go up to Kreebs as much as ever or have you quit going up since Dorothy came home? Say hello to your folks for me. It kinda sounds like in your letters your dad still has to have something to monkey with. I suppose them chickens will be just about the right size when I get home. What do you think? We don't get any too much to eat here. I guess they figure we aren't doing anything so they don't need to feed us to much. Glad to hear Earl Welsh is home. Has he been discharged or just on furlough? When ever you or the folks send a box, stick in a magazine or two because that is about all there is to do. Well, Marge, still loving and missing you.

All my love

Your Husband
Bill

On June 26, the United Nations Charter was signed.

June 26, 1945 - From Bill to Marge

Dearest Marge,

I'm a little late writing tonight because I just got back from the late show at Enbendrof (in Bavaria). Edward G. Robinson in "Mr. Winkle Goes to War." I got a letter from you of 17th, one from the folks, and one from Paulsons and 2 boxes from you with the stationary and hair oil. I don't think that candy ever tasted so good as it did tonight. All the boys said to tell you thanks. We ate all the candy before and after the show. I just had a cup of beer now that's about what I drink a day. We have a barrel of rum on tap too. We get 3 big shots a piece but I gave mine to one of the other boys. There aren't many of them very drunk yet tonight at least. I haven't seen any in our room.

Henpecked Mr. Winkle (Edward G. Robinson) is only too happy to go to war when he's drafted. Later his nagging wife (Ruth Warrick) and his neighbors are astonished when he returns home as a decorated war hero. *Mr. Winkle Goes to War* was released in 1944.

Boy but I sure needed this stationary you sent. I was wondering where I was going to get the paper to write you. I guess I got a pretty swell wife, eh? Sure love her to. I got your letter from Arlene and she said Bill had 3 stars and might get four. Well I know that is wrong because the last 2 stars haven't been issued yet and the way they work those stars are one - for over a certain period of time and for the time we have been overseas, there are only 3 stars for that period and the last two of *them haven't been issued yet.*

*If what LeMaster wrote me was true, Bill can only get 2 legally. Because you had to be assigned to a Division before the 26th of Jan to be titled to 3 stars and Bill and LeMaster were still in the replacement pool till the 1st of Feb. LeMaster said Bill was still there when he left and if he was cooking , well, the only action they get in on was a little artillery taking thru the roof and the likes. I sure got a kick out of LeMaster's letters. I've heard from him a few times now. He told me all about getting hit and that he didn't get much chance to even find out what it was all about.*

*I put in the day doing K.P. today. It's pretty soft here compared to in the States. I was sure glad to get the magazines to. As quick as the guys seen them, they all hollered 'next' on them. Well, Marge it is getting late and I guess I haven't anything else to say except I love you and take good care of yourself.*

*All my Love*

*Your Husband*
*Bill*

At last the victors met the German people. Not the Nazi Party, not the horror-masters of Buchenwald and Dachau, not the General Staff and the Wehrmacht, not Krupp's and I. G. Farbenindustrie, but the people, from whom all the evil and the vigor sprang.

The first consequence of this meeting was somewhat disturbing to the conquerors. In the inevitable amnesia of war, they had forgotten that they were fighting a people. It was easy to consider the German evil when Germany consisted of a tyrant and his tyrannies, of an army in impersonal battle, of bombs and submarines and, at the last, of the final anonymity - air attack without airmen.

Now, in the first long pause of peace, the conquerors found that Germany was 70,000,000 Germans.

http://www.time.com/time/magazine/article/

<u>June 27, 1945 - From Bill to Marge</u>

*Dearest Marge,*

*Well, Marge, I'm writing pretty early today because it will probably be late when I get back tonight. I am going to Amburg to a big U.S.O. show. There are 11 out of our platoon that get to go and I was one of them. I guess it is supposed to be pretty good. It has been raining most of the day and last night. I sure hope it quits before we leave. It's been cold today to. I see by that slips of Potratz's (bakery vendor) they are still getting a lot of stuff. How about the guy at Dorcester, Is he still getting much? Did you get a new girl yet? I sure hope you can find a good one.*

*We didn't do anything this morning because of the rain. I slept and read all morning. We have early chow at 3 o'clock and then we leave to go to Amburg. I've got the papers read and am starting on the magazines you sent. In a couple more days it will be six months since we were down in Kansas City. What a day and night, eh? It sure seems a lot longer than that but maybe it won't be that long before I'm home. We haven't heard any more about when we are going, but they are starting to plan trips for us to go to places of interest around here. So I guess we will probably be here all summer.*

Amberg lies on the Vils River, in the foothills of the Franconian Jura Mountains and the Bavarian Forest, southeast of Nürnberg. It was a distance from Bill's camp, the reason he had to leave in early afternoon.

A fortnight ago the House, led by Republicans and prodded by the Scripps-Howard press, cut OWI's (Office of War Information) appropriation from $42,000,000 to $18,000,000, a slash which would just about end OWI's activities in Europe and at home. But last week, as the Senate Appropriations Committee pondered this action, a galaxy of stars swooped to OWI's rescue.

President Truman flatly said that to abolish some of OWI's major functions now would "be a mistake." It was operating, said he, "in the interest of a nation still fighting a war which is far from over." Generals Marshall and Eisenhower pointed out that the Army's plans for information and education in Germany had all been based on OWI functions.

http://www.time.com/time/magazine/article/

Until Every One Comes Home.®

Unfortunately, the USO (United Service Organization) does not have detailed files on each individual who toured for the troops during WWII. During WWII, more than a million and a half volunteers and performers volunteered their time and talents to support the troops and gave more than 428,000 performances to a total audience of more than 200,000,000 G.I.s from 1941 to 1947.

You asked in your letter how I got a pass to go down and see Vernon. Well, I didn't. I just told Mac, that is one of our Lieutenants. He asked me when I was coming back so I told him probably Wed. So he said O.K. but if I got picked up or anything I would have been the same as AWOL. We didn't do any drinking except a little beer and that don't have any kick to it. So you see we were good boys. He's kept pretty busy most of the time, it looks to me. I haven't heard from him since I was down there so I kinda think maybe he has left. How's the young lad or lass is coming? Still kicking to beat hell? I suppose they annoy you plenty now. It sure is going to seem funny when I get home all the girls with young ones. I suppose Dorothy will get nice and fat like Maggie afterwards. I'll bet she'd burn if she could hear that. Well, Marge enough for now. I'll write you how the show is.

All my Love

Your Husband
Bill

P.S. You can send some more paper. I got plenty of envelopes so don't bother with them.

June 28, 1945 - From Bill to Marge

Dearest Marge,

Here it is 8 o'clock so I better be getting busy writing you. I didn't get any mail from you last night or tonight except the Democrat of April 4. Sometimes it takes a long time but it is better than not getting it.

The show was pretty good last night but I still think the Russian show we seen had better dancers. We rode about 100 miles to see it. I sure enjoyed the ride. We went through one place that was a big German training camp and airport. Boy, it was sure all bombed to hell. About every barracks was wiped out. Then we went though a couple factory towns. One of them was pretty well beat up with bombs but it was just the houses. The factories were hardly touched and probably can be started right up if they wanted to. Then I seen another place where they had crosses about fifteen ft high of Christ and the 2 thieves. A guy usually sees statues and crucifixes every little ways on the highways here. In town they are all over, even the houses have little grottos in the sides usually near the roof with the statues of the Blessed Virgin or some saint.

We got back from the show a little after 11. We didn't

*do anything today except one hrs march and we fucked off most of that. Then this afternoon I went to a show "Brewsters Millions" was the name of it with Dennis O'Keefe. Of course a show over here isn't like at home. The film usually busts 2 or 3 times during a show but it's sure something for amusement anyway. I hope you don't mind me writing on both sides of the paper. I figure it would go quick enough anyway. I think I'll write the folks yet tonight, if I don't get in a game of cards before then. There is only about 4 hrs darkness here now so it makes a long day of it.*

*One of the boys just got back from Paris and he is sure a mess. He's so all fucked out. He's hardly able to move. I guess he had a rough 3 days there. Do you suppose that will be all I'd be able to last when I get home? How about you? It hasn't been suffering, has it? I sure wish this war would end so we could be together again. Well, Marge, I'm still loving and missing you. Keep up the writing.*

*All my Love*

*Your Husband*
*Bill*

*Brewster's Millions* was released on April 1, 1945. In the movie, soon after his discharge from the Army, New Yorker Montague "Monty" L. Brewster learns that his long-forgotten uncle, who made a fortune in Bolivian tin, has died and left him eight million dollars. The unemployed Monty, who is engaged to secretary Peggy Gray, is ecstatic over his good fortune, but learns from his uncle's executor, Swearengen Jones, that the will stipulates that he must spend one million dollars by noon on his thirtieth birthday in order to receive the balance of seven million.

June 28, 1945 - From Bill to Jim and Amanda

*Dear Folks,*

*I'm getting around to writing again. I got a letter of June 17 from you the other night. I've been getting the Register, Democrat and Readers Digest right along. Sure glad to get them to. We haven't heard anymore of when we will be home but it will probably be late in the fall anyway. Probably in time to eat a few of them chickens, eh? But I'd sooner sweat it out over here than in China. We have quite a bit of entertainment now. Went to a USO show last night that was pretty good and then I went to a movie this afternoon. I see by the papers here they are getting pretty tight on the food rations. Well, it couldn't be much worse than over here. We don't get a hell of a lot to eat. Every now and then they break down and feed us good for a couple days but then we really go light on it the next few. I see in the papers where we are getting cigarettes and candy every day but for the last 20 days we got 6 packs of cigarettes and one little chocolate bar and 1/3 as big as a regular bar. I don't know where in hell it is all going to but us guys in the Infantry sure as hell aren't getting it. I haven't heard from Vernon since I was down there. I*

There is an order written on the outside of this envelope for the bakery. It must have been a phone order on Thursday that Marge took as she was reading the letter.

24 Sandwich
12 white
12 dark
For Golf Club

On June 28, the Polish Provisional Government of National Unity was put in place by the Soviet Union.

On June 29, 20.6 cm of rain fell in Litchville, North Dakota setting a state record.

Ruthenia, formerly part of Czechoslokavia becomes part of the Ukrainian Soviet State.

Generalissimo Chiang Kai-shek tightened up his Government in a threefold move last week.

As directed by the recent Kuomintang Congress (TIME, June 4), the Kuomintang Standing Committee ordered the abolition of all Party branches in the Army and schools, and the popular election of all provincial and district People's Councils. When & if executed, these orders would mark the end of one-party tutelage and the beginning of constitutional democracy in Free China.

In a move to check corruption in handling military supplies, a five-man military tribunal sentenced to death three high officers in the Chungking supply service: Major General Liang Lin (former mayor of Changsha), Major General Huang Yao, Colonel Pao Yunfei. Liang was convicted of "stealing military materials and of squeeze and extortion." Huang was convicted of receiving 4,100,000 Chinese dollars ($205,000 official rate) rake-off in purchasing military supplies. Pao had made 1,400,000 Chinese dollars from a building contract. All three were shot.

At the same time the Ministries of the Interior and Social Affairs cracked down on the press. New, strict regulations forbade Chinese newspapermen to write anything against the interest of the nation, required all Chinese newspapermen to join Chinese press associations, which are supervised by local representatives of the Ministry of Social Affairs.

Time Magazine

*don't know whether he is still there or not but I kinda doubt it.*

*Yes, I'm still using the cigarette lighter. It works good yet to. We have been in this town of Windischeschenbach, a town in Bavaria, for over a month now but we go to other towns to go to shows. One of the other Battalions have the theater here. I got a couple boxes from Marge the other day. They sure were good too. Of course, here everybody shares so a guy don't get to much out of one. I'm still figuring on going to Paris but they haven't been sending many only one or two a month and there are still 5 ahead of me to go. But if I get there and have any money, I'll try to send you something. We can't buy one thing in Germany here to send home. I could buy things but they wouldn't go through the mail here though. Well, say hello to the kids for me and don't forget to write.*

*Your son,*

*Bill*

June 29, 1945 - From Bill to Marge

*Dearest Marge,*

*I didn't get any letters tonight but I got 3 Registers. I guess the mail hasn't been coming in the last few days because there has only been about 6 letters for 50 some men in our platoon now. Sometimes in combat, we had about 15-20 men. We got our rations for the next few weeks. 6 packs of cigarettes. I hope whoever is getting our candy and stuff that we are supposed to be getting, is enjoying it. We got 7 qt. of Cognac to but I leave it alone. Some of the boys are a little drunk all ready.*

*I didn't do much today except a little close drill and a march. That's about all. I finished reading the magazine you sent this afternoon and played a little pinochle. There was a show tonight but I couldn't go because we have guard tonight and I've got 8 hrs. to pull. Long time, eh? It's our chickenshit Captain's idea of having formal guard post so there are only 9 men on and 3 posts to take care of so it makes it 8 hrs apiece but I guess we shouldn't kick because we have things pretty soft compared to some of the other outfits. I see by the Stars and Stripes where there are a couple more divisions going home for training. That makes 12 now.*

*I suppose you still listen for the news and read the papers yet, but I guess it took for me to get overseas to get you started reading them. (Bill was always a reader and enjoyed his daily paper). Every little magazine or paper that comes around here is sure well read. How's the money situation at the bakery. Still making it?*

*We get paid tomorrow. I guess but it don't do much good. There is nothing to buy with it. How are you coming by now? Getting mighty fat, I'll bet? I'd sure like to be home with you but I guess it won't be for a while yet but you had better take good care of yourself, if you do have to let the bakery go to hell. How old is Stan now anyway? I think it is sixteen but am not sure. You and John better try to talk him out of coming in the service but if he's going to, get him to get in the Navy because he will always have his meals and a fairly good place to sleep and he'll never get that in the Army.*

*Well, Marge, quitting for now. Still loving you.*

*All my Love*

*Your Husband*
*Bill*

June 30, 1945 - From Bill to Marge

*Dearest Marge,*

*Well Marge, I didn't get any letters tonight but got 3 Registers. I guess the mail must be coming by boat now because nobody is getting much. I sure miss your letters when I don't get them every day. I got a couple pictures here that were taken a few days after the war ended. The one is of our full squad. In the other picture this Harnist is the one who has his arm on my shoulder. Was about the best B.A.R man in the Co. He just got back from the hospital when it was taken. The other picture was taken when we're the only G.I.'s in a town. We were guarding a factory there. A girl at the factory took the picture that has her dog in the picture. One of the biggest German police dogs I ever seen.*

*The boys have one all talking about what they would be doing now if they were home on Sat. night. What do you suppose we'd be doing? Having a few nips probably. We had cognac rations again tonight but I gave mine to Harnist again. I haven't even taken mine yet. I see by our Regimental paper that we are going to get some wine and champagne, that's where I'll come in for a little.*

*Boy, but it was sure funny when I was standing guard last night. The guys were coming in at all hours, even some came in about 7 this morning, after laying up with Heiny cunt all night. If we stay here much longer, some*

On the White House appointment list were five notable callers - three marines, an Army private, and volcanic General George Smith Patton Jr.

Patton made news by going in unarmed. But he took his riding crop along, waved it rakishly at the cheering White House staff. When a reporter asked about his ivory-handled pistol, Georgie quipped: "Oh, that's my social pistol."

The other fighting men got the Congressional Medal of Honor, in a homey ceremony on the White House lawn. Reading the citations, Harry Truman got stuck when he came to "Peleliu Island," called on brown-haired, heavy-set Medal Winner Major Everett P. Pope of Wollaston. Mass, to pronounce it. Next time he reached the same name, the President got grins all around by ducking the pronunciation, substituting the phrase "on that same island named a while ago."

Said onetime Artilleryman Harry Truman to the medal winners: "I congratulate you. . . . I'd rather have that medal than be President."

http://www.time.com/time/magazine/article/

The US Army infantry squad of nine men was tactically organized around a single BAR (Browning Automatic Rifle). The US Marine Corp squad of thirteen men was organized around three fire-teams, each organized around a BAR. The much greater fire power of a Marine platoon with its nine BARs over the Army platoon with its four BARs was a great combat advantage.

*of them will probably want to be bringing some of them back to the States with them. I'll get to Mass tomorrow all right but I missed last Sunday for the first time in a long time. Well, Marge, I guess I better quit. The boys want the lights out but I'll be dreaming of you.*

*All my Love*

*Your Husband*
*Bill*

<u>*July 1, 1945 - From Bill to Marge*</u>

*Dearest Marge,*

*I got a letter from you today of the 19th and one from Veryle. She didn't have much to say except about the Radio Training. I never knew before what kind of a school she was in. She must be nuts to be taking up Radio with all that the Army and Navy have trained and will probably be releasing if this war ever ends. I told her if she decided she didn't like it, we could always find a job for her at the bakery. How's the bakery going now anyway? Have you found another girl yet? I sure hope so. I came back from Mass a little while ago. He sure gave a hot sermon about the guys out screwing everything. The choir sang a couple songs in English. They are sure good to. We have a collection box the same as at home only the money goes for rebuilding the churches in Belgium and France. I usually kick in a couple bucks because there is nothing else to spend the money for over here. I made about $20 playing pinochle this morning and then lost about 40 playing poker but still ahead over here. I've got about $120 bucks now. Of course have to buy a few cigarettes once in awhile. You can get from $1-5 a pack so you see money don't have much value to us guys here. A guy who don't smoke can do all right with his cigarettes.*

*One of the other Co's got their liquor ration last night and raised hell. One guy shot himself, another chased a G.I. down through town and shot a rifle out of his hands and I guess there was plenty more. Went on, I guess they won't get any more liquor from now on.*

*It has sure been cold here for the last week now. Lots of rain for the first of July. I suppose it is getting pretty hot there by now with the Fourth coming up. I suppose a lot of drunks too. Just wait till I get in the States again. I'll sure hang on a good one, been a long time now.*

*We are going to have General Ernest over tomorrow for inspection. I sure hope he don't show. Lot of the guys*

On July 1, Allied troops landed on Balikpapabn, Borneo in Indonesia.

The first of July, a story of a recent conversation between Generals Eisenhower and Zhukov went the rounds of the occupation forces last week.

Zhukov: "We have some German synthetic oil plants that we captured. . . . We have been unable to get them operating. I understand you have some running. . . . Could some of our experts come over and see. . . ?"

Eisenhower: "Certainly, send them over. We will show them how to do it."

Zhukov: "You mean you do not have to ask your Government?"

Eisenhower: "Of course not. Send them over."

Zhukov was astounded and pleased. He was also unable to return the favor.

http://www.time.com/time/magazine/article/

*are beginning to figure we will be one of the next divisions to go to embarkation but I don't think so, but if we are, we would probably be home in Sept.*

*Well I got to write to LeMaster yet, so I'd better quit. I never heard from Wyscover yet.*

*All my Love*

*Your Husband*
*Bill*

## July 2, 1945 - From Bill to Marge

*Dearest Marge,*

*Well, Marge, I didn't get any mail from you tonight but got 2 Registers. Didn't do much today except go out on the range and fire a few clips. I guess we will every week from now on to kinda keep in practice. My watch quit working today so I took it and one of my other ones down to the jeweler to get them fixed. They got a big "off limits" sign on the door but I had to get them fixed so I went in anyway. They'll be done Wed. If there isn't too much the matter with them. I just hope a Sgt "the same as M.P." don't catch me going in or it will cost me $75. I bought 5 packs of cigarettes last night for $5. The English are sure making money off of us guys. They get ammunition, cigarettes and candy for nothing and really get the price from us guys for it and the amount we get, they ought to shove it up their ass because it don't amount to anything.*

*I spend $35 for a P38 from one of the boys who went broke and I turned down $50 for it about 15 min. later. I'll probably wind up selling it yet, because we aren't supposed to have any pistols anymore and I've got 2 under my pillow now. I went to a show tonight "Till We Meet Again". I think that was the name of it with Ray Milland. Good show to. It's still cold and rainy here, but it looks like the people around here will all have big capes. They are starting to build the railroad bridges now. There are 3 of them that are blown. Our Division took all these towns around here about 3 weeks before the war ended.*

*I'm still about the same weight and every thing, I think, as when I left home. I was a little heavier about a month ago but I think I've lost a little since. They aren't feeding us so much. We had a good dinner tonight though. Chicken, potatoes and gravy, peaches, bread and coffee. How are you and the Kreebs getting along now? Do you still go up? I'll bet they're sure cozy with you now.*

Less than two months after the aircraft carrier Franklin had been hit off Kyushu by two Japanese bombs and turned into a floating inferno, the same fate befell her elder, more experienced sister, the Bunker Hill. The circumstances were astonishingly similar: the ship was at flight quarters (launching planes). The enemy aircraft dived through the Bunker Hill's own combat air patrol so suddenly that they could not be splashed by U.S. fighters.

A Zeke (old-type Zero) dropped a delayed-action bomb which penetrated the Bunker Hill's flight deck, went out through the ship's side and burst over the water. But the Zeke itself crashed on the after half of the carrier's deck, crowded with 34 loaded planes, ready to go. That kindled a raging fire. Then a Judy (dive bomber) dropped a 500-pounder through the flight deck, and crashed into the base of the island structure. The Bunker Hill's fight for life was on.

The Bunker Hill's fight for survival lasted through many agonizing hours. Part of the Marine detachment stayed in an ovenlike compartment, throwing bombs and rockets overboard. When the explosions ended and the fires were out, the chaplains led volunteers in a search for the dead; 352 men had died to save their ship. Time Magazine

During the filming of *Reap the Wild Wind* (1942), Ray Milland's character was to have curly hair. Milland's hair was naturally straight, so the studio used hot curling irons on his hair to achieve the effect. Milland felt that it was this procedure that caused him to go prematurely bald, forcing him to go from leading man to supporting player earlier than he would have wished. He was never in a film called *Till We Meet Again.*

There was a 1940 film by that name starring George Brent and Merle Oberon.

In historical accounts about the 90th Division, much is made in respect to the number of casualties from D-Day to V-E Day. Bill mentions in this letter that from the time he entered combat (January 13) until V-E Day (May 7) all but himself and one other soldier in his company were wounded or killed. (There were approximately 200 troops in his company F.)

Ray really has reason to call you fat-stuff now, eh? I'd sure like to be home with you in one way, but if I stay here for 3 months yet, I think we'll have a good chance of staying in the States (and not fight in the Pacific) unless things get bad like the breakthrough over here.

Boy, Marge I'd sure hate like hell to ever put in another winter like the last one. I don't know whether I ever wrote you this before or not but I joined this Co. at Bastogne and we went into the attack the next afternoon about 8 or 10 miles from there. So if you look on the map, you can see where it is at. Of all the guys I came in with, I don't think any of them were killed but Marquardt and myself were the only two that weren't evacuated.

I'm sure hoping I hear from you tomorrow. I suppose you aren't getting my mail very good either now. I guess most of it is going by boat. Still loving and thinking of you.

All my Love

Your Husband
Bill

July 3, 1945 - From Bill to Marge

Dearest Marge,

I didn't get any mail from you tonight but got a letter from Vernon. He's in Southern France, near Marseilles but has probably left for the South Pacific by now. Its sure rough that he has to go without a furlough in the States and he has about enough points to get out. He still hasn't got his Staff rating back. I sometimes think that our C. O. is chicken shit but he don't break his men for little things. There hasn't been anybody broke (reduced in rank) in our Co. yet that I know of. Well, tomorrow is the July 4. Dad's birthday. I suppose a lot of booze floating around. We have a parade about 30 miles from here in the morning and then I'm figuring on going to Regensburg, which is about 60 miles from here. I don't know if anything is going on there or not but I can see the sights anyway. We have to get up early in the morning because we leave here on trucks at 7:30 in the morning for the parade.

I had a drink of wine tonight. We had 1 1/2 qts for the squad, made about a drink a piece. Well it kinda looks like I won't get down to the cabin to do any fishing this summer. How are they doing? They catching any?

We didn't do anything today. It rained again and

Japan groped for a way to meet total disaster. In a "personal message," broadcast by Radio Tokyo, Emperor Hirohito told his people that they faced a crisis "unprecedented in scope in our national history."

A commentator declared it highly possible that the Emperor would invoke his supreme authority in the crisis. His powers would override all existing laws and exceed even the sweeping powers granted Premier Suzuki's Cabinet by the Imperial Diet (Parliament) last fortnight.

Said Radio Tokyo: "Personal government by the Emperor, based on the tradition and sentiment of the Japanese nation, is more deeply rooted than government by law and can meet more successfully what is occasioned by the gravity of the situation. [It is like] parental authority by which parents do anything they deem absolutely necessary for their children's welfare. . . ."

http://www.time.com/time/magazine/article/html

was pretty cold so we didn't have to go out. I played pinochle most of the day. Broke about even I guess. We get a lecture every night now on Venereal Diseases. I guess there is quite a bit of clap around now. Lot of the guys have girlfriends they are with about every afternoon and night. I suppose if they could, some of them would marry them and bring them back to the States. But you needn't worry about me. I've still been leaving them alone.

Well, Marge guess I better quit for tonight. I sure hope I hear from you tomorrow. Take care of yourself now.

All my Love

Your Husband
Bill

P.S. Send a box if you have time.

July 4, 1945 - From Bill to Marge

Dearest Marge,

I'm sure sorry you haven't been getting my mail very good. I got 3 letters from you tonight from the 19th, 22nd, and 24th. I knew you wouldn't think much of the idea of me asking for a transfer but I didn't think you realize what this Inf. is like in combat. Guys who never said a prayer before in their life find times when they do especially when they are throwing 88's or screaming mimies** at you. I don't think it will go through now, because they are on them to go to CBI. I'm sure glad to because I kinda doubt if we will see combat in the South Pacific unless things get really rough. The rumor is now we will be leaving here before long and be home in the last of Sept or early Oct but I don't think it will be quite that soon. It will probably be 2 months from the time we move from Germany until I get back in Iowa. So if I am writing before long that we are moving out of Germany, don't expect me home right away. In one way none of us boys are too anxious to get home because about the first 20 divisions or so will be heading for combat in CBI and there has been 12 left already that are already on the way.

It rained again today so we didn't have the parade or go to Regensburg so I played cards all day, pinochle, hearts and casino. Kind of unlucky day for me too. I lost about $70 so I have to get on their ass tomorrow. We had a cognac and champagne ration today. I traded my cognac for champagne but still only had about a glass.

*Screaming Mimi* is the nickname for the *nebelwerfer*, a piece of German World War II rocket artillery.

The *Nebelwerfer* ("Smoke Launcher") was a World War II German series of weapons designed to deliver chemical weapons. They were initially developed by and assigned to the Wehrmacht's Chemical Troops (Nebeltruppen). They were primarily intended to deliver poison gas and smoke shells, although a high-explosive shell was developed for their Nebelwerfers from the beginning. Initially two different mortars were fielded before they were replaced by a variety of rocket launchers ranging in size from 15 to 32 centimetres (5.9 to 13 in). The thin walls of the rockets had the great advantage of allowing much larger quantities of gases, fluids or high-explosive to be delivered than artillery or even mortar shells of the same weight. Nebelwerfers were used in every campaign of the German Army during World War II with the exception of the Balkan Campaign. One rocket was even adapted for air-to-air use against Allied bombers.

Wikipedia Encyclopedia

Marge is nearly seven months pregnant. Although we do not have any of her letters to Bill during June and July, it is obvious, from Bill's account, that the stress of her pregnancy and that of running the bakery, is taking its toll on Marge. Bill reassures her that he is excited about the baby....and that, if the stress is too much for Marge, "you can always lock it (the bakery) up".

On July 5, the US officially declares the liberation of the Philippines.

*Boy but that's the real stuff. This was bottled in 1927 so it should have been good - Some that the Hienies stole in France. The one thing the Germans took out of France was plenty of liquor. When we came through the Rhine and Moselle country, they had barrels of wine as big as gasoline storage tanks back in the States. I was in one wine cellar when we were cleaning out a town and myself and another guy were in it about a hour, sampling. They must have had about 20 of them barrels plus the bottled stuff. The same white wine is the only kind I like. I never could go to their sweet red wine.*

*The way you sounded in your letter, you must think I don't like the idea of the baby. Well, Marge I'll put you straight now. I'm just as glad as you are. I'm sorry I can't be home with you. If the baby worry's you too much, you know we can always lock it up or see if Ma won't help you out taking care of the money and making out the orders. You have sure been doing a swell job of it. How much are you paying the girls and John, Ray and Stan now?*

*I went down and got my watches back from the jeweler today. He put in a new crystal too. They are both running good now. Cost me 11 1/2 Heinie marks, which lots of the boys have that they accumulated coming through Germany. That would be $1.15 in our money. Pretty cheap, eh?*

*I don't know how I ever got along without a watch at home because I was sure lost without this one for a couple of days. I'm glad to hear it has finally warmed up enough to go fishing. Tell your folks to catch a few for me too. What do your folks think about the baby? Do you think they like the idea? When we build our house after the war, I'd like to have a statue of the Blessed Virgin built in over the doorway like some of them do over here. It sure looks nice. Well, Marge, I'll be dreaming of you and loving you more than ever.*

*All my love*

*Your Husband*
*Bill*

<u>July 5, 1945 - From Bill to Marge</u>

*Dearest Marge,*

*I didn't get any mail tonight except the Register but I'm hoping for some tomorrow. We didn't do much today except a little exercises and one hour march and we put in most of that laying in the woods. Pretty rough,* eh? Then this afternoon I watched the ball game. Our Co beat H. Co by 10 to 1. Tonight I went to a movie in the theater down town here. The first show was a German war film. It was sure good to but the shells coming in was just like it was when they were tossing them at us and then they had a regular show like in the States. Only all in German. These were German shows that they had before we took over here. It was a musical and everything - something like a show you see off Broadway at home. It had lots of good dancing and everything. We could make out, most of what was going on in the rest of it. They had one beauty in it that did a dance a little rawer than any you see in the States. Did the Hula and there wasn't much covering it either. The boys really went for it. There was a sound system and music in it just about the same as at home.

A few of our boys are going to the Field Artillery on detached service to train them Infantry tactics. The rumors are getting a little stronger and that we will be moving back out of the Germany the last of this month to do some training for CBI before we go home. I sure am hoping you are still all right but I'll bet you really look like you swallowed a watermelon. How about it? I suppose you hate to walk down the street or do you try doing a little camouflaging? Well Marge, I'll probably be home about the time the baby has a good pair of lungs and it will probably be playing with those tits instead of me. Or do you suppose I'll still be able to.

This place is like a madhouse tonight. One of the boys the bottom came out of his bunk and he nailed up the bottom. There are a few of them drunk raising hell with rifles but I don't think they will shoot anybody. Well, Marge, keep up the writing.

All my Love

Your Husband
Bill

The U.S. picked up some more Pacific real estate last week as troops landed unopposed on Kume Island (20 sq.mi.), 50 miles beyond Okinawa in the East China Sea, only 345 miles short of the China coast. Another airfield might be bulldozed out of Kume's forested hillsides, and Okinawa's left flank would be made more secure against attacking Jap planes. Radio Tokyo reported U.S. minesweepers clearing the way for an invasion of Okino Erabu (15 sq.mi.), 40 miles northeast of Okinawa. This suburban property would give similar protection to Okinawa's right flank.

http://www.time.com/time/magazine/article/

July 6, 1945 - From Bill to Marge

Dearest Marge,

I'm still doing okay. Got 4 letters from you tonight of the 21 to 25th and the Register. You mentioned in one of your letters of Pat Campbell coming home. I figured he'd be overseas by now because he came into the Army a month or so after I did. You also wrote that John Dotseth and Marcella (Robinson) said I probably could get out now but I've never seen any thing in the paper

On July 6, Nicaragua became the first nation to formally accept the United Nations Charter.

President Harry S. Truman signed an executive order establishing the Medal of Freedom.

Field Marshal Sir Bernard Law Montgomery last week noted a new form of German sabotage. He said that German women were wearing fewer & fewer clothes, thereby undermining the U.S. and British Armies' non-fraternization policy.

G.I.s and Tommies bore out the Field Marshal's story. German girls in brief shorts and halters systematically sunned themselves in full view of U.S. engineers building a bridge over the Weser River. Sometimes the girls shed the halters.

Military policemen under orders to arrest fraternizers had their patience tried by a girl who patted her backside and whispered "verboten" every time she passed.

Summer weather and human nature presumably had something to do with the national display of legs and skin. But the effect on U.S. and British troops was exactly what the Field Marshal feared. "If you leave your hat on, and don't smile," said G.I.s, "it's not fraternization."

http://www.time.com/time/magazine/article/.html

*about releasing them for business but you check on it and do what you can about it. I used to think we were fighting for something but don't anymore. They could of ended the war months ago if they wanted to because that was all that was on the radio in foreign languages about Japan trying to make peace terms. The German and Italians were telling us the news that came over about 3 times a day.*

*We are supposed to move to another building in the morning but the Colonel is seeing if he can't leave us here. I sure hope so because if we move, we'll be in a big factory with the whole Battalion and things will be a lot rougher. We didn't do much today because it rained most of the day. Played a little cards but didn't do very good, broke about even. I'm sure sorry to hear you have been having so much trouble keeping a girl. I guess there is no way I can help over here. I thought Hubert Dayton was dead or else I wouldn't have wrote about her. I can just see Riley strutting around next door. I suppose he puts in a lot of time to. Say hello to him for me the next time you see him. They must keep him pretty busy when he don't come in.*

*I quit for about an hour but am back again. We got arguing about different battles we were in, mostly on using white phosphorus shells. "Which is against the Geneva Convention." We were using a lot of them by the end of the war. See by the paper where the Japs and Americans are both using them in the CBI. We got our P.X. rations again today. A little better than before 6 packs cigarettes, 2 cans tobacco, 3 candy bars, 1 package of gum, 2 rolls of candy, 1 bar of soap, 1 cigar, 1 can of pineapple juice, Cost of $1.05 Cheap enough anyway. I hope we keep on getting this much. I got the stamps in your letter today so will start using them. Sometimes it's kinda hard to buy airmail envelopes. I don't know whether I'll ever make a baker again when I get home or not. This Army is sure makes a man lazy. Another one of our cooks is leaving for the States for discharge but I'm not going to try getting in the kitchen now because I don't think it would be permanent anyway and they do get a pretty good workout. I suppose you have a hell of a job making out my writing. I usually write letters on my knee sitting on the bunk and I can't write that way so it makes it all the harder.*

*All my love*

*Your Husband Bill*

July 7, 1945 - From Bill to Marge

Dearest Marge,

How are you and the little one coming by now? Is he still kicking hell out of you or is it going to be a girl. I guess it won't make much difference to me because you know how well I like kids anyway. I got 3 letters from you tonight, 2 of the 10th of June and 1 of the 25th and also one from the folks. Ma wanted to know if it was all right to try getting me out and I told her yes but even if they can, it takes quite a while to go through the channels. We are going to move tomorrow to the factory. On Sunday as usual, the Army always moves on our time. I don't see much sense to it, if we were going to be leaving here in a couple weeks, at least that's what the rumors are.

I sold the P-38 last night for \$60. I bought it for \$35 in the first of the week so I did pretty good on it. I went to a movie this afternoon but I didn't know the name of it. It rained again today. It seems like it does it about every day. You wrote wanting to know who to have for godparents for the baby, I thought you were going to have Stan and Marie Kreeb (she did) and they are sure all right with me. The folks have been godparents plenty of times already. You said in your letters that you kid Stan about just taking his girl friend home from skating. Do you mean to say that he still hasn't broke down and taken her to any shows or anything?

I'm getting plenty of tobacco now, so if you have sent any, don't send me more because I think I'll be able to get enough now. I guess us guys have been bitching so much they are loosening up with it. I wrote a letter to the folks and one to Jack Whittinger tonight. He wrote me a long time ago and I never answered it before so I thought I'd better. The folks said he is in Waukon for the summer. He's probably been in by now. He's a good baker if you could have him but I don't think he would work nights very long. I sure hope you have found a good girl by now. If you could find a woman who needed the job, it probably would be your best bet. I sure wish I was home so you wouldn't have to worry about it now.

Eitzen must have some big orders now to get that much stuff on a Sat. What time do you have to start packing it anyway? Well, Marge, I still pray that the Lord looks after you while I'm gone.

All my love

Your Husband Bill

Will the rationing of autos, refrigerators, and many other civilian items be necessary after Japan quits? Last week, the Wall Street Journal got its fingers on a confidential War Production Board report and announced that WPB is planning a postwar rationing system. Actually, WPB's survey was prepared for a special contingency: that Japan might be defeated in perhaps six months, before reconverted plants "are in full production and before military cutbacks have become fully effective."
http://www.time.com/time/magazine/article/

Corporal John C. Corbett of the 8th Marines had won a signal honor. He picked up a stone and hurled it with all his strength from the low cliffs of southern Okinawa into the blue waters which lapped the shore. That stone's splash meant that the eleven-week drive by U.S. forces from the center of the island had at last reached the southern tip.

The last-ditch Japanese defenders were split into pockets no more than a thousand yards square; Fleet Admiral Nimitz announced that organized resistance had ended. There was mopping-up still to be done: a few hundred of the enemy held out with machine guns, rifles and grenades. In the final pockets many of the enemy were killed; some committed hara-kiri with grenades or by jumping off the cliffs; some surrendered.

To the Japanese, the cost of defeat on Okinawa was staggering.

They had lost a base within 400 miles of their home islands, only 1,100 miles from Tokyo; this base would soon be the springboard for vast assaults on their homeland. They had lost (by preliminary count) 98,564 men killed and 4,500 captured.

http://www.time.com/time/magazine/article/.html

## July 7, 1945 - From Bill to Jim and Amanda

*Dear Folks,*

*I got a letter from you tonight of June 24th so will answer it right away. From the sound of your letter, you would think I didn't answer questions.*

*1. Well, I wrote you I was down to see Vernon and he was going to CBI.*

*2. He's left, I got a letter from him the first of the week and he was near Marseilles getting ready to leave.*

*3. I wanted to get in with him because it would be nice for us and to get out of this infantry.*

*4. It's all right for you to be getting me out if you think you can.*

*Well, I guess that is answering all your questions pretty well for now.*

*We are getting fairly good chow now. Plenty of tobacco again but not enough cigarettes. I've bought some for a dollar a pack. I go to about 4-5 shows of some kind a week. The Red Cross girls were here the other day with coffee and doughnuts. They come about once a month.*

*We are going to move in the morning but just to another building in this town. I hear we will be moving back out of Germany some time the last of this month. You can tell dad I was thinking of him on the fourth. I had a little champagne to drink but that was all. We have a bar downstairs where they have cognac and beer but most of the time I hardly every drink any of the beer anymore and I don't care for cognac. I'll bet he took on a few though. I'm glad you are getting a chance to go to Marshfield. I'll bet they will all be glad to see you. When I get out of this army, I would like to go up there again and go over to see Aunt Lydia.*

*I've been getting the full Register but its usually about a month old. Still all right though. I've been getting the Reader's Digest every month lately. I'll probably be getting the August one in a week or so. It comes fast. I'll have to write Jack Whittlinger in a letter tonight. I heard from him a while back but never knew where to write to.*

*Well you had better get them chicks growing and fattened up. I'll probably be home in a couple months. Do what you can about that other.*

*Love,*

*Your Son,*
*Bill*

July 8, 1945 - From Bill to Marge

Dearest Marge,

Well Marge, I'm getting busy and writing again tonight. No letters tonight but 2 Registers. I've been working to beat hell all day. We moved into our new home for a while. It is a big factory. Our whole Battalion will be in it which is close to a thousand men. I got done about 8 o'clock and went down, took a shower and changed clothes. We have nice showers here with plenty of hot water and I have really got a nice bunk for a change. I saw a nice spring setting outside and I thought it would just about fit mine so I carried it up and it fits swell. It's sure going to beat them boards all to hell but I'll bet somebody in Headquarters will be cursing. We're on the 3rd floor and in our room there are probably a hundred guys - 2 platoons. I was talking to one of the officers for a while tonight and he said we will be taking our training and maneuvers for the South Pacific over here instead of in the States so if that is the case, it will probably be December before we get home. I think we will have things a lot rougher here because the Battalion is all together and they will be lot stricter about every thing. I didn't get to Mass this morning but I'll try not to miss anymore.

I took my clothes up to a woman's house to have her wash them for me. Gave her 1/2 bar of soap to do it with and told her I would give her a pack of tobacco and package of gum to do it. She was all smiles then. Here is what I had: 3 towels, 2 sets of underwear, 2 sets of OD, 7 pairs of socks and a few handkerchiefs. Cheap enough, eh? I'm sure tired tonight but feel good for a change. This is about the first work I ever did overseas. A guy gets tired from marching and drilling but I have always hated it because I never could see where I was doing any good. I always like to work if it is something I liked.

Well, Marge, I am going to bed as quick as I finish this letter. Don't know whether I'll sleep or not because there are 3 radios going and a guy playing the piano so you can imagine what it is like. Say hello to your folks for me. I hope they have some good luck fishing this summer.

All my Love

Your Husband
Bill

Into New York Harbor last week steamed four Army transports carrying nearly 15,000 soldiers of the 86th Infantry, the first complete division to be shipped out of Europe for redeployment to the Pacific. For these men the war was far from over. But immediately ahead was home and a furlough.

Among 4,070 soldiers on the U.S.S. General Brooke was Pfc. Philip W. Small, 21, of Burnham, Me. It was early afternoon and hot before Pfc. Small finally staggered down the gangplank, bent under his barracks bag, sweating in his heavy O.D.s and battle jacket. By late afternoon —filled with anticipation and excitement—he was riding across the New Jersey flatlands with the rest of Company I of the 342nd Infantry Regiment.

His main and almost sole wish was for lighter clothes. At Camp Kilmer he got them: summer tans discarded by Air Forces cadets. Some of the caps even had Air Forces piping, which Pfc. Small and his pals promptly ripped off. "An infantryman can't ever look good," Small observed.

http://www.time.com/time/magazine/article/.html

Bill's perspective on the German people and on the taking of German prisoners is very interesting. As is evident in many letters, his feelings are not shared with a number of other occupation forces.

Last week the man who has been fighting the Japanese longer than any other world leader gave his answers to some of the war's persistent questions. In Chungking, at his first press conference since 1941, Generalissimo Chiang Kai-shek gave this estimate of the situation:

An Allied landing on the China coast is needed - the sooner the better. But when the Allies have successfully invaded Japan itself, then Chinese troops should be able to deal with any Japanese forces left on the Asiatic mainland.

Japanese surrender is unlikely, and the process of battering Japan into final, total defeat will probably take more than a year and a half, thus running on into 1947.

http://www.time.com/time/magazine/article/

July 9, 1945 - From Bill to Marge

*Dearest Marge,*

*I got a letter of Jun 28 and also a box with the magazines, fruit juice, tobacco and the box of Johnson Chocolates. They were sure good to and I got my share of them. I've still got the fruit juice. Will drink it tomorrow. How about having the girls fix me up a box like that every now and then but leave out the tobacco because I think we will start getting enough now. I've got some more news for you. It had a list of the Divisions in the Stars and Stripes and when we were going home and the 90th is listed to go in Dec. so I guess General Ernest told us the truth a while back. So it looks like I won't be home until Dec. or Jan unless they are able to move troops quicker than they plan. I'm sure anxious to get home but I'd sooner sweat it out here a little longer than go to CBI and most of the boys figure the same.*

*The Germans put on a show tonight that was good. Good dancing and also a good magician. I sure hope I never live to see the day when we were all living under some other country. You can't imagine what it is like. I don't think the Americans are any better than the Germans. These people have had about everything they own stolen from them. A lot of guys sent everything home. Watches, silverware and about everything. Most of them (Germans) will do about anything for you for nothing. All the women offer to wash your clothes and things like that. It is not uncommon to see some German standing along the creek and see some G.I. walk up and push him in and things like that. It sure burns me up. I guess I'm not what you call patriotic if that's what it is supposed to be. I never could see this kicking a man when he was down. I seen quite a few Germans get their faces lifted after they were taken prisoners and a few of them shot to.*

*I turned in quite a few prisoners but none of them got touched after they surrendered. Some of the guys got pissed off at me a few times because I wouldn't let them work them over but I always figured it was just getting some of your buddies killed because it was bound to get back to them. One time in the Siegfried line when about 20 of us were taking a pillbox, we got a bunch of prisoners out of it. We searched them and started to send them back when a bunch came off the side of us to surrender. They had machine guns trained on us all the time and waited to see how we treated their buddies before they opened up on us. They saw we let them keep their packs and grub and weren't treating them rough so they hollered " Surrender" and came a running. So Marge, don't believe like the papers say that they are all killers and like war. They could never convince me of it. From what I've seen the S.S. is altogether different. They could have saved a lot of trouble if they never turned them loose. They are devils all right. I've seen lots of these people who hated them worse than we did and I don't think they were putting it on either.*

*I got a few postcards here. I will send most of them, one of Austria, one of the boys just come back from there. I might get there by and by. One a week goes out of our platoon and they draw for it. There is about 50 in the platoon now so I don't know how my luck will be. I'm 4th on the list to go to Paris or the U.K. and they take 2 a month for there now so I should make it in August or Sept. Well, Marge, I'll start reading your magazines pretty quick. Still loving and missing you.*

*All my love*

*Yur Husband*
*Bill*

July 10, 1945 - From Bill to Marge

*Dearest Marge,*

*I'm writing a little earlier than usual tonight because we have another German movie. I guess they will show it outside up against the building. We had one last night after dark but I don't remember the name of it. Good show though. I didn't get any mail from you tonight but got the Readers Digest. Two of the magazines you sent me in that box, you had sent before so try not to do it again because I sure go for anything to read at all.*

*I was up and got my clothes from the woman who washed and pressed them. She did a nice job on them too. Her son was there who probably is about 20 - a good looking kid. He was telling me about getting hit at St. Lo (France). He was in the German tanker corps. He was telling how rough our artillery was. He got it in the arm but not to bad. He's luckier than most of them. You see a lot of one-legged farmer soldiers hobbling around over here. We had two guys murdered here in the last couple of days. They were out walking in the woods so we don't know how they got killed yet but I suppose it was some fanatic. We are not supposed to go out alone anyway but we got orders again tonight to always be*

When President James Garfield lay fatally wounded by an assassin's bullet at the White House in 1881, Vice President Chester Allen Arthur was dangerously ill. Had Arthur also died, there would have been no immediately available successor to the White House. The next in line was the Senate's President pro tem, but Congress was not in session and had elected no such officer. As a result of this and other crises, Congress in 1886 passed a new Presidential Succession Act, making the Secretary of State next in line after the Vice President.

Last week Harry Truman, as he took off for the West Coast on his first plane trip as President, asked Congress for another succession law. Its provisions: make the Speaker of the House first in line, and after him the Senate President pro tem. After them would come the Secretary of State and other Cabinet officers, as prescribed in the 1886 Act.

Said the President: The law should be changed because, in effect (by appointment of a new Secretary of State), the President could choose his own successor. He did not believe that the President should have such power. The two Congressional leaders, he said, were more logical successors because they came closest to being elected by all the voters of the nation. He did not have to remind Congress that the present Secretary of State is young Ed Stettinius, a personable and energetic man, but neither an experienced nor an elected official.

http://www.time.com/time/magazine/article/.html

On July 10, Admiral Marc Mitscher was named chief of the United States Navy staff.

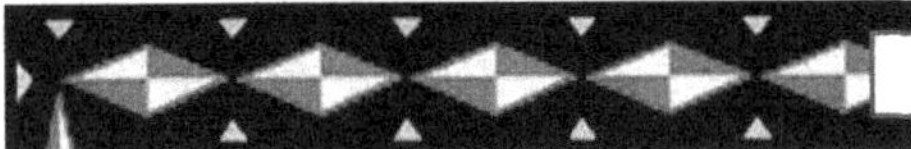



The ship's mail had just been thrown aboard, and throughout the destroyer there was that warm excitement, stimulation and laughter which always follows the operation.

The executive officer was a young one and he liked his men.

I saw him that morning as we lay off the beach at Tarakan leaning on the rail, an enlisted man beside him, a letter in his hands. He was reading. Then he folded the letter deliberately, put his arm around the sailor's shoulders, and handed him the letter. A moment later he appeared beside me on the bridge. He lighted a cigarette.

A signal man standing nearby whispered: "The smoking lamp is out, sir." He jerked into consciousness, rubbed out his cigarette. He turned to me: "That's the third one we've had this month. And this time it's the best man we've got on the ship. I've watched that kid change slowly from a Midwest farmer to the best machinist's mate I've seen in the Navy. When we wanted a job done we turned it over to him and that was like saying the job was done. But he's through now. He's through for a while anyway. We'll keep him busy. We'll keep him ticking. But we won't give him anything to do that has any responsibility connected with it."

He was mad. He just handed me the letter and said: 'This is the first I've had from my wife in six months.'

"I knew what it was. I didn't have to read it. It was short. They always are.

" 'Dear James,' it read, 'I know you will understand. I've met the only man in the world and I want you to give me a divorce.

Time Magazine
July 9, 1945

with a buddy and have enough ammo on us. Lot of the guys were getting where they never carried rifles or ammo and had dates off in the hills a mile or so where they would meet them. Another one of our boys just came back from the hospital. He had pretty tough luck in one way. He came to the Co in Feb. and was with us about a week and got hit. Then he came back and was with us less than 24 hour and got hit again. I sure hope he has better luck now.

Well how are you coming by now? Still getting hell kicked out of you? I'll bet you wouldn't be nice to sleep with now, eh? Have you been down to the cabin lately? I guess I won't be home for fishing or hunting either one if we don't leave here till in Dec. I just heard over the radio where Japan has been sending out peace feelers again. I sure hope it amounts to something this time. It will sure save a pile of lives if they don't have to go into Japan. Remember last year at this time, we spent a lot of it down to the river. What I wouldn't give for them times now. Does Emmet go down to his cabin yet? Well, Marge, write and let me know all the news.

All my Love

Your Husband
Bill

July 11, 1945 - From Bill to Marge

Dearest Marge,

I received 3 letters from you today and one from Sister Joseph thanking us for the donation. She also sent me a prayer book and medal with a nice long letter-five pages. She knew some of the Sisters that taught me and also was telling what a good worker and a good boy Stan is.

I'll try answer some of the things you had in your letters. One thing was about when I burnt my hair. I don't remember just how it happened but it was from candle I leaned over. You said you had thought Vernon hadn't seen that much combat to get 4 stars. I don't think he has seen any. You can be back in England and still get the stars. Just so you are over here during that period of time. It is for an assigned to an outfit. I wouldn't be afraid to bet that 80% of the guys you see wearing stars have actually never seen a day of combat. Lot of them might say they have but haven't. That article of Gammach about the combat badge is a lot of truth. It is one thing that not many are allowed to wear unless they saw

*combat but the guys like that in Div. Headquarters that have a fairly safe job get them. They are the only ones I know of who I don't think should get them. There was nobody any gladder than us guys on the line were to see the line medics get the combat badge. They just got it a while back and they earned it. Every time we advance they were right with us, one to every platoon and when hell broke loose, it kept them plenty busy patching guys up. Our platoon medic was one of the best. He would run out in machine gun and rifle fire to get guys. Some who thought they couldn't walk; he could convince them that they weren't hit bad and get them to get up and run back to a safe place.*

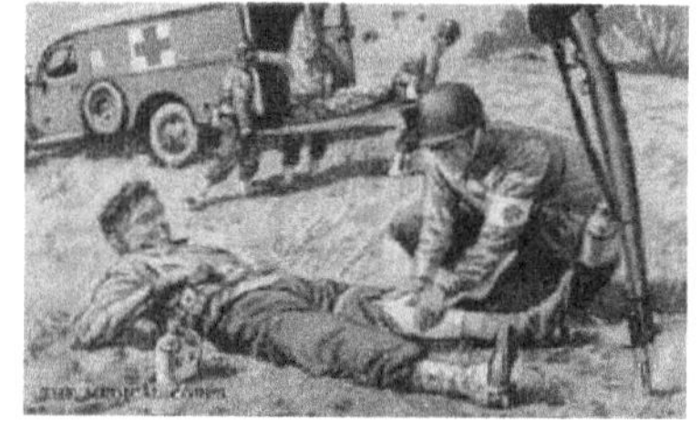

Combat Medics Badge

*We are supposed to have General Patton here tomorrow so they are getting things fixed up around here but I don't think he'll show up anyway so I'm not doing anything. I suppose I should straighten my things out a little. We are starting to get a few clothes issued now - I even got a sleeping bag but I use mine for a pillow. I never would sleep in one in combat so there is no sense starting now.*

*We have got about 60 or 100 P.W.'s (Prisoners of War) working around here. Good workers to but I'd sure hate to eat their meals. I thought ours were bad enough but I notice theirs today. It looks like all they get for the 3 meals is a little potato soup and a slice of black bread. They eat outside our mess hall, sitting around in the dirt and trash. Most of them have their mess kits they had when they were in the German Army but those that don't, use a can or something like that to eat out of. I guess they pick up enough butts around for smoking. That's one thing the civilians have very little of is tobacco but the German soldiers all used to have a lot of cigarettes. I smoked their cigarettes sometimes for a day or two at a time and they are sure lousy. Just about like an English cigarette but couldn't be choosey when I ran out and there weren't many days we didn't take some prisoners. Our P.X. opened today so I went over and got my ration for a week: 6 packs cigarettes, 1 coke, 3 candy bars and that's the ration for this week.*

*We didn't do much today. Had a little exercise and close order drill this morning and then we had a clothing inspection this afternoon and I slept all during that except for about 2 minutes while they checked my clothes. I usually listen to the news at midnight. That's when most of it comes over. It's been sounding pretty good but*

It is written in the Senjikun, Japan's code of battle ethics, that "I will never suffer the disgrace of being taken alive. ... I will offer up the courage of my soul and calmly rejoice in living by the eternal principles."

On Okinawa the unworthy soldier who had cooked for Lieut. General Mitsuru Ushijima, Japanese commander, told the story: on the night of June 21 he was ordered to prepare a No. 1 dinner for an important occasion. This he served at 10 o'clock to Ushijima and his chief of staff, Lieut. General Isamu Cho. Five hours later the cook was told that the ceremony was about to occur. Forty minutes after that Ushijima and Cho appeared, wearing dress uniform with medals, their boots highly polished.

On a narrow ledge overlooking the sea at the southern end of Okinawa the two Generals whispered to each other. They knelt side by side on a patchwork quilt covered by a white sheet (the color of death). Ushijima's aide stepped forward, bowed, handed each General a gleaming knife. The knives had been half covered with white cloth, so that the aide did not touch the sacred metal.

The Generals opened their blouses, unbuckled their belts. Ushijima leaned forward and with both hands pressed the blade against his belly. One of his adjutants did not wait for the knife to plunge deep. With his razor-sharp saber he lopped off his superior's head. General Cho leaned forward against his blade. The adjutant swung again. Orderlies took the bodies away.

General Cho had left his own epitaph: "Twenty-second day, sixth month, 20th year of Showa era. I depart without regret, fear, shame or obligation. Age on departure 51 years."

Throughout Japan there would be great rejoicing.

http://www.time.com/timeticle/

I sure hope the Japs surrender so our boys don't have to invade Japan because I think the amount of casualties will be terrible high. One of the boys was leaning over another one's shoulder reading the letter he was writing to his wife. Now they are razzing the hell out of him kidding him about getting ready to go on another honeymoon before going to CBI.

I wrote you it was in the Stars and Stripes that our Division would leave here for home in Dec. so don't figure on me being home for awhile yet. Maybe I'll make it for Christmas this year. I sure hope so anyway. I sure do love and miss you, Marge. I know you'll be just as happy as I will be when we get together again!!

All my love

Your Husband
Bill

July 12, 1945 - From Bill to Marge

Dearest Marge,

I received 2 letters from you today, dated the 29th of June. Sure good to hear from you so often. We get our mail in the afternoon now since the Battalion is all in the same town and building. It is sure funny you haven't heard from Marquardt yet. He should be out of the Army by now but maybe he's waiting till after he gets a little time at home before he comes down. I sure wanted to get that pistol home because I thought a lot of it. I see in one of these magazines you sent where they are the best pistols in the world today. Also a German Sauer pistol is one of the best. I've got one of them yet too. We didn't have the General here today, just as I figured but they tell us now he's liable to come tomorrow. Also hear we start taking basic again either this Monday or the next just like back at Camp Hood but I'm not as dumb about the Army now as I was then so it shouldn't be too bad. I see by the papers where the Japs are still sending out peace feelings. I sure hope our War Mongrels do something about it but to my notion I think there are too many cordian (?) men who are making a name for themselves to want to quit.

We aren't allowed to fire our guns except in self defense any more because a couple of the boys were drinking last night and shot a couple of krauts. Don't know what they do with them but they'll get a court martial. It kinda sounds like John likes his whiskey just as good as ever, just so he stays sober enough to work during

the week. Do you think he will ever settle down and get married? I hope he does before he gets much older. He should be saving some money by now but I suppose he spends it all. I'll sure get a kick out of seeing Stan doing the courting when I get home. He's got it pretty lucky with her working in the theatre. I suppose he's even got her talked into letting him in for nothing? How about it?

Keep up the writing.
All my Love

Your Husband
Bill

This letter was sent to Bill from Vesta, MN (located near Redwood City, MN) and then sent to Marge from Bill on July 23.

At long last Bill knows that Marquardt made it home and that his pistol is safe.

The letter does give some insight into conditions at home.

<u>July 12, 1945 - From Dennis Marquardt to Bill</u>

Hello, Bill

What are you doing, where are you and why? I wrote a few weeks ago but haven't heard from you yet. By god, you'd better write or I'll have to join the army and come back over there. You wouldn't want me to do that, would you?

Boy this civilian life is really rough. I get up at 11:30 just about every day. Next week I'm going to have to get up at 7:00. That's going to be rough.

Dad's going fishing for a week so I guess that leaves me with the hardware store. I've sure been hitting all the high spots since I'm back. I haven't had a chance to get down to your place yet. I still have the pistol and its in a safe keeping (place) until I get there or see you someway. I offered a woman $500.00 for a 1938 Chev Coupe a little while ago. Don't know if she'll sell it or not. You can't buy anything with tires on it unless it's a hell of a price. I can buy a V-8 for $300 but the tires are shot.

I don't know what else to write about. Take it easy and by, go, you'd better write or I'll be over and kick the ---- out of you.

A buddy

"Mark"

<u>July 13, 1945 - From Bill to Marge</u>

Dearest Marge,

I received a letter from you today of June 25th and you sure seemed hot about something I wrote about the baby but I can't remember saying anything. But if I did it was

just kidding because I want it just as bad as you do. I sure hope you aren't feeling to bad these days. How about the rear? Hasn't it widened out yet? I'll bet you get kidded plenty. Say hello to Dorothy and the rest of the kids for me. I got a letter from Marquardt tonight and he just got his discharge. He said he was going to drive down there as quick as he picked up a tire but was going fishing for a few days with his dad first. He sure is happy to be out and here's another guy who will be if the day ever comes. We didn't do much today except about 2 hours marching but we had our battle jackets on and shirt collars buttoned. We sure sweated our asses off because this was about the hottest day we have had. I see by the Stars and Stripes where 500,000 have left here for the States since V.E. day so I suppose by the time we leave, they will have about a million and a half or 2 million. Lot of men, eh? I seen a show again last night. "Janie" was the name of it. I don't know whether we are getting new shows now or not but the ones we used to get sometimes were 3 or 4 years old. I still like to see shows as good as ever.

*Janie* is the story of Janie, a scatter-brained and high spirited teenage girl living in the small town of Hortonville. World War II causes the establishment of an army camp just outside town. Janie and her bobby soxer friends have their hearts set aflutter by the prospect of so many young soldiers residing near-by. Produced in 1944 it starred Joyce Reynalds, Robert Hutton and Edward Arnold.

I was laying down along the creek or river this afternoon and it sure makes me lonesome when I think of all the good times we used to have at the river. Maybe next summer we will be able to spend them again. I'm sure hoping so anyway. I'm glad Freddy gets home with Dorothy once in a while now. Does she have any trouble keeping Mary away from him?

How's (illegible) doing anyway? Still screwing them all. Does she still hear from (illegible)? I've never heard from Paul Anderson. Why don't you send me his address and I'll write him. I'm getting so I write a few more letters than I used to because a guy sure likes to get them.

Well, Marge, still loving and missing you. How about having the girls fix me a box with something to read and some writing paper.

All my Love

Your Husband
Bill

July 14, 1945 - From Bill to Marge

On July 14, the Unites States battleship *South Dakota* becomes the first ship to bombard Japan.

Dear Marge,

I didn't get any mail tonight except 2 Registers. I guess I've been pretty lucky because I usually get some every day. I haven't had a Democrat for a month now. I wonder if they quit sending it or something. This is the *last 3 sheets of paper I got. I probably have to bum some for awhile. We didn't do much today - had inspections this morning and we usually have from Sat. noon till Monday morning off if we don't catch guard or detail. Monday we start taking basic training over for about 2 months and then we go on maneuvers. The training schedule isn't too bad the first week but lots of lectures and we have 8 hrs. training a day plus the time you spend cleaning up and retreat and reveille and then we have to wear these damn jackets if we go outside at all. It is getting hotter than hell here the last few days.*

*I went up town for a while this afternoon and had a few beers, beautiful tavern. It had a big nice backroom in it. We went in and they had one table all set up nice and the barmaid told us the officers were coming for beer and dinner and we had better come back after while but we had to stick around to see what officers and when they came. It was 3 Sgt's, then there were some M.P.'s but they couldn't do nothing to us because we caught them redhanded so we drank beer for about an hr. and left and they had theirs. The beer we got uptown is better than what we get but a guy could drink a barrel of it and never get a buzz on.*

*I had a chance to go to Austria tomorrow to see Hitler's hideout or Beurchesgardens. It's a 4 day trip but I let one of the other guys go in my place.*

*His brother is on the way to there and he'll get a chance to see him so I let him go in my place. I'll probably get to go a little later on because he's an old man (points-wise) and his turn should be coming up pretty quick. I took a shower a little while ago. It felt plenty good to. We have about 40 showers and plenty of hot water and they are going about all the time. We are going to have a 10 o'clock bed check now at night to have the guys in but it won't do any good because we keep the lights and radios on till about one. No shows now for a few weeks because they are working on the camera changing it over some way, I guess. I'll be going to Mass and Communion tomorrow. Say a prayer for you to. We have Mass at 1:30 now. He says Mass in about 3 other towns in the morning so it keeps him going.*

*These churches in Germany are sure beautiful. About every one I've been in is. How's everything going at the bakery now? Did you get another girl? I suppose if I ever get home to run it again, you'll never want to go near it. Can't say as I blame you because I know what*

In the daytime, as they rolled through the sweltering prairie heat, they ran out of water. The toilets wouldn't flush. At night, they curled up against green-plush, straight-backed seats, fitfully brushing at insects and soot that kept pouring in the windows.

Soon they learned to take the backs off the seats, improvise hot and prickly beds from two seats with the chairbacks in between. Another man would sleep on the other chairbacks—in the aisle. Some dozed on their luggage.

For six days and five nights they traveled in this fashion from Boston to California—500 veterans of the European war, now on their way to fight another war. When they got off the train at Camp Beale, Calif., they let out a G.I. gripe that could be heard all the way back in Washington.

Other trainloads of soldiers went through the same sort of experience—and they all griped. It did not cool them off to see civilians whizzing by in air-cooled Pullmans, or to hear a rumor that German prisoners of war were also riding in Pullmans. P.O.W.s ride in Pullmans only when they are certified as ill; Italian Service Units sometimes get Pullman service.

In Washington, ODT complained that the Army had grossly underestimated the flooding tide of redeployed fighting men. The Army denied it. But ODT's Colonel J. Monroe Johnson put his head together with War Department officials, swiftly worked out a program:

Beginning July 15, civilians would get no sleeping-car accommodations on trips under 450 miles, unless they are lucky enough to pick up reservations on trains making longer runs. This would rule out civilian sleeping berths on such heavily-traveled runs as New York to Washington, New York to Boston, St. Louis to Chicago.

http://www.time.com/time/magazine/article/.html

a hell of a job it is. How are John and Meikle getting along?

Well, Marge, I can't think of anything else so will quit for tonight. Still loving and missing you.

All my Love

Your Husband
Bill

July 15, 1945 - From Bill to Marge

Dear Marge,

Well, Marge, I didn't get any mail from you today and I probably won't till Wed. The guy who went to Berchtesgaden (Hitler's hideout) in my place was supposed to go on outpost this morning for 2 days so I took his place. I didn't get to communion but I went to the German Mass. The church was sure crowded to. It is just about the size of the church at home but a lot more beautiful inside. I think every one of these churches I see gets prettier all the time.

It seems like they (soldiers) have a few coming in late, just like at home. On this outpost we are on 2 hrs. and off 6 hrs for the 8 hrs. We check passes all kinds of people passing and bikes, cars, trucks, and walking and then there are all kinds of German soldiers going home. We have to check their discharge papers. The lucky bastards, them going home and us still sweating it out. There was one good looking girl who has been there all day waiting for a ride to a town about 40 miles from here. She came from Berlin and left as quick as the Russians got there. I asked her if she was a frau or fraulein and she said she was a frau but hasn't heard from her husband in 4 years. He was fighting the Russians. Most of these people haven't heard from their relations in the Army and don't know whether they are living or dead. That's one thing we do have, a pretty good mail service. I won't be able to mail this letter till Wed. but I'll write everyday anyway. We get 10 in 1 rations here so we have to do our own cooking. But this is a medic outfit stationed in this town so I had supper with them tonight. I hear over the radio last night where they have lifted the non-fraternization laws and where our Navy has been shelling hell out of the coast of Japan but I'm waiting and praying to hear that they surrender. This place we are staying in now was a big Radon factory. They got civilian guards on it so we don't have to guard it. There is a swell place to fish here if I only had the line and hooks but I've never

The War Department released some statistics last week on the personal conduct of U.S. soldiers, and they were shockers. Items:

Since war began, 101 have been executed for murder or rape (47 for murder, 43 for rape, eleven for both murder and rape).

One man was executed for desertion under fire. He was the first U.S. soldier to be executed since the Civil War for a purely military offense.

More than 200 others were condemned to death, but had their sentences commuted to life imprisonment or less.

A total of 33,519 have been under guard in the U.S. and overseas for various offenses.

Navy Department statistics were not quite so surprising. Some 22,000 have been confined. Executions of Navy men, Marines, Coast Guardsmen: none.

http://www.time.com/time/magazine/article/.html

seen any fish line and hooks around. They must not go for the fishing like we do back home. I sure hope you are taking good care of yourself these days. How is Lila coming along this time? Is she going to have the baby all right? She must be just about due, isn't she? Maybe if she has one, she'll get a few more brains. I often wonder how her and Jim are going to get along after he gets out of the Army.

Still loving you.

All my love,
Your Husband
Bill

July 16, 1945 - From Bill to Marge

Dearest Marge,

Well, Marge, I'm getting on the ball and writing again tonight. I should have a lot of mail when I get back tomorrow. I sure need a shave, haven't shaved for a week and I didn't bring my razor with me. So you can imagine what they are like. A Colonel sure looked at them today when he stopped to find out the way to a town. I suppose we probably had 500 civilians sitting around waiting for rides to different towns. They aren't allowed in American trucks unless they have a pass for M. government so we spend most of the time loading them in civilian cars and trucks going through whether they liked it or not. One truck came through with about 50 kids from Berlin on it. Then we put in about 20 more so they really had a load. A truck brought in a load of about 20 people and probably 15 or 20 babies and dumped them a little while ago so we sent the policeman up to get the Burgermeister, that's the mayor, and he bitched like hell when we told him he would have to find a place for them to sleep because there probably won't be any more trucks through and they aren't allowed on the streets after 9:30. At 9:20 they ring a bell and they sure run for home then.

This morning I went on guard at 5:30 and I knew some guys were sleeping in the house right behind the outpost so I went in, built a fire, and made a gallon of coffee for the other 2 guards and myself and the guy who went in with me. One of the women was sure surprised when she came downstairs and saw me making coffee. Couldn't you just see me doing anything like that back in the States?

We get a case of 10 in one rations a day but us guys

On July 16, the cruiser USS Indianapolis leaves San Fransciso, CA with the atomic bomb.

In a week when Under Secretary of War Patterson declared that battered Tokyo was no longer a primary bombers' target, the War Department announced the name of the man who will run the heavy bombers' assault on Japan to war's end. To no one's surprise, he was 54-year-old General Carl Andrew Spaatz. "Tooey" Spaatz will be chief of a new U.S. Army Strategic Air Force of the Pacific.

On the record, no one was better qualified to direct the aerial destruction of Japan than the onetime fighter pilot who was chief of the U.S. Strategic Air Forces in Europe. German propagandists hated West Pointer Spaatz, called him the "aerial bandit." Japanese propagandists would soon have their own ideograph for the precise, mild-mannered Pennsylvania Dutchman who is impatient to get the war over so he can go sailboating.

The man who directed the operations of Flying Forts and Liberators over Europe will have mostly Superforts in his new command. His assistant destroyers will be rough, tough, morose Major General Curtis LeMay, who last week became boss of the Twentieth Air Force, now based on Guam, Tinian and Saipan; and rough, tough, merry Lieut. General James H. Doolittle, boss of the famed Eighth Air Force, which is being transferred to the Pacific from Europe. Jimmy Doolittle's base will probably be Okinawa, from which MacArthur's Far Eastern Air Force began operating last week. Tooey Spaatz will direct his giants from head quarters on Guam.

http://www.time.com/time/magazine/article/.html

On July 16, the United States exploded the first Atomic Bomb at Trinity Site, Alamogordo, New Mexico. Using about six kilograms of plutonium, it succeeded in unleashing an explosion equivalent to that of 19 kilotons of TNT.

A train collision near Munich kills 102 war prisoners.

On July 17, at Postsdam, Germany, Truman, Churchill and Stalin began their final summit of war. The meetings ended August 2.

Bill writes about the I&E Program that was the *Army Troop Information and Education Program*. With the end of World War II, many U.S. troops in Germany remained to meet the new requirements of occupation. Staying with them was their own war-born radio network, the American Forces Network, Europe (AFN). Operating several powerful transmitters, AFN beamed news, information, popular music, and variety over a Western Europe otherwise bombarded by Cold War radio propaganda.

been eating with a medic outfit so we have plenty to eat and in the 10 in ones, there are cigarettes and candy so we are doing all right. I wouldn't mind staying on this outpost all the time. Have a lot of brass to salute but I don't mind to much. Got to go back again at 9:30 to 11:30 and then 5:30 to 7:30 in the morning.

Haven't read the Stars and Stripes for the last 2 days now so don't know how the war is coming but I'm sure hoping they make peace soon. I guess in our training that they started today, we are going to learn how to take our rifles apart and put them back together, how to shoot them, how to throw hand grenades and things like that. Our Lieut. was over last night and he was telling me about it. He said they were going to feel shitty as hell teaching us guys who had been on the line 5-10 months that stuff and he's only been with us about 3 months now. One of the other Lieut. came in the day after the war was over so you can imagine what it will be like for a while.

All my Love

Your Husband
Bill

July 17, 1945 - From Bill to Marge

Dearest Marge,

Well Marge I had 3 letters from you and one from Arlene Wyscover. The letters were the 5th, 6th, and 9th and also a box from you of tobacco. Boy, I'll have enough tobacco to smoke when I'm out of cigarettes and to have my laundry done, till I leave Germany.

We got back from the outpost this morning about 10 o'clock and then they expected us to go out and take the chicken shit training the rest of the day but none of us went. One boy is getting a court martial for refusing to go yesterday. I guess things are really getting chicken shit around here. They'll never be able to get any of the guys to even get their minds halfway on this stuff because lots of the stuff they'll be teaching, you know is wrong in combat. The oldest men it's the toughest on, because they have been through a lot of combat and are still here so they know the ways - couldn't be all wrong.

This big I+E program they are supposed to have over here is sure a laugh to my notion. That stuff and these big U.S.O. shows are just for the rear echelon.

We got a liquor ration tonight so I had a shot of champagne and a shot of wine. (That's what you and me will *have to have a party with sometimes.) Good champagne - there is nothing like it to my notion and surprising as it may seem, what we get is better than you could ever buy in the States.*

*I sure like to spend some of the times like we used to, just us two "Remember". Well, maybe it won't be to long, probably New Years. The war news sounded good tonight. Just heard it a little while ago. Sounds like the Navy is still shelling hell out of them.*

*In one letter you wrote you and your folks were fixing up the cabin and cleaning up around but you didn't say whether you put out your poles or caught any fish. That's the important thing when you write about being down to the cabin. Let me know whether you have any luck. You can tell John this is the place he would enjoy if he would have been in my place the last couple of days. All kinds of good-looking girls around and most of them like to go out with American soldiers. Lots of them speak enough English to get by but I still haven't monkeyed with any of them except talking to them. I started writing this letter about 4 hrs ago and I will just get a few lines written, and somebody comes over and sits on my bunk and then one or two more come over and have a bull session for a while before I get started again. Well, keep up the writing. Still loving and missing you.*

*All my love*

*Your Husband Bill*

July 18, 1945 - From Bill to Marge

*Dearest Marge,*

*Boy, Marge, I sure hit the jackpot tonight. Got 11 letters from you from 27th June to July 9 and also one from Ma. Keep me busy reading them for quite a while. You wrote about Vernon writing how heavy I was. I knew he was sure surprised to see me looking so good because I was pretty brown and heavy then. We just finished living off the fat of the land and I ate plenty then. Probably 10 or 15 eggs a day, half dozen big slices of brown bread and jam, sometimes a quart or two of strawberries or cherries and then some out of my K rations but I'll bet I lost 10 or 20 lbs since I've seen him because we don't get to much to eat. We can't loot any food like we could coming through Germany. I didn't do much today. Fucked off half the morning. Then I got caught so had to go out on the field with the rest of the Co. They were having lectures on mines, booby traps, and com-*

Kaiser Wilhelm had dreamed of the day when the world would be run from his ugly palace at Potsdam. Soon the world would be run from there—for a little while. The Big Three were headed there to draw some more lines on the future's blueprint.

Winston Churchill, had already left London. Tired out with campaigning, he rested at Hendaye, a pleasant town and international rumor factory on the Spanish-French border. President Truman planned to cross the Atlantic and then France without seeing Charles de Gaulle, who will visit him later in Washington. Since it would never do to give the impression of an advance Anglo-American caucus, Truman and Churchill decided not to meet before they reached Potsdam. Stalin was coming by train over rails recently changed, all the way to the Elbe, to the broad Russian gauge.

The British seemed to look to Truman to take the lead. Nobody knew what the Russians would bring up, but there was a general feeling in Moscow that they would undoubtedly take the initiative on such points as the early trial of war criminals and their own request for huge reconstruction credits.

Russia's need for postwar credit was one of Truman's bargaining points. What he might well ask in return from the Russians was: 1) as much cooperation as possible in Asia, during and after the Pacific war; 2) a pledge that Russia would not seek to communize all of Europe.

Long resigned to the creation of a tightly held Russian bloc in eastern Europe, Britain has sought to strike a balance with a western bloc. Washington last week talked in other terms. It recognized that a western European bloc would always be weaker than the Russian sphere, and hoped instead for a really unified Europe, in which both the western powers and Russia would have a say. (Time Magazine - July 18, 1945)

The shoulder patch of the 90th Infantry Division known as the Tough 'Ombres.

When the patch was created, the discernable "T" and "O" stood for Texas and Oklahoma from where most of the original soldiers came. As troops started coming in from all over the United States, the patch signified Tough 'Ombres, the name they fought under for the duration of the War.

Patton praised the 90th many times for doing as much, if not more, than any division to help win the war.

On July 19, the USS Cod saved 51 sailors from a Dutch sub in the only sub-to-sub rescue of the war years.

*pass reading.*

*This afternoon we had 2 hrs close order drill and then our Battalion Colonel gave us a big speech "he's leaving the Division", telling us to do as good a job for the new one as we did for him and then the old line of shit about being proud of being in Command of the best battalion in the Division and of the places we took, that even the General told him we wouldn't be able to do. The old shit's been thick the last few days. Patton toured all the 90th area and gave a big speech for the 357th telling how the 90th Division did as much if not more, than any Div. over here for winning the war. They printed his whole speech in the Division newspaper but left out most of the swear words. I suppose the folks don't think much of the idea of Vernon going to the CBI but his job wasn't very dangerous over here and I think he will probably get home quicker by going there. He only needs 5 points and if they open the points system up again, he'll be able to go home from there. But over here the guys with 80 points and above go to other outfits and will stay here till in '46. A few with 100 points or like that go home but most of them are getting transfers to the Division to leave in 1946. I think the 89th Div. is one of them that the high pointers are going to.*

*Is White still in it? I got a little thirst so went in and had a couple shots of wine, cost a dime. Cheap enough but that's all one guy can get. You tell Father Norton that I still haven't played around with any of these frauleins over here and there are a lot of nice ones. Well, Marge, take good care of the young lad and I still might be home earlier than New Years yet because they say they are a month ahead on redeployment already and that will probably get us home quicker.*

*All my Love*

*Your Husband*
*Bill*

*P.S. In regard to that money in the bank, you can take it out and put in postal savings.*

July 19, 1945 - From Bill to Marge

*Dearest Marge,*

*Well, Marge, no mail from you tonight but I guess I couldn't expect any after all I got last night. I got a letter from LeMasters and he said he thought he would be home for Christmas as the work would be done here in a couple months. He said he's wrote to Wyscover a couple of times but has never heard from him. They must be keeping him busy cooking. I'll have to make this short tonight because it is the only sheet of paper I could get ahold of. We have never been able to buy any since the war was over.*

*I see by the Stars and Stripes where the big meeting is on in Berlin and they figure it will either be Japan's surrender or Russia's entry into the war. We had bayonet training for 2 hrs today then 1 hr military courtesy, 2 hrs drill, and that was about all for today. The order came out today that we don't have to carry a rifle after retreat if we go up to town anywhere but I think I'll still carry mine while I'm in Germany.*

*We haven't got our rations for this week so that tobacco is coming in handy. I'm still loving and missing you more than ever.*

*All my love,*

*Your Husband*
*Bill*

July 20, 1945 - From Bill to Marge

*Well, Marge, I got a letter from you today of the 18th and one from Ma who wrote from up in Marshfield. It kinda sounded like they had a little tire trouble on the way up. I hope they have a good time up there.*

*I went uptown tonight with the little Dago to get some paper and every place was locked so he figured we wouldn't get any but I seen a bab (female) stick her head out of the window upstairs so I told her to come down and open up. We wanted some paper but she said nix, I'd have to wait till they opened in the morning. I had a gun and tobacco with me so I knew I'd get her to open up with one or the other so I told her I'd give her 2 sticks of gum to get it for me so she came right down and opened up. Then I got quite a bunch of paper and a couple pencils. Cost 3 marks and the 2 sticks of gum. Cheap enough, eh? They will do about anything here for candy, gum or tobacco. We got our P.X. rations tonight-6 packs cigarettes, 1 cigar, 1 plug tobacco, 1 can grapefruit juice, 2 candy bars and a pack of gum and that's about it. We didn't do much today. Had a little marching and a few lectures also had a class on taking care of our rifles. More bull shit. They got a big bunch of torches out here tonight. I guess we are going on a make believe taking a town. I suppose they figure we forgot how in the last 2 months. It will sure be a guy's ass if he kills one of these*

What U.S. and British authorities had dreaded ever since Italy's liberation—the organization of a Communist outbreak—was a fact last week.

Through the streets of Andria, in southern Italy, stalked Communist Leader Vincenzo di Gaetano, sporting a brace of pistols and a pair of huge knives. He had been sent to Andria by the Bari branch of the Communist Party. Round his neck on a string was a whistle, with which in recent weeks he has frequently summoned from their labor in the fields the 600 men and 500 women of his rowdy revolutionary "armed escort."

Armed with hand grenades and machine guns, Andria's Communists had disarmed the local carabinieri, looted a train carrying food, confiscated cattle from the farmers, replaced Andria's liberal mayor with a Communist laborer, evicted the Socialist leader of the local labor federation from his office, opened the jail and enrolled the inmates in the Communist ranks, kidnapped persons whose fate is a mystery, liquidated the family of the local forester who opposed them. When carabinieri were rushed in from Bari, two were killed. Comrade di Gaetano telephoned to demand that the others be withdrawn at once, that ten local carabinieri be put at his disposal. Meanwhile the unrest spread to nearby Corato, Trani, Barletta and Canosa di Puglia.

http://www.time.com/time/magazine/article/html

Many a U.S. citizen, pondering Japan's abject helplessness to defend its own shores asked: Must they fight it out to the end? In Congress, clamor for a clear definition of U.S. policy toward a defeated Japan would not calm down.

Under Secretary of State Joseph C. Grew found it time to set the record straight, at least in part. He told of indirect, unofficial Japanese peace feelers. He reminded the U.S. public that the Japanese militarists, like the Nazis before them, hoped to produce a cleavage of U.S. opinion over continuing the war, thus hoped to wriggle out with a defeat that would not mean the end of Japan's ruling military caste.

By Joe Grew's estimate, the time to tell Japan the price of peace was not yet. But the time had arrived to prepare to tell the Japanese people what unconditional military surrender will mean. This week such a statement was in preparation by one Administration group. Its present broad outline means that surrender must mean, unconditionally, the end of Jap militarism.

http://www.time.com/time/magazine/article/

Produced in 1944, *Dancing in Manhattan* starred Fred Brady, Jeff Donnel and Ann Savage.

Krauts now. The Lieut. says a guy would probably get 20 years for it. I'm going on outpost again in the morning and will come back again Sunday. I guess we have to check the discharges closer because they are forging a few of them. I guess there is one of Goring's high ranking men running loose in our area and is listed as a war criminal but the way they have things fucked up over here, I don't see how they can catch anybody.

I'm glad to hear Freddy is getting his discharge but I wonder how he is going to like going to work. Do you think they will live in Waukon? I'll bet Dorothy is sure happy about it. He'll be getting out in time to do a little fishing and hunting to. I've been sitting here sipping on a cup of beer ever since I started this letter. We have been having it every day but it isn't very strong. I drink 3 or 4 cups a week, I guess. I'll have to write a letter to Marquardt tonight to. He wrote and asked me a lot of questions about everything so I better answer them. He hardly ever took a drink until in March or April when we got hell shot out of us. He got disgusted and really started to hit the booze. We had a CO then that got us about 15 guys hit in a couple min by his not listening to the way our platoon leader and a couple more wanted to take a town. All of the guys where so mad. We could of shot him but yet we had to walk right out in the open field and let them blaze away at us with a half doz. machine guns. We had a movie last night, first one in a long time "Dancing in Manhullan." I didn't care for it to much but we do have some pretty good shows. We got a bunch of new officers in the Battalion now. They were transferred from the 99th Division. I think they only seen about a month of combat. Well Marge, I suppose I better quit for now if I ever figure on getting another letter wrote yet tonight.

All my love

Your Husband
Bill

On July 21, President Harry S. Truman approved the order for atomic bombs to be used against Japan.

July 21, 1945 - From Bill to Marge

Dearest Marge,

I just finished taking a shower and shaving so I guess I better get busy now and write. Didn't get any mail today except the Register. I wrote Vernon a letter this afternoon. It's been about a month since I wrote him but I suppose it will be a good 2 or 3 months before he gets it.

*I was supposed to go on outpost today but they called it off. We had a raid on a town about 40 miles from here. We got up about 2:45, ate breakfast and got there about 5:13. Caught most of them in bed. They posted guard all around the town and then our platoon searched the house for guns and ammo. Then ran the civilians down to the town square to have their papers checked. It was a lot of fun for a change again except we had to be a little easier on things than when we were taking towns. We got a case of 20 MM ammo is all I know of and I guess, about 6 people. I don't know what they were wanted for - whether they had forged the charges or what. I have 3 bottles of good beer while I was searching but I paid for it. I wouldn't mind it over here doing stuff like that and outpost duty. That's where a guy gets away from the chicken ----. Your time is your own and you can do whatever you want without somebody checking on you all the time. Here it is Sat. night - how I wish I was home with you. We had a lot of fun on Sat. nights. We have a show here tonight but I don't know what the name of it is.*

*In the Register I got tonight, there was a big article about them getting night crawlers in Des Moines. Do you remember how we used to do it and the nights Luther went with us. She got quite a kick out of it too. About 1/2 of the guys here never heard of them before or seen them. I guess they don't have them in Penn. That's where most of the guys I monkey around with are from. Some of our guys leave this week to go train Artillery and other outfits - Inf. Tactics. They will probably be gone in a month or so. Tomorrow it will be the 22nd again - a year and 5 months since we've been married and we have to spend the most of it away from each other. I sure hope it isn't that way in the next year.*

*How are the Kreeb's coming - do you still go up there? I suppose Ray still goes fishing every chance he gets. How about John and Stan - have they been catching any? We can't get ahold of any grenades anymore and ain't supposed to be firing our rifles around so I never go anymore. Well, Marge, that's about my limit for tonight. I'm going to try going to Mass and Communion in the morning if nothing comes up.*

*All my Love*

*Your Husband*
*Bill*

In five years (the Department of Agriculture reported last week) U.S. farm and food production had increased 35%. But the U.S. farm population as of Jan. 1 was 25,190,000; since 1940, more than 5,000,000 had left the farms for the city or the armed services. The U.S. farm population was the lowest it had been in 35 years.

Uncounted weeks in action had made Pfc. Devon Hunsaker a ragged, unshaven, mud-caked infantryman. Slogging wearily back from the lines north of Davao last week, dreaming of his home in Utah, he saw a vaguely familiar face in the column of replacements moving forward. "What's your outfit, buddy?" he asked. "Thirty-first Infantry," said the newcomer, and moved on. A quarter of a mile later, Private Hunsaker slapped his thigh and exclaimed: "I knew I had seen that guy before. He's my brother."

This is what the inglorious process of "mopping up" can do to the foot soldiers who wield the mop. It is a process dirty, bloody and exhausting, not easily distinguishable from any other kind of warfare. In the Philippines, it still meant mud and C-rations, belly-tightening fear and dog-tired homesickness, shooting Japs and getting shot at - and getting killed.

http://www.time.com/time/magazine/article/

The U.S. took over its section of occupied Berlin, death-ridden capital of a dead empire, last week. Along a road marked off by the Red Army, a column of 4,000 U.S. vehicles rolled toward the shattered city. As the Americans crossed into suburban Zehlendorf, a dismal rain fell. Cried some gaunt Berliners : "Gott sei dank — Thank God!" Others stood silent and sullen.

Next day, July 22, the Americans lined up in the courtyard of Lichterfelde's former SS barracks. Opposite them was ranged a Red Army detachment. Major General Nikolai Baranov, commander of the Russian garrison in Berlin, welcomed the newcomers. General Omar N. Bradley, commander of the U.S. Twelfth Army Group, replied. Bands played the national anthems of Russia and the U.S. The Stars & Stripes fluttered up a staff until it flew level with the Hammer & Sickle. A 48-gun salute was fired. Then the Russians marched smartly off.

In the rubble-heaped city, now fully opened to the Anglo-U.S. press for the first time since its capture ten weeks ago, two things at once impressed the Americans : the mark of death, and the mark of the Russians.

Death stared from the cadavers of mighty buildings; the smashed, charred bones of the Reichstag (see cut); the battle-broken Chancellery, where Adolf Hitler and his paramour, Eva Braun, may have died; the ruins of the Propaganda Ministry, Foreign Office, Kroll Opera House and almost every other notable Berlin edifice. The stench of death rose too from corpses still rotting under debris, from the corpse-clogged Liitzow Canal, from hasty, shallow graves dug in every park and Platz.

http://www.time.com/time/magazine/article/html

## July 22, 1945 - From Bill to Marge

*Dearest Marge,*

*Well, Marge, I didn't get any letters again tonight. That's what I hate about mail coming by boat. Got a lot of it in one bunch and then don't get any for a while. I suppose you are getting mine the same way. I hear over the radio that half of it is to go by boat.*

*I guess the 3rd Army is out of gas again from the papers. That's what they say. I think it was a good thing the war over here ended when it did because I kinda believe they ran out then. I know we were stopped the day before it ended because our tanks were about out.*

*I didn't do much today - got up about 7:30 this morning and had breakfast at 8. Then I came up and slept till noon. Went down and had dinner then went to church. Our chaplain didn't show up so the German priest said Mass. Had the Children's choir again. Then I slept till supper and now I'm writing you. It's about 7 o'clock. I'll probably read a while and if there is a show, go down. We don't have them till about 10 or a little after. Have to wait for it to get a little dark so we can see the show. Last night I went. It was "A Royal Scandal" a picture about Russians during the time of Katherine the Great. Most of the guys didn't like it.*

*I wonder what happened to the Democrat? I haven't got it for a couple of months now and I sure enjoyed reading it.*

*I suppose you probably went down to the river today if it is as hot there as it is here. Its getting time the fish should be biting now. I hear by the radio where the First Army will reach CBI by the first of Dec. They will probably make room for us in the States by that time. They tell us we can volunteer for CBI now but I don't think they will get many. There has been some who wanted to but I think most of them changed their mind by now. It sure looked like back home today to see the people all out walking all dressed up in their best clothes. The dress clothes they wear here are just the same as in the States, same colors and everything. See lots of girls with white dresses on now that the weather is warm.*

*The women are the ones who do the work over here. They start work about 5:30 or 6:00 in the morning and usually work in the fields till about 9 o'clock at night.*

*How do you suppose the women in the States would like to do that?*

*Well, Marge, guess I'll quit for now. Still loving and*

missing you. I hope I get some mail tomorrow.
All my Love
Your Husband
Bill

July 23, 1945 - From Bill to Marge

Dearest Marge,

I had a little better luck tonight. I got a letter from you of the 11th and also another one from Marquardt. He just wrote a few lines so I'll stick it in this letter. You wrote about Vernon hurting his hand, I'd forgot all about it. He showed me the place where it happened when we went by. Himself and another guy were on a truck holding stuff on and the driver clipped a tree knocking them off. The other kid got hurt too. Vernon's hand was bothering him then but he thought he might of busted a bone but the medic just wrapped it up, I guess. I kinda think Mason is nuts for taking a discharge with the rank he had. I'll bet he'll never make that kind of money in civilian life unless he gets on with one of these airline outfits. When you see Lila tell her to tell Jim to write. I've never heard from him except that once.

I didn't do much today. We were supposed to have bayonet training this morning but we just fooled around most of the time. Then this afternoon we had 4 hrs on weapons but we just crawled in the woods and slept.

They are having a hell of a job trying to make combat men do all this shit when they know it's just a waste of time - most of it anyway. They would be a hell of a lot better off if they gave us a little time to take care of our rifles and stuff inside because we get outside and we fuck off ever chance we get. We had a movie up town tonight so I went. It started at 6:15. - The Falcon in Hollywood. I liked it good to. I used to see most of the Falcon pictures in the States. On the way back, myself and a kid from Missouri "who came over when I did" went up and got in a strawberry patch. From there to a raspberry patch - some good too. Then we went a little farther and found a lot of nice peas. They were just about right so we filled our pockets and took off. I'll bet these krauts sure love us for it. Oh, we stopped in at the tavern on the way and had a couple of beers too. Nothing like the beer at home though.

The First Sergeant called me in today and told me that the transfer I put in for didn't go through because they were over strength. I'm sure glad it didn't now be-

On July 23, French Marshal Philippe Petain, who headed the Vichy government during World War II, went on trial for treason.

*The Falcon in Hollywood* was one of 13 Falcon movies between 1940 and 1946, starring George Sanders in the first three and Tom Conway in the following ten. The movie that Bill saw that night was produced in 1944.

One well-known gimmick in the Falcon series was tacking an epilogue onto one movie to act as a sort of tease to the next. This little "preview" often had little to do with the actual upcoming film, but it was meant to keep interest alive.

On July 24, the US destroyer Underhill was torpedoed by the Japanese in the waters west of Guam.

One typhoon had blown itself out off Okinawa, but a secondary storm of much greater violence was born from the original disturbance. It swung rapidly northeast toward the cruising U.S. Third Fleet. It was early June, only six months after Admiral William F. Halsey had lost three destroyers in a typhoon off the Philippines.

This time, the twister set a collision course for the task group commanded by Rear Admiral Joseph ("Jocko") Clark, and the Cherokee Admiral got it head on. Proud ships like the Hornet and Bennington (27,000-ton carriers) had as much as 25 feet of their steel-braced flight decks peeled back by the waves; parked planes were picked up and tossed aside in a jumble of wreckage; exposed gun mounts, built out from the ships' sides, were crushed.

Worst sufferer was the heavy cruiser Pittsburgh, a 13,000-ton yearling. Her bow began to quiver under the buffeting of mountainous seas; the forward compartments were cleared of men, and just in time. A huge wave threw her 10° to 15° off her course; the next tore off 104 feet of her bow.

Not a man aboard was lost; the forward bulkheads, bare to the buffeting seas, were shored up; the Pittsburgh fell behind the fleet.

http://www.time.com/time/magazine/article/html

*cause I'm hoping the war will be over before too much longer. Still loving you.*

*All my Love*

*Your Husband*
*Bill*

July 24, 1945 - From Bill to Marge

*Dearest Marge,*

*I got 3 letters from you tonight of the 11th, 12th, and 13th and also one from Paulsons. I was sure glad to get them. You must of misunderstood me in that one letter I wrote. I said the General told us we might stay in the States but of course, that all depends on the war. If they have a setback like the bulge, we will be there in a hurry and now we are supposed to be getting our training for there so if we are needed, they will just give us a furlough and ship us right out. You wrote Klemme was home and that he probably wouldn't be going to S. Pacific but a guy has to get hit pretty bad in the hand to keep him out of the Infantry. Boy, Marge, there is one guy in our platoon you ought to see. He came in after I did and spent about 3 weeks in combat and I'll bet he had 20 or 30 holes in him and the way the doctors sew them up, it really leaves the scars.*

*We were out on the firing range all day today and the doughnut girls came out with hot coffee and donuts. They asked some of the boys if they never get anything to eat the way they went at them and I guess they told the girls about the wonderful meals we get. They stayed until we got done tonight. They fired all the different guns: Carbine, M1. that's our regular rifle, B.A.R., that's an automatic rifle when you pull the trigger, it fires till you let go of it. I laughed at the one girl. She was firing the B.A.R. and one of the guys was putting in one shell at the time for her. Then he stuck in a clip and she pulled the trigger and about 10 shots went off before she could let go of it. They were pretty good shots. You could tell they have been firing the guns around at different places, because they didn't get banged up from it and they fired probably 50 or 60 shots a piece.*

*This new Colonel we got sure is getting disliked by everybody. I think he just came over from the States and he expects us to take the same chicken shit they dish out in IRTC (Infantry Replacement Training Center - Ft. Hood, TX). He came up to one of our best Lieut. today and started to give him hell. Then he said "How* long have you been with this outfit anyway". When the Lieut. told him that he came over with it, the Col. shut up like a clam and walked away. This Lieut. got a battlefield commission in Feb. and he don't believe much in all of this military courtesy. We are supposed to have 15 weeks of this training and our platoon Sergeants are going to turn in a thing to the Col. if they don't start feeding the men here pretty quick. They will be fucking off on all the training.

We have a bunch of damn Kraut civilians that work for our Co. and they get better food, cigarettes and I don't think the bastards do hardly any work. We tried to get rid of them once but it didn't do us any good.

Here is what we had for chow today. Breakfast: coffee and 1/2 slice of bread, a little dab of cereal and about 4 or 5 prunes. For Dinner: C rations meat and beans together, 1/2 slice of bread and about 2 tablespoons of fruit cocktail. For Supper: piece of cheese, a slice of cold meat, 1/2 slice of bread and coffee so you see we aren't getting all the food over here.

Every time I pick up a paper and see what all they say they are doing for the troops over here, I could rip it to pieces, it makes me so damn mad. They say every 3 months, we are supposed to get a trip out of Germany but it will be 6 months the 1st of Aug being in Germany for a lot of us, who have never been out. Well, enough bitching for tonight. I hope you don't mind it because we have to do something and that's one thing a guy learns in the Army. I can easily see where John gets it now.

Enclosed is a little article that was sure good. There were head and field glasses looking out of every window in the factory and pretty quick there were a lot of guys making for the hills.

All my love

Your Husband
Bill

July 25, 1945 - From Bill to Marge

Dearest Marge,

Well, Marge, here I go again tonight. No mail from you today but I got one from Beck. She just got the letters I wrote from here Jan. 9 - the 13th of July so I suppose there are a lot of letters I wrote you that are laying around that you haven't got yet. I don't think Vernon could ever put much in letters of what they were doing or anything like I've done all along. You remember

Because they suspected a fellow prisoner of war of writing a "traitorous" note, five sullen and shifty-eyed Nazis had brutally clubbed him to death; an Army court-martial had swiftly found them guilty. At Fort Leavenworth last week they were hanged for their crime.

For seven U.S. soldier-executioners it was a grim assignment. First they went to a makeshift gallows, built in an elevator shaft, and practiced with a sandbag dummy. Then, shortly after midnight one night, they carried out the verdict.

First to go was Walter Beyer, a 32-year-old sergeant still wearing parts of his Afrika Korps uniform. As he heard the sentence read and translated by an interpreter, his face was drawn, his eyes flicked nervously from one face to another. But he held his chin high. Said he: "I can't see why this is being done to me." When they placed the black hood over his head, he pivoted on his heel, marched smartly to the edge of the shaft, maintained his military bearing to the end.

Another of the condemned men started to say, "A wrong is being—" then his voice broke. He was silent as the hood was adjusted.

The others had nothing to say. But their military behavior was perfect; not a heel dragged.

A few days later, despite the Army's protestations that all is reasonably well in the prisoner-of-war camps, authorities at Fort Leavenworth hanged two more Nazis for the same kind of crime—murder of a fellow prisoner.

http://www.time.com/time/magazine/article/html

Training battle knowledgeable troops.

when I first came over, I wrote I was about 10 mi. from him and another time I wrote I thought he was back along the Rhine. Well, when I was down there I found out I was right both times. He was at Metz there once and I was in the replacements back a few miles from there and then when he was back at the Rhine, they built a big bridge there. Our Col. here is getting strict. He gave us hell tonight. I guess somebody broke into the officers mess last night and stole a lot of grub and liquor and if they don't start to feed us they will be having to place a couple guards there at night.

We played soldier all day today doing scouting, patrolling, throwing grenades and rifle positions and a guy knows damn well it don't do him any good because you don't do it any thing like it in combat but I guess we will have 13 months of this shit and when we get to the States, get 30 days and then get shipped out again. At least that's what they are trying to tell us but I think the Gen. knew pretty well what he was talking about in the speech he gave us. But I guess all we can do is wait and pray that this will end before then.

I thought when Roosevelt died, it would bring the war to an end a lot quicker but it don't look much like it.

Well, how are you and Junior getting along these days. Is he still kicking hell out of you?

I'll bet you will sure be glad when it is all over. I don't know what to think about the bakery. I don't want you to be working and worrying yourself about it all the time. I wish you could get some good woman that would take an interest in it. We could afford to pay her good money but if nothing else, we can always lock it up.

We can thank God for being as lucky as we are. I know lots of the boys who came over when I did who will never go back and lot more of them afterward. Well, Marge, better quit for tonight.

Still loving and missing you

All my Love,

Your Husband

Bill

On July 26, Winston Churchill resigned as the United Kingdom's Prime Minister after his Conservative Party was soundly defeated by the Labour Party in the 1945 general election. Clement Attlee becomes the new Prime Minister.

July 26, 1945 - From Bill to Marge

Dearest Marge,

Well Marge, it's getting around 9 o'clock so I thought I'd better get busy and write. Didn't get any mail today. There was only a few letters for the Co. When they come by boat we usually get a bunch all at one time.

Boy but I sure got the G.I.'s today. Started in about 3 this morning and have been running ever since just like when I went to Camp Dodge that time so I didn't go out with the Co. I guess there must have been 20 or 30 in our Co. on sick call today. Didn't eat anything all day till tonight. I ate a little supper and feel a little better now. We had a movie again last night "Bewitched" was the name of it. It don't seem like we ever get any first grade pictures.

We had shake down inspection about 5 o'clock this morning. They came through hunting for pistols and ammo. I guess they got quite a few but they missed mine. I got lots of loose ammo in my pack for a M1, 32 pistol and 38 pistol. I guess I wrote you we don't have to carry a rifle any more when we go uptown and yesterday they called in all our ammo. Today they started having a couple of kids and a couple local girls start working in the kitchen doing K.P. I guess they are going to make sure nobody misses any training. I'll bet there are sure a lot of guys coming home from over here now. The rumor is we will get home a month earlier than we are scheduled to. I'm sure hoping I'll be home for Christmas and New Years though. It kinda looks like they are not going to give the Japs anything but unconditional surrender. I still can't see any sense to it. If you could only see it over here, these Germans really have the laugh at us. A guy feels like busting them a lot of times but you'd probably get a few years for it. They start work at 8 and quit at 4:30 and we fall out at 6:45 and finish our day at 5:45 and then we are liable to catch guard detail after that.

What did Lila have to say when you went up to see her? I suppose she still is as much of a baby as ever. I wonder how her and Jim will get along after he gets back. How's John coming? Still getting drunk and having women trouble? He had better wise up and start saving some money because these kind of times aren't going to last forever. I've got quite a few letters I should answer but I just don't have the ambition. Say hello to your folks for me. There isn't much sense me writing them when I write you everyday. Keep up the writing.

All my Love

Your Husband
Bill

Released in 1944, Producer Darryl F. Zanuck had high hopes that Wilson would immortalize him, with *Bewitched*, in the manner that *Gone With the Wind* did for David O. Selznick. The notion of bringing the life story of Woodrow Wilson, 28th president of the United States, to the big screen was a labor of love for Zanuck, and accordingly the producer lavished all the technical expertise and production values he had at his disposal. Though Alexander Knox seems a bit too robust and overnourished for Wilson, his is a superb performance, evenly matched by those of Ruth Nelson as Wilson's first wife Ellen, Geraldine Fitzgerald as second wife Edith, Thomas Mitchell as Joseph Tumulty, Sir Cedric Hardwycke as Henry Cabot Lodge, Vincent Price as William Gibbs McAdoo, Sidney Blackmer as Josephus Daniels, and the rest of the film's enormous cast.

On July 26, the Potsdam Declaration demanded Japan's unconditional surrender. Article 12, permitting Japan to retain the reign of the Emperor, had been deleted by President Truman.

The Japanese government disregarded the US ultimatum.

The US cruiser Indianapolis reached Tinian with the atomic bomb.

Some Navy two-stripers, despairing of promotion to lieutenant commander, have taken matters in their own hands, they told a Pacific Fleet correspondent of the New York Times, July 27. Their straight-faced solution: the creation of the consoling rank, "Lieutenant Super Grade."

To qualify, officers must have been lieutenants senior grade for 24 to 29 months, "while their civilian contemporaries in the Army have become colonels and brigadier generals." They will be entitled to wear a neon star with blinker, and cap covers with a center rosette ringed with a one-half-inch band of phosphorescent material. Shirt collars and cuffs will be distinguished by a lacy fringe or fray and tinted a darker hue. (No pay increase is contemplated.)

According to the super lieutenants' charter, they "will rank with, but below, lieutenant generals of the Army, full generals of the Salvation Army and aviation cadets and midshipmen of the Navy."

Time Magazine
July 23, 1945

*The Whistler* was the first of eight Columbia 'B' thrillers based on the popular radio series of the same name. The Whistler, a shadowy figure, introduced each film as he'd done on radio: 'I am the Whistler...and I know many things, for I walk by night.' This time the Whistler tells the strange story of despondent Richard Dix, who, believing his wife dead, hires professional killer J. Carroll Naish to put him out of his misery. Then the wife suddenly shows up... and Dix can't locate his would-be assassin. Released in 1944, the title was actually *The Whistler* and *The Return of the Whistler* would not be released until 1948.

## July 27, 1945 - From Bill to Marge

Dearest Marge,

Well Marge, I sure hit the jackpot tonight. Got 6 letters from you and one from the folks. That was sure a dirty trick for Miekle to pull at a time like this. But in one way I'm glad you are rid of him. Nobody there ever liked him. I sure wish I was home so you wouldn't have to worry about things there. I'll bet I could still put out the stuff alone if I had to. I know Miekle will never find another job like he had there and if he does come back wanting his job back, I'd never give him over $25 a week if I were you. The only time he was ever any good was when he was getting $15 a week. $55 a week seems like a lot of money to be paying John and Stan but if they stay on the ball and put out the stuff, they are well worth it. I only hope John will stay sober.

The war news sure sounded good today. The Japs trying to get a little better peace terms. I sure hope they end it one way or another and then maybe we will be together again and you won't need to be worrying about the bakery all the time. You have been doing a swell job of it. I have a 2 mark piece here I'm sticking in a letter. I never seen many of them here and it is good money. I didn't have it too rough today. This morning we had a 2 hour march but we laid in the field most of that time. Then we had a couple hrs on map reading and this afternoon we had instructions on scouting and patrolling against the Japs but we spent most of that time laying around.

Tonight we have a movie again. I guess the reason you never see any of these pictures we see is because they don't have first rate pictures. Very few of the actors have I ever seen in pictures. I got 4 hrs of guard to pull tonight so I will get off all day tomorrow. Well Marge, I quit for a while and went down and seen the show. It was "The Return of the Whistler". I didn't care for it to much but it is something to pass the time. I guess I'd have to quit now because they'll be turning off the lights in a few minutes. They have lights out at 11 o'clock now. I'm sure loving and missing you more than ever.

All my Love

Your Husband
Bill

July 28, 1945 - From Bill to Jim and Amanda

Dear Folks,

Received your letter of the 14th yesterday so am answering right away. You must not be getting only about half of the letters I write. I wrote you before to keep sending the Register and find out how come they quit sending the Democrat. I haven't got it for a couple of months. I got a letter from Dad a couple months ago if that is the one you mean but none since. I haven't heard from Vernon since he left. The last I heard from him was when he was at Marseilles (France). I'm glad to hear that you've enjoyed yourselves up at Marshfield (WI--where Amanda was from)

Hated to hear about Miekle walking out but the bakery is probably a hell of a lot better off without him because nobody ever liked him anyway. I sure wish I was home and could take care of it so Marge wouldn't have to worry so much about it. From the way she writes, John and Stan must be really getting a good workout now. I'm glad business is still good. The Colonel told us this morning that we probably would get home in months sooner than scheduled so if that's the case, probably will be home in Nov.

Heard yesterday over the radio where Toyko told the peace terms (that) they would accept but I guess the US won't take nothing but unconditional surrender. Maybe the Japs will take it yet. I sure hope so anyway.

I'm supposed to go to Austria Monday on a 5 day pass. Go to Munich, then over to Hitler's Mountain. I guess it is a beautiful place. A few of our guys have went before but not many. I hope something don't happen that they cancel it.

I've still got a trip to Paris coming but have about given up on ever getting there. We are taking Basic training now, just about the same as what I had at Camp Hood except in a few weeks, we will be having a lot of Jap tactics. Of course, none of the guys take much interest in it because most of the stuff we got in Basic never did us any good over here. I learned more in the first couple weeks of combat than I did all during Basic.

We have movies about every other night here. You know how well I like shows so I never miss any of them. We are gradually getting all our clothes and equipment. I suppose by the time we get them all, we will get to carry them halfway to France. That's the way the Army usually works. Well, folks, I got a few more letters to write

On July 28, the United States Senate ratified the UN Charter by a vote of 89 to 2.

A United States Army Air Force B-25 bomber crashed into the Empire State Building killing 14 people including all on board.

Frank Sinatra got a cuffing from Stars & Stripes, which resented disparaging cracks he had made about the shows put on by the Army's Special Services and the U.S.O. Maybe, said S & S coldly, Frankie was just tired when he made the cracks: "He had just finished seven grueling weeks overseas, during which he sang several times every day."

Marjorie Lawrence, blonde operatic soprano stricken by infantile paralysis four years ago, arrived by plane in Germany after a swing through the Pacific, set out for a singing tour of British camps, still confined to her wheel chair.

so I'll quit for now.

Love,

Bill

P.S. If you get time how about sending me a box because we don't get to much to eat over here now.

July 29, 1945 - From Bill to Marge

Dearest Marge,

I didn't get any mail tonight but I guess I can't expect it every day. I wrote 3 letters already today, one to the folks, Ethel, and one to Marquardt. Doing pretty good, eh.

I didn't have to do anything today because I was on guard last night. The Col. told us this morning that we would probably be home in Nov. because they are one month ahead on redeployment already. I'm going to try going to Mass and communion tomorrow if our chaplain comes over. I'm supposed to go to Austria on a 5-day pass Monday down through Munich and then up to Hitler's home. Should be a good trip. I'll get out of a week of this training anyway. If we get home in Nov. they will probably be cutting this training short. We are supposed to have 15 weeks of it.

Well, how are things going at the bakery now? I'll bet it is kinda peaceful without all of Miekle's bitching around there. You asked if many of the married men go out with these girls over here. I suppose about 1/3 of them do but most of them don't monkey with them. Lots of the guys hate the Germans so much they don't want to have anything to do with them. I guess they figure they wouldn't be over here if it wasn't for them. We had to draw some more equipment again today. I suppose about the time we get everything, we will be able to carry it about half way back to France. Ma wrote that Lila and Dorothy both had babies now and said she was wondering who would be next, you or Sis. She said Sis is bigger than a balloon but she didn't say nothing about you being next. I can't understand how Pat Campbell has been able to stay in the states so long. What about Bud? Is he still in the States, too? Mike should have enough points for discharge by now I would think. He was overseas a long time.

Write and let me know what Beck has to say when she comes up. I guess she was figuring pretty strong on Vernon coming home before he went to the South Pacific.

On July 29, in Great Britain the BBC radio station was launched aiming at mainstream light entertainment and music.

Field Marshal Sir Bernard Law Montgomery's teetotalism, the town of Newport, England decided, is his own personal business. The Town Council rejected a proposal that all Newport citizens stick to orangeade and lemonade during the Marshal's visit there this month.

Colonel James Roosevelt, on active duty with the Marines since 1940, arrived at the Naval hospital in San Diego for a "rest and routine checkup" after seven months in the Philippines.

Louis P. Lochner, 58-year-old dean of A.P. newsmen in Germany, got a major bumping and minor injuries when a jeep he was riding in Berlin hit a Russian truck.

In reference to Sis being *bigger than a balloon*, she told Jan that her husband, Dale, was going to Japan when he got the word Sis had twins. The two babies were enough added points to his total that he got discharged instead.

Do Kosbau's ever here from Harold very often or where he is at? I've never heard from him. I wrote him once last winter but it is hard telling weather he ever got it or not.

It would sure be great to have one of those parties again like we used to with the whole gang together again. There isn't anything more I can think about so I guess I'll quit till tomorrow. I sure do love and miss you.

All my love,

Your husband,
Bill

July 29, 1945 - From Bill to Marge

Dearest Marge,

Well, Marge I'm getting around to writing again tonight . Here it is Sunday night. I wonder what we would be doing if I was home now. Probably be down to the cabin, do you suppose? I sure can't wait for the day we will be together again. How about you? I guess we will have a movie tonight so suppose I'll go. It will be out in the open against the building. We still don't have to pay for them yet but starting the 1st day of Aug, we pay for the Stars and Stripes, $.60 a month. I will still get it because I get a lot of enjoyment out of reading it and now it has all the news up to the day. Some of it we read in the Stars and Stripes before we get it over the radio. I went to Mass today but our Chaplain is gone to England on pass so we had our German priest again today and was I surprised when he gave us a sermon in English. You had to listen close or it was hard to understand him.

I never will get over how beautiful these churches are over here. Every part of them, even the place where they get baptized has a beautiful statue of St John the Baptist baptizing a person in the river and things like that. The pulpit where the priest gives his sermon is beautiful too. I've never seen anything like it in the States. It seems funny how people can build such beautiful churches and yet be having war all the time but I guess it because they don't have enough land. Hardly any of them have over 5 or 10 acres at the most.

I never will forget one church I was in. They had snipers in it and we had to blast it with artillery. When I went in it there were a couple dead Hienies laying there. All of the roof above us was gone, steeples and everything. One side mostly all in but the alter and the

On July 30, the heavy cruiser USS Indianapolis is hit and sunk by torpedoes from the Japanese submarine I-58 in the Philippine Sea. Her top secret mission, that of delivering the atomic bomb to Tinian, did not allow them to break radio silence. Some 900 survivors jumped into the sea and were adrift for four days. Nearly 600 sailors died before help arrived; most of them from shark attacks.

Captain Charles B. McVay III of the cruiser was later court-martialed and convicted.

Captain McVay was posthumously exonerated by the United States Congress in 2000, following years of efforts by survivors and others to have his name cleared of wrong doing.

Unfortunately, he committed suicide prior to Congressional action on his behalf.

Willys-Overland took the wraps off its civilian jeep last week. It looked just like the G.I.'s car-of-all-work.

But as a farmer's car-of-all-trades, the new jeep can pull a plow, harrow or load hay; by means of a power take-off at the rear it can run a saw, threshing machine, or drill post holes. Slicked up, with top, side curtains, and comfortable seats, it can carry farmer & family to town. Willys expects to make 20,000 civilian jeeps this year, expects to sell them in the neighborhood of $900.

http://www.time.com/time/magazine/article/

On July 30, 31,445 soldiers arrived in New York on seven ships from Europe; the huge Queen Elizabeth brought an entire division. In France, at shove-off camps named for U.S. cigarette brands, more thousands of men got their sailing papers, clambered aboard ships. By this week 532,258 shouting, cheering G.I.s had arrived back home in the States.

Redeployment was well ahead of schedule and still gaining speed. Speediest of all was air transport. Last week the Army Air Forces gave out some eye-popping statistics of history's biggest air passenger movement: in a 72-day period up to mid-July, 125,370 military personnel had been flown from the European and Mediterranean theaters to the U.S. They had come in 3,425 heavy bombers and about 600 Air Transport Command planes. The Army thought that virtually all the wounded would be home in a week or so.

On the average there had been a passenger-carrying plane over the Atlantic every six minutes. At New York, Miami, Washington, Bradley Field, Conn., and Hunter Field (near Savannah), Ga., as many as 100 aircraft turned up in a single flight. Proudly the A.A.F. pointed to its safety record: only three bombers had been lost; not one life had been lost in the A.T.C.'s transporting of 67,200 troops. Naval craft of three nations (U.S., Britain and Brazil) patrolled the three routes (via Iceland and Newfoundland; via the Azores; via Natal, Brazil, and the Caribbean). They were a chain of beacons, supplying weather data to the homing aircraft. Ashore, long range planes stood by for rescue missions.

Time Magazine
July 23, 1945

Regensburg, originally Castra Regina, meaning Fortresses, is located at the confluence of the Danube and Regen rivers.

*statues in it were never touched. You know some of the S.S. were great for using churches to snipe out of and it caused a lot of them getting destroyed. There are a lot of things been happening over here. I can tell you about it when I get home. I wouldn't care to write about them because they aren't according to the Geneva Convention.*

*I was sure surprised at Vernon, considering the time he was over here, how little he actually knew about what went on at the front. You remember when I left, I said I was glad in one way I was coming over here. I would never want to go through it again but I'm glad I did because I learned a lot. I never would of believed otherwise. I seen what it was like to watch men die and to dish it out. It's never bothered me much and I was sure glad because it can sure raise hell with a guy if it does. Some guys go off the beam from it but I was lucky not having any of my close buddies killed. Most of them got hit but I always figured they were lucky then, because they would get off the line a while. One guy I used to dig in with, used to stick his hand out of the hole when a barrage came hoping he would get it but he finally got a bullet in the back. He's back now and just as crazy as ever. I am going to Berchtesgaden (Hitler's Eagles Nest Retreat) in the morning if they don't cancel it, so I probably won't be writing for a few days. I sure hope you take my bitching in some of my letters serious because that is one thing a guy always does in the Army. I suppose I'll have to get over that habit when I get out, won't I??*

*Well, how's the little one coming? Still raising hell with you? Well, Marge be sure to keep up the writing. I'm still loving you and not playing around with any of these frauleins here.*

*All my love*

*Your Husband*
*Bill*

August 1, 1945 - From Bill to Marge

*Dearest Marge,*

*Well, Marge, I finally got away from the Company for awhile. I thought when I left it would be only five days but I guess I will have either 7 or 9 days altogether counting coming and going. We left Mon morning. Went to Regensburg. We crossed the Danube there, then went on to Munich and spent a couple hours there. I*

picked up a few postcards and was in Hitler's famous beer garden there. It's just a dump, to my notion.
I guess Munich was a beautiful city before the war but it has been sure all bombed to hell.

Nearly all the buildings were bombed and burnt. We got here to Berchtesgaden late Mon night. It is sure a beautiful place. Yesterday morning myself and another kid took a row-boat and rowed down the Lake to go to a little village called St. Bartholomew. The church there is 6 centuries old and is sure pretty. The only way the people can get in and out of the Valley is by boat. They even have to take their cattle in and out by boat. I bought a mess of postcards and 3 little round pictures (that) I will send home later. You can pick out what you want and give the rest to your mother and mine. Couldn't you just see me rowing 10 mi. at home? We got back from there about noon. Then in the afternoon we went for another boat ride on one of the big boats. They hold from 100-150 people. They have about 10 of them. I see Patton and some of the other Generals were here yesterday but of course, they had a couple special boats. I suppose they used to be Hitlers' or Gorings'. The best part is the only thing we have to pay for is postcards and things like that. The boats and boat rides were free and they have plenty of them. They must have a couple hundred now - boats, and all you have to do is sign for them. I sure wish I had some fishing equipment now because there are plenty big trout in here. Hitler never allowed any fishing here so they should be pretty big fish. But nothing around here to fish with. This lake has big high mountains on all sides. The water is the cleanest I've ever seen and I guess there is no bottom to it. This afternoon I'm figuring on going up to the Eagle's Nest, that's Hitler's home. It wasn't touched from the bombing but Goring and some of the others which were also the S.S. barracks had direct hits on them. Tomorrow I'm going to Salzburg, Austria. We can do any travels we want here or go any place we want to - plenty of good chow here to. There is no reveille or retreat or roll call. A guy don't have to stay

Above is one of the 3 little round pictures he writes about and the liquor decanter with a map of the region is shown below. Both were sent home.

Berchtesgaden is a municipality in the German Bavarian Alps. It is located in the south district of Berchtesgadener Land in Bavaria, near the border with Austria, some 18 miles south of Salzburg and 108 miles southeast of Munich. It is situated north of the Nationalpark Berchtesgaden.

Berchtesgaden is often associated with the fabled Mount Watzmann, at 8,139 feet the third-highest mountain in Germany (after Zugspitze and Hochwanner), which is renowned in the rock climbing community for its Ostwand, and a deep glacial lake by the name of Königssee. Another notable peak is the Kehlstein mountain (5.505 ft.) with its ever popular Kehlsteinhaus (Eagle's Nest), which offers spectacular views to its visitors.

Berchtesgaden's neighboring towns are Bischofswiesen, Markt Schellenberg, Ramsau and Schönau am Königssee.

One of the postcards that Bill sent back home. This one shows the Konigssee that he writes about - it is the lake below the Eagle's Nest and the only route into the Berchtesgaden area.

here at all if he don't want to. The only thing I'll sure miss not getting your mail here, but then I should have a lot of it when I get back to the prison. It gets cold as hell here at night. That's the only bad thing about it. I went around to the German barber to get a shave and haircut this morning and just had to sign for it. I guess they have some fund to pay them out of. Well, Marge, I'll write in a couple days again because I only brought along 4 sheets of paper and two envelopes.

All my Love

Your Husband
Bill

August 2, 1945 - From Bill to Marge

Dearest Marge,

Well Marge, I just came back from Salzburg, Austria. It's only about 15 mi. from here. We left early this morning and got back tonight. I've got a bunch of postcards of some of the places I was. I sent some in this letter and the rest later on. We went all through the Archbishops big castle and was it ever big, about a 1,000 years old. We were in the rooms where the Nazi's kept the Governor of Austria. A big room up on the top, with chain shackles and everything like you see in the pictures of centuries ago. This place and the Church, which is also 1,000 years old was built by St. Rupert. In the Church all of the bishops and archbishops of Salzburg are buried, Also some great musicians. So many altars, I'd hate to begin to count them. The main altars were painted by Michael Bank (?) some great painter of that time. I guess that we were in the catacombs that were built in 377 by St. Maxium. It's tunnels and rooms all are carved out of solid rock in the Mts.

We went in the room where the first Christians in Europe had Mass. The altar is supposed to be copied from St. Peters altar in Rome. Then we were in the room where St. Maxium and 50 followers were caught and killed by orders of some king. Also

Berchtesgaden - Königssee vom Malerwinkel aus

*saw the place where they dumped the bones. As you go into the catacombs it has a big iron gate as you get through so that there is an altar with lots of skulls of Christians along the side of it and in front of the altar is supposed to be buried the bones of forty Christians and lots of other things to numerous to mention. Also at the Archbishops surrounding's, there is the most modern theatre in Europe with a revolving stage and everything. In one big room upstairs there used to be a fireplace all of gold and silver but I guess the Nazi's took them. Salzburg is about the first city I have been in that wasn't all bombed to hell. Lot of the houses were hit but not so much of anything else. I also went to Mozarts home and went all through it and Mozart Museum. We had guides that took us to all the different places. I'm not very good at describing things so when I get home, I'll try telling you about most of these places that I've been to. I guess this will be the last letter I write till I get back to camp because this is all the paper I've got and none of the other guys brought any. I seen a stage show last night put on by the Germans. It was supposed to be Marie Actnerbes. They sang American songs and everything. It was pretty good. These rear echelon guys sure get the breaks to be stationed in a place like this and Salzburg. There are shows going all the time and plenty of sights to see. The only thing I sure miss getting your mail down here. Still loving and missing you.*

*All my Love*

*Your Husband*
*Bill*

#### <u>August 4, 1945 - From Bill to Marge</u>

*Dearest Marge,*

*I sure don't know where to begin. I got back a little while ago. First thing I had to do was read your mail. I*

**Nazis in Berchtesgaden**

The area of Obersalzberg was purchased by the Nazis in the 1920s for their senior leaders to enjoy. Hitler's mountain residence, the Berghof, was located here. Berchtesgaden and its environs were fitted to serve as an outpost of the German Reichskanzlei office (Imperial Chancellery), which sealed the area's fate as a strategic objective for Allied forces in World War II. The Berchtesgadener Hof Hotel was a hotel where famous visitors stayed, such as Eva Braun, Erwin Rommel, Josef Goebels and Heinrich Himmler, as well as Neville Chamberlain and David Lloyd George.

There is the Kehlsteinhaus (nicknamed Eagle's Nest by a French diplomat), which was built as a present for Hitler's 50th birthday in 1939. The remnants of homes of former Nazi leaders such as Adolf Hitler, Hermann Göring, and Martin Bormann were all demolished in the early post-war years.

< < > >

Salzburg, Germany is also the home of the Von Trapp family and where *The Sound of Music* was filmed - Jan says that this was one of the only movies she remembers Dad 'having to see' when it came out. That and *To Hell and Back*, the autobiography of Audie Murphy, which is the only movie she remembers Bill taking Denny and her to see when they were kids. Sue remembers going to this movie and *Patton* with Bill.

Potsdam Conference ends on August 4. Truman doesn't tell Stalin about the atomic bomb.

Four thousand miles from Independence, Mo., Harry Truman threw a wet blanket over fellow Americans' eagerness to travel. Congressmen who wanted to widen their horizons by trips overseas during the recess were told by the President they would have to pay their own expenses ($725.65 via A.T.C. New York to Paris).

Thousands of soldiers' wives, who recently got a halfway promise from the War Department that they might be allowed to join their husbands in Europe if their husbands were going to be stationed there for any length of time, had their hopes blasted by another Presidential ukase. He said he was against it. The best solution is to get U.S. soldiers back to the U.S., said Harry Truman, who does not want Americans "to settle in Europe."

Time Magazine
August 6, 1945

*get 6 letters from the 20th to the 25th. I'm glad you finally got to the cabin for a few days. I'll bet you would sure like to have had me there with you, eh? I also had a letter from the folks. Ma says she sure hopes the baby has brown eyes. I'll bet if it does it will sure be her favorite. (Her one other grandchild so far is Jimmy and he lives out of town.) I got a letter from Vernon to and he didn't go to the South Pacific. He is staying at Marseilles. They took all the guys with 75 points or more out of his outfit just before they left. He also got his staff rating back.*

*Here is his new address in case the folks haven't heard from him yet:*

*S/Sgt. V.W.*
*676 Port Co. 382 Port Bn.*
*APO 772*

*I really enjoyed myself on the trip down to Berchtesgaden. I guess I never told you about being to Hitler's Nest. It is on top of the mountain, a beautiful place. The bombing never touched it. We drove all the way except about 1/2 of it and then we had to walk the rest of the way. It has a big elevator going up but that was for officers, same as with most of the best things to see: For Officers only.*

*Down about 3 miles was where Hitler's big house was, Goring and a few more big shots were also there and they had S.S. barracks. They were pretty well blown up. I went through everything an enlisted man could. It must have cost a big fortune to build, the roads alone up to these places are through solid rock in the mts. and everything. These mts. are called the Bavarian Alps.*

*Last night I seen a stage show put on by the Germans. Really good, lot of the mountain dances, folk songs and things like that. Everybody went wild over it. The guys would have kept them going all night if they could. They sang some American songs in English too. The guys stationed down there really have a paradise.*

*We left there about 8:30 this morning and stopped at Munich for a couple hrs on the way back. It is about 1/2 destroyed, they say, but people come and go just like on a street in a city in the States. They live in a room or two fixed up. Most of the walls of the buildings are still standing, some all*

The Munich Museum was spared destruction by Allied bombers and was one of the few government buildings that was. Postcard from Bill's trip.

burnt out inside, others probably 1/2 of it burnt out. I see when we come back tonight they are having a dance here. They brought in a lot of beautiful girls from Czech. But I don't think I'll go down. Well, there is going to be a movie down here to so I guess I'll go down and see it. Still loving you and leaving the girls alone.

All my Love

Your Husband
Bill

August 5, 1945 - From Bill to Marge

Dearest Marge,

I sure hope I get some mail tomorrow. I didn't get any tonight. Most of the mail has been coming slow. Some guys still get letters wrote to them last winter. How long is it taking my letters to get there now? How is my little fat wife coming now? Getting bigger all the time, I'll bet.

How are you coming with the name situation? You should have plenty of help around there to help you pick one. What does Stan have to say? I'll bet he don't razz you any, does he? Is he still taking out the Hegeman girl? I suppose you thought I quit my letter in a hurry last night but the show started and I wanted to see it. Bob Crosby in something, I don't remember the name. It wasn't very good anyway. The Colonel kind of spoiled the boy's fun at the dance last night, I guess. He was kicking the guys out who didn't keep their shirt collar and pockets buttoned so I guess lot of the guys took off for walks with the girls. They ate in the mess halls today and went back tonight. There were some nice looking ones but they had a few tough looking old blisters. I got up about 8 this morning, had breakfast and went to church. Our chaplain isn't back yet so I went to the German Mass this morning. Had dinner when I got back and then played a little pinochle for the first time in a long time. Lost about $10.

I missed getting paid this month because I was at Berchtesgaden on payday so have to wait till next month. I got about $30 and a $110 loaned out. I think if I figured it up, I haven't spent any of my own money since I left the States. Do you still get your allotment checks and war bonds okay? I hope Marge, that you buy whatever you want for yourself and things for the baby without thinking you spend too much money. We are lucky compared to a lot of these guys wondering what they will do after

August 5, 1945 - No U.S. military man now predicted an immediate surrender by Japan: Admiral William F. Halsey's ill-considered 1943 forecast—"Victory This Year"—was not forgotten. But an astonishing number of military men last week joined in a propaganda barrage designed to bring about an early surrender.

Deliberately, they wooed the enemy by talking tough. Potsdam provided the lure; the military men spelled out the harsh alternative. Boomed the big brass:

This is "the beginning of the final plunge into the heart of the Empire. . . . If the Nips do not know they are a doomed nation, then they are stupider than I think they are."—Admiral Halsey.

"The Japanese . . . are asking for invasion and they are going to get it."—Rear Admiral Arthur W. Radford. CJ Redeployment and retraining of U.S. troops will be speeded to permit the delivery of "a single crushing blow. . . . There's no use doing it piecemeal."—General Jacob L. Devers.

"The biggest massing of air power the world has ever heard of" will soon throw 7,500 bombers and fighter bombers, and later 10,000 of them, against Japan.—General George C. Kenney.

"Japan eventually will be a nation without cities—a nomadic people."—Lieut. General James H. Doolittle.

The Sun & the Wind. With regular broadcasts in Japanese by the Navy's Captain Ellis M. Zacharias, the OWI hoped to persuade the enemy to surrender now and not delay until the situation was "complicated" by other possibilities—obviously a reference to Russian entry into the Pacific war.

http://www.time.com/time/magazine/article/html

The Army finally gave the public a look this week at the plane which Army Air Forces chief General Henry Arnold called the world's fastest fighter plane - the Shooting Star (P-80), which Lockheed has been producing since February.

With a service ceiling of 45,000 ft., it can thunder along at 550 m.p.h. Stories of its fast speed include one that a P-80 was flown from California to New York in three hours and 57 minutes. (Best previous nonstop time: six hours, 39 $\frac{1}{2}$ minutes). Its power is a kerosene-burning jet engine: it has no propeller. Its round nose houses six 50-cal. machine guns. On its wings it can carry either bombs or fuel tanks. Wings and torpedo-like fuselage are painted and polished to the slickness of a wet eel.

http://www.time.com/time/magazine/article/html

OPA (Office of Price Administration) magnanimously dropped rationing of about 6,000 new 1942 cars still in the nation's stock pile, scarcely enough to meet one day's prewar demand. Many dealers, to avoid argument, simply went right on selling cars only to holders of top priorities. OPA also announced that, when the new cars roll off production lines, they will be rationed at first to the same eight classes of essential drivers who previously got stockpile cars.

http://www.time.com/time/magazine/article/

they get out and if they can get their old jobs back and things like that. You see in this Div., I think about half of them got over 60 points and they will probably have enough to get out when they figure up the points again. Lots of guys who came in the Army the same time as I did got from 65-75 points. They got hit once or twice and have 2 or 3 kids. It really puts them up there.

How old is Stan now anyway? Will he be 17 or 18 this fall. I sure hope he don't get any ideas of coming into the service. We have quite a few kids 18 and a couple of them, you would think were about 15 by the way they act and look but they did pretty well in combat. But don't think any of them got over one star so they were in just long enough to get a good taste of combat. Mother wrote that Bud Gowen is home to see now. Did you get a chance to see him? I think he came over about the same time as I did but he should have enough points to be out. He's been in the army five or 6 years now.

It will be kind of rough falling out for training again in the morning after the week vacation. Have you seen anything of Miekle since he left? I suppose he got some big job or has an interest in someplace by now. I'm sure glad you are finally rid of him in one way. Have you found anybody to help out yet? Anyway, don't be killing yourselves. Make what you can, try taking care of Eitzen and let the rest go. I know you have had to work like hell there and I guess it's about enough to drive you nuts sometimes, eh? I remember how disgusted I used to get with it sometimes and I had a good girl working then to. I don't think we'll ever get another one like Dorothy, do you? How is Riley coming? Still the busy lover man? Well, Marge, guess I quit for now. Sure missing you more that ever. I think a lot of all the good times we used to have and hoping it won't be too long before we have them again.

All my Love

Your Husband
Bill

August 5, 1945 - From Bill to Jim and Amanda

Dear folks,

I had a letter from you the other day and better get busy and answer it. It sure sounds like all the boys are getting home now. I wrote Marge with Vernon's address if you haven't got it yet, she'll give it to you.

I'm sure glad he didn't go to the Pacific. He's stationed

*in Marseilles, France. He's going for enough points for discharge now, I think, because I guess they are counting them again. I just came back from Berchtesgaden. That's where Hitler's home was. I went all through it and places around there. I went to Salzburg, Austria to. Went through the big Archbishops castles there. It is a thousand years old. Also the church, which is a 1,000 yrs old too. Sure is beautiful. The main altars were painted by some painter from that time. I suppose there are probably 20 or 30 altars in it. All the Archbishops of Salzburg for the last 1,000 years are buried there.*

*I was also in the catacombs built in the year 377 by St Maxium. The original altar and rooms they had mass in are still there. Also seen where they buried him and the first 50 Christians in Europe who were killed there by the kings men when they were having mass. It is all tunneled out of solid rock in the mountainside. I also spent a little time in Munich, Regensburg (capital of Bavaria) and Nuremberg. Those 3 cities sure had hell bombed out of them. There isn't much left that didn't get it but they have the streetcars running in all of them now. When I get home I'll be able to tell you better of the things I seen. I'm not much good writing about them. I'll stick in a few post cards I picked up there.*

*How's everybody at home, all well, I hope. Are they getting along all right at the bakery without Mieckle? I suppose it's a little quieter around there without his griping. How is little Marie coming? I suppose she is getting so big I will hardly know her when I get home. We haven't heard anything more about when we get home so it (will) probably be Nov or Dec. Well, there isn't much else to write about so I guess I better quit for now. Write and let me know the news.*

*Love, Bill*

August 6, 1945 - From Bill to Marge

*Dearest Marge,*

*I got a letter today from you of the 26th. Sure glad you enjoyed the couple days at the cabin but you didn't say whether you did any fishing or caught any fish. Don't keep me wondering like that where it is any good fishing or not! I guess the lights will be going out here in a few minutes so I probably have to go down to the can to finish this letter. Didn't do much today. We kept practicing for the General. I'm on a demonstration team to demonstrate scouting and grolnting (patrolling?) in*

Winston Churchill II, almost-five-year-old grandson of the former Prime Minister, had his own idea of the meaning of the British elections. When his nurse asked him if he had heard about them, he replied: "Yes, I have a new grandpapa."

Grace Moore, returning from a U.S.O. tour of Europe, had an idea about faithless G.I. wives. Said the fizzy blond cinemactress and Metropolitan Opera soprano: "They ought to shave the heads of these women. . . ."

Henry Ford hailed his 82nd birthday with his customary optimism and plug for unhampered private enterprise. The entire world, said he, is "on the threshold of a prosperity and standard of living that never before was considered possible." He admitted that "there are problems, human, economic, and political, that must be solved."

Admiral William F. Halsey, who had already been promised a saddle for his projected ride on Hirohito's white horse, heard that a pair of handmade spurs were in the offing. Vernon L. Fertig, Machinist's Mate 3/C, had been working on the spurs for more than four months, wrote wistfully from the Aleutians: "I'd like to be there to saddle the horse for you."

On August 6, the United States dropped an atomic bomb, nicknamed *Little Boy*, on Hiroshima, Japan at 8:15 a.m. (local time).

On August 7, President Harry S. Truman announced the successful bombing of Hiroshima with the atomic bomb, while returning from the Potsdam Conference aboard the US Navy heavy-cruiser *USS Augusta* in the middle of the Atlantic Ocean.

*front of the General and some more Brass so I'll get out of 3 days training and practice today and tomorrow yet and then put it on for him Wed. Of course, we don't do much practicing - spend most of the time laying around. Of course, the Colonel had to come out this afternoon to watch and changed a few things. I think he would have us marching at attention doing it if he could. Somebody will probably take a pot shot at him yet if he don't watch out.*

*I went down and took a good shower tonight. Was dirtier than a pig - sure felt good. We had a movie tonight - something about the life of Chopin but the sound didn't work and then only could get about half the film run so everybody left.*

*We had the rumor today that the advance party to the States for the Div. is going to leave this area the 15th of August so if it is true, we probably will be moving back out of Germany the first part of Sept. I sure hope so because I hate to think of taking these maneuvers over here. Although I guess we will spend a night or two a week out in the county any way.*

*I hope I'll be able to spend Christmas home this year.*

*Well, still loving and missing you, quit for tonight but will write a longer letter tomorrow.*

*All my love*

*Bill*

## August 7, 1945 - From Bill to Marge

*Dearest Marge,*

*I got two letters from you tonight 24th and 26th of July and I finally heard that you didn't get any fish. Tough luck, eh? I'm glad Paulson's like it down there - may be that way your folks will go down a little more often. I hope the fish start biting because I know your Dad and Mother like to catch them as well as I do. You wrote ---- and ---- didn't get along too well. I always knew he had a mean streak in him. His dad is the same way. Where is he at now anyway? Has he started to hit the booze any yet, I wonder? Some of the guys are sure lucky staying in the States as long as they do.*

*Is Swede still in the states? So he's still figuring on going into the chicken business after he gets out. It's going to be quite a letdown from a Major to working in a garage, isn't it?*

*We had the youngest Battalion Commander of any outfit in the ETO during the last 3 months of combat.*

*He was only 26 years old. The Lieut. that used to censor my mail, Bill Foster, was only 22. He was our Co. commander for awhile.*

*I don't know whether I ever wrote you this before or not but that concentration camp of Flossenburg is only a few miles from here, part of our Regiment is guarding 9,000 SS they have in it. When our Div. took it, they had dead bodies stacked up all over the place. I guess lots of guys went up to see it but I never did. Our Regt. Com. was over today and gave us a speech. I guess we start with maneuvers the 15th of Sept till Middle of Oct. I sure hope they change the schedule and send us home earlier but he said we were to arrive in the States about the 15th of Dec. So if we do, I'd be spending Christmas and New Years at home. Do you suppose we will enjoy it as much as last New Years? I was sure happy to get to spend it with you.*

*Has Sis ever heard from Dale yet? He's liable to make it home before the baby is born yet, eh? I'm sitting here sipping on some wine while I'm writing. This is the first we have had in quite a while and we got about a pint a piece - 40 cents, cheap enough, eh?*

*This sour wine is a lot better than any wine I ever drank in the States. This is probably about the same as John used to get in Africa. We get cognac too but I always give mine to somebody who feels like getting full. I don't know what whiskey would be like anymore. I think the last whiskey I drank was in Kansas City but I'll bet I'll still be able to put away my share when I get home. How about you?*

*I got my 3 stars for my ETO ribbon yesterday and I lost them all ready. I think I was sure lucky getting into the 90th Div. when I came over because it is supposed to be one of the best Div. over here. We got pretty near all new officers after the war was over and they had the pick of going to the 1st, 4th, 9th. Or 4th Armored and took the 90th because of its reputation. At least that is why they tell us they took it. I think I'll have to write Marquardt after awhile. He has surprised me writing as much as he has because he hardly ever wrote any letters when he was over here.*

*I didn't do much today - Played pinochle most of the day. Cost me about $15 but I'll be making that back again and probably a little besides. How long before we have one of those games in the back of the bakery again, do you suppose? I'm sure glad I sent that pistol home with*

Broadway and Hollywood have also gone to war in U.S.O. Camp Show uniforms (Army o.d. or khaki). Last week some 250 entertainers invaded Europe, the largest group yet in a great push that began shortly after V-E day. The Army prescribed it as a cure for the G.I. doldrums.

The supreme commander behind U.S.O.'s army of entertainers is chunky, chubby Abe Lastfogel, 47. Affable Abe, who worked his way up from office boy to senior partner of show business' Wm. Morris Agency, was asked to organize U.S.O. Camp Shows in 1941.

Working without pay, he operated on the premise that entertainment for servicemen was not only "desirable but essential." He had a big job recruiting entertainers, who were leary of the hardships and pay (the U.S.O., which is subsidized by the National War Fund, pays run-of-the-mill entertainers $100 a week, topflight volunteers $10 a day). But by hook & crook, Lastfogel rounded up thousands of smalltime entertainers. These troupers, formed into small variety companies, were (and still are) the backbone of U.S.O. Camp Shows.

http://www.time.com/time/magazine/article/html

On August 8, the United Nations Charter was ratified by the United States Senate and the US became the third nation to join the new international organization.

On August 8, the Soviet Union declared war on Japan.

To most, Ulithi means no more than Ailinglapalap, another Pacific atoll. But to U.S. Navy men Ulithi for nearly a year has been a home, a grocery store and an arsenal. Until last week it was also a military secret.

Ulithi is a series of flat, palm-dotted islands. It is 110 miles east of Jap-held Yap, 400 miles southwest of Guam—and 4,000 miles nearer the war than Pearl Harbor. Ulithi was captured without opposition last September by the 321st Regiment of the 81st Infantry Division. The Japs had just left. Ulithi's great, 112-sq.-mi. anchorage could hold nearly 1,000 ships of the U.S. Fleet—something neither Guam nor Pearl Harbor can do.

When the Americans turned up at Ulithi, the 300 primitive natives and their paralytic King Ueg (pronounced Weg) agreed to move from Mogmog to mile-long Fassarai, one of the atoll's southern islands. The result was something new in naval history: a vast service station enabling entire fleets to operate indefinitely at unprecedented distances from their main, landmass bases.

*Time Magazine August 6, 1945*

*Earl Carroll Vanities* (1945): Royalty from a small European principality come to New York City to arrange for a loan to prop up their country's troubled finances. While the queen mother attends to the negotiations, Princess Drina strikes up a friendship with Tex Donnelly, who owns a nightclub and gives her boogie-woogie piano lessons.

Starring Dennis O'Keefe, Eve Arden, Constance Moore and Pinky Lee.

Marquardt because I'm afraid there is going to be a little more red tape taking them home by the time I come. Well Marge, keep up the writing and have Ma see how come they quit sending the Democrat.

I'll bet you really fill out a dress now, eh.

All my Love

Your Husband

Bill

August 8, 1945 - From Bill to Marge

Dearest Marge,

Well Marge, I didn't get any mail from you today but I hope I do tomorrow. The news of that new bomb sure sound good. Maybe it will bring the Japs around to surrender. That's all the guys have been talking about here the last couple of days.

The General and some more brass were here all morning. He thought our demonstration was excellent and gave us the old line of bull (about) what good men we were. But tonight after retreat our Captain gave us quite a lecture. It seems the Colonel was uptown this afternoon checking to see if any of the guys were slipping out and of course, he rounded up quite a bunch and of course, they all had to be out of F. Co! So the Col. told the Captain as long as F. Co had the best record in combat, they should be the best garrison soldiers. So the Captain was telling us to try doing a little better as it is now F is the Co which is always fucking up. We sure have some naughty times in our little concentration camp here.

What do Luthers ever hear from Junior now? Is he back on line duty? I sure hope the guys never have to invade Japan. It will probably be 50,000 more casualties if they do. We are supposed to have a show tonight, Earl Connols Variety I hope they have the projector working tonight. I hardly ever leave the area except to go in town to church or shows, something like that. I see by the papers where some of the Senators are trying to have the size of the Army cut. I don't see where they will every use all of them in Div. Because over here the most they ever had was 3 million and that was when the war ended.

It is just 7 months today I have been overseas. Sure seems a lot longer. What do you think? I sure can't think of anything to write so guess I'll quit. Still loving and missing you.

All my love Your Husband Bill

August 9, 1945 - From Bill to Marge

*Dearest Marge,*

*I got 4 letters from you tonight of July 29 and 1st August. That's coming in pretty good time.*

*Sorry to hear that ---- is treating her baby the way she does. I'll bet if Jim was home he would knock some sense in her head. You said it was 8 months since we were in Kansas City but it was only 7. I don't know what you did about that lot (of land) but do whatever your Dad thinks. I think a person would always be able to get their money out of it and it don't do much good in the checking account.*

*Anything like that ever comes up, its all right with me whatever you do. What are you paying for flour and lard now anyway? And how much flour are you buying at one time? I haven't been able to watch the markets any since I've been over here. I always thought when the war ended I would book (order) quite a lot but I'm not so sure now because I think Russia has a big crop this year and all over where I've been in Bavaria and Czech. They're getting big crops so don't think the Germans will starve this winter like they were afraid of. They probably won't be shipping the wheat out the States like I figured to make it higher than hell. You asked about the bowl for the doughnuts. Well, it is in the bottom of that cabinet where we keep all the spices and extracts right at the end of the bench.*

*Say, it kinda sounds like you are really mixing with the nice people, the Whites and Masons. Where is Pink working or is he taking it easy for awhile?*

*Does Dorothy have any idea what Freddy is going to do when he gets out? I think most of the guys will probably try to get jobs at home. Most of our guys are figuring on going back to live in their hometowns. We didn't do anything today except a clothing inspection. They checked all our equipment and then I lost about $100 playing poker. Rough, eh? They are cutting our Co. down to regular strength now for some reason or another so a lot of the guys who came in the last 5 or 6 months will be getting shipped out but I'm not in that bunch. There are still a lot more come in after I did even when they get it cut to regular strength. Boy, but us guys were sure glad when we heard the news last night that Russia was to declare war on Japan today. That will sure save a lot of G.I. lives.*

*Every time the news comes on, there is always a bunch*

On August 9, the United States dropped the second atomic bomb on Japan. This one, nicknamed *Fat Man* destroyed Nagasaki at 11:02 a.m. (local time).

In the estimation of US Military Planners, dropping the atomic bombs on the Japanese mainland would save as many as 1,000,000 wartime casualties.

The Soviet Union began its army offensive against Japan in the northern part of Japanese-held Chinese region of Manchuria.

August 1945 - A new era was born—the age of atomic force. Like many an epoch in man's progress toward civilization, it was wombed in war's destruction. The birth was announced one day this week by the President of the United States. His words:

"Sixteen hours ago, an American airplane dropped one bomb on Hiroshima, an important Japanese army base. That bomb had more power than 20,000 tons of TNT. ... It is an atomic bomb. It is a harnessing of the basic power of the universe. . . . What has been done is the greatest achievement of organized science in history. . . ."

Thus to the U.S., already great in military and scientific prowess, had come man's most destructive weapon. To the U.S. Army Air Forces had been given the means for complete destruction of Japan. General "Tooey" Spaatz and his Pacific flyers could now blow the enemy into the sea, for one atomic bomb dropped from one plane can wreak the same destruction as 2,000 B-29s.

http://www.time.com/time/magazine/article/html

Unconditional surrender—the victory theme of the U.S. and her Allies since 1943—was replaced last week by a more daring formula for ending the war with Japan.

From Potsdam to Tokyo went a declaration (by the U.S., Britain and China) offering concrete, unalterable terms upon which Japan could end the war. The phrase "unconditional surrender" was still used. But it applied only to the armies in the field. The terms were for the nation. Their gist:

Defeated Japan could have industries, but not a war industry.

She could have a government, but not a government of militarists.

She could have a home—the four main islands, and such little ones as the Allies might let her keep—but not a Greater East Asia.

The occupation of Japan need not follow the German pattern. But the declaration's promises to limit occupation to "points designated by the Allies" obviously could mean anything: Tokyo alone, or every city and hamlet in Japan. The significant provisions were that 1) there would be an occupation; 2) it would end as soon as Japan had effectively disarmed and had established a peaceful government.

All mention of the Emperor was omitted, possibly because the Allies are still debating what to do with him.

http://www.time.com/time/magazine/article/html

On August 10, Japan offered surrender to the Allies, *provided this does not prejudice the sovereignty of the Emperor.*

*right there. Maybe before many more days we might get the news we have all been waiting to hear. If that bomb is as good as they claim, I hear they used it again today. Boy when this war is over, nobody could ever get me to live in a manufacturing town in a city after seeing the way it did over here. If there was another war, the cities in the States will sure take a pounding.*

*The people who lived on farms are the fortunate ones. Most of them had a lot of stuff put away out in the hills that the G.I.'s didn't get in their looting going through. You wrote once about sending a cable when the baby is born but a letter would be faster because it takes cables a couple of months before the guys ever get them.*

*I sent my clothes up with a kid to have them washed a little while ago. Just about every thing I got was dirty so the old lady will earn her soap and whatever else I find to pay for it with. You asked about the women bothering me - not much. I've never monkeyed with one, yet and don't intend to but I tell you if I was single, I wouldn't pass up some of them and I've had plenty of chances.*

*Well, Marge, take good care of yourself and the young one. I'm sure waiting for the day we can be together again.*

*All of my Love*

*Your Husband*
*Bill*

<u>August 10, 1945 - From Bill to Marge</u>

*Dear Marge,*

*I thought I'd better get busy and write you this afternoon, because we have a night problem from 6-11:30 or 12 tonight, scouting and patrolling. I suppose they try to have us going through all their woods and they will probably succeed tonight because it is raining and cold on that hill this afternoon so a guy will get cold if he don't keep moving tonight. We didn't do much today. This morning we had a couple min. to wash up equipment and things like that. Then of course, we had a short arms inspection again. It must be a couple weeks since we had one. I guess you know what they are, don't you?*

*Then we had some close order drill and Co. mass drill. This afternoon haven't did much, just got done sweating out the P.X. line for an hr. Got 6 pack of cigarettes, 1 cigar, 1 plug tobacco, 4 bars of candy, 2 rolls mints, 1 bar of soap and a Coke.*

*That's the week's supply. It is getting a little bit better than it was at first. We are even getting a little snow today so you know it isn't very warm. I kinda am figuring on catching a couple hrs. sleep as quick as I finish this letter.*

*We've only had a few real hot days over here since I've been here. Haven't heard much war news to amount to anything today except the Pres. saying they were going to continue to use the atomic bomb till they finish this war. Boy, it must be hell to be near that from what I've read about it.*

*The rumor is going around here now that we are liable to be Occupational now that the Russians entered the war.*

*Of course a guy never knows from one minute to the next what he is going to do. That the old Army gave up keeping you guessing. The news will be on in about 15 min. so I'm going to listen to it before I catch some sleep. Sure hope everybody is all right at home and things are going pretty good at the bakery. I've been lucky since I've been over here never missed any time on account of being sick. How are you and the Kreebs been coming? Still go up to see them?*

*I sure hope I get some mail from you again today I sure look forward to it. Still loving and missing you.*

*All my Love*

*Your Husband*
*Bill*

In one of the greatest dragnet roundups of all time, the U.S. Army in Germany arrested 80,000 Germans last week. To prevent alarm-spreading, a half-million G.I.s first isolated the target communities by cutting their outside communications, then searched all houses in the U.S. zone, stopped every person moving on the streets and roads. Some 15,000,000 Germans were sifted through the screen.

The raid had multiple purposes: To ferret out illegal material such as weapons, ammunition, radio transmitters, U.S. uniforms and rations, gasoline; to catch Nazis; to turn up U.S. AWOLs (only a handful); to inhibit black-market operations. A secondary purpose was to test the occupation army's security machinery. It tested very well. Orders for the raid (Codeword: "Tallyho") were distributed three weeks in advance. There were no leaks.

http://www.time.com/time/magazine/article/

<u>*August 11, 1945 - From Bill to Marge*</u>

*Dearest Marge,*

*Well, Marge, I thought I'd better get on the ball and start writing. We've been sitting around talking about the news and listening to all the news broadcasts. About 10 minutes after I wrote to you yesterday, we hear the news where the Japs offered to surrender and then got the news tonight that the four powers now are all (agreeing), now all we are waiting about is the cease firing for it to become official and then I'll collect $50 bucks. I didn't write you about that part because I thought you would think I was nuts but I bet a guy 50 bucks that the war with Japan would be over before Sept. and it looks like I'm going to collect it. Tonight at chow everyone went wild when they heard that the four powers accepted it. Now we will have to sweat out getting home. I*

On August 11, the Allies replied to the Japanese surrender offer by stating that Emperor Hirohito would be subject to the authority of the Supreme Commander of the Allied Forces.

The *Four Powers* Bill writes about was The Allied Control Council or Allied Control Authority, known in German as the Alliierter Kontrollrat and was the military occupation governing body of the Allied Occupation Zones in Germany after the end of World War II in Europe; the members were the United States, the United Kingdom, and the Soviet Union. France was later added with a vote but had no duties. The Allied Control Council was based in Berlin-Schöneberg.

Back in Washington after 32 days away from his White House desk, President Truman found the capital hot, humid and in the doldrums, and the country's domestic problems piled up in stubborn, mountainous stacks. The first 100 days had come & gone. Now President Truman faced problems which could not be solved by a mere reference to his predecessor's policy. New decisions had to be made - and had to be made by Harry Truman alone.

First & foremost was an all-out row over the size of the Army. Civilian officials were clamoring for release of soldiers to mine coal and help out in the transportation jam. Almost everybody in the capital thought the Army was too big - except the Army. Last week, the scrap was brought to a head by Colorado's angular, crinkly-haired Senator Ed Johnson, a constant thorn in the War Department's side.

Senator Johnson accused the Army of "blind and stupid and criminal" failure to provide an orderly discharge of soldiers.

The point-discharge system he branded a "mathematical monstrosity." He charged that the Army could transport and supply no more than 3,000,000 at the Japanese front, not the 7,000,000-man Army as presently called for.

*Time Magazine August 13, 1945*

On August 13, the Zionist World Congress approached the British government to discuss the founding of the country of Israel.

*sure hope we come home earlier now. They should have plenty of planes to fly them home with.*

*They just brought in a lot of booze from Pilsen a while ago. I guess they will have them Sat. night dances again tonight but you needn't worry about me because I never go anyway.*

*I don't know whether I'll get to church in the morning or not. I'm to go on outpost for a week guarding a D.P. (Displaced persons) camp over to Weines and get out of all the training and only have to stand a little guard but I don't suppose I'll be able to get any mail while I'm over there. Most of the guys all want to go but only 3 (get) to go from our platoon and we can't let anyone else take our place. I just tried to fix it for another kid could take my place but no dice. The reason they all want it mostly is they can get laid all day and night there if they want to. I didn't get any mail the last 2 days so I suppose there'll be some tomorrow when I'm not here. I'll bet they are really celebrating in the States now but I think I'll still wait till I get home and then we will sure make up for lost time.*

*I suppose by the time you get this letter the baby will be born or awful close. Sure wish I could be there with you but maybe now when I get home it will be to stay. It sure is going to seem funny after the way I've been living this last 7 or 8 months.*

*Well, Marge, better quit for now. Sure missing and loving you.*

*All my Love*

*Your Husband*
*Bill*

August 13, 1945 - From Bill to Marge

*Dearest Marge,*

*I got 2 letters of July 30th from you yesterday and one from the folks. I sure hated to hear about the steam boiler going on the bum. If you haven't bought a new one yet, try to get a small one heated by fuel oil or Skelgas, that's what I always planned on getting. If you don't get one right away, a little hotplate or small oil burner with a pail of water on top will furnish plenty of steam. I sure wish I was home to take care of it but there's nothing I can do about it over here. Oh, if you get one, have it so the pressure don't go above 25 lbs.*

*I'm over on this outpost for a week now. We left yesterday afternoon. We were supposed to leave in the morn-*

*ing but us guys keep disappearing till after the mail got in so we got our mail before we left and I put my stuff on the wrong truck so I'm without anything for a couple days. Left my rifle, blankets, shaving and washing articles, change of clothes, cigarettes and writing stuff so if I don't get it back they will really be socking it to me. We are supposed to pay for any equipment we lose now. We sure have a nice place to stay here - in a big house well furnished. I guess there are about 5 or 6 girls that do the cooking and keep the place clean, serve us just like we were in a restaurant in the States. We do 2 hrs guard duty and then we have 6 hrs off. We are guarding about 600 Poles. They have a big dance every night. I was on guard there last night so I walked in and watched a while and one old gal came over and started talking to me. Then she asked me to come upstairs a minute so I did, thinking she was going to show me something - instead she wanted to lay me but I turned it down and sent her to one of the other boys. I guess he will take care of her the week he is here.*

*If I wasn't a married man I could get pretty well fagged out here but I think their girls will suffer a little bit more with the guard this week because there are four of us guys married who don't monkey with them.*

*I sure enjoyed watching the dance each night though. Well, Marge, I'll probably write again tonight so will close for now. Still loving and missing you.*

*All my love*

*Your Husband*
*Bill*

So far as any discernible, immediate effect on Japan last week was concerned, the Potsdam offer of surrender terms (TIME, Aug. 6) was a flop. The Suzuki Cabinet had specifically rejected the terms. Admiral Kichisaburo Nomura, the dry old man who was talking peace in Washington on Pearl Harbor day, called the terms "the height of impertinence." The controlled Japanese press and radio played them up as though they were good for home morale. An "extremely indignant" civilian letter-writer to a Japanese newspaper denounced the Potsdam declaration for "scheming to alienate the military and civilians." Said he: "The war's responsibility rests upon the shoulders of the nation's 100,000,000 subjects."

But the offer was not necessarily a failure. Its authors had not expected an instant success; it was a slow-burning fire. And it had been timed to precede the shock of the new atomic bomb, a weapon which would hit Japan and the Japanese as no land or people had ever before been hit. Soon the survivors might be more receptive.

http://www.time.com/time/magazine/article/html

<u>August 14, 1945 - From Bill to Marge</u>

This letter is postmarked, Kerson, Germany

*Dearest Marge,*

*I just got off guard so I thought I better write. I didn't get any letters from you today but got a box you sent around July 11 with the tobacco, cigarettes, magazines, tomato juice and candy in it. Thanks a lot - the candy sure went good and the magazines make the guard go by lots faster. I suppose the Lieut. would eat my ass out if he caught me.*

*Last night when I was on from 2 to 4 I brought my blanket along and myself and another kid crammed in a command car and caught a couple hrs sleep. A guy wouldn't mind pulling guard if there was any sense to it but there isn't. Here where we are, there hasn't been much going on around except this morning a little boy*

On August 14, Japanese Emperor Hirohito accepted the terms of the Potsdam Declaration and accepted unconditional surrender as per those edicts.

From Solid Fuels Administrator Harold L. Ickes came a chilly prediction last week: unless the Army quickly releases some coal miners from the service, U.S. citizens will have the most uncomfortable winter of the war.

"I am not a prestidigitator," said Honest Harold, "and neither are any of the members of the Solid Fuels Administration staff. We have no magic wands and we cannot produce coal without coal miners. No one else can."

Then he gave the figures: in the present fuel year (which began last April 1) the manpower now in the mines can produce 575,000,000 tons of soft coal (estimated need: 600,000,000 tons) and 43,000,000 tons of hard coal (estimated need: 55,000,000 tons). "These figures," said Ickes, "point definitely to a worrisome deficit of 37,000,000 tons."

http://www.time.com/time/magazine/article/html

was playing around where I was on guard and fell and got quite a cut in his head. By the time I got him to the doc, I was just covered with blood. He's all right though as quick as he got it bandaged. The people where sure thankful and nothing doing but they had to wash my clothes for me. Four of us ate that bag of candy so I got a lot more out of it than I usually do. Sure good to.

The 9 o'clock news should be on in another 15 or 20 min. so I'm supposed be in at the radio listening. The quicker it ends the sooner we will be together for good again.

In this town there are four storks. Some young ones have a big nest right up a top of the priest' home. It is the first time a lot of the guys ever seen them but I have noticed them in quite a few homes coming through Germany. I guess it is supposed to be some good omen if they live on top of your chimney according to what I gather from the people.

I guess most of the boys are to the dance or having pussy tonight. There are only 2 of us that have not anyway. Aren't you glad your man don't have this stuff over here! When I get home, I'll have to make up for the lost time eh? Don't you think you will be in the mood!

We had a couple of American girls here for supper but I wasn't talking except to say Hello. The Burgermeister of this town is an American citizen. I guess he got caught over here when the war started. We ran into some of them that lived in one American city and some who lived in all different cities in the states.

I hear they are still continuing the training for Japs back at camp even with the war about over. One good thing to get out of all that training and formations this week anyway. The Lieut. told us this was supposed to be sort of a rest for us.

Well, Marge hope you are taking care of yourself. Still loving and missing you and praying it won't be to long before we are together again.

All my love

Your Husband Bill

<u>August 15, 1945 - From Bill to Jim and Amanda</u>

This letter is postmarked, Weisan, Germany.

Dear Folks,

Received a letter from you of July 29 the other day so thought I better get busy and write. We just heard last night where the war ended (Victory in Japan) and we sure are a happy bunch over here. I'll collect $50 when

*I get back to camp for it. I had 50 dollars bet with a guy the war would be over before Sept. and it looks like I'll collect. I'm on an outpost now. Guarding D.P. (Displaced Persons). Those Poles and Ukrainians, they loot the hell out of these towns if they ain't watched. But I'd never stop them from bringing things in because the Germans brought them here, so they can suffer a little for it.*

*We stay in a nice home here. There are just 18 of us guys in this town. We have 3 different posts we have to guard. Have 2 hrs. on and 6 hrs. off and so on. We are here for a week. It is supposed to be kinda a rest for us, I guess. It's good to get away from all that chicken shit training we've been having but I haven't got in on much of it. Down to Berchtesgaden a week, then last week was on a demonstration team for the general and this week over here so am getting out of most of it. Maybe they will quit it now that the war is over. I wished to hell they could get me home as quick as they brought me over.*

*How is everybody coming at home. I suppose all the kids have grown a lot since I've left. Just a year ago today I left for the army and I put most of it in overseas - going on 8 months now.*

*Well, Vernon should get home in a month or so now. I hear where they are sending all the high pointers home first but I think our Div. will all go home together because most of them are fairly high pointers.*

*I'm down quite a ways. I've got 36 now but I think they will discharge them with less points than that.*

*I'll sure be glad when I get home. I don't know whether I'll be worth a damn around the bakery or not. It has been so long since I've did a day's work.*

*I can see now why John couldn't take it when he got out.*

*I hope Marge will be able to find somebody before school starts. It's only a couple weeks off.*

*Was not doing any thing today. The Lieut. gave us the day and night off on account of the war ending. I went to Mass and benediction here this morning. I forgot about it being a holy day till I seen all the Krauts going to church and I asked one how come. He told me it was a holy day. Well, better quit for now. Write and let me know the news and how everything is coming.*

*Love,*

*Bill*

On August 15, Japanese Emperor Hirohito announced Japan's surrender on the radio. The United States calls this day V-J Day (Victory in Japan). This ends the period of Japanese expansionism and begins the period of Occupied Japan.

Korea gained independence following Japan's surrender.

On August 17, Indonesian nationalists Soekarno and Mohammad Hatta declared the independence of the Republic of Indonesia, with Soekarno as the president. Dutch colonial authorities did not approve.

The novel *Animal Farm* by George Orwell was published by Fredric Warburg.

On August 18, scheduled demonstrations at the Polo Grounds and Ebbets Field to end segregation in organized baseball were called off.

On August 19, the Viet Minh, led by Ho Chi Minh, took power in Hanoi, Vietnam a French colony at the time.

Mao Zedong and Chiang Kai-shek met with Chongqing to discuss an end to hostilities between the Chinese Communists and the Nationalists.

On August 21, President Harry S. Truman ended the *Lend-Lease Program*.

Republic of Mauritius (French: République de Maurice) is an island nation off the coast of the African continent in the southwest Indian Ocean. Jews who had been freed from German concentration camps had gathered on this island nation and on August 25, the government of Britain permitted them to leave and enter Palestine.

On August 26, Japanese diplomats boarded the USS Missouri to receive instructions on Japan's surrender.

On August 27, US troops landed in Japan after the surrender.

On August 29, Great Britain liberated Hong Kong from Japan.

General MacArthur was named Supreme Commander of Allied Powers in Japan.

On August 30, General MacArthur landed in Tokyo, Japan.

August 25, 1945 - From Bill to Marge

Dearest Marge,

Well Marge this sure isn't anything like the way I used to spend Sat night. Just came back from uptown and walking around. We were walking around for the last couple hours raiding a few apple, pear, and plum trees. Pretty well filled up on the stuff now.

I didn't get any mail from you again tonight but had a letter from Vernon dated Aug 17. He's still at Marseilles and figured he will be there a while yet. One thing over here nobody is sure of anything. The rumors are the 90th is going home in Oct but it's hard to tell if many of us guys will be with it but we still haven't heard anything from the General about it. But I suppose he'll be around one of these days telling us how things are going to be. I'm hoping I go home with them though I didn't do anything today. Slept all morning while they had the inspection and then this afternoon I played casino about all afternoon. We haven't had any wine or anything to drink here all week so I suppose the first of the week we will have another ration coming in.

I'm going to try going to communion tomorrow if the chaplain is there and I don't get stuck on anything to do. Been going to go for quite a while now but something always comes up. DeMarco and myself are both sitting here writing. He always writes his wife every night.

Well how is everything going at the bakery now? Is the new help coming along pretty well? I'll sure be glad when I'm back there taking care of things. Maybe you won't have so much to worry about then. Did you ever get rid of the doughnut machine? It is sure an eyesore there. I hope to hell somebody buys it. How's John and Stan coming with their romances? They aren't figuring on getting married yet are they?

Well Marge I'm sure waiting for the Sat. nights when we can go out tipping a few again.

Still loving and missing you.

All my love,

Your Husband
Bill

COMPANY "F" 357TH INFANTRY
APO 90, U.S.Army

29 August 1945

SUBJECT: Non Table of Organizational Weapons.

TO : Adjutant General, 90th Infantry Division, APO 90, U.S.Army.

The following named Enlisted man is being transfered from this company and he has the following non T/O weapon in his possession.

Waldron, William, 37772525 Sauer, 32, No. 404690

CLIFFORD E. PENROSE
Capt., Inf.,
Commanding

Why wait to make your pipe-dreams come true?

The minute the whistle blows—make a date with Model. Get that special kind of deep-down happiness only a pipe-smoking he-male can know!

Make a date—

The pistol mentioned in this transfer is probably the one pictured on Page 134 earlier in this narrative.

Captain Clifford E. Penrose, Bill's CO, was quite a soldier. Cliff was born Oct. 4, 1918, on a farm near Udall in southeastern Kansas. He grew up in Wichita, Kan., and attended the University of Wichita (now Wichita State University) before joining the Kansas National Guard.

He entered active military duty Dec. 20, 1940, before the U.S. entered World War II. After having served in the last working unit of the U.S. Horse Calvary, he graduated from Officer Candidate School in the 60th Armored Infantry Battalion of the Ninth Armored Division, where he was awarded the Silver Star Medal for Gallantry in Action during the Battle of the Bulge. He was also awarded the Bronze Star Medal and Oak Leaf Cluster to the Bronze Star Medal for Bravery, Combat Infantry Badge, Purple Heart and various Campaign Medals. He was twenty-six when he was Bill's CO.

On December 15, 1944 (the night before the Battle of the Bulge commenced) he wrote to his wife, "I'm living in a dugout and the damn thing is starting to leak tonight. So don't let a few blurred spots bother you, it isn't beer. We had Spam for supper tonight. And then your package came. Thanks a lot, but next time don't send Spam."

From 1946 to 1949, he served on the Hiroshima and Okayama Military Government teams as public health and welfare officer during the occupation of Japan after World War II.

Cliff served in the Far Eastern Command during the Korean War from 1952 to 1953. He retired from the U.S. Army in November 1965.

He died on March 18, 2010.

Quote from *Battle: The Story of the Bulge* by John Toland, Random House, 1959.

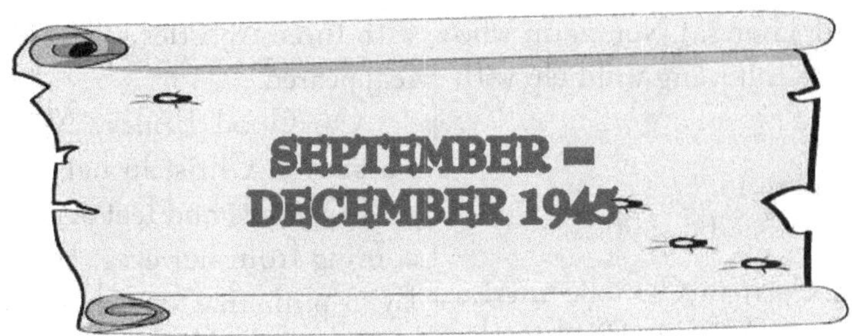


The world has changed. In April, Adolf Hitler with his wife of one day, committed suicide and caused their bodies to be covered with gasoline and burnt. Less than a days fight away, Soviet troops were in Berlin and making their way toward the Fuhrerbunker. A few days later, the German government accepted unconditional surrender. They first attempted to make a separate peace with the United States, Great Britain and France; the thinking being that such an arrangement would allow the Wehrmacht, cleansed of the Nazis, to join with the Allies and take on the Communist Soviets. Many in the highest echelons of the German war machine were surprised when the overture was declined.

Once peace was achieved in Europe, the Potsdam Conference edicts began to take affect. Berlin, and the country as a whole, were divided into Sectors obstensibly to insure that a unified Germany would never again be able to mount war on its neighbors. Before long the country becomes East Germany, administered by the Soviets and West Germany, under the supervision of the rest of the Allies. Potsdam virtually ensured the creation of the Cold War.

Meanwhile in the Pacific, fanatic Japanese, in control of the government, continue to push for victory when sanity would dictate surrender; old people, women and children were being trained by the govt to use pitchforks and spears and they intended to defend the homeland at all costs. Allied forces were bombing major cities, Japanese strongholds were falling against overwhelming odds (in spite of suicidal defenses) and wartime resources, always in short supply to the island Nation, had all but disappeared. Against this backdrop it was estimated that millions would die if the Allies were required to take Japan's home island by force; the vast majority of these would be Japanese civilians. The decision was made by President Harry S. Truman to use the atomic bomb.

The first atomic bomb was dropped on August 6 (Japanese Time) and the world entered The Atomic Age. Almost a footnote but for the impact it would have, on August 8 the Soviet Union declared war on the Empire of Japan. The second atomic bomb was dropped on August 9 and Japan asked for peace on August 10; their sole preoccupation was the future status of the Emperor. The Allies responded the next day that the Emperor would be subservient to the Supreme Commander of Japan. On August 14, Japanese Emperor Hirohitio accepted the peace terms as per the Potsdam Conference.

The defeat of the Axis Powers sowed the seeds of future conflict. Korea gained independence, China lacked a power base with two competing factions, Indonesia sought independence as would Vietnam and, among others, Israel was in the throes of birth and being.

Closer to Bill's world, the point system remained a constant preoccupation. While scuttlebutt had it changing on a daily basis the larger picture was that moving the troops home was an unimaginable task; it would be impossible to find fault with men wanting to return home and being impatient to see that happen.

Frustrating to this narrative, in this time period there seem to be missing letters. Bill is on guard duty at some outpost on August 14. He has commented that he thinks he will remain with Company F, 357th Infantry, 90th Division for the duration and that they will be returning "probably" in December. He has further discounted his MOS of cook/baker and prefers his present duty - although not as much as he would prefer returning to Marge, Waukon and the bakery. After his letter to the folks on August 15, we have nothing until a single letter to Marge on August 25 in which he says nothing about a transfer. Then, on August 29, he was transferred and sent to Headquarters Company to become again a cook/baker. Would that we had more background on how this came about, but perhaps future letters will illuminate that which occurred.

While en route to Headquarters Company, Bill made

a visit to Therese (pronounced Theresa) Neumann who very much impressed him. The following will help with our understanding of why:

Therese Neumann
April 9, 1898 - September 18, 1962

Therese Neumann was a German Catholic mystic and stigmatic. She was born on April 9, 1898 in the village of Konnersreuth in Bavaria, Germany, where she lived all her life. She was a member of the Third Order of St. Francis.

On March 10, 1918, Therese Neumann was partially paralyzed after falling off a stool. She sustained more falls and injuries during this period. In 1919, she was blinded completely. Bedridden, she reportedly developed horrible bed sores that sometimes exposed bone.

Therese reported that her eyesight was restored on April 29, 1923 - due to the blessing of Therese of Lisieux; Therese Neumann said the saint later called to her and cured her of her paralysis and bed sores as well.

On November 13, 1925 Neumann was diagnosed with appendicitis. She asked her family to take her to the church to pray immediately. She then announced that she had been cured of all traces of appendicitis.

Therese would later develop the stigmata. On March 5, 1926, the first Friday of Lent, a wound appeared slightly above her heart, but she kept this secret. However, she did report a vision of Jesus at Mount Olivet with three Apostles. On subsequent Fridays the wound reappeared.

On Good Friday, Neumann witnessed the entire Passion of Christ in her visions. She displayed wounds on her hands and feet accompanied by blood apparently coming from her eyes. Blood poured from the wounds. By 3 p.m. that day, her parish priest Fr. Josef Naber was summoned to give Neumann the Last Rites. By 4 o'clock, her condition improved. The wounds on her feet and hands were observed when she was bathed.

By November 5, 1926, she displayed nine wounds on her head as well as wounds on her back and shoulders. These wounds never healed or became infected and were found on her body at death.

From the year of 1922 until her death in 1962, Therese Neumann consumed no food other than The Holy Eucharist, and claimed to have drunk no water from 1926 until her death.

During the Third Reich, Therese Neumann was the target of ridicule and defamation, as the Nazis knew about her dissenting views and feared her growing popularity. She was observed by the Gestapo. She was never physically harmed, though her family home, parish church and priest's house all received direct attacks. She encouraged Fritz Gerlich to continue his opposition to Hitler and his national-socialist party. Mr. Gerlich was subsequently killed for his opposition.

*Wikipedia, The Free Encyclopedia*

---

September 3, 1945 - From Bill to Jim and Amanda

*Dear Folks,*

*Well, folks, I thought I would write again tonight. I wrote a couple nights ago. Things look kind of bad around here lately. I think I'll get transferred to occupational army but don't know for sure yet. I'm working in the kitchen now I was transferred to HQ. Been doing a little baking. Here is my Inf. (illegible) --address? (Can read 357 Infantry.)*

*I went over to see Theresa Neumann today. That's the woman who has all the wounds of Christ and bleeds from them every Friday. She hasn't ate or drank anything for 17 years and looks just as well as anybody. I seen the wounds on her hands. They are blood clotted about the size of a dime. I got a holy card from her with her signature and was also in a picture taken of her that*

Therese Neumann

goes to the Bishop of Regensburg. I'm going to try getting one but don't know whether I'll have any luck or not. Well, I suppose Vernon should be home soon. I'll bet there will be the celebrating around there then. I suppose the fair will be starting in a couple days there. Do you suppose you'll be able to keep John working then? I just hear over the radio when they are going to be along all right at home. Well, better quit for now. If I get transferred out, I'll write as soon as I do.

Love,

Your son
Bill

On September 2, Japanese general Tomoyuki Yamashita surrendered to Filipino and American forces at Kiangan, Ifugao on the Phillipines.

World War II ends. The final official surrender of Japan was accepted by the Supreme Allied Commander, General Douglas MacArthur and Fleet Admiral Chester Nimitz for the United States and delegates from Australia, New Zealand, the United Kingdom, The Netherlands, China and others from a Japanese delegation led by Mamoru Shigemitsu on board the American battleship USS *Missouri* in Tokyo Bay. In Japan, August 14 is recognized as the day the Pacific War ended; that was the date Emperor Hirohito accepted the terms of the Potsdam Declaration.

September 4, 1945 - From Bill to Marge

Dearest Marge,

Well Marge, no mail tonight but maybe I'll get some tomorrow. Things have sure been happening today. The 2 cooks I'm on shift with are leaving in the morning so the Mess Sergeant is going on with me in the morning but he will probably be gone in a week or so. Things are really going to be fucked up around here before long. The Major told one of the boys tonight that maybe the low pointers would go back with the 90th. I'm sure hoping so anyway. I think they are trying to keep all the cooks with under 45 points anyway. I guess all we can do is hope and pray. We had a little Swedish kid for supper tonight who was only 12 years old that could speak English, Swedish, German and Danish. We had quite a time with him. Some of the boys are pretty happy here that are leaving tomorrow. I guess they go home with the 16th Armored. There are a lot of mosquitoes around here now but they haven't been bothering me yet.

I just got done shaving up about 200 steaks for dinner tomorrow. They eat better down here than they do in F. Co. but I don't eat regular like I did before. I guess it is working around food. I kinda lose my appetite. I suppose I better get to bed pretty quick - have to get up at 4:30 in the morning so I don't get so much time to lay around and read and visit. I sure hope you are all right yet. I bet it will seem a lot different when I get home to have a family, eh? Well, say hello to your folks and every body for me. I better get to bed now. Keep up the writing. Still loving and missing you.

With all my love,

Your Husband Bill

On September 4, Japanese forces surrendered on Wake Island after hearing word of their country's surrender.

At the bottom on this letter Bill gives his new address which was HQ Co 2 Bn. 357th Infantry APO 90 so the transfer was not out of the 90th but simply out of F Company and to Headquarters. When he writes about *go back with the 90th*, he is referring to his Company and out of HQ, officer land.

September 5, 1945 - From Bill to Marge

Dearest Marge,

I got one letter from you tonight of the 27th of Aug. Glad to hear that Kreebs bought the house but what are they using for money? I don't think they ever saved any, did they? I can just see the way he'll have the place fixed up by the time I get home!

I just seen in the Stars and Stripes where in the re-counting of points, children count too so if the baby was born by Sept 2, I'll have enough to go home with the Div. The Div. is scheduled to sail from here the 1st of Dec. but I might get to go with them anyway if they don't transfer in a bunch of cooks. 3 more of the cooks out of this kitchen will go home in the next couple of weeks. I guess there are 4,000 (men) to leave the Div. Soon.

I'm glad to hear the folks might buy the house. They should have quite a little in bonds by now and I think Ma probably has a few dollars salted away. I played a little pinochle this afternoon and lost $10 bucks but am still pretty well fixed. I hope I collect a little of the money I've lent out before all the guys go. I got some payday!

Do you know, Marge, I've only missed writing to you a couple days, when I was down to Berchesgarden, since the war ended here. Pretty good for me, eh? I owe quite a few letters but I'm going to find a lot less time to write them now than I ever did. I think this working for a change is agreeing pretty good with me. My hands are starting to harden up again. Don't have to fall out for retreat, no patrol or drilling or any of that shit. The mail clerk picks up our mail every morning. I sure wish I had a good big bottle of Lucky Tiger for my hair. We don't get anything like that over here so if you send me a bottle. Keep on writing. I'm sure hoping and praying I'll be home for Christmas.

All my Love

Your Husband
Bill

September 6, 1945 - From Bill to Marge

Dearest Marge,

I sure can't figure out what is happening to my mail. I only got 1 letter all week. Should have a bunch by tomorrow.

Our Mess Sarg. and 2 more cooks are leaving tomorrow so this kitchen will be a mess till they get some new

On September 5, Iva Toguri D'Aquino, a Japanese-American suspected of being wartime radio propagandist *Tokyo Rose* was arrested in Yokohama.

The Russian code clerk Igor Gouzenko came forward with numerous documents implicating the Soviet Union in numerous spy rings in both Canada and the United States.

ones in. I've been baking every day, I guess. Before I came I guess they never got any baked goods. I got a bunch of pictures I am sending but I couldn't get one that I was in - had to take what I could get. One of Thersa Neuman and the priest, one of our factory here, and the gate coming in, also battalion retreat. I marked an "F" by our Co and a few more. I got an extra picture I think I'll send to Father Mac (Father MacDonald who was pastor of St. Pat's in Waukon). I think he'd like a picture of her (Therese Neumann.) If you notice in her hand you can see the blood clot. I'm sure glad I got the chance to go see her.

The Catholic Church has confirmed neither Therese Neumann's inedia nor her stigmata and has in the past discouraged pilgrimages to Konnersreuth. The "Resl", as she is colloquially known, nonetheless attained a place in popular piety - a petition asking for her beatification was signed by 40,000 people. In 2005, Gerhard Ludwig Müller, Bishop of Regensburg, formally opened the proceedings for her beatification.

I'll keep myself shaved up a little better now than when I was with F. Co. A guy pretty near here is working in the kitchen and there's one about 35 min. (that) is leaving out of the Co. tomorrow so it will make that many less to cook if we don't get in a bunch of new men. Well, Marge, I hope you are all right and things are still going all right at the bakery but I suppose John had to go on one during the fair, how about it?

We are trying to get a couple more Krauts to work in the kitchen and then we won't need many cooks because they work harder than any G.I. would. We got 5 good ones doing the K.P. and they really do a good job of it. Well, Marge, there isn't much to write about so guess I will quit for tonight. Still loving and missing you and praying I'll be home for Christmas.

All my Love

Your Husband
Bill

September 8, 1945 - From Bill to Marge

Dearest Marge,

Well, Marge, no mail tonight but I guess I can't expect it every night. Got along all right on my shift this afternoon. Have to get up early in the morning. Don't know whether an alarm clock will wake me anymore or not. It better or they won't get any breakfast in the morning. I just came back from uptown. The Dago and a kid who just got back from Berchtesgadens wanted to go up and have a beer so I went along. We were only up there about 1/2 hr though. Sure a lot of guys and there was a woman walking around and a few in the tavern we were in. One of the boys in this Co. is marrying a girl from Pilsen. He went with her in the States from '38 to '40. Then she came back here and got slapped into a

On September 8, American troops occupied southern Korea while the Soviet Union occupied the north with the dividing line being the 38th parallel.

Hideki Tojo, Japanese Prime Minster during most of World War II attempted suicide to avoid facing a war crimes tribunal.

concentration camp till we came. I guess he had a hell of a time finding her. He's just waiting for his papers to come back now till they get married. I suppose there will be lots of boys getting married when they get home now too. I'd sure like to see Swede's girl. Do you suppose they will be married when he gets home? From the way the S. and S. (Stars and Stripes) read today it might be a long time before us low point guys get home but I'm hoping I get to stay with the Div. (It was) 8 mo today I left the States and it looks like I'll be wearing at least 2 overseas bars by the time I get home. I know I was turned in to stay with the Div. but its hard telling whether it will do any good or not. I sure hope you are getting my mail better by now but I suppose they have things pretty well fucked up by now with all the guys going home. Guys getting cables now are getting them a little quicker than they used to but not a hell of a lot. Well, Marge, I'm hoping I'll be home for Christmas. Still loving and missing you. Keep up the writing.

All my Love

Your Husband
Bill

On September 9, 1945 the first actual case of a *computer bug* is documented. A moth was found lodged in a relay of the Harvard Mark II computer at the Naval Weapons Center in Dahlgren, Virginia.

September 9, 1945 - From Bill to Marge

Dearest Marge,

Well Marge no mail again tonight except about 6 old Registers from the first of Aug. I never have got the Democrat since the war ended over here. How come they quit sending it?

Cessation of *The Democrat* may or may not be indicative of the feeling at home that the War was over.

Haven't got much of anything to write about tonight. I got to Mass this afternoon.

I went to the movie tonight. Claudette Colbert and Fred McMurray. I don't remember the name of it but it was pretty good. It won't be long before I won't be able to see any of the old gang here any more from what they said today. The men left in E and F after the transfer's are done are going to First and Third Battalion so it will only leave the whole Second Battalion about the size of a Co or a little bigger. I still don't know whether I'll be able to stay with the outfit or not but am sure hoping. I hear over the radio today where they are going to send 2,000 a month home on furlough out of the army of occupation. At that rate 24,000 out of 400,000 is all that will get home a year. Not very good, eh? I sure hate to think of getting transferred because it takes about a month for a guys mail to catch up with him and I sure

Fred MacMurray was in four movies released in 1944 but only one, *Practically Yours,* with Claudette Colbert. In the movie, Bellamy (Fred MacMurray) returns from action over the Pacific as a war hero and stays with Mr Meglin (Cecil Kellaway) for 2 weeks before he returns to war. However, the whole country believes that he is going to marry Peggy (Claudette Colbert) because of a transmission of what were seemingly his last words before he decided to sacrifice himself for his country. Needless to say, he didn't die and Peggy wasn't who his final message was for. It was for Piggy, his dog.

General MacArthur's command decided to make a fresh start on a fraternization policy for U.S. occupation troops in Japan. Indoctrination material prepared in advance of the surrender had contained sharp warnings against fraternization (TIME, Aug. 27); this was squelched last week.

The experience of commanders in the European Theater was a guide for MacArthur's advisers. G.I.s might not want to fraternize with Japanese men, but it was a foregone conclusion that they would find Jap children cute; as for Japanese women, they have appealed strongly to most westerners who have lived in the country. When doughfeet crossed the Rhine, they went from countries where they had enjoyed the attentions of Allied women; many of those crossing the wharves of Yokosuka would be going from miserable, womanless mid-Pacific "rocks."

G.I.s arguing among themselves were as divided as the high-command councils. Some thought there should be an immediate ban, which might be lifted "when we see how we get along with the Japanese." (It had been that way in Germany, and the Allies had wound up looking ridiculous.) Whatever is decided, the command would be criticized. Politics, military discipline and biology were hard to balance in one equation.

*Time Magazine September 3, 1945*

On September 11, the Batu Lintang camp, a Japanese civilian and POW internment camp, in Sarawak, Borneo was liberated by Australian forces.

look for them letters of yours.

I'd sure like to have a couple of these Krauts working for me at home. They could get the work done. You ought to see the way they work around here, nobody has to call them in the morning and they never leave till everything is done after supper. Well think I'll read awhile and then go to bed. Still loving and missing you.

All my love,

Your Husband
Bill

September 10, 1945 - From Bill to Marge

Dearest Marge,

Well, Marge, no mail again tonight. It looks like it is getting more screwed up all the time. I sure haven't got anything to write about tonight but thought I better anyway. I know you look for my letters as much as I do for yours. I was over to the Dispensary and got a shot this afternoon so my arm is a little stiff. We just took them about 4 months ago and we are supposed to have them every 6 months. I guess they figure giving it now will hold most of them till they get home. A few guys left again today and another big bunch going Wed. so this Battalion is getting smaller every day. Oh, Marge, by the way, when the baby is born, send a copy of the birth certificate so I can have the allotment made out. I sure hope you are still all right and getting my mail all right. But any time you don't, don't get thinking, I'm coming home because I'll write all the time up till I get on the boat. I'm sure hoping I don't get transferred because the guys we got from the 16th Armored a couple weeks ago still haven't started getting their mail yet. I suppose Vernon is on his way home now because all the guys with over 70 points have left this Div. already. Well, I got to get up early in the morning. Things have been going good in the kitchen. There are only 2 of us on each shift but we have been getting it done. Well, Marge, keep up the writing and I sure hope I'm home for Christmas.

All my love

Your Husband
Bill

September 11, 1945 - From Bill to Marge

Dear Marge,

Well, Marge I got 8 letters from you tonight from the 30th to the 4th of Sept. Sure glad to get them but I *wished I got them every day instead of in a bunch like they come. I don't see why it takes so long for my mail to get there but I have still been writing every day. There was sure a pile of men left here today for home and transferred. I suppose I'll be transferred to occupation pretty quick now. Because they will probably have enough cooks. They are cutting out G and F Co. so that will leave 2 less kitchens in the Battalion.*

*From the sound of your letters Kosbau must be as big a cunt hound as ever. I'll have to write him a letter, might get there before he leaves. I'm not surprised about (deleted) out with Pat's wife. Well, he should be able to keep her satisfied anyway. What do you think? I'll bet the gang really has some big times at the Berg (Heidelberg, Spillville, IA)*

*How I would like to be there to go with them but I guess it will be a long time yet from the way things look. I feel like going over the hill lots of times but it don't do any good over here. You can't get home anyway. They have really got us fucked. There was a show up town this afternoon but I was too lazy to go up. The little Dago is on outpost and most of the rest of the guys I partied with have left so it sure seems funny around here. It sure burns me up, there are guys coming in after the war was over a month before and all going home already and the rest of them (going) with the Div.*

*Well, Marge, take care of yourself. I sure hope I get home by Christmas but have about given up home now from what they tell us. Keep up the letter writing.*

*Still loving and missing you,*

*All my love*

*Bill*

September 11, 1945 - From Bill to Jim and Amanda

*Dear Folks,*

*I got a letter from you a couple days ago and a package of Aug 3 - sure glad to get it too, thanks a lot.*

*I don't see where my letters have been going to because I write at least once a week and sometimes twice. I'm first cook now but I think I'll get transferred before long into Army of Occupation. I'm lacking 9 points to go home with the Div. in Dec. Most of the old men have left already for home. Lot of guys who came in after I did. I guess there will only be about 4,000 left in the Div. when it goes home, about half of it is gone already.*

*Marge writes that Donny, Swede, and Harold are all*

September 11: The shape of things to come in the peacetime U.S. was still forming hazily, like ectoplasm at a spiritualists' meeting. But U.S. citizens, staring with a séance-sitter's skeptical fascination, began to nudge each other last week. Government and industry really seemed to be conjuring a facsimile of normal living.

After 43 months of drawing up blue laws for industry, the War Production Board threw all but two score of its war time restrictions to the winds, giddily told startled U.S. manufacturers to make all the automobiles they wished. The same went for washing machines, ironers, pots & pans, electric razors, pottery, Kleenex, toys, radios, suits, dresses, storage batteries and photo graphic film.

Few of these items would be available in any quantity before Christmas, but the words rolled on the tongue like bubble gum. Some U.S. citizens even enjoyed knowing that there were no more restrictions on cotton linters, natural resins, green bone glue, horse mane hair and an insecticide named pyrethrum.

http://www.time.com/time/magazine/article.html

City bus lines, which had been forced to use the skip-stop system, a wartime innovation apparently designed to facilitate passing up passengers, would this week be allowed to halt under virtually every street light if the driver was in the mood.

The Federal Housing Administration resumed its prewar program of insuring mortgage loans on housing. The new houses would come later.

Radio "hams" who were ordered to dismantle their sets and get off the air on Dec. 7, 1941 began putting their sets together again. They were once more free to stay up all night hoarsely calling "CQ CQ CQ" into a microphone, without being suspected of espionage.

President Harry Truman prepared to give Montgomery Ward & Co. back to Sewell Avery and his stockholders, other seized plants back to private management. And with an eye on the clock, he vowed to ask Congress to repeal War Time.

http://www.time.com/time/magazine/article/html

On September 12, the Japanese Army formally surrendered to the British in Singapore.

*home. I'll bet they are sure having a big time. Sure wish I was there with them. I suppose Vernon is home by now. I've lost a lot of weight since I've been here, working in the kitchen took it off. I've been lucky never being sick or anything since I've been over here. You ought to see the way the Krauts K.P. work from morning till night, 7 days a week and then there is one who does my washing every morning so I usually have a clean pair O.D. to wear every day. Pretty nice, eh? 2 of them are only 15 and real nice kids. I sure feel sorry for them having to pay for what a lot of the big shots did. The one kid don't believe me when I tell him he'll get home before I do. And I think he will because when the Div. leaves, they will probably discharge all of them.*

*How is everybody coming at home? All right, I hope you can tell Marie it will be quite a while before Bill is home yet. Marge wrote you have a chance to buy the house. Are you going to? How much does he want for it?*

*I hear Stan is getting to be quite the lover since I left. When's he planning on the big wedding? Tell him he better wait until I get home. Well, there isn't much to write about so guess I better quit for now. Keep up the writing.*

*Love,*

*Your Son*
*Bill*

September 12, 1945 - From Bill to Marge

*Dear Marge,*

*Well, Marge here I go again. Not much to write about. I hardly ever leave the building except to go to church or up to see a show once in awhile. Not much new around here except a few low pointers left today for 3rd Army Headquarters and the call for 60 pointers and above so they will be leaving in a few days. It's hard to tell, maybe this Div. will stay here as Occupational yet. I'd a hell of a lot sooner stay in it as Occupational than go to some other outfit. I just come down from F. Co. and there isn't hardly anyone left in it.*

*What haven't shipped out are on outpost but they still got 4 guys with over 80 points they are holding for court martial. They took 1500 P.W. to France a while back and missed the train coming back but still got here 3 days ahead of time. They think they'll get 6 mo and 2/3 of their pay taken away for it though. We had 10 in 1 ra-*

*tions to feed today so I made a bunch of cakes so the boys were pretty well satisfied. We have a good breakfast in the morning - oranges, cornflakes, toast, bacon and fresh eggs and coffee. Then steak for dinner so we are feeding pretty good. Today I ate the first banana I've had since I've been overseas with a big dish of ice cream. Sure was good too. I got the Reader's Digest again yesterday and am about half through with it. I'd sure love to be home with you (for) Christmas but I'm kinda giving up hope of it now the way things are going. I wrote to Harold and Swede last night. I hope the letters get there before they leave. I don't see why it should take over 8 or 9 days. I hope you are getting my mail better now. I guess you will have to get the folks and kids something for Christmas because I don't think I'll get to any place where I can buy anything for them. Well, Marge, still loving and missing you and still haven't played with any of these women over here.*

*All my love*

*Your Husband*
*Bill*

September 13, 1945 - From Bill to Marge

*I've been sitting around upstairs mostly all evening talking with the little Dago. He came in off outpost today. He sure is disgusted though when he heard the news yesterday that they are keeping everybody with under 60 points. He said he just about fucked one of them Krauts over on the outpost but he didn't. I told him he better transfer to Headquarters Co. and I'd look after him whenever he's with me. He won't even talk to the women except some slams at them. We've been trying to figure out someway we could take off and get home but they have things pretty well sewed up according to what came out in the paper today. We'll be here a year or two yet.*

*Marge, I sure wish you would do what ever you can to get me out because if the people in the States don't put up (a large) enough holler, these fucking generals will be able to keep their large armies and keep us guys over here. Every time I pick up a paper, it pisses me off more. Read how bad the Krauts treated all the prisoners and shit like that but they don't tell about all the good corps they had, and about them killing (just) a few American P.O.W but you will never read of the thousands of Germans that were shot by our troops after they gave up*

One of Bill's best friends was an Italian guy named DeMarco – he calls him the little Diego (Dego); sounds like they pretty much depended upon each other.

On September 13, the arrival of the first U.S. troops at Atsugi Airdrome was world-wide news last week, and plenty of newsmen were on hand. But they were all Japanese. (U.S. reporters who wanted to go along were entangled in Army red tape on Okinawa.) Result: Japan's Domei news agency scooped the world.

http://www.time.com/time/magazine/article/html

September 13: After the Army transport had taxied to a halt on Atsugi airfield one day last week, the first man to climb down was a tall, loose-jointed officer with the three stars of a lieutenant general gleaming on his shirt collar. Said the General, grinning:

"This is the beachhead where I was supposed to land. General MacArthur gave me this area. I never expected to reach it in a plane without a shot being fired at me."

Lieut. General Robert Lawrence Eichelberger, 59, newly appointed commander of the Tokyo area, already had on hand his own crack 11th Airborne Division, commanded by Major General Joseph M. Swing, and some infantrymen of the 27th Division. This week tens of thousands more (including the dismounted 1st Cavalry Division) landed from transports, swelling the body of troops toward the 500,000 or more who will land in weeks to come on the sacred soil. The occupation of Japan had begun.

http://www.time.com/time/magazine/article/html

*and I've seen that myself.*

*When and if I ever get home, I'll tell you a few of the things that went on over here that you will never see in the papers. They have us so fucked up now, we are never sure from 1 hr. to the next how long we will stay in the Div. Some of the guys are just getting a couple hrs. notice that they are leaving.*

*I haven't done much today - worked this morning and was off this afternoon so went up town to the movie, Stan Laurel and Oliver Hardy in "Nothing but Trouble". Then I stopped in to the Kraut barber and got a hair cut. Cost a dime. Pretty high priced, eh?? After supper I went over and took a shower. Felt good, nice hot water. I haven't got any mail the last 2 days now but will get a bunch pretty quick again. How is everything going at home, OK, I hope. Gosh, Marge, I sure miss you more and more every day. And when they come out with this 60 points stuff, it about got me. Combat men get fucked again. Out of most of the high point men, very few of them saw much action on the line. Well, Marge, I guess we better just keep hoping and praying for the best. Still loving and missing you.*

*All my Love,*

*Your Husband*
*Bill*

September 14, 1945 - From Bill to Marge

*Dearest Marge,*

*I got one letter from you today of Sept. 4 and one from the folks and a box from Ethel. I suppose it will take a little longer for me to get my mail now because tomorrow is the last day for E and F. Co's. All the men are getting transferred to H, Hqs, G and Third Battalion. The Dago was down to see me this afternoon and he goes to G. Co. so that ain't so bad. He also is going to the Riviera on furlough in a few days. Took him a long time to get it.*

*Well, the news isn't any better today. I still can't see what the hell they need with 400,000 troops to occupy the section of Germany we got. I suppose when I do get home, I'll hardly (know) the Kreebs house the way they will have fixed it up. I suppose there is getting to be a pile of guys around home now on furlough and discharges. If Congress puts up enough squawk, maybe some more of us guys will get home. Haven't heard anymore what they are going to do with our Div. They might even break it* up for all we know. Nothing is sure here from one day to the next. It wouldn't be so bad if it weren't for that I got my rations today. We are still getting 7 packs a week although the Stars and Stripes said we were to get 10, but I got enough now anyway because we get 10 in 1 rations to feed the men every 10 days and they have cigarettes in them so I take what I want out of them.

Have you found anybody to work in the back end yet? I sure am hoping you have anyway. There should soon be a lot of bakers loose with the war plants all closed and discharging.

Well Marge, keep up the writing. Still loving you and missing you.

All my Love,

Your Husband
Bill

September 15, 1945 - From Bill to Marge

Dearest Marge,

I just stopped up to see if I had any mail but didn't have any. This was the last day for F. Co. We got about 30 men from there and all the cooks and the Mess Sarge. from there. I guess our kitchen will be moved up there in a few days.

Gave an order today - anyone having brass knuckles to get rid of them. It seems a few guys have been spending their nights beating up Krauts with them and they spoiled a few of their faces. It seems like all some of the guys like to do is raise hell with them.

I went up to the show this afternoon. Pretty good but I never remember the names of them. I just got a package of Aug 13 from you, 2 letters - 4th and 5th, and one from Beck. I gave the Dago one box of the cookies because he sure likes them. Then I still got the fudge and other box of cookies. I don't have anybody to share them with here. Most of the cooks don't care for sweets and myself and another guy have a room to ourselves. I've sure been waiting for the news about the baby being born. When the hell is it going to happen anyway? I'll bet that ass is really wide by now. How about it?

I sure wish you wouldn't work so hard, Marge. If nothing else cut down on what they are making. We have trucks going to the Red Cross clubs around here every night. They have dances and stuff like that but I guess I'll still wait till I get home with you before I go to any of the dances and stuff, eh? I don't know whether

The psychological lessons of war, gathered by a committee of the National Research Council, were available last week in Psychology for the Armed Services (Infantry Journal, $3). Some of them turned out to be more or less useful tips for peacetime behavior. Samples:

To hear conversation despite a loud background noise (e.g., of guns or machinery), put fingers in ears or wear earplugs.

To see in the dark, wear special red glasses for a while beforehand. Wearing a black patch over one eye and then shifting it to the other eye just before stepping into darkness works pretty well, too.

Slowest way to get drunk: highballs while standing at a bar. Quickest: straight whiskey or cocktails lying down.

*Time Magazine September 10, 1945*

On September 15, a hurricane in southern Florida and the Bahamas destroyed 366 planes and 25 blimps at the Naval Air Station.

The 90th Patch referred to in this letter is shown on the front cover and Page 215.

you have seen the 90th Div. patch so I'll send you one in this letter. We are only issued 3 but I managed to get a hold of a couple more. I thought I better finish this letter before I start looking at the papers you sent or I never will get it finished. Well, Marge, better quit for now and I'll still be looking for your letters.

All my Love

Bill

September 16, 1945 - From Bill to Marge

Dearest Marge,

I just came back from the show. They had a German show tonight with about 20 or 30 entertainers. Sure was good to. Most of them speak English - mostly singing, dancing acrobatics, and a good magician.

I didn't get any mail today but maybe I will tomorrow. I didn't get to church today. Went on shift this noon and we have Mass in the afternoon. I got the Kraut K.P.'s each a pair of pants today and they sure were happy about it. All they have is the one pair they have on. You see the supply Sgt. gets along pretty good (with me). He likes a little lunch once in awhile so I asked him for a few extra pairs and he got them for me. I've got quite a few more than I'm supposed to have so I don't need to worry much about that. I usually work in O.D. all the time. I guess there are a bunch more men leaving the Battalion this week but don't know whether they will be high points or low points. I sure hope I don't get transferred. From the looks of the papers, the bastards are trying to make us permanent over here. There are a bunch of us who decided to wait till the first of the year and if it don't look like we're going to get home, we are taking off. As far as doing any good here, having this many does more harm. I know if I were these people I think I'd be hating the G.I.s. In this town of probably 3 or 4 thousand, there are still about 7 or 8 hundred of us and there were about twice that many. Well, Marge, I sure hope you got by the fair (Allamakee County Fair) all right and you better let up on the work. I sure wish I could be home with you Christmas but everyday it looks like I'm getting farther away from getting home. Still loving and missing you more than ever.

All my Love,

Your Husband
Bill

September 16: As he walked out, gaunt and shaken, to surrender Corregidor, Lieut. General Jonathan M. Wainwright did not feel like a hero. As a prisoner of Japan he did not feel like one, either. "Skinny" Wainwright, who could remember the bugle-bright traditions of the U.S. cavalry, learned a dingier drill—to remove his shoes when entering buildings, to bow to his captors. He was allowed no news. Lonely and aging, he could only wonder about how the war was going, and what the nation and the Army thought about him—if they ever did think about him.

Last week, five days after his 62nd birthday, after three years and three months of isolated captivity, he found out. Rescued from his prison camp at Sian, 100 miles northeast of Mukden (TIME, Aug. 27), he flew into Chungking and a warm and wonderful welcome.

There were messages of congratulation from home, an autographed wirephoto from his wife, his back pay, summer khaki uniforms to replace his worn clothing, good food, and the stirring atmosphere of a U.S. Army post. And, better than all these, he found that his country remembered him with sympathy and pride.

http://www.time.com/time/magazine/article/html

September 17, 1945 - From Bill to Marge

*I got 2 letters from you, Sept 6 & 7, your birthday card and a box of candy with writing paper. Sure glad to get them. The box was mailed from Clermont. The fudge was good but the peanut butter was a little moldy so I gave it to the Krauts. They liked it, mold or not. Don't send me any more writing paper because we get plenty here but you could send me a bottle of Lucky Tiger and a bottle of hair oil. I don't care for sweets as much as I used to now (that) I'm working in the kitchen. I get plenty to eat and we feed better than they did in F. Co. We're sure feeding a pile of men now that we got in a bunch from F. and E. Co's. A few more men with over 64 points are leaving tomorrow and some (are leaving) the last of the week so that will take it down a ways again. It sounds like Wiedeman likes this Army life, eh? Well I think if he ever gets any sense, he will change his mind. Of course, the officers do have a pretty nice thing of it even over here. Most of them have their women and I think they stay nights with them most of the time. They have quarters to themselves and here they have one of the most beautiful bars I ever saw and I guess they get plenty of liquor. We don't even get any beer anymore. I suppose you are sure disappointed in my letters lately but it looks like they are planning to keep us here. Nobody is sure of anything. Div. don't even know what the hell is going on. Things get changed around so much. Most of the boys all went out to a party tonight. They buy schnapps from the people uptown and they get plenty drunk off of it. I went up to the movie this afternoon but it wasn't any good and was an old picture.*

*I got a birthday card and letter from Lula today so I'll have to write them. I sure hate to hear the old man is hitting the bottle again. I wonder if he will ever learn. I know how it makes Ma feel. I suppose when Vernon gets home they will hit it up more than ever. Well, Marge, I guess all we can do is keep hoping and praying (that) I'll get home before too long. Still loving and missing you.*

*All my Love*

*Your Husband*
*Bill*

September 18, 1945 - From Bill to Marge

*Dearest Marge,*

*Well, Marge, I just finished work so I think I'd better write. No mail today. It's sure funny, me being the*

The outlines of a Fourth Reich emerged in Russian-occupied Germany last week. The Russians announced that they had organized a complete German government for their zone.

The new German Premier: Marshal Georgi Zhukov. His deputy prime minister: one Leo Skrzypczinsky, described as a former German factory owner who spent four years in a concentration camp. A political unknown, without party affiliation, Skrzypczinsky was recommended by the Communists. Under Premier Marshal Zhukov were twelve ministries (one for each division of the Soviet Military Government), each headed by a Red Army officer. Under each Red Army officer was a German state secretary (selected from lists submitted by the four "antifascist" parties). As state secretaries, the Russians picked five Communists, three Social Democrats, two Christian Democrats, one Liberal Democrat, one nonparty member.

http://www.time.com/time/magazine/article/html

On September 18, typhoon Makurazaki killed 3,746 people in Japan.

1,000 white students walked out of Gary, Indiana schools to protest integration.

The world might have forgotten the fact, but Berlin was something more than international military-government headquarters. People still lived there. This week TIME'S Berlin Correspondent John Scott cabled:

One afternoon about a fortnight ago, I was taking leave of a German acquaintance on Limastrasse in front of my Zehlendorf house while a spry, blond boy about three and a half feet high stood gaping at me, as his kind in Berlin will. When I had said goodbye and turned to walk toward the mess, he came up, grinned, took my hand and said, "Du sprichst doch Deutsch. Hast du kein Kaugummi für mich?"

I gave him some of the American chewing gum he asked for and asked him why he wasn't in school. "School? Oh, I'm on the morning shift now, and besides, the Americans took our school and I have to go to another one very far away, and anyhow I am busy." At that point we came to the mess and as I had to go in if I were going to get anything to eat, I left him with an invitation to come and see me.

He came next morning; I gave him a chocolate bar and we had a long talk. His name was Dietrich. He was eight. He wore clean but patched clothes, was lean as a wolf and just about as quick. He spent a lot of time around the press camp, particularly in front of the enlisted men's mess, picking up butts. "My mother smokes the long ones and we exchange the others for potatoes," he explained seriously.

Dietrich lived in a small, neat, almost undamaged house. He, his six-year-old sister Heidi and his mother had two rooms; the four others were occupied by a grey, staring-eyed woman of 40-odd with six children, one of whom, a boy of 16, had just returned from a British P.O.W. camp.

http://www.time.com/time/magazine/article/html

*only guy in again tonight. The rest of the guys just left with the women. They were in fooling around the kitchen about 1 hr waiting for them. Pretty good looking to - most of them are getting to speak pretty good English by now. I think lots of the boys will be marrying these Kraut girls if they get a chance. Just think if a guy brought one back to the States with him and bought 10 or 15 acres, she'd make him a good living.*

*I see by the paper today where they are trying to stop the draft and let those out (that have been) in over 2 years. It's beginning to look like the bastards are going to try keeping us over here forever. The General was here again today so maybe we might know something in a day or two. I guess the Div. is still going home in Dec. as scheduled but it will be awful small. There is still a chance of us low point men going home with the Div. but it is awful small. I think if they hold the 90th for Strategic Reserve in the States, we might go home with it. I'm sure hoping and if I do, why I guess we'd either have to get somebody to look after the bakery or something because I sure want you to be with me. Boy, Marge, I just got done writing a few minutes ago. I was the only one here. Well, in comes one of the guys with a girl. Wanted to know if he could use the room across from me to sleep with her and I told him to go ahead and then in comes one of the cooks with another and he got himself a room. I'll bet at least once or twice a week I get propositioned and I've still been turning it down. It's a good thing I'm not single or I'd sure be taking care of my share but I made up my mind before I come overseas (that) I was leaving it alone so it hasn't bothered me much. Well, Marge, guess I'll get to bed - have to get up at 4:30 in the morning. Still loving and missing you. Hope I'm back with you before too long.*

*All my Love*

*Your Husband*
*Bill*

September 19, 1945 - From Bill to Marge

*Dearest Marge,*

*I got two letters from you today of Sept 9th and 10th. It sounds like you kinda figure I'll be home before long but I guess you know better by now. Before 800 low point men could go home with a Div. but starting now they have cut it out. So I guess there isn't much chance of going home with the Div. I see by the paper where*

*MacArthur says he won't need over 200,000 for Occupational (in Japan) there, so maybe they will start sending some men over here. We are hoping Eisenhower cuts the Occupational forces over here because they sure don't need all they have. God, but they are still keeping us all fucked up so we don't know how in the hell we stand.*

*I'm sure sorry to hear about Dad having to have the operation and I hope its nothing serious. I suppose there goes their chances of buying the house to, eh? We moved our kitchen upstairs today so I have to go on shift again in the morning until we get things straightened out. They got a pretty good bunch of guys in this Co so I'm getting to like it better all the time. I was a little short on handkerchiefs and socks so I went in today and got a bunch from the supply Sgt. We are supposed to pay for clothes now but I don't need to worry. I've got about 3 times what I'm supposed to have. Went uptown to the show this afternoon. Stan Laurel and Oliver Hardy, pretty good to. I still like the movies as well as ever. Gosh, Marge but I'd sure give anything to be home with you but it looks like I'll be here quite a while yet. It sure pisses me off when all these guys come over after I did, get home and I'm stuck. I guess we have a few more men leaving the last of the week. I hope the new Mess Sgt. that we got from F. Co is one of them. Well, Marge, I'm sure praying I get home with you soon. Keep up the writing.*

*All my love*

*Your Husband*
*Bill*

Laurel and Hardy starred in 106 films. The two in which they appeared in 1944 were *The Big Noise* and *Nothing But Trouble*. Bill mentions seeing *Nothing But Trouble* on September 13. Their career together ran from 1921 through 1945.

*September 20, 1945 - From Bill to Marge*

*Dearest Marge,*

*I got a letter from you today of Sept. 11. It sound like it is still taking my mail quite a while to get home. I get part of your letters in 8 or 10 days. I sleep about all afternoon so I've been sitting around reading most of the evening. I guess I wrote you (that) we got a new Mess Sgt. and he sure is a prick. I told him to stick his kitchen up his ass last night. So the First Sgt was down this morning and asked me to stick it out for a few more days and maybe they can get rid of him. He don't know a damn thing but he got a staff rating so he was stuck in for Mess Sgt., but maybe things will work out O.K.*

*That's pretty good about Helen Baxter but I thought she'd probably be getting her shoes (?). How about Lu-*

On September 20, Mohandas Gandhi and Jawaharial Nehru demanded that all British troops depart India.

The switchover to peacetime production was farther along in many lines than many a businessman had thought possible.

Last week the National Industrial Council rosily reported a brighter outlook for 1945-46 jobs than had been expected.

There was still much slack. Government and private business analysts agreed, in the main, on the immediate trend: business in general would slide downward for about six months, then climb. The optimistic guesstimaters were almost unanimous: 1947 and 1948 will see national income on a high level — perhaps about $135 billion (wartime peak: $165 billion).

Beyond that, some prognosticators foresaw a deep depression, perhaps beginning in 1949. Most private analysts were more confident, believed that housing and foreign trade would help maintain a high level. There was no mistaking the bullish enthusiasm of most businessmen.

http://www.time.com/time/magazine/article/html

*ther or is Freddy home for good now? You never ever mentioned Mary, who's she going with or is she still taking care of all she can.*

*I was over talking to the Sgt. In charge of the Motor pool a while ago and there are 58 more men leaving here tomorrow. None out of our Co. though. I guess part of the Fourth Armor is going to take over the Occupation of this area pretty quick. I guess the Div. still goes home in Dec. as scheduled but it will be awful small. They still haven't transferred many low pointers out of the Div. so I'm still hoping there might be a chance of going home with it. One thing I sure like about working in the kitchen is we don't have to pull any guard, detail, reveille or retreat or do any drilling. And then the time goes by faster too.*

*Got my ration today - about twice what we usually get - 12 packs cigarettes, 2 bars soap, 2 cigars, 10 candy bars, pack of gum. Cost $ 2.15, cheap enough.*

*I was put in for a rating this month but the little deal I had last night will kinda fuck it up but I don't give a shit any way.*

*Boy, Marge, but it sure pisses me off to see the way some of these married men with kids take out these Heinie cunts. I guess that's about the biggest reason I don't like the Mess Sgt. He's got 2 kids and is out about every night with some cunt. Well, Marge guess I'd better quit for tonight. Still loving and missing you.*

*All my love*

*Your Husband*
*Bill*

September 21, 1945 - From Bill to Marge

*Dearest Marge,*

*I got one letter from you today of the 12th and one from Ma and one from Ethel. Ma didn't have much to say. She just got back from LaCrosse so she just wrote a short (one) but I guess Dad is all right from the sounds of it. That article you clipped out of the Register is about true but I heard today where the guys are going to be able to marry them. They say there are 28 knocked up so far in this town by G.I.'s. They are checking all the women from 14 to 45 to see if they have V.D. now.*

*It is sure quiet around here at night. I usually am alone every night because the rest of the cooks have something they are shacking up with. I'll be glad when the Diago gets back from the Riviera because we always spend a lot of time together cursing the army. I see by the Stars and Stripes where Truman said they might cut the Occupational forces over here. I sure hope so anyway.*

*How much longer are you going to keep us in suspense anyway? I am anxious to here whether it is a boy or girl. You said if it is a boy, you were going to name it little George. What's the name if it is a girl?*

Bill doesn't know but Marge delivered a girl today and will name her Janice.

*I went up to the show this afternoon but I'd seen it before so I came back to work. I was supposed to be working this afternoon. From the sounds of your letters that romance of John's must be getting pretty serious. When's he going to marry the girl anyway? Or does he still say he's not going to. Well, still haven't heard anything definite on when I'll go home or go to Occupational forces but I'm sure hoping I go home with the Div. but I don't think there is much chance of it.*

*If they ever inspect my room down here, I'll sure catch hell because my clothes are all over and I never make my bed. I've been sleeping in a fart sack (sleeping bag) the last couple months. Well, Marge, keep up the writing. Hope to be home with you soon. Still loving and missing you.*

*All my Love*

*Your Husband*
*Bill*

September 21, 1945 - From Bill to Jim and Amanda

*Dear Folks,*

*Received your letters today so am answering right away. Glad to hear that dad is getting along all right. If you buy the house, how much will you have to pay for it and how much down? It will cost quite a lot to build a new foundation and move it, won't it? I still haven't any idea when I'll get home but from the sounds of things, I'll be stuck over here for Occupational but heard today they might cut the occupational forces. Sure hope so anyway. Well I suppose Vernon is home by now. If he isn't he must be going pretty quick. I haven't heard from him for quite a while now. I like it pretty good working in the kitchen. It makes the time go by a little quicker. Our Battalion is getting pretty small now. All these guys with over 65 points have left for other outfits to go home and then some went to 3rd Battalion at Flossenberg. They have about 10,000 SS troops they are taking care of and discharging. I don't think I'll get any*

Crackdown followed Allied crackdown as the Allies turned the screws on Germany.

In the Russian-occupied zone, eastern Europe's sweeping Communist-sponsored land reform hit the big landowning Junker, and that stiff-necked class that had long been one of the world's worst curses stood in imminent danger of dissolution. Saxony took the lead. There the Provincial Government issued a decree: all Junker estates of more than 100 hectares (250 acres) were expropriated.

Confiscated also was all land owned by the Nazi Party, active Nazis, war criminals, Reichstag deputies under Hitler. Three days later Brandenburg and Mecklenburg followed suit. The land would be divided among the landless peasants, farm workers and refugee German farmers. Said Communist Party Chairman Wilhelm Pieck: the bloodless revolution may be completed by October.

In the British-occupied zones, the blow fell on German industrialists. In a sweeping move to denazify the Ruhr industries, the Control Council arrested 40 leading officials of the powerful Rhine-Westphalian coal syndicate. Biggest fish in the British net: Tycoon Hugo Stinnes, 48, son of Germany's onetime greatest financier and powerful figure in the Ruhr coal and steel industries. Said the British: "Such men represent the worst in Germany . . . never hesitated to use their vast power to support dubious political movements . . . assisted in the growth of the National Socialist Party."

In the American-occupied zone, control authorities kicked out 40,000 Berlin block, street and house leaders. They had originally been appointed by the Russians to search out known Nazis, handle ration cards, report on available labor. The American report was that the small-fry German leaders had begun to wield power in their neighborhoods just as arrogantly as their predecessors in Germany's notorious block organizations had done under Hitler; some of them had actually worked under the Nazi regime. (The British still held to the block leaders, warned them not to consider themselves little kings but servants of the people.)

In Berlin the U.S. Army got tough with municipal officers. A month ago the Army had told city officials to get the people out rounding up wood to heat their homes this winter. Berlin's Oberbürgermeister dallied, spoke of combining wood-gathering with regular forest thinning. Last week U.S. soldiers rounded up laborers in Berlin, packed them off to Grunewald. There they were given saws and axes, told to get busy. They did.

http://www.time.com/time/magazine/article/html

*place to buy any Christmas presents so I wish you would buy something nice for Marge for Christmas. Write a check on my account.*

*If you run short of money with dad sick now, you can get it from Marge or let me know. I'm sure hoping I get home before long but don't think there is much chance of it. They ordered overcoats for us the other day so I suppose we'll be getting them before long. The weather has been nice the last few weeks here, been pretty warm every day. I don't know what we'll do when it gets cold. There isn't a stove in the whole damn place except the big furnace for hot water. Well, Ma, write me about all the news and I wish you would send the Democrat.*

*Love,*

*Your Son*
*Bill*

<u>September 22, 1945 - From Bill to Marge</u>

*Dearest Marge,*

*I got one letter from you today of the 13th. I've been lucky lately getting it everyday instead of all in a bunch. Glad to hear you are still all right. You said in your letter about me being on 24 and off 24. Well, here is the way it works. Go on at noon and then get done about 7 or 8 Pm and then go on again next morning about 4:30 AM till noon. Then we are off till the next noon.*

*Just heard over the radio again where all under 45 points are going to stay for Occupational and won't get home before next June, but I'm sure praying they change that before long. From the sounds of it, they don't plan on sending any more men over here but if they think I'm going to stay here, they are crazy. From a guy who don't monkey around, there isn't a damn thing to do; but lots of these guys (that) are out screwing these Heine cunts every night have a lot of fun. They get plenty of whiskey and schnapps now but I still don't drink any of it. It will sure seem funny when I get home again to taste whiskey again. I always turn it down ever since I've been overseas and there's a quart sitting in the room here now if I wanted any.*

*I asked the First Sgt today for a pass so he said as quick as they have another quota, he will try sending me which probably will be in another month from now unless I have my ass shipped to some other outfit. I sent a box today with a little junk I had in my pack so don't throw it away when it comes. The belt I wore all during combat, it's a German machine gun belt but I carried my ammo for my 38 in it.*

*There are also a bunch of postcards in it and a picture of Therese Neuman's house and a map of the path of the 90th Div. Also a Kraut Shelter half. I just stuck it in to fill the box (to keep it) from rattling. They have finally got all the bridges in and the trains running here this week. We had about 6 or 8 engines and a bunch of cars out here all the time but they are finally putting them to use.*

*I've sure been missing you more and more every day. I think I'd give about anything to be able to see you soon. I can't say as I've ever been homesick. I wouldn't mind it at all if it weren't for you. That is why this country is no good for any normal guy if he is going to be true to his wife. I hardly ever go up town or am around any women so the pussy hasn't been bothering me any, but if anybody would of ever told me before I came in the Army, I would go this long without any ass, I would of though it pretty near impossible. There are quite a lot of guys who don't chisel on their wives and some guys who have girls in the states don't monkey with these girls either. Well, Marge, better quit for tonight. Still loving and missing you.*

*All my Love*

*Your Husband*
*Bill*

*P.S. This is sure a hell of a place and a way for a guy to spend his birthday, eh?*

Bill writes in this letter about having a German shelter-half. Each infantryman was issued one in which he rolled his belongings that he wanted to keep dry. At night, two guys would get together, clip the two halves together forming a shelter that was almost big enough to sleep under.

Today was Bill's 25th birthday.

September 23, 1945 - From Bill to Marge

*I didn't get any mail from you but I got Stan's letter. He was telling me you are going to have triplets because you are lot bigger than Mary Campbell was. Holding out on me, eh? He also wants to buy my suit but nothing doing, I might get home someday yet.*

*He was telling about the little boys in Lansing getting castrated. How come you never mentioned it? Bashful, eh?*

*He said John Dotseth would help put in the flue's. I'm sure glad of that but you better be sure you have the right ones before they tear it down.*

*I see by the Stripes today where they are going to let all the guys out of the Army that aren't essential. At that rate, it is hard telling when they will ship us home. They still haven't sent any replacements overseas since*

President Truman sent his first peacetime message to Congress. In 16,000 workaday words—the longest Presidential message since Theodore Roosevelt's 20,000-word document in 1901—he laid out his program for peace and prosperity.

Had he read his message himself, Harry Truman, who speaks at the rate of no words a minute, would have taken more than two hours. Instead, he turned it over to House and Senate reading clerks.

http://www.time.com/time/magazine/article/.html

Right back in the groove after getting out of the Army, 132-lb. Ben Hogan, the man with the delayed wrist-lash, still could belt a golf ball out of sight. On the fairways, he never made a careless shot. His ability to concentrate was hard to believe. Once again he was a man to beat on the pro circuit.

After romping home first in the Nashville Open, 19 strokes below par, the wasp-waisted Texan headed for Dallas. En route last week, he came down with flu, gobbled some sulfa pills, decided to play anyhow. Despite a 102° fever, he fired a 68 to tie for the first-round lead in the $10,000 Dallas Open. But next day, woozy from sulfa, he slumped to 74. After that he could not catch Sam Snead (lately recovered from a broken arm), Jug Mc-Spaden or Byron Nelson. Hogan finished fourth with a 3-under-par. In the longer run he was a good bet to succeed wartime golf's king of the links, fast-greying Byron Nelson, now 18 lbs. underweight after the nerve-wearing grind of winning 16 tournaments within a year.

http://www.time.com/time/magazine/article/html

the war ended in May. There were supposed to have been 40 some low point guys shipped out today for Occupational but it was called off for some reason. I'm hoping maybe we will go back to the States with the Div. I see where the 82nd Airborne is leaving Berlin this week for home and they don't know yet whether low pointers will go yet or not. If they do, maybe we'll have a chance. I haven't been to Mass the last 2 Sundays now because I've been on the afternoon shift when we have Mass. We had a big shake down for pistols and brass knuckles today. Bunch of guys were shooting up the town and beating up Krauts last night. I heard the shooting after I went to bed but didn't pay any attention to it.

We sure had a good dinner today - steak, French fries, cake, ice cream, onions, peas, coffee, bread and butter. Pretty good, eh?

Well Marge, keep up the writing and I'm sure missing you more and more.

All my Love

Your Husband
Bill

September 24, 1945 - From Bill to Marge

Dearest Marge,

I didn't get any mail from you again tonight but hoping I do tomorrow. It is sure getting cold here the last couple of days. Have to be finding a stove to set up in my room before long. I see the Krauts have a hell of a big pile of wood cut for us. Uptown they got it all piled up high ready for us to use. This is sure going to be a cold place if we are here in the winter. I think it's probably about the coldest part of Germany. I see by the Stripes where MacArthur might not keep any troops in Japan. I hope it is true because what I've seen of Occupation, I can't see where it does any good. If they keep Ford, Standard Oil and a few of the money men out of these countries, they will never build up enough for another war.

There are a few more high pointers leaving again tomorrow. One of them got a girl knocked up who is 3 months along now so he is pretty glad to get out of here. Did you ever get those post cards I sent of here and of Theresa Neumann?

I suppose it won't be long before you will have the snow and cold weather there. I sure been wondering how my feet are going to take it again after freezing there last winter. My feet don't sweat anymore like they *used to. Even on the hottest day this summer my socks always stayed dry. I suppose we'll be getting overshoes and overcoats pretty quick.*

*How's everything going at the bakery now. I suppose Stan is so busy with basketball that it is hard to get any work out of him. I suppose Dale (Goltz) will get a discharge soon after he gets back off furlough. I think he will probably have a job supporting a wife and 2 kids because he never ever would stick to a job.*

Sis Goltz had twins.

*Well, Marge, be sure and keep writing. Let me know all the news around there. Still loving and missing you.*

*All my Love*

*Your Husband*
*Bill*

September 25, 1945 - From Bill to Marge

*Dearest Marge,*

*I got a letter from you today of the 14th. Sounds like everything is still going all right at home. I wish I could say the same about over here. From what the papers say, I won't have a chance of going home before next June at the earliest with 36 points. Everything under 45 is Occupation and from 45 to 59 clear up, they go home from Jan. till June. It said in our Div. paper today that the 90th and 11 more other Div. are to be Occupational so will probably be sometime before the 90th goes home. I'd sure hate to think of spending another year in this hole but maybe the people in the States will raise enough hell to get us guys home and send over others or turn the Occupation over to their other countries because the Americans are sure fucking up on it.*

At this stage, Bill figures he has 36 points and that it would take 45 for him to be able to be shipped out with the Division.

*Our Battalion is going out to raid the towns again in the morning so I suppose there will be a lot of looting done as usual. I have to have breakfast ready at 3:30 AM so I'll probably have to start about 1:00 AM. One of the cooks is going on pass in the morning so will have to work a little harder, I suppose. Been having it pretty easy. Don't send me any more boxes with stuff to eat because I get or can make about anything I want in the kitchen now but you can send me some magazines. Course don't get too much to read.*

*We had a movie upstairs this afternoon. I slipped up and seen about half of it but it wasn't much good. Gosh, Marge, I'd sure give about anything to be home with you or to know I was going to before long but it looks like the army's got us fucked.*

*Still loving and missing you. All my Love Bill*

Nowhere did the expected "pockets of resistance" develop. The Japs quit as unanimously as they had fought. Did they all suddenly realize the hopelessness of the struggle? Or all bow to the will of the Emperor? Or all share a hope of their power's revival? Anyway, they quit.

At Wake, Redemption. When the Stars & Stripes went up on Wake Island, the U.S. redeemed the second territory (after Guam) to be occupied by a foreign foe since 1814.

The Japs had eaten all the island's gooney birds, and most of its rats. Everywhere were relics of Major James ("Send us more Japs") Devereux's stand: U.S. ammunition was stacked in neat piles; rusted machinery was everywhere.

http://www.time.com/time/magazine/article/html

In determined and confident tones, the powerful United Automobile, Aircraft and Agricultural Implement Workers (C.I.O.) read out the declaration of war. Said the union: the auto industry must raise wages 30% to make up for the loss in take-home pay caused by the return of peace, i.e., the loss of eight hours of overtime when the week was cut from 48 to 40. The industry, said the union, must raise wages without raising auto prices,* which have not yet been fixed.

If the pay raise is not granted, said the union, it would strike one automaker and close all his plants and keep them closed. The spectacle of those tight-shut, silent plants, said the union, should be a lesson to the rest of the industry.

http://www.time.com/time/magazine/article/html

The *Waffen-SS* (German for "Armed SS", literally "Weapons SS") was the combat arm of the *Schutzstaffel* ("Protective Squadron") or SS. In contrast to the *Wehrmacht*, Germany's regular army, the Waffen-SS was a combat unit composed of volunteer troops with particularly strong personal commitments to Nazi ideology and initially selected on racial basis. As stated by Himmler, the primary goal of SS formations was to fight Jewish people, people considered subhuman by the racist Nazi ideology(i.e Poles, Jews, Roma people) and communists.

http://en.wikipedia.org/wiki/Waffen-SS

September 26, 1945 - From Bill to Marge

Dearest Marge,

I got one letter from you again tonight of the 15th. It kinda sounds like you are still holding out, eh? I'll bet you are really getting big by now, eh? I suppose you don't like the news I've been writing lately but that is about all we ever get. There sure isn't anything to do here. It's been plenty cold the last few days now and we still haven't got any stoves yet. I slept most of the afternoon. Pretty tired. I got up at 1 o'clock this morning. Started feeding breakfast at 2:30 and fed the last about 9 o'clock, I guess. When I went upstairs tonight, two of the little Kraut K.P. were waiting to ask me about if I thought they would leave. They heard over the radio about the German PW going to France and Russia to work and they thought they might have to go, but I told them I didn't think they would and would probably get their discharges from 2nd Battalion when it leaves here. If it ever does, they most likely will.

I guess Div. got 10,000 more S.S. so that will make more guard duty and work for the boys. I guess all told the Div. must have 30, or 40,000 prisoners. We have some working here who have their discharges. It's getting so I hardly know anybody around here any more. All the old guys and officers have left. I'll sure be glad when the Dago gets back because we always spend a lot of time together. Haven't played any cards for a month now. I suppose Vernon is home by now. I think I'll write Beck a letter tonight. I heard from her a week or so ago and she sent a few pictures of the baby. I'm glad to hear Dad will be home and is getting along all right.

I'm still hoping they do something about getting us guys home. There still hasn't been any replacements sent over here since V.E. day. Well, Marge, keep up the writing and I'm hoping and praying, we will be together again before to long.

All my love,

Bill

September 27, 1945 - From Bill to Marge

Dearest Marge,

Well Marge, no mail tonight except a Register of the 24th of August. I guess you have cut down on your writing, eh? Well, after the baby is born maybe you will step it up again. I just read your last letter again, it kinda sounds like you get a little disgusted too, but no more *than I do, I don't think.*

*It is getting colder than hell here. I guess we will be having snow before long from what the Krauts say. Our Colonel left for home today. That's sure a blessing. His old man died, I guess. He's been trying to get a furlough for 2 or 3 weeks.*

*I just came from the movie "Frisco Sal" - it wasn't bad. We have them up where F. Co. used to be now instead of uptown. I guess there was a USO show uptown but I was working so I couldn't go. It's beginning to seem like about half of the guys are drunk around here most of the time. They are getting a lot of cognac and schnapps. I guess they pay from 8-12 dollars a qt. for it. I suppose there are more and more guys coming home every day. I see the points system is cut to 60 by the first of Nov. I'm just hoping they count the points again in Dec. but it is doubtful. I sure hate to think of staying over here till next year at this time. I'm afraid the Army is going to have a rough time of it. Some of the guys have been so pissed off, they've been beating up Krauts, knifing them, and everything else. I sure do miss and love you, Marge and am praying we will be together one of these days again.*

*All my Love,*

*Your Husband,*
*Bill*

In this movie, Sal comes to the Barbary Coast from New England to find out who murdered her brother. She gets a job singing in Dude's saloon, falls in love with Dude, then wonders if he might be involved in the murder. Starring Andy Devine, Susanna Foster and Alan Curtis.

September 28, 1945 - From Bill to Marge

*Dearest Marge,*

*Well, Marge, I didn't get any mail tonight but am hoping I do tomorrow. My little pal, the Dago got back today so we both have been sitting down here shooting the bull. I got a bottle of good sour wine so that helped a little. Things still don't look very promising but if the people back in the States keep raising hell with the Congressmen, we will probably get there by and by.*

*The little Dago got back from the Riviera without getting fucked but he said a few of the French babes propositioned him but he was still saving it for his wife. He came over last Nov. and has 45 points. Got a purple heart or he would only have 40. It's getting just colder than hell here so I went upstairs and got one of our kitchens gas stoves and brought it down here so (its) pretty warm in my room now. We got rations again today - a carton of cigarettes, 10 candy bars and a few other things. I gave one of the Krauts a few packs of cigarettes and candy*

In the U.S. and British zones of occupied Germany, Germans had little say in the reopening of their schools. Allied occupation officers did it all: organizing courses, screening teachers, printing new books and destroying the old.

Last week the Russians went at it differently. Marshal Georgi Zhukov summarily ordered the Germans themselves to open all schools (except universities) in the Soviet zone by October 1. German officials were "warned" to prepare buildings and books in time. All private schools were told to become public ones. The German zone administrator was given two days to submit a list of courses and books for Soviet approval. German school directors were told to go out and find non-Nazi teachers. Teaching, said Marshal Zhukov, must "reveal the reactionary character of Naziism, fascist race instructions, and the military character of the former German Reich." His instructions were typical of the Russian way: make the Germans do the work themselves, police them while they do it.

http://www.time.com/time/magazine/article/html

Would that we had Marge's letters. Much of the following is conjecture.

In three of his letters, Bill has written to both Jim and Marge that anything they could do to secure his discharge was okay with him.

On September 28, this document was prepared; it is on onion skin paper, delicate and difficult to read. It is probable that Marcella Robinson was instrumental in crafting these letters that were then sent to the local Congressional Representative requesting a Hardship Discharge for Bill. Marcella worked for a local attorney (Maury Hart) and Marge had her write and send the request to Washington DC.

This we do know: (1) Marge needed Bill home to run the bakery, especially since she had given birth to their first child on September 21 and (2) it was apparent that Bill was not going to accumulate enough 'points' to get sent home. Actually, it was looking as if he was going to have to remain in Germany for up to another year! Further, that the War was over, he had done his job and could see no reason for being made to stay where he was.

As per above, this document was prepared on September 28 but for some reason was not mailed until October 10. There is a reply from Congressman Henry O. Talle, Second District of Iowa, on October 12 who had already started working on the appeal and who wrote that he would support this effort.

Jan seems to remember hearing that Bill went to his own headquarters where he knew an officer who confirmed that a Hardship Discharge was possible; one soldier had been discharged early to return to farm work. So he told Marge to get Marcella to help and see if that would work because he didn't have enough points and knew it would be a long time going thru channels on his side.

APPLICATION FOR DISCHARGE

TO THE COMMANDING OFFICER OF PFC WILLIAM WALDRON, 37772525, Headquarters Co., 2nd Bn., 357th Inf., A.P.O. 90, % Postmaster New York, New York.

STATE OF IOWA
ss.
ALLAMAKEE COUNTY

Undersigned affiant, being first duly sworn, says that:-

She is the wife of PFC William Waldron. That PFC William Waldron was inducted into the Armed Forces on the 17 day of August, 1944, and was sent overseas on or about the 8 day of January, 1945. That he is an experienced Baker and the owner of a Bakery in the City of Waukon, Iowa, which is the County Seat of Allamakee County, Iowa, and prior to his induction into the Armed Forces had been doing the baking in said Bakery for several years.

That since Pfc William Waldron entered the Army I have been operating said Bakery with hired help, but since school has commenced it has been impossible for me to secure any competent help.

That on the 21st day of September, 1945 I gave birth to a baby girl so in the future it will be impossible for me to work at or look after the Bakery myself, and unless Pfc William Waldron is discharged from the Army it will be impossible for me to keep the Bakery open, and as it is the only Bakery in Waukon, Iowa it would be a great hardship if same was closed. It is impossible to hire experienced Bakers at this time, and I believe that Pfc William Waldron would do more towards the reconversion effort if he were discharged and allowed to come home and operate his Bakery, and I hereby make application to you to discharge him from the Army.

That there are attached to this Application the Affidavits of two local residents who are not members of my family.

This Application for discharge is made because of special importance to the reconversion effort.

Dated this 26th day of September, 1945.

Mrs William Waldron

This is Page 2 of the appeal. Each of the submissions were notarized by E. C. Sullivan, Notary Public of Iowa, in and for the County of Allamakee.

AFFIDAVIT

STATE OF IOWA
ss.
ALLAMAKEE COUNTY

Undersigned affiant, first being duly sworn, says:-

That he is the physician of Mrs. William Waldron, whose husband is a member of the Armed Forces, that she gave birth to a daughter on September 21st, 1945, and it will be impossible for her to look after and take care of the Bakery owned by her husband, as she has in the past, I have read the attached Application for Discharge, and I am familiar with the facts set out therein, and the statements therein contained are true as I verily believe.

C W Rominger MD

Subscribed and sworn to before me, a Notary Public of

In support of Marge's endeavor, this is Page 3 and was signed by C. W. Rominger, MD who was the doctor who delivered Jan.

AFFIDAVIT

STATE OF IOWA
ss.
ALLAMAKEE COUNTY

Undersigned affiant, first being duly sworn, says that:-

He is a resident of Waukon, Allamakee County, Iowa, and the Manager of the Eclipse Lumber Company in said City. I am well acquainted with William Waldron and his wife. That I have read the foregoing Application for Discharge of Pfc William Waldron, and I am familiar with the facts set out therein and the statements therein contained are true as I verily believe.

Ray H Kreeb

Page 4 of the Affidavit was further support and was signed by Ray Kreeb.

There were leis for everybody—some made of ginger flowers, some of paper. Planes flew overhead. Bands played Aloha Oe. WAVEs kissed sailors. A hula dancer performed on the flight deck. The Saratoga, biggest U.S. aircraft carrier left in World War II was sailing for home.

The Sara's hangar deck, the pilots' ready rooms and even the admiral's flag office had been turned into quarters for over 2,000 sailors, who tossed their leis in the water as the big carrier weighed anchor from Pearl Harbor. Soon 35 smaller escort carriers would be similarly transformed into Navy transports.

Back in the U.S., the Army released 14,121 soldiers in a single day. The number of men returned to civilian life since Germany's defeat had risen above 700,000. The Army now expected to discharge 400,000 in September (an earlier estimate had been 250,000). By Christmas, the Army hoped, the total of discharged soldiers would stand at 2,000,000.

Nevertheless, Congress was on edge to get demobilization going even faster. The public had put the heat on Congressmen, and they passed it on to the War and Navy Departments.

http://www.time.com/time/magazine/article/.html

Eschenbach Bavarian China now considered antique china is available on Ebay and china websites.

The company is in business today and makes magnifying glasses and lab equipment.

Jan remembers that Marge was mad because Bill sent home guns and never a set of china.

*because he is a good worker. We bought a cow today for 3500 marks. We've been getting about half enough meat to feed the men so we fixed things today so they will have enough.*

*Father Murphy ate with us today. He's sure a good Joe. Every time he comes to the Battalion, he usually stops in to see me. They are sure getting a lot of guys up for Court Martials here now for looting, beating up Krauts, and things like that. I sure wish they would get us home before long because it's bad leaving guys here to long. I'm still behaving though and am going to keep it up. I sure do love and miss you, Marge and hope and pray I get home with you one of these days again.*

*All my love,*

*Your Husband*
*Bill*

September 29, 1945 - From Bill to Marge

*Dearest Marge*

*Well, Marge I got 3 letters from you today of the 7th, 8th, and 9th and one from Veryle. Sure glad to get them too. I got a kick out of Veryle's letter. She said in her letter about being out with Ralph and they pitched a bitch and he really got polluted. She must have sure learned the language since I left. I'll have to write her and ask her if she still got her cherry or if she's using it for a tail-light, eh?*

*I sure wish I was as hopeful as you about me being home by Christmas but I don't think there is a chance now. Some of the low point men signed up for 1 1/2 yrs over here so they will go home for furlough and then come back. Maybe that would be one way of getting back, eh?*

*I think that is a lot of shit about the gov't stopping the Democrat from coming because I've been getting the Register all along and other guys been getting their home papers. You asked what kind of a factory this was. Well, at the end of the war they were making radar parts but before that they made dishes. Some of the best in the world, they say. Eschenbach is the name of them. They are going to start up again now. We can order them if we want from $40 - $120 a set but fuck these Krauts, I ain't spending any more money here than I have to. I'm glad you got the pictures I sent but I thought it would take them longer to get there.*

*We were supposed to have a bunch of high point-*

In this letter, Bill mentions sending home pictures. This oil is one he purchased while in Germany and it now hangs in the bedroom of one of his daughters (much to the chagrin of her loving husband).

*ers leaving this week but the order came down stopping them so there is something up. Lots of rumors flying around again but nothing good. From the looks of the paper, they are still figuring on keeping us guys here with under 45 points permanently no matter how much combat time we had or overseas time we have. One of the boys got a letter from a kid that had 60 some points who is back in the States now. I wrote you about him - after the war one of the guys getting killed and a couple wounded fooling around with a pistol? Well, this was the kid that pulled the trigger. He got it in the hand and is back in the States now. I get more pissed off at this fucking army every day, I guess. Keep up the writing.*

*All my love*

*Your Husband*
*Bill*

September 30, 1945 - From Bill to Marge

*Dearest Marge,*

*I didn't get any mail from you today but got a box from my mother and one from yours. Tell her thanks a lot for me, will you? Haven't did much today. Worked this morning and then went to church this afternoon. Myself and the little Dago are sitting here writing a letter. We had a bottle of wine a little while ago. Good to. One of the Krauts was in and we were kidding him about the American soldiers fucking his girl. He says he don't think he will ever marry now because all the women have been screwed too much by the Americans and Russians. I guess there are not many virgins left over here. I read the Stripes a while ago but there is nothing that sounds like I'll get home any quicker in it. It is sure cold here now. Still haven't got any stoves in the building the kitchen is about the only place that is warm.*

*It sure don't make any sense leaving all us guys here doing nothing. There is no training going on any more. About all half the guys do is get drunk. I guess they were really raising hell with the natives again last night.*

*I read the articles in the Readers Digest this month about Theresa Neumann. Our chaplain always gets some extra ones for us guys. That Major Bradley that*

Joseph Patrick Kennedy, now 57 and with red hair greying, came out of self-imposed political exile last week and went back to work for his native state of Massachusetts.

At the behest of young, earnest Governor Maurice J. Tobin, Joe Kennedy had become chairman of a "special commission relative to establishing a state department of commerce." His job was to prepare legislation to rejuvenate Massachusetts' rapidly deteriorating industry.

Joe Kennedy had taken the job reluctantly. His last public service, as U.S. Ambassador to the Court of St. James, had ended badly when he told newsmen that democracy was through in England. Then he had broken with his good friend Franklin Roosevelt and retired to write a book (still unfinished) to prove that he was right in the beginning about the war and the world.

was mentioned in one article is the guy I tried to get a pass from to go see Vernon that time. All the men mentioned were in the 90th. I'm sure hoping they start sending some men over here before long and maybe we'll get home. Quite a few guys are signing up for 3 year hitches now and get a furlough from 30-90 days in the States.

Well, Marge, keep up the writing and still loving and missing you.

All my love

Your Husband
Bill

<u>September 31, 1945 - From Bill to Marge</u>

Dearest Marge,

Well, Marge, no mail again tonight so I should have some tomorrow. Still nothing new around except lots of rumors - mostly bad though so I won't mention them. We got paid today and I won a watch for 9 bucks on a P.X. drawing. I suppose there are still more and more guys coming home every day now. I sure hope I do before long but guess I have quite a while to sweat out here yet. They are having quite a recruiting drive. Getting quite a few guys to sign up for a hitch too.

I seen a movie tonight, pretty good to. We have them in the building here instead of uptown. It makes it a lot better too - saves that long walk uptown.

I was called up before a Colonel today. They were checking up on a guy in J. Co. who looted $75,000 back when the war was on. The other kid who was in on it got killed in April so they are having a hell of a job getting the goods on this kid. Of course, I said I didn't know anything about it and I guess most of the other guys said the same thing. I sure hope they don't send him up for it but it is hard to tell. I hope things are still getting along at the bakery and everybody is all right. Say, when's John got to marry that girl of his anyway?

Well, Marge guess I'd better quit for tonight. Have to get up early in the morning. Still hoping and praying I will be home with you soon.

All my love

Your Husband
Bill

<u>October 3, 1945 - From Bill to Marge</u>

Dearest Marge,

I just received the good news tonight. Sure glad you

The big news from Japan was what had not happened. A desperately small force of U.S. troops (100,000 by last week) had landed in a previously uninvaded country populated by the most fantastically nationalistic people on earth; yet not an American had been killed, not a demonstration had occurred.

Terrorists still sought some of the leaders who had surrendered Japan. Efforts persisted to preserve Japan's national pride against the admission of full defeat. But these were not typical of occupied Japan. Cabled TIME Correspondent John Walker from Tokyo:

"I can only conclude that we considerably underestimated their exhaustion and willingness to cry uncle. One may legitimately doubt the sincere willingness of the national leadership to embrace the permanent role of a peaceable fourth-rate power, but here in the midst of it one can scarcely doubt the sincerity of the people's relief over the war's end and their willingness to obey the government in submission to the occupation."

http://www.time.com/time/magazine/article/html

On October 1, Heavyweight Champ Joe Louis was discharged from the US Army.

The US Office of Strategic Service (OSS) was disbanded by President Harry S. Truman who *didn't trust spies*.

News of Jan's birth finally makes it's way to Germany.

and the baby are all right. I got a letter from you of the 20th, one from your mother and a card from mine and a letter from Marguardt. Really did all right, eh.

Ma wrote that her and Veryle were helping John in the back end. Damn but I sure wished I could be home. But maybe there will be plenty help around with all the guys getting discharge now. They stopped all the high-points from leaving. They say the Div. is still going home with everybody from 55 points and up but it is probably just another rumor. I hardly ever even get outside the building now. It is cold. Work, eat, sleep is about all. There sure isn't a hell of a lot to write about. I suppose it's really a big relief to have it all over with, eh. I sure hope the baby isn't as old as Vernon's before I get home. I suppose you really gave Stan quite a let down by not having triplets like he had it all figured out, eh? It will probably be harder than hell to keep the bakery going now. I suppose that if nothing better, we can always lock it up. Course I find out over here that money don't mean a hell of a lot. I was glad to hear that Veryle came up to help out a few days; maybe you can talk her into staying eh? Or is she still figuring on going back to school. They tell me I'll be going on pass pretty quick but I think something will come up to put a stop to it.

Well Marge, I sure hope I get home with you before long. Still loving and missing you.

All my love,

Your Husband, Bill

October 3, 1945 - To Marge from Helen

Dear Marg,

Ever since I read of the shower held for you I've been waiting impatiently for Janice's arrival, so now I mustn't be tardy in my congratulations. I hope you're feeling fine. How much did she weigh? The paper didn't say. I hope your husband will be home to see Janice soon. Has he prospects yet of his trip home? I like your choice of name incidentally; I've a cousin Janice I like a lot. One's association with a name always seems to make a difference.

When Vonnie comes to see you, tell her I'm going to write to her one of these days. I've been wondering about Bob's coming home too. I guess I haven't written to either you or Vonnie since we came down here nearly six months ago. Bob's at Frederick, Okla. But we couldn't find a closer place to live than this - 27 miles

On October 1, Arthur C. Clarke put forward the idea of communications satellites in a *Wireless World* magazine article.

Henry Stimson went home with his wife to West Hills, L.I., on his 78th birthday. The crowded week had brought him the Distinguished Service Medal, awarded by Harry Truman for 40 years of work, "exceptional in the history of the nation." There had been the big reception at Dumbarton Oaks, the farewell press conference, the final Cabinet meeting. Henry Stimson, correct and courtly as ever, loved it all.

Longer than most men, he had seen and feared the conflict that brought him back to Washington five years ago. Sooner than most, he had learned that there was no passive defense against aggression. As Herbert Hoover's Secretary of State in 1931, he had spoken out almost alone against the Japs' first thrust at China. From then on he had refused to recognize Axis conquest, even when it was unpopular to refuse.

http://www.time.com/time/magazine/article/html

On October 3, Elvis Presley made his first public appearance at the age of ten years old.

"It seems as if everybody in the country was getting impatient to get his or her particular soldier out of the Army and to upset the carefully arranged system of points for retirement which had been arranged with the approval of the Army itself."

Henry Stimson

There was, in dreadful truth, such a thing as the atom bomb. But strategists went on planning armies and navies as if it did not exist. Diplomats bickered away without ever mentioning it. To plain people it was a horror shoved in the back of the mind on the vague assumption that somebody would work out a way to subdue it for man's good.

At a U.S. Cabinet meeting, Henry Wallace and others cited scientific opinion that the secret could not be kept, argued that the bomb be made available to the United Nations Organization. Said Britain's Sir Stafford Cripps: "The thing I fear is that as the months and years pass the story of Nagasaki and Hiroshima will fade into the background and that . . . this new power of destruction . . . will cease to have its compelling force upon our political actions."

http://www.time.com/time/magazine/article/html

away. We have a large four-room apt (also a bathroom.) It's upstairs but we liked it better than either of the two smaller apts. downstairs. It's wonderful to have so much room. We'd lived cooped up so long we felt like rabbits. We have a huge yard, a garden which died to the last bean, and a three-car garage, which we never use. However, Bob's Lizzie has withstood the elements for so long that she gets claustrophobia in any enclosure. Mickey also has a playpen in the backyard. We're really thrilled to have this place.

I'll very likely be going home in a couple of weeks, for the field is to be closed. We don't know when Bob will be discharged. He has 57 points, not enough for a November discharge.

Mickey will be two the 29th of this month and really is changing. He talks a lot now-sentences even-mostly with essential words only. He'll say to Bob when he comes home, "Mommy reading paper" and "Judy crying" if he hears the girl downstairs. He's very heavy - weighed 39 pounds a couple of weeks ago.

Isn't it wonderful to have the war over and be able to plan for a civilian life! Bob's plans still are quite hazy - I hope he doesn't go back to Baltimore. I kind of have roots in Iowa. I guess though I thought I was footloose and all that, you know.

If we get to Waukon after Bob gets his discharge, we'll certainly make it a point to see you and Janice - and I hope, Bill too. You'll be living in Waukon, won't you?

Well so long for now. I hope you're both getting along first rate. Write

Love, Helen

October 3, 1945 - To Jim and Amanda from Bill

Dear Folks,

I got your card today of the baby being born. Sure glad it is over with and they are both doing all right. I hope dad is up and around before long. I suppose it's been pretty hard on him to stay in bed.

How are the kids coming? I suppose they will be so big when I get home I'll hardly know them. It still don't look like I'll be home very quick. They haven't sent any replacements over here yet. Lot of the boys are signing up for a hitch in the army. They go home for furlough and then come back for 1 1/2 years. I suppose there's 3 - 4 hundred signed up in the Div. already. I got the squirrel you sent. So me and a couple of the boys are going to *have a nice feed with it. I never ever seen any squirrels in these countries. Lot of deer though - they are pretty tame to. I suppose the boys are spending lots of time in the woods now. I'd sure like to be home to go. I don't suppose dad will be able to go though, eh?*

*I hope those congressmen stay on the ball back there and get us home before long because the army sure as hell wants to keep us over here. The guys here don't do any training any more, just lay around and do a few details now and then. Well, Ma, think I better quit for now. Have a couple more letters to write yet. I suppose Vern is home with Beck and the boy by now. Well, write me and let me know how everything is going.*

*Love, Bill*

October 3, 1945 - To Marge from Bill

*Dearest Marge,*

*Well, Marge, I didn't get any mail today but I guess I won't be able to expect any for a few days, eh?*

*Sure been a lot of rumors flying around the last few days. A bunch of guys supposed to go on pass tomorrow had them all cancelled. They gave a big recruiting talk today also. Told us anybody with 9 months or so over here might as well enlist because they would probably be here 21 more anyway. Sure encouraging, isn't it. But I don't think I would enlist if I had 2 days over here. DeMarco and 30 more are supposed to be transferred to 3rd Army QM Friday but I'm hoping they cancel that to. I'm sure anxious to hear what the name is going to be. I sure hope I'm home with you before she gets very big. I'm still hoping I stay with the 90th. Some say it's going home and others say it is going to Austria so we don't know where in the hell we are at as usual. One thing this army sure keeps a guy fucked up all the time. We were supposed to have a movie tonight and after waiting an hour and a half, they finally decided there was a piece missing to the projector so we didn't have any. I got a box from you with candy and magazine in it. Mailed Sept 4 and the candy was moldy but I was sure glad to get the magazine. I got a little clipping I cut out of the Stars and Stripes that we thought was sure good so I will send it.*

*Well, Marge, I sure can't think of any thing else to write about so I guess I better quit for tonight. I sure hope you and the daughter are getting along all right. I'll say a prayer for you both. Still loving and missing*

The U.S. defeat at Pearl Harbor, already twice investigated and shortly to be reviewed once more, this time by a Congressional committee, was still a live political and military issue. Last week, in an article by John Chamberlain, one of its editors, LIFE added a new note to the political side. Said Chamberlain:

Through the Jap code (which the U.S. had in its pocket before Pearl Harbor), President Franklin Roosevelt and the Washington high command knew, hours before the attack, that Japan was breaking off negotiations, that this meant a surprise attack somewhere in the Pacific.

By the time the 1944 Presidential campaign had rolled around, G.O.P. Candidate Thomas Dewey knew what his opponent had known in December, 1941.

Out of patriotism, Dewey kept silent on that vital fact in his campaign.

"Dewey was in a position," wrote Chamberlain, "to charge that the President had 'betrayed' the interests of the U.S. in failing either to forestall or mitigate an attack for which we were . .. not yet ready. The political impact of such a charge . . . might well have landed Dewey in the White House."

http://www.time.com/time/magazine/article/html

you and sure hope I'll be home soon but it don't look much like it.

All my love,

Your Husband, Bill

October 4, 1945 - To Marge from Bill

Dearest Marge,

Well, Marge no mail again tonight. I thought I'd have a letter from Ma but didn't get any. DeMarco is leaving at 8:30 in the morning for a quartermaster outfit near Nuremberg. 210 more are leaving the Battalion either Monday or Tues for Munich to the Military Gov't. I suppose I'll be in that bunch. They are taking everybody with under 60 and over 70 points out of the Division. I guess the Div. will leave here this month then go home in December so I probably won't be getting any mail from you for about a month after I leave here. I got fucked out of my pass again so I've kind of given up all hope of ever getting one. It is sure cold and raining here today. We got our overcoats a few days ago so I got mine pressed by the Heine tailor. They looked like some we threw away on the line the last week.

Damn, but I think when you sent me this paper, you planned on me writing long letters. It don't seem like there is any end to a page. (big sheets) You can tell dad that I finally got him a German razor. I got two of them today for 5 bucks and 5 packs of cigarettes from the barber in town. They sure don't want to sell them because they can't get anymore. I offered one guy 20 bucks for one and he wouldn't sell it. I got a nice ashtray today to, with 357th and 90th Division wrote on it. Also had the 5 campaigns wrote on it. They were made in one of the towns a few miles from here. Now if I can keep it without busting it. I sure hope you and the baby are doing all right by now. I suppose it will be a while before I know her name.

I'm sure glad I'm in the kitchen now because I sure hate standing guard in this kind of weather. The guys are pulling guard every other night now. Well Marge, better quit for tonight. Still loving and missing you.

All my love

Your Husband, Bill

October 5, 1945 - To Marge from Bill

Dearest Marge,

I was sure glad to hear from you again. Got a letter

General George S. Patton Jr. had kept mum for quite a while. It was unlike him. Last week, in Bavaria, where he is U.S. military governor, he broke the irksome silence, brandished his riding crop and informed the press: "Well, I'll tell you. This Nazi thing. It's just like a Democratic-Republican election fight."

The fact that General Dwight D. Eisenhower had just instituted an investigation of Bavaria's Nazified German bureaucracy did not seem to cut much ice with George Patton. In his opinion, too much fuss was being made about denazification. Said Patton: "I'm not trying to be King of Bavaria."

He hated Nazis as much as anyone else, he said. But one of the first things he had learned about military government was that "the outs are coming around saying that the ins are Nazis. . . . More than half of the German people were Nazis and you'd be in a hell of a fix if you tried to remove all Party members." Most Nazis had merely been forced into the Party, anyway, he said, or had joined it because it was a good thing at the time.

Patton's ideas on how to run Germany were shared by many of his subordinate officers. The ideas: 1) restore normal conditions to prevent anarchy; 2) get German industry back into shape so that the U.S. taxpayer will not have to foot the bill; 3) show the Germans "what grand fellows we are."

Said Patton in his best grand-fellow manner: "To get things going, we've got to compromise with the devil a little bit."

http://www.time.com/time/magazine/article/html

*from you of the 25th. One from Ma and a long letter from Swede. Sure was good to hear from him again too. I guess you must have wrote a letter or two since the baby was born that I've never got. I gather from this letter the baby's name is Janice but still don't know the middle name. Not bad. I've sure been wondering what you were going to name her. Maybe by the time I get home, I'll probably be able to take her on a good drunk with me, eh?*

*They told me today that I leave Tuesday for Munich to go to the Military Gov. All the guys with less than 55 points are leaving to different places. The Dago left this morning for QM (Quartermaster Corp) in Nuremberg. I sure hated to see him go, we have been together for so long now. I had a long letter from ma today that she added a little every day for 3 days. She said Harold helped one night and that he would be getting discharged before long. It would sure be good to have him back but I doubt if he would go back to work in the bakery. Swede said he was getting married in Nov. and that he would be back in the chicken business in four or 6 months. I sure wished I could expect something like that, but it don't look that way. They've been having a lot of trouble around Munich. I think that is why they are transferring combat riflemen there. All of the guys going there are combat men. Those who have seen combat are going to a medic outfit. I've kinda got the Krauts upstairs sweating. My room was looted a couple days ago. Cigarettes, candy and clothes. I told them I was going to kill the bastard if I found out which one it was.*

*Marge, be sure to send Janice's birth certificate so I can have the allotment made out. Ever since the 15 of August, about 20 times a day somebody would ask me if I was a papa yet. Even the damn Krauts got asking me every time I'd get mail. So don't worry, I get my share of kidding to. One guy's a pal of mine, Ray Ilg. is his name. As quick as he heard it, he came running in. " Come on Bill, we got to figure out how long you've been over here." So after he got done, he thought it was OK. They always are wanting to know when I am going to break down and take a crack at one of these Heines. Most of the married men are playing them but there are still a few of us that aren't and I don't even intend to if they keep me here 10 years. Gosh, but I sure hated to pass up some good American whiskey a few times but I ain't drank any of that stuff over here yet either. But wait*

When Bill writes about the Swede he is referring to Paul Anderson, life long friends from Waukon.

Married: Shirley Temple, 17, cinema's dimpled goldilocks who grew up to bobby-sox roles (Kiss and Tell); and Sergeant John Agar, 24, tall, handsome A.A.F. physical instructor; in Los Angeles.

In his letter of October 4, Bill mentions this ashtray.

The Council of Foreign Ministers, established at Potsdam to carry on for the Big Three, had scarcely warmed the red leather chairs in London's Lancaster House before the members began wrangling over procedures. They stayed in session a fortnight, progressed only in the sense that they strangled over progressively more important matters.

When China's Wang or France's Bidault was in the chair, the going was relatively smooth. Table-thumping began when one of the other three took the gavel. Byrnes and Molotov did not get along well, and Molotov disliked Bevin.

http://www.time.com/time/magazine/article/html

On October 5, *Meet the Press* premiered on radio.

After a six month strike by Hollywood set decorators, *Hollywood Black Friday* occured when a bloody riot broke out at the gates of Warner Brothers' studio.

On October 6, General Eisenhower, arriving on Hitler's train, received a warm welcome in Hague.

A memorial for those who had been executed by the Nazis was unveiled at Terbregge.

*until I get home. I don't think I'll be able to get enough. Well Marge, got to get up early again in the morning so better quit. Still missing you more every day and hope to be home with you before too awful long but till then you'll have to keep up the writing and let me know how that little daughter of ours is doing. You think you'll keep her a virgin as long as you were?*

*All my love, Bill*

<u>October 6, 1945 - To Marge from Bill</u>

*Dearest Marge,*

*I got a letter from Veryle and 2 from you today of Sept. 22. Having the baby must have been hell, eh. I'm sure glad it is all over with and you are both all right. I was over to Regt. today to make out the allotment but they said you would probably have it made out by this time and I see by your letter tonight that you know what to do. In case you haven't got my last letter yet, I'm shipping to the M.G. (Military Government, Army of the Occupation) at Munich Tuesday. Gosh, but it is sure going to be hell not getting any mail from you for about a month or so. I suppose it will take that long anyway. All the men with 56 points are leaving the outfit. I guess you will have to give up hope of me being home for Christmas because it is liable to be quite a lot longer than that now. You sure have enough company at the hospital anyway so I suppose you still get in on all the gossip, eh?*

*This is getting to be a worse hole every day. In one way I'm glad its not to another Inf. Outfit I'm going to because during --- (?) I think they are more chicken shit. But that's one good thing working in the kitchen. I get out of all of that. I had another little run in with the mess Sarg. We ran short of chow today and he told the boys he couldn't help it if we weren't getting enough rations and of course, I had to tell him if he and a couple more of the cooks would quit lugging it up to them Heine cunts, we would have plenty. You can imagine how he liked that. Well, I've only one more shift to put up with him so I won't mind. There's been quite a few guys enlisting. I hope they keep it up but I think they need their heads examined, but I guess for these guys in love with these Krauts, it's a pretty good deal. They can live pretty cheap here and some of these guys are making 3 - 6 hundred a week doing a little black marketing on liquor and cigarettes and the like. But all I ever did was trade cigarettes for the razor. I don't think I'll make any of this easy money. I think some of the boys in the kitchen been making plenty to because the Krauts give about anything for coffee and sugar. Well, Marge, better quit for tonight. Still loving and missing you. Take good care of that daughter.*

*All my Love, Bill*

October 7, 1945 - To Marge from Bill

*Dearest Marge,*

*Well, Marge, didn't get any mail tonight but am sure hoping I do tomorrow because it will be my last chance to get any for quite a while because I leave Tuesday. Boy, Marge, if there are any 'strings' to pull on or any way you can get me out of this Army, I sure wish you would do it. From the looks of the Stripes today, I'll be here another year yet. I'm getting so I hate these bastards more every day I'm here. I had my room looted again today and the officers didn't know if they could shake them down or not so I borrowed a 45 from the supply room and myself and another guy really shook them down. Bed, bags, mattress and everything they had and we sure found the shit. Then I went and got the officer of the Guard and had them all thrown in the jug.*

*They were supposed to get their discharge tomorrow but they're fucked now. I should of shot the bastard, and then they wouldn't have to bother trying them. Tomorrow morning will be my last morning cooking here. I sure wish I could go home with the Div. but every thing is by points now and by the looks of the Stripes today, those having under 45 points as of VJ day will stay for occupation or will go home from January to June.*

*I guess the army figures we should forget we have wives in the states and settle down living with these Kraut cunt like most of the guys are doing. I wouldn't mind staying over here if I knew that it was guys going home who came over before me, but lots of them going now came over after I did. Tell Stan if he believes any of that recruiting shit they are probably handing out in the states now, he ought to have his head examined.*

*Well, Marge, I probably shouldn't be writing at all tonight the mood I'm in. I better quit before I start writing to much about this army.*

*Still loving and missing you.*

*All my love,*
*Bill*

With each new mail delivery, Congressmen got more jittery. The angry letters, pouring in last week from the folks at home and the boys abroad, were all but unanimous: speed up demobilization, or else. Sweating under the mounting pressure, Senate Military Affairs Committeemen talked nervously of "passing a bill." When General MacArthur, in Tokyo, guesstimated he could police Japan with 200,000 men, the pot boiled.

In this situation there was only one thing for the Army to do. Sad-eyed General George Catlett Marshall, chief of staff, stepped up to explain. At the Library of Congress he faced 350 members of Congress, half a hundred G.I.s and WACs whom Alben Barkley, Senate majority leader, had told to come on in.

For an hour, General Marshall spoke with his usual even assurance, as usual without notes. Highlights: the point score for discharge will be down to 60 by Nov. 1; everybody with two years of service can hope to get out this winter; separations are running 17,000 a day, will shortly exceed 700,000 a month; the demobilization rate has nothing to do with the postwar Army's size.

When he finished, there was not a single question. The pressure went down, visibly. The Gallup poll found that most people were satisfied with the rate of discharge. But before long, Congressmen expected the heat would be on again.

http://www.time.com/time/magazine/article/html

On October 8, President Truman announced that both Canada and Britain had been told about the atomic bomb secret prior to the explosion.

On Aug. 31, 1944, Adolf Hitler spoke his mind to a group of German generals at his secret headquarters. According to a stenographic transcript found last week in the resort town of Wiesbaden, the Führer said:

"This war is no convenience to me. For five years I've been shut off from the other world. I've not visited the theater, I've not heard a concert, and I've not seen a film.

"I live only for a single mission, to lead this battle because I know if there is not iron will power behind it, the battle will not be won.

"I blame the General Staff because they, instead of always exhibiting iron will, have weakened the front officers, for when General Staff officers come to the front they spread pessimism."

Latest Hitler rumor, circulating in Bavaria: he is alive and plotting another war against the western Allies—in collaboration with Generalissimo Stalin.

October 8, 1945 - To Marge from Bill

*Dearest Marge,*

*I didn't get any mail from you again tonight. I guess there were only about a dozen letters from the Co. I'll sure miss getting your letters for the next month. I hate that worse than anything. I'm going to the 3rd Army. My APO is 403 but you will have to wait a day or so and I'll send the right address. Of course, they tell us here that it will only take a week or so for us to get our mail there from here but I don't believe any of this army bullshit any more. I see by the Stripes today they are letting guys out with 2 yrs service in the States and they passed the 1-year enlistment bill. Got my bag all packed except my blankets and foot sack. Supposed to leave at 8 o' clock but that will probably mean 10.*

*I sure hope everybody is fine at home and things are going a little easier in the bakery. I suppose you are really taking good care of that daughter of ours, eh.*

*I suppose it is getting cold at home now too. It seems I am going to be stuck in the coldest part of Germany this winter. I'm sure glad there are quite a few guys going along that I know. How is Max? Does she ever help out at the bakery?*

*I sure wish I was back there now instead of in this fucking country. But I don't know as whether I'd ever go back to working nights except occasionally. I'll sure have a lot of homework to catch up on, eh. How about you?*

*Well, Marge, I sure spend a lot of time thinking about you and hope I'm back with you before long and get a chance to see that daughter of ours.*

*All my love,*

*Your Husband, Bill*

October 10, 1945 - To Marge from Bill

*Dearest Marge,*

*I didn't write last night. Am writing early this morning. Am in a replacement pool at Augsburg with about 300 of us guys from the 90th. We are only here for reassignment and they tell me it won't take over 4 hrs. It sure is a nice city. I went uptown last night and went to a movie and then stopped into a bar on the way back and had a few beers. They had 12% beer and there was plenty boys drunk. Looks about like the Landmark only on a little longer scale. Guys sitting in every booth and loving the babes. I just sat around and drank beer and watched them for an hour and a half. This is about the best sleeping deal I've seen. We have Army cots to sleep on and in the mess hall, they bring our meals to us on the table so no chow line to sweat out.*

*We all get interviewed this morning and maybe some of us 'go out' yet today. I probably won't be able to mail this for a day or two till I get my new address. This is the address I sent you only it's Augsburg instead of Munich. We can get shipped anyplace in Bavaria from here even back where we came from. A lot of these boys got girls back around Wieden and Wiedenbach and want to go back that way but I sure hope I don't because I never cared too much for it around there. Well, Marge, I'll write again as quick as I find out where in the hell I go.*

*Sill loving and missing you.*

*All my love*

*Your Husband, Bill*

October 11, 1945 - To Marge from Bill

*Dearest Marge,*

*Well, Marge, I finally got assigned today and am I ever glad. I was sure getting tired sweating out these lines. I got assigned to this Co. right here so I won't have to move my stuff far and hope I'll get my mail a little sooner now. Here's my address:*

*HQ Sv. Co. 3rd Mil Gov Regt, APO 403, % P.M., NY, NY*

*I guess all these rear echelon guys have gone home so we have to fill their places. Quite a few guys from the 90th are getting assigned here but most of the guys I knew are getting shipped out. I went down town last night and stopped into the Red Cross Club and had coffee and doughnuts and then went down to one of the theaters but I seen the shows playing at all 3 theaters so went up to the bar and had a few beers. Then went back to the Red Cross and read for a couple hrs. They seem to get all the magazines and everything. It sure pisses me off to take this rear echelon job. When the war was on, these guys used to say they would have to stay here a couple years but we would go home when the fighting was over but it looks like its just the opposite. This looks to be a pretty nice city. It don't seem to be as beat up as most of them and quite large too. I hear by the radio where they are going to start sending over a few replacements. I hope they send plenty so we can all go home. Boy, Marge, but I sure miss you more and more every day but I guess we'll have to make the best of it*

This letter is postmarked Augsburg, Germany.

The U.S. wartime policy of allocating surplus air transports to foreign airlines paid a fat dividend. The Royal Dutch Airlines (K.L.M.) bought 16 surplus transports and The Netherlands Government granted U.S. airlines cabotage (the right to land and embark cargo and passengers en route to any destination in the world served by American flag lines in Holland). Thus the Dutch subscribed to the "Five Freedoms" drafted (but not adopted by all the countries) last year at the Chicago International Civil Aviation Conference. Result: American Airlines Overseas, Inc., formerly American Export Airlines, certified to fly to Amsterdam, may begin a survey flight next week.

http://www.time.com/time/magazine/article/html

Two recently isolated giants, the U.S. and the U.S.S.R., were suddenly everywhere. Russia was claiming colonies in Africa, making friends among the Arabs, gripping eastern Europe, regaining its economic position in Manchuria, actively concerning itself with the control of Japan. The U.S., which five years ago seemed half-indifferent, was now insistently expressing its views on the internal politics of Balkan countries, expanding its influence in the Middle East, preparing to keep great island bases opposite Russia's back door.

When the giants came together at the ill-tempered, ill-prepared London Council of Foreign Ministers, each seemed to the other aggressively expansionist. The U.S. was stronger, so the Russians talked tougher.

The President received two gifts last week: 1) an autographed photo of the late Frederic Knight Logan, modernizer of The Missouri Waltz (one of Harry Truman's favorite songs); 2) an old Sioux pipe of peace, said to have been smoked by Chief Crazy Horse when he decided (after the Custer massacre in 1876) to surrender and return to the reservation.

The gifts were ill-timed. The six-month waltz of Congress with the Missourian in the White House was definitely over. Democrats (notably Southerners) had boldly walked off the reservation and joined Republicans on the warpath. Last week the House Ways & Means Committee (14 Democrats and ten Republicans) voted 18-to-6 to reject the President's reconversion proposal: unemployment compensation up to $25 a week for 26 weeks. Then the Committee voted 14-to-10 to shelve further consideration of aid to the jobless, including the bill the Senate had chopped out of the Truman recommendations.

http://www.time.com/time/magazine/article/html

*until they finally decide to send us home.*

*I suppose there are more and more guys coming home everyday. Damn, but I would sure give plenty to be in one of those bunches going before long. Well, Marge I still haven't monkeyed with any of this cunt. Doing pretty good, don't you think? But I tell you there are not many of the married men who aren't playing them. Lots of them have their steadies that they shack up with every night. Well, Marge, I better quit for now. I hope I start getting mail from you pretty quick. Still loving and missing you.*

*All my love*

*Your Husband, Bill*

October 11, 1945 - To Marge from Bill

*Dearest Marge,*

*Well, Marge, I thought I might as well write again tonight seeing how I missed writing one night. How are you and the little daughter doing by now? Fine I hope. Sure wish I was there with you.*

*It don't look like I'll have to do much work here. They have all Kraut cooks and women waiting tables. About all we have to do is seat the guys, watch over the Krauts to see that they don't run off with everything but they say we will move to Munich shortly. I sure hope not anyway because they have a nice kitchen here now. We feed all the way from 500 to 1500 men a meal so you can imagine how big it is.*

*I think I'll write the folks yet tonight. It's been a week or so since I have. I suppose Vernon must surely be home by now. I'll bet Beck don't need to worry anymore about him planning on staying in the Army. I think he's had his fill of it by now but for a young single guy, this is sure a good deal over here. All the pussy he wants and don't cost nothing to live. They say this Mil. Gov't is the best deal a guy can get into now. It isn't as chicken shit as most parts of the Army. I haven't saluted an officer here yet and don't intend to. They don't seem to mind either.*

*I sure hope everything is going all right at the bakery and that you have found some help for the backend by now. John has sure surprised me how well he has been sticking it out. We'll have to buy him a swell wedding present when he gets married, eh? Have you asked him when it is going to be? From the sounds of your letters he must have it pretty bad. I think by the time I get home,*

I'll have to learn to dance and drink all over again and screw to, eh? Well, I sure hope they keep changing things and get me home. Course I sure get more lonesome for you all the time. Well, Marge, take good care of the little daughter and I hope she don't get to big before I get a chance to see her.

All my love

Your Husband, Bill

October 11, 1945 - To Jim and Amanda from Bill

Dear Folks,

Well, Ma, I suppose you know by now I'm not coming home with the 90th. I got transferred here a few days ago. All the guys under 55 points left the Div. I guess this is going to be a pretty good deal for being in Germany. I see by the paper where they are sending a few men over here. I sure hope they step it up for all us guys to get home before long. But I guess I'll be stuck the winter here anyway. I got your card about the baby being born about 3 days before I did the letter. I'm sure glad Marge and the baby are both all right. I sure hope to hell I get home before she gets too big. I suppose by now Vernon is probably home with Beck and his son, eh? I've got the same APO now that he used to have. I'm in the kitchen here but I guess I won't have to do much except watch. They have a bunch of German cooks and women working. Feed from 500-1500 a meal so you can imagine the size of the place.

I'm in the city of Augsburg about 40 miles from Munich. Pretty nice city, too. It isn't beat up as bad as most of the cities over here are. I hope dad is better by now. Have you decided whether you're going to buy the house yet or not?

It will probably be 3 - 4 weeks before my mail catches up to me now. Well, keep up the writing and let me know the news home.

Love, Bill

October 12, 1945 - To Marge from Bill

Dearest Marge,

Well, Marge, another day and work is done. I haven't decided whether to go up town for a while or not. There should be a show on by tonight that I haven't seen yet. Went to bed early last night but I think it was midnight before I went to sleep. The radio was going till then and still no news when the hell we will ever get home. We

Before the Council of Foreign Ministers met in London, Britain's Ernest Bevin told a friend: "If Molotov bangs his fist on the table and yells at me, I will bang my fist and yell right back at him." This childishness, not to be confused with toughness, befitted neither the great tradition of British diplomacy nor the dire necessities of 1945.

Foreign Commissar Molotov was tougher than ever before, and more tightly bound by his instructions. U.S. Secretary of State Byrnes offered him a compromise (virtually excluding France from Balkan discussions) which was generous to the point of humiliation. Molotov cabled home for instructions, got an answer: "Stick to your brief."

At a dinner party, one of the conference's few pleasant interludes, Molotov said of Byrnes: "He doesn't need to persuade anyone. He just has to hold up a little bomb." A delegate who heard him remarked: "Mr. Molotov never makes jokes just to be funny." Undoubtedly, Mr. Molotov did not think the atomic bomb was funny.

More than at any former conference of World War II and its unpeaceful peace, the negotiators struck attitudes and took extreme positions for the sheer sake of bargaining. Quibbling over details had vastly increased. Molotov won no friends by arguing for an hour and 40 minutes over the wording of a conference communiqué, later issuing his own statement.

http://www.time.com/time/magazine/article/html

In response to Marge's petition for a Hardship Discharge for Bill (see Pages 273-274), Congressman Talle wrote this letter.

HENRY O. TALLE
SECOND DISTRICT OF IOWA

HOUSE OFFICE BLDG.
SUITE 1420

HOME ADDRESS:
DECORAH, IOWA

COMMITTEE:
BANKING AND CURRENCY

**Congress of the United States**
**House of Representatives**
**Washington, D. C.**

October 12, 1945

Mrs. William Waldron
Waukon, Iowa

Dear Mrs. Waldron:

Thank you for your letter postmarked October 10 and enclosures.

I have already contacted the Adjutant General of the War Department in support of your appeal, and you will have further word from me at the earliest opportunity.

I earnestly hope that the Department may grant your appeal and that your husband may be permitted to return home to his family and to his business without undue delay.

With good wishes, I am

Sincerely,

Henry O. Talle

Henry O. Talle, M.C.

Talle:sc

Our news sheet tells us that Congressmen are being "troubled" by two questions from their constituents: 1) "Why isn't my Johnny getting home faster?" and 2) "Why are they drafting my Johnny, now that the war is over?" . . . Mother No. 1 should be among the most enthusiastic supporters of a peacetime draft law. Mother No. 2 should thank God that her little darling was born too late to fight in this war, and is only being asked to serve now, in perfect safety, to relieve a man who has, perhaps, already gone through months, or years, of hell.

http://www.time.com/time/magazine/article/html

*don't have so many to feed today, about 500, and I hope it don't get any more. I helped a little with the meat today and placed the guys at the table. That was about all I did. Sit around the rest of the time.*

*Well, I suppose you are gradually getting back into shape, eh? Or are you still a pretty good sized chunk? Is Veryle still helping out or has she gone back to school? I see by the Stripes where the strikes are slowing down the reemployment. It's funny some of the guys coming home don't raise hell with them. If I feel ambitious enough I think I'll write Veryle and Swede today. Don't have as good a bed to sleep on here as I had in Eschenbach. Regular cot here, canvas and a little hard but think I'll get used to it quick enough. Just about all the boys from the 90th have been reassigned, quite a few of them are here but not many I knew.*

*Damn but I sure hope it don't take too long for my mail to catch up but everything is pretty well fucked up over here so it's hard telling when I will get it. The paper says they are turning the government over to the Krauts on Nov 5 so I don't see why they need so many men here. That clean up force is just an alibi to keep men in the Army. Thousands and thousands of troops are lying around idle here now, and all that stuff could be gotten rid of. But I guess they are saving it so it can be done in the winter or they should let the Krauts pick it and clean it out. Well Marge, better quit for now. Still loving and missing you.*

*All my Love*

*Your Husband, Bill*

October 13, 1945 - To Marge from Bill

*Dearest Marge,*

*I thought I better get busy and write. Was over to the mail room this morning and got some envelopes and saw they've got a 'Tough Hombres' boy as mail clerk. He said he's waiting for the mail from the 90th as much as any of us but thinks we should get some in another week. This place got so many new men that things will be a mess for quite a while. I went up town for a while last night and seen the show, "God is my Co Pilot". Pretty good to. Stopped in and had a couple of beers before I came back out here. This is about 5 miles from town and sometimes you have to wait an hr or so to catch a ride. One of the girls in the kitchen makes our beds and sweeps out every morning so we don't have any cleaning to do in our rooms.*

*Every time I read the damn paper it makes me madder. I see today where the redeployment is to be slowed up by the British taking back a couple of their ships and they still figure on keeping a lot of men over here after the first of the year. But I'm still hoping they will change things before long and make a time limit for being overseas. I'll sure be glad when I start getting your mail again because I sure miss it. It will probably be a month or so old when I do start getting it again. We are getting in a couple hundred more men again Monday. I guess. I hope that is all because it just is getting down to morale now. Well I suppose you and the baby are pretty well acquainted by now eh? Do you suppose she gets as ornery as her mother used to get sometimes? Well Marge I think I'll quit for now. Still loving and missing you. Hope I start getting your letters soon.*

*All my love*

*Your Husband, Bill*

October 14, 1945 - To Marge from Bill

*Dearest Marge,*

*Well, Marge I better get busy and write again but*

*God is My Co-Pilot* was released in 1945. It is the story of Robert L. Scott who dreamed his whole life of being a fighter pilot, but when war came he finds himself flying transport planes over The Hump into China. In China, he persuades General Chennault to let him fly with the famed Flying Tigers, the heroic band of airmen who'd been fighting the Japanese long before Pearl Harbor. Scott gets his chance to fight, ultimately engaging in combat with the deadly Japanese pilot known as Tokyo Joe. It starred Dennis Morgan, Dana Clark and Richard Loo as Tokyo Joe.

Field Marshal Sir Bernard Law Montgomery, according to a now-it-can-be-told story, bamboozled Axis spies with a double, Lieut. Clifton James, peacetime actor. The double made a noisy departure for Africa, got a big official welcome in Algiers, set the spies to reporting the Marshal's absence from his invasion base just before D-day.

http://www.time.com/time/magazine/article/html

General of the Army Dwight D. Eisenhower sent home his first report on the occupation. In 20 pages, it cited the facts & figures of a defeated nation's life.

Most of the report, written in August, dealt with Germany's desperate economic exhaustion. The details:

Less than 10% of the industry in the U.S. sector was working.

Mines would produce no coal for house-heating this winter.

The average German diet was one-third below subsistence level.

The pressure of inflation was increasing, revenue from taxes was down, currency volume up.

There was virtually no trade.

Eisenhower's part of Germany was in a political coma. Everything Nazi had been outlawed, but denazification was progressing against great obstacles. The details:

80,000 Nazis had been arrested, 70,000 dismissed from office in the U.S. sector (the Nazi Party and affiliates had 10,000,000 members throughout Germany).

Germans were taking more responsibility in local and regional government.

There were some party-political stirrings, mostly leftist. Labor unions were springing up rapidly.

The population was generally orderly and obedient.

Re-education of the people was proving extremely difficult. A great "intellectual void" remained to be filled.

http://www.time.com/time/magazine/article/html

there isn't a hell of a lot to write about. We got in a hundred or more men today who all have 80 points. They are going home from here. They probably will leave out in the morning. Hell, I thought they were rid of guys with over 70 by now but guess not. The truck just left a few minutes ago with the cooks and girls who work in the mess hall. They make 2 trips with them.

I didn't get to church this morning. Haven't found out where they are yet. There are 3 or 4 within a few miles from here but they are all Kraut but I'll probably find out in the next few days where there is a good one. I rode down town last night and had a few beers and then came back about 9 o'clock. There is one guy on the shift I'm on who is married and has one kid. He don't monkey around with any of these women either but there sure aren't many guys who don't. It is nice and warm in our room here. We have one big radiator and it sure kicks out the heat although I think it is a little warmer here than at Eschenbach.

Well Marge, I suppose the daughter is getting along pretty well, eh? Damn but I sure would give anything to be home with you.

How is business anyway? Are they still turning out the stuff? I suppose John is getting to be quite the baker by now. I hope he is still leaving the booze alone. Do you ever ask him when he is going to marry that gal of his? I suppose he is still spending every cent he makes though?

We didn't get any Stripes today so I didn't get a chance to read anymore of the bad news. All of these men over here are sure a joke because 1/2 of them don't do anything and besides none of the guys care too much about doing anything. It seems the more you do the more the army fucks you up. Well, Marge, I'm still waiting for your mail to start coming again. I hope it does before long. Still loving and missing you.

All my love

Your Husband, Bill

October 15, 1945 - To Marge from Bill

Dearest Marge,

I think I should get some mail from you in the next day or two. One of the boys who came from #357 with me got 3 letters today so I'm going to go over in the morning to see if they haven't some for me. I went up and seen the show tonight but I think I seen it a couple years ago.

*My Pal Wolf was the name of it.*

*I'm getting to know a few of the guys so don't have much trouble getting a ride anymore. I suppose you have read all the bad news in the papers lately the way the redeployment is getting slowed up. I hope the people keep on raising hell with the Congressmen because that's about the only way we will ever get home. The war department sure is doing every thing possible to keep them in. This life is sure soft here. We don't do too much work and I guess the guys out to the small detachments really have a soft life. Have nice hotels to stay in just for probably 15-30 guys. They have their own private rooms and everything but I guess there is nothing over here to satisfy me except if I had you here. I think a lot of the boys found a home over here.*

*Well, Marge I hope everything is going good there and you and the little daughter are getting along fine. I sure wish I could be there with you. Still loving and missing you more than ever. Hope I get some mail soon.*

*All my Love*

*Your Husband,*
*Bill*

<u>October 16, 1945 - To Marge from Bill</u>

*Dearest Marge,*

*Well, Marge, I still didn't get any mail yet today but some of the other boys from the 90th did so maybe I will in the next day or so. There sure isn't anything to write about. Same old thing, day in and day out. I still haven't ever monkey'd around with any of these Heine Cunts. We have about 40 working, some good lookers to. It's a good thing I am married or I would probably be taking plenty of it because its there for the asking.*

*I see by the paper today where the redeployment has been slowed up a month by strikes and losing the British ships. It also said there are over 2 million left here. So they have sure been lying about how many men they have over here. They claimed at the end of the war in May, they had a few over 3 million boys.*

*Marge if the women back in the States are getting anything like over here, I don't think I would ever want to get home. Lot of these Germans (are) coming home now and finding some G.I. living with their wives. I guess they keep right on shacking up with the G.I.'s . There is sure going to be a lot of trouble if they keep on having as many guys here in Germany.*

*My Pal, Wolf* was released in 1944. Fun movie with nice story: Gretchen finds a dog that has fallen into an abandoned hole in the ground and brings him home. The dog befriends and protects her and Gretchen wants to keep the new friend she's found. Turns out the dog is a war dog scheduled to leave right away for the front in Europe and the DOD sends a jeep to pick the dog up at Gretchen's house. Gretchen and a few of her more daring friends decide to go find Wolf at the Army training grounds close by. They find Wolf and ask as to whether they can buy him. The private there tells them that they need to talk to the Secretary of War in Washington DC. This might deter a lesser soul, but Gretchen sets out on foot for Washington. Ultimately the Secretary of War tells Gretchen that Wolf has his part to do in the war effort and that she needs to let him go and do the job he was trained for. All's well that ends well, however, and the Secretary sends Gretchen a puppy to hold her over until Wolf returns from war. We never find out if he does.

Alois Hitler, Adolf's half brother, released by the British after questioning, turned up at Hamburg's town hall to ask a favor: He wanted his name changed.

Adolf Hitler himself may still be lurking somewhere, according to the Netherlands radio. It quoted General Dwight D. Eisenhower as saying that there was "reason to believe" Hitler was still alive.

I'm the only one in tonight. The rest of the guys are either to the show, bar, or out with some cunt.

Well, Marge, I suppose you realize by now I've got quite a while to put in over here yet and nothing I can do about it either. Well, guess better quit for now. Sure hope I will find out someday when I will go home. Still loving and missing you.

All my love, Bill

October 17, 1945 - To Marge from Bill

Dearest Marge,

I didn't get any mail yet but I'm still hoping I'll get some soon. I guess nobody is getting much now with the ships all being tied up. I just came back from the show "Woman in Green". Good picture to. I thought I'd seen it before but guess I didn't. Stopped up and had a couple beers afterwards. I was sure tempted to dance. One of the gals that works in the kitchen asked me to but I told her I didn't dance. I think the farther I keep away from these cunts the better, eh? You wouldn't want your husband playing with any of this stuff, would you?

*Woman in Green* was released on July 27, 1945. It is the story of Holmes (Basil Rathbone) and Watson (Nigel Bruce) investigating a series of bizarre and apparently unconnected murders, and the death of a possible suspect. The trail leads to a society of hypnotists and a mysterious, glamorous woman. The fiendish Dr Moriarty, though reported hanged in Montevideo, is believed to be involved.

I finally found out where the church is for Catholic mass so I think I'll be going Sunday. Only about a mile from here. From the looks of the Stars and Stripes, it will be a hell of a while before I'm home or out of the Army. It said by the middle of winter they are dropping the points system and going by just when I would have enough points when they quit it. If I ever join any of these reserves and shit like that when I do get out, I hope somebody puts a bullet through my head. This army is sure no place for a married man if he intends to stay true to his wife. And it is sure plenty hard to do over here.

I sure do miss you Marge and would give anything to be with you again. I wouldn't miss being away from home if it weren't for you. I guess being with you is being home for me. Still loving you more than ever.

All my love, Bill

Major General Claire Chennault, finding himself being talked up as next Governor of Louisiana, effectively deadpanned: "I'm an honest man; I know nothing about politics."

October 18, 1945 - To Marge from Bill

Dearest Marge,

I got my first letter from you today since I was down here (of Oct 13). You can't imagine how glad I was to get it. From the sounds of things you and the baby are both home and doing all right. Sure was nice of the baker from Guttenberg to send the blanket. That must have

Lieut. General James H. Doolittle, who was quite a showman himself in his earlier air-race days, braved the hazards of an Olsen & Johnson show in Chicago, did all right.

*been a good 2 years ago I gave him that sugar. From the sounds of things you have been having plenty of company. I suppose Paul Kosbau is sure glad to be home again, eh? I don't think he ever had a furlough did he?*

*Our Mess Sarg. here was born in Germany. He came to the States in '35. Today his father came to see him. Came all the way from the Holland border. He has lost about 65 lb. in the last 4 years, he said. You see most of the border people had it pretty rough. Most of them were for the Allies. We had some boys from the 79th Div. in tonight. They were supposed to go home this month but the schedule is moved back a month now with the ship shortage*

*Well, Marge, I'm sure hoping I get mail again tomorrow. Most of the guys are uptown again tonight so I think I'll turn in early.*

*Take good care of that daughter till I get home. I suppose we will be able to celebrate our birthdays together, eh?*

*Still loving and missing you and praying I'll be home soon.*

*All my love*

*Your Husband, Bill*

October 19, 1945 - To Marge from Bill

*Dearest Marge,*

*I was sure glad to get so much mail from you today - 8 letters from you and one from Ma. I sure wish I was home with you and then you wouldn't have to worry so much about the bakery. Did Harold say whether he was coming back to work again or not when he gets out? I sure hope he does. Oh by the way before I forget, don't buy any more bonds because I think its just to loan the fucking Limi's (British) and the bastards used to charge us guys 5 bucks a carton for our own cigarettes.*

*That's too bad about Helen Sweeney's baby dying. From what you say having a baby must be quite an experience. Maybe when I get home you can tell me all about it. How long do you have to wear the girdle now? Remember the way I used to kid about them.*

*I see by the Stripes where they will cut the points to 50 in Dec. If they have a recount again, I'll have enough. I'm sure hoping they do. That would make me 54 in Dec.*

*From the sounds of your letters (deleted) must really be out getting her share. What will she do if she got it*

Nuremberg, October 19: The faces told the story. For all their bestial apathy, for all the unfolding record of their deeds at Belsen and Oswiecim, the men and women in the dock at Luneburg were human, and theirs were human crimes.

It was generally true, as Joseph Kramer, Irma Grese and their lesser co-defendants said, that they had obeyed orders ("Anyone in the SS is as guilty as anyone else"). A corollary truth, hard for the occupiers to grasp, was that the basic crime—Naziism—was not an individual but a national crime. Since this was so, the German people could never really be convinced that the national crimes of Naziism were crimes at all.

At Lüneburg, undeterred by such considerations, the British prosecutors last week rested their cases against Kramer & Co. For reasons and in a fashion totally incomprehensible to the Germans, British defense attorneys then did their human duty.

http://www.time.com/time/magazine/article/html

Lieut. General George Smith Patton Jr. said: "All good things must come to an end. . . ." Erect and sad, he handed his beloved Third Army flag to his successor in command, Lieut. General Lucian K. Truscott Jr., a General who had fought with his mouth closed. The band played Auld Lang Syne. Some 400 soldiers and WACs, also erect and sad, watched him march stiffly away.

Thus last week, in Bad Tölz, did George Patton close a great if occasionally troubled combat record and a distinctly poor record as Military Governor of Bavaria. For comparing Germany's Nazi problem with U.S. Republicans v. Democrats, and otherwise flouting the orders and policies of General of the Army Dwight D. Eisenhower, General Patton had been summarily dismissed and relegated to a particularly galling desk job (command of the almost nonexistent Fifteenth Army, now writing a history of the German campaign).

http://www.time.com/time/magazine/article/html

Bill receives word of Marge's effort regarding the Hardship Discharge. In that his morale is so low, his response is to be expected.

broke off in her? I suppose her husband would really appreciate it when he gets home. I've read your letters over a couple times and probably will read them again in the morning. I don't think you need worry about me being like Neal Weidman when I get home because I think we'll spend most of our time together.

Ma sent a picture of Marie and Butch and I sure wouldn't know them, they have grown so much especially Butch. He didn't even walk yet when I left. I'm glad your mother is so good to you and the baby. Remember I always used to tell you (that) you shouldn't talk to her the way you did. Maybe you'll appreciate her a little more now, eh?

I wrote you about this occupation before but you asked in your letter about having so many men and so few in Japan. Well, they are not needed but it is just a way of keeping men in the Army and making jobs for officers that couldn't make a living in civilian life. Most of the guys in this outfit don't do anything and in different outfits none of them do anything. Well, Marge better quit for now. Still loving and missing you.

All my Love, Bill

October 20, 1945 - To Marge from Bill

Dearest Marge,

I got 4 more letters from you today. Sure good to get them. The mail clerk of the 90th is really on the ball. We get our mail as quick as they separate it. I sure hope the discharge papers you are making out go through all right but I think they usually take a long time. We got orders today to move to Munich within two weeks. I sure don't like that because we will have a crummy place there but the new General wants us there and we will still be about 10 minutes from 3rd Army HQ.

The cooks and waitresses here get from 8-16 dollars a month. How do you suppose anyone in the States would like to work for them wages? 2 of our cooks worked in the States and most of their relations live there. One guy gets packages and letters from them every day. You ask whether I still have my hair short or not. Most of the time it is long but the last time I had it cut a little shorter. I've lost weight since I've been in the kitchen because I don't care for food like I did before. I was the heaviest at the end of the war I've ever been or I suppose I will ever be. We took a few pictures today so I'll send you one as quick as they are developed.

*A couple of the old boys from MG just came back off pass and couldn't figure out what happened. They wondered if the (symbol for 90th Division, the Tough 'Ombres) took over the M.G. Most of the M.G. is 90th Div. boys now and they are kinda showing the civilians around here who is boss now. Before we came they (the civilians) got by with a lot of shit they don't now. I've knocked half a dozen off the sidewalk now. The bastards expected us to walk out of the way for them but they are learning the way the Inf. does it if they don't move. But they are learning quick to.*

*I've given up hope of getting any place to buy you anything for Christmas in Germany. Here there is nothing much to buy. That was about the only reason I wanted to get to Paris. Please don't work around the bakery any more than you have to now. Let them make what they can and let the rest go to hell.*

*How are Stan and John getting along with their women now? I suppose John will have her taking instructions pretty quick, eh?*

*I suppose the guys will be coming in pretty quick. They usually get in about 10 or so. I'm all alone again tonight. I think I better write the folks yet tonight before I turn in. I would think all the guys getting discharges now there would be plenty of help around but I suppose they are all spending the money they have saved up.*

*Well Marge take care of that daughter and hope I get home before she gets much older. Still loving and missing you.*

*All my Love, Bill*

The Holy Land was tight with unholy tension. Jews talked of a showdown, Arabs of a holy war. A division of British air borne troops patrolled streets and country roads. Two more divisions were on the way.

Police in armored cars cordoned off Jerusalem's central section, searched the crowds in public buildings. In the narrow area between the Jewish city of Tel Aviv and the Arab city of Jaffa, panic flickered among scores of jittery Jewish families. Plumbing signs marked on walls by sewer workers had been mistaken for Arab threats, and had raised visions of another St. Bartholomew's Eve. This week, Jews staged a general strike; Arabs planned to follow suit.

As always, the fate of Jews and Arabs alike would be decided elsewhere.

http://www.time.com/time/magazine/article/html

<u>October 20, 1945 - To Jim and Amanda from Bill</u>

*Dear Folks,*

*Thought I'd better write you a few lines before I went to bed. Got a letter from you of Sept 30 and R and S of 25th. Sure glad to get them both. Marge tells me that you have been working pretty hard at the bakery. I sure do appreciate it, Ma. Maybe when I get home, I'll make it up to you. It's sure hell to just waste my time over here doing nothing when I could just as well be home. I suppose you know by now it is just the*

army stalling to keep men in the army that is keeping us over here. We have all civilian cooks and waitress's here so there isn't much for us guys to do. I'm in Augsburg, nice city - it isn't beat up as bad as most of them but we are moving to Munich in a couple weeks. I'm glad to hear you are finally going to buy the house. How much have you got to pay down and what percent interest for the rest? How about answering my questions now? You say I don't answer yours but you sure slip up on mine. Read this letter when you write your next one.

When is John going to marry that babe of his? Better tell him married life is a hell of a lot better than single. I'm sure glad John has been sticking to the bakery the way he has. Maybe me coming in the army was a good thing, course I don't think he would have settled down if it weren't for the responsibility. Marge writes that he sure has been swell.

The only thing I'll miss here in Germany when I get home is sour wine. I usually drink a bottle or so every day. It is nothing like the wine in the states.

Well, Ma, think it don't look very promising but I hope I'm home with all of you. Sure couldn't get over the size of Butch in the picture you sent. He wasn't even walking when I left but Marie don't look much bigger. Well, better quit for now.

Love, Bill

Long Island's Grumman Aircraft Engineering Corp. performed the neatest reconversion trick of the week. It went into production of a brand-new commercial product: an aluminum canoe. Designed by President Leroy Grumman, who turned out the Navy's Wildcat and Hellcat fighter planes, the canoe weighs one-half to two-thirds as much as wooden canoes. A 13-footer weighs only 38 pounds, yet the thin skin is tough enough to deflect anything up to a bullet. When capsized, the canoe automatically rights itself in the water with the help of air tanks in the bow and stern. Grumman is now turning out the first order for 1,000 canoes, has orders in the offing for another 5,000. The price: slightly higher than a wooden canoe's.

http://www.time.com/time/magazine/article/html

October 21, 1945 - To Marge from Bill

Dearest Marge,

Well Marge, just came back from downtown so I thought I better write before I went to bed. Didn't get any mail today. No mail service here on Sunday. I was on a shift this morning so I didn't get to go to Mass. I'll sure be glad when I get out of this Army, I'll be able to go every Sunday.

Went in to see the show but after it started, I'd seen it before, so I went up to the bar. One of the girls that works in the kitchen asked me to dance so I did once. She was a stage dancer before the war ended and dances just like girls back home. Sure enjoyed it to. The bar is where we always catch a ride home from. One of the drivers is always there so when he leaves he tells us. Otherwise we have to wait on the street for a bus or to catch a ride. I still carry my pistol every time I go out because I don't trust some of these people to much. Of course, we are not allowed to but I have carried a gun ever since I've been *in Germany and I will till I leave.*

*Damn, Marge but I would sure give anything to be home with you but maybe the day will come yet. The days go by pretty fast. I think every day it is one more closer to being with you. Some of the boys are down in the kitchen so I think I'll go down and have a sandwich before I go to bed. Still loving and missing you. Hope to be home with you and our little daughter soon.*

*All my love*

*Your Husband, Bill*

October 22, 1945 - To Marge from Bill

*Dearest Marge,*

*I didn't get any mail today except the Readers Digest so I should have some again tomorrow. I hope by now you have my new address. Then I'll get your letters quick again.*

*I guess we are going to move to Munich next week. I sure hate that because about every place is burnt out. I'm all alone again tonight. All the fellows went to the show or bar. I've still never met anybody from Waukon over here yet and I should have. We have guys coming in eating from about every outfit imaginable. We got orders today to move our patch (symbol for 90th Div. Tough 'Ombres) over to our other shoulder and put the 3rd Army patch on our left.*

*I suppose you are feeling pretty good by now and the daughter is growing some. Sure wish I could be home with you. Wrote a letter to Marquardt this morning. First time I've wrote to him for quite a while. Did Harold say whether he wanted to come back to work in the Bakery or not after he is discharged? Sure hope so anyway. I wonder if Goldie and him will ever get married. Ma wrote he had some other babe out as quick as Goldie left.*

*Well, Marge can't think of any thing more to write about so will quit for tonight.*

*Still loving and missing you.*

*All my Love*

*Your Husband, Bill*

October 23, 1945 - To Marge from Bill

*Dearest Marge,*

*I got one letter from you today of Sept 26. Kinda old, eh? But I expect to get some later one's tomorrow. I hope anyway.*

"For the first time since assuming this office six years ago it is possible for me to report that the security of the United States of America is entirely in our own hands."

With this matter-of-fact statement, General of the Army George Catlett Marshall this week delivered to the nation what may be his valedictory as Chief of Staff. In a "Biennial Report to the Secretary of War," he told how that security had been won. But mainly—and most earnestly—George Marshall warned the U.S. of the certain consequences of future unpreparedness and of how the U.S. might be destroyed in another war.

The long report was the story of disaster narrowly averted, when the security of the nation rested dangerously in hands other than hers. Said George Marshall: "The refusal of the British and Russian peoples to accept what appeared to be inevitable defeat was the great factor in the salvage of our civilization."

http://www.time.com/time/magazine/article/html

As rapidly as it could, the U.S. was stripping away its military strength.

With no postwar directive from Congress, but pushed by individual Congressmen and public demand ("Get the boys home and out of the service"), the War Department was turning out thousands of able, war-trained officers and noncoms who might have stayed to backbone the peacetime army if permanent rank and other inducements had been offered to them. The Army had already discharged more than 1,000,000 men and would soon be tearing itself down at the rate of 1,000,000 a month. Draft and recruiting supplied replacements at the rate of about 86,000 a month.

By March 15, the world's greatest air force (2,385,000 in 1944) will be down to 165,000. To A.A.F. generals who have been planning for a postwar air force of 400,000, the size of the force they will have will not be as disconcerting as the force's lack of balance. Approximately 60,000 of the A.A.F. next spring will be gunners. Pilots, who have generally collected the most points, are leaving in droves. The smart, self-reliant youngsters whom A.A.F. would most like to keep are the quickest to leave; they are not afraid to try civilian life.

So far the Navy has resisted public clamor; only 255,000 of the Navy's 3,000,000 have been released. But under growing pressure, and aware of the damage its policy has had on the morale of its reserves—both officers and enlisted men— even the Navy is beginning grudgingly to relax, will raise its discharge rate to 280,000 a month by January.

http://www.time.com/time/magazine/article/html

We are moving to Munich Tues I guess. Sure going to hate that because there isn't much left of Munich and I'm just finding my way around here. Went to the show tonight and went up to the bar a few minutes afterwards. Got in quite an argument with some of the 9th Air Force boys. High pointers, they started kidding me and another kid from the 90th about not having many points and don't think we didn't pour it back about the rear echelon. It was about 8 against two but I think we came out best. One of them was an Inf. Man who got hit and transferred to the Air Corp and he told them off to. That they didn't even know what the fuck it was like till they spent a day on the line.

I very seldom ever say anything to anybody about combat except old buddies but like tonight when some of these rear echelon cocksuckers shout off about being beginners and good for another couple years here, it burns me up. One of them was pissing because he didn't get the Purple Heart back in England when he cut himself on one of our planes. I suppose you see by the papers where the Army is still fucking up and doing everything they can to keep the guys here. If they would of wanted to, they could have had everybody out of here by the end of this month. I sure hope those discharge papers you made out go through because once they do, it don't take long to get out of here now. At least that is what the Stripes says but can never believe anything we read in it. I sure do miss you more all the time. I'm still leaving the women alone over here so you don't need to worry about me stepping out on you. I'm glad I've got a good wife at home or I probably would be taking them out. Loving you more and more. Hope to be home with you before to long.

All my Love

Your Husband, Bill

P.S. You said you didn't know my X number. I didn't get what you meant because my serial number you have on all my letters.

October 24, 1945 - To Marge from Bill

Dearest Marge,

I didn't get any mail from you today but got a letter from Ma of Oct 7. I don't suppose you have been getting my mail very good either. I see by the S & S where it got all held up for a couple weeks. Army fucking up as usual. I don't know whether I ever wrote you or not but *there are guys here every day wanting to buy cigarettes for $25 to $35 dollars a carton. Can you imagine paying that much for cigarettes? Some of the guys are making good money off of them but I sooner give them away than stick any body that much for them. We get a carton a week and that is just about what I smoke.*

*I am sitting here all alone again tonight. Got a good bottle of wine I'm drinking. Cost 36 m, cheap enough, eh?*

*Got a box from Paulson's today. Don't send me any more boxes now because I can get whatever I want to eat in the kitchen. We get about everything. I sure hate to think of moving Tues. I guess we will have an apartment house and a restaurant for a mess hall and will have P.W.'s instead of women for waiting on table. I guess about 10 of the girls here speak good English.*

*This has been a swell day here, nice and warm. I'm out all day. Days like this sure make me wish I was down to the cabin instead of in this God forsaken country. I can get a 3 day pass and a jeep now anytime I want it but there is no place in Germany I care to see. I suppose you must have got the package I sent by now with that junk I had. There is a map that shows the battle route of the 90th in it. This new General the 3rd Army got has been kinda fucking things up here. If it wasn't for him, we wouldn't have to move. This is a beautiful place but Munich is no good. They are moving most of the people*

Like every other soldier, General Ike was thinking about going home. He knew that he was to be the U.S. Army's next Chief of Staff, a job big enough to take any soldier's mind off the dreary chores of occupation. But last week he still had a big job and plenty of trouble on his hands in Germany.

Speaking to the press, General Eisenhower vigorously defended his Army against growing criticism from back home. The bulk of the occupation job had been done well, he snapped. Mistakes had been made, but they would be corrected. Nazis would be weeded out, would not be permitted to vote in the coming German elections. Growled Eisenhower: "A Nazi is a Nazi, and I hate Nazis."

But there was more at stake than the U.S. Army's efficiency in getting rid of Nazis. In the Allied Control Council's debate on reparations, the whole question of What To Do With Germany suddenly seemed wide open again.

Most people had the notion that Potsdam once & for all had turned Germany into a country of fields and pastures, with a factory here & there to relieve the bucolic monotony. Actually, under the general terms of the Potsdam Agreement, Germany could have a substantial light industry. The Potsdam objective was to slash Germany's heavy industrial war potential. The Germans were to live at a level "not exceeding" the European average. Potsdam specifically provided for German imports to meet "Germany's approved postwar peacetime needs." What were the approved needs? What was the average living standard? Obviously the Potsdam policy needed interpretation.

http://www.time.com/time/magazineticle/html

**CERTIFICATE**

Oct 25,1945
(Date)

1. I certify that I have personally examined the items of captured enemy equipment in the possession of William Waldron and that the bearer is officially authorized by the Theater Commander, under the provisions of Sec VI, Cir 155, WD, 28 May 1945, to retain as his personal property the articles listed in Par 3, below.

2. I further certify that if such items are to be mailed to the US, they do not include any items prohibited by Sec VI, Cir 155, WD, 28 May 1945.

3. The items referred to are: Sauer, 32 No. 404690 Pistol
Camera 6x18

A.S. Keller (Signature)
A.S. KELLER
MAJOR, A.C.
Su. Co, 3d Mil Govt Regt.
(Rank, Branch and Organization)

(This certificate will be prepared in duplicate)

AG USFET Form Nº 33 Lel. 8-46 5,000,000 78,920

*out for the winter. Well, Marge, I'll write again tomorrow.*

*Still loving and missing you and praying I'll be home with you soon.*

*All my Love*

*Your Husband, Bill*

October 25, 1945 - To Marge from Bill

*Dearest Marge,*

*I got quite a few letters today. One from you of Oct 10, one from Paulsons, Vernon, and Marcella (Robinson). I took the copy she sent and went right over with it but I guess I got some more forms to fill out now. Probably be a day or two before they get them ready. Sure wished those papers would have come when I was back at the 90th. Would have saved a lot of time and trouble. Our CO there was a good friend of mine. I never seen the one here yet but probably will in the next day or so.*

*Vernon wrote Oct 12 and was at a staging area and said not to write because he would be leaving for home soon. Sure hope he is on his way by now. Got the foot-prints of the baby in the letter of yours now. I'll be waiting for a picture. From the way Stan figures, it don't look like I'll be home in time for John's wedding, eh? Is he saving any money yet? He should be if he is ever going to.*

*Well, I guess I'll have to quit for now. One of the cooks wants me to make some icing for cakes. I'm off now but I usually ice them for him on his shift. Keep up the writing. Still loving and missing you and hope to be home with you before to long.*

*All my love*

*Your Husband, Bill*

October 26, 1945 - To Marge from Bill

*Dearest Marge,*

*I got 2 letters from you today of Oct 9th and 11th and also a package with the paper and cookies. You can't imagine how glad I am to get them. I go over about 3 times a day for mail because there is no set time when they get it in. We had a party here tonight for our CO and they had dancing and beer, eats and women. One of the girls wanted me to take her out and I tell you I was really tempted. She is a beaut. She works in the kitchen here and was a stage actress before the war was over. But I told her I had a good wife at home and was never*

The copy and forms that Bill writes about in this letter is regarding a Hardship Discharge. Apparently Marcella Robinson has suggested that, in addition to the civilian political appeal already started by Marge, Bill should also be working for the discharge through the military.

A thousand clamoring Englishwomen crowded London's small Caxton Hall. They demanded immediate transportation to the U.S. They were brides of U.S. servicemen, and they spoke for 40,000 others, all necessarily left behind in the redeployment rush. Many had babies. Many were hard up. Many were just desperately lonely. All wanted space on westbound ships.

"A lot is being done," Commander Herbert Agar, U.S.N.R. said gently. He assured the wives that they had not been forgotten. Mrs. Louis Sherman, jiggling a baby over her head, broke in to ask why at least a few wives could not be put aboard every troop ship.

U.S. troops, Commander Agar explained, had to be sent home first. But his words were lost in the high-pitched storm. In peroration he assured them: "You have been reasonable and sincere—I thank you for your kindness." He sidled to a side door, and fled.

http://www.time.com/time/magazine/article/html

*going to take out any of these girls. She says, "Ya, but I bet your wife goes out" and I told her my wife trusts me and I do her. In the kitchen the girls call me the quiet one because I never fool around with any of them. There are only two of them I even talk with all the time. I figure if it weren't for these fucking Krauts, I wouldn't be over here and it burns me up more all the time.*

*The guys were kidding me tonight about not taking Doris out after we got in and I said if I ever took any of these Heine Cunts out or monkeyed over them, I would have to write and tell my wife no matter how bad it hurt and that was one thing I never wanted to have to do. Every day I stay in Germany I realize how much more I love you, Marge and hope you believe me and never regret the day we got married. I only wish it would have been sooner. I'm sure glad I got to know my wife pretty well before we were married. One of the boys here got a letter from his mother the other day that his wife is about 5 months along and he's been over here for 14 months. He about went nuts when he got the letter. From your letters I'll bet (deleted) will have a lot of explaining to do now. I sure hope (deleted) finds out about it but she will probably give him the patriotic line. I'm sure glad the baby is getting along good but wish you would take it easy and not work any more than you have to. The First Sgt. told me today he is waiting for the papers from the CO before he mails out any forms but he said even so, it takes a hell of a while to get a discharge approved. So I'm not building my hopes up much. I would sure give anything to be with you again.*

*I'm not surprised to hear that Freddie is not trying to find a job because he always was lazy. I told Dorothy that before they were married.*

*Well, Marge, loving and missing you more than ever and praying to be with you soon.*

*All my love, Bill*

<u>October 27, 1945 - To Marge from Bill</u>

*Dearest Marge,*

*I got two letters from you today and also a box from your mother. Tell her thanks for me but don't send anymore now because I get plenty to eat in the kitchen. The letters were of the 6th and 9th. Got the (baby's) birth certificate, don't need it now but might some time or another. I sure spend enough of my time running over to see if I have any mail from you. We are getting ready to*

Not since the London mob cheered gaudy Lord Nelson had any sailorman returned to port from victories so vast. But Americans were inclined to be a little vague about the U.S. Navy's white-haired, pink-cheeked Fleet Admiral Chester W. Nimitz, who had directed the Battle of the Pacific from a desk. He had never courted publicity. He had accumulated stiff titles like CINCPAC or CINCPOA instead of nicknames. And he had spent most of the war at Pearl Harbor and Guam.

Also the public had been welcoming Army heroes on a production-line basis and was a little throat-weary. Nevertheless the Navy was determined to see that its senior hero got his due.

When the Admiral arrived in Washington, D.C., the Navy had gathered up 5,000 troops, a half-dozen bands, artillery and captured Japanese equipment for a parade to end parades, had gassed up a thousand airplanes to fly overhead. The show pulled a bigger house than either Generals Eisenhower or Wainwright—more than a million people cheered from the sidewalks.

In New York, 3,000,000 more people roared a welcome, threw 274 tons of ticker tape and letterheads (on account of the paper shortage General Eisenhower got but 77 tons). A huge ship's bow with five stars, hawsers, other seagoing gizmos was built in front of City Hall, and vast mobs gathered to watch the Admiral go aboard to the shrill of bosuns' calls. In the evening 2,000 people paid $15 a plate to attend a posh Waldorf-Astoria dinner where Admiral Nimitz was introduced by Nelson Rockefeller.

http://www.time.com/time/magazine/article/html

Although they had a car, gas was rationed and impossible to get, so Marge walked to work at the Bakery from her parents where she was living. They lived up the street from the Waukon Bowling Alley down on Spring Ave. Not much fun to be to work at 2 AM or so to do the baking.

In the Philippines, the first weak steps along the road of reconstruction were taken. In bombed and burned Manila the Rotary Club began its weekly Thursday luncheons. In the Manila Hotel socialites and dressmakers staged the capital's first fashion show and ball since 1941 against a background of charred greystone walls. The Islands' top dressmaker, Ramon Valera, turned out 24 gowns in two weeks (with material at $50 a yard), then collapsed from overwork. The first trickle of civilian goods had arrived from the U.S., tumbling black market prices 50%. And the Islands had shipped their first large load of hemp (2,000,000 lbs.) to the U.S.

But the basic economy of the Islands, still largely controlled by the U.S. Army, was still very sick. Little had been done to solve the Islands' biggest problems: 1) shattered transportation lines; 2) the lack of money to rebuild homes and industry.

http://www.time.com/time/magazine/article/html

move now. Will move Monday and supposed to be set up to feed Tues. morning. Don't know yet whether we will take our cooks with us or not. Sure hope so though. We won't have only about half as many men to feed there though.

From the sounds of your letters the Dr. must of did quite a job of sewing you, eh? The papers still haven't come to the CO yet but probably will in the next few days. But I guess it takes a long time for the discharge to go through over here.

I sure hope the car works good for you now but I suppose it's just as bad on gas as ever, eh? The guy that does our baking brought his little daughter up with him this morning. She is about 4 yrs and cuter than hell. I got a letter from Marquardt today. Still isn't married. Still working for his old man and said he sure hopes I get up there before long. I hope you are starting to get my mail all right by now. They say they have the mess cleaned up for it is going through again.

I am giving up all hope of ever getting home by Christmas but sure hope I can make it not to much later. I'll probably get transferred again in another month or two because I think this outfit will break up after they turn running the gov't. over to the civilians.

Well, Marge still loving and missing you and hope I can get home to you before to long.

All my love

Your Husband, Bill

October 28, 1945 - To Marge from Bill

Dearest Marge,

No mail today. We don't get any on Sunday. I suppose you think I'm really getting to be a heathen. I didn't get to church again today. I sure hope when we move, it isn't too far from the church. I guess we are supposed to move tomorrow and I guess the place is plenty crumby. I hope you and the baby are fine and wish you wouldn't work nights. I hope there soon starts getting to be some help around.

I'm just hoping they figure up the points again in Dec. If they do I'll have enough to get out but if not I'm stuck for a long time I think. I suppose when I get home Kreebs will have their house fixed pretty swell, eh? Does Ray still go downtown nights as much as always? I can just see you drinking the beer now. Don't suppose the baby will get a jag on off of it, do you? I should soon start get-

*ting your letters direct. It's been 3 weeks we have been here now. I suppose Swede (Paul Anderson) is getting all ready to get the knot tied, eh? He said in the letter I got from him, he hadn't tried it out yet. I see by the papers where a Navy Air Corps pilot with 20 points can get discharged the first of Nov so I suppose Harold will get out. I hope he goes back to the bakery. I guess we could sure use him.*

*Just heard the news and it still don't help me any getting home when I see all the guys with 80 to 100 points around, I wonder if they are sending any body home.*

*Say Hello to your folks for me. I sure hate to write anybody any more except you. Just can't get up enough ambition, I guess and there isn't a hell of a lot to write about. I'm sure hoping they pass that training bill because it might mean us guys will get home then. I think about all the good times we used to have and I hate these Krauts all the more. Still loving and missing you.*

*Love, Bill*

October 29, 1945 - To Marge from Bill

*Dearest Marge,*

*I got a letter from Ma and two from you of Oct 18th and 20th with my new orders. I'm sure glad it went through so fast. I'm sorry to hear about Dad being sick again. I hope he isn't laid up to long. Damit it, burns me up laying around here doing nothing when I could be home doing a little good. I sure wish you wouldn't work so much. Let them make what they can and the hell with the rest.*

*From what I hear about getting discharges here, it takes 6 months to a year so I'll probably get home as soon without. If a guy could once get in the States, he is all right.*

*I suppose Janice is growing quite a lot already and developing a good pair of lungs, eh? I wrote you we were to move today. Well, I had the Krauts load all the ration stores and pretty near everything and about 10 min. before we were going to pull out with the fresh food, they called it off. We move next Monday now to a different place in Munich with the 3rd Army near Echolan. Things will probably be chicken shit there but I hope not.*

*Last night we got a little hungry so a couple of us cooks fixed our selves some fried chicken and fresh fudge. Sure was good to. I went down to the show tonight. Earl Can-*

All over the U.S. the housing situation was so tight that people were almost ready to move into abandoned chicken coops. Last week the Federal Public Housing Authority offered them something a little better than that. FPHA is ready to sell the Government's 320,000 temporary, jerry-built housing units around shut-down war plants. They were not houses that would last a lifetime, said FPHA, but they would be good enough until the shortage eases.

First to go on the block will be the 300-unit clapboard project at Wichita, Kansas. As fast as other units become surplus, they too will be put up for sale, along with 35,000 trailers. When these units were built, Congress provided that they be torn down within two years after the war emergency was over, lest they become slums.

Now FPHA believes that it can conform to the law, and maybe help ease the housing shortage, by selling the units to private builders who agree to: 1) demolish the units and move them from present sites; 2) use some of the salvaged material for entirely new houses. FPHA will show the method of recovery at a 20-acre "showcase" exhibit to be erected at Silver Springs, MD, in mid-December.

http://www.time.com/time/magazine/article/html

Through the Panama Canal last week steamed 48 heroic ships of the U.S. fleet carrying 57,000 veterans of the Pacific war—and one historic metal table.

The table was an ordinary folding mess table. On the September morning, in Tokyo Bay, when Japan's representatives were due aboard the Missouri to surrender, somebody discovered at the last minute that there was no table on hand big enough for the ceremonious signing. A table from the enlisted men's mess was carted topside and set up on the Missouri's teak-planked veranda deck. The ceremony over, the table was taken back to the mess where it belonged. A dozen men had eaten spaghetti at it before the ship's officers shouted, "Where's the table?" They retrieved the now historic object and stowed it reverently away in an officer's room. *Time Magazine*

This picture was taken after the war but shows Amanda, Jim and Butch.

nolls in Vanities. I seen it once before but didn't mind sitting through it again, good show.

I sure can't figure out so many getting discharges and still no help around (Waukon). I suppose by the time I get home, they'll be a dime a doz. I sure don't know what I would do if it weren't for your letters about every day. They caught 5 Krauts today who stole 1,000 packs of cigarettes from the P.X. I hope they burn their ass good for it. The girls here all know how well I like the Germans to. I don't make any bones about it anymore. Well Marge, I sure miss you and wish I could be with you. Hoping to get home someday before long.

All my Love

Your Husband, Bill

October 29, 1945 - To Jim and Amanda from Bill

Dear Folks,

I got your letter of Oct 17, today. Glad to get it. Sure hated to hear dad is sick again. Hope he ain't laid up too long. We ate that squirrel you sent a couple weeks ago. Sure was good to. I got the papers Marcella sent but the C.O. still didn't get the ones to fill out yet but he probably will before long but I guess it takes a hell of a long time even if they approve it. I sure can't imagine Butch talking. He couldn't say a word when I left home but guess he's getting to be a pretty big boy now, eh.

I had a letter from Vernon a few days ago and he's in a staging area waiting to go home so probably is on his way now. Told me not to write anymore because he would be gone by the time he would get it.

I guess there isn't much of anything you could send me for Christmas. We get most anything we need here but if you can get any good Lucky Tiger, I could sure use a bottle. We were all packed ready to move to Munich today but they put it off till Monday.

I'm sure glad John has been sticking to the bakery the way he has. I hope you will soon be able to find some help. It burns me up laying around here doing nothing when I could just as well be home.

Well, Ma, say hello to the kids and dad for me. I hope dad is better soon.

Love, Bill

October 30, 1945 - To Marge from Bill

Dearest Marge,

No mail today but I guess I shouldn't expect it every day. There sure isn't much to write about. We have the same thing day in and day out. I just locked up the kitchen a little while ago. I usually do every other night because the other boys on my shift want to go out and one drives the truck taking the help downtown. We usually lock up between 7 & 8. Went over and got a ham out this afternoon and then shaved and took a shower so I didn't work too much this afternoon. I bought a roll of film yesterday so will take some pictures one of these days. The last I took were no good at all. The weather has been staying pretty nice here. I sure hope it keeps it up to. I suppose it is starting to get pretty chilly at home now.

How's John coming with his love affair? Tell him he better marry the gal and then he won't have to be going to Decorah all the time. I sure hope he keeps on working and lets the booze alone till after I get home anyway.

The guy who drives just came back and is sitting here writing a letter to. We've been talking about the way these young guys who never touched a woman till they came overseas will act when they get around women in the States. Be pretty rough on them, I bet. He's Italian and don't monkey around with any of the women. Married, but no kids - been in the Army about 4 years but never came over till March.

How are things going at the bakery? I hope they soon get better. I hate to think of you having to work now with the baby also to take care of. I hope your folks are still both OK. I better quit for now - will be looking for some mail in the morning. Still loving and missing you.

All my love,

Your Husband, Bill

October 31, 1945 - To Marge from Bill

Dearest Marge,

I got 2 letters from you today of Oct 15th and 23rd and one from Veryle. I must still have a lot of back letters coming from you yet. I hope anyway.

I just came back from the show "10 cents for a Dance" was the name of it, wasn't bad either. I just came out of the theater when I seen a street car heading this way so I hopped it. Had to switch once and then walk about 1/2 mile but it was better than waiting till 10 for a ride

In Berlin's high-ceilinged Kammergericht last week the International Military Tribunal formally indicted 24 top Nazis as war criminals. For 50 solemn minutes the session proceeded in English, Russian, French and German. The presiding judge, Russian Major General I. T. Nikitchenko, quoted from the 25,000 word indictment: the U.S., France, Britain and Russia "hereby accuse [the defendants] as guilty . . . of crimes against peace, war crimes and crimes against humanity and of a common plan or conspiracy to commit these crimes. . . ."

Next day Allied officers handed copies of the indictment to each of the defendants in the lightless cells of Nurnberg prison.

http://www.time.com/time/magazine/article/html

Released in 1945 the film starred Jane Frazee and Robert Scott. The story is that while on a thirty-six hour leave, soldiers Billy Sparks and Ted Kimball, III go to the Merryland Dance Hall in search of female companionship. Billy buys ten minutes worth of dances for everyone in the hall in order to get a dance with Jeannie, who becomes more interested in Billy when he brags about his wealth. Although Jeannie is not a fortune hunter, she needs five hundred dollars for another taxi dancer, Joyce, who was injured in a car accident and needs surgery.

The pride-bound U.S. Marine Corps dove into its statistical records last week, came up with the announcement that nearly 90% of its 589,852 officers and men had served overseas in World War II. Marine officers, who had long sung "We are proud to claim the title of United States Marine," could be proudest of all: 98.3% of them had seen active duty overseas.

Messerschmitt AG, later Messerschmitt-Bölkow-Blohm (MBB) was a famous German aircraft manufacturer, known primarily for its World War II fighter aircraft, notably the Bf 109 and Me 262. The company survived in the post-war era, undergoing a number of mergers and changing its name from Messerschmitt before being bought by DASA and is now part of EADS.

Many immigrants with the surname Messerschmitt changed it to Smith in the US.

This letter was written to Bill's little sister Jeanne sometime in the Fall. It is not dated.

Jeanne gave this letter to Jan in 2009.

out with one of the boys. The streetcars here are a little slower than in the States though. It don't cost us anything to ride them. There is a big concert at the Ludwickban downtown tonight. Lot of the fellows went but I don't think I would care to much for it.

We still don't know for sure when we move now but I hope we don't. The only move I want to make is go home but I guess that will be a long time off. I sure wait for the end of every month. It's one month closer to getting home.

We got paid today. I got $4.10 but I threw the 4.10 in a kitty that they have to buy ice cream beer and liquor with. We have ice cream 2 or 3 times a week and have beer or wine now and then for supper, all depends how much they have in the funds. Tomorrow is a big Holy Day in Germany here (All Saints Day). I haven't found out what it is yet but I guess every place is closed downtown.

Went for a little ride with one of the fellows this afternoon and we went out by all the Messerschmidt plants. They must of really had quite a layout here at one time but now every one of them is wrecked. The bombers really had the direct hits on them.

How is the car working now since you have got it fixed? I hope it isn't burning the gas it used to.

Well, Marge, I think I'll write Veryle a few lines before I go to bed. Still loving and missing you and leaving these Krauts alone. Praying I get home with you soon.

All my love

Your Husband, Bill

November, 1945 - To Jeanne from Bill

Dear Jean

I got your letter in with the folks so I had better answer or you will be getting mad at me like you did at Vernon.

How's Marie coming? I suppose she kinda misses Bill a little don't she? Now that school is started, I suppose she will be coming over there someday. I don't suppose you have been down to the river with Marge yet, have you? They had better save some of the hunting and fishing for when I get home. They have a kid about your age working down here in the P.X. That is a store where they sell candy, beer, pop and everything like that.

Brother Bill

November 1, 1945 - To Marge from Bill

Dearest Marge,

I didn't get any mail today. I guess there wasn't much come in. The C.O. got the papers that Marcella (dad's lawyers office) sent but he said they would never get through channels. So the First Sgt is typing some up for me to sign tomorrow. He said (he) didn't know weather it would do a hell of a lot of good or not but would try anyway. There are two of us staying in again tonight, both writing letters. I just went down and fixed up a couple drivers something to eat. They got in late. It is just like a summer night here. It rained bad for a couple hours and turned out really nice now.

I sure hope Dad is better by now. I'll bet it is keeping Ma pretty worried, eh? How's things going at the bakery, any smoother?

I guess today they cut the points to 60 for discharge. We have some guys with 60 and a few points are going to try getting a discharge and civilian job here now. I think maybe in another few months they might do something about getting us guys home. Just listened to the 9 o'clock news but there wasn't much.

Well, Marge, still loving and missing you-take care of that daughter.

All my love, Bill

On November 1, John H. Johnson published the first issue of *Ebony* Magazine.

Telechron Incorporated introduced the model 8H59 called the Musalarm that was the first clock radio.

Tire rationing may end Jan.1. But this will not mean tires for everybody. By the end of September, rationing boards had issued 780,000 more certificates than there were tires available.

November 2, 1945 - To Marge from Bill

Dearest Marge,

I got one letter from you today of Oct 21. My mail has been coming through in pretty good time, eh? But I guess you are getting mine better now to. I have to go over and sign some papers in the morning but that probably will be the last I hear of it for quite a while.

HQ had a party tonight - beer, wine, cognac, rum but I had a couple small glasses of wine that was all, I didn't stay very long. The guys are all starting to come back now though except those who are shacking up.

From the sounds of your letter, the Kreebs must be getting their house fixed pretty nice now, eh? Has Freddy O'Reilly started to do anything or is he still loafing. I'll bet Dorothy will have a hell of a job trying to keep him working. I see by the Stars and Stripes today where they might get the shipping speeded up a little. I sure hope so anyway.

I think I would give about anything to be home with you again but all we can do is hope and pray it won't be

At Des Moines Iowa Packing Co., one H. Shapiro, a veteran who wanted to return as an .83-an-hour sausage stuffer instead of going back to his job as a .74-an-hour check sealer, provided a test case for his union. After a four-day strike of 1,000 workers, the union won its demand that returning servicemen receive all promotions granted to colleagues in their absence.

http://www.time.com/time/magazine/article/html

Henry I. Modell, president of the National Federation of Army and Navy Stores, appealed to Navy Secretary James Forrestal for more speed in releasing surplus merchandise. Modell had his eye on the Navy's estimated surplus of six million dungarees, nine million chambray shirts, 1.8 million utility shirts, 1.3 million suits of heavy underwear, 500,000 pairs of galoshes.

The era of blood and tears and anger had ended. Sooner than any other people who had felt German bombs, Britons felt pity for the defeated enemy. Last week a united House of Commons protested hotly against the continuation of Germany's misery - and against the chaos into which a destitute Germany would drag Europe.

"Shame! Shame!" There was passionate talk of starving German children, of unnecessarily cruel treatment, of the "greatest catastrophe the human race ever experienced." Cried Labor's Michael Forte: "We are protesting against the wanton and deliberate creation of a new sore [in Europe]." Charged Independent Sir Arthur Salter: "If . . . millions during this winter freeze and starve, this will not have been the inevitable consequences of [war]." The implication was that Russia, Poland and Czechoslovakia were deliberately creating chaos in Germany. One M.P. accused the U.S. of the same "lunatic policy."

Some suggested that Britain send food from her own scarce stocks to Germany. A lone dissenter, thinking of Germany's hungry neighbors, said that he did not care "two rows of pins" what happened to German men, women & children. Tories and Laborites alike shouted: "Shame! Shame!"

http://www.time.com/time/magazine/article/html

*to long. Still loving and missing you.*

*All my love,*

*Your Husband, Bill*

November 3, 1945 - To Marge from Bill

*Dearest Marge,*

*I sure did all right on the mail today. Got 6 letters from you of Oct 12-18th and one of the 26th and one from my little Diago pal. He is in a Quartermaster outfit near Nurnburg.*

*I'm enclosing a money order for $100 in this letter. I give up on going to Paris before Christmas. I signed the paper for Discharge today but will probably take quite a while to go through channels but I think the 1st Sgt got them okayed here today. You asked about M.G. so I'll tell you. There are 3 Regiments that have control of the Government in Germany here and this is one of them. I'm in Regt. HQ so am probably pretty lucky. The Detachment from the Regiments are in all the cities around Weider, Regensberg, Neremburg, and a lot of the smaller cities but I think by Dec. they will turn the government over to the civilians in a lot of the smaller places so this outfit will be pretty small then. I was sure surprised to hear Mrs. Swan is working at the bakery but you have never mentioned it since. Is she still working there? I'll bet she is a good worker to, isn't she? It sure seems funny to hear you write about Butch talking because when I left, he couldn't talk at all.*

*Ma sent me a picture of him and he looks pretty good in it. A little better looking. I hope that daughter of ours isn't as homely as Butch was when he was a baby but from what you say, she must be really all right. I can just hear you talking to her all the time. I'll bet Tao (Mom's Pekinese dog) is sure losing out now, eh? Or has he kicked off by now?*

*When you wrote about being up to Eitzen and being down to Butch's, sure brings back old memories. Remember when you were teaching school and we used to bus up there now and then and you usually got a little on the way back. I wasn't the guy to hold out on you, eh? I'll bet them kids will never know how well their teacher liked her ass, eh or didn't she? You wrote how you sure do miss your loving, it isn't starting to suffer a little, is it? Boy, I'll bet the first night we are together when I get home will be kinda rough, eh and remember you can save the nightgown for about a month, don't you think*

or do you suppose you will wear me out before that? I'm sure hoping and praying that the day we will be together again won't be to long. I don't know whether you believe me or not when I tell you I'm not playing any of these women but I sure hope you do. If anybody would of told me a year or so ago that he could pass it up when it was thrown at him every day, I would think they were nuts but I'm sure finding out different. We have some pretty girls working here to but two of us don't monkey with them at all. It is nothing to have them ask us to take them out but they are gradually learning we aren't weakening. Two of the other guys who are married are shacking up about every night now with them. They only get $12 a month working here, cooks and all and it cost them about $10 for a pair of Black Market shoes. The people here are about the same as back in the states. Some of these girls must have had a hell of a lot of stockings on hand, because most of them wear silk stockings.

I'll bet its kinda rough on (deleted), when she can never get away from her husband as well, as she likes her fun. Do you suppose he has found out about all the cocks been in her before he ever got her or does he think he got a virgin?

I guess the Army has kinda taken Chuck Berg down a notch or two, eh? Does she know yet weather he will come over here or go to the Pacific? Have Luther's heard from Junior? He should have enough points to come home by now.

Well, Marge, I better quit for now and as we say here, it sure eats my heart out when I have to stay here instead of being home with you. Still loving and missing you.

All my love

Your Husband, Bill

November 4, 1945 - To Marge from Bill

Dearest Marge,

Here it is Sunday again and I didn't get to church. This is one hell of a place to find a place to go to church. I was on shift this morning but was off this afternoon. Didn't get any mail today. I guess the mail clerks don't work on Sunday here.

Went down to the show tonight. "Hangover Square". Didn't care to much for it. I got a ride a few minutes after I got out so got back here about 9:30. I see a notice up on the bulletin board that all men with fifty points

*Hangover Square*: In fin-de-siecle Victorian London (date 1899 shown in the opening scene), the police suspect that a composer who suffers from periods of amnesia may be a murderer.

The period setting creates a dark mood, especially in the key scene when Bone (portrayed by Laird Cregar), having strangled Netta (Linda Darnell) on Guy Fawkes Night, carries her wrapped body through streets filled with revelers and deposits it on top of the biggest bonfire.

The final scene shows Cregar as Bone, playing his piano concerto (composed by Bernard Herrmann), unmindful of the conflagration around him, as flames consume all.

Britain's Foreign Secretary Ernest Bevin for the first time openly regretted that Germany had been split into occupation zones, in effect admitted that the system was not working: "It might be said that we were wrong to develop zones. . . . Probably . . . it would have been better if we had not done it." He reported that some 15 million German "displaced persons" were being chivied back & forth across Europe; that some ten million Frenchmen, Italians and others were also waiting to go home. Telling of how he watched the misery-laden procession of refugees in Berlin, he said: "I felt, my God, that is the price of man's stupidity. ... It was the most awful sight. . . ."

This generous outburst, a credit to British decency, swept Bevin and others of like mind into one historical error. When Bevin said of the Sudeten Germans and the Czechs that they "had lived together in perfect harmony until Hitler's stooges and agents broke up their democratic state," he was falling back on the old, dubious view that Hitler's New Order had been the work of only a few Nazi gangsters. The 3,000,000 Sudeten Germans, now joining Europe's miserable displaced millions, had risen in a mass to betray the Czechs.

http://www.time.com/time/magazine/article/html

On November 5, Columbia joined the United Nations.

*can apply for civilian jobs here now and I guess there are quite a lot of them doing it. I hope they keep it up because the more that sign up, the quicker I'll get home with you. We still don't know where the hell we will move now. I guess we wait until the other outfit moves out of the place we move into. It sure don't seem like the G.I.'s are getting any thinner around. Go downtown here and see thousands of them on the streets. I suppose they are getting pretty thick around home to. Oh, be sure to write and let me know if you got the money order I sent yesterday. I sure wish I could get you something for Christmas here but there isn't much to buy that's any good.*

*How is John coming with his girl? Are they still getting along all right?*

*Has Lila hear anything about when Jim is coming home? He should soon have enough points. I sure hope Dad is getting along okay by now but I'll bet it is hard on him to have to stay in bed. I suppose your Dad takes it a little easier now than he used to or does he still work around the houses and buildings up town?*

*Well, Marge, I bet you and the daughter are getting pretty well acquainted by now. Haven't been getting her full on that beer you drink, have you?*

*I guess I better quit now. Hoping I hear from you tomorrow. Loving and missing you more than ever.*

*All my love,*

*You Husband, Bill*

*P.S. You can send me some magazines to read if you get time.*

November 5, 1945 - To Marge from Bill

*Dearest Marge,*

*I got one letter from you today of the 24th. From the sound of it, things are going pretty good. I didn't quite understand what you meant when you said you weren't getting back into shape right and that you had better see the Doc.*

*Nothing much new around here today except one of our guys is going to Officers (Quarters) to be Mess Sgt. He sure hates to go too. There are two guys leaving for the States on furlough, one has been over here 22 months and the other a little over a year. They only got 50 points. No battle (experience). The furlough works by time in the Army and overseas time. Combat time isn't worth shit but I think I'll still get home quicker than what the papers say yet. Civilian jobs are open to guys with fifty points here now and they were supposed to be in the clean up force and that is sure a joke because they can clean out everything they are going to in a month if they want to.*

*The rest of the boys are all gone to the show or the bar tonight so I'm here all alone. Just got my laundry back at suppertime. I had 4 sets of OD's, 2 towels, 6 pairs socks, 2 sets shirts and pants and one field jacket. Gave her a candy box and a pack of cigarettes. Cheap enough, eh? Sure don't cost much to get anything done here but they don't want money, always want cigarettes, soap or candy. From the looks of the Stars and Stripes, today they are planning on quitting the points system and discharge on 2 yrs service. That will help a lot of guys in the States but fuck a lot of them over here. I can just hear DeMarco cussing when he reads it today. He has 45 points but only a little over a year's service. Well, Marge, keep up the writing because I sure wait for them. Still loving and missing you.*

*All my love,*

*Your Husband, Bill*

On December 6, HUAC began investigation of seven radio commentators.

The House Committee on Un-American Activities (HUAC or HCUA, 1938–1975) was an investigative committee of the United States House of Representatives. In 1969, the House changed the committee's name to "House Committee on Internal Security". When the House abolished the committee in 1975, its functions were transferred to the House Judiciary Committee.

The committee's anti-communist investigations are often confused with those of Senator Joseph McCarthy. McCarthy, as a U.S. Senator, had no direct involvement with this House committee. McCarthy was the Chairman of the Permanent Subcommittee on Investigations of the Government Operations Committee of the U.S. Senate, not the House.

November 6, 1945 - To Marge from Bill

*Dearest Marge,*

*I got two letters from you today of Oct 20th +26th. The first was mis-sent to the 3rd Inf. Regt. But I got it finally. I'll have to cut this kind of short tonight. The boys will be wanting the light out pretty quick. I went to the show tonight "The Falcon in San Franciso" I guess was the name of it. I met the boys at the bar afterwards and got a ride out so we all fixed a good lunch and sat around shooting the bull. Nothing new around here, same old shit every day.*

*Oh, you wrote about drinking the 12% beer. Well, 12% beer here is about the same as 3.2 beer in the States. It would take a pile of it to get drunk on. They have some beer they call 6% which is just a little over 1%. Besides I don't drink much beer. I have a little wine about every day though. Maybe a glass in the morning and one or two when I sit down to write you. I never drink any water any more. When I'm thirsty I drink wine or juice which we get plenty of. It will sure be good to get home where they have good water and milk. I don't know weather I could drink much whiskey anymore or not.*

*I suppose by the time I get home the baby will be*

*The Falcon in San Francisco* (1945): On vacation, Tom Lawrence--The Falcon--and his Brooklyn-born sidekick 'Goldie' Locke meet with a cute little girl named Annie whose nurse has just been murdered. Accompanying Annie home, The Falcon is arrested for kidnapping, but bailed out of jail by a mysterious woman (Helm). A labyrinthine plot then unfurls involving silk smuggling, a steamship called the S.S. Citadel and an ex-bootlegger named Duke Monette.

Stars were Tim Conway and Rita Corday.

When genial, chubby-faced Jim Lucas joined the Marines, he left a reporting job on the Tulsa Tribune's courthouse beat. He became a crack combat correspondent, got out the first story of the landing on Tarawa—and was threatened with court-martial for writing that "something suddenly appeared to have gone wrong." He covered eight Marine landings.

Like many another newspaperman derricked out of his old job by the war, Jim Lucas had no desire to go back. He came home a lieutenant, surprised to find a flattering array of jobs thrust at him. He took the best one—roving columnist for the Scripps-Howard Newspaper Alliance —and went at it like a marine. Last week his first column kicked up a fine fuss.

" 'Little people' like to believe they don't make wars," he wrote. "After three years in the Pacific some of us reject that as rank escapism. We think you little people had a hand in making the war we just finished.

"It's not that we like military life. Most of us don't. We've been scared, uncomfortable, unhappy, lonesome. We've wanted to come home. But . . . we've always taken it for granted someone would take our place. . . . We are surprised to hear it seriously argued that we've always been able to train an army after we are attacked . . . and wouldn't . . . recommend telling it to the boys who were on Wake or Bataan.

"It comes as a shock that a segment of the public . . . [is] campaigning noisily against universal training. . . . Okay, mother. Okay, professor. Okay, parson. But are you willing to take the consequences, if you lead us into World War III?"

The ex-marine's opinions were frontpaged in 18 out of 19 Scripps-Howard papers. When Lucas promptly got 227 letters, all but three damning him, Scripps-Howard was sure that their marine had landed. *Time Magazine*

*changed a lot from now. It will be kinda hard to get used to at first. I suppose you think she will like her old man all right? That is pretty good about Billy McCormick. That's one kid I never could stand. He worked in the bakery a couple days when I first had it but I get rid of him in a hurry. I don't think it was safe to leave anything laying around with him around. I hope John don't get running around with him. Well, take good care of yourself and Janice. Sure am hoping and praying I'll be home with you before too much longer.*

*All my love, Bill*

November 7, 1945 - To Marge from Bill

*Dearest Marge,*

*I didn't get any mail today. I guess there wasn't much come in. I see by the paper today where M.G. will fold up here in June and maybe there (Munich) at end of Feb. but the rumor here is that all our detachment will be broke up Dec 15 and there will just be HQ for a couple months. It sure seems foolish to move to Munich just for a couple of months but I guess we are still going to. They say next week, but the officers are still trying to stall it off. I hope we don't have to go. The only move I want to make is home. It will be 10 months tomorrow since I left the states and sure seems like a lot longer. Still haven't seen any of the replacements that they are supposed to be sending over here. I hope they start coming pretty quick.*

*I'm the only one in again tonight. The rest of the guys are all downtown. I think I'll write a letter to the folks yet tonight. I haven't wrote them in about a week now. One of the guards just came up for me to get their lunch for them. We always fix them sandwiches and a few cans of juice for lunch at night. It is the only place I ever seen it but it is pretty nice for them. There sure isn't much to write about it. The same old thing every day here. How about sending me the Republican or Democrat? Ma sent me one by air mail and it came in no time. The guys over here are trading American money for German marks now, 6 to 1. One kid had a $1.00 and traded for $6.00. Pretty good, eh? We aren't supposed to have any though.*

*Well, Marge, keep up the writing. I would sure give anything to be home with you again and to get a chance to see the baby before she gets very big. Hope you are getting that tummy back in shape by now. Still loving and missing you.*

*All my love, Bill*

November 7, 1945 - To Jim and Amanda from Bill

*Dear Folks,*

*I haven't heard from you for quite awhile but thought I better write. I'm glad dad is getting better. Marge wrote that he is working a little again now. I hope he don't try to overdo it though. I'm still waiting to hear when Vernon gets home. I hope it is soon. I'll bet he hangs on a good one then, eh. Or do you suppose he'll be so glad to be with Beck and Jimmy to.*

*I sent in the papers for discharge here a few weeks ago but it takes a long time for something like that to go through, even if they pass it. But the 3rd Army Headquarters is only about 30 miles from here but I don't think that will help much either.*

*It burns me up to lay around here doing little or nothing and can't go home. I suppose about 1/2 of the guys they have over here really do anything.*

*I hear over the radio that the civil war is still going on in China. I hope they put a stop to it before they start dragging other nations into it.*

*I sure hope you'll be able to find somebody to work in the backend (of the bakery) pretty soon. I know it's too hard on you to be there at night and then work around the house in the daytime. I guess John must be getting pretty good by now, eh? When is he going to marry that babe he's going with now or won't he say yet?*

*It don't look like I'm going to get outside of Germany to buy any Christmas presents. I sent Marge $100 I had and still got about $60 but I took my name off the pass list so know I won't go anyplace. 10 months overseas now and didn't get any (leave). Lot of these guys here have wives in England and get furloughs there right along. And some who reenlisted went to England instead of the States. Well, Ma, hope it isn't too long before I get home. Keep up the writing.*

*Love, Bill*

November 8, 1945 - To Marge from Bill

*Dearest Marge,*

*I got one letter from you today of Oct 28th. I hope I get some more in the morning. It is sure a miserable day here. Cold and raining, the wind is a blowing to beat hell and this is about the first night we haven't had any heat*

Congress displayed a soggy lack of enthusiasm; the public was remarkably silent. So it seemed possible that the debate over peacetime conscription, touched off by President Truman's message to Congress, might sputter out like a damp fuse in the fogs of the first postwar autumn.

For this pallid reaction the President was partly to blame. He had shown courage in delivering his message in person, braving the uneasy reception his advisers had urged him to avoid. Yet out of deference to Congressional sensibilities—or perhaps merely out of the traditional American preference for euphemism—he insisted that his plan for universal military training was not conscription at all.

Fleet Admiral Ernie King joined him in this bootless exercise in semantics, based on the technicality that trainees would not be in the armed forces. But details of the training plan (see below) made clear that the 18-year-olds, if not actually in the Army & Navy, at least would have a hard time staying out or getting out.

Using soft words for hard ones did not ease Congress' problem. The U.S. might be willing to buy a year of training just as a gigantic—and highly expensive—national health program. It was even more likely to buy a tough program of future military security, based on the discovery in World War II camps that the value of training depends on how closely it approximates the conditions of battle. But confusing the two products helped the sale not at all.

Whatever the label, Congress was faced with a hard choice. Few Congressmen relish the responsibility of leaving any stone unturned in the quest for U.S. security. Yet there are a few dissenters even in the high command of the Army, Air Forces and Navy (e.g., Admiral Nimitz) who question the effectiveness of a year's peacetime training, however arduous it may be.

www.time.com

Out on the Montana range, rattlesnakes were unusually plentiful, and the old men predicted a long warm fall and a short easy winter.

In Chatsworth, Ill. First Lieut. Billie Wittier, an Army nurse, made Page One of the weekly Plaindealer when she got back home: "She has seen much front-line active duty in the European sector, including Italy and Germany. She was able to see the Alps in all their beauty and says Switzerland, especially, is beautiful."

In Manhattan, a nobly decorated veteran of the Pacific was passed along by a junior executive, who was unfavorably impressed by his willingness to take "anything," to a junior executive who told him, kindly, "You know, I don't think this is exactly the job for you." Upon hearing this, the young hero burst into tears.

Happy days, more or less, were here again. Despite prodigious achievements at home & abroad, the nation had not been essentially changed by war. Now, returning to peace rather than struggling through it nine-tenths dead, the U.S. was more like itself than ever—in a world which would never again be remotely the same.

http://www.time.com/time/magazine/article/html

in our room. I guess just because it is cold.

The Mess Sgt. had to fire 2 girls today, old lady and her daughter. I sure felt sorry for them. They are Russian and the order came out that we could hire no Russians and had to fire what we had working for us. The Russians want them all back, I guess, so they are going to get them one way or another. The girl got down on her knees and begged to stay but there's nothing we can do. They are Catholic and all the Catholics sure hate to go back but they have to or starve, one or the other. I sure do hate it more every day I stay here and I see more new stuff the army pulls every day. There was supposed to be a riot downtown tonight but I haven't heard weather it came off or not. A bunch of Poles were supposed to raid some German warehouses but the M.P. were tipped off about it so maybe it blew over. I think it will be rough here this winter because the people won't have much to eat. They are only allowed about 1/2 lb. of butter and fat a month, not much, eh? It is good for a lot of them but I hate to see some of the innocent ones suffer.

From the sounds of your letter John and that babe of his are getting pretty serious. Do you think he's getting a little of it yet? ANSWER or don't you think he had as good as luck as me?

Let's see, how many times we were out together before I put the make on you? Well, Marge, what I would give to be with you and praying I will be before long.

All my love,

Your Husband, Bill

November 9, 1945 - To Marge from Bill

Dearest Marge,

I got one letter from you today of the 27th. I think by tomorrow I should have one of the first. That's pretty good about Riley kidding you about me but Marge, here is one of the few married guys who's going to come home and be able to say he never monkeyed with any other women and be telling the truth. I see by the Stripes where all the guys in the states with 50 points can get discharges. That sounds better but it still don't help us any but maybe it won't be to long. I see where they are getting a few more ships but there are still lot of guys with over 100 points.

The rumor is we move next Wed. or Thurs and we will have a beautiful Mess hall but we will have inspection by a Brig. General every day and I sure ain't going to care much for that kind of shit.

Well, how is our little daughter coming. Still taking good care of her?

I sure can't wait for the day I get home with you. I hate it more every day I stay here. This would be a wonderful deal for anyone who was single or didn't care much about his wife. It makes me sick to see a couple guys here who have kids at home shacking up every night. Well Marge, I have to get up early in the morning so I better quit for now. Still loving and missing you will all my heart.

All my love,

Your Husband, Bill

November 10, 1945 - To Marge from Bill

Dearest Marge,

I didn't get any mail today so I suppose I won't get any till Tues. I don't suppose there will be any Mon on account of Armistice Day. We are sure getting the snow here now. It started last night and been snowing steady ever since. Not much of it sticking though - about inch deep. It sure is warm for snow but I'm sure glad I'm not sleeping in foxholes now. I'd sure hate to ever go through that again, went down to see the show "Story of G.I. Joe". I liked it pretty well but I think the Army censored it pretty good before they ever made it. I've seen German training films that were a lot more realistic. Of course after we came back from the show, we had to pick out the faults of it but a lot of it is like regular combat except the artillery fire don't sound like that coming in on you.

I don't know weather you seen it or not but for the looks on guys faces, whiskers and dirt, it was just like combat.

I got a snapshot I'm sending here. It was taken out beside the mess hall. We took some more but they aren't ready yet. As quick as I get them, I'll send them. I guess I sent that $100 bucks home just in time. They stopped all money orders now. I guess they are going to keep tabs on our money. A lot of boys are making a fortune here and I'm in a good setup for it but I never did any yet and don't intend to. Well, Marge, I'm sure praying your man gets home with you soon. Course, I sure miss you more every day and still loving and missing you. Keep up the writing cause I sure do wait for them.

All my love, Your Husband, Bill

On December 10, General Enver Hoxha became the president of Albania with the approval of the Soviet Union.

Heavy battles break out in Surabaya between Indonesian nationalists and former colonists returning from World War II.

Story of G.I. Joe (1945): War correspondent Ernie Pyle (Burgess Meredith) joins Company C, 18th Infantry as this American army unit fights its way across North Africa in World War II. He comes to know the soldiers and finds much human interest material for his readers back in the States. Later, he catches up with the unit in Italy and accompanies it through the battles of San Vittorio and Cassino. He learns from its commanding officer, Lt. (later Capt.) Bill Walker (Robert Mitchum) of the loneliness of command, and from the individual G.I.'s of the human capacity to survive drudgery, discomfort, and the terror of combat.

If Bill had not been a man of character, in his position as cook, he could have made a fortune himself. In a country that was starving, stealing food and selling it on the Black Market would have been a snap. As these letters have shown, not drinking hard stuff and not cheating on his wife, Bill was a very moral man.

November 11, 1945 - To Marge from Bill

*Dearest Marge,*

*Well, Marge, no mail again today. Didn't do very well on mail this last week. Two of us are sitting here writing letters having a little wine in between writing. The rest of the guys went downtown. I finally made it to church this morning. The M.P.'s have a little chapel a couple blocks from here and I went there so I'll be getting there more often now. I'll be glad when I get home and be able to go every Sunday again. I hear over the radio where Patton is taking over Eisenhower's job for a while. Sure hope it isn't permanent. Lot of news today about getting the guys home but it don't look like they are getting any thinner over here. You wrote about Fitz getting married. How about, does the guy know it yet? I suppose she is just as big a pain in the ass as ever, eh? Do you remember the night in the bakery I told her off? Long time ago, eh - that was before I ever had any intentions of shipping you out.*

*Say Stan and that gal of his must be getting pretty serious. Does he spend any money on her yet? You know he used to say he wouldn't waste any money on girls or has he got her paying the way.*

*I'm glad you are finally getting rid of that donut machine. It has been an eyesore there for a long time. You never wrote weather Pratt even made that counter for the front end or not.*

*I had a chance to make T/4, or Sgt. but told the Lieut. I didn't want it or if he put me in for it, I would fuck up to get busted. I don't want anything to keep me from getting home if I ever get the chance. I'm the headman on our shift and it calls for a T/4 rating. So I don't know weather he will put somebody else in for it or not. Lot of these guys want ratings but I sure as hell don't. The guy I wrote you about who went to officers mess, well, he didn't like it so he fucked up and is back here again. Sure glad to. He don't monkey with any of the girls.*

*Have you picked out the spot where we are going to build our house yet when I get home? I'm glad we live in a small town because if there is ever another big war, the cities in the States will feel it. Well, Marge, enough for tonight. I hope you and Janice are still doing all right + what I would give to be with you both. I'm still waiting for a picture of her. Still loving and missing you. Keep up the writing.*

*All my love, Your Husband, Bill*

The fog had lifted and a sharp autumn wind whistled past the skyscrapers, quickening the pulse of the city. In the Navy Yard in Brooklyn lay the spanking new carrier Franklin D. Roosevelt, ready for a presidential commissioning. Across Manhattan, in the brackish waters of the Hudson, an impressive fraction of the U.S. fleet rode at anchor, ready for a presidential review. There would be a parade for Harry Truman up Fifth Avenue, past the flags and the glittering shop windows. He would make a speech before hundreds of thousands on an open meadow in Central Park.

It was Navy Day for the greatest Navy of the world in the greatest city in the world. The President's speech had been heralded in advance as the most important of his career. It was time for such a speech: relations between the victorious Allies had steadily worsened.

*Time Magazine November 5, 1945*

Revolution really came to England. Its symbol was a new taxicab—the sleek, shiny prototype of 3,000 which will eventually take the streets of London beside the vanishing hacks of the past (see cut). Age, the blitz and the robombs have halved the peacetime ranks (8,000) of the veteran models. Though pernickety and anachronistic, their comfortably high doors and maneuverable wheelbases were admirably suited to their purpose. Wheezing their way through two World Wars, they have been as much a part of London as St. Paul's or the oystermen of Billingsgate. With their passing London will be a little less London.

*Time Magazine November 5, 1945*

November 12, 1945 - To Marge from Bill

Dearest Marge,

I got 3 letters from you today of Oct 27th, 29th, and 30th and one from Ma. It kinda sounds like you are getting my mail faster than I get yours now, eh? Sure glad it is going through fast. The Stars and Stripes looked pretty good today. If they do everything it says they are going to, we should get home quicker. There are supposed to be 400,000 leave here this month but I still don't believe it.

I don't think I'll bother writing to that guy about the donut machine. If he don't want it, the hell with him. That was pretty good in your letter about Helen but I think less of her than any girl I ever went with and I never cared much for any of that family. You could turn your back to any of them and they would knife you.

I guess you know how much I think of you by now, Marge because if I didn't I probably (would) be doing like a lot of these other guys. Went down town for a while tonight. Went to the show but it was lousy. Went up to the Circle Bar afterwards and had a few beers. I wish you could just see the place and see the guys sitting around mugging the girls right in front of any body. It makes me mad as hell every time I go up there. I hardly ever play any cards anymore. None of these guys play pinochle. I don't care much for poker.

Sure was surprised to hear that John's girl is a Catholic. Well, maybe it will save him a little time then, eh? You asked about that lot next to our cabin. Bill Schaffer was planning to build a cabin there. I suppose your dad figured it wasn't even worthwhile to bring the boat down to the river this past summer. I never heard you mentioning them catching any fish. Will I ever be glad when I get a chance to go down there again. Maybe next summer we will be able to. I sure hope I get home before that anyway. If they count the points once more, I'll be all set but I doubt now if they do. It kinda sounds like Dorothy is having a rough time. Remember I used to tell her before she was married that Freddy didn't care much for working. I'm sure hoping you get somebody to work soon so you won't have to be working at night. Well, Marge, keep on loving me and pray that I'll be home with you soon.

All my love,

Your Husband, Bill

On December 12, the Nobel Peace Prize was awarded to Cordell Hull for his part in establishing the United Nations.

After his return from China a year ago, Robert W. Prescott, 32, a former Flying Tiger (six Jap planes) and Hump-hopper for the China National Aviation Corp., began writing unsentimental letters to his old buddies. His letters made one point: he was looking for money and talent to build a U.S. counterpart of the C.N.A.C.

Shy, baby-faced Robert F. ("Duke") Hedman, who had shot down six Japs, and had flown the Hump 350 times, had an unemployed $10,000. Joe Rosbert (six Jap planes), who once crashed in the Himalayas and walked out in 46 days, threw in $10,000, took a job as chief pilot. J.R. ("Dick") Rossi, also a six-plane man, got his letter in India after his 600th Hump crossing. Wrote Prescott: "Rossi, put that drink in your left hand and tell me what you're doing." Rossi joined up.

By July 1945, Prescott had raised $87,000 from flyers, another $87,000 from businessmen. In Washington he had used his veteran's priority to buy a DPC-owned fleet of 14 surplus Conestoga twinengine cargo planes for $401,000 ($90,000 down). He promptly got most of his down payment back by selling six of them for a profit of $80,000. Then National Skyways Freight Corp. took off.

*Time Magazine November 5, 1945*

If Congress acts, the Army & Navy are ready. They have a blueprint for training the nation's 18-year-olds, in greater detail than has yet been announced.

Out of the 1,200,000 youths who reach military age each year, the Army & Navy expect to reject about 225,000 for serious physical or mental disabilities. Of the rest, enrolled for training through local boards, the Army will take 700,000, the Navy 275,000. The Army holds that trainees should receive $30 a month pay, cheap Government insurance, some sort of dependency benefits if needed.

As far as possible, trainees will have their choice between Army & Navy, among different branches inside the services. Like World War II's selectees, they will take aptitude tests, be assigned—within the limit of quotas—to training and jobs for which they are best fitted. They will probably wear some sort of cadet uniform, not yet designed, to distinguish them from regular soldiers & sailors.

All medical care will be provided by the services. Whatever his physical condition at the start, the trainee would end his year with teeth in good shape, hernias and similar defects repaired, eyeglasses if needed.

*Time Magazine November 12, 1945*

On November 13, Charles De Gaulle was elected head of the French provisional government.

November 13, 1945 - To Jim and Amanda from Bill

Dear Folks,

Received your letter of the 22nd of Oct. so thought I better answer right away. The mail has been coming through slow again for some reason.

I'm still taking things pretty easy over here. We still don't know when the hell we will move. They change their minds about every other day. I'm sure hoping Marge has got somebody to work nights by now. John has sure been sticking to it pretty good, eh. It's getting about time you get him married off, isn't it? Marge writes that he has a hell of a nice girl. You asked me what I wanted for Christmas. I guess you better put it off till next year. There is nothing I need in clothes or food. Haven't heard nothing from the papers I sent in but that takes a long time, I guess. I see by the Stars and Stripes where the 90th is going home next month. Sure wish I was back in it.

There are sure a pile of guys reenlisting over here now. I hope they keep it up and maybe I'll get home sooner. I bet there are getting to be a pile of guys at home now, eh. But most of them probably don't want to work. I'm glad dad is all right again. I suppose it made it kind of hard to make both ends meet with him laid up. How are the kids coming? I suppose Marie has forgot all about me by now or thinks I'm never coming home. Well, I suppose Vernon will be home for Thanksgiving this year. I suppose he'll go back to work for that cheap Schultz store, eh'.

Well, keep writing. I'm waiting for those papers to come you sent. That one you set airmail come in about 10 days.

Love, Bill

November 13, 1945 - To Marge from Bill

Dearest Marge,

Didn't get any mail from you today. It kinda looks like they are fucking up on it again somewhere but I hope mine are still getting to you O.K. The news in the paper looks better the last few days. If the people in the states keep up putting on the pressure, we will get home yet. Lot of the boys are enlisting now and maybe that will help to. You and getting home are about the only things I ever think about.

I went down and took a bath a little while ago. The shower run was full, so I grabbed the tub, first time I've been in a bathtub since I've been in the Army, I guess. Felt pretty good. I can still see you sitting in the tub at home on Sat. Remember the way I pestered you a few times when you were taking a bath. I sure think a lot of the good times we had at home and down in Texas. When they start letting wives come over here, the guys who have them here will have it nice. I think they will be able to spend most of the time with them and this country is really something to see.

I guess Patton is a big boy here now but I hope they don't keep him because he's no good for the enlisted men. I wrote a letter to the folks tonight so when I finish this one, if I can't find anything to read, I'll probably go to bed. I am anxious to get that picture of Janice and you that you are going to send. I think I've lost quite a bit of weight since the war ended, about the same now as I was in Texas but there are no scales here so don't know for sure.

The weather has turned out nice again. All the snow is gone. I hope it stays this way. The jeeps look funny around here now. The guys are getting steel tops and sides put on them now for the cold weather.

How's the ford working anyway? You wrote you had it all overhauled but never said if it was any better or not. Well, Marge take care of that daughter of ours and hope I get to see her soon.

All my love,

Your Husband, Bill

November 14, 1945 - To Marge from Bill

Dearest Marge

Well Marge, didn't get any mail from you again today but got one from Marcella of Nov 2nd. She said she wrote to Washington again. Sure hope it helps.

I was talking to one kid in my old co. back in the 90th today. He's going home tomorrow on a dependency discharge. He only got 30 points, come in Feb. and is only about 20 or 21. Sure hope mine goes through. We had 155 shipped out today for home and there is another bunch going tomorrow.

I guess the packages coming now are slowing down the mail but I hope mine keep going through to you O.K. Went down to the show tonight "Blonde Ransom" was the name, wasn't bad either. Stopped in and had a beer and then came back here. The rest of the boys were at a dance over at the Red Cross club so I had to catch a ride

Among Army and Navy officers the hottest question of the week was not the atomic bomb but the merger of the armed services. It was so hot, in fact, that burly Admiral Jonas Ingram, commander of the Atlantic Fleet, angrily declared that the proposed single department was "too much in line with Hitler." The U.S. Army, favoring the merger, still had the offensive. The slower-moving, more conservative Navy, although it had had ample warning of the Army's intentions, had to fall back on denunciation while it looked around for more effective weapons.

There was a case to be made against merger. But the Senate Military Affairs Committee, listening to Navy's witnesses last week, heard no convincing arguments against the unified department.

http://www.time.com/time/magazine/article/html

When Duke Randall, owner of the Paradise Gardens nightclub in Manhattan, loses $63,000 to gangster Ice Larson in a rigged poker game, he promises to have the money in one week or give up the club in exchange. While driving home, Duke crashes after swerving to avoid the speeding car of heiress Vicki Morrison, and she then takes the unconscious Duke home and nurses him.

Two days later, Vicki entreats Uncle William to advance her $63,000, and when he refuses, she moves on to her next plan. Soon after, Duke sees a newspaper report that Vicki has been kidnapped, thus the name *Blonde Ransom*. Stars were Donald Cook, Virginia Grey and Pinky Lee.

back. Hear tonight we might not even move to Munich. I sure hope not anyway, every thing is getting in good shape here. Have a beautiful kitchen and our room is usually pretty warm. Marcella (Robinson -his first cousin) wrote her and Stella (Dad's aunt) were down Sunday but you and the baby were out. She said Stella is getting pretty fat. I'll bet Stell won't like that if she heard it.

Hope everything is going good there and both you and Janice are all right. I've still never been sick since I've been over here.

Well, Marge better quit for tonight. I say a prayer for you and the baby every night. Sure hope I'll be home with you before long.

All my love,

Your Husband, Bill

November 15, 1945 - To Marge from Bill

On November 15, Harry S. Truman, Clement Attlee and Mackenzie King called for the creation of the United Nations Atomic Energy Commission.

Dearest Marge,

I got your letter today of the 2nd of Nov and also 2 papers. Ma sent the first. I never hear nothing back on the paper I sent in yet but if I don't in a couple weeks, I'm going to see the Regt. Commander. Was talking to a lieut. today who's discharge just come through. He had a printing shop and he's getting out to run that. He said his Uncle kept working on them till it went through. I see by the papers they are gradually sending more ships over here. Hope they keep it up. I suppose there will be lots of guys signing up for the civilian jobs here now. Course no matter how few points you have, you can get a discharge and civilian job.

Has Lila heard from Jim lately? He should be getting home before long or hasn't he got enough points yet? I think he went overseas about the same time as I did, didn't he?

Swede (Paul Anderson) did take the fatal step with Theresa Wetzel.

I'll sure be glad when we can get all the old gang together for a party again. Harold, Swede and Jim. Have you heard when Harold and Swede are getting out? I suppose Swede is taking the fatal steps about now.

It sounds like you are getting my letters faster now than you ever did, eh? Mine are coming a little slow though, I think.

Every time I read any thing about the Atomic Bomb, I know I never want to live in any city or manufacturing area. I'm sure glad I've got a good wife waiting for me at home or I'm afraid I'd be like a lot of these other married men over here. Sure hoping and praying I'm *home with you before long. Do you think we will be able to make up for all this lost time we have had? Sure do love and miss you.*

*All my love, Bill*

November 16, 1945 - To Marge from Bill

*Dearest Marge,*

*Well, Marge, didn't get any mail today and I sure do miss it when I don't. Just came back from the HQ party. They have one every Friday night. It is a beautiful place where they have them. I just had a few beers was all. Didn't dance any. Didn't want to go but they practically dragged me. There were five of us guys at our table and three girls. A couple of the boys got a little mad at me because whenever I talk about these girls, I usually call them pigs or sluts and one of them talked good English and understood me but I shamed one guy out of taking one home. I keep kidding him about what his wife would say if she ever seen him out with a slut like that so he finally got rid of her. One nurse was over to our table for a while. I think they are just about as bad as these pigs here. I sure wish I was home with you. It sure makes me sick to go to something like tonight and not have you. About all I do is sit around and remember the places we used to be together and the more I see of these sluts, the more I know I'll never chisel on you.*

*See by the paper today where they are starting to break up this outfit. The other two Regt. have been pretty well busted up all ready and now they are going to start on this one but I don't think it will affect us guys in HQ for a couple months yet.*

*Well, Marge, waiting to here from you and loving and missing you more every day.*

*All my love,*

*Your Husband, Bill*

November 17, 1945 - To Marge from Bill

*Dearest Marge,*

*I received your letter of Oct 30 and one from Paul Anderson and Ethel. Sure sorry to hear you are working so hard. Think you better just have John make what he can and let the rest go to hell. I got some bad news for you tonight to. Got the answer back on the papers I sent in. Says DISAPPROVED. Evidence presented is insufficient to establish enlisted mans importance.*

*The First Sgt. told me there wasn't much I could do*

On November 16, the United States imported 88 German scientists to help in the production of rocket technology. The move was heavily contested by the Soviet Union.

The motion picture *The Lost Weekend*, starring Ray Milland, was released. This was the most realistic film portrayal of alcoholism up to that time and it won several Oscars in the following year.

Yeshiva College was founded in New York City becoming the first Jewish College in the United States.

The United Nations Educational, Scientific and Cultural Organization (UNESCO) is founded.

On November 17, a new world recoed air speed of 606 mph was set by WJ Wilson of the Royal Air Force.

It appears that Plan B has, for the present, failed but Plan A is still working it's way through the halls of government.

From one-legged, Russian-born Alexander de Seversky (*Victory through Air Power*) came a declaration intended to be heartening: the atomic bomb is just another bomb.

After surveying Hiroshima and Nagasaki, the self-chosen priest of omnipotent air power told U.S. newsmen in Tokyo:

1 - Much of the effect of the atomic bombs in Japan was due to flimsy construction. In a steel-and-concrete U.S. city, one of the bombs would have done no more damage than a ten-ton TNT bomb.

2 - The bomb was a great step, but only a step, in "the science of demolition."

3 - Two hundred Superforts with old-style bombs could do as much damage as the atomic bombs had done in Japan.

De Seversky's conclusion was the same one he had reached in every other strategic argument: Air power is the answer.

"Of course," de Seversky admitted, "we cannot judge what the future will bring. There may come a time when we can deliver atomic bombs without the use of planes. But under the present set-up we must have control of the air."

http://www.time.com/time/magazine/article/html

now unless you could get it through from that side. He said there are a lot of them going home with less points than I have but have got the pull in the states to put them through.

Damn but I've been so pissed off all day. Lay around here and do little or nothing and they say they need us here.

Here it is Sat. night again. Nothing like Sat. night at home - just another day here. I'm all alone here tonight. Rest of the guys are downtown. Oh, by the way, you probably won't get a few of my letters because I read in the paper today where 4,000 lb of our mail burnt up the 10th of Nov. near Frankfurt so write and let me know weather you got that $100 money order I sent.

If you want to you can send me a few cigarettes and some magazines to read. Usually I have enough cigarettes but sometimes I run a pack or two short a week and they cost $3.50 a pack on black market. From the sounds of Swedes letter he is probably out of the Navy by now. He said the Hound would be to. I hope Harold comes back to work in the bakery. I guess we could sure use him, eh? I think I'll write Swede a letter yet tonight. Course, I got plenty of time. Sure am loving and missing you Marge and hope I get to see the baby before much longer.

All my love, Bill

November 18, 1945 - To Marge from Bill

Dearest Marge,

Well, Marge no mail today as it is Sunday and we don't get any. Hope I have some in the morning. I got to Mass again this morning. I was working but I took off for an hour. Played pinochle for the first time tonight since I've been down here. We just played for fun - no money involved. The 71st Div. is shaking down the town here today for poss. and everything. I guess they probably won't finish until tomorrow. Do you ever have any pinochle games any more? I suppose I'll have to get home to get them started again, eh? And what I wouldn't give to be with you. I wrote to Swede and Marcella last night. I sent Swede's letter to Waukon because he said he'd be out about the middle of Nov. and getting married right after. Then he will take her to Waukon. He said he hopes she don't have the flag out when they get married. I suppose you will get a chance to meet her before long from the sounds of his letter. Harold should be out now to. I'm sure hoping he goes to work in the bakery.

Has Freddy broke down and took a job yet? I think Dorothy will probably be having to make the living yet.

Have you still got Mrs Swain there? Does she put in many hrs. or work part time? Well, Marge I sure hope this letter finds you and Janice all right.

How are your folks? Say Hello to them for me. Well Marge, I'll be waiting to here from you. About all I do is wait for your letters. Still loving and missing you.

All my love,

Your Husband, Bill

November 19, 1945 - To Marge from Bill

Dearest Marge,

I sure got the mail today. 6 letters from you from the 3rd to 8th and one from the folks, Veryle and DeMarco. Veryle didn't have much to say. Asked what I thought of the babies names and a few things like that. Said she had a little whiskey once in a while. DeMarco got transfered again and is near Wurzburg and is still as disquieted as ever.

I got the snapshots you sent. Couldn't see much of the baby in them but I thought the picture of you and the buggy was good of you. You don't look any heavier in it than when I left. I sure like it anyway but I'll still be waiting for the other picture of the baby.

Sure glad to here Vernon got home. I'll bet there will be some party at the house when he gets there. John and him will probably have hung on a good one by this time, eh?

I'm sure sorry to hear that Dad is still sick. I guess the money Ma had saved up is about gone now. I was talking to a Major today and he told me he didn't think there was much chance of the discharge going through while I was over here. He said you should put in for an emergency furlough for me and then I could apply for discharge in the states but I guess we will just have to wait and see how things turn out. If they only count the points again, I'd have enough for discharge but I don't think they will. I see where they can get a discharge now if they have 3 kids and 4 yrs service.

I'll bet John don't like Ralph Anderson coming in every night. I know he never used to like him before he went to the Army. Do Luther's ever hear much from Junior? He should be getting home before long. I would

In preparing the way for new car ceilings, OPA boss Chester Bowles last week hinted that car manufacturers may be granted a small price increase. But auto dealers would be expected to absorb the increase, sell cars at 1942 prices.

Anticipating a protest from dealers, Bowles explained that the auto retailers' prewar mark-up of 22-25% on cars was cut to 12-13% by losses on high trade-in allowances. For the next few years Bowles thought that dealers would be able to keep trade-in allowances low. Thus they could get along with a smaller new car markup, more than make up any difference by greater volume. Last week the Ford Co. added weight to Bowles's argument. It announced that it already has orders for 300,000 cars.

http://www.time.com/time/magazine/article/html

Vernon made it home. He's shown here with Jimmy and John.

Internationalism's grand old man, Jan Christian Smuts, had evidently pondered the recent upsurge of British pity for defeated, miserable Germany (TIME, Nov. 5). Last week, in a speech at Capetown, Field Marshal Smuts said what pitying British M.P.s had neglected to say in their House of Commons debate:

"You see today a ruined Europe. If tomorrow you hear of suffering, disease, starvation and death on a large scale unknown before in times of peace, remember that that was in the first place the curse of Hitler and in the second place the dreadful responsibility of the German people who allowed such a monster to become their master.

"The dreadful responsibility rests on us to do all we can to save what can still be saved. But do not forget where the chief responsibility lies."

http://www.time.com/time/magazine/article/html

*think I suppose Mona Knieble will be back before long. I'll bet you miss her since she's been to Marte (?) eh? I think I'll write to the folks tonight and DeMarco if I get enough ambition. Stan must be quite the lover, eh, if he's with that gal of his every night. Ma said he even was with her at Iowa City. Do you ever ask him if he is getting a little of it? I'll bet John does.*

*Does Max ever help out in the bakery any? Sure hope we start getting our mail spread out again instead of getting it all in one bunch. We are having lots of guys redeployed home through here everyday. Most of them are hoping they make it before Christmas.*

*I see by the paper today where a few replacements finally came over. 800 went to the 90th Div. area. I guess that 90th goes home in Dec. with guys from 60 to 70 points. Sure wish I was with them.*

*Well Marge hope you keep on writing so good cause I sure don't know what I'd do without your letters. Sure glad I got a wife I can trust at home.*

*Still loving and missing you.*

*All my love,*

*Your Husband*

November 19, 1945 - To Jim and Amanda from Bill

*Dear Folks,*

*I got your letter of Nov. 4th today so am answering it right away. Sure glad to hear Vernon is back. I'll bet you will have a time when he gets there, eh.*

*Sure hate to hear dad is sick again. You asked about the papers. Well, I got an answer back - Disapproved. I was talking to a Major today and he told me it is pretty hard to get a discharge when you are overseas but if anyone was sick or anything and, an emergency furlough would go through and he could get a discharge on that side (of the ocean.) But I don't know what to think. Maybe the last letter Marcella wrote will help. I'm just laying around here doing nothing. That's what burns me up. If they recount the points again, I'll have enough, but I don't think they are going to. Marge sent me some snapshots of the baby today but I couldn't see the baby very good in them. But they were sure good of Marge and Stan. Stan must be getting to be quite the lover, eh? Even taking her to Iowa City with him. I suppose he and John will be having a double wedding before long? You wrote Mike Campbell is getting married. Who to?*

*I got the 2 Democrats you sent and was glad to get*

*them to.*

*I've been getting to church the last couple Sundays now again. Well, Ma, write when you have time again. I suppose John and Vernon probably went on a good one by now, eh?*

*Love, Bill*

November 20, 1945 - To Marge from Bill

*Dearest Marge,*

*No mail today but guess I couldn't expect any after yesterday. Went down to the show tonight. Wasn't bad but don't remember the name of it. Is our room ever cold tonight. Seems like when we need the heat, there is never any. It has been cold here for the past week or so now. I suppose you are starting to get a little snow at home by now eh? They say it don't go below zero here. I'm sure hoping not anyway cause it looks like I'll be stuck here this winter. I hope you are still getting my mail fast. I think ours is coming by boat again cause it is taking 2 weeks or better for mail to come.*

*In those pictures you sent Stan looks like he's filled out a little more. I've been having to look at them over quite often. That's sure a good picture of you beside the buggy. So you think when I get home we'll probably make another eh? Well never can tell. We both should be in good shape. I'll bet Vern's been giving Beck hell ever since he got home eh?*

*I slept most of the afternoon today. That's one fast way of passing the time. Tomorrow Janice will be 2 months old eh? I suppose she's growing more all along, probably be walking by the time I get home. Well, Marge, better quit for tonight. Sure as hell wish I was home with you but guess all I can do is keep hoping and praying it won't be to much longer. Still loving and missing you.*

*All my love,*

*Your Husband, Bill*

On November 20, trials against 24 Nazi war criminals of World War II started at the Nuremberg Palace of Justice.

Kenneth McKellar, President of the U.S. Senate, last week temporarily yielded his chair, stepped down to the floor and informed his astonished colleagues that he had solved the problem of the bomb. Outlaw it, said the gentleman from Tennessee.

For a very few minutes a very few Senators beamed. Then skepticism set in. Snapped Colorado's Edwin C. Johnson: "If it is possible to outlaw the bomb, why not go the whole step and outlaw war?"

http://www.time.com/time/magazine/article/html

November 21, 1945 - To Marge from Bill

*Dearest Marge,*

*Well Marge just finished work at 10:30. Getting that big dinner ready for tomorrow. The cooks really worked their asses off today so it shouldn't be bad for in the morning. We only have two meals tomorrow from 9-1 and 3-4.*

*Remember the big meal we had out to camp last Thanksgiving. Sure wish I had you here with me and I'd*

On November 21, General Motors workers went on strike demanding higher wages and better benefits.

Was everybody out of step but Wall Street? Last week it seemed so. As news of strikes and wage demands clogged the tickers, the market reacted to it almost as if it were good news. Not for months had there been such a scramble to buy. By week's end, the Dow-Jones averages had climbed up to 188, close to the highs of the last big bull market in 1937.

The reason why Wall Streeters kept buying in the face of such news was plain. They were betting on an upcoming business boom, plus a heady dose of inflation. Ever since V-J day they had kept their eyes, and staked their cash, on this. Short-term troubles, which may well cut earnings, were discounted.

The biggest political news in Europe was the rise of a new Opposition. It was the Opposition to Communism and to the occupying Red armies, and it was rising in the countries where any opposition was a miracle. The might of the Red armies, the vigor and vigilance of the Communist parties had not been enough to prevent this phenomenon in Hungary, Austria, Rumania, Bulgaria, Poland, Yugoslavia.

There were signs that the Russians themselves, usually astute in such matters, had recognized the existence of a genuine, popular Opposition and were adjusting themselves to the facts of political life in their European sphere.

http://www.time.com/time/magazine/article/html

*enjoy it a lot more. Didn't get any mail from you today again but got 2 Democrats Ma sent. Still don't see any chance of getting home for quite a while yet. There is lot of shit in the papers every day. I see after this month they are pulling all the fast ships away from here and going to use them in the Pacific. Also see where MacArthur is planning on having only 200,000 men there by spring. Sure wished they would do the same over here.*

*We were supposed to have wine for dinner tomorrow too but we couldn't get any. Haven't been able to for a couple weeks now. I got a couple bottles of cognac yet I never drink it. Usually let the boys have it when they are going to have a party. I get a bottle every week for nothing so am not going to turn it down.*

*Well, Marge, I sure hope you have found some help by now and are having things a little bit easier. I guess we will be spending our Second Christmas and Wedding Anniversary apart too but I'm hoping it isn't to much longer after that before I get home. I guess we'll just have to keep hoping and praying eh? Well, Marge, I'm still being true to you. Loving and missing you more every day.*

*All my love, Your Husband*

November 22, 1945 - To Marge from Bill

*Dearest Marge,*

*Got one letter from you today of Nov. 8th. I was surprised to get any - this being Thanksgiving. Not many are working.*

*I sent the menu what we had for dinner. Sure looked nice with everything all set up. We had 2 Colonels and 4 Captains for dinner and of course a Colonel and Captain had to give a speech. We had a civilian orchestra playing during the meal. We had about 350 seated all at once for the meal so you can imagine how the girls had to work serving them. I think there are about 12 or 15 girls serving. This is the first big meal I've ate in a long time. I usually go down and fix a little lunch about 9 or 10 every night though.*

*The rest of the boys are all out tonight so I'm in alone.*

*We let the help eat in the dining room here tonight because the tables were all set and everything. I believe they were glad to get such a meal. I suppose it's been years since they have had that good a meal. Sometimes I feel sorry for them. You know it is the moneymen that make wars and start wars. I think they should have Ford and a few more of the big money men in the states standing trial here at Nuremberg too because the German army had more Ford trucks, tanks, half tracks, jeeps than any other kind. Most of them made before '41 to so he sure as hell helped promote this war.*

*I think most of their people hated to go "Heil Hitler" as bad as I hate to salute an officer. You would think by this time I wouldn't mind it but I still do and I've never saluted once since I've been here except to get paid and not very often at the 90th. I could stay in the army years and I still would never make a garrison soldier. It's too much like Hitler's system. They run their little camp the same as he did, I think.*

*Sure am glad Vernon got home. I hope the folks don't blame Beck to much for keeping him to herself so much because I know when I get home, I'll want to spend most of my time with you. If at all possible I wished we could have a week or so together before I did get to Waukon or wouldn't you like that? I miss the folks and the kids to but you're the one I really miss. Wouldn't mind staying over here if I had you with me. These guys who come over here next spring will really have a life and if they don't bring their wives over afterward, they are crazy because they'll be able to go about any place they want to and they'll never travel any cheaper. I could get a jeep or car whenever I wanted to now but there is nothing more I want to see here. I've been pretty well all through Germany and I haven't missed much except Berlin and that's like Munich and these other cities. This is the nicest city I've seen here yet. All the big Messer Schmitt plants are here but they didn't hurt the city much. I suppose all together it would be about homes and factories of about 10 or 15,000 wiped out. People at home will never realize what hell war is until they see it. You go downtown here and on the way you will see hundreds of guys going along with just one leg. There's a hospital here and I guess that all they have in it is one legged guys. Kids 6 yrs old and older, guys 50 or 60. It's hell staying here but I guess we can just thank God that I'm all in one piece. I know lot of the boys I was with aren't and a lot of them won't see Thanksgiving.*

*Well, Marge, I suppose you had a big dinner at home and will have again Christmas. Sure wished I was there with you but we will be next year. Hope you realize I won't be able to send you nothing for Christmas cause*

"The Hun," said Winston Churchill, "is always either at your throat or at your feet." Definitely at the Allies' feet when they invaded Germany, "the Hun" last week showed signs of getting up again.

Perhaps catching on to democratic ways, Germans began to gripe—at Allied "inefficiency," at the coming Nurnberg trials of big war criminals. Thousands of unemployed men had ample time for mischief. Here & there, snipers were still active. At night, G.I.s found wires strung across highways, intended to decapitate motorcyclists. U.S. Army cars were looted. German girls suspected of fraternizing were waylaid and warned.

In the U.S. zone, anti-U.S. organizations began to crystallize. Most of them consisted only of a dozen or so young men who just seemed fond of playing cops & robbers. So, in their early days, did some of Adolf Hitler's brown shirts.

http://www.time.com/time/magazine/article/html

On November 23, most United States wartime rationing of foods, including meat and butter, was ended.

*there's nothing to buy but I'll make up for it when I get home. I guess Ma figures they have stores going here just like at home where you can buy everything but they don't. Everything is rationed, what they do have.*

*Still loving and missing you. Hope to hear from you again tomorrow.*

*All my love*

*Your Husband, Bill*

<u>November 23, 1945 - To Marge from Bill</u>

*Dearest Marge,*

*Got one letter from you today of the 12th and one from the folks and also one from Veryle and a box from Livingoods. I've been sitting here eating the chocolates. The rest of the boys all went to the party tonight but I don't care much for them. I told them I didn't feel good to get out of going. HQ CO has one every Friday night. Glad to here Vernon stayed over a few days longer. I suppose that made the folks pretty happy, eh? Does Vernon know what he is going to do yet? I suppose go back to work for Schultz Bros, (variety stores) eh?*

*You wrote a few weeks ago that you and Janice were supposed to go see the Doctors but you never wrote since weather you went or not. In the letter I got from Ma, it kinda sounds like they liked John's gal pretty well. Maybe he will bring her over a little more often now, eh?*

*That romance of Stan's must be pretty serious if he is with her all the time. Did he forget all about being a priest now? Suppose he is taking a little of it?*

*What did your folks think when they seen him playing cards for money and you to?*

*I got a couple snapshots I'm enclosing. We are going to take some more when we get a nice day but the sun isn't out very often lately. These were taken along side the mess hall. I can just see John holding the Baby. I suppose he's waiting for her to start calling him Uncle John.*

Under the collar of Moscow censorship, the necks of frustrated American and British newsmen grew hotter & hotter. Most of them were very, very tired of the stalls and rebuffs they met in trying to send out what news they could get under Russia's peculiar "freedom of the press." The New York Times's able, soft-voiced Brooks Atkinson found "humorous stories ... especially difficult to get approved. [They] arouse inordinate suspicion." And it was not that the correspondents were anti-Russian; one of the complainers was Anna Louise (I Change Worlds) Strong, onetime editor of an English-language Communist paper in Moscow. Against Russia's box-rigid censorship, they found it hard enough to get at the truth; they found it impossible to get the whole truth out.

*Time Magazine November 12, 1945*

*Well, Marge the days are gradually slipping by. It won't be long now and it will be Dec. Sure wish I had some idea of when I'll go home but haven't any. When they cut to letting them out with 2 years service then it will let a lot guys go home for here with way less points than me.*

*Well Marge, better quit for tonight. Have a couple more letters to write yet. Still loving and missing you.*

*All my love, Your Husband, Bill*

November 24, 1945 - To Marge from Bill

Dearest Marge,

Received one letter from today of 11th and a box from Paulson's. Glad my mail is still going through fast to you. I've been about half sick all day. We got influenza shots yesterday and I had a cold when I took it so that didn't help any either. Lot of the boys were sick from them. I think it's the first time any shot ever made me sick. I was sure surprised to hear Vernon isn't doing much boozing. I sure hope he keeps on and don't start hitting it very hard.

Most of the guys are in tonight. If we stay over here much longer, I think we will all be nuts. There sure isn't much to write about. Same old shit every day going on here. I think I'll get to Mass again in the morning. I've made it the last 2 Sundays now so I'm getting back in the habit again. I slept just about all day today so don't suppose I'll sleep much tonight.

Ma writes that Janice is getting to be quite the little doll. She must think she is alright, eh? I hope Dad gets better before long. He's sure been sick for a long time now hasn't he. I know it bothers Ma a lot about being able to make ends meet. Well, Marge keep up the writing. Still loving and missing you.

All my Love,

Your Husband, Bill

November 25, 1945 - To Marge from Bill

Dearest Marge,

Well here it is Sunday and no mail today. I got to Mass again this morning. All the guys in the kitchen went. We had a Lieut. Colonel say Mass. That's about the highest ranking chaplain I've seen around yet.

We've got 450 replacements coming in tomorrow or Tues. just fresh from the states. I bet the boys sure give them the old run around. I'll have to look them all over to see if I know any of them. All the guys that go through here, I never seen anybody I knew yet except the 90th boys. The 90th pulled out from Weiden yesterday and started to move to POE (Port of Embarkation) so I suppose they probably won't leave till the last of Dec.

We took a few pictures again today but it takes a couple weeks to get them developed now. We can get plenty of films now cause the photographers are making them here again. The town is off limits here again today and tomorrow. Guess they are having another civilian

In China the U.S. Marines were busy at a traditional chore: carrying out a tidying-up expedition on a foreign shore. The forces involved numbered some 53,000 - almost three times the size of the whole Marine Corps in 1939. They were the Third Amphibious Corps, who had landed on the coast of northern China.

The Corps' commander, rugged 57 year-old Major General Keller Emrick Rockey, veteran of World War I, Haiti, and Nicaragua, had bossed the 5th Division at Iwo Jima. His China mission, as he saw it: clean out the Japs, secure the ports for the arrival of U.S. ships with Chinese Nationalist soldiers, open the railway which feeds coal from the northern coalfields to resurgent Shanghai. He made his headquarters in sprawling, ugly Tientsin.

With him in Tientsin was the famed 1st Division which invaded Guadalcanal, New Britain, Peleliu and suffered its worst casualties at bloody Okinawa. Few if any veterans of those grisly days were still on hand, but the new men were the same kind of businesslike Marines. Under Rockey and grey-haired, peppery Major General Dewitt Peck, who commanded the famous 4th Marines at Shanghai before the war, they cleaned up and settled down.

http://www.time.com/time/magazine/article/html

This is Bill's second reference to Lima (Limey) wives being shipped back to the US in place of waiting troops. The plan created a lot of dissatisfaction from both the folks back home and the troops.

The nickname Limey comes from the lime juice formerly served to the crews on British ships to prevent scurvy.

This is one of the items Bill sent back home. Must have been one of his favorites as it shows three gentlemen playing cards.

shakedown.

How is our little daughter getting along? I'm still waiting to get that picture. The snapshot you sent about all you could see was her mouth wide open. Sure wish I would be home with you before long but as yet nothing been in the papers about us getting home any quicker. They got down to 64 points in this outfit and I guess the next shipment will be from 55 up. That still is a long way from me.

There are a pile of guys applying for discharge and furlough now but not many of them are going through except the furloughs. Well, I suppose by the time ... I just heard the news over the radio and it sounds like they are going to take the Lima (British) wives back to the states in Dec. and leave us guys over here. Boy if the people back in the states let them get by with that shit. There's nothing we can do about it here. It is just like having our hands tied and I guess they only going to send home 100,000 guys in Jan. so at that rate, I guess I might be home by '47. Boy I get pissed off every time I hear the news like this. So guess I better quit for tonight.

All my love

Your Husband,
Bill

November 26, 1945 - To Marge from Bill

Dearest Marge,

Didn't get any mail from you again today and guess I won't for a while. They say all the mail planes have been grounded the past week. I got a letter from Harold and one from Marqardt today that went to the 90th. I got a few things here I'm going to send tomorrow. You keep the ashtrays and one box of perfume. Give one to my mother and the box of hankies to yours. I've been trying to get hold of something for the past couple of months. If I can get a hold of any thing later on, I'll send it.

It started snowing about 8 o'clock here and in a couple hrs there is an inch or two already so we'll probably have plenty by morning.

I went to the show tonight "Royal

*Scandal." I saw it once before but didn't mind seeing it over again. Things sure don't look very promising for us guys with low points. From the looks of the papers they are still planning on keeping us over here. In the letter I got from Harold, he said he would have his discharge in a week or so and that was mailed on Nov 6 so I suppose he is home now. Hope he's working in the bakery by now. From the sounds of his letter, he must think I'm probably playing these cunts. He would sure get a surprise if he was over here.*

*Well, Marge, can't think of anything else to write about so I better quit for tonight. Still loving and missing you.*

*All my love*

*Your Husband, Bill*

<u>November 27, 1945 - To Marge from Bill</u>

*Dearest Marge,*

*I got 2 letters from you today of 11th and 13th and one from Frank Gregory.*

*Glad to hear you had a good time at the 'Berg.*

*I suppose it is about the same as ever there. I think if I stay over in this fucking county much longer I'll be nuts. I guess I just got the blues tonight. Today reading in the paper all the guys going home and a lot of them came over after I did. We got in 150 guys who just came from the states and I talked to one who had 32 points and 2 kids. We get in about 400 more tonight around midnight that we have to feed so probably won't sleep much tonight.*

*If there is anyway at all you can just put in for an emergency furlough for me, do it because I should have a good chance of it going through now. Did you ever find out from the draft board about it? I know a lot of guys getting out that have a business. I sure hope things are going a little better for you at the bakery by now. I wrote last night I was sending a box but I guess I've got a little red tape to go through before I can send it. The Captain's got to see all the stuff and Okay it.*

*I still can't see Vernon leaving the booze alone but I hope he keeps it up. You wrote about Freddy working but never said what he's doing or anything. I'll bet Dorothy sure hates it when he keeps such good track of her but I suppose she needs it, eh?*

*Well Marge I sure as hell don't feel much like writing*

*A Royal Scandal,* also known as Czarina, is a 1945 film about the love life of Russian Czarina Catherine the Great. It stars Tallulah Bankhead, Charles Coburn, Anne Baxter, and William Eythe. The film was based on the play Die zarin (The Czarina) by Lajos Biró and Melchior Lengyel.

Directed by Otto Preminger.

On November 27, General George C. Marshall was named special United States envoy to China.

The trial against NSB-leader Mussert begins. Mussert was the chief of the Dutch Nazi party, NSB (Nationaal-Socialistische Beweging).

The *'Berg* is the Heidelberg Dance Hall in Spillville, Iowa.

In Britain, winter lay ahead, but autumn lingered. In a Kentish garden figs ripened, scores of Red Admiral butterflies swarmed over beds of chrysanthemums. Beneath clean-picked apple trees strawberries bloomed again. Farmers harvested late crops as daffodils poked their shoots out of the soil. The season was just a little queer.

London's overworked bus conductors and conductresses (clippies) decided to enforce a "no standing" rule during rush hours. Clerks and M.P.s trudged to work, tempers flared. Goaded by a bossy clippie, 60 medical students shooed her off her own bus while they sang "Oh, why are we waiting?" (to the tune of Oh, Come All Ye Faithful). Hastings fishermen protested against the encroachment of an amusement park on their fishing grounds. In London's St. Bartholomew's Hospital, 40 night nurses, peeved with their frugal fare, staged a lie-down strike. They stayed in bed an extra hour.

http://www.time.com/time/magazine/article/html

On November 28, an earthquake in Balochistan, Pakistan caused a tsunami that killed more than 4,000 people.

The Church has bungled its job of religious education. Such is the verdict of Protestant chaplains who met in Washington, D.C. last week at the invitation of the Federal Council of Churches.

The chaplains had all been in war theaters and their battlefront experiences had convinced them that the Church needs renewed warnings: Organized religion has allowed church members to remain religious illiterates. The trouble probably lies in an indirect way of teaching with high-sounding theological terms instead of plain talk, which the chaplains found more effective. Henceforth, civilian clergymen will have to be better trained in modern educational methods.

Returning servicemen are coldly undenominational. They are hungry for religious faith; but denominational hair-splitting only confuses and bores them.

*Time Magazine November 19, 1945*

On November 29, the Socialist Federal Republic of Yugoslavia was declared; this day was celebrated as Republic day until the 1990s. Marshal Tito was named as the first president.

Assembly of the world's first general purpose electronic computer, the Electronic Numerical Integrator and Computer (ENIAC) was completed. It covered 1,800 square feet of floor space. The first set of calculations was run on the computer that day.

tonight so guess I better quit.

All my love

Your Husband, Bill

November 28, 1945 - To Marge from Bill

Dearest Marge,

Didn't get any mail today or get much of anything done. I slept most of the day from 10 this morning till 3 this afternoon.

Fed 400 men this morning at 3 o'clock. They were supposed to be in at 10 or so after we fed them, we had the cooks start on breakfast. A hell of a pile of them are from Iowa but didn't know any of them. Dubuque, Newton and all over. Mostly guys who were in defense plants and lot of them figure they'll be home by July. They sure got high hopes anyway. Went downtown and saw a show tonight. Stopped in at the Red Cross on the way back and had coffee and donuts. They had a dance going on there to but we watched them about 10 minutes and then came on back to the Cavern. That's what this place is called on account of so many different outfits being in here. It used to be a big German post.

The weather turned out pretty nice again. Our snow is about all gone again.

I hope it stays warm. One of the boys and me have been sitting here cursing the krauts. He likes them about as well as I do so they caught hell.

We've been working the hell out of them the last couple days here. We will be feeding a 1,000 men a meal now or over. Do you imagine the dishes and staff it takes. Well, Marge, here is hoping I get home before to long. I guess I miss you more ever day. Well, take good care of everything. Loving you more than ever.

All my love

Your Husband, Bill

November 29, 1945 - To Marge from Bill

Dearest Marge,

Well no mail again today. I guess they just aren't sending it through. We got rid of 150 of our Rookies today. They sent them out to detachments. They tell us we are going to move to Munich again but I got to see it first. They have been stalling it off so long now, they might as well leave us stay here. I got a couple snapshots here I'll send. They were taken the day before Thanksgiving. We were out getting some branches for trimming the dining room.

We have sure been getting bad rations here lately. For the next 4 days all we have is canned meat to feed to them and the guys sure bitch about it. They had a little trouble here the other day. I guess some GI told some civilian that MG was going to sell a bunch of jeeps one afternoon and quite a few came over here trying to buy them.

Well Marge, I bet you sure get tired of my letters never any news or anything but can't be helped. Things go about the same here every day. I suppose Swede and his frau must be home by now, eh? And he's probably back in the chicken business. These replacements sure figure strong on going home in 5 or 6 months. I wished I had as high hopes as they do but yet I'll bet there will be a lot of them going home before I do. Well Marge, I got a letter to write to the folks yet tonight so think I'll quit. Still loving and missing you.

All my love

Your Husband, Bill

November 30, 1945 - To Marge from Bill

Dearest Marge

I got 4 letters from you today of Nov 1st, 11th, 14th, and 15th. Also the Democrat of the 13th. On the letter of Nov 1st you had the right address except you put APO 90 instead of APO 403. Sure good to hear that Dale is working but I hope Harold does, but it isn't to good to let Dale use the car because I can tell you if you keep on letting him, he'll get where he won't even ask and take it anyway. I see by the paper where Clare Duggan got a discharge. That sure was quick. How long was he in the army - 2 months?

Just was downstairs and had a little lunch. We usually do before going to bed. You asked about the points. No they are not still counting them. If they would I'd have enough for discharge. I know the guys with 3 campaign stars in the states are getting discharges weather they got enough points or not. Sure would give anything if I could be home with you and get a chance to see the baby.

Well this is another month going by but they still don't go fast enough for me. Well, Marge, better quit for now. Still loving and missing you more than ever.

All my love

Your Husband, Bill

Marshal Georgi K. Zhukov was entertaining General of the Army Dwight D. Eisenhower at a lavish Hohenzollern palace in Potsdam. Sergeant Harold Kempner, a Russian-speaking Philadelphian on the staff of the A.M.G.'s weekly Grooper, crashed the gate and accosted Zhukov.

Mindful of the U.S. Army's eagerness to get home, Kempner asked when the Allied occupation should end. Answered Zhukov: "In less than ten years, if the Germans are cooperative." Any message for U.S. soldiers? Said the Marshal: "Give them my regards."

Rudolf Hess crouched in the darkened auditorium, impassively listening to the Wagnerian crash of the talkie's sound track. Suddenly he half rose: before him on the screen was Rudolf Hess, Deputy Fuhrer of the Third Reich, in the center of the triumphant 1934 Nazi Party Congress. Next to him, Adolf Hitler capered with joy.

For a moment, Hess stared at Hess. The man in the newsreel, young and strapping, screamed "Sieg Heil!" The real man, haggard and old, sank back into his seat. Psychiatrists watched him closely.

The Nürnberg of 1934 faded from the screen and the lights of Nürnberg, 1945, went up. Colonel John Harlan Amen, who once helped Bill O'Dwyer clean up Brooklyn's Murder Inc., softly asked: "Do you remember? Hess tried to brush his hand against his eyes, but the handcuffs stopped him. Said he: "I must have been there ... I don't remember."

http://www.time.com/time/magazine/article/html

## December 1, 1945 - To Marge from Bill

Dearest Marge,

I didn't get any mail today. I sure hope you are getting my mail better than I'm getting yours. I guess with so many guys going home it probably helps screw it up a little more.

We have a bunch of guys with between 60 and 65 points leaving Tues for home. They are supposed to be in the States Dec 21. They will sure be lucky if they do get them that far. They are transferring into the 80th Div.

We are gradually getting rid of our Rookies. We got about 200 of them assigned here to HQ and senior Co.

I sold a watch today for $80 in Russian marks, which I bought for $9.00 just 4 or 5 months ago. It didn't keep good time or anything so did pretty well on it. Sold it to one of the Spanish guys who works for us. They sure hate me, there are five of them. Before I came they didn't do nothing hardly but I've been working the hell out of them the last couple weeks. To my notion they are nothing but Nazi Collaborators or else they wouldn't be here in Germany.

So Stan's gal hangs around the bakery now like you used to eh? Do you suppose he's getting a little of it yet? But I'll bet she isn't as hot as the first night or day I had you out. How about it. Remember up at LaCrosse you sure creamed your pants that night on the way back when we parked along the road. Or isn't your memory as good as mine?

Don't you wish we could have some of those times again. I would sure give anything up to be home with you again.

I have a couple of snapshots here I'll send. One is of the dining room Thanksgiving morning. I'm all alone again here tonight. The guys sure kid me a lot about staying in at night. Most of them figure anything to get away from here and take your mind off being stuck over here but I hate it worse at the Red Cross or bar than sitting around here reading or writing. It makes me so damn mad watching guys loving up these pigs that I don't care about going out except to a movie.

By the way how much stuff (product at bakery) do you make now? You never say how much stuff you make or how much in checking account or things like that.

I sure thank God I've got a good wife at home. Maybe some day Marge, I'll be able to make it up to you for as

At 10:04 one morning last week big, bluff Senator Alben Barkley rose in the caucus room of the Senate Office Building and rapped for order. Spectators filled the hall to the corners. Senator Barkley asked for absolute quiet; the acoustics are notoriously bad. The Congressional committee's investigation of Pearl Harbor had begun: in the days & weeks to follow, history would be dragged up from the dark corners, dusted off and laid out on the committee table for the world to read.

Seated with Senator Barkley were four other Senators and five Representatives. Klieg lights glared on the witness chairs. Cameramen were poised for action; there were seats for 100 reporters.

In the front row of spectators sat two men with a special interest in the proceedings: big, heavy, Admiral Husband E. Kimmel, in a grey business suit, and lean, bronzed Lieut. General Walter C. Short, also in grey. Their careers were already wrecked. Now other men would feel the stab of fact as well as the bludgeon of political innuendoes.

"Exhibit 1." In the first few days, the most interesting evidence came not from the witnesses, but from a 253-page printed booklet introduced as "Exhibit 1." This was a complete dossier of coded Japanese messages intercepted by U.S. Army and Navy Intelligence between July 1, 1941 and Pearl Harbor Day. It showed conclusively, if further proof were needed, that official Washington was intimately aware, long before Dec. 7, 1941, of the warlike intentions of the Jap Government. It also showed that matters were coming to a climax in Japan by the end of November and that a deadline for war had been set.

http://www.time.com/time/magazine/article/html

*good as you've been and you need never worry about me going out with these pigs over here because I won't.*

*Well Marge I'll be waiting to here from you. Loving and missing you more every day.*

*All my love, Bill*

December 2, 1945 - To Marge from Bill

*Dearest Marge*

*This is Sunday so no mail again today. I made it to Mass again this morning. Getting pretty good about going to Mass again, eh? I was thinking about when we were down in Texas we had to go to Temple to Mass and still made it ever Sunday.*

*I was downtown for about an hr tonight but I'd seen the show so caught a ride right back. Lot of the shows here we seen at the 90th before coming down here. I guess the 90th isn't going home on schedule. They got quarantined for the scurvy and the 80th Div. is going in their place.*

*It turned out fairly warm here again. It rained for about an hour today.*

*How's the little daughter coming. Growing like a weed, I suppose. She'll probably be walking by the time I get home. I suppose you are getting ready for Christmas. Don't forget to get the kids and folks something. I would sure give anything to be home with you then but I know I won't so we can hope I can make it for our Wedding anniversary but don't see anyway I'll get home by then either.*

*Do you know that I've got about 65 days furlough time coming but I doubt if I ever get it. Well Marg, there isn't much to write about so will quit for now. Keep up the writing. Still loving and missing you more than ever.*

*All my love*

*Your Husband, Bill*

December 3, 1945 - To Marge from Bill

*Dearest Marge*

*No mail again tonight. This makes about a week now without any mail. I guess they must be fucking it up someplace because I know you are writing.*

*We have about 300 men leaving out the Regt tonight for the 80th div. They are sure a happy bunch of guys. We had to feed them all for supper. I see by the papers where there are generals over here raising a stink about*

On December 2, General Eurico Gaspar Dutra was elected president of Brazil.

In one respect, at least, Adolf Hitler got exactly what he deserved: his devoted Eva Braun was as mean-spirited a doxy as his worst enemy could have wished.

U.S. intelligence officers culled these bits from a 1935 diary:

"It seems as though I'll never get rich. I can't do anything about that. . . . He [Hitler] was just here but no dog and no cupboard. He didn't even ask me if I had a birthday wish. So now I bought myself some jewelry. . . . Hope he likes it.

"When he says he loves me he takes it about as seriously as his promises which he never keeps. ... I have just sent him a letter. ... If I don't get an answer by 10 o'clock I'll take my 25 pills and lie down peacefully. . . .

"The weather is gorgeous and I, mistress of Germany's and the world's greatest man, have to sit at home and look at it through a window. . . .

"If only I had a dog. . . ."

http://www.time.com/time/magazine/article/html

On December 3, communist demonstrations in Athens presage the Greek Civil War.

It has got to be an Iowa thing - The noontime meal was often called *dinner*, evening meals *supper* and the late night (sometime late afternoon) snacks, *lunch*. Bill uses these designations often in his letters.

What Bill couldn't know was that many in the upper echelons of the Army were convinced that our next foe would be the USSR and that Germany would play a major part if such a conflict should it occur. Many wanted to increase troop levels in Germany.

*so many men going home. They are worrying about their jobs. There are over 200 generals in ETV here and they only need about 50 so it is easy to see why they are trying to keep the men here.*

*From the sounds of things they will be quitting the points system pretty quick. Sure surprised tonight all the guys stayed in but two. They tell us we will move to Munich Wed but I still don't believe it. The Mess hall is supposed to be all set up there with help and everything. I sure hate to move again. The only move I want to make is to go home but don't look very promising yet. How about it - do you still miss your Husband?*

*I think every day I stay over here I miss you that much more. Well Marge I'm hoping everything is going good at home and sure hope I get home soon. Still loving and missing you.*

*All my love Your Husband, Bill*

SAVE

gJr/4134

WAR DEPARTMENT
THE ADJUTANT GENERAL'S OFFICE
WASHINGTON 25, D. C.

IN REPLY REFER TO:
AGPE-A 201 Waldron, William K.
(10 Oct 45)

4 DEC 1945

Mrs. William Waldron
Waukon, Iowa

Dear Mrs. Waldron:

I refer to your letter of 10 October 1945, with inclosures, relative to the discharge of Private first class William K. Waldron, 37772525, from the military service, due to hardship.

I am pleased to inform you that instructions have been issued returning this soldier to the United States for discharge for the purpose stated provided he so desires, signs statement of such desire and there are no military reasons to the contrary.

Due to the great distance involved and the uncertainty of transportation, no statement can be made as to the date of his arrival in the United States.

Sincerely yours,

Edward F. Witsell

EDWARD F. WITSELL
Major General
Acting The Adjutant General
By: [illegible]

December 4, 1945 - To Marge from Bill

*Dearest Marge,*

*I got 5 letters from you today of 16th, 17th, 18th, 19th, and 20th but they were all postmarked the 19th or 20th. Also one from Ma and the Democrat you sent Nov. 18th. That's fast for a paper but our letters are coming slow. I suppose I won't get any more now for a few days. I should be getting those pictures of Janice in the next few days if you mailed them on Monday. Are you still nursing her any or is she strictly a bottle baby now? Say but wouldn't I have fun sitting watching you nursing her.*

*From the sounds of your one letter you and Dorothy must have had quite the conversation. From the sounds of it, I guess I'll have to leave it alone if I ever do get home. I didn't quite get what you meant when you said you would have to go through a lot of misery the first month or two when I get home. You wrote about Sis and Dale using rubbers. Dale always used them before they got married, I knew that for sure because he used to ask me where to get them. You knew that (deleted) was knocked up a few times before she was married, didn't you? And had to get them knocked.*

*How much do you have to pay Dale for working? Maybe he'll get better after he's worked a while. You know, John wasn't very good when he first got out of the Army. John has sure been swell but I suppose Stan is more interested in his woman than working now, huh? Does John even let him use the car to take her out? Or does he pester you for ours?*

*I was up to the show tonight "Tarzan and the Amazons". It wasn't bad, anything to pass the time. I caught a ride back as quick as it was over.*

*I sent that box today I wrote you about. Hope you get it soon. I see by the papers where they are trying to stop the draft but I hope they don't for a year or so yet before some of us guys get a chance to get out. There are very few guys left in this outfit now entitled to wear 3 stars on their ribbon but I'm one of them stuck. I'm still hoping the war department comes out with something to send combat men home. You asked about the 50 points getting civilian jobs. Well, guys over the Army points mark can put in for discharge and take a civilian job here or driver and interpreter with UNNRA and lot of jobs like that. Our Mess Sgt. put in for one but it hasn't gone through yet.*

*I am glad Marie is home and feeling pretty good. Say hello to them for me and wish them a Merry Christmas for me. I'm just hoping I get some mail from you over Christmas and that will make mine a lot better. Course I sure love to get your letters. What kind of an operation did Marie have anyway?*

*Well, Marge, be waiting to hear from you and take care of that daughter. I suppose you will have her talking pretty quick. I can just hear you talking to her all the time. Still loving and missing you more than ever.*

*All my love*

*Your Husband, Bill*

December 5, 1945 - To Marge from Bill

*Dearest Marge,*

*No mail today. Guess there wasn't much come in.*

On December 4, by a vote of 65 to 7, the United States Senate approved the entry of the United States into the United Nations.

*Tarzan and the Amazons* (1945): A group of archaeologists asks Tarzan to help them find an ancient city in a hidden valley of women. He refuses, but Boy is tricked into doing the job. The queen of the women asks Tarzan to help them. Starring Johnny Weissmuller and Brenda Joyce.

UNNRA stood for United Nations Relief and Rehabilitation Administration.

The U.S. was mighty close to rationing coffee again. Sad-faced Judge John C. Collet, Economic Stabilizer, sadly admitted as much last week. He announced a new subsidy program designed to get more coffee into the U.S. during the next three months. Said he: U.S. coffee supplies are so short that a subsidy is "the only alternative either to a return to rationing or to a price increase to consumers of 5% or more per pound of roasted coffee." Thus the RFC will pay about $25,000.00 to Latin American growers.

On December 5, a flight of USAF Avenger torpedo bombers, known as Flight 19, disappeared on a training exercise in the Burmuda Triangle.

After a year and a half as a combat dog in the South Pacific, Rex was carefully retrained by the Army for civilian life. Then he was turned back to his owner. For a while the German shepherd seemed as friendly and tractable as ever. But one day his front-line viciousness flared up again. In his master's backyard in Albany, Calif., Rex suddenly rose with a snarl, leaped a seven-foot fence, set upon 65-year-old Ume Akazi, a woman of Japanese descent. Before his master could pull him off, Rex gashed her knee severely.

With K-9 demobilization about half complete last week, such incidents were happily rare. Out of nearly 9,000 demobilized war dogs returned to their civilian owners, fewer than a dozen have been reported as troublemakers. Army, Marine, and Coast Guard trainers have received hundreds of letters praising the model behavior of canine veterans since their return to civilian life.

http://www.time.com/time/magazine/article/html

*Sure miss it when I don't get it. I'm enclosing a money order for $80.00. You can buy yourself whatever you want with it. I hope you buy yourself something with it cause there isn't much I can get over here and I don't think I'll ever take a furlough now. I hear by the news where they are starting to take a bunch of the ships away from here now and move them to the South Pacific. It's beginning to look like they are not going to change the occupational scene.*

*Well, I suppose by the time you get this letter it will be just about Christmas time and I'll sure be wishing I was home with you.*

*Our move to Munich was postponed again till the 15th of Dec. They keep on stalling it off. Maybe we will never move. We just came up from the kitchen a few minutes ago. Again had steak, onion, French fries and toast. Really tasted good to.*

*I hardly ever eat at mealtime but I really enjoy a lunch at night. Well, Marge, not much to write about so will be waiting to hear from you. Still loving and missing you.*

*All my love*

*Your Husband, Bill*

December 6, 1945 - To Jim snd Amanda from Bill

*Dear Folks,*

*Well, just finished a letter to Marge so thought I better get busy and write you. Got a letter yesterday that you wrote the 18th. I suppose you had a big dinner Thanksgiving and are getting ready for Christmas. Sure wished I was there with you but I know it will be quite a while yet. As yet they haven't come out with anything to let low point combat men go home. Lot of these noshier who just came over figure they will be home before us. That's sure good letting Claire Duggan out of the army. He couldn't have been in over a month or two, was he?*

*Stan and that little gal of his must be getting it pretty bad. I suppose he is pestering John for the car all the time now or don't he let him use it?*

*Has Vernon started back to work for Schultz Bros yet? How are all the kids coming? Getting bigger every day, I suppose. I bet when I get home, I'll hardly know them any more. Still got the dog yet?*

*I'm glad dad is getting better and back to work. If you don't have enough money for the down payment on the house, be sure and let me know how much you need.*

*I think that's about the first thing Marge and me will do when I get home is build a house. That is if we can get the stuff then. I think I picked out a pretty good wife, don't you? There aren't many girls who would take as good care of things when her husband is gone as she is doing, is there?*

*Well, Ma, I hope you all have a merry Christmas and hope to be with you next year. Don't forget to write and let me know the news.*

*Love,*

*Your Son, Bill*

On December 7, a patent was issued for the microwave oven.

December 10, 1945 - To Marge from Bill

*Dearest Marge,*

*Well, Marge, did pretty well today. Got 3 letters from you of 20th, 21st, and 26th. Also one from the folks and a card from Veryle. Ma wrote about the mistake I made on her address and you did to. Boy that happens so damn often but I usually catch myself. Lots of times I just start addressing it to you when I notice it and lay it aside and take another.*

*It even makes me mad when I hear of Andy getting out and me stuck here. I know if I was in the States I could get a discharge easy but getting there is the stickler. We have a bunch leaving again Wed or Thur with from 56 - 60 points. Going with the 94th Division but they won't get home till the last of Jan.*

*See by the paper where part of the 90th left for home. What I wouldn't give to be still with them. Some of the boys are downstairs frying steak now so think I'll go down as quick as I finish this letter. I usually get stuck with the job of fixing them. We get mostly canned meat all the time and it's sure lousy. We get about one fresh meat for 2 or 3 days and that's just enough for one meal.*

*I've sure been getting some of these girls that work in here pissed off at me. Had the Mess Sgt. by on the other day and I told 3 more of them they are going to get it if they don't get the lead out of their ass. We've got a bunch of pretty good workers but there are about 4 or 5 chickens and I'm giving them a rough time.*

*I suppose you can just hear me cursing them in English and most of them understand when I do. I can talk just about enough German to make them understand me and that's about all.*

*Well, Marge, getting hungry so will quit for tonight.*

Another lapse in letters with four days missing, but doesn't sound like they have moved the Company.

It's obvious in this letter that Bill is running the kitchen and that the Mess Sargeant is posted somewhere else.

As he has related earlier, his job is supposed to be filled by a Sargeant or higher grade.

On December 10, Preston Tucker, movie star, revealed plans to produce a new, 150 mph car, *The Torpedo*.

From Berlin last week, TIME Correspondent Alfred Kornfeld cabled:

"I watched the following incident in Berlin's swankiest nightclub, the Femina. At the end of a set of dances a SHAEF-patched U.S. Army captain staggered drunkenly off the dance floor. 'Is there any son-of-a-bitching Russian in the house?' could be heard all over the suddenly quiet club. His bleary eyes fell upon my guest of the evening, Russian Senior Lieut. Anton Pablov. Making his way towards our table, the American officer shouted at the top of his lungs: 'Come on out and fight, you raping bastard.'

"The club manager persuaded the captain to retake his seat, then came to our table to apologize. The Russian officer cut him short: 'It's you Germans who are the cause of all this. Get away from here.' Lieut. Pablov then walked over to the American captain, said in perfect English, 'Don't worry about it, I wish I were back home myself.' Pablov offered his hand. The American captain took it, turned back to his bottle. Red-faced, the German manager retreated to the kitchen."

http://www.time.com/time/magazine/article/html

On December 12, the Special Court of Justice sentenced NSB leader Mussert to death.

*Still loving and missing you more than ever. Keep writing.*

*All my love*

*Your Husband, Bill*

December 11, 1945 - To Marge from Bill

*Didn't get any mail today except the paper of Nov. 20 and still didn't get around to reading it. We been sitting here playing casino for the last 3 hrs and I thought it was getting time for me to write you.*

*I sure hate these bastards here more every day I stay here and they are beginning to know it to.*

*Well, how are things going at the bakery. Did you try to hire Harold yet? I suppose Swede is getting his woman pretty well broken in by now eh? I would sure like to be home to kid him but I bet the boys will enough anyway. Does Bob still go with the barber or has she got somebody else on the string now. Sure wish I had some hope of getting home but as yet there isn't a thing says I'll ever get there. I see by the paper today where they stopped these rookies just coming over from Weinlisten. I guess as quick as they were getting off the boat, they were signing up for 1 1/2 years and getting a boat right back for a 30 day furlough at home.*

*Well, Marge, take good care of that daughter of ours and maybe I'll get to see her before she gets to big yet.*

*Still loving and missing you. Keep up the writing.*

*All my love*

*Your Husband, Bill*

December 12, 1945 - To Jim and Amanda from Bill

*Dear Folks,*

*Well, thought I'd better scribble a few lines before I went to bed. Sure as hell isn't much to write about. Still haven't any idea when I'll go home. I'm still classed occupational. We've been getting quite a bit of snow and cold weather here the last couple of weeks but not near as cold as it gets at home.*

*I'm enclosing a snapshot I had in my pocket. I meant to send before.*

*Well, how are Stan and John coming with their romances. They haven't got married off yet, have they? Marge writes that John has quite a case on his gal and hardly does any drinking anymore. How is Dad coming? Is he better yet or is he still sick some? Sure hope he gets along OK.*

Well, I suppose the town is getting pretty well filled up now with all the guys getting home.

Well, Ma, better quit for now. Write and let me know all the news.

Love, Your son, Bill

December 16, 1945 - To Marge from Bill

Dearest Marge,

Well, Marge this is Sunday so no mail today. Made it to church again this morning.

Went to the show tonight, "My Reputation" with Barbara Stanwick and George Brendt but I'd seen it a few months ago at the 90th.

It's raining and freezing here tonight so I suppose there will be a lot more wrecks here tonight and tomorrow. I see by the Stars and Stripes where they are closing the port, Marsailles, the first of the year so they must not be figuring on sending many home.

Also said there would be 60,000 replacements here by the lst. It seems like they are cutting down all the time and a hell of a lot of the replacements disembark and then go right back home.

One of the boys had a pint of Bond and Lillard Whiskey today. Sure was tempted to have a few but guess I'll still wait till I get with you. Getting pretty close to a year now since we've been apart. I'll sure never forget the last night we spent together at Kansas City and how cold it was the morning I left. I suppose a lot of these guys that left there are home with their wives now and still lot of them left over here who'll never go home. I sure wish they would count the points again but don't think they will. If they would I'd have enough for discharge and to go home in Jan or Feb.

Well, Marge hope and pray I won't have to stay here much longer and can go home to you and Janice. Still loving and missing you more than ever. Keep up the writing.

All my love

Your Husband, Bill

December 17, 1945 - To Marge from Bill

Dearest Marge,

Well Marge didn't get any mail from you today but got one letter from the folks of Nov 30. Ma must sure figure I'm on my way home or am coming soon but there is no need for her to get her hopes up because it will be a

*My Reputation* (1946): Tongues begin to wag when a lonely widow becomes romantically involved with a military man. Problems arise when the gossip is filtered down to her own children.

This movie wasn't released in the US until January 16, 1946.

*Bond-Lillard* is a straight bourbon whiskey distilled in Kentucky. It was one of the few distilleries that operated throughout prohibition as it claimed to produce *medicinal spirits*.

Man was still fighting hard against the machine last week. In Chicago, seasoned liars were still holding out against the lie detector.

The machine had won the first round. When the lie detector was introduced, its grim little pointer spotted surprised liars almost as soon as they opened their mouths. Hardened virtuosos who could fool a cop, a clergyman—or even a wife—were no match for the polygraph.

But the machines and their operators both had weaknesses. The liars, gaining experience, became so accomplished that Policeman John E. Reid, Chicago's lie-detector expert, has had to modernize his machines to cope with trickier lying.

*Time Magazine December 10, 1945*

long time yet. From the looks of things now they won't have the guys with 55 points out till after Jan. None of the guys here with 55 points or less have been transferred to other outfits yet and it takes at least a month after transfer to get to the boat.

I'm all alone tonight. A couple of the boys are staying out to the airport with some friends. This outfit was supposed to be breaking up before long but it looks like they will keep it going. I guess it is just to good a thing for the officers to pass up. Our CO left for the states today. Suppose we will get a new one in a few days.

Have you heard any more about Dotseth selling the building? Sure hope he don't anyway. I don't think he will ever find a sucker to pay 14,000 for it. I think he paid 9,000 for it when he bought it 15 or 20 yrs ago.

Well Marge, I hope everything keeps on going OK there. Sure wish I was there with you. Still loving and missing you.

All my love

Your Husband, Bill

The building that Bill is writing about was where the bakery was located during this time. It was across the street from the theatre where *Main Street Pizza* is now located.

<u>December 17, 1945 - To Jim and Amanda from Bill</u>

Dear Folks,

Received your letter today of Nov. 30th. You sure were mistaken by thinking I was on the way home, eh. I guess you had better not expect me for another 6 months or so from the way things look over here. They still haven't cut the points for Occupational yet and it looks like it will be the first of Feb. before they get the 55 pointers out of here. There are a few replacements coming over but they are very few. I'm still working in the mess hall but don't have much work to do. Heard today we are supposed to move to Munich again but I still doubt it but then it will be about like them to have us move Christmas or the day before. There sure isn't a hell of a lot to write about. I hardly ever leave the post except to go down to a show and a lot of them I've seen before I came here.

From the sounds of your letters Stan must not help at all hardly at the bakery. How about that girl of his. Has he got her paying the way? This will be the second Christmas and New Years I've missed being home.

Well, Ma, write and let me know all the news.

Love, Bill

December 18, 1945 - To Marge from Bill

Dearest Marge,

I can't tell you how happy I was today to get the news about the approval. I got 7 letters from you and one from Marcella. It will probably be a week or so for the papers for me to sign will come, but there are a couple catches in it that can hold me here, transportation especially. But after January there should be plenty if they let the English women go to the States but I guess we can just hope and pray until it does go through but you keep on writing till I write and tell you to quit.

I'm glad you got a good Christmas present for your mother because nothing could be to good for her. She has been swell to us. That is sure good the way Dale is loafing around but he's always been that way and don't suppose he will ever change. You wrote about you never getting mad or ornery any more. Boy, I guess I will really have a wonderful wife to come home to, eh? But with that 130 lb. you must be like little jumbo again like when you were teaching school that winter.

From the sounds of your one letter you would like the idea if we could be together for a few days before I get home so we'll have to try doing it eh? I know Ma wouldn't like it but that will be tough shit. As long as you and me want it, that's what counts. I know for sure I won't put in for that pass to Switzerland now. I ain't going to take a chance on staying here a couple weeks longer. The only reason I wanted to go was to get a watch for you and call you anyway.

You asked about if Vernon chiseled over here. Yes, I know he did but don't think very much and I'm pretty sure he wrote Beck about it because we talked about that when I was down there. He said Beck didn't care but I still couldn't see it.

You wrote about getting the cash register cleaned up. I guess it was about time. They should be checked over once a year anyway and I guess it was about 2 or 3 years now. No, I've never ever heard from Jim since I've been overseas. I wrote him once last winter but never heard from him so haven't wrote again. I guess he don't like to write any better than I do. I suppose Lila is figuring on them living in Milwaukee after he gets home. Remember a few good nights we spent up there?

Say, John must really be reforming. Maybe he won't even have a few drinks with me when I get home if his girl gets him to quit smoking and drinking. I'm sure

Letters from both Marge and Marcella let Bill know that Plan A, working through the congressman, has worked and that the petition for Hardship Dischage has been approved. It's now up to the Army to get the paperwork processed.

On December 18, Uruguay joined the United Nations.

Nothing fascinates a Texan so much as 1) Texas; 2) another Texan. Thus, when news reached Austin a fortnight ago that the "Shooting Bull Detachment" of the "Texas Expeditionary Force" (both dreamed up by bored Texas flyers in Manila) had named Lone Star Governor Coke Stevenson CINCTEF, the homefolks called the whole thing mighty rich.

Governor Stevenson, who once promised the U.S. that Texas would make no separate peace, promptly informed the Shooting Bulls that as soon as the Army had the Far Eastern situation in hand, he would send the Texas Navy to fetch them home.

The idea tickled Texans. But they were also unhappily reminded that the Texas Navy (Honorary Commander: Admiral Chester W. Nimitz, of Fredericksburg, Texas) has no ships at the moment.

http://www.time.com/time/magazine/article/html

Not all of them want to come home. In the past two months, nearly 5,000 highpoint G.I.s in Europe have asked to be discharged on the spot. By last week about 15,000 had applied for civilian jobs with the Army and UNRRA in Germany and France.

Reasons for staying ran from A to Z. Some of the men wanted to avoid breaking off with local sweethearts or mistresses. A few were idealistically inclined to help finish the job and decided they could do more as civilians.

Another attraction lay in the prospects for graft and black-marketeering. But most of them, looking homeward with critical eyes, were prompted by the feeling that the U.S. was too confused a place to come back to just now. Whatever the job prospects at home, they knew they could save money in the jobs at hand, with salaries ranging from $1,704 to $5,800 a year, with all expenses paid. And those who joined UNRRA could also be sure of getting their fare home paid if they stayed for at least a year.

So far only a small percentage of the 15,000 have been placed—1,654 with the Army and 270 with UNRRA. Since military rank does not figure in the qualifications, many a former enlisted man has turned up in an upper-layer job. The head of UNRRA's motor pool, at a salary of $5,000, is an ex-corporal. UNRRA's chief clerk, at $4,600, is an ex-sergeant.

For the same reason, few of the officer applicants have been accepted. One young lieutenant colonel was beaten out by a more experienced ex-sergeant for the top job in a branch of the Army's Criminal Investigation Division.

http://www.time.com/time/magazine/article/html

On December 20, rationing of tires ended in the United States.

*glad to hear he has cut out the boozing, like he was doing before I left.*

*Well, Marge, I'll sure be hoping and praying that those papers come through quick and I'll get back home with you before long. Maybe our prayers are going to be answered. Keep up the writing. I've been getting the paper right along.*

*Still loving and missing you.*

*All my love Your Husband, Bill*

December 19, 1945 - To Marge from Bill

*Dearest Marge,*

*Well, Marge no mail today but guess I couldn't expect any after all I got yesterday. I'm sure sweating out those papers coming thru now. Well I guess the Regt. is finally moving. They got all packed today anyway. I guess every thing is moving except officers, this mess hall and Special Services. And we probably will be here till the first of the year so if the papers come now, I'll have to go to Munich to sign them. And our mail will be a day later because the post office and everything is moving their outfit around here that were supposed to leave this week for home have been postponed. Guess they still haven't got the ships to take care of them.*

*Boy, Marge, I'm sure hoping and praying I'm home before our wedding anniversary but that would be pretty hard to do because they keep stalling around so long. Most of the boys went to the dance at the Red Cross tonight but 2 of us are sitting here writing letters. I've got a few snapshots we took I'll enclose in this letter. Well, suppose by the time this letter reaches you, it will be New Years and we'll never forget what a happy one we spent together last year and how lucky I was finding you after I came back from the airport. Had a bottle of wine tonight. First one in a long time. We aren't getting any more beer either. 3rd Army stopped all the bottled beer so have to buy a barrel now and that's to much. Well, Marge, take good care of our daughter and maybe I'll get to see her before she gets to big yet. Still loving and missing you.*

*All my love,*

*Your Husband, Bill*

December 20, 1945 - To Marge from Bill

*Dearest Marge,*

*Well, Marge no mail today and guess it will be a few*

*days till I do. They had 25 mail bags full this morning but didn't sort it out. A lot of the men got moved today but not all of them yet.*

*I was talking to the Personal Sgt. this morning. He's the one who has a lot to say on discharges and furloughs and he told me if I had the copy with the signature on it, he could start it rolling right away but he said if the papers didn't come before next Thursday to come in and see him and he'll try to get things going for when they do come. He's got 55 points so I hope the papers come before he ships out because he can speed it up a lot. When I told him I only had 36 points he said it would take quite a while. Then he asked me how much overseas time I had and how many battle stars. I told him and he said he thought he could rush things at that rate.*

*I went down to the show tonight but had seen it so came back here and we fried steaks. Were they ever good. We still aren't certain when the kitchen moves but hope it is soon as long as everything else is up there. I know you are just as anxious for me to get home as I am and maybe if they cut orders, it won't take long. See in the paper today where the first of Jan, the points are cut to 55 for discharge.*

*Well, Marge, isn't much else to write about except still love you and hope and pray I'm home with you soon.*

*All my love, Bill*

In the nation's biggest strike, President Truman's cooling-off proposal was a hotfoot that brought instant action —but the result was not what he had called for. After 16 days of stalemate, General Motors Corp. and the C.I.O.'s United Automobile Workers' Union promptly sat down again at the collective bargaining table.

The protagonists met in Pittsburgh, and also in Detroit. The upshot was another stalemate.

Biggest news was that C.I.O. President Phil Murray and U.A.W. President RJ. Thomas took some of the play away from Strike Leader Walter Reuther. They seemed to want the strike settled in a hurry, but not on G.M.'s new proposal of a 13 1/2¢-an-hour increase. At week's end the U.A.W. Council of G.M. workers flatly turned down President Truman's request to return to work immediately. It was, in effect, a vote of confidence in Walter Reuther.

http://www.time.com/time/magazine/article/html

December 21, 1945 - To Marge from Bill

*Dearest Marge,*

*Well Marge, no mail again today. Still don't know how in the hell we will get our mail from Munich. Mess Sgt told us today that when our kitchen breaks up here, we will be reassigned. So I hope we don't move till after those papers come. If I only had the original copy the adjutant sent you, I could get it started right away but here's hoping and praying it comes in the next couple days. The Mess Hall in Munich feeds about 1500 a meal and they have it all staffed.*

*We are only feeding about 150 men here now and they are waiting for reassignment and a few going home and reenlistments. I heard over the radio tonight that Patton died today so I suppose there will be a big funeral in the states for him.*

*I'm going downtown in the morning to have my picture taken but don't know whether they will have it done before we move or not. I'll have to give him a couple*

On December 21, General of the Army George S. Patton died from injuries sustained in a car accident on December 9.

*packs of butts to hurry him up. I suppose it is impossible to get anything over here without cigarettes or candy to go along with the money. I ordered 4 baskets from the one legged soldiers at the hospital here today. Cost about 10 marks and a cartoon of butts. They are made from paper but they are nice. I'll send them as quick as I get them. I've got about 80 bucks more money that I'm supposed to have so I have to find some way of getting rid of it before I go home.*

*Well, Marge, sure hope everybody's is all right at home and I'm home with you soon.*

*Still loving and missing you. Keep up writing.*

*All my love*

*Your Husband, Bill*

December 22, 1945 - To Marge from Bill

*Dearest Marge,*

*I got 5 letters from you today of 7th, 8th, 9th, 10th, and 11th. Also one from Ma and a few Christmas cards and was I ever glad to get your letters, but don't figure on me being home to quick because even if the papers do come next week, I still wouldn't leave this outfit till around the last of Jan.*

*That is pretty nice stationary you get at the bakery, eh? Sorry to hear you still have trouble with the Ford but maybe after I get home we will trade it off and get another one. So you finally heard from Arlene again and Bill isn't coming home till next summer. At that rate he must have had under 45 points. That's what I was thinking but you wrote he had 3 stars and that would mean over 45 points but I don't see how he could when he stayed back behind till in Feb. I wouldn't doubt but Arlene goes out and does a little.*

*I'll be glad when I get a chance to see Pat's wife. Do you suppose she will be any fun on a party?*

*I'm sorry to hear Barb is no good but I'm afraid when I get home she won't stay long if she don't snap shit. I've sure got so I can chew ass since I've been here. We had a little trouble here today. One of the guys ran one of the other fellow's gal out of our room and he got pretty mad about it so finally Mess Sgt. and I got into it and finally I told the Mess Sgt. and this other guy they could love their fucking Krauts but if I find cunts fucking off on my shift, I'd have them on their hands and knees swabbing down the dining room. They all know I hate them and I've seen more combat that any guy in the kitchen*

On December 22, the Catholic People's Party was established in Utrecht, the Netherlands.

Few of the 250,000 U.S. soldiers, sailors and marines who lost their lives in World War II had ever said where they wanted their bodies to lie. Of the combat troops polled on the question early this year by TIME Correspondent Robert Sherrod, the great majority hoped that they would be buried near the scene of their last battle, with their comrades-in-arms. But war widows and parents, by & large, do not share these sentiments; by last week, the War Department alone had received nearly 90,000 letters from next of kin who want their soldiers' bodies brought back to the U.S. for reburial.

Congress heeded the expressed views of the quick, who have votes, rather than the imperfectly known wishes of the dead. Assured of passage in the House before Christmas was a bill directing the Secretary of War to return the body of a member of any of the armed forces, on request of the next of kin.

http://www.time.com/time/magazine/article/html

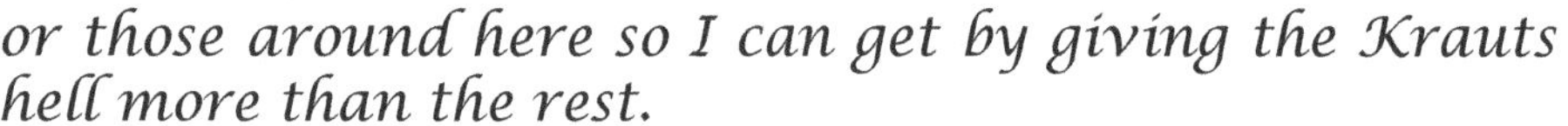

*or those around here so I can get by giving the Krauts hell more than the rest.*

*I sure hope I get over this before I get home or it probably will be rough around the bakery. I sure wish we could get Veryle working back at the bakery. From what I get she probably won't be able to find a job for the schooling she took, so maybe we can get her back. She is a good worker.*

*So I'm supposed to expect a pretty fat wife, eh? Well, maybe I can knock off a few pounds of that when I get home or will you take them off of me?*

*Well, Marge keep up the writing. I'll let you know as quick as I hear anything. All my love, Bill*

December 23, 1945 - To Marge from Bill

*Well Marge this is Sunday so no mail today but I made it to church again today. We have midnight mass downtown for Christmas so I'll try going to Mass and communion. I don't remember but I don't think I ever got to mass last Christmas. We will just have to make up for it next year. I was downtown yesterday and had my picture taken. I'll get it next week some time, I think. Also got some baskets from the one legged soldiers. I'll send them as quick as I get the picture.*

*We sure don't have many men here to feed any more. From 70 to 200 but we will probably have a bunch for Christmas. Did you find out yet what Vern is going to do or where he will be at if he works for Schultz Bros? I suppose he would like to be at Monticello.*

*Be sure and write and let me know if John gave his gal a ring for Christmas. I hardly even go downtown anymore at night. I guess I was down once last week to the show. I see in the Stars and Stripes today where the English women are going to the States between the 10th and 20th of Jan. and looks like it will stop a lot of high point men from going home. The 94th Div., which is in Augsburg, have from 55 to 59 points and they don't leave Augsburg till in Jan. I'm sure hoping I go home soon so we can be together on our wedding anniversary. Ma writes that she is sure disgusted with Stan anymore. She says that damn girl and basketball take up all his time but maybe if business is dropping off enough by now, John is able to make cookies and cakes. He should be plenty fast by now because he worked fast when I left. Well Marge, keep up the writing.*

*All my love Your Husband, Bill*

In the great square before Berlin University the new barbarians screamed "Down with un-German trash and smut!" Brownshirted students paraded by torch light, singing the Horst Wessel Lied. At midnight, May 10, 1933, when they lighted a bonfire of 20,000 books, as "subversions that strike at the root of German thought," Joseph Goebbels rhapsodized:

"These flames . . . light up the new era. . . . Spirits are awakening, and oh, century, it is a joy to live!"

Last week, Berlin's new anti-Nazi municipal government decreed a "literary cleanup." It proposed to ban from the city's libraries and bookshelves three categories of Nazi propaganda: I) the entire output of 63 publishers; 2) all the works of certain authors (Historical Novelist Bruno Brehm, Historian Werner Beumelburg) ; 3) specific books (like Hans Fallada's Iron Gustav, Hans Grimm's People Without Room).

Prime movers in the new book "cleanup" were the Russians. The British and Americans had objections in practice, but not in principle. They favored a ban "only on books containing I) Nazi, pan-German, militaristic, racial or anti-democratic ideas; 2) material tending to create popular unrest, undermine the Allied military government or divide the United Nations.

It was not quite like Goebbels' book-burning; but yet it was quite like it.

http://www.time.com/time/magazine/article/html

Captain Sam Harris, 33, of New York, a handsome, uniformed, confident figure, stepped to the microphone in Nürnberg's courtroom last week and read seriously from the first page of his brief: "The noise you hear is my knees knocking. They haven't knocked like this since the day I asked my wife to marry me." To cover their embarrassment, the British lawyers smiled. The Russians shrugged; such naiveté was just one more thing they did not understand about Americans. But the Russians were not surprised when Harris went on to make a highly effective argument. They have become openly enthusiastic about the way Prosecutor Robert H. Jackson and his assistants are conducting the U.S. case against the Nazis.

Individual defendants were inexorably linked to definite crimes against humanity. Field Marshal Wilhelm Keitel was not always engrossed in high strategy; he assisted in rounding up slave labor by ordering Polish homes burned. Alfred Rosenberg, the philosopher, was involved in an order that babies born to Russian women on slave-labor trains be thrown from the windows. Albert Speer, Director of War Production, urged more SS brutality to accelerate the working pace of the slaves.

http://www.time.com

*Over 21* (1945): Despite his age (39), Max, against the wishes of the newspaper's Board of Directors headed by owner Robert Drexel Gow, enlists in the army to do what he considers his patriotic duty during World War II. Paulie decides that once Max is in Officer's Candidate School in Florida, she will move there temporarily into a small bungalow to be close to him, despite the fact that he will have to live in the barracks and will have little time to spend with her. The film starred Irene Dunne and Charles Coburn.

December 24, 1945 - To Marge from Bill

Dearest Marge,

I got only one letter from you today of the 12th. I was talking to our First Sgt. tonight and the papers still haven't come. Sure wished you would of sent the one you got but maybe they will come soon.

I'm figuring on going to confession about 10:30 tonight and then go to Midnight mass. We got a jeep this morning to go with. Was downtown looking around and got one of these Bavarian pipes, cost me a buck and a few candy bars. Also bought an oil painting which cost me $60. They are higher than hell. I'll have to send it without the frame because it is too big to send with the frame and all (See Page 276). I guess frames are plenty cheap in the states. It is pretty near impossible for civilians to get this stuff.

I have quite a time trying to barter with them in my poor German and they try sticking you if they can. I can understand them pretty well but I can't talk it worth a damn. The only trouble now we have to go to Munich to mail packages. I hope you got the perfume I sent by now. Be sure and write and let me know if you did.

One of our Captains was telling us today when our mess hall breaks up, we were going to supervise at the General mess. I guess he's sure a Jerk. One of the guys went there about a month ago but guess he is going home now. I'm sure hoping by the time I get home, we'll be able to get some help because I hate to think of working nights again but I think if I get on the yeast man's ass, he'll find a baker.

Well, Marge think I better get ready to go to church. I'll sure be thinking of you.

All my love

Your Husband, Bill

December 25, 1945 - To Marge from Bill

Dearest Marge,

Well Marge, the big day is over. Just came back from the show "Over 21". Pretty good to. We had a swell dinner today. About everything anyone would want. I went to Midnight Mass last night. They had it at the Ludwickbon. That is a big theater that holds about 2,000. When we came back we had turkey sandwiches before we went to bed. They called tonight and told me we move Thurs morning so I suppose I will have to start *packing again in the morning. I told them it would take about 3 2 1/2 ton trucks with trailers so they said they would send them from Munich to be here at 8:30 so it kinda looks like we will move this time. The other fellows are all still out yet. Don't know where the hell they went tonight. It seems like there is getting less all the time to write about. I'm sure hoping I hear something this week on those papers. Know as quick as they come, the First Sgt. and Personnel Sgt will push them through as fast as they can for me.*

*I went to confession and communion last night. The first time I've been there in quite a while but one of the boys I went with said it was the first time in 4 years for him. Before he went, I was sitting telling him what to say when he walked in. I guess the guys around us didn't know what the hell to think. He said he would of went before only he was scared to go after so long being away. I'll bet his wife will be happy when she hears because she knows he hadn't been going the last few years and guess she is a good Catholic.*

*Well, Marge, better quite for tonight. Still loving and missing you.*

*All my love*

*Your Husband, Bill*

<u>December 26, 1945 - To Marge from Bill</u>

*Well Marge no mail again today so I should be getting quite a bunch tomorrow. We got things pretty well packed to move in the morning. So I guess we are finally going to move this time. It seems every time I pack my bags to move, I have more clothes. A year ago at this time, I was on my way home. Sure wish I was now but it looks like it is taking those papers a long time to come. I went down to get our pictures today but they won't be finished till next week so I'll have to get back to Augsburg someway.*

*If we are in the kitchen system, I'll be able to get a jeep. We haven't been getting any Stars and Stripes the last couple days. Guess they took a little vacation over the Holidays.*

*I'm sure hoping and praying I get home before our Wedding anniversary. It sure would be wonderful to spend it together this year. A couple of the cooks are pretty blue here today having to go off and leave their pigs here. I guess the kitchen up there has all men working in it.*

May the Infant Christ Child shower His choicest blessings upon you and your loved ones, this day and throughout the coming year.

Father Doyle
Father Podbielski
Father Rush

— MIDNIGHT MASS —

Augsburg, Germany

1945

Fiorello LaGuardia, New York's outgoing Mayor, Liberty magazine's incoming radio commentator, had in hand 1) a shiny new Packard sedan, free, from the U.S. Conference of Mayors; 2) two more jobs. Beginning Jan. 6 he will do a local broadcast for a dairy firm, and write a weekly Sunday column for the leftist Manhattan tabloid PM, which took a proud half-page to announce the news.

This letter is postmarked Munich, Germany.

HEADQUARTERS COMPANY
THIRD MIL GOVT REGT

Waldron, William K.
(Name)

Te c 4 37772528
(Rank) (ASN)

The bearer is assigned to this headquarters and authorized to work in and circulate within the city of Munich from 0500 to 2300 hours.

Expires__________

Signature__________

Clayton B. Doughty
CLAYTON B. DOUGHTY
Capt., CAC,
Commanding

*How's our little daughter coming? Still growing? Maybe I'll get home before she starts walking and talking yet. I hope you keep on writing till I write and tell you to quit because a guy's never sure of anything here. The 94th Div. was supposed to leave here quite a while ago to go home and they are still in Augsburg. I got a box today. I'll probably send it after I get to Munich.*

*Well Marge, I'm still loving and missing you more than ever and hope I'm with you soon.*

*All my love*

*Your Husband, Bill*

December 27, 1945 - To Marge from Bill

*Dearest Marge,*

*Well Marge no mail again today but I'm sure hoping I do have some tomorrow. Well, we finally got moved to Munich. We are in with 3rd Army rear. I thought M.G. had a setup in Augsburg but this got it beat all to hell. They have 31 women who just take care of the kitchen personnel's room, make their beds, shine their shoes, and everything like that. 5 of us guys got the same room together so it will be pretty nice. The only thing I don't like is we will be transferred to this outfit and it is a detachment that will be here after the first of the year. I'm hoping they won't put us to work for a day or two yet so we can find our way around here. We've got nice beds, with springs and clean with white sheets on them. Can't get over it. Probably won't be able to sleep tonight. It's been so long since I've slept in a soft bed.*

*Well, Marge, I think getting transferred will slow me up a little getting home but not much if those papers would only come. I sure hope things are going a little better for you at the bakery now. I suppose when I get home it will probably take me a couple months before I can start taking on work. Sure haven't did any since I've been overseas, even made the Krauts load and unload my kitchen, barrack bags and other shit I brought along. Well, maybe tomorrow I get a chance to see what everything is like around here. Still loving and missing you.*

*All my love*

*Your Husband, Bill*

December 28, 1945 - To Marge from Bill

*Dearest Marge,*

*I got one letter from you today of Dec. 13th and also*

one from DeMarco. He's still in Germany here to. I went over to see the Sgt. Major today and had a talk with him and he took me in to see the officer that takes care of Discharges when they come through. He told me the papers go from Washington to 3rd Army HQ and Co just a few miles from here and from there he will get them. He said as quick as he gets it, he will let me know and try getting me out of here a few days afterwards so I'm sure hoping it don't take much longer.

*Nuremberg Palace of Peace*
Pictured on a postcard that Bill sent home.

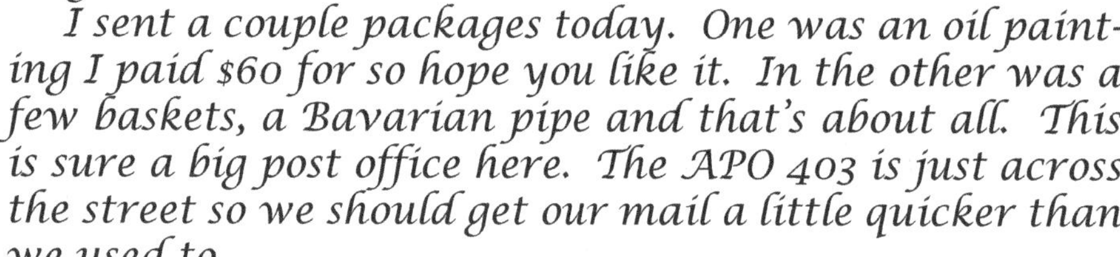

I sent a couple packages today. One was an oil painting I paid $60 for so hope you like it. In the other was a few baskets, a Bavarian pipe and that's about all. This is sure a big post office here. The APO 403 is just across the street so we should get our mail a little quicker than we used to.

I start working in the morning. Work every day but only at meal times. Take count of how many are eating and see if they are all in proper uniform. I guess I'll put in about 5 hours a day. I told the Mess Sgt I was waiting for a discharge to come through. He gave me the softest job there was there. I went down to the show tonight. Its about 3 blocks from where I sleep. "Paris Underground" was the name of it. Wasn't to bad but they have a poor projector there.

You never mentioned what you have to pay Dale for working or any of the rest so I kinda been wondering. Oh, Marge, but I'm sure praying they get the papers here pretty quick. Still loving and missing you and hope to be home with you soon. Keep writing.

All my love Your Husband, Bill

December 29, 1945 - To Marge from Bill

Dearest Marge,

Well Marge another day gone by and no mail but I guess you probably aren't getting mine very good either from the looks of the Stars and Stripes. See by it no mail has gone to the States for a week on account of bad weather. Tomorrow is Sunday so nothing then either. I'll have to find out where the church is in the morning.

The rumor is going around pretty strong that the 90th will get another battle star for Czech so if they do it will make 4 for me and 5 more points. The 71st Div. called HQ here today to find out if it has been confirmed

On December 27, Twenty-eight nations signed an agreement creating the World Bank.

Terror strikes were carried out against British military bases in Palestine by Arabs.

*Paris Underground* (1945): Among the terrified refugees jamming the roads out of Paris in 1940 are Kitty de Mornay, a rich American divorced from her French husband, and her companion Emmeline (Emmy) Quayle. A German patrol orders their car back to Paris and, en-route, they stop at an inn where they find a wounded RAF flyer, Lieutenant Gray. They hide him in the luggage compartment of their car. Starring Constance Bennett and Gracie Fields.

On December 28, Congress officially recognized the Pledge of Allegiance.

Three members of the German Social Democratic Party drove through the evening rain. Near the Neukölln Rathaus an American Military Police jeep halted the car. Party Chairman Max Fechner, Secretary Fritz Schreiber, Committeeman Herman Schlimme followed the MPs into their headquarters at the Hermannplatz.

Inside, a sergeant brusquely asked why they had been speeding. Schreiber, the driver, replied that he had driven at a moderate pace. Grey-haired, austere Fechner then produced his identity papers to show that he was party chairman, holder of Card No. 17 from the Committee for the Victims of Fascism, and authorized to drive a car.

What happened next was the subject of an Army investigation last week. According to Schreiber, the sergeant shouted: "Shut your trap, you swine," punched Fechner in the face.

Two hours later another shift of MPs took over. The new sergeant made Fechner stand motionless with his face to the wall. After an hour and a half, the old man, an ex-concentration camp prisoner, collapsed. The sergeant ordered him up again. "You Nazi pig," he yelled, "for twelve years you raised your hand in the Nazi salute, and here you don't want to stand up!" At 2 a.m. the three Germans were turned over to the German police.

While U.S. military authorities investigated the complaint, other U.S. officers and civilians continued their task of teaching Germans to like and respect democracy.

http://www.time.com/time/magazine/article/html

yet. I sure hope it is. I guess I'll go to bed early again tonight. It is raining out now but it's been just like spring the last couple of days. I suppose with the mail tied up you probably figure I'm on my way home but don't get your hopes up to high of me being home for a while yet, because I'm liable to be here a month yet. But I'm hoping I'm not. The quicker I leave here the quicker I get home. I hope you have sent the papers you got from the Adjutant General in case the other don't come through. They can send a trace with yours.

Well, Marge better quit for tonight. Think I'll write a quick letter to the folks yet. Still loving and missing you and praying I'm home with you soon.

All my love

Bill

December 29, 1945 - To Jim and Amanda from Bill

Dear Folks,

I haven't been getting any mail the last week. Sure hope you are still writing and not thinking I'm on the way home yet. Course it's hard telling how long it will take the papers to come yet. They go to the 3rd Army HQ. and then here. We have finally moved to Munich. Have nice beds here. Clean white sheets. The P.W. make our beds, shine our shoes, and clean up our room every day. The only bad thing about this place, they have a colonel or general inspecting it every day. I work about 5 hours a day here. Count how many eat and see that they are in proper uniform so I have in-between meals off but there isn't much to do. They have a big Red Cross club a few blocks away and a theater. We feed over a thousand men a meal. You would think in that many, I would see somebody from around home but don't. See a lot of guys I knew back in the 98th but that's about all.

I'm sure hoping I get home in time for Marge's and my wedding anniversary but if the papers don't come pretty quick, I won't because it takes a couple months to get processed and get home from here. A lot of boys here are supposed to get to some other outfit next week to go home. Probably the 102th Div. It's supposed to go home the first part of Feb.

We have been having swell weather the last couple days, just like spring. I suppose you have plenty of snow at home by now. How is Dad and every one else? I hope everybody is all right.

I suppose the kids are getting so big I'll hardly know

*them. I am sure anxious to get a look at my daughter. Marge writes she sure is a good girl. Well, folks, guess I better quit for tonight. As quick as I hear anything, I'll write and let you know. Keep writing.*

*Love, Your son, Bill*

December 30, 1945 - To Marge from Bill

*Dearest Marge*

*Well Marge sure hope I get some mail tomorrow. Only got one letter from you in a week and a half now but don't suppose you are getting mine very well either. I found where the chapel was this morning and made it to Mass on time. They have it way up on the fourth floor of one of the buildings here.*

*I went to the show today "Shady Side" I think was the name of it with Ginny Simms. Went by the P.W. cage on the way. It was all closed in with high barbwire fence. When we went by, a couple of them were just getting in. They have a buzzer on the gate to get in. I think that's about the best I have ever seen. Sure miss out on my night lunches here. I guess they don't monkey around the kitchen at night here.*

*See by the paper today where the 94th is supposed to leave on the 9th of Jan but they are still around here yet so they will have to go in a hurry to make it.*

*I hear on the radio where they are still going to send the Lima (Limey) women to the states this month. Sure makes a lot of guys mad who are still stuck here with enough points for a discharge. Well Marge sure hoping and praying to see you soon.*

*All my love*

*Your Husband, Bill*

December 31, 1945 - To Marge from Bill

*Dearest Marge,*

*No mail today and guess I won't get any till Wed. The mail isn't coming in or going out for today and tomorrow. I guess nobody is working. I'm sure spending a lot different New Years Eve this year than last. Do you remember how happy we were we got to spend it together in that little room in Kansas City. What a night. I know I'll never forget it.*

*I guess I'll stay in and read tonight. Most of the guys are going over to the bar. I guess they have beer, wine and a little hard stuff there. I see by the orders that came out yesterday I made Sgt. but don't think it will*

On December 31, ratification of the United Nations Charter is completed.

If Bill is right about the star being Ginny Simms, the movie he saw had to be *Broadway Rhythm* released in 1944 as that's the only movie she was in around that time. In the movie, George Murphy plays a successful Broadway musical comedy producer named Johnnie Demming. He needs a star for his new show. He's smitten with the glamorous film star, Helen Hoyt (Ginny Simms), and offers the part to her, but she turns him down because she wants to be sure she's in a hit.

Ginny Simms shown above with Robert Walker.

In Nürnberg, enterprising reporters had interviewed Hermann Göring and other Nazi defendants by relaying questions through defense attorneys. The war crimes tribunal last week told counsel to cut it out; the Russians had complained.

In Le Havre, biggest port of embarkation for homebound G.I.s, the U.S. Army port area commander demanded to look over all correspondents' stories. His reason: dispatches reporting friction between the French and the G.I.s had caused "embarrassment."

In Tokyo, General MacArthur talked about "unfettering" the Japanese press—but still kept it on a leash.

Censorship was still news—and still impeding the news.

*Time Magazine December 31, 1945*

*hold me here any longer than being a T15. I've sure been sweating out those papers coming ever since I've heard from you. If they only come before they transfer the Sgt. Major and Personnel Sgt. out to go home, it will help a lot. Cause they have more say about how you go home than the officers and I know they will do me a favor if they can. They have been all after me to try to straighten things out in the kitchen here so they get better food but I'm keeping my nose out of it this time. Back at Augsburg I changed menus and everything else to fix the meals better and they all know it, but I'm not going to do it here in case I'd be liable to get stuck. A couple of the boys just come in with some cognac and wine so I'm having a glass of wine. I think when I get home if I can buy good wine, I'll hardly ever drink whiskey cause I like the wine a lot better. But the wine I drank in the States is all together different than the wine we drink over here.*

*Oh, Marge but what I wouldn't give to be with you and the baby now but maybe it isn't to far off. I sure do love you or else I wouldn't be sitting in here tonight.*

*Loving and missing you more than ever.*

*All my love*

*Your Husband, Bill*

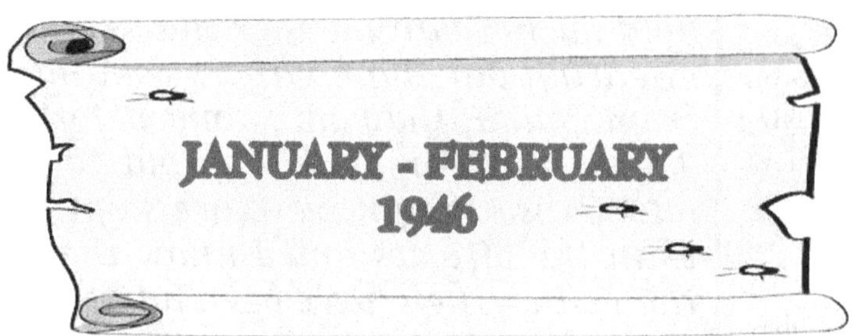


Certainly American military service is an honorable means of Duty to Country. There is the ever-present sense of "duty and service" plus the military protocol that permeates every hour of the day. For every American serviceman the "hurry-up-and-wait" essence of military life creates both boredom and resentment at times during their term of enlistment.

Bill certainly is revealing another side of his personality throughout his tour of Occupational Forces service. For one, the war is over - since the end of May in the European Theater of Operation and since August in the Pacific. Also, there seems to be an excess of troops in Europe. Many of them are waiting and waiting for discharge orders. There is much anticipation for orders of transfer which could mean, prior to August, being sent to the brutal combat going on in the Pacific Theater. At the same time many of the high ranking officers in the Army were convinced that the next war could be in the near future, that it would be against the Soviet Union and that Germany would be central in that conflict. Further, means for transporting men back home were being used beyond capacity.

Marge and Jan

At the troop level, Bill was an excellent combat infantryman but the inaction of the Occupational Forces is another thing. By November, Bill knows he is soon to be discharged but the US Army seems to him to have adopted the ultimate waiting game.

Bill seems to get more "testy" in that the anticipation of his discharge orders being received is high. Yet the uncertainty of the orders actually arriving is creating a great deal of angst. This is noticeable in the tenor of his letters to Marge. His letters are short and cryptic. He is trying to emit a calm yet it is obvious he is anxious. Plus he is trying to not create stress in Marge's own anticipation of their re-uniting.

From what we can discern from Bill's letters, Marge's letters show unrestrained excitement. She states that she is mindful that Bill may not get home to her (and to baby Jan) until March but one can feel the unbridled hope that she wants him home sooner than later.

In spite of the lack of transport ships and the possibility of another war, at the troop level it appears to Bill that the military is dragging its feet in terms of their obligation to cut orders for his discharge. He urges Marge to try civilian lines of communication and she contacts Congressman Henry Talle about the delay. As we have seen, the Congressman was sympathetic to their plight and pushed the Army to act in their behalf.

Marge sent a copy of her letter of inquiry to Representative Talle to Bill (received by him on January 22). Bill, in turn, submitted the letter to his Headquarters Personnel Sergeant. Anytime a Congressman gets involved in a military matter and that involvement includes communication from the Congressman to the soldier's unit, it usually results in immediate action.

Finally!! On January 23 the orders for Bill's discharge will arrive. He will be on his way, heading west from Germany on his way to the United States and Illinois (Camp Grant) for discharge and into the arms of his long waiting wife.

Marge will make plans to take the train to Camp Grant to be with Bill upon his discharge.

And, certainly, the Irish were celebrating!

January 1, 1946 - To Marge from Bill

Dearest Marge,

Well Marge I'm sure hoping I get some mail tomorrow. I got in the mailroom this morning but there wasn't any for me but a few of the other guys got some. I sure hope you haven't quit writing figuring I'll be home. I'll write and tell you when not to write anymore.

We all went to Mass this morning. They even had a pile of officers there this morning. I went to the show tonight. "Love Letters" with Jennifer Jones. Sure thankful that it is over too!

Well Marge, ain't much else to write about so guess I'll quit for tonight. Still loving and missing you.

All my love,

Your Husband
Bill

What a great way to spend New Years Day. *Love Letters* is a story about WWII and a British soldier (Joseph Cotton) who has been writing love letters for a friend, but finds himself falling in love with the woman (Jennifer Jones) from afar. When his friend is killed, the letter writer tries to find out more about the woman, but finds his way obscured by a scandal no one will talk about. As he investigates he discovers that the disappearance of the woman is related to the mysterious circumstances of his friend's death.

January 2, 1946 - To Marge from Bill

Dearest Marge,

Another day without any mail. I thought for sure I would get some today but didn't. The last letter I got from you was the 13th. It seems like it takes mail longer every day to get here.

They say they are changing the APO system now. We will get our mail from one to three days sooner but I have to see it first. See by the paper where a big mail plane crashed bringing up all our mail in France so I might have had a letter or two on that.

Haven't done anything all day. Went over to get paid and had a short inspection. Our old Mess Sgt. back in Augsburg shot himself today with a pistol. Guess it isn't very serious. So he probably won't be laid up very long. I sure hope you got the first box I sent and will get the picture and the other box all right. Sure wished there was something I could buy around here but you have to get a pass to get out of here so I never bother leaving the post. I guess I still have about a hundred bucks more than I'm supposed to. I sure can't wait until the day I get home with you but as yet, I haven't heard a thing about going. Well, Marge keep up the writing,

Still loving and missing you.

All my love

Your Husband
Bill

This letter is postmarked Munich, Germany.

On January 1, Emporer Hirohito of Japan announced that he was not a god.

In Budapest, the National Assembly proclaimed Hungary to be a republic. This, over the objection of the Soviet Union but with the backing of the other Allies.

January 3, 1946 - To Marge from Bill

*Dearest Marge,*

*Well Marge I finally got some mail from you again of the 17th and 18th. They sure have the mail system all fucked up now but maybe they will have it straightened out in a few days. You wrote about John going on his vacation as soon as I get home but I think he'll have to wait awhile till after I get used to things again. You know it's been a long time since I've did what you call 'a good days work' and it's been 1 1/2 years now since I've done work like in the bakery. Sorry to hear about Stan not wanting to do nothing. If he don't snap out of it when I get home, he just won't work there at all. In another 6 months I don't think jobs and money will be so plentiful. I think the boys pulled a fast one on you when they said something was wrong with the big boiler and ran water all over everything. The only thing that could do that is leaving all of the valves open.*

*We got a new Colonel here from the states and is he ever chicken shit. Boy, he's been raising hell with all the officers and everybody else but maybe somebody will take a shot at him and put him where he belongs.*

*Well, Marge the days are gradually slipping by and I'm still in Germany. I'm beginning to doubt whether I'll make it home in time for our wedding anniversary now. I'm going to wait another week and if I don't hear nothing, I'll see the Colonel - maybe he'll take me to 3rd Army and find out if they ever sent the orders from the States or not. I just read an article in the Stars and Stripes where the War Department wrote a kid's folks he was on the way home and then never sent any order for his return. So mine could be the same deal but I hope not. I'm sure praying every day that it comes through pretty quick and I know you are just as anxious as me. Better try to get Veryle to go back to work for us if she is still there yet.*

*Well Marge, still loving and missing you more than ever and hope to be home with you and Janice soon.*

*All my love,*

*Your Husband,*
*Bill*

January 4, 1946 - To Marge from Bill

*Dearest Marge,*

*I got one letter from you today of the 21st and one from Marquardt, Beck and the folks and a card from*

A boy and a girl stood before an elderly clergyman in an 18th-Century, bomb-damaged Berlin church. The girl, blonde, in her late 'teens, was well dressed, well fed, carefully made up. She spoke for the two: "Will you marry us?" The silent youth, in his early twenties, looked better fed than most Germans, although his blue suit did not fit him well. The girl readily produced her identification papers, but he said: "I lost mine in the bombing . . . she can vouch for me."

The Pfarrer noticed his accent and began to question him. The boy admitted: "I am an American." He pleaded: "But please marry us. I'll pay 200 cigarettes and 20 candy bars. How about it?" Although soldiers in the U.S. Army of Occupation are forbidden to marry German girls, the German minister knew of no law which would bar him from performing the ceremony. He married them.

The bridegroom was a member of the 78th ("Lightning") Division. He knew that if U.S. authorities learned of the marriage they would probably annul it and punish him. But with only 23 points, he faced another year in Berlin, so the chance seemed well worth taking.

In another year, he also figured, the marriage ban might be relaxed. U.S. authorities might even be transporting German wives of G.I.s to the U.S.

For last week's secret ceremony was neither the first nor the last of its kind. Clandestine G.I.-Fräulein marriages are expected to increase this winter. A G.I. husband can provide his Frau with extra food, fuel to heat her room.

http://www.time.com/time/magazine/article/

Johnny Angel (1945): Johnny Angel (George Raft) sets out to learn who hijacked a gold shipment from his father's ship and killed his father, the captain. He is joined in the search by Paulette (Claire Trevor), whose own father has been killed by the hijackers.

The first commercial all-freight flight across the Atlantic took off from LaGuardia Field for London with $41,000 worth of merchandise. The pioneering Pan American DC-4 hauled a 3,520-lb. cargo: 1,900 lbs. (1,000 meals) of frozen food; 225 lbs. of mink and Alaska lynx furs valued at $36,000; consumer staples, such as pipes, tobacco, fruit cake, fresh pineapple, clothing, cosmetics, books, stationery, radio equipment.

The nose is no respecter of perfume price. Tests taken among students at the University of California showed that expensive brands ran about nose-&-nose with inexpensive. Another conclusion: after eight hours, there's no difference in lasting quality between expensive and inexpensive brands.

The first shipment of crude rubber to the U.S. from the Far East since 1942 arrived in New York. The Canton Victory brought in 8,100 tons. Another 275,000 to 350,000 tons of natural rubber are expected to reach the U.S. this year.

http://www.time.com/time/magazine/article/

Jean Ann. I haven't got any of your letters from the 13th to the 18th. You mentioned Dale saying John paid too much for the ring so from the sounds of that John must of broke down and bought his girl a ring, eh?

Ma didn't say anything in her letter about it so she must not know it yet, eh? Did you ask him if he has tried it out yet? I went to the show tonight: "Johnny Angel" with George Rafft and Ann Sheridan.

Our POW's have really been working today getting the rooms all cleaned up. I guess the Colonel is making an inspection in the morning and everything is supposed to be just like in the States. I wish they'd sent the old bastard back because all he's doing is fucking up things here. We are supposed to have all our clothes with the shoulder patches, stripes and everything else on but my jacket is the only thing I got patches on and no stripes on anything. The First Sgt told me the other day it's about time I sew some on.

I was talking to some boys from the 94th today and they were supposed to pull out tomorrow for the States but its been postponed again till the 9th. They have from 56 points on up.

Well think I'll drop the folks a line yet before I go to bed, so I'll be waiting to hear from you.

Still loving and missing you.

All my love,

Your Husband
Bill

<u>January 4, 1946 - To Jim and Amanda from Bill</u>

Dear Folks,

Well, Ma, got Jean Ann's card and your letter today. Tell her thanks for me. I hope she is over the flu by now. I suppose you hate to get my letters saying I'm still here but still haven't heard anything yet about going home. From the sounds of things, they are still short of ships. Some outfit that was supposed to go home a week ago is still here and has been postponed till next week. They haven't got down to taking the 55-point guys out of the outfits to send home yet. You gave me Clem Sweeney's address. I suppose I could get a jeep and go out to see him. It isn't far from here but guess I'm not that anxious to see him. I never cared too much for him anyway.

Glad to hear Vernon is working but is he going to get pretty good money or will they screw him again? It is about the coldest here now that it's been yet. Probably *about zero. I'm sure taking life easy. Have a PW to make my bed, shine my shoes and everything like that. We have a good barber who cuts our hair and shaves us. Don't cost nothing. All I do is check the men coming in at mealtime, 2 meals every other day. See that they are in proper uniform and make out a report how many eat a day. But I'm afraid it's too good to last, if I don't get out of here pretty quick they'll probably find something else for me to do.*

*The mail has been coming through awful poor lately. Well, Ma, I sure hope I get home pretty soon. Say hello to everybody for me*

*Love,*

*Bill*

January 5, 1946 - To Marge from Bill

*Dearest Marge,*

*I didn't get any mail today. Sure hope I do on Monday. If those papers haven't been passed by the 3rd Army yet, it looks like I'll be stuck here for quite a while yet.*

*Everybody is sure mad and down in the dumps here tonight. We just got the news over the radio where General MacNarney told the press that after Feb, only 90,000 a month will leave here whether they are eligible for discharge or not. And if they keep cutting the points or let guys out any length of service, they will still stay here for 3 months afterwards because the War Department hasn't been sending over hardly any replacements. So Marge maybe you better have Marcella write them and find out whether they even sent the papers here and if so why they aren't coming through.*

*According to the radio tonight guys with under 50 points will be here till next July. This fucking Army is doing everything possible to keep the guys in and to get them to enlist. I have sure found out our American Army is one of the biggest political machines in the world. I hear this new Colonel we have is going to issue guns to everybody here. I sure hate to think of it if he does because most of the boys in M.G. are Infantry men and they will sure be shooting things. I sure feel the lowest tonight I have in a long time.*

*Lot of the boys are sure getting drunk and I suppose they'll be uptown beating the hell out of the Krauts. But I'll still leave the booze and the Krauts alone. I've hardly even left this place since I've been here. If the people at home don't keep putting on the pressure, they are li-*

New York's Governor Thomas E. Dewey, mouse-quiet since the Democratic sweep in the New York City elections, suddenly spoke up in a voice that had loud tones of renewed hope.

First he proposed a state rent-control law to replace OPA ceilings if Congress lets them expire this year. Such action might not endear Tom Dewey, titular head of the G.O.P., to those Republican Congressmen who take the view that price controls are an unnecessary evil born of the New Deal. But it sounded like smart long-term politics for wooing the man who might be in the street except for rent controls. It also sounded realistic to most economists, who agree, however reluctantly, that the free supply-&-demand economy which was an inevitable war casualty could not return full-blown the day war ended.

Next, rumors began leaking from the State Capitol that Governor Dewey, who can boast a $500 million war-accumulated treasury surplus, would soon announce a new cut in taxes - possibly reducing state income taxes to half the prewar level.

Finally the Governor showed up in person on Staten Island, where his administration is starting a $5 million project for converting Army barracks into temporary housing for veterans. Wearing his inevitable Homburg with the preciseness of a toy soldier, he accepted an honorary membership in the A.F. of L.'s United Brotherhood of Carpenters & Joiners, thereupon took six hammer strokes to drive the first nail into a two-by-four. The resulting picture looked for all the world like candidate-with-Indian or candidate-with-dead-fish, only a little better.

http://www.time.com/time/magazine/article/

able to keep us here forever.

You can't realize how many guys are going to hell since they have been over here and in a way, you can't blame them because there is nothing to look forward to. Well Marge, guess I've bitched enough for tonight so better quit. Still loving and missing you.

All my love,

Your Husband
Bill

January 6, 1946 - To Marge from Bill

Dearest Marge,

Well Marge starting another week. Went to church again this morning and then myself, First Sgt. and our supply Sgt. went uptown to put in calls for home but they are all booked up till the 14th. They open up to book calls again on Thursday for the 14th on so we are going up early Thursday morning and wait for them to open up and maybe we'll get a chance to call. They can only book 48 calls for every 4 days so maybe we'll have to get there a couple hrs before they open. Maybe I'll have called you before this letter gets there but if not, be expecting me to call. I went to the show a little while ago "Tender Grapes" with Edward Robinson.

There sure isn't anything to write about here. All we have been hearing the last couple days over the radio and in the papers is the bad news about redeployment. We are having the coldest weather here now that we have yet. Close to zero the past week. Well, Marge I sure hope I get home with you and Janice before long but it don't look very good now. Still loving and missing you more than ever.

All my love,

Your Husband
Bill

January 7, 1946 - To Marge from Bill

Dearest Marge,

I got one letter from you today that you wrote on Christmas eve. Sure sorry to hear that you aren't getting my mail but mine isn't coming through very good either. I went over and seen the Regimental officer about my discharge today so he wrote a letter to Third Army to find out if they got any word on it. We are supposed to go through channels to see the Regimental officer but I knew that would take a couple more days so I didn't. I

*Our Vines Have Tender Grapes* (1945): Life in small town Wisconsin. Selma (Margaret O'Brien) and Arnold (James Craig), aged 7 and 5, pal around together between their two farms. Selma has a newborn calf that her father gave to her which she named 'Elizabeth'. Nels (Edward G. Robinson) is the editor of the Fuller Junction Spectator and the kids just call him 'editor'. Viola is the new school teacher from the big city. While Nels wants to marry Viola, Viola does not want to live in a small quiet, nothing happening town. The biggest news is that Lars Faraassen has built a new barn.

wouldn't be surprised if they don't have a riot among the soldiers over here if they don't do something about getting the guys home. The Stars and Stripes sure blasted Patterson and MacNarney and I guess they have been organizing the Non Coms to raise hell with the General.

You still only see about one out of 10 guys working over here, so it looks like the officers are just trying to keep the men here so they will keep their rank. You can't imagine how well an officer lives over here and he can save every cent he makes, most of them get their liquor and everything else for nothing. I still am taking things pretty easy in the mess hall. I guess I must work at least 4 hrs every other day. Rough, eh? We got about 25 or 30 guys working in the mess hall plus about 150 Krauts and Hungarians and it would only take about 5 or 10 men at the most. I'm sure hoping and praying I'll make it home by our wedding anniversary but I kind of doubt it now.

Keep up the writing. Still loving and missing you.

All my love,

Your Husband
Bill

On January 7, the Allies recognized the Austrian Republic, with the borders established in 1937, and divided the country into four occupation zones.

Cambodia became an autonomous state within the French Union.

A network-manager was hired last week as a station-manager. Both the station and the man were outstanding, and both he and the station felt lucky. The manager was young (35), shrewd Lieut. Colonel John S. Hayes, who built and bossed the crackajack American Forces Network in Europe. The station was the New York Times' 10,000-watt WQXR, which devotes 80% of its broadcast day to "the best in music," the rest to frequent news and infrequent commercials.

http://www.time.com/time/magazine/article/

January 8, 1946 - To Marge from Bill

Dearest Marge,

Well Marge, no mail today and the news still isn't any better. Sure hope things improve pretty quick. I think things will get bad around here if they don't. We had a few guys quit work today that are eligible for discharge and say they aren't going to do anything till they send them home.

I guess our old Mess Sgt. is going to get a court martial for shooting himself and for having ammo on his person. I sure hope you are getting my mail by now and don't get the idea I'm on my way home yet for awhile. Sure wish I was. I hope everybody is all right at home and everything is going good at the bakery. You haven't found out from John when the big wedding is going to be? Has he been out to the farm since the first time? We haven't got a radio here anymore. The guy that had it figures he's going home so he sold it for $2.00 today.

The sailing koster was hardly bigger than a lifeboat; she seemed even smaller when she left the Swedish coast and beat out into the foul weather and seam-starting seas of the Skagerrak. The 16 Estonian refugees - seven men, five women, four little children - who had wedged themselves into the Erma's tiny cabin had no visas, no charts of the Atlantic, no food but potatoes, cereal, bread and canned fish. But they did not complain. After years of war and wandering, they were going to America.

They had fled from their Baltic homeland after it was taken over by Russia, refused to go back to their Communist-dominated country. It had taken virtually all their money to buy the Erma's 36-ft. hull, to install an old marine engine, and equip her with sails and stores. The Erma was small but she was seaworthy. And the leader of the expedition, tough, blue-eyed Harri Pahlberg, was a master mariner. So was the first mate, leathery Arvid Kuun.

http://www.time.com/time/magazine/article/

On January 10, the first meeting of the United Nations was held in London, England.

*Project Diana*, under the authority of the U.S. Army, bounced radar waves off the moon, measuring the exact distance between the earth and the moon and proving that communication is possible between earth and outer space. This effectively opened the space age.

Well Marge, I sure hope I get home with you soon.
All my love,

Your Husband
Bill

January 9, 1946 - To Marge from Bill

Dearest Marge,

Didn't get any mail again today except the paper of Dec 4, sure can't see what the hell is the matter. Without mail the guys over here are getting more disgusted and pissed off every day. It said in the paper today the guys with 50 to 54 points won't get home till the middle of April so I suppose 3rd Army won't let my papers come through.

I'm going down in the morning to book a call to you. We are figuring on getting there a couple hrs before it opens so we'll get our's booked. I'm still taking things pretty easy but the new Colonel is sure raising hell around here. Did you ever get that last money order I sent or the packages? I've got a little more shit laying around here yet. I'll pack it and send it one of these days but I'm still waiting for the picture I had taken in Augsburg. It isn't finished yet but maybe I'll get over to get it the last of the week. How are Swede and his wife getting along? I see by the paper I got today where he pushed her down the street in the wheelbarrow. I suppose he's working for the old man now. Well, Marge, I'm sure hoping and praying I'm home with you soon.
All my love,

Your Husband
Bill

January 10, 1946 - To Marge from Bill

Dearest Marge,

Well Marge finally got some mail today but is pretty old - 21st and 22nd of Dec. Sure hope you are getting mine. We were suppose to be having better mail service this month but it looks like it is getting worse. All the guys are bitching about mail and redeployment. From the radio it sounds like Truman is siding with the War Department on it. If so, when election comes around again, he'll never get any votes from the men overseas now. I think I heard a hundred of them cursing him around here today. The boys are getting pretty hot over this new slowdown and I guess this is holding up my papers now too.

WAR DEPARTMENT

AGPF-A 201 Waldron, William K.
(12 Oct 45)

MSR

10 January 1946

Honorable Henry O. Talle
House of Representatives

Dear Mr. Talle:

Further reference is made to your communication of 12 October 1945 with inclosures from Mrs. William Waldron, Waukon, Iowa, relative to the discharge from military service of her husband, Private First Class William Waldron due to hardship.

I am pleased to inform you that instructions were issued on 4 December 1945 directing the return of Private Waldron to the United States for discharge for the reason stated.

We cannot anticipate the precise date when this soldier will return because of the distances involved but I hope that he will be returned in the near future.

The delay in making final reply to you was unavoidable and is regretted.

Sincerely yours,

EDWARD F. WITSELL

EDWARD F. WITSELL
Major General
Acting The Adjutant General

4 Incls.

This letter from the War Department was written to Representative Talle in answer to his petition for discharge mailed October 12, 1945.

According to this letter, "instructions were issued on 4 December 1945" for Bill to be discharged due to hardship.

It's been more than a month and it can only be assumed that those orders are working their way through the military structure.

The man on trial before a U.S. court-martial in London was Sergeant Judson H. Smith - one of twelve men charged with cruelty to G.I. prisoners in the guardhouse of the 10th Reinforcement Depot at Lichfield. But last week, as the story of repeated brutalities continued to unfold, lowly Sergeant Smith became almost the forgotten man at his own trial. The accusing finger pointed higher & higher up the chain of command.

Handsome, dignified Major Richard E. LoBuono, onetime provost marshal at the depot, had been called as a defense witness for Smith. Under triphammer questioning LoBuono began to amend his answers. Among the cross currents of his testimony was one which swirled close to Colonel James A. Kilian, the depot's bespectacled former commandant. LoBuono testified that he had been shaken by Kilian's threats. One of them: "I made you what you are today and I am going to hang you." Later, LoBuono said, he "had gained the impression" that Kilian "was trying to control witnesses for his own protection - to keep this off his own doorstep." www.time.com

*I went out to see the movie tonight but had seen it, so stopped at the Red Cross on the way back. They had a good orchestra and an acrobatic troop there. Sure good. Lasted a couple of hrs. Sure sorry to hear that Dad is hitting the booze again but guess he will never learn. I'm glad you sent Patratz something cause he has sure been a good customer. So Jean Fitz has finally got engaged, eh? I wonder if the guy knows what a lemon he's getting or is she a little better than she used to be?*

*Well Marge the days are gradually rolling by but it*

still don't look much like I'm getting home.
Loving and missing you more than ever,
All my love
Bill

On January 11, Enver Hoxha declared the People's Republic of Albania and installed himself as prime minister and dictator.

January 11, 1946 - To Marge from Bill

Dear Marge,

I didn't get any mail today except a radiogram the folks must of sent at Christmas time. Sure took long enough to come. Took 2 weeks for it to get here from Nuremberg.

I suppose you are hearing the stink back home now that this slowdown in redeployment is causing. There are a pile of guys right here that refuse to work since it happened.

This was sure a beautiful day - just like spring. Nice and warm with all the snow gone but don't suppose it will last. A year ago at the time I was just pulling into Scotland. We had a few guys leave for home today. They reenlisted. It seems like that's the only way they can get home. I sure hope I get my call through all right to you Monday. Read in the paper where the telephone co. is having a big strike in the States.

I slept all afternoon so don't suppose I will sleep much today. Sure wished I had you here in bed with me. All of these Hungarian P.W. we have here are supposed to leave for home on Tuesday. Lot of them are pretty happy about it but some want to stay here to work.

Well Marge, sure hope I start getting your mail a little quicker. Still loving and missing you. Hope I get home with you soon.

All my love,
Bill

"Just after sunset, by the light of a young moon, the helpless Americans were led from their barracks. . . . When they reached the beach, their hands and feet were tied, they were blindfolded and finally ordered to face the ocean. Japanese soldiers, three platoons strong, stood six paces to the rear with rifles and machine guns. . . . Then the command was given that ended the lives of 96 Americans."

Thus last week, in a U.S. Navy court on Kwajalein atoll, a Japanese war crime on Wake Island in October 1943 was officially detailed for the first time. The victims: U.S. civilians, most of them from western states, who had been building a Navy base when the Japs took Wake four years ago.

Just before the verdict was read, sharp-nosed Rear Admiral Shigematsu Sakaibara, who had ordered the mass murder, had a request to make of the court. He asked "that the people who planned and carried out the dropping of the atomic bomb on Japan should be regarded in the same light as we." The court ignored his plea. The sentence: death, by hanging, for Admiral Sakaibara and ten other Japanese naval officers under his command.

http://www.time.com/time/magazine/article/

January 12, 1946 - To Marge from Bill

Dearest Marge,

I didn't get any mail again today and tomorrow is Sunday so can't expect any tomorrow. It seems like we only get any mail about one day a week any more. Just heard the news tonight and it was worse than ever. These fucking Generals are trying to soft soap us more. They got such a good deal over here they are going to do everything they can to keep the men here. This M.G. is really a joke over here. They have about 15 men where they need one. We are starting to have Major's for C.O.'s now to make more jobs for the officers. It used to be they had a fixed list - no Captains but now they have a Major, Captain and a few Lieut. I don't know what the hell happened to my papers but I doubt if the War Department will ever send them.

Well Marge there sure as hell isn't anything to write about. I hardly ever leave this building except to go over to see if there is any mail. Don't do a hell of a lot of work - a couple hours every other day. The Mess officers have an order - no eating at night here but I went down and had the night cook fry me a steak tonight and I told him if the Lieut. said anything, I'd take the blame for it.

Well Marge, sure hope I get home with you soon but it don't look like it.

All my love,

Your Husband
Bill

January 13, 1946 - To Marge from Bill

Dearest Marge,

Well Marge, thought I better get busy and write before I go to bed. Just finished taking a shower. It's snowing to beat hell out tonight but we have been having too nice of weather to last. Made it to church again this morning. I haven't heard from the folks for close to a month now. This mail is sure all fucked up here now.

A few of the boys went to Augsburg this afternoon and didn't get back yet so they will probably stay there all night now. I guess they had a few black market deals that they wanted to get done. Yesterday I got a letter back I wrote to Vernon in July. How is he doing in his new job anyway?

Well Marge better quit for now. Still loving and missing you more than ever.

All my love,
Bill

January 13, 1946 - To Jim and Amanda from Bill

Dear Folks,

I thought I better write you again. Haven't been getting hardly any mail for the last month now. It seems like we only get mail once or twice a week any more. I'm going to phone Marge tomorrow. We have to put in for calls four days ahead of time but then it is quite a job, getting the money order and finding a ride downtown twice to make it. Sure hope everybody is fine at home. I

Any kind of merchandise at fair prices, especially clothing, is a rarity in rackety-rax Rome, Italy. So is Swiss-born George Bloch. Last week the combination produced a riot on the Corso Umberto I.

Two years ago Shopkeeper Bloch had put up a sign: "This firm has closed its doors because it cannot get goods at proper prices. Rather than go to the black market, we retire temporarily from business." Just before Christmas he put up a new sign: "We open Jan. 2. All goods at prewar prices until we are sold out. . . . Please buy as little as you can - think of others."

http://www.time.com/time/magazine/article/

Shown in this 1946 photo are (couples left to right) Beck, Vernon and Jimmy with Ruth and John.

This week, 26 years to the day after the League of Nations, brave in its new motley, took its first bow, a bright and gaudy United Nations calliope will call the faithful to order in London.

Drafty Central Hall, Westminster, was all spruced up for the meeting. Its walls had been painted a chaste cream; new fawn carpets had been laid. In approved conference formation, 40-foot-long refectory tables, each of which would seat three delegations, were ready for the delegates of the 51 convening nations.

The Americans and French will put up at swank Claridge's, the Russians in their own Embassy in Kensington Palace Gardens ("Millionaires' Row"). Last week one hotel requested more Scotch "for the Americans." Ruled the Foreign Office: "They'll get enough at the various receptions."

All the Scotch in the world would not wash away the probability that UNO was heading into a rough maiden voyage. The original intention was to confine the first meeting to first matters like establishing the Security Council and electing a Secretary-General. But the world was too full of controversy to keep the agenda antiseptic.

http://www.time.com/time/magazine/article/

*still haven't been sick or anything.*

*We have been having nice weather the past week but it has started to snow tonight. I suppose you have read in the papers where they have about stopped redeployment so it is hard telling when I'll get home. As yet those papers never came through from Washington. I'm still taking it easy working about 3 hrs. every other day. Don't know what I'll do when I get home and have to work again. It will take me a while to get used to it again. I suppose the kids are getting so big I will hardly know them when I do get home.*

*I'm sure anxious to see what my daughter looks like. I suppose she will be walking if I don't get out of here pretty quick. In the last week here a pile of guys have quit work entirely because they aren't sending them home.*

*Well, folks, will be waiting to hear from you and sure hope I go home pretty quick.*

*Love,*
*Bill*

January 13, 1946 - To Bill from Amanda

*Dear Son Bill,*

*Well, have been intending to write the last couple days. Thought sure I would get at it yesterday. Marge got the box you sent and thanks very much for the perfume. It sure was nice. And were we ever sick your call didn't come through. Marge wasn't here. Maybe that is the reason the game at Lansing was so exciting for it was a wild game. Had 2 referees and sure needed them. Saw Bob McDonald last night. He sure looks good. It sure feels cold tonight - will be below zero, guess it is now. The boys won another basketball game this afternoon at Ossian 46-20 but the Lansing game really was a game. See by the paper Jean Davis broke her back. Just wonder if the telephone strike will be settled so your call will go through in the morning. Would I ever love to say "Hello Bill, how are you." Did you get the cable Christmas greeting? Got your letter of the 19th Dec. wondering when Stan worked. Well, he worked Friday night and 1:30-3:30 Sat. afternoon.*

*Heard Bud Campbell called Sat morning from Seattle, Wash. Oh, did you ever send the razor you said you got Dad? He is OK, I guess. He's getting a fellow in the shop to help him. Decker worked for Jones a few years ago (illegible).*

*There was a fire at Marquette Friday night. Burned*

*the bank and 4 other buildings. They didn't seem to be able to check it. They had the Prairie and McGregor fire trucks.*

*Well, still had 2 chickens saved for you - great big rooster and hen. Something happened to one of them.*

*Allamakee St has 2 beer taverns now. Cunningham moved his up where Coleb's grocery was. Colebs went out of business. No building. Cut O'Brien is in where Owens used to be. Cunningham was there. They say there is going to be a change on Spring Ave. There is a clothing store going in down there either where the Coast to Coast or Snow White is. The paper said that Walt Stove was going in business for himself. Had a letter from Vernon the end of the week. Said Beck went back to Monticello after she went back with Vernon. The day after Vernon's stayed till the day after New Years. Said it seemed funny her not being there again. But they just couldn't find a place to live. Gerry is still sick, she hasn't been out of bed since before Christmas. The boys got a real thrill out of the Lansing game - the Archbishop was there and gave them $10.00. Well, must write Vernon and Beck yet.*

*Thanks very much again for the perfume. Arny Buntruck was home at Christmas time, he had broke his back in a jeep accident. Had it in a steel brace of some kind. He looked good and waited on trade at Hausmans one afternoon. Write and hope soon you get home.*

*Lots of Love*
*Mother*

<u>January 15, 1946 - To Marge from Bill</u>

*Dearest Marge,*

*I sure did all right today. Got 6 letters from you from 16th, 27th, 28th, 29th, 30th, and 31st. I was sure glad to get them to. Got a little more bad news today. I wrote you I had the officer write to the Third Army about the papers, but they gave me the old run around and said it wasn't in their department so the officer sent it on the NSF ET at Frankfort. I sure hope something comes out of it then. But I'm hoping by now you have wrote to Washington to find out about it. He told me that would be the best.*

*I heard the new redeployment news tonight and its just as bad as ever. Boy, Marge, from the sounds of your letters you want your new home pretty bad. Well, I guess I do just as bad: so you can kinda keep your eyes*

Tall Ellis M. Zacharias, a Navy captain with a flair for the unorthodox, was one of the first skippers to go after the Japs, ended up as an intelligence officer, making highly effective propaganda broadcasts in near-perfect Japanese. Last week he showed up in a particularly unorthodox light - the Pearl Harbor Committee discovered that here was one Navy man who had been 100% right about the time and place of the attack.

A memorandum was placed in evidence showing that Captain Zacharias had personally warned Rear Admiral Husband E. Kimmel, in the summer of 1941, that the Japs would start war with a sneak air raid on Pearl Harbor on a weekend—"probably Sunday morning."

http://www.time.com/time/magazine/article/

**Receives Phone Call from Germany**

Mrs. William Waldron, nee Marjorie Leet, of Waukon, received a call last Monday morning from her husband, Sgt. Waldron from Munich, Germany. The connection was very good, and Mrs. Waldron was able to hear her husband very plainly. Sgt. Waldron has served in Germany for the past year, and is a chef at the present time. He has no diea when he will be home.

An article that appeared in the *Waukon Democrat* about Bill's phone call of January 14, 1946.

In a seach of military acronyms, there is nothing that seems to fit with NSF ET. One that describes the situation but is probably incorrect is *Not So Fast European Theater*.

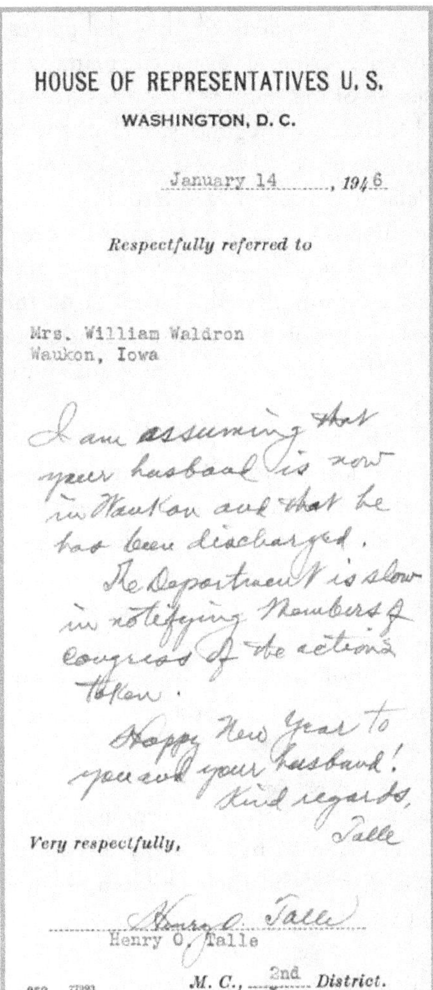

HOUSE OF REPRESENTATIVES U. S.
WASHINGTON, D. C.

January 14, 1946

*Respectfully referred to*

Mrs. William Waldron
Waukon, Iowa

I am assuming that your husband is now in Waukon and that he has been discharged.
The Department is slow in notifying Members of Congress of the actions taken.
Happy New Year to you and your husband!
Kind regards,
Talle

*Very respectfully,*

Henry O. Talle
Henry O. Talle

*M. C.,* 2nd Iowa *District.*

This handwritten note was mailed to Marge by Representative Talle on January 14 along with the letter from the War Department shown on Page 364.

*open for a good place to build one. It kinda sounds like Sweeney got stuck for that shack he bought. It will cost him a lot of money to fix it up. So you went to Prairie New Years Eve. I was wondering if you wouldn't be going someplace with Kreebs. Well, when I get home and we go to Prairie, I'll bet you will have a few more drinks than 3, eh? I can just hear Harold feeding you a line. I think Harold and all the rest of the guys figure I'm chiseling but someday they might get a chance to talk to some of the guys over here that know me and they all know I don't monkey around at all. They even have a hell of a job to get me to go over to the Red Cross. I sure can't picture Dorothy looking so tough and her hair turning gray. What does Freddy think about it anyway? He must really be rough on her.*

*I finally got those pictures I wrote you I had taken. Got 6 of them. I'll stick a couple of them in this letter and a couple more in a few days. Sure took me long enough to get them.*

*So our daughter is getting to be a pretty good girl, eh?*

*I think I get more lonesome for you every day I stay over here. Well, Marge, better quit for now. Sure hoping and praying I get home with you soon. Still loving and missing you.*

*All my love,*
*Bill*

<u>January 15, 1946 - To Bill from Dennis Marquardt</u>

This letter is postmarked Vista, Minnesota.

*Dear Bill,*

*I got your letter the other day, was sure glad to hear from you again. I'm sure glad to hear your getting out. Boy we're going to have to get together after you get back.*

*I think I told you in my last letter that Drum and I finally got together. We fought the whole damn war over. We had to have a few short ones to make it move interestingly. That bastard is just like he always was.*

*All I've done this evening is sit here and listen to the radio. Well, I guess a guy should stay home once in a while.*

*You know tire rationing went off the first of the year but shit, tires are a damn sight harder to get now than they ever were. I've been trying to get a set for my car.*

*With the deal you've got over there, I would think*

you'd want to stay in. You're living like a king having those Krauts bring your breakfast to you in bed. Write and let me know when you get out.

Your pal,

Mark

January 16, 1946 - To Marge from Bill

Dearest Marge,

Didn't get any mail from you today but got one from Marquardt and 2 from Ma. From the sounds of her letter, the kids must have had quite a party up there New Years. Ma sure thinks I'm on my way home but I guess she knows different now.

We are getting a taste of winter here again today. It turned out pretty cold today. I haven't been out of the building the last couple of days except to go after the mail. A few of our guys are shipping out tomorrow with 55 points and next week they say 53 + 54 point guys leave but it will take them a month or more to leave here. This mess hall here is sure a screwed up affair. They got a chicken shit mess officer now and he don't know nothing and thinks he knows everything.

I see the new redeployment schedule is in the paper today and it is the same old shit as before. From the looks of it I'm stuck here till Sept. if those papers don't come through. I'm beginning to see more every day what a crooked political machine this Army is.

Well Marge, I hope everything is going all right at home. I think I'll write the folks a few lines before I go to bed. Still loving and missing you.

All my love,

Bill

January 16, 1946 - To Jim and Amanda from Bill

Dear Folks,

Well, Ma, finally got a couple of letters from you again -29th & 31st. I suppose you know by now I'm not on my way home. I guess those papers must of got screwed up on the way if they even sent them. I called Marge the 4th and told her to check up and find out if they sent them. A guy sure has to go through a lot of trouble to make a phone call over here.

The boys must have had quite a party there on New Years. Stan sure picked out a lemon for Donnie though, didn't he? So John bought his gal a ring, eh. Well, I suppose pretty quick you will hear he's getting married, eh?

As president of the Philippines, Manuel Quezon accepted many evidences of his country's regard. Officials of the Quezon regime gave him a yacht and the use of 100-year-old Malacanan Palace, named new streets and buildings for him as fast as they were constructed. When the Philippines Congress met last autumn, after the liberation of the islands, it voted his widow a pension of 1,000 pesos a month, almost automatically.

But when the first check was delivered last week, delicate, greying Mrs. Aurora Aragon de Quezon immediately sent it back. With it went a letter which demonstrated why thousands of Filipinos regard her as a combination queen-mother and patron saint.

"I feel that on account of ... countless war widows and orphans ... I should waive collection of a pension . . ." the letter stated. "I cannot, in good conscience, receive ... Government assistance when so many of my less fortunate sisters and their children are not yet taken care of. . . ."

http://www.time.com/time/magazine/article/

On January 16, Charles de Gaulle resigned as head of the French provisional government. He would be replaced by F. Gouin on the 20th.

Sgt. Bill Waldron

On January 17, the United Nations Security Council held its first session.

Senator Dennis Chavez (D-NM) called for a vote on a Fair Employment Practices Committee bill that calls for an end to discrimination in the work place. A senate filibuster prevented it from passing.

*I've got a couple pictures here I had taken. I'll stick them in the letter. I sent Marge a couple last night. Sure hope everybody is all right at home. I'm still all right but I hope to get the hell out of this country pretty quick. A year ago at this time, I was in Belgium.*

*Our mail sure comes through poor now. It is taking from 2 weeks to a month.*

*Well, guess I'll get to bed now. Sure hope I get home with you soon.*

*Love,*
*Bill*

January 17, 1946 - To Marge from Bill

*Dearest Marge,*

*I got one letter from you today of Jan 2nd. I sure wait for them everyday too. The boys are going to 3rd Army to try to find out whether we are getting a star for Czech or not. The rumors are pretty strong we will get it. It will make me 4 stars and 4 points so I sure hope we get it. So you went on a little spending spree to Decorah, eh? Well I guess you are sure entitled to it. There isn't much of anything I can buy over here to send you. So Marie thinks Dale and Sis are a little jealous because we are pretty well set for our age. Well, guess they aren't the only ones. I knew a few in business that didn't like to see the bakery going all right either. One thing, nobody gave it to us. So Leona finally hooked Tiny Hanson, eh? Sure didn't think he would ever get married. He'll have to loosen up with his money a little more now. I suppose you have the Income tax about ready now. Should be a lot less this year than last with the baby and us being married. That should knock off a bit.*

*I'll bet you had quite a job getting everything fixed up, eh? I've got a Hungarian bill here that I'll stick in this letter. I don't think I ever sent any before. I suppose Ray has their house in nice shape by now. Sure be glad when I get home for us to go out with them and maybe go fishing. It will probably be fishing time by the time I get home the way things look. I still can't get over how tongue-tied you were the other day when I called you up.*

*I still haven't got the letter yet you wrote about John giving his gal a ring. When I wrote Ma last night I told her pretty quick she'll be hearing he's getting married but she won't like that.*

*Well Marge hope I hear from you tomorrow. Hoping and praying those papers come soon.*

*All my Love,*

*Bill*

The reason *she won't like that* is because John lived at home, paying rent and Amanda needed the money to help raise the family.

January 17, 1946 - To Bill from Marge

*My dearest Bill,*

*I didn't get any mail today but I got a letter from Talle. Of course it isn't in reply to the ones I sent yesterday. I took it up to Marcella and she said that it is evidently your commanding officer over there that is holding it up but the letter we sent yesterday should get action again. All we can do is hope and pray anyway.*

*I have to go up and help Marie for awhile. I made chocolate cakes again this morning, but there isn't any icing so if they get iced today, I'll have to go up and make some but I don't know much about it. It is almost 1:30 so I have to get going soon.*

*Lu and Byron (Livingood - her sister and husband) were up today. He thought I should have spanked Janice to have her cry when I was talking to you. I don't think you could have heard her anyway, do you?*

*See, every time I get a gov't letter, I think I get my hopes up just that much higher. Sure wish I could talk to you again. That was just too wonderful. I'll copy the letter from Talle and send it to you and write again tonite. Gee I do love you, honey - more than ever. Keep writing and loving me as much as I do you. I dreamed last nite that you came home and when I went outside to meet you, you didn't even kiss me. Just shook hands. I'm sure glad it was only a dream though, because I was about heart broken. Crazy isn't it?*

*Bye now.*

*With all my love,*
*Your wife,*
*Marge*

Britain was treading warily in awakened India.

For two taut months the country had watched the Raj's court-martial of three "Indian National Army" officers who had fought with the Japanese against Britain. More than 30 had been killed in protest riots (TIME, Dec. 3). A severe sentence might make these men martyrs, and touch off another nationalist explosion.

When the three officers were marched into the Delhi courtroom last week, their faces were grave. Colonel E. K. Squire, resplendent in ribbons and scarlet collar tabs, began to read the verdict: "All three of you are guilty ... of waging war [against the State]. . . . The sentence of the Court ... is transportation for life, cashiering and forfeiture of arrears of pay and allowances." One prisoner blinked, another swayed, the third looked fixedly ahead.

The Colonel droned on: "No finding or sentence by court-martial is complete until confirmed. . . . The Commander in Chief has decided ... to remit the sentences of transportation for life. . . ." (The three men smiled faintly.) The Colonel added dryly that the three were now free men.

http://www.time.com/time/magazine/article/

January 18, 1946 - To Marge from Bill

*Dearest Marge,*

*I didn't get any mail today. Just came back from the show "Captain Eddy" - life of Eddie Richbacker. I enjoyed it pretty well. I suppose you probably seen it*

Captain Eddie (1945): WWI flyer Eddie Rickenbaker remembers his life which brought him from a car salesman, race driver and pilot in WWI, to an important person in the early years of civil airline service, after his plane crashed in the South Pacific in late 1942. Starring Fred MacMurray and Charles Bickford.

months ago. The days are gradually slipping by pretty quick. It will be another payday and month gone by and I'm still in Germany. It was a year ago today I got assigned to the 90th Div.

I sure hope you have wrote to Washington to find out about those papers cause if we don't keep on their ass, I'll never get home.

I had them write to Frankfort to see if they could find out anything there so it will be a week or two before I find out whether the papers even came there or not. But I don't think they ever came from Wash. Or I would have heard something before now.

I sure hope we can have a little time to ourselves after I do get home. I'm sure hoping that we will be able to spend a lot of time down at the river this summer. I suppose Stan is too much in love not to even think about going fishing any more. We are still having the winter weather here but I'll bet it's not as cold as back home.

I just listened to the redeployment news and it's just as rotten as ever. According to it I can figure on staying here another year. I hate this Army more every day. Well Marge, better quit for now. Still loving and missing you.

All my love
Bill

On its New Year's Eve program the Berlin City Opera included selections from Johann Strauss's frothy Fledermaus. Orchestra and vocalists, whirling through the three-quarter-time Second Finale, finally reached the lines:

" . . . Dass ich sehe, wer mich besiegt Und wer meine Uhr gekriegt!" (". . . That I may see who conquered me And who got my watch!") The audience roared, clapped, stamped, and the conductor had to oblige with two encores of the passage. The handful of Russians in the auditorium, well-aware that their habit of appropriating any watch they can lay their hands on is a pet German peeve, were more hurt than annoyed. Said one much-decorated Red warrior after the concert: "I did not think it was at all funny. If these people only knew that I shall be able to buy two cows with a good watch back home. . . ."

http://www.time.com/time/magazine/article/

<u>January 19, 1946 - To Marge from Bill</u>

Dearest Marge,

I didn't get any mail today again and won't tomorrow cause it is Sunday so will be hoping for some on Monday. Things here sure been popping today. The Colonel was in and wanted to bust a few of us guys for not having this mess run right but it all wound up where the Mess Officer is getting canned.

I went over to see the Major after it was all over and told him what was all wrong so it fixed it for a couple of us. Could see the General but in the meantime, I guess the Colonel found out what a good mess hall we ran in Augsburg so he sent over a new mess officer. Their mess hall is about as screwed up as anything I ever saw but could be straightened out easy enough. I've been trying to keep my nose out of it but the last couple days, Sam and myself been trying to straighten out some things but the mess officer tries blocking everything we do.

Three of us decided we are going to get the hell out of here for a while and go on a tour of Switzerland and

HENRY O. TALLE
SECOND DISTRICT OF IOWA

HOUSE OFFICE BLDG.
SUITE 1420

HOME ADDRESS:
DECORAH, IOWA

COMMITTEE:
BANKING AND CURRENCY

**Congress of the United States**
**House of Representatives**
**Washington, D. C.**

January 19, 1946

Mrs. William Waldron
Waukon, Iowa

Dear Friend:

The time has come again when I must call on my friends for service. And, I hasten to add, it is a service which I deeply appreciate.

I am, therefore, enclosing herewith a nomination paper with the request that it be properly signed, notarized and returned to me in the enclosed stamped and addressed envelope.

The excellent service given me in the past has been a source of genuine encouragement, and I am most grateful.

The war years made severe demands upon our people and upon the Congress. The job that lies ahead is, in the words of Lincoln, - "to bind up the nation's wounds." This task will require thought, work and sweat, and I want you to know that I stand ready to do my part.

Thanking you for your service and with good wishes for the New Year, I am

Gratefully,

Henry O. Talle

Henry O. Talle, M.C.

Enclosures: 2

One favor deserves another.

Congressman Talle, Republican, was first elected to Congress in 1939. Soon after his election, the census caused Iowa to lose one of its seats in the U.S. House and the district lines had to be redrawn, Talle's District 4 was broken up.

He faced a difficult election in fall of 1941 against three-term Democrat Bernhard Jacobsen. Talle, however, was aided by the continued decline in support in Iowa for Democrats and won with a considerable margin.

The letter to the left is asking for Marge's support and was probably preceeded by a phone call.

Congressman Talle represented Iowa in Congress from January 3, 1939 to January 3, 1959 and then served in the Eisenhower Administration. He is buried in Arlington National Cemetary.

*Italy so if those papers don't come before the first of Feb. I'm going to try going the first week in Feb. and get back the middle of last of Feb. I'll write you more later if I do go.*

*I got transferred into service Co. yesterday but I won't use my new address yet for a few days. Well, Marge, nothing else I can think of so will quit for tonight. Hoping and praying I'm home with you soon.*

*All my love*
*Bill*

<u>*January 20, 1946 - To Marge from Bill*</u>

*Dearest Marge,*

*I just came back from the show - Fred McMurray and Joan Leslie - don't remember the name but it was sure screwy. I thought I better write before going to bed. It's been a long time since I have missed writing to you.*

*Where Do We Go from Here?* (1945): In the movie a guy named Bill wants to join the Army, but he's 4F so he asks a wizard to help him, but the wizard has a slight problem with his history knowledge, so he sends Bill everywhere in history, but not to WWII. Starring MacMurray and Leslie.

Bill at work while waiting, waiting, waiting.

I guess when I moved from the 90th to Augsburg was the last time. I sure hope I get some mail from you tomorrow. I hope things are running pretty well for you there. I suppose it will take me quite a while before I'll be able to get back in the swing of things and be able to do a good day's work. In the past four months, I don't think I've even lifted a pan in the kitchen so you know how much actual work I've done. I met a couple kids from my old Co. today. They came down from one of the detachments but left right after supper to make it back yet tonight. It was good to see them again but I would sooner see DeMarco than any of them. I write to him all the time but it takes his letters about 3 weeks to come and mine about the same time. Sam and myself have been sitting here running down the Army and wondering if we will get home by Easter. I don't think there is much chance of getting there by our wedding anniversary but I'm still hoping it might be this week. Well, Marge keep up the writing. Still loving and missing you.

All my love,

Bill

January 21, 1946 - To Marge from Bill

Dearest Marge,

I got one letter from you today of Dec. 25 and one from Veryle postmarked Jan 9th. It sounds like she is back to Omaha. She must like it pretty well.

We have sure been having the brass around the mess hall here today. At noon General Mueller was here looking around and tonight we had a two Star and a one Star General looking things over. I guess they were well enough satisfied with the way things were going. I was waiting to get my ass chewed for not having on a tie but they didn't say anything. Nobody is supposed to eat here unless they have one on.

The baby is four months old today. I suppose she is getting to be quite a big girl, eh? And only a month away till our wedding anniversary. It don't look much like I'll make it when I'm still here. I was over to the Red Cross for a while tonight. Drank a couple cokes and listened to the orchestra. They were pretty good.

These Krauts are getting so they can play American music pretty well now. I hear a few of them German tunes are making hits back in the States. I know the guys here like Lil Marlene as well as any American piec-

U.S. statisticians tidied up their books for 1945, produced an adding-machine report on the state of the nation.

In twelve months, U.S. citizens tossed off 190,000,000 gallons of whiskey, gin, brandy, rum and cordials, tying 1942's national, post-repeal record for drinking. They had trouble at home - in Reno a record 8,590 divorce suits were filed; in Hamilton County, Tenn., there were five times more marital split-ups than marriages; all across the nation the divorce rate boomed to new levels.

The U.S. also had more crime—in Chicago, barometer of the national mood for larceny and gunplay, the law was broken on 38,533 occasions, 10% oftener than the year before. There were 29,000 traffic deaths, the highest national total since 1941's alltime record of 39,969.

http://www.time.com/time/magazine/article/

*Lili Marlene* was sung by Marlene Dietrich and was a Number One song on the Hit Parade in the U.S.

*es.*

*Do you suppose we will still be able to dance together when I get home? It's been a long time since we have. It warmed up a little here today - hope it keeps on. The weather usually breaks earlier here than at home but it rains then so it is pretty near as bad. I'll stick this other picture I have here in this letter. I have one left. I'm sending to Marquardt. I'll have to get enough ambition to writing him yet tonight. Still loving and missing you and hoping I am home with you soon.*

*All my love*

*Your Husband*
*Bill*

January 22, 1946 - To Marge from Bill

*Dearest Marge,*

*I really hit the jackpot today. Got ten letters from you from the 4th to the 12th and one from Ma and was I ever happy to get them. The pictures of the baby sure are swell. I showed them to all the guys and they all think her mouth and smile is the same as mine.*

*I got the paper you sent and turned it into the Personnel Sgt. Maybe I'll get some action now. I also wrote a letter to the Stars and Stripes, which I'll mail tomorrow so maybe I'll get some action soon. I think the Per. Sgt. is taking my papers to the General.*

*We are having a big shakeup of the mess here tomorrow. Most of the mess personal will lose their jobs. I guess us guys from Augsburg will take over. They tell me I'm supposed to have charge of one shift and that I was put in for Staff Sgt. tonight but I'm really hoping my papers go through now before the Staff ratings come which will be about the first of Feb. It seems like a bunch of guys even went to the General bitching about the mess and told him if he put us guys in charge we could straighten it out. So I guess tomorrow the mess Sgt and a few more get canned.*

*I just came from the show "Captain Kidd". I liked it pretty well too. Sure will be glad when we start going to shows together again. Dorothy must be having quite a rough time of it if Freddy won't even let her go through town alone. You sure can't imagine how glad I was to get your letters today and the pictures of the baby. I sure like them but it just makes me realize all the more what I'm missing out on at home.*

*Well Marge, I'll have to read your letters again in the*

On January 22, in Iran, Quzi Muhammad declared the independent people's Republic of Mahabad in the Chuwarchira Square in the Kurdish city of Mahabad. He would be the new president and Hadschi Baba would become the new prime minister.

*Captain Kidd* (1945): In this unhistorical account, Capt. William Kidd is already a clever, ruthless pirate when, in 1699, he tricks the king into commissioning him as escort for a treasure ship from India. He enlists a crew of pardoned cutthroats and Orange Povey, whom Kidd once abandoned on a reef and hoped never to see again. Of course, Kidd's intentions are treacherous. But there's more to gunner Adam Mercy than meets the eye. Starring Charles Laughton and Randolph Scott and nominated for an Oscar.

The Army, which has been turning men loose at a steadily accelerated rate (1,000,000 last month), abruptly jammed on the brakes. As if realizing it for the first time, the Army announced last week that the problem was no longer how to bring the boys home and get them out of uniform, but how to keep intact a force big enough to meet the nation's global commitments.

These commitments would compel the Army, as of next July 1, to have 335,000 men in Europe, 375,000 in the Pacific, 87,000 in other areas overseas, 360,000 manning U.S. installations, 343,000 in training or transit. Total: 1,500,000.

But at the rate the Army has been tearing down its establishment, it would have nothing like that number next July 1. After January, declared the slightly confused Army, the U.S.-bound legions will be reduced to less than 300,000 a month—although there is shipping available for twice as many. The new order means that a G.I. eligible for discharge may nevertheless be kept overseas until a replacement arrives.

http://www.time.com/time/magazine/article/

*morning. Still loving and missing you more than ever.*

*All my love*

*Your Husband*
*Bill*

<u>*January 23, 1946 - To Marge from Bill*</u>

*Dear Marge,*

*I got 3 letters from you today of 12th and two of the 14th and also got some good news. My papers came today. Two sets! One that I got from you yesterday was approved here today by the General and also they came from Frankfort. Now all I'll have to do is sign them tomorrow then I start turning in my stuff. The Personnel Sgt. told me he would put me on shipping orders direct to LaHavre (Belgium) the last of this week or the first of next week. I guess it really pays to know the right guys in the Army. I sure can't tell you how glad I am that I'll be going home but don't think I'll make it quite in time for our Wedding anniversary but not much after.*

*I just got started on my new job this morning and I think it would have been a headache. You see, I would have about 200 men or a few more working under me and have to see that everything runs smooth all in this one building. Under us we have a large kitchen, bakery, meat shop, ice cream shop and three dining rooms that hold close to a 1,000 men so you can imagine how many you have to be giving hell to all the time but in each department there is a G.I. supervising and them in the basement. We have about 10 big walk-in refrigerators plus all the storerooms and a laundry room. We also*

RESTRICTED

HEADQUARTERS
THIRD MILITARY GOVERNMENT REGIMENT

APO 403
25 Jan 46

SO 21

EXTRACT

1. So much of par 36 SO 15 this hq cs 18 Jan 46 as relieves PRESCOTT, BRYANT 0 913 100 [illegible] and assigns 0 to 976th F. Bn, APO 403 is revoke[illegible]

2. Fol name[illegible]

[illegible] Warba, Julius E 36 954 [illegible] Pfc
Lowell, Donald E 31 454 603 Pfc

9. Waldron, William K 37 772 525 Tec 4 Sv Co this regt is reld fr pres asgmt and atchd unasgd Camp Herbert Tareyton, APO 568, LeHavre Port of Embarkation, for return to the US for disch. on account of hardship, under the provisions of Sec III AR 615-362, 15 Dec 44. WP w/o delay. Correspondents and publishers will be notified to discontinue mailing letters and publications until they receive notification of new address. Appropriate WD AGO Forms may be used for this purpose. Rail T atzd. TDN. Auth: Msg form Mil Pers Div, EM Sec, SPXPE-[illegible] file AGPE-A 201 Waldron, William K (10 Oct 45), dated 4 Dec 45. [illegible]: 29 Jan 46.

10. BLOCKER, TOM B 0 177 183 LT COL FA hvg been asgd this regt fr Hq Third US Army per par 4 SO 14, Hq Third US Army 14 Jan 46, is asgd this hq for dy w/O of [illegible] EDC[illegible]: 18 Jan 46

The Personnel Sargeant did as he said and in just two days, orders were cut and Bill was on his way home via Belgium.

*have a big laundry here but we don't have anything to do with the running of it, thank God.*

*I wrote a letter to Marcella and the folks already tonight - lot of ambition, eh? I couldn't hardly believe it today when the Pers. Sgt. called and told me the papers were there and he was getting them ready to send to the CO. He said the CO would probably make sure if it didn't go the rest of the way through channels. We had the General in again today. He seems like a hell of a good guy. Me without a tie again and I didn't go up and salute and report to him but just showed him around. He walked through all the dining rooms seeing how the table looked and the food and said it was better than what they were getting.*

*Well Marge, sure hoping I see you soon.*

*All my love*
*Bill*

January 23, 1946 - To Jim and Amanda from Bill

*Dear Folks,*

*I got a letter from you yesterday of Jan 7 and got 15 from Marge yesterday and today. The paper's finally got here for me to go home. Have to sign them tomorrow and probably will be out of Munich the last of the week or first of next week. I don't know how long it will take them but at least I'll be on the way and I sure can't wait till I get there though. I got the pictures Marge sent of the baby. They were sure swell. I suppose it will take me a while to get used to the baby. I still can't believe I'll be going home.*

*Well, folks, sure hope I will be seeing you before long.*

*Love,*
*Bill*

January 24, 1946 - To Bill from Marge

*My dearest Bill,*

*Hi, honey, how is my husband coming? Hope you are O.K. and have some news on coming home.*

*Just got home from Lansing and the basketball game. St. Pat's got a reaming by Lansing Public - 62-29. Of course we expected too but the boys really played a nice ball game and I'm proud of them. Lansing has a whale of a good ball club and are pretty dirty players. They probably will go all*

Douglas MacArthur's first detailed account of his stewardship in Japan and Korea ran to some 100,000 words and had the usual MacArthur attributes. It read well; detailed facts punctuated its sweeping perspective. And it boiled down to one basic fact: General MacArthur had done a bang-up job of occupying Japan.

He had also looked the future in the eye. Last month's meeting of the Foreign Secretaries had put an eleven-nation Far Eastern Commission (FEC) and a four-power Allied Council for Japan over the General, at the same time leaving him in operational control. MacArthur, who had worked largely on his own since the surrender, promptly said that, although he did not like it, he would obey orders. His report was calculated to show that he should be allowed to continue with a minimum of outside interference.

http://www.time.com/time/magazine/article/

On January 25, the United Mine Workers rejoined the American Federation of Labor.

The goings-on at St. Albans Naval Hospital on Long Island were enough to make any Navy captain blink. Sailors and marines were involved; so were WAVES and civilians. It was happening in phone booths, on the ladders, even in the middle of the corridors. To tough-minded Captain C. F. Behrens, executive officer, it was a matter for emergency action. He drafted a stern, four-paragraph memorandum: "Lovemaking and lollygagging are hereby strictly forbidden. . . ."

Then he got right down to cases. "The holding of hands, osculation and constant embracing of WAVES, corpsmen or civilians and sailors or any combination of male & female personnel is a violation of naval discipline. . . "

Time Magazine January 14, 1946

On January 26, President Harry S. Truman established the Central Intelligence Group. He had not trusted Wild Bill Donovan and the power of the Office of Strategic Services and had disbanded that organization at the end of the war. It became immediately evident that such a group was a necessity and he begrudgingly established the CIG with limited powers. In 1947, the CIG evolved into the Central Intelligence Agency with Rear Admiral Roscoe H. Hillenkoetter appointed as the first Director. Truman never achnowledged his initial error.

*the way toward the State. Wish you could get home in time to see them play a game.*

*It is sort of cold out and I've got a hell of a cold, too. All I do is cough and cough. Janice is fine and full of the devil - think the pictures are sort of cute.*

*Your Mother and Dad and Pete Stiebstad went to Lansing with me is all. Marcella and Earl were going but ended up going with Kreite. Asked Char to go but they were going to Postville to a dance. Paul was telling me that he had asked McGowan over for dinner today but didn't tell Ruth till almost noon so she made him take them down town to eat. He was laughing about Jim and the baby - said it was a scream to see Jim carrying it. Said guessed he'd trade it off for a dog - a dog wouldn't be near so much work and you wouldn't always have to get someone to take care of it. Acted like he was sort of ashamed of it. Can't see Jim's being that way but suppose you have to sort of get used to it. Hope you won't be ashamed to carry your daughter around, honey. She's pretty nice, I think and getting sweeter every day. Don't you think she looks like the Waldrons? But then if I don't think she is nice, who would?*

*Didn't hear too much on the demobilization program this week but people in the States sure think they should get home right away.*

*Well, darling, all for tonite, Sure love and miss you more all of the time. Hope I hear from you again soon.*

*With all my love*

*Your wife*
*Marge*

January 26, 1946 - To Bill from Marge

*My Dearest Bill,*

*Well, honey, I didn't get any mail from you today. Of course, those last letters came thru so fast that I can't expect any for a while.*

*Boy, is it ever getting cold out - supposed to be 20 below in the morning and snowed about four inches this morning and is blowing something terrible so see where tomorrow won't be anything.*

*Marie came down after me to go to church and then I went up there. She put up my hair and her own. Ray is jacking up the floor so he was in the cellar most of the time. Came up for coffee and then he gave me a ride home. I wore my sweater and skirt and did I ever get razzed about the bumps. But then Marie always*

HENRY O. TALLE
SECOND DISTRICT OF IOWA

HOUSE OFFICE BLDG.
SUITE 1420

HOME ADDRESS
DECORAH, IOWA

COMMITTEE:
BANKING AND CURRENCY

Congress of the United States
House of Representatives
Washington, D. C.

January 31, 1946

Mrs. William Waldron
Waukon, Iowa

Dear Friend:

The promptness with which you raturned the nomination paper I sent you is most gratifying.

It is not possible for me to thank the signers individually, but perhaps you will express my appreciation to them whenever you have the opportunity.

I am deeply grateful for your cooperation and support, and with your continued assistance I am confident we can speed the return of sound, constructive government.

Cordially,

Henry O. Talle

Henry O. Talle, M.C.

Talle:vs

Apparently Marge followed through for the Congressman and this letter shows his appreciation. As can be discerned from the letter, he was not a fan of what the Democrats had done to the country during Roosevelt and Truman.

*reminds him that you made them. That's a lie tho, isn't it?*

*The Ford is running perfect since Frank put the electric fuel pump on. Dad bet me a quarter that it won't start in the morning so I'm waiting.*

*This is the kind of nite I'd sure like to have my husband to love up. Think you'll care if your wife wants to love you up honey? You used to get pretty mad at me.*

*Gee, January is about gone. The time is going faster this year. Last year I worried so from minute to minute about you - then some days I was so darn sick too. I sure waited for news reports and papers then.*

*John Dotseth and Lou Hanson were in getting warm this morning. John said he looked at his papers after he got home that day and that I was right - 47'. I'm glad he mentioned it so I don't have to.*

*Hattie's sister called Marie today and said Hattie had lost her baby. She would have been about two months along. I sure feel sorry for them cause she wanted one so badly and this is two she has lost. Guess she'll have to have an operation to have any. I'm sure glad we got our little stinker even if we probably will have a dozen. Oh, no - I told Stan when we had 11 you'd have to sleep*

On January 31, the last session in Germany of the Permanent Court of International Justice was held.

Yugoslavia's new constitution, modeled after the Soviet Union, established six constituent republics - Bosnia and Herzegovina, Croatia, Macedonia, Montenegro, Serbia and Slovenia.

On February 1, Trygve Lie, a Norwegian socialist, was selected as the first United Nations Secretary General.

"The army," said Lenin of the collapse of Russia's land forces in 1917, "decided the question of war and peace with its feet." Last week a nervous U.S. Government heard an impatient scraping of other feet - the G.I.s of a once-great U.S. Army. It had won a war with dashing gallantry but it still had a precarious political front to hold. G.I. Joe wanted to quit - and to hell with winning the peace.

There was little violence; it was more like a Union Square demonstration. But the noise spread around the world. Fueled on homesickness and low morale, the ruckus was touched off by the Army's abrupt announcement that it would be some time before a lot of U.S. soldiers got home, because many would have to carry on for a while as occupation troops.

In Manila, where G.I.s started sporadic demonstrations several weeks ago, the noise was loudest. Disintegration of the soldierly virtues had shown in drunkenness, reckless driving, carelessness in dress. Then demonstrations became organized.

Mass meetings booed the top command, collected funds to buy space for protests in U.S. papers. They promised: "We are marking the names of Congressmen who are interested in our welfare."

http://www.time.com/time/magazine/article/

upstairs and me down cause I won't have 12. Stan stays so damn innocently and then laughs -"What difference would that make?"

Well, honey, guess I'll go to bed and see if I can keep warm. Sure think of you always and love and miss you more than ever.

With all of my love

Your wife,
Marge

February 1, 1946 - To Bill from Marge

My Dearest Bill,

Well the County tournament is over with the Lansing boys and Waterville girls as Champions. I sure hated to see Lansing win. Bet you think I'm quite the basketball fan this year, don't you? I always did like basketball and when you follow teams, it is more interesting.

I went to church first with Marie and Ray's sister so when I got to the game there was standing room only but I got a seat before the end of the game.

I didn't hear from you today. Gee, honey, it is now going into the fourteenth month we have been apart. Remember it was the first of January we left each other in Kansas City. Honestly, Bill, sometimes I get so lonesome for you I could scream and tonite it is worse than usual. I always feel sorry for myself. You'll laugh when I tell you this but whenever I see Stan and Mary Ann together, I get more lonesome for you than ever and they were at the game. He reminds me of you in so many ways and it always makes me lonesome to see him loving her up. Believe me, he doesn't care where or who sees him do that either.

Well, Kosbau and Goldie take the final step tomorrow. Finally making it legal, eh? Dirty, aren't I? They are being married at the little Brown Church. I haven't gotten a gift yet but will in the morning. What, I don't know.

Boo, is it ever cold out tonite. Hate to think of tomorrow as it probably will mean a trip to Eitzen.

Your Mother came down this afternoon to see the things you sent. Took the razors up to your Dad so he was going to sharpen them and see if they can use them. His has a straight end on and these have a curved end.

Janice is fine but full of the dickens. I'll be glad when you can see her and I do hope you'll like her. Course there's not much else you could do now that she's here, is *there, HA.*

*I feel OK again today. Went up and worked this morning but didn't this afternoon. Seems like they don't get much done if I'm not there tho. Finished cleaning out the steel cabinet and you'd never know it was the same thing.*

*Well, Bill, I haven't much to write about. I love you so terribly much but all we can do is keep praying, I guess. Oh, how I hope you can get home soon. I miss my husband and my loving, honey. Keep writing*

*With all of my love*

*Your wife*
*Marge*

February 6, 1946 - To Bill from Marge

*My Dearest Bill,*

*Oh, honey am I ever happy to hear that you really are coming home. You probably won't get this letter but I'll keep writing until you write for me to stop, just in case you don't leave as soon as planned.*

*I thought if they ever did get the papers thru that it wouldn't take long for you to get home. I can hardly wait, honey and know you can't either. I won't be expecting you till the last of the month or the first of March though.*

*Your mother and Shar said you got the babies pictures. I hope you like them and her when you get here. That is my biggest concern, I guess. Bill - I still can't believe that you are coming. It is too good to be true.*

*The weather is so bad out today. I hate to go out again but must. Haven't been good for much since I got your letter. There is a lot to do here too.*

*Boy sounds like you would have had a lot to do there now. No labor, eh? Glad you've got used to giving orders anyway cause there will be a lot for you to do when you get here. Suppose we'll have . . . (missing rest of letter)*

February 1946 - To Viola and George from Marge

*Dear Folks,*

*Well, arrived safely - aren't you surprised? Ha. The train was a little late getting in but the conductor told me how to get to the hotel so I walked - only three blocks.*

*This is a huge hotel, what I have seen of it but my room hasn't a bath is the only disadvantage. Maybe we can get one later with the stool. I couldn't have gotten*

On February 5, the Chondoist Chongu Party was founded in North Korea.

From a junket through Germany, a refugee reporter (Gerhart H. Seger) brought back a "secret document"—a directive to Germany's Communist Party workers. In essence it is a restatement of worldwide Communist strategy. It appeared last week in Manhattan's liberal-labor, violently anti-Communist weekly, the New Leader. Excerpts:

"Comrades! . . . We have to begin anew and to learn from our mistakes. . . . Which forces can we consider on our side? The still unorganized, suffering labor groups . . . part of the middle classes and the youth . . . part of the bourgeoisie which was cheated under the Nazi regime and is now afraid of being swallowed by American imperialism. All these forces must be combined for the struggle to reach the next partial goal, a democratic Germany...."

Democracy in Germany, the directive hastened to point out, is only a tactical maneuver in the fight for the strategic objective: "the dictatorship of the proletariat." To that end some "retreats, zigzags, and marking time" would be necessary.

http://www.time.com/time/magazine/article/

Feb. 1946. There is no stamp or postmark so she must have not mailed it. The return address is Camp Grant, Ill. and it is noted Wed. nite, 9:00

The outside of the envelope has notes on the train itinerary
Milwaukee
Janesville 8:49 – 12:55
Burs. To Rochele 2:57
Burlington 9:00

in if I hadn't called and reserved a room.

How is my girl? I surely do miss her a lot. I hope she is good for you Mother and doesn't keep you up at nites. I surely could play with her if I had her here now but hope she is sound asleep.

I'll go right to bed, I think. Could sure go for a cup of coffee but guess I'll wait till morning. Sure wish there was some way of letting Bill know I got in here tonite but then it won't be much longer and he'll be here.

Don't worry about us Mom and try not too about Ethel either. Hope we can get home to see Veryle.

I had one change at Janesville, Wisc. Didn't leave from Prairie after all but from Marquette at 3:00. I didn't have any wait at Janesville either but the train from there to here was terrible.

Hope Dad is feeling better. Maybe I'll have called before you get this.

Hope Janice is O.K. and love her for me. I sure do miss her even if I never was with her very much.

Lots of love,
Marge

Postmarked Omaha, Nebraska.

February 8, 1946 - To Marge from Veryle

Dear Marge,

I got your letter tonite and darling, I'm so happy and glad for you that Bill is coming home. It's been so long.

Doris and I were talking about coming home the weekend of my birthday and if Bill is home, I'm sure we will. Then Mom would be home and I could see her too.

The snaps of Janice were darling. Bet she is sweet and lively. Sure anxious to see her.

Well, let me see what have I done that would be interesting. Jim called last nite so we went to the Music Box again. He brought me a valentine box of candy. His soldier friend and girl met us and we had a swell time. Bob Berkey's orchestra too! Got home about 1 o'clock. Oh yes, we also had our pictures taken - you know, ones like Bill had taken in Minneapolis with Stall? It isn't so bad.

Tomorrow nite Doris and her boy friend and Bruce are coming over. I imagine we will have a pretty good time. Last Saturday nite I got pretty high on wine and beer!! What a combination. You can imagine. He brought bottles of beer and a fifth of wine. It seems to me I've written this before. I know I've written it and you're the only one I'll tell, so I must have. Unless I just imagine I've written it. Anyway I'm getting to be an

With the hurly-burly and posturing of the public hearings over, legislators and brass hats got down to work together last week on a plan for the merger of the Army and Navy. After so many months of pull & haul, it was a relief even to Navymen, who still opposed the merger.

In hopes that the threatened reorganization would be made only on the topmost Government level, the Navy had offered the Eberstadt plan (for Army, Navy and Air Departments, all tied in at the top by a National Security Council). The Army had won President Truman's backing for outright merger with the Air Forces as a third and coequal branch. The Navy recognized that in any case there was virtue in getting together on the lowest level—down where procurement, recruiting, training and transport services overlapped.

www.time.com

*awful boozehound. It all goes down so easy. Guess I'd better stick to Jim. Nothing stronger than beer and no smoking for him!! Me and my men, they're not worth the time I spend talking or writing about them so guess I'll just forget them all. Isn't that a good idea?*

*Mrs. Singer flew to Minneapolis this morning for a 10 day vacation and shopping trip. She is going to redecorate the house soon too. Her sister is here with us so it isn't so bad but she doesn't know much about keeping house or cooking. I fed Mr. S. lamb chops, potatoes, peas, salad, and chocolate pudding for supper. How's that?*

*I had more fun at work today. One of those crazy days, you know.*

*After supper I mopped the kitchen floor and washed my clothes. I also wrote a letter to Ruth Baxter.*

*I'm very surprised at Harold and Goldie's wedding in a way. Where are they going to live and what does he do?*

*I bet Marie's house will be darling. I'm so anxious about this one too, she has such great plans for it. I'll tell you about them some other time.*

*I want to see "The Harvey Girls" Sunday. I'd like to have Doris go along but I imagine Frank will still be in town. We do good if we get to S.S. on Sunday mornings anymore.*

*What's the matter with John? Did you two disagree about something? The last time I talked with him, he said that since you had been working nites he'd gotten to understand and like you more that he did before. Guess you 2 never did agree too well anyway, did you? Is Dale any faster? Has he beaten your record for fryings yet?*

*How's Grandma & pa? Tell them hello and give them my love. Mom always sends her letters on down to me too.*

*We finally have 2 clocks in the house again. Mr. Singer brought one home tonite. A real nice electric.*

*How's the weather? Boy, it is really swell around here. Beautiful out east tonite, a little colder today. No snow or water just about like spring.*

*Guess I'm running out of chatter for tonite. Guess I'll go to bed and just as sure as I do Doris will call. Anyway I guess I'll try it. It is about 10 o'clock*

*Good nite and keep well.*

*Love Always*
*Veryle*

*PS Forgot what I was going to say now.*

Ahead, as far as the eye could see, the black pavement of Fifth Avenue lay smooth and empty between the towers of Manhattan. Millions of people, jammed along the sidewalks, stood waiting to welcome the 82nd Airborne Division. In 42 side streets below massive, grey Washington Arch, 13,000 soldiers waited too.

The division's proud, rugged commander, tall, slender, 38-year-old Major General James ("Slim Jim") Gavin, marched out into the avenue. The 82nd's bayonet-tipped phalanxes moved out behind him, and the cold wind sent a contagious roar of applause rolling for miles through the great city.

The U.S. Army was parading again in victory.

The 82nd Airborne had come a long, hard way to Fifth Avenue and the honor of marching for all U.S. foot soldiers, living and dead, who had "walked through the mud" of World War II. They had jumped and fought from Casablanca to Berlin. Now, in the biggest U.S. victory parade, they marched as though they heard the bugles of Gettysburg and the Little Big Horn, of San Juan Hill and Château-Thierry, sounding with their bands.

http://www.time.com/time/magazine/article/

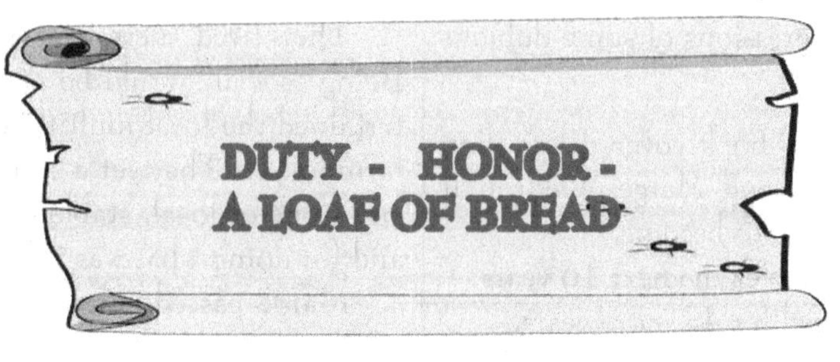


The odyssey, these past two years, is over in terms of a serviceman who placed himself in harms way and returned home with honor. A wife, Marge, is now able to share a daughter with her husband and a marital and a professional union for another 40-plus years.

DUTY - Bill completed his military duty on February 23, 1946, 18 months and 6 days after his August 17, 1944 induction. The over-riding compunction to enlist following D-Day was met with serious trepidation by his spouse, yet the desire to place himself in harms way was a patriotic decision steeped in what military veterans of the WWII era (The Greatest Generation) considered as a responsibility to defend their country's birthright to freedom.

Bill discarded his exemption from military call-up, from his "essential" bakery profession, and enlisted. Plus, he had been assigned an MOS as cook/baker that was an occupation that most likely would have kept him off front-line combat duties. He rejected that to volunteer as a scout for his company, one of the most dangerous of all infantry duties.

HONOR - All military men are taught to defend themselves and their comrades. They are also taught to defeat the enemy. In the vanquishing of the opponent, destruction and death become collateral elements. Yes, Bill had to kill German soldiers. In conversations, years after the war with selected children, Bill sadly stated that there were occasions when they got orders to dispose of captured German prisoners because of the impossibility of transporting them to American lines. However, Bill obviously served with honor. His devotion to Marge is intimated in nearly every letter home.

The love he expressed for Marge is stated in every one of those letters. Too, he made certain that he never placed himself in a position to *chisel* on his wife; often he was left to himself as his comrades made the evening rounds of nightspots where soldiers plied themselves with alcohol and tested the waters for favors from the opposite sex. He served his Country and his family well.

In addition, Bill expressed his disgust about how many American soldiers treated German nationals after V-E Day. He stated in several letters that he held no grudge toward German citizens. He felt most Germans had national pride and they disliked the war as much as American troops disliked fighting it. Bill tried to respect the rights of those German citizens. He felt too many soldiers showed disrespect and displayed cruel and inhumane actions to the defeated German citizens.

A LOAF OF BREAD - Marge's role certainly was not forgotten in this book nor diminished by her husband's participation in the world's greatest military conflict. She dealt with and performed her responsibility as spouse, mother, and business operator in a manner that established a foundation that transcended to the lives of her ten children. She was the wife of an American soldier. She had to be constantly fearful that one day she could receive a telegram from the United States government stating that "We regret to inform you that....". Bill could have been injured, missing in action, or, worse, killed in action!

Marge was obligated to go through nine months of pregnancy, leading to the September 21 birth of her first child, alone. She was also tasked with operating the bakery business enduring the long, tir-

ing hours and frequent transgressions of some dubious employees.

Although the narrative of this book covered less than two years of the lives of Bill and Marge Waldron it formed a backdrop for what was to become.

-Nine more children born over the next 16 years.

-A marriage that flourished for 42 more years.

-Successful operation of the Waukon Bakery and Catering business throughout their marriage together.

Bill and Marge never strayed far from Waukon, Iowa. They took frequent vacation trips, but always set a timetable to get back home in short order.

They lived their lives with vigor and enthusiasm. Being "social" would be an understatement. They entertained the local multitudes at their large acreage and farmhouse. They set a sterling example for their progeny - one of loyal, stable marriage, strong faith in God and for doing what was "right and honorable".

Marge passed away in 1987. Bill followed her in 1992.

Their children, grandchildren, and great-grandchildren need only read their wartime letters and the narrative of this book to glean what should be important facets for their own lives. Duty, Honor, and a Loaf ("It ain't store bought!") of Bread.

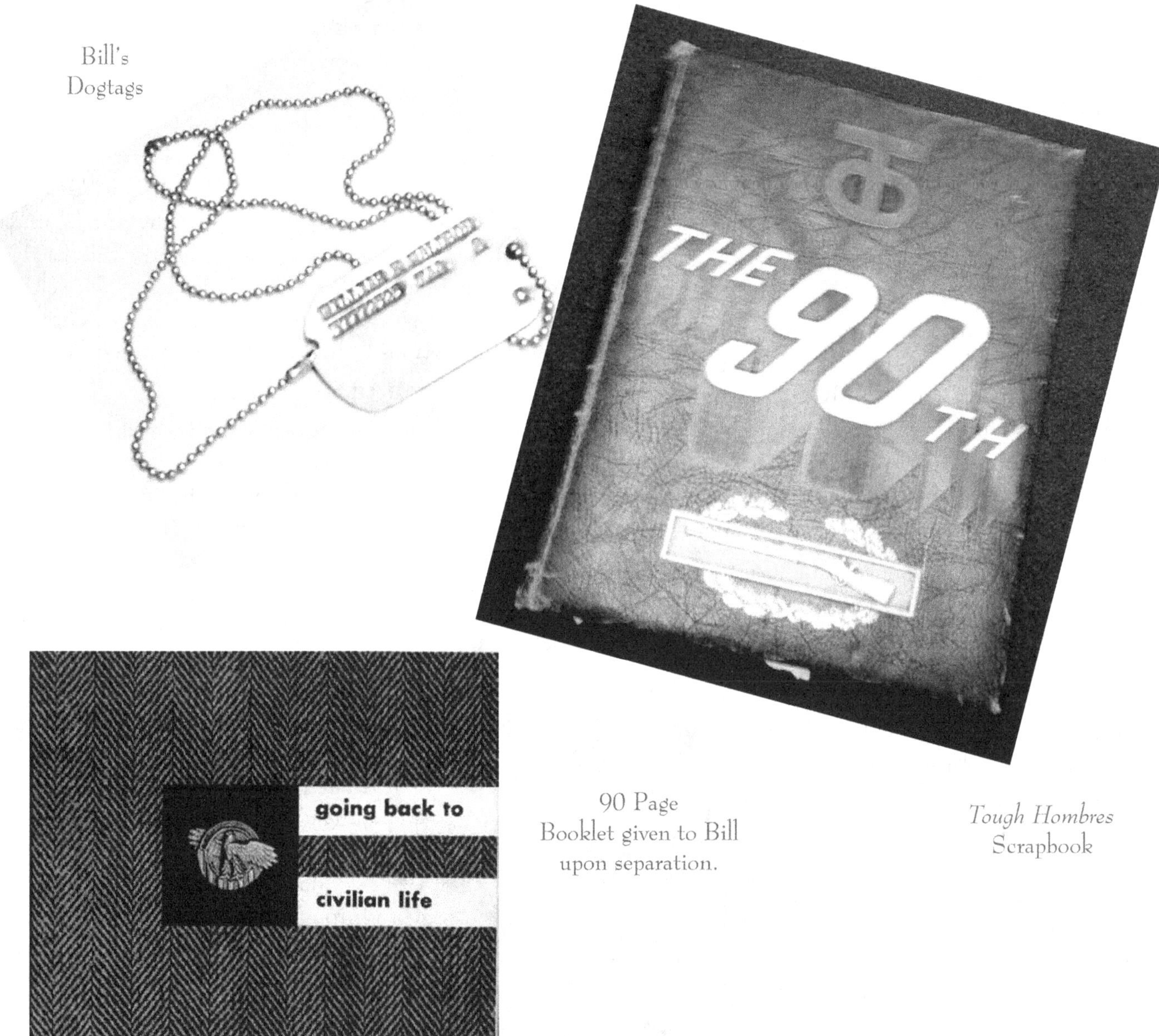


Bill's Dogtags

90 Page Booklet given to Bill upon separation.

*Tough Hombres* Scrapbook

# Discharge Record, No. 3, ALLAMAKEE County, Iowa

Form 104-10B3 P-F4290 — Official Form W. D. A. G. O. Form 53-55 November, 1944

Filed for Record the 4th day of March, A. D. 19 46, at 11:20 o'clock A. M.

No. 782 — Lillian Meierkord, Recorder.
Fee xxx

ARMY OF THE UNITED STATES — HONORABLE DISCHARGE

THIS IS TO CERTIFY THAT

WILLIAM K WALDRON

37772525 TEC 4 CO F 357TH INF

ARMY OF THE UNITED STATES

is hereby Honorably Discharged from the military service of the United States of America.

This certificate is awarded as a testimonial of Honest and Faithful Service to this country.

Given at SEPARATION CENTER CAMP GRANT ILLINOIS

Date 23 FEBRUARY 1946

A. F. LaRouche
A. F. LA ROUCHE
MAJOR, INF.

## ENLISTED RECORD AND REPORT OF SEPARATION
## HONORABLE DISCHARGE

1. Last Name — First Name — Middle Initial: WALDRON WILLIAM K
2. Army Serial No.: 37 772 525
3. Grade: TEC 4
4. Arm or Service: INF
5. Component: AUS
6. Organization: CO F 357TH INF
7. Date of Separation: 23 FEB 46
8. Place of Separation: SEPARATION CENTER CAMP GRANT ILLINOIS
9. Permanent Address for Mailing Purposes: WAUKON IA
10. Date of Birth: 22 SEP 20
11. Place of Birth: WAUKON IA
12. Address From Which Employment Will Be Sought: SEE 9
13. Color Eyes: BLUE
14. Color Hair: BROWN
15. Height: 5' 8"
16. Weight: 129 Lbs.
17. No. Depend.: 2
18. Race: White X
19. Marital Status: Married X
20. U.S. Citizen: Yes X
21. Civilian Occupation and No.: FALIER 4 01.400

## MILITARY HISTORY

22. Date of Induction: 17 AUG 44
23. Date of Enlistment:
24. Date of Entry into Active Service: 17 AUG 44
25. Place of Entry into Service: FT SMELLING MINN

SELECTIVE SERVICE DATA
26. Registered: Yes X
27. Local S. S. Board No.: 1
28. County and State: ALLAMAKEE IA
29. Home Address at Time of Entry into Service: SEE 9

30. Military Occupational Specialty and No.: COOK 060
31. Military Qualification and Date (i. e., infantry, aviation and marksmanship badges, etc.): COMBAT INFANTRYMAN BADGE
32. Battles and Campaigns: ARDENNES RHINELAND CENTRAL EUROPE
33. Decorations and Citations: 2 OVERSEAS SERVICE BARS EUROPEAN-AFRICAN-MIDDLE EASTERN CAMPAIGN MEDAL W/3 BRONZE BATTLE STARS GOOD CONDUCT MEDAL WORLD WAR 11 VICTORY MEDAL
34. Wounds Received in Action: NONE

35. LATEST IMMUNIZATION DATES

| Smallpox | Typhoid | Tetanus | Other (specify) |
|---|---|---|---|
| IM AUG 44 | STIM SEP 44 | STIM OCT 44 | |

36. SERVICE OUTSIDE CONTINENTAL U. S. AND RETURN

| Date of Departure | Destination | Date of Arrival |
|---|---|---|
| 6 JAN 45 | ETO | 13 JAN 45 |
| 6 FEB 46 | USA | 16 FEB 46 |

37. TOTAL LENGTH OF SERVICE

| Continental Service Years | Months | Days | Foreign Service Years | Months | Days |
|---|---|---|---|---|---|
| 0 | 5 | 28 | 1 | 1 | 9 |

38. Highest Grade Held: TEC 4

39. Prior Service: NONE

40. Reason and Authority for Separation: DEPENDENCY SEC 111 AR 615-365 DTD 15 DEC 44

41. Service Schools Attended: NONE

42. Education (Years)

| Grammar | High School | College |
|---|---|---|
| 8 | 4 | 0 |

## TROOP LEVELS

The following is an explanation of the troop size and commanding chain for various military elements. In Bill's letters are the words *squad*, *platoon*, *company*, etc. The following description should help.

Squad: 9 to 10 soldiers, typically commanded by a sergeant or staff sergeant, a squad is the smallest element in the Army structure.

Platoon: 16 to 44 soldiers, led by a lieutenant with an NCO as second in command, and consists of 2 to 4 squads.

Company: 62 to 190 soldiers, three to 5 platoons commanded by a captain with a first sergeant as the commander's principle NCO assistant.

Battalion: 300 to 1,000 soldiers in four to 6 companies normally commanded by a lieutenant colonel, with a command sergeant major as principle NCO assistant.

Regiment: 3,000 to 5,000 soldiers. A regimental headquarters commands the tactical operations of 2 to 5 organic or attached combat battalions. Normally commanded by a colonel with a command sergeant major as senior NCO. The term *regiment* can be interchanged with the term *brigade*.

Division: 10,000 to 15,000 soldiers. Usually consisting of three regiment (brigade) sized elements and commanded by a major general (one star).

Corps: 20,000 to 45,000 soldiers. Two to 5 divisions constitutes a corps, which is typically commanded by a lieutenant general (two stars).

Army: 50,000 + soldiers. Typically commanded by a lieutenant general or higher, an army combines two or more corps.

While Bill was actively engaged in combat from January 13 through May 7 (VE Day), the 357th Regiment was made up of 12 front line companies. At full strength Bill's rifle company would have approximately 190 to 200 men; just before the Battle of the Bulge there were sometimes as few as 80 men in company F. Bill was sent to Europe as a *replacement* troop and, because of the attrition in numbers from the time the 90th Infantry Division landed at Normandy until the commencement of the Battle of the Bulge, Bill became one of the troops to bolster the numbers needed to bring the level of assignment for Company F to an acceptable number. Bill entered his combat duty exactly in the middle of some of the most fierce fighting Allied forces had thus far experienced in World War II. Plus, the weather conditions were some of the most extreme with which American fighting men had to deal.

## ACRONYMS USED IN BILL'S LETTERS HOME

AAF Army Air Force
APC Armored Personnel Carrier
APO Armed Forces Post Office
AWOL Absent With Out Leave
BAR Browning Automatic Rifle
C-5 Military transport plane
CBI China, Burma, India Theater of Operations
CO Commanding Officer
CQ Charge of Quarters
COL Colonel (officer rank)
CPL Corporal (enlisted rank)
CPT Captain (officer rank)
DP Displaced Person
Dragons Teeth - Tank traps/obstacles along the Siegfried Line
ETO European Theater of Operations
ETV European Theater of Victory
Fart Sack - Sleeping Bag
GP General Purpose
HQ Headquarters
IFV Infantry Fighting Vehicle
IRTC Training military handbook
KP Kitchen Patrol
LT Lieutenant (officer rank)
M.G. Military Government
M.P. Military Police
M-1 Basic infantrymen rifle
MAJ Major (officer rank)
Messerschmitt - German fighter plane
Mess/Officer/Sergeant - In charge of food/meal facilities
Non Com (NCO) - Non Commissioned Officer
OD Officer of the Day
OD Officers Dining
OD Olive Drab
OM Operations Manual
PFC Private First Class (enlisted rank)
POE Port of Entry/Port of Embarkation
PTA Primary Target Area
PVT Private (enlisted rank)
P.W. Prisoner of War (POW)
PX Soldiers store
Per Sgt - Personnel Sergeant
QM Quartermaster - distributes military supplies
Rep Depo - Reinforcement Depot where GI's waited for reassignment.
Stars and Stripes - newspaper distributed to troops
SGT Sergeant (enlisted rank)
TD Tank Destroyer
T-4 Tech Sergeant
3rd Army OM - Operations Manager
UNNRA - United Nations Relief and Rehabilitaion Administration
USO United Services Organization
VD Venereal Disease
V-E Victory in Europe

## BIBLIOGRAPHY

Some books that further document this era

*Citizen Soldiers* by Stephen E. Ambrose

*The Complete History of World War II* by Francis T. Miller

*Battle of the Bulge*, Veterans of Foreign Wars Magazine, December, 1944

*Illustrated World War II Encyclopedia* Volume 1, H.S. Stuttman Inc. (Publishers)

*90th Sustainment Brigade* (United States); Wikipedia, the free encyclopedia.

*90th Division History Book*; 90th Division Association.

*History of the 90th Infantry Division: Tough Ombres* Texas Military Historical Society.

www.savingprivatesheridan.com

www.gov archives/holocaust/nazi gold/merkers mine treasure.com

## THE WALDRON BROTHERS

Vernon (Vern) Waldron gave this information to Marie Waldron in 1955:

He was drafted in December of 1942, sent to Camp Cadray, a new camp in Ill.

Vernon was a member of the 359th Engineers. They built bridges to bring in artillery equipment after the foot soldiers had gone ahead.

Early in 1944 he was sent overseas and landed in England. His outfit was part of the Normandy Invasion in France, however, he wasn't involved because he was transferred to the 1301st.

Vernon was overseas for twenty months and his son, Jim, was eighteen months old before Vernon saw him.

At the end of the war Vernon was in Munich, Germany and went to Czechoslovakia to see his brother, Bill. It sounded like Bill had been with the American troops when they went into Germany and Poland at the end of the war. He witnessed some of the atrocities that were committed against the Jewish people in the concentration camps.

Vernon waited for two months after the war to return home and during that time he made himself a ring from a silver dollar. He had the ring up until this summer when he lost it in his front yard.

John Waldron gave this information to Marie Waldron in 1955:

In 1941, John, age eighteen, tried to enlist in the Navy but they wouldn't take him because of his teeth. So he enlisted in the Army. When he finished his basic training in October he came home on leave for a short visit.

In early November, with $3.00 from Mom and Dad and $2.00 from Frank Hager, he hitchhiked back to base. When he returned to camp he received a telephone call telling him that he had a new baby sister.

In October 1942, as an infantryman, John was sent overseas and first landed in Fedela, North Africa. He was part of the 3rd Infantry Division, 10th Field Artillery, under the command of General George Patton. A short time after arriving in North Africa, John was wounded with shrapnel in the knee. In this same invasion three of his buddies were killed.

The 3rd Division marched through North Africa and into Italy, pushing back the Germans all the way. His division was the most decorated of the war and was the honor guard for Stalin, Roosevelt and Churchill in French Morocco. One of the most decorated and better known persons in his division was Audie Murphy, who later went on to become a motion picture star.

While in North Africa John also contracted Malaria and was sent home in August of 1943 with an honorable discharge. He tried to re-enlist two months later but was rejected. After John recuperated at home he moved to Chicago. He lived and worked there until Bill joined the Army. At that time John returned to Waukon and agreed to run the Bakery so that it could remain open. Bill volunteered and was sent overseas in 1944.

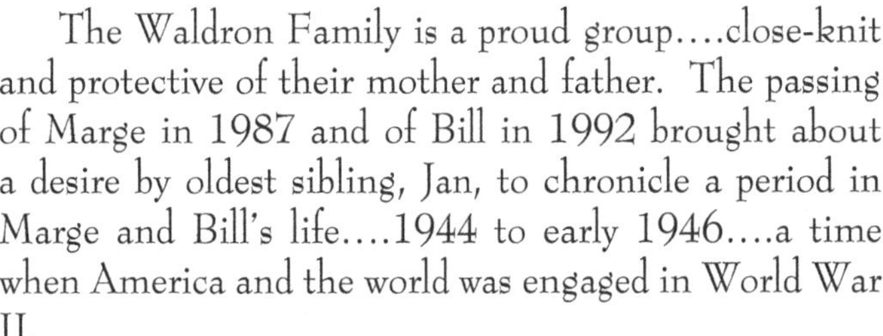


# POST SCRIPT

The Waldron Family is a proud group....close-knit and protective of their mother and father. The passing of Marge in 1987 and of Bill in 1992 brought about a desire by oldest sibling, Jan, to chronicle a period in Marge and Bill's life....1944 to early 1946....a time when America and the world was engaged in World War II.

Following Marge's passing, Bill decided he no longer wanted to live in the large farm house east of Waukon. Here Marge and Bill spent the bulk of their marriage, raising ten children. Bill moved back to Waukon, and took up residency at the duplex he and Marge had owned for nearly 40 years. Since there were a lot of collectibles that Marge had accumulated, and the duplex certainly was unable to become a storage area, Bill allowed his children to draw lots for these treasures. In a box were several hundred faded, worn, tattered letters that Marge and Bill had written to each other during Bill's military service. Any of the siblings who wanted received a stack of these letters. Fortunately, nearly all of the letters were kept safe (stored away because they were articles of importance that reflected a time in the parents marriage).

A few years after Bill's death in 1992, Jan was going through packing boxes (probably during one of our many moves) and began reading the letters. She decided to gather the letters that other siblings had. She, painstakingly, began a project to transcribe these letters to the computer, as another way of preserving some history of Marge and Bill. Intrigued by the discourse between Marge and Bill, Jan also began researching the 90th Infantry Division on the internet during the period of the Normandy landing through February, 1946 (Bill's discharge from the Army). On one of our trips to California we stopped at the George Patton Museum near Palm Springs and purchased a book about the 90th. At that time we began an odyssey to find out as much as we could about Bill's company and regiment during his service.

We came to realize that the narrative we had begun to put together was much more than about Bill's wartime experience. It also magnified the trials and tribulations of what Marge was enduring during this time frame. Bill, in the midst of some of the most difficult combat American troops could possibly face, trying to reassure Marge that all was OK with him. And Marge, newly married (six months before Bill entered the Army), soon to understand that she and her husband would have a child, having to operate the bakery business (sometimes with honest to goodness employee issues), and constantly experiencing the stress of not knowing the safety of her husband.

For Jan, the driving force behind this project is that the current Waldron family grandchildren, all 24 of them, and great grandchildren, currently 10 of them, and, certainly future generations within the Waldron family will have a record from which they can glean a better understanding about why Marge and Bill are so respected and loved.

Along with Marge and Bill's letters to each other, there are also letters to and from Jim and Amanda, to and from siblings, and from several friends of Marge and Bill.

As you read the letters enclosed, we have provided a narrative based on our perceptions, and, most importantly in respect to research we have done on World War II.

Ed and Jan (Waldron) Votroubek